D0536370

Keep this book. You will
need it and use it throughout
your career.

CONTEMPORARY HOSPITALITY MARKETING

A Service Management Approach

Educational Institute Books

UNIFORM SYSTEM OF ACCOUNTS FOR THE LODGING INDUSTRY
Ninth Revised Edition

RESORT DEVELOPMENT AND MANAGEMENT
Second Edition
Chuck Y. Gee

PLANNING AND CONTROL FOR FOOD AND BEVERAGE OPERATIONS
Fourth Edition
Jack D. Ninemeier

TRAINING FOR THE HOSPITALITY INDUSTRY
Second Edition
Lewis C. Forrest, Jr.

UNDERSTANDING HOSPITALITY LAW
Third Edition
Jack P. Jefferies

SUPERVISION IN THE HOSPITALITY INDUSTRY
Second Edition
Raphael R. Kavanaugh/Jack D. Ninemeier

ENERGY AND WATER RESOURCE MANAGEMENT
Second Edition
Robert E. Aulbach

MANAGEMENT OF FOOD AND BEVERAGE OPERATIONS
Second Edition
Jack D. Ninemeier

MANAGING FRONT OFFICE OPERATIONS
Fifth Edition
Michael L. Kasavana/Richard M. Brooks

STRATEGIC HOTEL/MOTEL MARKETING
Revised Edition
Christopher W. L. Hart/David A. Troy

MANAGING SERVICE IN FOOD AND BEVERAGE OPERATIONS
Second Edition
Ronald F. Cichy/Paul E. Wise

THE LODGING AND FOOD SERVICE INDUSTRY
Fourth Edition
Gerald W. Lattin

SECURITY AND LOSS PREVENTION MANAGEMENT
Raymond C. Ellis, Jr., & the Security Committee of AH&MA

HOSPITALITY INDUSTRY MANAGERIAL ACCOUNTING
Fourth Edition
Raymond S. Schmidgall

PURCHASING FOR HOSPITALITY OPERATIONS
William B. Virts

THE ART AND SCIENCE OF HOSPITALITY MANAGEMENT
Jerome J. Vallen/James R. Abbey

MANAGING COMPUTERS IN THE HOSPITALITY INDUSTRY
Third Edition
Michael L. Kasavana/John J. Cahill

MANAGING HOSPITALITY ENGINEERING SYSTEMS
Michael H. Redlin/David M. Stipanuk

UNDERSTANDING HOSPITALITY ACCOUNTING I
Fourth Edition
Raymond Cote

UNDERSTANDING HOSPITALITY ACCOUNTING II
Third Edition
Raymond Cote

CONVENTION MANAGEMENT AND SERVICE
Fifth Edition
Milton T. Astroff/James R. Abbey

HOSPITALITY SALES AND ADVERTISING
Third Edition
James R. Abbey

MANAGING HOUSEKEEPING OPERATIONS
Second Edition
Margaret M. Kappa/Aleta Nitschke/Patricia B. Schappert

CONVENTION SALES: A BOOK OF READINGS
Margaret Shaw

DIMENSIONS OF TOURISM
Joseph D. Fridgen

HOSPITALITY TODAY: AN INTRODUCTION
Third Edition
Rocco M. Angelo/Andrew N. Vladimir

MANAGING BAR AND BEVERAGE OPERATIONS
Lendal H. Kotschevar/Mary L. Tanke

ETHICS IN HOSPITALITY MANAGEMENT: A BOOK OF READINGS
Edited by Stephen S. J. Hall

HOSPITALITY FACILITIES MANAGEMENT AND DESIGN
David M. Stipanuk/Harold Roffmann

MANAGING HOSPITALITY HUMAN RESOURCES
Second Edition
Robert H. Woods

FINANCIAL MANAGEMENT FOR THE HOSPITALITY INDUSTRY
William P. Andrew/Raymond S. Schmidgall

HOSPITALITY INDUSTRY FINANCIAL ACCOUNTING
Raymond S. Schmidgall/James W. Damitio

INTERNATIONAL HOTELS: DEVELOPMENT AND MANAGEMENT
Chuck Y. Gee

QUALITY SANITATION MANAGEMENT
Ronald F. Cichy

HOTEL INVESTMENTS: ISSUES & PERSPECTIVES
Edited by Lori E. Raleigh and Rachel J. Roginsky

QUALITY LEADERSHIP AND MANAGEMENT IN THE HOSPITALITY INDUSTRY
Robert H. Woods/Judy Z. King

MARKETING IN THE HOSPITALITY INDUSTRY
Third Edition
Ronald A. Nykiel

CONTEMPORARY HOSPITALITY MARKETING
William Lazer/Roger Layton

UNIFORM SYSTEM OF ACCOUNTS FOR THE HEALTH, RACQUET AND SPORTSCLUB INDUSTRY

CONTEMPORARY CLUB MANAGEMENT
Edited by Joe Perdue for the Club Managers Association of America

CONTEMPORARY HOSPITALITY MARKETING

A Service Management Approach

William Lazer, Ph.D.
Roger A. Layton, A.M.

EDUCATIONAL INSTITUTE
American Hotel & Motel Association

Disclaimer

This publication is designed to provide accurate and authoritative information in regard to the subject matter covered. It is sold with the understanding that the publisher is not engaged in rendering legal, accounting, or other professional service. If legal advice or other expert assistance is required, the services of a competent professional person should be sought.

> —*From the Declaration of Principles jointly adopted by the American Bar Association and a Committee of Publishers and Associations*

The authors, William Lazer and Roger A. Layton, are solely responsible for the contents of this publication. All views expressed herein are solely those of the authors and do not necessarily reflect the views of the Educational Institute of the American Hotel & Motel Association (the Institute) or the American Hotel & Motel Association (AH&MA).

Nothing contained in this publication shall constitute a standard, an endorsement, or a recommendation of the Institute or AH&MA. The Institute and AH&MA disclaim any liability with respect to the use of any information, procedure, or product, or reliance thereon by any member of the hospitality industry.

©1999
By the EDUCATIONAL INSTITUTE of the
AMERICAN HOTEL & MOTEL ASSOCIATION
2113 N. High Street
Lansing, Michigan 48906-4221

The Educational Institute of the American
Hotel & Motel Association is a nonprofit
educational foundation.

Printed in the United States of America
1 2 3 4 5 6 7 8 9 10 04 03 02 01 00 99

Library of Congress Cataloging-in-Publication Data
Lazer, William.
    Contemporary hospitality marketing : a service management approach
  / William Lazer, Roger A. Layton.
     p. cm.
     Includes bibliographical references and index.
     ISBN 0-86612-158-7 (pbk.)
       1. Hospitality industry—Marketing. I. Layton, Roger A.
     II. Title.
TX911.3.M3L39 1998   98-50023
647.94'068'8—dc21   CIP

Editor: Timothy Eaton

Contents

Preface

Contemporary Hospitality Marketing differs markedly in both approach and content from many available books used in hospitality marketing courses. It is not a basic marketing text adapted to hospitality simply through the addition of hospitality cases, examples, and illustrations. From the outset, it was developed as a *hospitality* marketing book. As a result, some topics normally covered in basic marketing courses are not included. Conversely, attention is given to some topics that are important to hospitality but are not addressed in basic marketing texts. Examples include entrepreneurship, "moments of truth," service quality, service gaps, hospitality networks, travel and tourism operations, and creativity. The concepts, theories, and issues covered reflect marketing areas that we feel are most germane to hospitality businesses.

The book's contents also reflect some of the radical changes that have occurred in the industry in the past two decades. While small, local hospitality enterprises were typical of past hospitality businesses, they have been eclipsed by large conglomerates that operate globally and comprise increasingly important economic sectors. The pace of hospitality operations has quickened considerably, the windows of market opportunity close more rapidly, and market dynamics are often unpredictable. Hospitality decisions involve major commitments of resources contending with significant domestic and international risks. In such a management setting, marketing concepts, tools, information, and approaches become ever more integral components of effective hospitality management.

Contemporary Hospitality Marketing adopts a managerial approach along with a service management focus to the study of marketing activities. In our quest to determine what should be included, we went well beyond the usual appraisal of books that are currently on the market. First, extensive interviews and discussions were held with knowledgeable and involved staff members of the American Hotel & Motel Association's Educational Institute. The Institute is recognized as a leader in hospitality education worldwide. Their personnel are in continuous contact with both practitioners and educators in hospitality around the globe.

Then, numerous interviews were held with hospitality executives in the hotel and restaurant industries in the United States, Australia, Japan, Thailand, Singapore, Indonesia, Malaysia, Turkey, and Hong Kong. Both the trade and research literature were scrutinized and information was gathered from fellow academicians and industry contacts. As a result, a list of topics that should be addressed in hospitality marketing courses emerged which was then modified by our own insights, ideas, and preferences. That formed the basis for developing a detailed proposed book outline which was submitted to the Educational Institute for their review and reactions. The Institute's staff and advisory groups, which include both industry executives and professors, then shared their insights and comments. These inputs proved invaluable in extending and modifying our ideas and approaches, leading to a revised outline that guided the development of the manuscript.

We approach marketing as much more than a functional activity. It is an activity that extends well beyond sales, advertising, promotion, and merchandising activities. Marketing is seen as the driver of every hospitality business, as a philosophy of hospitality operations, as a way of hospitality business life, as an activity that pervades all hospitality decisions and actions, be they front office, reservations, guest relations, engineering, services, food and beverage, accounting, merchandising, pricing, or housekeeping. Hospitality marketing represents that important point of view that considers companies and their operations through the eyes of guests, and is directly associated with revenue-creating activities—sales and profits. We address hospitality marketing issues from a strategic perspective, taking into consideration both national and global orientations, and practical and theoretical considerations.

Essentially, hospitality businesses are first and foremost marketing businesses. The ultimate marketing challenge is satisfying guest wants and needs at a profit, while the essence of hospitality is rooted in serving guests profitably. Hospitality marketing is concerned with managing marketing resources and processes effectively to create and maintain profitable guests. It involves a variety of functions, decisions, and activities that are intellectually and professionally challenging. Properly carried out, marketing brings satisfaction to providers and guests alike.

Contemporary Hospitality Marketing is divided into four main sections. Part I, Marketing in the Hospitality Setting, consists of four chapters: Marketing's Role in Hospitality Management; Service: the Centerpiece of Hospitality Marketing; Hospitality Marketing Strategies; and Strategic Hospitality Marketing Planning. Part II concerns the focus of hospitality marketing efforts—guests. Chapters 5, 6, 7, and 8 deal with Individual Guest Behavior, Business Guest Behavior, Guests of Tomorrow, and Segmenting and Targeting markets, respectively.

Part III comprises chapters 9 through 14, which deal with the components of the marketing mix and cover a wide range of strategic concerns related to marketing decisions and action. The specific topics covered are Marketing Data and Information Systems, Product/Service Mix, Distribution Mix, Pricing Mix, Advertising, Public Relations, Selling, Promotion, and Merchandising.

Part IV, Achieving Hospitality Marketing Leadership, presents three main leadership challenges. Chapter 15 deals with the Service Challenge. Chapter 16 pays attention to Entrepreneurship, Creativity, and Innovation. Chapter 17, the concluding chapter, points to the future and discusses some likely future perspectives.

Contemporary Hospitality Marketing is designed to meet the needs both of hospitality managers and college students. The major objective is to provide readers with an understanding and appreciation of the scope and importance of marketing in hospitality businesses, to familiarize them with marketing perspectives, concepts, approaches and tools, and to help in the quest to manage hospitality marketing more effectively. We also hope that it will prove helpful to readers trying to make up their minds about career decisions. One of the most important personal questions for those considering careers in hospitality is whether they really want to make hospitality their life's work. That issue should be raised often as experience is gained with different sectors of the industry. Success and happiness truly depend on whether people enjoy what they are doing. That is particularly true in an industry that is all about serving guests well. Unless providers receive enjoyment from extending hospitality, it will be difficult to excel. As an experienced successful hotelier stated, "This is the 'feel good' business," and a leading restaurateur emphasized, "In this business, you derive satisfaction from serving customers—treating them as you would guests in your own home."

We are deeply indebted to many members of the hospitality industry, both academicians and practitioners, who contributed so much to the development of *Contemporary Hospitality Marketing*. They shared their ideas, insights, and experiences so generously, making very important contributions to the book. Although it is not possible to single each of them out, nevertheless, we express our deepest thanks and gratitude and gratefully acknowledge their splendid contributions. We would be most remiss if we did not acknowledge the major contributions of several people who were very directly and intimately involved with the development of the *Contemporary Hospitality Marketing*. Included are Mr. George Glazer, Vice President of Academic Publications, and Mr. Tim Eaton of the Educational Institute. Mr. Glazer encouraged us and assisted with the initial development of this project, while Mr. Eaton's insightful questions and careful editing added immeasurably to the contents and readability. Dr. Ron Cichy, Director of *The* School of Hospitality Business at Michigan State University, was a continuing source of support and encouragement. We are indebted to Ms. Joanna Simpson of the University of New South Wales, Australia, whose assistance in gathering data and conducting interviews is reflected throughout the manuscript. In Australia, we particularly thank each of the following for giving several hours of their time to detailed discussions of many aspects of hospitality management – Margaret Armstrong, Nicholas C. Baker, Beth Barclay, Sharon Beavon, Michele Bribosia, Jenny Jane Carpenter, Angela Clarke, Philippa Close, Bernadette Dennis, Jean D'Souza, Ellen DuBois DuBellay, Kim Dutton, Barbara Farris, Catriona Fraser, Janie Hicks, Juliet Hudson, Paul Iacovino, Kim Knudsen, Keith Lamb, Anne S.Lewinski, Janet McGarry, Julianne Newell-Usticke, Daniel Oesch, Richard Perram, Margaret Powell, Philippa Russell, Macy Still, Vicki Stone, Linda Sweeney, Robyn Thurston, Max Turpin, Robert Webb, Katie Wilson, Tracey Wood, Jon Wooller. In addition, we are deeply indebted to Frank Arthur Banks, Ricardo Castaneda, Daniel Forge, Masatoshi Ito, Mehmet Önkal, and George Petkoff, for their generous sharing of ideas that are reflected at various points throughout the book.

Above all, we appreciate greatly the continuing contributions of our wives Joyce and Merrilyn, whose support and understanding contribute immeasurably and in so many *important* ways to this and our other professional endeavors. We dedicate this book to these two exceptional partners in life.

William Lazer, Ph.D.
Professor Emeritus, Michigan State University
Distinguished Research Scholar and Sensormatic Chair,
Florida Atlantic University

Roger A. Layton, A.M.
Dean, Faculty of Commerce and Economics
University of New South Wales

About the Authors

William Lazer, Ph.D., Professor Emeritus of Michigan State University, is Distinguished Research Scholar and Sensormatic Chair in Marketing at Florida Atlantic University. He holds a Bachelor of Commerce (University of Manitoba), M.B.A. (University of Chicago), Ph.D. (Ohio State University), and an Honorary Doctor of Laws (University of Manitoba).

Contemporary Hospitality Marketing: A Service Management Approach is the latest of 18 books. He has lectured at scores of universities throughout the world and has published more than 150 articles, many of which have been translated into various languages. As Consulting Editor, Dr. Lazer developed the Wiley Marketing Series. He is a member of the editorial staff of numerous academic and business journals.

He is the recipient of the prestigious Irwin/American Marketing Association Award, Michigan State University's Distinguished Faculty Award, and Sales and Marketing Executive's International Outstanding Faculty Award. He is a Past President of the American Marketing Association and has served as a National Science Foundation Visiting Scholar, a Beta Gamma Sigma Distinguished Scholar, and an Embassy Scholar. Dr. Lazer is an Honorary Fellow of the Academy of Marketing Science and of the Marketing Institute of Singapore, as well as an Honorary Director of the Japan Marketing Association and a Fellow of the Royal Academy of Arts. His scholastic honors include Beta Gamma Sigma (Business), Sigma Xi (Scientific), Phi Kappa Phi (Scholastic), Alpha Iota Delta (Decision Sciences), and Mu Kappa Tau (Marketing).

Dr. Lazer consults, lectures, and serves as an advisor for many Fortune 500 companies and professional associations in the United States and abroad. His clients have included: Singapore Airlines, IBM, Dentsu, Ford, GTE, Caterpillar, Monsanto, PepsiCo, Chrysler, NEC, General Motors, Whirlpool, General Mills, Ito-Yokado, American Institute of CPAs, National Restaurant Association, American Management Association, Japan Management Association, and the College Entrance Examination Board. His government service includes the Blue Ribbon Committee on Trade Negotiations under three Presidents; Official Delegate to several White House Conferences; Chairman, Census Advisory Committee; Fulbright Commission; and Advisor to the Office of the Price Commissioner. He is a Past President of the Lansing Symphony Association and has been a member of the boards of directors of The Ansul Company, Bio-Detectors, and several non-profit associations.

Roger A. Layton, A.M., Dean of the Faculty of Commerce and Economics, joined the University of New South Wales in 1958 as a Lecturer in Economic Statistics. In 1967, he was appointed Professor of Marketing, filling a chair that had been created by donations from the Sydney business community.

At the time, marketing was in its infancy as a management discipline, and Roger Layton played an important role not only in Australia but also in the United

States in encouraging high standards in research, teaching, and practice in this emerging field. He contributed through books on marketing in Australia, through editorial participation in leading international journals, and through the introduction of new degree and certificate programs. In conjunction with Hoover Australia, he adjudicated the annual Hoover Marketing Awards until 1981, in this way encouraging Australian managers to set high standards for their own marketing initiatives.

Roger Layton has held senior academic positions at Purdue University, Ohio State University, and Keio University, Tokyo. He has consulted widely, with current interests ranging from the provision of expert evidence on sampling and related statistical issues to strategic management and marketing practice and the emerging field of service management. His publications include several books, including a co-authored book on the fundamentals of marketing, now in its third Australian edition, and he has contributed a series of papers on macro-marketing systems that have provided new analytical tools for the design and operation of societal macro-marketing systems in developing countries.

In 1998, Roger Layton was made a Member of the Order of Australia for services to marketing in both research and teaching.

Part I

Marketing in the Hospitality Setting

Chapter 1 Outline

The Hospitality Industry
The Development of Hospitality Marketing
    The Provider Orientation Phase
    The Sales Orientation Phase
    The Promotional Orientation Phase
    The Marketing Orientation Phase
The Marketing Orientation as a Management Philosophy
    The Marketing Philosophy versus Traditional Approaches
    The Marketing Philosophy in Operation
    Transition in Management Thinking
The Logic of Marketing
    Marketing Mix
    Marketing Mix Perspectives
The Functional Perspective
    Conceptual Connections
    How Is Marketing Organized?
    Coping with Functional Structures
Toward More Effective Hospitality Marketing
    Marketing as a High-Risk Necessity
    Guests as Assets
    Hospitality Marketing Checklist
Concluding Comments

Marketing's Role in Hospitality Management

"In the hospitality industry, marketing is the name of the game... After all, a hotel room is a hotel room is a hotel room. Hotel managers are challenged to differentiate their rooms from everyone else's... Marketing is the key."

—Frank A. Banks, General Manager,
Rihga Royal Hotel, New York[1]

"The customer is the foundation of the business and keeps it in existence... There is only one valid definition of business purpose: to create a customer... Because it is its purpose to create a customer, any business enterprise has two, and only these two, basic functions: marketing and innovation."

—Peter F. Drucker[2]

"I firmly believe that those companies that succeed in the times ahead will be those who understand marketing in its broadest definition and application."

—J.W. Marriott, Jr., Chairman, President, and CEO,
Marriott International[3]

HOSPITALITY LEADERS like McDonald's, Pizza Hut, Disney, Hilton, and Marriott understand well that success and effective marketing go hand in hand. They know from experience that success involves more than simply providing superior products and services. Exceptional marketing plays a pivotal role in distinguishing hospitality leaders from the rest of the pack.

Marketing is critically important to managers of hospitality enterprises. The goal of marketing is guest satisfaction, which is the very essence of hospitality. It is also the key to growth and profits. Marketing is all about guests, both actual and potential. Management thinking among industry pacesetters places guest concerns at the most fundamental levels of hospitality strategies, decisions, plans, and programs.

What does marketing mean? There are three basic ways of thinking about contemporary hospitality marketing. First and foremost, we can look at marketing as a philosophy or fundamental orientation of management. We can also see it as a logical approach to strategic and operational business challenges. Lastly, we can see it as a major functional area within the hospitality organization. It is important to understand each of these perspectives to appreciate the real nature, scope, and role of marketing in hospitality.

In some parts of the hospitality industry, marketing is often *wrongly* used as a synonym for sales. While marketing includes sales, it encompasses much more. Marketing involves designing, managing, and pricing products, services, and guest experiences and planning the wide array of communications that promote these offerings. It includes decisions about location, facilities, and operations and deals with one of the most important choices the hospitality business makes—the choice of guests. At one end of the spectrum, marketing addresses such strategic issues as:

- What is our property actually worth?
- Where should we expand or contract?
- What new markets are emerging?
- Where should new units be located?
- Which properties should be closed?
- What alliances should be made with other companies?
- What products and services should be added?
- What advertising and sales strategies should be used?
- What pricing, promotional, and merchandising strategies should be adopted?

At the other end of the spectrum, marketing also deals with such day-to-day decisions as determining what items to feature on menus; what hours to observe in dining rooms, coffee shops, bars, and room service; what prices to charge for rooms, parking, health clubs, cabanas, lounges, and valet services; what personal care items to offer in bathrooms; and myriad other operating considerations.

Ultimately, marketing refers to a total management commitment to serving guests, to a culture that stresses satisfying customers. It is a management philosophy that sees business as a system responsive to a changing market environment. Within this context, we offer the following definition:

> **Hospitality marketing** is a total system designed to plan, price, promote, and make available to selected markets hospitality products and services in the form of benefits and experiences that create satisfied guests and achieve organizational objectives.

By this definition, marketing is more than just another business function. It is a philosophy of operation that sees the hospitality business as a system of activities extending well beyond the walls of a property. Marketing embraces a network of alliances with external partners, such as suppliers and agents, working to satisfy guests and achieve company objectives. This definition stresses the interdependence of the hospitality company's internal and external partners as they seek to satisfy guests while generating company profits.

This definition embodies the approach to marketing taken by today's leading hospitality companies, and it is one of the key factors that separates these leaders from everyone else. Yet, this "state-of-the-art" marketing approach is available to anyone who chooses to use it. By describing this state of the art, we intend to prescribe ways in which effective marketing can raise company performance in today's market environment.

> "Marketing is really about managing change… At Marriott, we address change by committing ourselves to offering quality products at every price level, treating our employees fairly, providing consistently good service, and really listening and responding to our customers. These commitments drive our marketing efforts."
> —J.W. Marriott[4]
>
> ≈
>
> A popular anecdote highlights the importance of thinking in terms of guests. While addressing thousands of employees at an annual meeting, the president of a large restaurant chain asked rhetorically, "Whose restaurants are the best?" The employees shouted "Ours!" He then asked, "Whose food is the best?" Again, the crowd yelled "Ours!" "Whose service is the best?" Right on cue, the employees roared "Ours!" The president continued, "Then why are our sales and profits so poor?" A lone voice from the back of the room shouted loudly, "Because the guests don't like them!"

In this chapter, we provide the historical and contextual basis for examining hospitality marketing as it is practiced by today's hospitality industry leaders. We begin by very briefly sketching an outline of the hospitality industry. We then examine phases in the development of hospitality marketing and advocate the adoption of the marketing philosophy as the basic guiding principle for conceiving and managing hospitality businesses. We also discuss contemporary marketing from the three basic perspectives mentioned earlier: as a philosophy, as a business logic, and as a major functional area. We conclude with some suggestions for improving the conceptual and practical application of marketing in the hospitality industry.

The Hospitality Industry

Before we address hospitality marketing, we want to set the context by briefly sketching the outlines of the industry that will be our focus. The hospitality industry spans a spectrum of travel-related businesses large and small, global, national, regional, and local, independent and chain, economy and world-class. Despite their variety, all share the common focus of providing hospitality products and services that deliver guest satisfaction. The hospitality industry is a service business providing food and lodging to those traveling for business or pleasure.

Hospitality has become increasingly important to the economic well-being of societies worldwide. Estimates are that the hotel sector alone generated more than $247 billion in revenue worldwide in 1994.[5] Moreover, hospitality is a growth industry characterized by dynamic change. Markets for hospitality services continuously veer in new directions, reflecting changing technology and socioeconomic environments, different lifestyles, and rising guest expectations. Indeed, the industry that existed just ten to fifteen years ago has changed fundamentally—consider, for example, the emergence of ecotourism, the growing national involvement in the tourism industry, the growing intensity of destination and airline competition, pressures on costs, and the increasing importance of women as a hospitality market. These changes and others not yet apparent will inevitably lead to dramatic change in the way the industry operates today.

The hospitality industry is part of the tourism industry. Hospitality comprises two main business sectors, lodging and food service. It includes those institutions and activities involved with providing short-term or transitional lodging and food services. Lodging encompasses hotels, motor hotels, motels, resorts, parks, pensions, bed and breakfast facilities, and camps. Food service includes commercial and institutional establishments such as restaurants, bars/taverns, snack bars, contract food companies, cruise ships, catering, lunch counters, dormitories, nursing homes, lodging properties, and so forth.

The Development of Hospitality Marketing

Hospitality marketing has received its greatest attention in just the past ten to fifteen years.

> "When I was in the hotel business in New York twenty years ago, there was no reference to marketing at all, just sales. I look at sales as providing the volume for the hotel. The vital job of marketing is to raise the average room rate, to get the maximum value out of the property, and to provide the image for the hotel. It takes a lot longer to market a hotel than it does to sell it."—Frank A. Banks[6]

Hospitality marketing has progressed through four identifiable (though overlapping) phases, each with its particular orientation: a provider phase, a sales phase, a promotional phase, and a marketing phase. The marketing orientation approach that we advocate (and that is currently used by leading hospitality companies) often represents the last step in a sequential progression through these four phases. This does not mean, however, that all hospitality companies have followed this progression. Many companies still approach marketing from provider, sales, or promotional orientations that are ultimately less effective than they need to be for those companies to hold their own in the increasingly competitive marketplace.

Let us outline the development of hospitality marketing by briefly considering each of these four phases or approaches to marketing.

The Provider Orientation Phase

For many years, marketing in hospitality was largely ignored. The industry was provider-dominated—that is, it focused on internal operations, activities, and procedures such as housekeeping, menu engineering, and front desk operations and on controlling labor, food, and beverage costs. General managers of hotels were drawn from food and beverage operations, and restaurant managers were steeped in food preparation and related experiences.

In considering provider needs, this traditional perspective looked inward, resisted change, and focused on producing standardized lodging and food services and products. Decisions were based on owner/manager/employee considerations, and guests were expected to adjust to the hospitality offerings made available to them.

The provider orientation evolved under conditions of high market demand or periods of shortages, particularly in the lodging sector. In the latter 1970s and early 1980s, however, market conditions in the United States and elsewhere changed markedly. Shortages dwindled, excess capacity emerged, hospitality alternatives multiplied, and keen global competition arose. A different management orientation was necessary.

We should note, however, that even during the provider orientation phase, leading industry members such as Ray Kroc, Conrad Hilton, Kemmons Wilson, E.M. Statler, and J.W. Marriott were well attuned to guests and developed their businesses accordingly. These leaders had two important industry influences. First, they developed profitable organizations that are still with us today. Second, they led the industry from the "mom and pop approach" with its provider mentality to today's sophisticated market-oriented approach.

The Sales Orientation Phase

As industry competition increased and excess capacity developed, many in the hospitality industry changed their focus to volume. Businesses turned to increasing sales by selling more aggressively, paying less attention to profit than to volume. This still reflected an inward-looking, short-term perspective that focused on selling what businesses had available, often on a price basis. The sales approach, which became quite prevalent in the late 1970s among many companies, was supported by the growth of hotel, motel, and restaurant chains that emphasized selling standardized products and services assertively to mass markets. This approach was reflected in the actions of such companies as Holiday Inn, Denny's, Burger King, Taco Bell, Best Western, and Pizza Hut. During the sales orientation phase, hospitality businesses featured competitive pricing, convenient locations, drive-through windows, fast service, readily prepared standardized food items, and uniform lodging facilities.

In implementing the sales approach, chains first added sales staffs and later employed experts in advertising, merchandising, promotion, market research, direct mail, and other marketing areas. It was this emphasis that helped foster the incorrect industry perception that marketing is the same as sales, which regrettably too often carries over to this day.

The Promotional Orientation Phase

In the early 1980s, as markets evolved and became more competitive, the need for short-term results led to a broadening of the sales orientation to encompass a promotional emphasis. Recognition was given to the importance of such mass marketing activities as advertising, public relations, direct mail, and merchandising to communicate with markets, generate favorable images, and support sales activities. Specialized staffs were hired to carry them out. While this expanded the promotional emphasis, other significant hospitality marketing activities were still ignored. The orientation remained short-term, focusing on sales volume, existing company offerings, and company needs and desires. It still neglected the primacy of guest wants and needs.

The Marketing Orientation Phase

The **marketing orientation phase** describes the approach now being used by the leading hospitality companies. It is the management perspective that we prescribe. It identifies a major difference in focus from sales. Sales focuses on what a hospitality business wants to sell its guests, on what the business wants and needs. Marketing focuses on guest wants and needs.

Two main factors drew many managers in the hospitality industry toward a marketing thrust. First, they recognized that other businesses were benefiting significantly from adopting marketing approaches and techniques. Second, hospitality markets changed radically, becoming more competitive. Profits were being squeezed, excess capacity was multiplying, global competition was appearing, and guests were becoming more knowledgeable, informed, and demanding than ever.

Leading food and lodging enterprises became more attuned than ever to what guests wanted and expected. Many hospitality managers changed their focus from internal to external, from their business routines and systems to their guests. In the process, they became more flexible, change-oriented, and responsive to markets. They targeted market segments, differentiated their offerings, and used the logic and approaches of marketing to gain competitive advantage, increase market share, and enhance profits. The marketing orientation began to attract more attention.

As more marketing-trained and -experienced people entered the hospitality industry, along with sophisticated investors, business approaches and operations were altered to emphasize marketing. Existing sales departments extended their activities and responsibilities, becoming full-fledged marketing departments. Marketing research was used regularly to gather and analyze guest data and monitor market developments. Managers turned their attention to strategic hospitality marketing planning and to developing coordinated marketing systems. Marketing activities related to promotion, distribution, product/service offerings, pricing, alliances, and affiliations became integral components of effective hospitality management.

The Marketing Orientation as a Management Philosophy

We have already begun to discuss how marketing may be thought of as a basic management philosophy for the whole hospitality business, as a way of thinking about the challenges the business faces. This orientation is expressed in a fundamental commitment to putting guests first in management's thinking, and then letting all else flow from that.

In the marketing philosophy, thinking about hospitality businesses begins not with buildings, facilities, or strategic alliances—important though these are—but with guest needs, interests, desires, and expectations. Hospitality businesses that truly understand guest needs, interests, desires, and expectations are better able to achieve high levels of guest satisfaction, develop guest loyalty, create and retain a talented, service-oriented staff, and build a strong competitive market position yielding long-term profitability.

> "The view that an industry is a customer-satisfying process, not a goods-producing process, is vital for all businessmen to understand. An industry begins with the customer and his needs, not with a patent, a raw material, or a selling skill."—T. L. Levitt[7]
>
> ≈
>
> "Marketing starts with the customer; it starts with credibility; it starts with developing relationships; it starts with people. Not budgets, not dollars [but rather with] opportunities to do more for the customer, inform the customer, get customer feedback.... Probably the number one thing we work on...is learning more about our customers."—Denise Fugo, owner, Sammy's Restaurant, Cleveland[8]

In practice, guest concerns are all too often subordinated to the concerns of managers and employees. Consider the following news clipping:

> "Complaints from passengers wishing to use the Bagrell to Greenfields bus service 'that the drivers were speeding past queues of up to 30 people with a smile and a wave of the hand' were met by a statement pointing out that it is impossible for the drivers to keep their timetables if they have to stop for passengers."[9]

The marketing philosophy leads to a management mindset or orientation different from the internally focused one that was widespread and may still be found. Essentially, it becomes a way of business life centered on the importance of meeting and exceeding guest expectations.

Stated another way, a manager inside the four walls of a business facing increasing change in external markets has three basic options. The first is to ignore change, hoping that it will pass. The second is to attempt to change the way things are developing, perhaps through intensive sales activity, perhaps through lobbying government for protective measures, perhaps through informal or formal agreements limiting competition. Experience suggests that these tactics will not prevail in the long run, but are useful in buying time. The third option is to change internally, to respond to the external challenges with a reorientation of the company toward the new markets and their needs. This option has proven successful on countless occasions.

The Marketing Philosophy versus Traditional Approaches

Exhibit 1 contrasts two orientations, the marketing philosophy and the more traditional approach to starting and operating hospitality enterprises. The traditional way to start a food or lodging business began by considering personal abilities and desires, such as enjoyment of cooking or baking, desire to have a restaurant, knowing how to run a catering service, having spare rooms in a large house that could be used for a bed and breakfast business, or working in a motel and accumulating some money to branch off on one's own. The hospitality offerings may or may not be what guests want. (Of course, guest reactions will finally determine success or failure.)

In contrast, the marketing philosophy relies on guest wants and needs to drive the process well before any business is established. Company goals and missions are first considered in terms of satisfying guest wants and needs and identifying opportunities to better serve guests. Companies match their capabilities and resources, both actual and potential, with perceived market opportunities and identify those target markets and segments that they wish to serve. As guests respond by making purchases, not only are their wants and needs satisfied, but hospitality providers achieve their goals: sales, profits, margins, image, reputation, and market position. Feedback is gathered throughout, permitting appropriate adjustments to serve guests better. Profits are seen as a measure of how well a hospitality business meets guest expectations.

Does the marketing philosophy make sense in practice? Perhaps the strongest evidence for this comes from the experiences of many highly successful service businesses who have found that a strong commitment to customer satisfaction through service excellence is the key to their success. The many examples include Marriott Corporation, Four Seasons Hotels, McDonald's, Walt Disney Company, Nordstrom Inc., SAS, American Express, Club Méditerranée, Ritz-Carlton, and others. In each case, the marketing philosophy translates directly into an overwhelming concern for the customer, seeking to build sustained habits of loyalty based on high perceived quality and value for money. An example of this commitment comes from the Ritz-Carlton Hotel Company, whose service led the President of Racing Strollers, Inc., to comment, "At the Ritz-Carlton Hotel…customer devotion is done right.... Every Ritz-Carlton employee I've ever met acts as if it is the high point of his day to help us."[10] Her praise was inspired in part by an incident in Atlanta, where she needed to find a grocery store that carried a special goat cheese she needed to make pizza for her allergic son. The concierge located the store and, when no cabs were available, summoned a door attendant to drive her in a hotel car at no charge. When we look at the truly successful hospitality companies, a common factor that stands out is the primacy of guest wants and needs.

The Marketing Philosophy in Operation

Operating under the marketing philosophy involves a fundamental transformation in the way many hotels, restaurants, and recreation/leisure companies should

Exhibit 1   Traditional versus Marketing Orientation

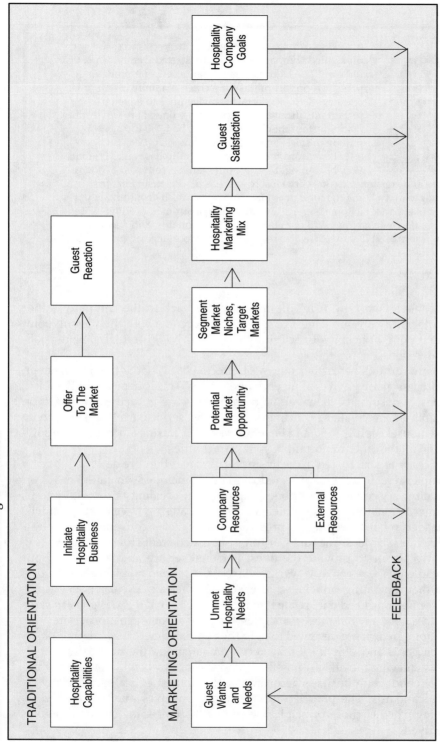

TRADITIONAL ORIENTATION

Hospitality Capabilities → Initiate Hospitality Business → Offer To The Market → Guest Reaction

MARKETING ORIENTATION

Guest Wants and Needs → Unmet Hospitality Needs → Company Resources / External Resources → Potential Market Opportunity → Segment Market Niches, Target Markets → Hospitality Marketing Mix → Guest Satisfaction → Hospitality Company Goals

FEEDBACK

Mr. Masatoshi Ito, the founder of the very successful and diversified company Ito-Yokado, started Denny's Japan Co. Ltd. in 1973 as a franchise operation. At that time, Mr. Ito perceived opportunities for a chain of family restaurants and negotiated a contract with Denny's to develop restaurants throughout Japan. Now one of Japan's leading family restaurant chains, Denny's had 480 units, $944 million in sales, and 11,700 employees in 1996.

The reasons for its success? Mr. Ito has said, "From its very beginning, Denny's of Japan has followed evolving business and consumer trends very closely and has placed customers first. We endeavor to drive home the fundamentals of our business by continuously striving to enhance customer service and to reinforce our menus with a wider selection of items that appeal to our customers. Taste, quality, and friendly service are top priorities at Denny's. We also recognize the importance of atmosphere and cleanliness."

be run. It means working from the marketplace back to the company rather than the other way around. Guest considerations become both the starting point and the end point of hospitality activities, directly driving strategies, plans, policies, and decisions.

But how can this be carried out most effectively? What is the management thought process involved in dealing with operations? This is depicted in Exhibit 2. The actions of hospitality managers and employees are guided by or based on policies. Policies are created regarding reservations, service levels, pricing, room standards, housekeeping, food and beverage services, business accounts, empowerment, and all the other important hospitality activities.

Policies are in turn rooted in the business principles they are designed to carry out. Principles refer to a company's credo and might include such guidelines as offering quality service, providing good lodging value, dealing fairly with guests, serving international business clientele effectively, catering to celebrity clientele, being a leader in housekeeping, or providing unparalleled convention and meeting facilities and services. The Ritz-Carlton's published credo, for example (stating in part, "We pledge to provide the finest personal service and facilities for our guests, who will always enjoy a warm, relaxed, yet refined ambience"), tells us a lot about their operating principles. To check whether a particular policy is appropriate or not, one need only relate it to the principles that it is designed to carry out. If it does not carry out those principles, the policy may be inappropriate.

Principles in turn are designed to help the company meet its goals and objectives. Such goals and objectives may focus on satisfying the most discriminating tastes, achieving the highest possible standards of excellence, never being undersold, or conducting business according to the highest ethical and socially responsible standards. The propriety of operating principles may be checked by determining whether those principles do in fact help meet the company's goals and objectives.

Exhibit 2   From Marketing Philosophy to Operations

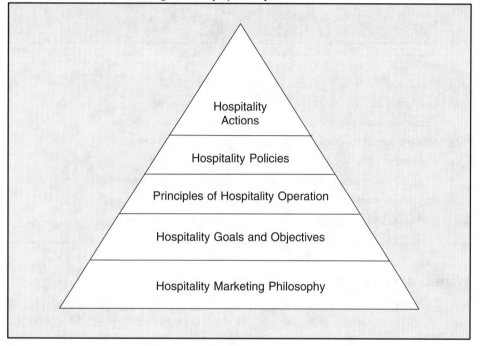

Hospitality
Actions

Hospitality Policies

Principles of Hospitality Operation

Hospitality Goals and Objectives

Hospitality Marketing Philosophy

But how does the marketing philosophy tie in? The marketing philosophy is the basic underpinning for conceiving and managing hospitality businesses. The propriety of hospitality goals and objectives may be checked by determining whether those goals and objectives are based on guest wants and needs. Guest wants, needs, and expectations serve as the guiding business values, as the foundation upon which hospitality goals, objectives, principles, policies, and actions all ultimately must stand.

Hospitality businesses still too often ignore the implications of the marketing philosophy, making decisions and taking actions for the convenience of managers, employees, or administrative systems. The focus is on internal efficiency, cutting costs, and short-term profits, not guests.

The commitment to a marketing philosophy starts at the very top of an organization. Information about guest satisfaction (of both the company's and the competitors' guests) is a good starting point in assessing how effectively the marketing philosophy has been put into place. This approach stimulates managers to raise such important questions as: Is our hospitality business truly catering to targeted guests and satisfying their wants and needs? Are guests brought directly and immediately into our decisions and operations? Are procedures being carried out for the convenience of guests or the staff? Are we serving guests more effectively than our competitors? What changes can be made in policies and procedures to serve guests better?

Exhibit 3   Marketing Orientation Shifts

From	To
1. Product centered	Market centered
2. Past	Future
3. Negotiation	Competition
4. Opportunistic search	Focused search
5. Accumulation	Resource management
6. Mechanistic structures	Learning organizations
7. Carrot and stick	Empowerment
8 Transaction-based information systems	Relationship-based information systems
9. Traditional markets	Benefit-based markets
10. Self-contained business	Network membership

Transition in Management Thinking

It is easy to state that the marketing orientation involves a complete rethinking of the hospitality business. But just what does that mean? It implies the shifts and transitions depicted in Exhibit 3. Each of these shifts involves a change in the way hospitality managers think about themselves and their business.

For example, a marketing orientation challenges existing power holders. The shift from a focus on product to a focus on markets inevitably leads to a power shift away from those managers who understand operations to those managers who understand and are comfortable with the uncertainties, risks, and opportunities of the marketplace. The abilities that matter most concern problem-solving skills and obtaining knowledge about likely future developments. A marketing orientation also challenges the value of experience because, in a time of change, the future is unlikely to be like the past.

Traditional views of management have often advocated the virtues of agreements among competing firms to hold back the forces of change. However, resisting the forces of change will not work in today's hospitality world, where competition is the key and the search for best global practice exemplifies the intensity of the drive. Part of this drive leads marketing oriented managers to actively search for new services and products with a clear view of the end user in mind, rather than waiting for new opportunities to suggest themselves. These managers focus not merely on accumulation of assets or expansion, but on the most effective management of resources.

Traditional hospitality organizations with mechanistic and clearly defined hierarchical lines of command and functional arrangements worked well when the same basic set of tasks was performed over and over. But that is hardly the situation today. Market-driven hospitality enterprises are challenged by unpredictable changes that call for flexibility at all levels. These companies operate more effectively with a flatter organizational structure that facilitates a built-in capacity to learn, to use a team approach, and to be open and to respond quickly to market changes. Traditional hierarchies can do many things, but moving quickly is not one of them.

Not surprisingly, in market-oriented companies, the "carrot-and-stick" philosophy of people management is inappropriate. Rather, managers are experimenting with empowering employees to determine appropriate guest service actions on their own. For employees to do this effectively, they need timely, comprehensive, and relevant information. Obtaining such information calls for a conscious effort to research guest needs. Regrettably, in too many hospitality firms, such information is just not available. Information systems tend to be built around the needs of traditional accounting for transactions rather than information about guests. Marketing oriented managers want to know about the profitability of various categories of guests, services offered, networks used, and benefits provided. This situation is further complicated by a move away from the traditional ways of categorizing guests (corporate, individual, airline, public sector) and toward labels that point more strongly to the benefits that different groups of guests are seeking.

Hospitality managers are beginning to see themselves as part of a network of enterprises dedicated to serving guests and not merely as self-contained businesses. Cooperation and coordination extend well beyond the boundaries of individual hospitality businesses.

Each of these shifts or transitions is part of the move toward a marketing orientation. Given such implications, it is little wonder that implementing a marketing orientation is one of the most challenging tasks facing hospitality managers. Hospitality marketing efforts sometimes fail not because they were inappropriate, but rather because the commitment to make them work was inadequate.

The Logic of Marketing

To this point, we have generally focused on the perspective that sees marketing as a management philosophy. The second hospitality marketing perspective is to see marketing as a logic—a clearly structured way of thinking through the issues raised by an external or internal challenge in order to reach decisions and take action. The marketing logic is concerned with developing hospitality offerings that will better satisfy guests. It focuses on creating and effectively delivering the right hospitality services and products, when and where guests want them, at prices guests are willing to pay. The logic involves assessing changing market environments, gaining a good understanding of consumers' wants and needs, segmenting and targeting markets, positioning the company, and developing appropriate offerings that both satisfy guests and achieve company objectives. Such thinking helps match a company's assets and capabilities with changing market opportunities, and ties together decisions about products, services, pricing, distribution, and communications.

The logic of marketing affects all operating hospitality decisions, such as:

- Developing new menus and food items

- Using demographic, attitudinal, preference, and lifestyle information to improve lodging facilities and food, beverage, and service offerings
- Advertising to attract new customers or increase customer satisfaction and loyalty
- Merchandising activities like special gifts, clubs, points and services to attract and hold good customers
- Using promotions to attract conventions, professional meetings, and international business travelers and to increase the demand for food and beverage offerings
- Pricing lodging and meals to maximize profits and counter slow growth periods
- Creating, developing, and marketing franchises
- Developing cooperative advertising programs
- Designing integrated travel packages: air, hotel, restaurant, rental car and other ground transportation
- Identifying new locations
- Developing data bases that incorporate guest records
- Monitoring competitors' actions

Marketing Mix

The **marketing mix** comprises the mix of controllable marketing variables that companies offer to guests to satisfy those guests' wants and needs. It refers to the totality of a hospitality company's offering to the marketplace. The marketing mix is the mix of choices in each of the four primary decision areas that lie at the core of a hospitality marketing system. These are the product/service specification (including location), pricing, network partnership, and promotion. While the choices made by managers in each of these areas are to a large extent controllable, they *are* constrained by external environmental factors and the resources or capabilities of the business. The choices are all interrelated as well. The choice, for example, of a five-star product/service package must be matched by appropriate choices in pricing, network partnership, and promotion.

Developing a marketing mix is among the most fundamental responsibilities of marketing executives. The basic challenge is to develop, offer, and adjust unique and differentiated hospitality services and products in a superior manner—to beat what is on the market. The concept highlights critical marketing decision areas such as advertising, promotion, pricing, distribution, personal selling, and merchandising. The marketing mix is a vehicle for increasing marketing efficiency and productivity, gaining market share, and increasing profits. By altering marketing ingredients, hospitality businesses can come up with quite different mixes that are better attuned to guests and thereby gain competitive advantage.

Developing an effective marketing mix is complex and difficult. It requires analysis, planning, and creativity. Both those marketing variables controlled by an enterprise and those that lie outside its control must be considered.

Exhibit 4   Hospitality Marketing Mix

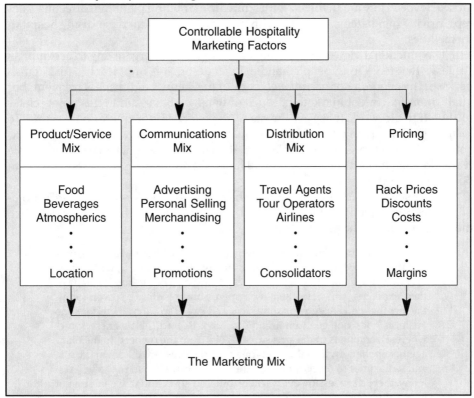

Marketing Mix Perspectives

Two perspectives come into play in designing a hospitality marketing mix: that of the overall marketing mix, and that of each of the individual submixes (see Exhibit 4). Conflicts and tradeoffs are involved at both levels. The overall objective is to optimize the *total* mix, sometimes at the expense of the individual components. For instance, to enhance the overall mix, it may be necessary to raise prices so that advertising expenditures can be increased, or to reduce marketing research expenditures so that more money can be directed to personal selling efforts.

Unfortunately, hospitality marketing decisions are often made on a piecemeal basis. Attention is directed to individual components such as advertising, pricing, distribution, or personal selling, rather than to the whole marketing mix. The result is that the marketing mix is not as effective as it could have been if the same resources had been used differently.

The Functional Perspective

The third perspective is that of marketing as a function. As such, it is both an activity—something that people do—and a name for part of the organization.

Marketing departments carry out marketing activities at strategic, operational, and tactical levels. They are involved with strategic marketing planning, directing sales reps, pricing menu items, working with travel agents, and merchandising hospitality facilities.

The functional view of marketing explores ways of organizing to accomplish the tasks that marketing people handle. In so doing, it is important to distinguish between the everyday or *operational* work of marketing and the less frequent, but vital, *strategic* work of marketing. Much of what we have said to this point relates to the strategic work that sets the stage for everyday or operational work. To see just what is involved at the operational level, consider the following three examples of people practicing marketing. If marketing is what marketing people really do, then these three examples will help add depth to our insights into operational marketing.

The first is an interview with Jenny, the Regional Sales Manager for an international chain located in Sydney, Australia. She spoke about the early 1990s, when the industry was in the grip of recession.

> I came in at a bad time. It's terribly hard, for very little reward, because half the time people aren't traveling anyway! But the thing is, with hotels, of course, the management companies, the owners of the hotels still have their expenses, still have their repayments and overhead; so you know, the fact that you shrug your shoulders and say "I'm sorry, there's just no business," it's not good enough. You have to find the business somewhere. Everyone is under pressure. It goes from the owners, to the management company, the GM, everyone puts the pressure on down the line and so it comes to me as far as Australia is concerned, and they say, "Yes, Jenny, there's a recession everywhere, but you gotta find it, we've still got to pay our overhead!"

The second example considers the sales challenges faced by the Francisco Grande Resort in Arizona as it attempted to build occupancy in the middle of the desert.[11] Building occupancy meant contacting and educating potential guests in Phoenix and Tucson. The resort was looking for a sales manager. Candy, a "people person" who lived there and worked in sales, was the only applicant.

Management focused Candy's activities on a program of "Chamber of Commerce marketing." Her target markets were five chambers of commerce, three in nearby communities, plus those in Tucson and Phoenix. The core strategy was to develop personal relationships with chamber directors and through them develop company contacts.

The approach worked well, the reception was great, and the results exceeded all expectations. Candy capitalized on personal relationships established, became the hotel's member in each chamber's activities, and cultivated a unique relationship with them.

Our third example concerns Ted and Judy Blair, who own four small properties totaling 340 rooms in Cody, Wyoming, a small town that traces its history back to Buffalo Bill.[12] They discovered that the American West has great appeal for overseas tourists as the following indicates.

Recently, the Blairs blitzed operators in Tokyo and Osaka in Japan, and Taipei, Taiwan....They made their first trip to Taiwan seven years ago under the sponsorship of United Airlines. That following summer, they received 2,500 room nights from international visitors, primarily from Taiwan and Hong Kong.

Today, traveling with their U.S. partners (including ground, air, and attraction operators), they blitz overseas wholesalers and conduct press conferences for the overseas trade press and use the cooperative marketing programs of Foremost West, Go USA (the public-private overseas tourism promotion partnership) and the airlines.

The payoff: about 90% of their summer high season business now comes from overseas markets.

As you think about these examples and review your own perceptions of marketing, you may well wonder where they fit into our broader scheme of things. If marketing is what marketing people do, then it seems to be very different from the conceptual thinking we have been describing. Is there a connection?

Conceptual Connections

Marketing, as we have emphasized, is first of all a management philosophy that stands for a total commitment to guests. For Jenny, Candy, and the Blairs, this commitment establishes the context in which they work, defining for each of them the nature of the sales tasks they are undertaking. As a logical approach, it begins with guest needs affecting all of the decisions of the marketing mix, and establishes an organized, planned foundation that positions Jenny's, Candy's, and the Blairs' sales activities in a broader marketing context. As a function, marketing involves Jenny, Candy, and the Blairs in much more than sales. For example, the Blairs are involved with trade shows, press conferences, overseas tour operators, and the programs of Foremost West in their hospitality marketing activities.

All three examples illustrate some of the real day-to-day work of marketing as marketers interact with guests, suppliers, wholesalers, and others in a search for mutually profitable business. That is part of the nuts-and-bolts context of marketing. Although we are much concerned with the broader or conceptual aspects of marketing (doing the right things), it is essential to keep in mind the implications of our choices for the day-to-day practice of marketing (doing things right).

How Is Marketing Organized?

Generalizing from the above examples, it is not surprising that marketing is often equated with sales or promotional activities. But this captures only part of marketing. In considering how marketing is organized in a hospitality context, let us begin with typical organizations, and then identify what these typical structures tend to leave out.

Where is marketing positioned in hospitality organization charts, and what does it do in smaller as well as larger enterprises? In most small businesses, the owners or managers do the work of marketing. A typical structure for a mid-size organization is shown in Exhibit 5. You can see the clearly defined hierarchy of positions beginning with the General Manager (Chief Operating Executive) and

Exhibit 5 Typical Organizational Structure for a Mid-Size Organization

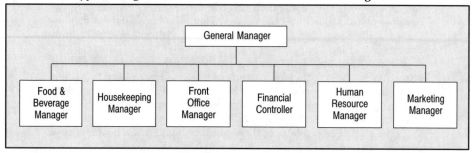

Exhibit 6 Typical Marketing/Sales Organization Chart for a Mid-Size Property

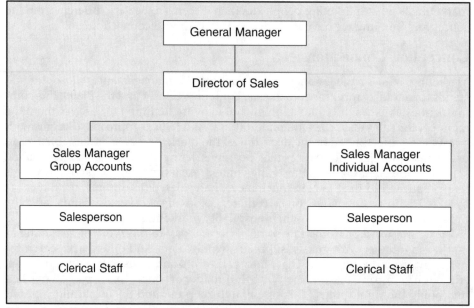

Source: James R. Abbey, *Hospitality Sales and Marketing*, Third Edition (Lansing, Mich.: Educational Institute of the American Hotel & Motel Association, 1998), p. 86.

continuing down through the major functional areas of food and beverage, housekeeping, front office, finance, human resources, and marketing. Exhibit 6 presents a typical marketing/sales function for a mid-size property. For a larger or more sophisticated operation, the chart might take the form shown in Exhibit 7. In both cases, the marketing function is largely sales and promotion. A slight variation on this structure is used in a Sydney hotel, where the marketing and front office activities are brought together, reflecting the selling responsibilities of front office staff and the need to coordinate sales, reservations, and front office systems.

As we look at these charts, questions arise about where some important marketing decisions are actually made. Decisions about new services or products do

Exhibit 7   Typical Marketing/Sales Organization Chart for a Large Property

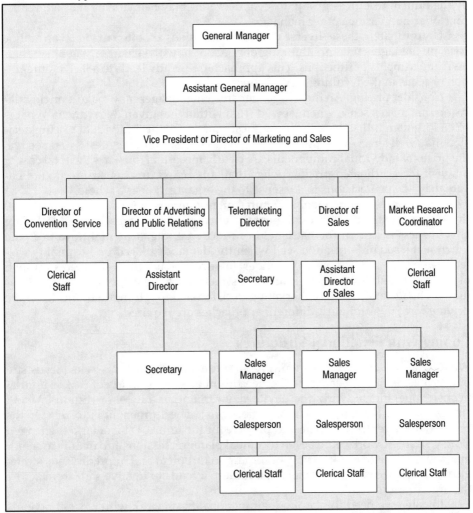

Source: James R. Abbey, *Hospitality Sales and Marketing*, Third Edition (Lansing, Mich.: Educational Institute of the American Hotel & Motel Association, 1998), p. 87.

not seem to be any single person's direct responsibility. Instead, various marketing decisions are spread throughout an organization.

   For example, decisions about the availability, location, and time of service are partly made by food and beverage (room service), housekeeping, and the front office (check-in times). Strategic choices relating to how services are delivered flow from the sales office or from senior management. The whole range of communication decisions, such as advertising and promotion, often falls to sales. Guest relations, however, may be placed in the front office or with the General Manager. Public relations is often located in sales, but can also be under the General Manager.

Staff relations (training and internal marketing programs) will usually be handled by the human resources group. Pricing decisions may be made by marketing, the controller, and various other managers.

Unfortunately, these diverse marketing decisions are often made on an ad hoc basis by managers who are thinking only about how the changes will affect their own departments or functions. This approach frequently leads to a lack of integration or focus in the resulting service concepts.

Consider pricing. An individual department manager may make a pricing decision that makes sense when viewed from within that given department. What is often forgotten is that, by affecting a guest's *total* cost, this individual pricing decision may well affect every other department. That is, from the guest's perspective, the prices of individual components are clearly important, but so is the total cost of the visit. A coordinated pricing policy that cuts across functions is needed to ensure that pricing decisions make sense to the organization as a whole.

Unfortunately, functional structures often interfere with the cross-functional thinking needed to provide a coherent variety of products and services. Marketing effectiveness is lost on the battlefield of functional (departmental) loyalties. The functional structure did quite well when the demands placed on hospitality systems were more predictable and routine. However, today's markets are losing much of their predictability, and the functional structures that enforce routine responses inhibit change and effective marketing decision-making. If marketing is to be the driving force in hospitality, different approaches are required.

Coping with Functional Structures

What organizational format should replace functional structures? The jury is still out. Problems arise because of the need to manage two kinds of tasks simultaneously: operational work (the day-to-day running of a hotel or restaurant) and strategic work (having longer time horizons). The former aims to master the present, the latter to anticipate and prepare for the future. When markets changed slowly, strategic work could be left to annual planning sessions and mainly to senior managers. But with markets now becoming so turbulent and unpredictable, strategic work has become continuous. In addition, it tends to involve staff from across the organization.

To cope, we need to overlay the functional framework with cross-functional teams and working alliances through which strategic work can be tackled. It is not possible to show this new organization in a simple diagram; in any event, formal organization charts tell only part of the story.

Where does this leave us? The sales and promotional work that is usually done under the name of marketing is clearly operational in nature and is captured in the functional charts that we have considered. The broader aspects of marketing decisions such as product and service planning, pricing, distribution, opportunity assessment, availability planning, and so forth tend to cross functional boundaries. They require coordinating mechanisms, such as committees, working parties, project teams, and so on. The extended view of marketing that we have been considering leads frequently to strategic work, and as such, it fails to gain a clear foothold in the functional structure.

Exhibit 8   Options for the Marketing Function

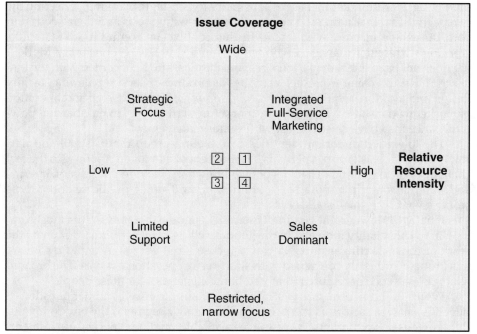

Adapted from Nigel Piercy, *Market-Led Strategic Change* (London: Thormann, 1991), p. 148.

To explore the broader issues of organizational design raised here would take us too far afield. Our main concerns are to alert you to the ramifications of a strong commitment to marketing and thus to guests and to point out that, in designing functional marketing departments or groups, several options exist, as is suggested in Exhibit 8. In Exhibit 8, the horizontal axis shows the resources allocated to marketing, including staff, time, and money, relative to other hospitality businesses of similar size. The vertical axis shows the range of issues dealt with by the marketing team. For a small business, the relevant resources include the time that the owner/manager is able to spend on marketing activities, relative to similar small enterprises. Thus, for example, the Blairs of Wyoming, who own four small properties, may well spend a higher proportion of their time in sales activity than do the owners of comparable properties. The vertical axis deals with the range of issues to which marketing is expected to make a substantial contribution. This reflects the view of marketing as a business philosophy and as a logic, with the capacity to integrate ideas and issues that touch many other functions.

Using this chart, we can identify four different forms of marketing organization. In the upper right quadrant lies the integrated full-service marketing group. Responsibility for sales and promotion is only part of its work. Its involvement extends to the full range of marketing factors and alternatives, with substantial strategic and operational components. It has significant resources and real clout in the firm.

The upper left quadrant suggests a very different view of the formal role of marketing. Here, marketing has responsibility for strategic planning, reflecting the perspective that marketing is concerned not only with guests and their needs, but with the whole macro environment. In this context, marketing has a staff role, working with senior managers who have overall strategic responsibility. Marketing does not have direct operational responsibilities, but is concerned with the longer term issues arising from such activities as product or service planning, facility design and location, acquisition or takeover options, and the design and operation of marketing data bases. Typically, the marketing staff is small in number, but powerful, since they have close contact with senior management.

The lower left quadrant identifies a marketing group that is small and narrowly focused. This group is perhaps best thought of as a token response to the real challenges of marketing. Their responsibilities may include analysis of internal and external data, planning sales promotion, and other public relations type work—typically a small staff service role.

Finally, the lower right quadrant identifies a model that is by far the most common in the hospitality industry. In this model, selling responsibilities dominate the work of the marketing group. Narrowly focused, but with substantial resources, this group is primarily concerned with short-term, operational issues. The broader strategic matters that require integrated handling are not for these people!

Which of these formats is best? There is no simple answer to that question. It depends on such factors as the particular hospitality segment, the environments, the demands of key markets, the resources available, and the experience and talents of management. What is important is simply that *the critical work of marketing has to be done somewhere in the organization.* If the marketing function is narrowly defined, the broader marketing work associated with the marketing philosophy must still be performed by someone. This work has to be coordinated and integrated with the work of all functional areas, and the right balance must be sought between managing the present and creating the future. When strategic marketing matters are neglected, hospitality businesses pay a high price.

Toward More Effective Hospitality Marketing

We conclude this chapter with a few comments directed at making hospitality marketing more effective both in terms of management's conception of marketing and in terms of practical application.

Marketing as a High-Risk Necessity

Putting guest needs first is much easier said than done. In the short term, hospitality businesses face relentless pressure to reduce costs. This pressure invites a trade-off between costs and service that can work against the needs of the guest. In the long term, putting guests first opens the door to change because guest needs and priorities change, competitors change, and hospitality environments change.

Building hospitality enterprises that are truly responsive to guest needs means willingness to go where they go, which is ultimately a commitment now to an uncertain future. It involves risk, uncertainty, and self-doubt. But the value of this commitment to an uncertain future has substantial empirical support, for research indicates that outstanding successes in services are inevitably customer driven. While successful managers do indeed keep a very careful eye on productivity and costs, they also understand customer priorities and are dedicated to optimizing guest satisfaction.

In fact, studies show that outstanding service companies achieve exceptional levels of customer satisfaction, create strong staff and customer loyalties, and use them to build high levels of profitability. The three interrelated elements of people, customer satisfaction, and profits appear time and again as the central themes in the strategies implemented by highly successful service enterprises. Marketing may be high risk, but going where changing guest wants and needs lead is a key to success.

Guests as Assets

We do not normally think of guests as assets. Yet, according to the philosophy and logic of marketing, guests rank among the most important of all assets. Loyal guests are reflected in market share, sales, and profitability. They truly bestow value on company assets and ultimately determine what a company is worth. Yet, guests do not appear on the balance sheet. The assets that *do* appear (such as computers, furniture, equipment, supplies, and buildings) attract significant management attention. Our point is that the care and maintenance of the customer base is at least as important as the care and maintenance of physical assets.

What creates asset value? Computers, buildings, furniture, and supplies have value when they create or support hospitality products and services that guests buy. In other words, guest reactions make items valuable or worthless. When guests refuse to purchase hospitality offerings, the ingredients and products used to make them lose value.

Similarly, under the logic of marketing, expenditures on marketing activities such as advertising, selling, and merchandising are not merely costs as accounting statements suggest. They are investments in generating loyal guests, developing market share, and creating repeat purchases. As such, they are often pivotal determinants of hospitality success. They can directly affect the worth of a hospitality business. Compare the asset value of a local McDonald's, which has benefited from extensive marketing, with that of any number of competing local hamburger outlets. The additional value of the McDonald's is largely a marketing creation.

Guests are indeed important hospitality assets and should be treated as such. It is far less expensive to maintain loyal, satisfied guests than to attract new ones. While problems will inevitably arise, every effort should be made to anticipate and prevent them. When prevention fails, guests should be offered reasonable redress.

Hospitality Marketing Checklist

How can hospitality businesses determine whether they are using marketing to good advantage? Exhibit 9 offers a practical, convenient management checklist. We shall comment briefly on each of the guidelines.

Effective hospitality marketing starts with guests and then works back to designing the enterprise and its offerings, rather than simply offering guests what the company has or can produce readily.

Exhibit 9   Hospitality Marketing Checklist

- Work back from guests to the hospitality enterprise.
- Clearly state and communicate company values.
- Set high service standards.
- Remain close to guests.
- Develop an innovative climate.
- Value employees and empower them.
- Focus on action, not analysis.
- Seek organizational clarity and simplicity.
- Maintain flexibility.
- Be future-oriented.
- Diversify carefully.
- Rethink the enterprise.

Company values should be clearly stated, understood, and communicated to all. They provide realistic guidelines for daily operations and actions. Employees should understand what the company is all about, particularly its perception of the primacy of guests.

Management should set high but achievable standards. Companies should strive to extend themselves and improve continuously. Accepting mediocrity breeds decline. Once a company is on the down slope, reversing the trend can be difficult, time-consuming, and costly.

Maintaining close contact with guests furnishes valuable information and guidance. It provides an understanding of how well the company is serving guests and what it should be doing. Close contact provides a feel for markets and opportunities.

Hospitality companies should strive to develop and maintain a climate that encourages employee creativity, innovation, and entrepreneurship. This implies empowering the staff and accepting reasonable market risks, which, of course, means some failures. Innovation is the engine of change, the very lifeblood of hospitality ventures.

Hospitality providers must accept the fact that employees make the difference. Employees can either make or break guest service encounters as they implement marketing programs. They are among the most important of all hospitality assets and should be trained and empowered to deal effectively with guests.

The analysis of markets and marketing data, and the resulting information and knowledge, are important assets. However, they must not be confused with results. Research, computers, guest profiles, market trends, and financial statements are very useful management *tools,* but they are not substitutes for marketing *action.* Marketing actions yield results—market analysis does not.

Similarly, marketing organizations are not ends unto themselves. They exist to facilitate effective marketing actions. Marketing organizations should be kept lean.

Adding poorly conceived marketing activities and the staff to carry out those activities adds costs and complexities without increasing effectiveness. Marketers should strive for clarity and simplicity in developing organizations, adhering to the architectural dictum that form follows function. Too often, marketing activities and departments just seem to grow, taking on self-perpetuating bureaucratic lives of their own.

Centralization induces rigidity, the antithesis of the organizational flexibility necessary to meet opportunities quickly in dynamic markets. Centralizing marketing activities should only be done with great care, because hospitality businesses need the freedom and capacity to deal with local needs. To the extent possible, flexibility and decentralization are the preferred organizational guidelines.

marketers should keep their sights firmly fixed on the future: ᴵre guests, future markets, and the future opportunities they t year's sales and profits, all we can do is learn from them. Marᵇility is to enhance future profitability.

ifying, whether regionally or functionally, hospitality enterprises ᵉe that they understand the new markets or business involved. or joining other companies, the guideline is to "bring something ᴵis means such things as being better able to capitalize on assets, efficient, or doing some things better than competitors. An examᴵopment of networks of cooperating hotels that create guest conveᵉncy, and savings through common reservation systems, joint ᴵampaigns, and coordinated vacation packages.

ᴵg managers should play a leadership role in getting hospitality busiᴵink, reorient, and reinvent themselves continuously. In that way, they ever more guest driven, reflecting changing guest needs, new environrent technologies, and emerging market opportunities. This is all part ng a change culture.

tality marketers may assess how well their businesses are carrying out the marketing philosophy by applying the above guidelines and realistically evaluating their situations. By making such assessments regularly and honestly, hospitality managers will have a good idea of what improvements might be in order.

Concluding Comments

Success and leadership in the hospitality industry and effective marketing go hand in hand. Marketing's goal of guest satisfaction is the essence of hospitality. Hospitality marketing is much more than sales. We define hospitality marketing as a system designed to plan, price, promote, and make available to selected markets hospitality products and services in the form of benefits and experiences that create satisfied guests and achieve organizational objectives. The marketing orientation represents a fundamental approach, a way of life, for effective hospitality companies.

Over time, various approaches to hospitality marketing have been developed. The provider, sales, promotion, and marketing orientations approach marketing from different perspectives and focus on different elements. The marketing orientation is the most recent development and the most effective in today's marketplace. Here management thinking starts not with bricks and mortar, but with such considerations as guest needs, desires, interests, and expectations. Hospitality businesses are seen as guest-satisfying processes rather than goods-producing processes.

Marketing may be considered from three perspectives: as a philosophy of operation, as a logic for hospitality businesses, and as a business function. Operating under the marketing philosophy means a fundamental transformation in the way that many hotels, restaurants, and recreation/leisure companies are run. The commitment to do so starts at the very top and involves shifts in the way managers approach their decisions, how organizations function, and the manner in which people carry out their responsibilities.

The marketing logic focuses on creating and effectively delivering the right hospitality services and products when and where guests want them at prices they are willing to pay. It is involved with the decisions and actions that design a company's marketing mix, its offering to the marketplace. Developing a marketing mix is one of the critical responsibilities of marketing executives. It is a complex and difficult task involving two perspectives—the overall mix and each submix.

Marketing as a function is both an activity and a name for part of an organization. In smaller hospitality organizations, owners often do the work of marketing, while in large organizations, extensive marketing departments exist involving various marketing specialties and specialists. The place where important marketing decisions are actually made depends on the specific situation and company. Generally, marketing decisions are spread throughout an organization. Functional structures often interfere with the cross-functional thinking so necessary for marketing effectiveness. Marketing decisions benefit from coordinating mechanisms such as project teams, working parties, and committees.

Four different approaches to the formal role of marketing in organizations can be identified. They are the full-service marketing group, the strategic planning focus, the small and narrow focus, and the selling domination. The best approach for a specific hospitality business depends on many factors, such as the environments, hospitality segments, key markets, resources, and management talents. Regardless of the organizational approach and formal marketing role adopted, truly outstanding hospitality companies work at achieving exceptional levels of guest satisfaction and loyalty.

Endnotes

1. Personal interview, August 1994.

2. *The Practice of Management* (New York: Harper & Row, 1954), pp. 37–39.

3. *Marketing News*, 29 February 1988, p. 2.

4. *Marketing News.*

5. Glenn Hasek, *Hotel and Motel Management,* 19 February 1996, pp. 1, 33.

6. Personal interview, August 1994.

7. "Marketing Myopia," *Harvard Business Review,* July–August 1960.

8. "Marketing Roundtable," *Restaurant Management*, March 1988, pp. 32, 34.

9. Patrick Ryan, "Get Rid of the People and the System Runs Fine," *Smithsonian*, Sept. 1977, p. 140.

10. *The Wall Street Journal*, 25 October 1993, p. A20.

11. This story is told in Bill Scatchard, *Upsetting the Applecart* (Tampa, Fla.: First Effort Books, 1992).

12. *The Successful Hotel Marketer*, January 1993.

Key Terms

hospitality marketing—a total system designed to plan, price, promote, and make available to selected markets hospitality products and services in the form of benefits and experiences that create satisfied guests and achieve organizational objectives.

marketing mix—the totality of a hospitality company's offerings to the marketplace to satisfy guests' wants and needs.

marketing orientation phase—the management perspective approach now being used by leading hospitality companies, which places the emphasis on guest wants and needs. This phase was brought on by a significant increase in other businesses adopting marketing approaches and hospitality markets becoming more competitive.

promotional orientation phase—a phase during which the hospitality industry broadened the sales orientation to recognize the importance of mass marketing activities, yet still neglected the primacy of guest wants and needs.

provider orientation phase—a phase during which the hospitality industry was focused on internal operations, activities, and procedures, and guests were expected to adjust to the hospitality offerings instead of the offerings being adjusted to the guests.

sales orientation phase—a phase during which the hospitality industry concentrated on aggressively increasing business (paying less attention to profit than to volume) and featured such things as competitive pricing, convenient locations, and drive-through windows.

Review Questions

1. What is hospitality marketing? What is its main goal?

2. What are the three fundamental ways of looking at hospitality marketing? Why is each perspective important?

3. What are the four phases of hospitality marketing? What approach do leading hospitality companies use today?

4. What is the purpose of the marketing philosophy? How does it differ from traditional marketing approaches?

5. What is marketing logic and what is it concerned with?

6. What is the marketing mix? Why is the marketing mix among the most fundamental reponsibilities of marketing executives?

7. How are marketing functions organized is hospitality businesses? How can functional structures interfere with marketing effectiveness?

8. How can hospitality businesses determine whether they are using marketing to good advantage?

Internet Sites

For more information, visit the following Internet sites. Remember that Internet addresses can change without notice.

Denny's
http://www.dennysrestaurants.com

Hilton Hotels Corp.
http://www.hilton.com

Marriott International
http://www.marriott.com

McDonald's Corp.
http://www.mcdonalds.com

Pizza Hut
http://www.pizzahut.com

Rihga Royal Hotel New York
http://ny.rihga.com/

Rihga Royal Hotels
http://www.rihga.com/

Ritz-Carlton Hotel Company
http://www.ritzcarlton.com

Walt Disney Corporation
http://www.disney.com

Chapter 2 Outline

2

Service: the Centerpiece of Hospitality Marketing

"It used to be location, location, location! Now it's service, service, service! We're fulfilling the promise; we are doing what hotels are supposed to do."

—Frank A. Banks, General Manager,
Rihga Royal Hotel, New York[1]

HOSPITALITY MARKETING is closely related to services marketing. Understanding services marketing provides valuable perspectives and guidelines for hospitality managers.

In services marketing, company personnel are the critical factor in seeing that targeted guests receive quality services. They are determinants of success or failure. As J. Willard Marriott, Sr., stated, "If you take care of your people, they will take care of your customers, and your business will take care of itself."[2]

Marketing's major concern is to satisfy customers at a profit, and exchange is its central concept. This underlying logic is the same for both services and products. Despite this similarity, however, product marketing and services marketing differ greatly. In product marketing, tangible products dominate. Although product marketing may involve services, it does so only to a limited extent (even when products are customized). Moreover, product decisions are often made by managers who are remote from final consumers—who are separated by "supermarket shelves." Product marketing often reduces or eliminates human interactions through such techniques as automation and self-service.

In contrast, services are intangible (although they are usually offered in conjunction with tangible products). Services are experiences rather than physical products. Service-dominated exchanges are quite different from product-dominated exchanges. While products can be (and usually are) created in a location separate from customers, services cannot be separated from customers. Services involve interactions of at least two people—the provider and the receiver. Service providers—whether door attendants, bell persons, concierges, or food and beverage servers—are often the ultimate determinant of a service organization's marketing effectiveness. Successful services marketing lies in the occasions in which service providers and customers interact in the course of transactions. Services marketing must take into account complex sets of people-related skills that

Exhibit 1   The Product/Services Marketing Spectrum

Tangible	Intangible
Products	Services

Frozen Foods	Airlines	Restaurants	Travel Agents
Fast Food Outlets		Resorts	

are often absent from product-marketing settings. The variables involved in services marketing are generally more complex and less predictable than those of product marketing.

> Although many hospitality businesses *talk* about the importance of their staff, few actually conduct their businesses accordingly. Chick-fil-A, the rapidly-expanding Atlanta-based fast-food chain, is one that does. Recognizing the critical importance of employee commitment and loyalty to extending good service and pleasing guests, Chick-fil-A shares productivity gains with employees. Its operators earn 50 percent more than its competitors do, and its employee turnover is a low five percent, compared with 35 percent for its competitors.[3]

Exhibit 1 presents marketing as a spectrum bordered by pure product marketing (involving only tangible elements) at one end and pure services marketing (involving only intangible elements) at the other. These endpoints are more abstract than real because in practice most marketing activities deal with a mixture of both products and services. Hospitality marketing falls toward the services marketing end. In other words, while hospitality exchanges may involve both tangibles and intangibles, intangibles dominate and guests often take away from their exchanges little other than their experiences. Getting the exchanges right, time after time after time, is the ultimate hospitality marketing task.

All of the marketing activities performed in marketing products also pertain to marketing services. In addition, services marketing always entails an important "people" element that is not as prevalent (and may be lacking altogether) in product marketing. In this sense, the marketing of services is more challenging and demanding than marketing products. Since services marketing embraces both the marketing of tangibles and intangibles, product marketing may be thought of as a special case of the more general and complex subject of services marketing. That perspective, while unconventional, points out the importance of service and personal factors in hospitality marketing.

In the eyes of guests, hospitality enterprises stand or fall on the cumulative impact of the many **service encounters** in the course of a visit. In the world of hospitality, *the service encounter is the basic marketing building block.* These encounters are essential in designing and implementing effective hospitality marketing programs. Seen from this perspective, marketing touches almost every aspect of the hospitality business through its fundamental concern with the success of each service encounter. Hospitality marketers—that is, service providers throughout an organization—are challenged to ensure that every service encounter is a winner for both guests and providers. The important point is that hospitality marketing is indeed everyone's concern.

This chapter focuses on service encounters and on how to manage them. In discussing hospitality services, we shall work toward developing an understanding of how the service encounter leads to competitive advantage and underpins long-term marketing strategies. With this in mind, we will analyze the service encounter, evaluate its components, and determine the elements necessary for successful, profitable hospitality operations.

> "SAS [Scandinavian Airlines System] is not a collection of material assets, but the quality of the contact between an individual customer and the SAS employees who serve the customer directly. Last year, each of our ten million customers came in contact with approximately five SAS employees and this contact lasted for an average of fifteen seconds each time. Thus, SAS is created fifty million times a year, fifteen seconds at a time. These fifty million moments of truth are the moments that ultimately determine whether SAS will succeed or fail as a company. They are the moments when we must prove to our customers that SAS is their best alternative."—Jan Carlzon, CEO, Scandinavian Airlines System[4]

Service Encounters and Service Chains

To illustrate the complexity of the task facing hospitality marketers, consider two recent examples in our experience:

> We were tired. After a long flight to reach a remote resort, we wanted nothing more than to settle into a comfortable room and begin to relax. We emerged from the air terminal as dusk was falling and found ourselves overwhelmed by an enthusiastic young woman who sorted arriving guests and their luggage into groups by resort. After ten minutes of confusion, a bus pulled up and we boarded and prepared to depart.
>
> But the bus wouldn't start for another thirty minutes because of mechanical problems. When we eventually arrived at the resort, there was only one person working at the front desk and it seemed to take forever to register. We were offered a glass of orange juice, but what we wanted was privacy, relaxation, and a beginning to a holiday. After twenty minutes in line, we registered. Our luggage was nowhere in sight, but we were told it would be delivered to the room.

> The resort was beautifully laid out with canals, bridges, and ponds. We rapidly became lost, but a *guest* helped us find our room, which was beautiful. We anxiously waited for our luggage, which didn't arrive for more than forty minutes.

Did it *have* to begin that way? Successful marketing of hospitality services requires careful planning and proper implementation of each service encounter in the total sequence of activities and systems that each service provider deals with. The problems we encountered were not with the staff we met, but with inadequate supporting systems, procedures, and training.

On a more positive note:

> A few years ago, we stopped overnight at a hotel in San Jose. That evening in the hotel restaurant, we had the salad to end all salads—and our vivid memory of it remains. The server built the salad from a trolley with an enormous range of options. He advised us of our choices while carefully tossing the salad and adding ingredients. The salad was an event in itself, a culinary feast unexpectedly presented with touch of theater. We felt the urge to applaud. The memory of an unexpected pleasure has remained with us over the years.

This example illustrates flexibility, innovation, and creativity in satisfying guest wants and needs. It shows how powerful the service encounter can be and how one service provider can make such a great difference.

Similar examples are part of the repertoire of any traveler. While individually memorable, they add up to overwhelming impressions of superb or disastrous service, of met and unmet expectations. Unfortunately, most of the service encounters remembered and talked about refer to things that have gone spectacularly wrong. Guests do not seem to recall readily most of their ordinary service encounters where things went pretty much as expected. Moreover, each successful encounter confronts hoteliers and restaurateurs with a short, never-to-be-repeated opportunity. Unlike situations involving the repeated purchase and use of standardized branded products, the provision of services results in unique interactions and situations, making it more difficult to reinforce positive experiences in guests' minds.

Jan Carlzon, soon after he became CEO of Scandinavian Airlines System, visited the CEOs of many U.S. airlines and found that they fell into two groups. There were those who almost immediately discussed aircraft planning, focusing on the utilization of tangible assets. Then there

> "were those who, even if you pushed them, after one hour ... didn't want to talk about ... aircraft. They talked about the business in the marketplace, the customer. They talked about human resources in their companies as their tools to create ... good service."[5]

The latter focused on the use of intangible assets, especially their staffs, and saw customers as the income-generating assets of great potential value. Moreover, Carlzon found that the airlines with CEOs in the second group were the only ones that were profitable!

That insight has rich meaning for the hospitality industry. The conventional perception of a hospitality property is to consider the building, its site, furnishings, and specific features—the tangible, visible assets—as the business. Indeed, the very language we use in talking about a hotel, restaurant, or resort as a *property* or *site* supports this way of thinking. We use words that connote visible, tangible assets, reflecting the image of hospitality businesses that we carry around in our minds. Instead, we should view physical or tangible assets merely as frameworks within which the really important business of hospitality marketing—the provision of intangible services—takes place.

In other words, the physical features of hospitality offerings, however distinctive, provide only the context within which services are rendered. It is largely services that differentiate the hospitality offerings of competing providers, although the physical aspects may support or enhance services through design, atmosphere, imagery, space, color, information, or data systems. Sometimes they help by simply moving, carrying, feeding, or bedding guests efficiently. Nonetheless, physical infrastructures, organizations, and information and other systems, while important, assume supportive or ancillary roles. This concept is central to effective hospitality marketing.

What this means is that hospitality marketing's focus is not just towering atriums, lakes, lobbies, and golf courses. Rather, it is carefully conceived concepts of services delivered consistently to all guests, especially those from strategically selected target markets.

Hospitality Services

It is important to distinguish between the *types* of hospitality services offered and the *quality* of the services delivered. All hotels and restaurants offer certain types of hospitality services; the types and number of services may vary by property. Beyond these differences, however, the quality of service extended by hospitality institutions varies greatly. The outstanding service that guests receive in the Regent, Oriental, and Peninsula hotels of Hong Kong, long recognized as among the best in the world, eclipses similar services offered by most other hotels. The manner in which similar services are carried out, whether registration, housekeeping, or concierge activities, is an extremely important marketing component. Small things and attention to detail make for great differences.

Quality service means satisfying guests by meeting and exceeding their desires and expectations. Superior service is fundamental to superior hospitality marketing. However, achieving and maintaining high service quality is a demanding hospitality challenge.

The fact that even good service is not all that common gives excellent service providers an important marketing edge. Service is a most important factor in generating hospitality differentiation for it bestows market uniqueness, builds customer loyalty, and pays long-term dividends. To achieve truly effective hospitality marketing, guest service must become an obsession, a passion.

A service philosophy embodies the basic management conviction that outstanding service pays off. Top management must believe that quality service is directly related to the bottom line. Unless this is so, an organizational commitment to excellent service will not exist. Top management, by signaling its desire to invest in

Exhibit 2   Elements of the Service Chain

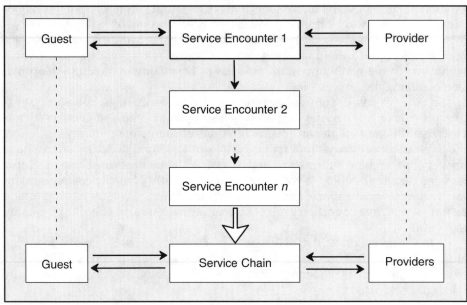

outstanding service and to continually improve service quality, sets the tone for the whole organization.

Despite the supposed industry-wide recognition that service quality is important, surveys and guest complaints suggest that hospitality service may actually be deteriorating. Guests commonly complain that they can't get quality service anymore and that hospitality service standards are being eroded.

Planning the Hospitality Service Encounter

We have emphasized that service involves interactions between hospitality service providers and guests in a series of service encounters. These encounters make up a **service chain** (see Exhibit 2). At each stage of the service chain, interactions occur between guests and hospitality providers. These experiences are affected by such factors as attitudes, skills, expectations, desires, and personalities. Guests bring a sense of anticipation to the encounter. Hospitality providers bring people, training, and other resources, along with an understanding of management hopes. When the actions of hospitality providers meet or exceed guest desires and expectations, the service encounter is successful. If a gap exists between anticipation and reality, then guest attitudes change for the worse.

When a gap occurs, hospitality marketers must turn negatives around. Since it is much harder to reverse negative attitudes than to reinforce positive ones, each service encounter needs to be a winner. The service goal is to offer the level of service that leaves guests wondering why other hotels or restaurants can't achieve a similar level of service. (Keep in mind, of course, that the advantage of outstanding service can be reduced or negated by inferior products.)

Recently, we encountered a gap between anticipation and reality during a dinner visit to a well-known restaurant chain that features a "bottomless salad bowl." According to restaurant policy, guests are greeted with a large bowl of salad and warm bread sticks when they order. This particular evening, our server arrived with a salad bowl that was about one-third full. When we commented on that, he replied forcefully, "I gave you more than I should have. It's a good thing that the manager didn't see me." As he continued, we noticed full salad bowls at the two nearby tables. He asked, "Do you know how expensive lettuce is now? The manager thinks that people are wasting too much salad." Just as he was making that point, another server passed with a heaping salad bowl for the table behind us. We looked at each other and just smiled. Neither our server's words nor his actions met our desires or expectations. A large gap existed that management may not have even been aware of.

To illustrate, consider the process of checking into a hotel. There will be a chain of service encounters that might break at any point. It might go something like this:

- Arrival at the front entrance
- Greeting
- Luggage handling
- Reception
- Trip to the room
- Entry into the room

Each of these events could easily be broken down into a more detailed list of activities. For the time being, however, these broad headings will suffice and we can consider how they are perceived by both the guest and management.

We recently spent two nights at an award-winning resort hotel that we were considering for a series of management development workshops. The five-year-old resort, part of a hotel chain, contained 55 suites, a range of function rooms, and a wide assortment of leisure and health facilities. A brief description of each encounter follows:

- *Arrival at the front entrance.* We had some difficulty in finding the resort as signs on the main road were limited and the resort was not marked on our maps. When we found the hotel and drove in, the single car space in front of the main door was occupied by an empty car—probably waiting for someone to move it to a parking spot.

- *Greeting.* There was no one at the entrance. My wife went inside to wait and with some difficulty found a seat.

- *Reception.* I approached the front desk and asked about our booking and luggage handling. The young woman behind the counter was most helpful and welcomed us to the hotel. We were told a little about the resort and our room in particular.

- *Luggage handling.* After some delay, during which I unloaded our baggage, a bell person appeared and moved the car ahead of us in the entrance. He then returned, found a trolley, and picked up our baggage.

- *Trip to the room.* The room was some distance from reception and, because the floor levels were uneven, the luggage trolley could not reach our room. The last stage of our trip to the room required carrying baggage up a flight of stairs and along a passage. During our walk, the bell person told us quite a bit about the resort and advised reserving a table at the restaurant if we intended to eat there.

- *Entry into the room.* The room was well prepared and much nicer than we had expected, with a very pleasant view across a small park. The bell person showed us where all the relevant controls were located and left.

Looking back over the impact of this chain of service encounters, our initial impressions were very negative. After we had settled into room, our initial perceptions of limited service were largely overtaken by the unexpected pleasure associated with the room we had been given. However, in a keenly competitive environment, too many things were allowed to go wrong. The resort could ill afford all of those early negative impressions, particularly given the ultimate reason for our visit.

What should be done to optimize guest satisfaction? As we will discuss in the following section, each service encounter must be analyzed in detail. Detailed analysis is time-consuming work, but it should be done to ensure that hospitality investments and the marketing activities and expenditures involved in bringing guests to the front door are not squandered because of poor attention to the service encounter once the guests arrive.

Consider the following situation. A major national restaurant chain developed a new pasta dish, engaged in extensive television advertising, and conducted a merchandising program involving a $5 off coupon. This part of the marketing program drew us to the restaurant. However, when we were seated, our server did not arrive, although several servers were standing around chatting. When our server finally approached us to take our order, he had a basket of buttered bread sticks, which we did not want. We requested the plain variety along with some water, and gave him our order. The server did not return for an inordinately long time, only appearing when our soup was ready. The unbuttered bread sticks did not arrive, and our entrée was taking a very long time. After an extraordinarily long delay, we asked another server, and eventually the hostess, about our order. Finally, our server arrived with our entrées but without the bread sticks. When asked, he mentioned something about a mix-up in the kitchen, explaining that the bread sticks would be out soon. They arrived with the check just as we were finishing our meal. On presenting the check, the server asked in a very perfunctory manner, "Was everything all right?" The service chain had broken down badly.

Guest perceptions of service translate into either repeat business or disappointment and perhaps bad word of mouth. Service encounters have the power to reinforce or destroy the effectiveness of hospitality marketing programs. Ultimately, managing services means managing service chains, which in turn involves managing details. The big picture matters, but attention to detail is the hallmark of superb hospitality marketing operations.

Taking the Service Encounter Apart

Hospitality service encounters vary in importance from the trivial to the critical. However, even trivial activities such as greeting guests in a hotel corridor may become less trivial when service providers refer to guests by name and engage them in conversation. Sometimes service encounters can be instrumental, as with checking in or out of a hotel. But such services can also be emotion-laden, as is the case with flattering service, name recognition, and the personal deference of the maître d' at a prestigious restaurant.

Hospitality service encounters may be simple or complex; standard or custom; low tech or high tech; remote or friendly; low or high skill; frequent or occasional. Such characteristics have a direct bearing on the success or failure of specific encounters. The challenge is to select those attributes that are most important to guests.

Marketers need a systematic way to identify critical components of each encounter in a service chain. This means raising questions and gathering information to deal with service situations more effectively. Examples of pertinent questions include:

- Exactly what happened?
- What are the guest reactions?
- Should it be done differently?
- What resources would be needed for optimal performance?
- What changes should be made?
- How can these changes best be put into effect?

Service Encounter Analysis: The Six S's

To improve service chains, we suggest gathering, organizing, and analyzing pertinent data according to the "six S's":

1. Specification
2. Staff
3. Space

4. Systems

5. Support

6. Style

Hospitality managers can ask questions about each factor in order to improve service. Below we briefly indicate the kinds of questions managers might ask. This list is merely suggestive, not exhaustive.

1. *Specification.* Specification means clearly describing the what, when, where, and how of service encounters. It requires careful thought about the links between particular service encounters in the service chain. Service encounter analysis begins by specifying clearly the overall service strategy and what it is designed to achieve. Does it focus on cost or service-quality leadership? Does it aim to provide unique service values, customized or standardized, complex or simple, frequent or occasional? Is the goal to provide service at any reasonable cost? Is service limited to luxury packages or does it include budget travelers?

2. *Staff.* Which staff members are involved in providing the service? What skills do they need? What training has been provided? How committed are they to service goals? Is team cooperation or individual empowerment required? What attitudes are appropriate—friendly, open, helpful, warm service or efficient, unobtrusive, uninvolving, nonthreatening service? What staff members deal with guests? How close are the backroom staff to guests? Are staff presentations and appearances appropriate? To what extent are guests involved in the provision of service? What skill, knowledge, information, or experience do guests need to fulfill their roles? What are likely guest expectations? What communication occurs between guest and service provider? Do the dynamics of the exchange proceed smoothly? Do any language and cultural barriers exist?

3. *Space.* Where will the service encounter occur? Is the space appropriately designed to facilitate the service encounter? Is there adequate space to handle each activity such as waiting, completing forms, storing or handling luggage, and assembling tours? Is signage appropriate? Is the decor attractive to guests and supportive of necessary activities that have to be carried out?

4. *Systems.* Is the information necessary to respond effectively to guests' needs readily available? Is the appropriate technology being fully used? Are the interfaces between different functions such as housekeeping, sales, and the front office fully operational? What measures of quality or performance are used? Are they the most helpful for both service providers and managers? Are the criteria for success clearly defined? Is everyone involved aware of guest needs and concerns?

5. *Support.* Are the service providers given the facilities and financial and human support needed to do the job? Is the technology appropriate? Have employees been given the training they need? Are incentive and reward systems

geared to the tasks to be performed? Is supervision supportive? Does the organizational structure help or hinder performance? Are the suggested procedures appropriate?

6. *Style.* How should the service encounter be conducted, given the organizational culture? Are the management styles and marketing orientations appropriate for the tasks? Do service providers have the appropriate attitudes? Is the right emphasis being placed on service quality?

Managers should develop their own checklists to guide and assess performance within specific service chains. These service chains should be considered from the perspective of major guest categories because the relevance and importance of specific factors may differ by groups of guests.

A challenging practical concern is how finely to deconstruct a service chain into its separate components—how much detail is needed? Too much detail not only takes excessive time and resources, but results in confusion rather than clarity. Conversely, when activity categories are too broad, they can disguise or minimize important problems. Achieving the right balance is a trying task.

As a general guideline, analyze the service chain to the extent that service encounters of operational and strategic significance are highlighted. To do so, four criteria may be used:

• Value creation

• Factors driving costs

• Effective differentiation

• Competitor innovation

Value creation relates to the perceived importance of service encounters to actual and potential guests. Where an activity creates significant aspects of total guest value, it should be treated as a separate encounter in a service chain. In our example, the failure to provide covered parking for more than one car and the absence of a door attendant would have become quite dissatisfying if the weather had been inclement.

Factors driving costs in a possible service encounter include what it costs to get the service encounter right and whether the cost is reasonable. Relevant cost factors should be analyzed separately when some elements are reasonable and others are prohibitive.

Differentiating one's service encounters from those of competitors may be very important. When a hospitality business does things that can be differentiated particularly well, or when its service encounters are unique and differentiable assets, they should be analyzed separately.

Competitor initiatives in performing the service may be analyzed. If one or more competitors have found particularly attractive or low-cost ways of handling a certain service, then it is worthwhile to examine that service encounter as a separate element.

When the encounters comprising a service chain are identified and the analysis suggested above is completed, management can then address the following three issues regarding each specific service encounter and the whole service chain.

1. Can we reduce costs and still maintain guest values?

2. Can we increase guest values while keeping costs constant?

3. Can we reduce the investment in required resources without increasing costs or reducing guest value?

Practical suggestions relating to these issues highlight possible productivity gains and profit opportunities.

Enhancing Service Quality—Bringing Managers and Guests Together

So far, we have tacitly assumed that management has an accurate understanding of guest needs and desires. But studies consistently show that this is not the case. The challenge is to bring guest perceptions and expectations into the management of hospitality service encounters and service chains. This requires linking management views and decisions to the service levels expected and received by guests. In this way, guests become active participants in decisions about both the quality of overall service encounters and the service chains.

The quality of hospitality service is quite difficult, but not impossible, to measure. Problems arise because hospitality services are heterogeneous, vary from guest to guest, server to server, and situation to situation, and as a result are exceedingly difficult to standardize. Moreover, since guests play an active role in service specification and delivery, hospitality service quality depends not only on service providers but also on their interactions with guests.

Despite these difficulties, research has identified five common dimensions of service quality that apply to hospitality situations, as well as measurable factors pertaining to each. They are:

1. The appearance or presentation of tangible elements that are part of the service

2. The reliability or dependability of the service

3. The responsiveness to guest needs

4. The assurance of those providing the service

5. The ability of those providing service to empathize with guests.[6]

The choice of which dimensions to use in investigating the service quality of a particular hotel or restaurant really depends on the specific situation. For example, in some cases, performance efficiency may be primary, while in others the ability to empathize may be paramount. Since these dimensions are a useful starting point for analysis, we shall detail various elements that contribute to each.

The general approach is to identify and measure service gaps. Service quality shortfalls arise where gaps occur, such as between guest expectations and services received, or between management and guest perceptions. The following discussion pinpoints where hospitality service gaps tend to occur.

The gap between guest expectations and management perceptions. In reality, many hospitality managers are too remote from guests or front-line service providers, lack research data about guest needs, and rely heavily on their personal experiences and observations. The resulting gap often translates into an overemphasis on certain hospitality factors, such as costs, and the neglect of others that are important to guests. This occurred recently when Continental Airlines's management, in an effort to reduce costs, stopped carrying aspirin on its flights, saving an estimated $20,000 a year. Customer complaints, however, were so numerous that the decision was reversed. An airline spokesperson commented, "The lesson [is]...that we listen to our customer...instead of focusing so heavily on costs."[7] When management accurately understands the service expectations of guests in a specific service chain, the resulting gap will be small.

The gap between management perceptions and the specification of service quality standards. Simply understanding guest interests, desires, and priorities is not enough. That understanding must be translated into clear specifications of service quality standards. Difficulties ensue when management fails to specify its expectations. Problems may also arise when the existing resources are inadequate to deliver the service quality specified. Examples include lack of parking space, not enough staff, inadequately trained staff, inadequate security, mediocre food, and so on. Technology may be helpful in both setting and applying appropriate standards. For example, guest databases may be used for improving front desk operations, equipping housekeeping operations, planning food and beverage offerings, designing fitness facilities, engineering menus, and scheduling operations.

The gap between specification of service quality and the service actually delivered. Specifying service quality is one thing; delivering it is quite another. Where staffs are unwilling or unable to meet management's service quality specifications, a gap occurs in service performance. The causes may include such factors as lack of training, misunderstanding, conflicting or unrealistic staff expectations, poor staff selection, poor supervision, and lack of empowerment. Service quality specifications must be based on realistic service delivery capabilities.

The gap between service delivered and service promised. Hospitality managers are challenged to live up to the service levels promised. An overenthusiastic sales campaign (perhaps initiated by those having little involvement with or awareness of the day-to-day delivery of service and the difficulties of living up to promises) can cause such a gap. Part of marketing's task is to manage guest desires and expectations so as to meet or exceed them. This task should bring marketing considerations and activities directly into daily involvement with each of the service delivery issues at each stage of service delivery processes.

Since marketing's task is to create satisfied guests, marketing is intimately concerned with quality service. But creating satisfied guests is a shared responsibility. Every staff member should appreciate the overriding necessity of creating satisfied guests through service quality, as well as the important role each staff member plays therein.

Concluding Comments

This chapter focuses on marketing of hospitality services and the critical service encounters. That is where all the marketing thought and planning meets the ultimate test—the delivery of hospitality services to guests.

While the marketing of tangible products and of intangible services have many similarities, service-dominated exchanges must take into account complex sets of people-related skills and embrace both tangibles and intangibles. Thus, service marketing can be more challenging and demanding than product marketing.

The delivery of hospitality service is an outcome of a managed service system designed to achieve desired objectives. An important component is top management's commitment to developing outstanding service. Given appropriate management and staff dedication, truly breakthrough service is possible. But that requires a focus on intangible assets such as customers and their needs and expectations, rather than on the usual tangible aspects such as buildings and physical infrastructures.

Service encounters, the interactions between guests and hospitality providers, are the links of service chains. At each stage of the service chain, guest expectations may be met, exceeded, or unmet. When they are unmet, management is challenged to turn negative situations around. To do so, analysis of the six "S's" of service encounters (specification, staff, space, systems, support, and style) can be helpful.

To enhance service quality, a clear understanding of guest needs and desires must be kept in focus. Managers can analyze five dimensions of hospitality service in their search for improvements: the tangible elements involved, reliability of service, responsiveness to guests, assurance of service providers, and guest empathy. Since hospitality marketing's task is to create satisfied guests, delivering quality service is a crucial component.

Endnotes

1. Personal interview, August 1994.

2. Roger Dow, "Motivating Employees Through TLC," quoted in *The Quality Service Handbook,* Eberhard E. Scheung and William F. Christopher, eds. (New York: American Management Association, 1993), p. 248.

3. *The Wall Street Journal,* 4 March 1996, p. A10.

4. Jan Carlzon, *Moments of Truth* (Cambridge, Mass.: Ballinger, 1987), pp. 2-3.

5. Cited in James L. Heskett, W. Earl Sasser, Jr., and Christopher W. L. Hart, *Service Breakthroughs* (New York: Free Press, 1990), p. 18.

6. Valarie A. Zaithaml, A. Parasuraman, Leonard L. Berry, *Delivering Quality Service: Balancing Customer Perceptions and Expectations* (New York: Free Press, 1990).

7. *The Wall Street Journal,* 14 May 1996, p. A8.

Key Terms

service chain—a series of service encounters between hospitality service providers and guests.

service encounter—an interpersonal exchange between a hospitality provider and a guest.

Review Questions

1. How do product marketing and services marketing differ? Where does hospitality marketing fit on the product/services spectrum? Why?

2. Why is the service encounter considered the basic marketing building block?

3. What is a service chain? How can it be positively and negatively affected?

4. What is the purpose of service encounter analysis? What are some questions hospitality managers might ask?

5. What are the five common dimensions of service quality that apply to hospitalty situations? How are they useful?

6. Where do hospitality service gaps tend to appear?

Internet Sites

For more information, visit the following Internet sites. Remember that Internet addresses can change without notice.

Chick-fil-A
http://www.chickfila.com

Marriott International
http://www.marriott.com

Rihga Royal Hotel New York
http://ny.rihga.com

Scandinavian Airlines System
http://www.sas.se

Chapter 3 Outline

Planning for Strategic Decisions in Hospitality Marketing
    A Case Study—The Russell Hotel
Marketing Mix: A Framework for Marketing Strategies and Decisions
    The Marketing Mix and Systems Thinking
    Marketing Mix Levels
Framing the Marketing Mix: Coping with Complexity
    SWOT Analysis
    Putting the ESC Grid to Work
Hospitality Marketing: Two Strategic Views
The Ethical Dimension
Concluding Comments

3

Hospitality Marketing Strategies

"No company is going to succeed without a clear set of tough-minded strategies grounded in a clear understanding of what's happening in the marketplace."

—Louis Gerstner, Jr., Chairman and CEO, IBM[1]

GENERAL BUSINESS STRATEGIES may be thought of as comprehensive guidelines or commitments that deal with the general thrust of a business and guide it toward its objectives. Similarly, hospitality marketing strategies can be seen as the blueprints that direct the marketing plans and actions of hospitality businesses. They are the master marketing plans, the overarching designs for achieving long-run success in marketing. Marketing strategies guide the allocation of marketing resources in the long run.

General business strategies and marketing strategies are closely related. Most business strategies have their roots in marketing because they are inextricably linked to marketing opportunities. Since marketing opportunities are always changing, reflecting dynamic market conditions, marketing strategies must also reflect basic shifts in market conditions. This requires management vision and creativity. In a sense, marketing strategies provide stability within change. They deal with basic general thrusts and directions that are relatively stable, while at the same time accommodating changes signaled by likely future developments and opportunities.

This chapter focuses on thinking strategically and developing and formulating effective marketing strategies. We will investigate the process of formulating effective hospitality marketing strategies and present tools and approaches for dealing with the complex and detailed information involved in developing successful strategies.

Planning for Strategic Decisions in Hospitality Marketing

We begin by looking at the steps involved in developing and implementing a hospitality marketing strategy. Typically, this process begins with a conceptualization stage. In this stage, managers try to understand their current business situation,

Exhibit 1   Strategic Planning Process

Marketing Audit
1. Corporate Objectives, Mission
2. Situation Analysis
   Environment
   Strategy
   Capability
3. Strengths, Weaknesses, Opportunities and Threats (SWOT) Analysis
4. Strategic Issues Identified

Choosing a Strategy
5. Options, Priorities

Building Marketing Plans and Budgets
6. Working Assumptions
7. Marketing Objectives, Mix
8. Estimated Outcomes
9. Functional, Project Plans, Budgets
10. Implementation and Measurement

how this situation is likely to change, and what might be done in the event of likely changes. At the second or implementation stage, ideas for action are turned into strategic (long-term) and tactical (shorter-term) plans that can be put into effect. These two stages deal with important questions underlying strategy formulation, such as where are we now, where do we want to be, and how can we get there? The **strategic planning process** (see Exhibit 1) answers these fundamental questions by leading hospitality managers from a consideration of their corporate mission and objectives to the implementation of plans and the measurement of the results.

The first five steps of the strategic planning process are concerned with developing the necessary understanding and analysis, with identifying the high-priority issues and finding the right strategic response. The search for strategy usually begins with a consideration of the business mission, corporate objectives, and policy commitments. The focus is on such business concerns as profit, market share, growth rate, markets to be served, alliances formed, resources acquired, skills developed, funding, the images of the business held by key stakeholders (guests, agencies, suppliers, wholesalers, employees), and social responsibility. These five steps deal with developing a clear understanding of the forces at work in each of the markets of interest, reviewing current strategies, and identifying the capabilities needed for the business to do what it hopes to do.

The first four steps of the strategic planning process are often undertaken as part of a **marketing audit,** which is a systematic, unbiased analysis of the environment and of the company's operations. This audit provides information for identifying market opportunities as well as company capabilities and deficiencies. (An important part of the process, commonly known as a SWOT analysis, is discussed later in the chapter.) As a result of the audit, strategic issues are raised and methods of dealing with them suggested. Internal analysis might point to various strategic issues such as those concerned with establishing a guest-driven information system, building a strong working alliance with a major tour wholesaler, restructuring the pricing program, or developing approaches to increase sales to local businesses. External analysis might consider issues like those arising from a natural disaster, a major change in legislation, a special tourism event, or the aggressive actions of a competing firm. Dealing with the challenges arising from both internal and external issues is part of the strategic planning process.

As a result of the marketing audit, management is able to identify options, establish priorities, and choose an appropriate strategic response. The creative insights of managers and staff are critically important here. As managers focus on a situation, consider the essential issues and challenges, assess company resources and capabilities, and think creatively about future possibilities and options, alternative strategic responses become clearer. Effective strategies to deal with the issues can be formulated. Sometimes the responses lead to the development of new strategic approaches or new ways of doing business that break through the limits imposed by conventional thinking.

The next five steps of the strategic planning process deal with translating these strategies into marketing plans and budgets that can be implemented directly. While arriving at the actual plans and budgets is not the focus of this chapter, we are interested here in the steps dealing with the assumptions, the marketing objectives and marketing mix, and the estimation of outcomes.

Strategic plans require specifying the important assumptions guiding units or managers. Working assumptions deal with such factors as an assumed rate of inflation, market growth, food and labor costs, the expected political climate, government actions, and competitive moves. When specified, such assumptions give managers at all levels a common starting point for their specific plans and budgets. In this way, the strategies of various departments can be translated into shorter-term actions that reflect company assessments of overall conditions.

The next step—a crucial one for our purposes—centers on developing specific marketing objectives and making decisions concerning products and services, pricing, promotion, communication, and networking links that, taken together, constitute the marketing mix or hospitality offer. Marketing objectives, of course, should complement both the overall company objectives and those of other critical hospitality functions. They deal with desired performance outcomes—profit contribution, sales, market share, growth rates—for the business as a whole and for each major product/service or market area.

Once these objectives are determined, decisions must be made about each aspect of the marketing mix. This important and demanding task reflects the strategic priorities identified earlier. Broad ideas must be translated into specific hospitality marketing programs and actions. To the extent possible, it is important to estimate the likely outcomes of adopting the programs being considered. This is always a difficult aspect of planning, because no one can predict with certainty what will happen if an action is taken or a program is instituted. The best that can be done is to consider the important factors carefully. Given management's best estimates of both risk and performance, marketing strategies can be selected, and the plans to carry them out can be specified.

At this point, the detailed work of preparing working plans and budgets, which we do not address in this chapter, begins. Specific subobjectives, actions to be taken, resources needed, and timing issues are stated. Plans may relate to specific markets, customers, services, projects, or functional areas, and they may lead to the development of short- or medium-term budgets.

The final step—implementing plans and budgets—is one of the most critical in the strategic planning cycle. This is where strategies and plans to carry them out are tested in the marketplace. In many situations, implementation involves change and adaptation to establish new routines and relationships. It also involves careful thinking about how a plan's success will be measured. Information gained from such measurements is used to adjust plans and to improve the strategic planning process itself.

These ten steps each play an important part in creating and implementing marketing strategies. Although we have presented them as a sequence, that is not how things always work in practice. In the dynamic world of hospitality, strategic planning systems must cope with the unexpected. Change will not wait until a system is ready to deal with it. When strategic issues arise unexpectedly and require immediate responses, management may enter the sequence at step 4 (strategic issues identified) and consider steps 1, 2, and 3 only to the extent feasible within time and resource limits. Management establishes the issue's context, importance, and priority and develops a basis for a planned response. Sometimes steps 5 to 10 may be carried out merely as adjustments to existing specified plans and budgets, rather than as an extensive process.

In practice, the strategic planning process sometimes works in reverse. It may move forward from the present to the future, rather than work through the usual process of going back from the future to the present. Managers may begin by considering whether what they are doing will continue to work and then develop a strategy around it. They evaluate whether current approaches will capitalize on business strengths, meet threats, address weaknesses, and build capabilities. If so, they may conclude that present strategies are in line with emerging issues and opportunities and are likely to lead to acceptable performance.

Regardless of the approach adopted, hospitality managers need to give specific attention to each step in the planning model. While the order of the activities may vary, the care and attention given to the details of the business and its environment must not waver.

A Case Study—The Russell Hotel

Strategic hospitality marketing decisions are concerned with two basic sets of choices: those that identify the guests whose wants and needs are to be served and those that determine what a hospitality business will offer in response to guest wants and needs. These choices lie at the heart of marketing strategy. Both are illustrated in the Russell Hotel case that follows. As you read through it, identify the guests whose needs are being served by the hotel and list the specific management decisions made to create their offer in response to the needs of their guests. Try to think of ways in which their offer could be improved from the point of view of guests, management, and owners. Consider the tradeoffs that have been made and whether they are justified.

The Russell Hotel is a 30-room boutique hotel located in the midst of one of Australia's premier tourist districts, The Rocks, in Sydney. It is within walking distance of the Sydney Opera House, the ferries, and trains and close to the central business district. About half of the hotel's guests come from overseas, and 70 percent of this half are Americans. The other half are Australians, usually on a repeat visit to the hotel. The following is an edited interview with Ms. Robyn Thurston, General Manager of the hotel.

RT: The hotel opened in 1982. We offered a service that was very different from what the Hilton or the Regent offered. The Sydney public got used to somewhere different to stay and they rather liked it.

Q: Do you think maybe they prefer the familiarity and personalized service and a kind of more friendly atmosphere?

RT: Oh yes. In regard to the service, there will always be both international and domestic guests who choose to stay in places like this. We have people here who have been coming for their wedding anniversary every year since it opened. As an example, the second weekend in August, we have four couples who come down from the country every year. They just love the hotel. They like us and they like the service we offer. Really, all we are offering is bed and breakfast, but we do it very well. We know all the guests who come in regularly and make the guests feel at home. We recognize them and know them and they don't need to fill out registration forms—we'll do all that for them. Guests get to have their favorite rooms. We keep guest history cards so that we know what their favorite rooms are. We send them information on specials and Christmas cards. That sort of thing is important and people like it.

Our housekeeper is really friendly, and all her staff are terrific. The room attendants say "Good Morning" to everyone, and "Did you have a nice day yesterday?" or "I hope you enjoy your day out today."

Q: Is this very nice restaurant downstairs part of the hotel?

RT: Yes. But we are only really offering bed and breakfast here. They get a nice room and breakfast downstairs. We sub-let the restaurant, which is run by a very nice fellow. Guests can use it and charge their dining bills to their room. He keeps our brochures downstairs, we keep his cards up here. People will have a look at the brochure and come upstairs to wander around. All our vacant rooms are left open so people can come in just off the street and look at the rooms. I don't need to take them around. People who are celebrating their honeymoon or wedding night or whatever can come in and chose a room they like without me standing in the background holding the door open.

Q: And I see that you have got a very nice electric kettle and a nice coffee maker. Are they in all the rooms?

RT: Not all of the rooms have teapots, but they have fresh coffee makers and Twinings tea bags. We have fluffy bathrobes in the wardrobes, the beds are turned down at night, chocolates on the pillow, fresh water put in, papers are complimentary, and there are fresh flowers in the rooms. The breakfast is a larger version of a continental breakfast with a large selection of fruits, tea, coffee, croissants, pastries, toasts, jams, marmalades, juices. Those sorts of things are standard and I think that's what the regular people really like. The international people who come here think, "Wow! Look at this location!" and then they think about the room. We have been getting 35 percent of our guests from North America. I'm sure that half of that is word of mouth!

Q: How do you go about marketing this place? For example, if you've got 35 percent North American guests, do the bookings come through travel agents?

RT: The majority come through travel agents. The Russell has pretty well honed its reputation and most travel agents who know the hotel feel quite confident in sending their clients here. We work very closely with the Australian Tourism Commission. They support us very well. We support them with advertising in their magazines that they distribute such as *Destination Australia, Travel Agents Manual*. When they have visiting journalists, we take part in their program so we get lots of journalists staying with us and of course that helps a lot.

Q: Because they will go back and write it up in *The New York Times* and so on?

RT: They might be from the *Iowa Times* or the *Florida Sun Sentinel* doing an article on alternative accommodation in Australia, or on Heritage Australia, or whatever.

   The reason we don't advertise in newspapers is that it virtually costs you the same amount of money for a one-day newspaper as it does for a magazine ad. A newspaper is thrown out after one day, whereas a magazine has a longer life. We don't have a huge advertising budget, so we can't afford to keep advertising in newspapers. However, in Canberra [about 300km from Sydney], which is booming, it's worth it because every weekend we sell four or five rooms to Canberra residents.

   But getting back to service, we are more about looking after the guest and the people who choose to stay here. That is why the business market is something we don't go after. Business men and women are usually quite demanding. You know, they'll want to come to the desk and check out immediately and fast, fast, fast and you don't have time for pleasantries. You are courteous, but you are becoming like a receptionist and always saying, "Thank you very much, Mr. Smith, just sign here." There's none of that thing here. When people check out here, it's "Hello, how are you, where are you off to today, and I hope you enjoyed Sydney." You can have a conversation with them.

Q: So it's a very relaxed mode?

RT: Yes, people who come here are usually on holidays and we nurture that with them. We tell them about Sydney. All of the people on the desk eat out regularly in Sydney and eat out very well, and we do not pass on information about dud restaurants, touristy restaurants. We tell them about the places we go to, whether it's the theaters and obscure pubs, bookshops, and places on Oxford Street that they might like. We are only doing as much as the concierge in a large hotel would do, except that it is more personalized because we are talking to them. We then ask them the next day, "How was it?" We pass on anecdotes from other guests. They know that I'm the manager and Michael is the assistant manager and they get to know the staff here. If they are here three days, we might see them ten times; in an international hotel, they might walk past the desk and see ten different people.

So if I can put them on to something that I would go to, they come back and say, "Thanks, that was just fantastic!" It's always gratifying when they enjoy it. I don't feel any reservation about doing it because I know what they are going to have is good, whereas I couldn't feel the same about sending them to some of the touristy places. It's not what The Russell is about! We are good Australian, honest, looking after people who have come for an Australian experience, but not the "G'day, mate."

Who are the customers of this hotel? It certainly does not appeal to all prospective guests, for many choose the Regent just up the road. It probably would not appeal to families with young children, to business travelers looking for efficiency, or to backpackers. It does appeal to a narrow market of older people, from Australia and overseas, looking for something personalized, special, and almost otherworldly.

In your list of the marketing decisions that made this hotel really special and a continuing success, you probably picked the following:

- The product/service concept—individualized, focused on a specific market, strong on service, with rooms that are "different" and with unexpected features that are valued by guests, located in a highly attractive area, with a great breakfast included.

- Networked links with travel agents, official tourism agencies, and other tourist facilities.

- Promotion through word of mouth, official tourism bodies, magazines, newspapers, journalist visits, but on a low budget.

- Market segment—individual guests and small groups, not business guests.

These decisions are integral parts of the marketing mix or market offer of the Russell Hotel. It is time to consider the marketing mix in more detail.

Marketing Mix: A Framework for Marketing Strategies and Decisions

The **marketing mix** provides a useful framework for understanding hospitality marketing strategies and decisions. It refers to a company's total offering to the markets it chooses to serve—its mix of controllable marketing variables that are directed to these targeted markets. We can think of hospitality executives as mixing marketing ingredients as a result of their decisions, and thereby creating a unique offering to the marketplace. Thus, the marketing mix is both a way to designate a firm's combination of marketing factors (such as advertising, pricing, and personal selling) and, by focusing attention on questions of "have we the right mix?", a means of increasing marketing efficiency and productivity.

Four important areas of decision making are involved:

1. *The product/service mix:* decisions about the benefits that will be provided to guests, including location, rooms, restaurants, menus, services provided, and airline connections.

2. *The pricing mix:* decisions about what these benefits will cost the guest, in terms of both money and time. Includes room rates for different categories of guests, service and other charges, decisions that determine the ease with which a guest can use the facilities, and such issues as the time spent waiting for service.

3. *The distribution mix:* decisions about how the guests will gain access to the benefits offered, perhaps through travel agents, airlines, tour wholesalers, or other packagers. Refers to the networks developed to bring prospective guests into a purchasing relationship with the hotel conveniently and efficiently.

4. *The promotion mix:* decisions about how guests will learn of the available benefits (an emphasis on word of mouth, television or other mass media, direct mail, personal selling, public relations activities, trade fairs and shows).

The marketing mix is the mechanism by which a hospitality enterprise, or part of it, serves targeted markets. It focuses on marketplace dynamics and ways of linking companies closely to guests and markets through market offerings. By altering the ingredients of the mix, organizations can adjust to changes in the marketplace.

Developing a marketing mix is one of the fundamental responsibilities of hospitality executives. It involves formulating and carrying out marketing strategies about the mix, developing marketing plans to put the mix into effect, and then developing the actual mix as a result of decisions about combinations of marketing factors. This basic responsibility concerns allocating and adjusting marketing inputs to create unique offerings that satisfy guest wants and needs and also achieve company goals.

While the concept is simple, the challenges of developing effective hospitality marketing mixes are complex and difficult. They involve consideration not only of controllable marketing variables, but also of influential external factors, such as economic, technical, social, and political factors, that lie outside a company's direct control.

The Marketing Mix and Systems Thinking

Developing an effective hospitality marketing mix is rooted in systems thinking. That is, it focuses on the effectiveness of the overall mix, which, as we noted earlier, comprises four interrelated subsystems or submixes: the product/service mix, the pricing mix, the distribution mix, and the promotion mix. Each of these subsystems must be developed so that it supports and complements the others, so that synergy occurs and the impact of the total mix becomes greater than the sum of the parts.

Two perspectives are always in play in designing a hospitality marketing mix: the overall marketing mix and each of the individual submixes. Conflicts and tradeoffs are present at both levels. For example, at the submix level, choices may be made among expenditures on advertising, personal selling, public relations, and merchandising. Across the submixes, choices may be made between raising prices or reducing service, or between increasing advertising or offering price discounts. The objective is to select those tradeoffs that will optimize the *overall* mix. This means that some components benefit at the expense of others. While optimizing submixes at the expense of the overall mix should be avoided, in practice it occurs regularly. When it does, some marketing mix elements are unwisely neglected while others receive larger budgets than they merit.

Regrettably, hospitality decisions are too often made on a piecemeal basis. Attention is directed to one specific ingredient (such as pricing, direct mail, or personal selling) that is treated as a separate or unrelated entity, rather than as a component of a total system. The specialists responsible for individual departments or activities, like advertising or direct mail, often strive to maximize the output of their area rather than that of the whole mix. This narrow view is a reason that some marketing components are overused while others are neglected.

Marketing Mix Levels

The marketing mix can be viewed at several organizational levels. It can be applied to a conglomerate, to a single hospitality business, or to a single product or service. For example, companies like Ritz-Carlton, Hilton, and Hyatt that own and operate several hotel and food service companies worldwide will have a global corporate marketing mix. There is also a corporate marketing mix for a company that owns and operates various kinds of lodging properties such as full service hotels, suite motels, and lower- and higher-priced properties. And there is the marketing mix for a single property, such as Jim's Diner or the Lakeshore Motel.

From a corporate perspective, the marketing mix may comprise many diverse offerings and marketing ingredients covering an extensive array of services and products. Overall corporate mix decisions shape the mix decisions of its business units and their specific offerings. Included are decisions about product and service design, price level, value choices, positioning, images, alliance, and networks.

Chains that are themselves part of conglomerates may be thought of as strategic business units with their own marketing mixes. Their products and services, prices, promotion, sales, distribution, and merchandising policies and activities may differ significantly from those of other strategic business units in the company.

At the specific service/product or single enterprise level, hospitality marketing mix decisions are made with a focus on a specific entity or activity. The resulting advertising messages, content and themes, rack prices, discounts and allowances, or service and product features that constitute the unique mix will differ from others in the same organization.

The concept of the marketing mix offers an apt framework for reminding managers that guests ultimately determine what hospitality services and products will be produced and how they will be marketed. In a sense, the marketing mix operates as a change agent. The mix is changed to meet new market conditions and, when properly implemented, provides effective links between an organization and its environment.

The systems perspective we have been exploring is well illustrated by the corporate marketing mix of the Marriott Corporation. Over the past few years, Marriott has been developing a portfolio of hotels and resorts tailored to meet the needs of several carefully specified customer groups, including the following:

- *Marriott Hotels and Resorts* provides the outstanding facilities and services expected by the five-star business, leisure, and convention markets.

- *Marriott Suites* offers two-room suites with first-class hotel services for the frequent business traveler.

- *Courtyard by Marriott* offers smaller mid-price hotels for guests looking for well-located, sensible accommodation with some amenities such as a restaurant and swimming pool.

- *Residence Inn* provides moderately priced suites with kitchen facilities for guests moving interstate or on business who are looking for long-stay accommodation.

- *Fairfield Inn* offers budget-priced rooms with limited amenities.

Each of the above hotel brands must develop a unique marketing mix to appeal to its targeted markets. Its market offerings reflect the specific needs of guests in the target markets. Decisions must be made about the four major marketing mix components. In appealing to different markets, companies have both their unique overall total company marketing mix and the individual marketing mixes of separate units.

Framing the Marketing Mix: Coping with Complexity ———

In framing the marketing mix, hospitality managers must cope with a complex array of data, sort out the essential details, find sensible patterns, and work toward developing a marketing mix that will both satisfy guests and meet company objectives. An important and difficult step centers on reducing the complexity of the mass of information about guests, markets, and hospitality businesses. This entails the search for order and pattern in company data that will help managers determine the appropriate actions to take. But how is this done? By way of illustration, we shall explore the general process of moving from identified problems and issues to the development of hospitality marketing strategies through the use of a valuable tool—the **environment-strategy-capability (ESC) grid**. Consider the following scenarios based on actual hospitality marketing situations.

1. The General Manager of a new Asian hotel is considering a strong push into the incentive travel market directed toward regional business houses. He wonders whether the market will grow and whether it will behave like the American market, where incentive travel is an important concern of many major hotels. However, he is also aware that a recent speaker at a conference in Hong Kong suggested that the profitability of such business is low. The General Manager wonders whether Asian businesses would indicate a growing interest in travel incentives.

2. The president of Omni Hotels Asia Pacific, in discussing his company's plans for expansion in Asia, said, "We're not here to be second best. We're here to be the leader. We're here to win the war." As the *Asian Hotelier* put it, "The campaign about which he speaks is for rooms, rates, and customer loyalty. It's not going to be a quick victory. Short term, he talks of expanding from four to 20 hotels in five years. Long term, he speaks of 100 hotels in China in 20 years."

3. An accountant in a major hotel is considering a consultant's proposal to upgrade the existing computer system to include provision for guest history data. A substantial cost is involved, and it will take some time for guest histories to accumulate to the point where they might be useful to front desk staff. She wonders how she should respond.

4. In the Bangkok market, a price war is breaking out following extensive construction of five-star properties and a downturn in demand. A manager of one of the properties is trying to decide whether to lower prices to match competition or to hold the line. He wonders what factors should be considered in making a decision.

5. The new General Manager of an old but recently refurbished 400-room Sheraton inner-city hotel wonders whether to follow the lead of the ITT Sheraton mission, which clearly states: "At ITT Sheraton, we are committed to being the best lodging company in the world by attracting and retaining the best employees and focusing on total customer satisfaction as the means to improving long-term profits and value for our owners and ITT." As a consequence of this commitment, ITT Sheraton is questioning traditional hotel practices, processes, and structures, and the Asia-Pacific Division has adopted the slogan, "There are no rules." The GM wonders what she should do.

6. The food and beverage manager of a major hotel recently attended a seminar in which the speaker said, "If we had our way, we would demolish every hostess stand in America's restaurants. Why? Because all too often, restaurateurs allow their hostesses to hide behind these fancy podiums, forcing the guests to open the front door themselves and approach the hostess to be formally greeted." She wonders whether the hostess stands in each of her restaurants should be removed.

In looking over the six examples, one is struck by the diversity of the situations that these managers must resolve. Each raises issues that challenge the strategies being pursued by the company concerned. A common element in these situations is that each identifies a challenge that begins with change, sometimes in the external environment and sometimes within the business itself. In each case, management should be concerned about the "fit" between what might be done and what is needed in each of the particular market situations. Failure to act appropriately could close off important long-term markets, turn away prospective guests, and risk the loss of market share and profits.

In order to help us develop appropriate marketing strategies, we are going to use the ESC grid. This focuses our attention first of all on identifying the nature of the issue(s), and then goes on to highlight the implications of the issue(s) for both strategic and operational decisions. With a clear picture of the immediate challenge and its implications for the hospitality business, the grid uses the idea that there should be both a fit between strategic response and marketplace and a fit between strategic response and the capabilities of the business. In commonsense terms, the strategies chosen must be appropriate to the market and must make use of the resources or capabilities of the business. The closer the fit, the greater will be the chance of success.[2] Let's see how this would work with our six situations.

Our first step is to deal with the environment of each of the circumstances. We might first identify whether the source of the issue lies outside or inside the business. Is it external or internal? We can classify the six scenarios as follows:

External	Internal
1. Incentive travel	3. Guest history data
2. Expansion into Asia	5. Culture change
4. Price war	6. Restaurant podiums

Whether the challenge is external or internal affects the kind of management responses that might be considered. The external situations are largely outside the direct control of management. The internal issues relate to a company's capability to respond directly to challenges through its actions.

The second step addresses the scope or level of the decisions required. Is it a macro-, mid-, or micro-level situation or decision? *Macro-level situations* are wideranging and strategic in character, deal with the big picture, and arise from broad market trends or changes that can affect many areas of the business. *Mid-level situations* deal with more immediate and less comprehensive situations, such as the challenges arising from specific market conditions that require a competitive response. *Micro-level situations* are issues that arise at the day-to-day level of activity because of shifts in such factors as customer behavior patterns or changes in everyday routines. We can classify our six situations as follows:

Level 1: Macro (the big picture)

      2. Expansion into Asia

      5. Culture change

Level 2: Mid-level (specific market factors)

      4. Price war

      3. Guest history data

Level 3: Micro (customer or service encounter factors)

      1. Incentive travel

      6. Restaurant podiums

We can now combine both classifications into an environment/level matrix like the following one.

Exhibit 2 The Environment-Strategy-Capability (ESC) Grid

	Environment	Strategy	Capability
Macro-Level	E1: Macro Forces	S1: Vision	C1: Culture
Mid-Level	E2: Competition	S2: Market Mix	C2: Resources
Micro-Level	E3: Guests	S3: Service Encounter	C3: Skills

	External	**Internal**
Macro-level	2. Expansion into Asia	5. Culture change
Mid-level	4. Price war	3. Guest history data
Micro-level	1. Incentive travel	6. Restaurant podiums

Now we can take the analysis a little further using the logic of the **strategic success hypothesis**.[3] Basically, the strategic success hypothesis states that businesses achieve optimal performance when their strategies and internal capabilities are in line with the challenges of their external environments. The core idea is that *strategy must match environment, and capability must match strategy.* To be effective, management strategies must satisfy these two principles. In so doing, the strategy chosen will first be responsive to market conditions. Second, it ensures that companies are formulating strategies that they have the internal capability to implement. There is little point in proposing strategies for which companies do not have the financial resources or people skills to implement. The ESC approach links company capability and environment through the idea of strategy.

Let us now take the basic scheme to the final stage of developing an ESC grid. In the ESC grid (see Exhibit 2), external environmental issues fall into the Environment column, while internal environmental issues fall into the Capability column. The grid is then completed by adding the Strategy column. The ESC grid can be a very valuable strategic marketing planning worksheet for two important reasons. First, it leads management to collect, summarize, and focus relevant information. Second, it helps management develop and explore the plausibility of various strategies. In this way, the ESC grid helps management work through the mass of data that typically arises in dealing with strategic marketing situations and ensures that important factors are not overlooked.

Let us briefly note the general kinds of information that would be placed in the nine cells of the grid. *E1* would include material describing the major changes taking place in the relevant market environments. *E2* would present information about the competitive behavior of each of the markets—who the competitors are, how they compete, and why they win (when they do). *E3* would summarize information relating to customers—who they are, how they buy, what benefits they are looking for. *S1* would focus on corporate strategy, commitments, vision, mission, and policies. *S2* would describe the current marketing mix, setting out information about products and services offered, the prices being asked for each, where and when they are available, and how they are being promoted in the markets of interest. *S3* would state how day-to-day interactions with customers are handled. *C1* would list crucial data on corporate capabilities, including assets, locations, and facilities, as well as information on corporate culture and the ability to change with the times. *C2* would look at systems including product development, financial and accounting data, and staff development. *C3* would deal with how staff are trained and supported as they go about offering the services that customers are seeking.

To deal realistically with each of the above cells, managers need large amounts of detailed data. Although some managers may resist doing the grid because of the detailed information they need, they should do it anyway because of the benefits it provides. When detailed worksheets are completed, managers develop a good grasp of the strategic situation and a number of critical questions are raised. Consideration is given to whether the approaches in the strategy column are appropriate to the market forces described in the environment column. If there are gaps between the strategy choices required by the market and the alternative strategies listed ("strategy gaps"), then performance (sales, market share, profit) will suffer. The greater the gap and the longer it persists, the greater the undesirable impact on overall performance.

Similarly, strategies must also be assessed with respect to current and potential capabilities. The capability column identifies how present business resources and capabilities relate to the strategy choices being considered. When the capability to support strategy options is lacking, a "capability gap" exists. As with strategy gaps, the wider the capability gap, the greater will be the negative effect on performance.

Strategy must be matched to environment and capability for each of the three decision levels. At the macro or corporate level, top management is concerned with choosing the long-run strategies of the business and with taking steps to ensure that the capabilities exist to support the chosen strategies. Here, strategic choice will be concerned with such considerations as vision and mission, facility design and location, corporate culture, and human resource strategies, as well as the overall positioning of the enterprise in terms of price-quality tradeoffs.

At the mid-level, where specific markets are a primary focus, strategy is concerned with the competitive struggle and the skills needed to succeed. At this level, strategic considerations include product and service design, the choice of rates and discount schedules, relationships with travel agents, tour operators, and wholesalers, and a wide range of promotional or communication options. Here, strategy considers options relating to designing service systems, specifying information gathering procedures, developing quality management systems, and organizing marketing efforts.

At the micro or customer level, strategy focuses on guests making up a market segment. The choice of strategy may involve determining what will be done in specific categories of service encounters. The capability question then involves training for the needed skills.

Failure to define a convincing mission or to create a supportive culture is a well-recognized path to business failure. So is failure to respond to competitive challenges through a lack of creative insight in choosing strategies or the lack of ability to implement appropriate strategies. And well-conceived hospitality marketing strategies often run aground because the details of service encounters were not addressed carefully, resulting in dissatisfied guests. Guest satisfaction is, of course, the ultimate test of all the detailed planning. It requires informed and capable managers—not just technicians and operators, but people who can apply principles and precepts that flow from education, experience, training, discussions with other managers, reading, meetings, and conferences.

In generating and selecting their strategies, managers try to produce a flow of pertinent ideas and alternatives so that they can choose those with greatest value. Sometimes, the choices are almost self-evident and suggest themselves. At other times, however, where the approaches are less obvious, alternatives may be suggested by focusing on how to:

- Achieve increased customer satisfaction through outstanding service.

- Build sustainable competitive advantage.

- Create the capabilities needed for future success.

Thinking about how their company might change to accomplish the above can help managers pinpoint effective strategic approaches. Achieving outstanding service in critical markets is an obvious starting point in the search for strategy. Building outstanding service concepts and then designing and implementing the systems to deliver them reliably are among the most important steps that any service enterprise can undertake.

SWOT Analysis

SWOT (strengths, weaknesses, opportunities, and threats) analysis is a widely used approach to formulating marketing strategies that flows directly from the construction of an ESC grid. The strengths and weaknesses of a business can be seen in a comparison of strategies and capabilities, and the opportunities and threats tend to flow from a comparison of environment and strategy. A SWOT analysis focuses on the important strengths and weaknesses when a business is compared with major competitors, and highlights key opportunities and threats that exist in changing environments. It can help managers differentiate their company from those of their competitors and can furnish a clearer understanding of the strategic thrust of their business.

In a SWOT analysis, consideration is given to guest needs and reactions to current market offerings, competitors' decisions and actions, and company opportunities for improving strategic approaches. The key to an effective SWOT analysis is to identify important related issues and to keep in focus the fact that the most important company strengths and weaknesses spring from a clear understanding of guests. A strength is a strength only if guests see it as such, and not because management says it is.

When an assessment of strengths, weaknesses, opportunities, and threats has been completed, managers are in a position to think of appropriate strategies. An opportunity without the strength to respond or a strength that has no opportunity to be exploited is of little strategic benefit. Either situation requires additional management consideration and action. Both weaknesses and threats are limiting factors that may need long-term attention. Management is challenged to convert weaknesses into strengths and to counter threats or convert them into opportunities. In considering strategies for building sustainable competitive advantage, a useful step is to perform a SWOT analysis for each important competitor. Such evaluations should be based on a sense of how guests, not management, see competitors. Competitors are competitors when guests see them as viable alternatives.

SWOT analysis is a way of summarizing some of the issues that flow from the more extensive ESC analysis. When managers evaluate environments and strategy, and assess strategy and capability, they consider not only strengths, weaknesses, threats, and opportunities, but also other strategic aspects.

In addition to the immediate and shorter-term strategic needs, such as service design and competitive challenges, there are the longer-term concerns of capability creation. Typically, they center on such tasks as culture change, like changing a traditional hotel management viewpoint to guest-centered thinking or redesigning organizational structures and operating systems from responding to management preferences to responding to emerging market needs. And strategically, in the long run, management can change all of the aspects of a hospitality venture under its control, including management, location, offerings, and operating systems.

Putting the ESC Grid to Work

To see how the ESC grid can be used to deal with strategic challenges, let us apply it to one of the situations we briefly described earlier. Consider the breakout of a price war in the Bangkok market and its impact on the management of a major five-star property. As we have already noted, the initial problem is confined to a local market, so we classify it as a mid-level environmental issue (*E2* in Exhibit 3).

Before noting possible strategic options, management should pay some attention to the factors precipitating the price war. A primary cause lies in a boom in the construction of five-star properties, itself a consequence of changing economic perceptions, improving tourism, and speculative investments. While these conditions are unlikely to go away in the short term, their impact may wax and wane over time, suggesting that there is a high degree of volatility in the basic market situation. Some of these factors are noted in the macro-level environment box (*E1*) for further consideration. In addition, management will wish to identify the specific market segments or customer groups most likely to be affected by discounting of room rates and to assess just how much of the hotel's business stems from these groups. In any event, their expectations or perceptions of the competitive offers being made will be important factors to consider in putting together a sound marketing response. This element is noted in the micro-environment box (*E3*).

Possible responses are then noted in the mid-level strategy column (*S2*) opposite the environmental issue—the impending price war. Management's initial response is to consider changes to the pricing structure in parallel with reductions in service. A key question that arises here concerns the importance and expectations of those guests most likely to be attracted by the discounted room rates. A related issue centers on the availability of hard cost data on service components, generally or specifically for certain customer groups. This data would in turn raise

Exhibit 3   Environment-Strategy-Capability Grid: The Price War in Bangkok

	Environment	Strategy	Capability
Macro-Level	Over building in Bangkok Trends in tourism [E1]	Corporate policy? [S1]	Flexibility [C1]
Mid-Level	Price war [E2] Travel agents, Wholesaler reactions?	Review price-value offer by segment [S2] Initiate advertising campaign Productivity review	Cost system capacity? [C2] Forecasting system? Identify repeat customer?
Micro-Level	Guest expectations? [E3]	Reinforce loyalties [S3]	Service specifications? [C3] Training capacity?

questions about cost and productivity: could equivalent service levels be provided at a lesser cost? Similar concerns arise in forecasting the demand levels likely to be encountered with different price-service options. Is the forecasting system up to the task? Can the hotel database identify repeat customers as a separate group and explore their pricing sensitivities? If there are problems here, then the possibility of a capability gap exists at this level with important decisions being taken on the basis of a mix of emotion, guesswork, and experience.

Assuming that a discounted rate structure is introduced with some matching reductions in service levels, both macro and micro strategy issues need to be considered. There will be some concerns about the implications of a local discounting strategy for corporate-wide policy on pricing. These concerns may be greater if a wide-ranging advertising campaign is planned using international media and working through global travel networks. These are examples of macro-level strategy considerations (S1). Turning to the micro-level strategy (S3), the change in service specification and the matching changes in discounts will have an impact on many regular guests, who will perhaps wonder whether they are really valued by management if the benefits are seen to go to non-regular customers. At this point, there will be a need to think through ways in which individual staff in day-to-day service encounters can reinforce guest loyalties. The little things may become central here—for example, the use of the guest's name in greetings, the offer of a pre-specified room, perhaps with individualized touches in flowers or facilities.

If these actions are to be successful, they must be backed up by careful planning of capability (C1–C3). We mentioned earlier the need for supportive information systems in designing the appropriate mid-level marketing strategy. The consequences of the macro- and micro-level choices will require flexibility in the way the enterprise runs (a question of culture, style, and organization), as well as detailed attention to staff training, recognition, and rewards.

The preceding discussion highlights a critically important point: *You can never change just one thing.* We began with a single issue—a price war in a local market. As we began to consider the kinds of response, it quickly became evident that it was not just a matter of changing the discount strategy of the property we were assessing. There were effects both at the level of corporate or group strategy and at the level of the staff involved in daily service encounters. Questions emerge about the capability of a business to design and implement the appropriate strategy. Doubts may arise about the research costs, or the quality or reliability of the market data being used. There may be worries about the ability of the business as a whole to handle a discount strategy, as well as the skills of individual staff in dealing with both old and new guests.

We can map onto the grid the sequence of steps taken to explore the issue as shown in Exhibit 3. We began with the price war, which was generated by a conjunction of longer-term trends and which will affect the way current and prospective guests will view the hotel. Management's response involves a close look at the products and services provided to guests at each pricing level. Perhaps when choices are made, they will be supported by a carefully constructed communication campaign—internal as well as external. All this in turn will require trained staff, the availability of relevant and timely data, and a culture that is supportive of changes in the service offerings. While this list is not the only sequence of responses, it serves to point out the complex links between actions that are often seen as marketing decisions with a wide range of initiatives in related management areas. All of them are essential for market success. The dimensions of marketing strategy extend well beyond conventional marketing boundaries, requiring a systems view of the hospitality business concerned.

Hospitality Marketing: Two Strategic Views

We may distinguish between two entirely different perspectives of hospitality businesses that affect how managers function and arrive at strategic decisions. The first we term a Newtonian perspective. Here, managers perceive the business climate basically as rather stable and mechanistic, made up of very predictable inputs and outputs. Managers think in terms of cause and effect. Their approach is to measure, analyze, predict, and control. This approach reflects a basic Newtonian concept that a body remains in a state of rest until it is hit by a force, and then it moves in the same direction as the force that hit it. From this perspective, hospitality enterprises tend to remain as they are until they are affected by market forces that move them in a different direction. Then they go with the flow.

Second is a more contemporary perspective of hospitality businesses as existing in continuously changing, somewhat unpredictable environments sometimes affected by random events. As a result, market developments can be somewhat disorderly and messy, exhibiting irregular tendencies. At the same time, however, some order exists within the disorder. Patterns and configurations can be discerned. Sometimes, the patterns appear only in a larger global context. This perspective suggests that managers cannot manage simply by following mechanistic rules and guidelines. The fact is that market environments differ, and the same kind of situation in one organizational setting or location may have vastly different manifestations in another.

In the contemporary perspective, unexpected changes are to be expected, even though they cannot be predicted. Irrational changes are now a way of business life in the hospitality industry. Moreover, irrational market changes, just like rational ones, offer extensive opportunities for growth through creativity, innovation, and change.

Hospitality managers must be ever sensitive to the inherent opportunities to change their strategies that are signaled by continuously changing environments. It is a key to staying ahead of the pack, which can be very profitable. But doing so depends on informed, insightful, and proactive management. It implies a change orientation. Managers are continuously challenged to reinvent, reorient, and reestablish their businesses. Doing so has far-reaching impact, for it deals with changing visions, missions, goals, and objectives, reorienting market positioning and the marketing mix, and changing such organizational factors as training, empowerment, motivation, and compensation.

In changing strategies, management can never change just one thing. A single issue such as a price war in a local market, a specific change in government regulation, or a competitor's move may necessitate a strategic response. But as management starts to consider appropriate responses, it quickly becomes evident that more is involved than simply changing an action in a single property. Consideration must be given to the impact of the proposed strategy on the rest of the organization—its staff, its capabilities, its daily service encounters. Management must assess the capability of a business to design and implement proposed strategies.

It is clear that in formulating and implementing strategies, effective hospitality businesses in the future will have to be responsive to dynamic business environments. They will need to be more flexible, improvement oriented, innovative, entrepreneurial, and comfortable with risk. They will have to be better prepared to deal with change.

The Ethical Dimension

So far, we have implicitly assumed that, in selecting strategies, hospitality managers are interested only in economic concerns such as occupancy, sales, costs, and profits. But there are other important factors to be considered in our assessment of matching strategies, capabilities, and environments, such as ethical concerns. While the pressures to ignore ethical issues can be nearly overwhelming when those concerns seem to interfere with achieving profit and sales goals, hospitality managers can find that ignoring ethical dimensions is not easy.

Ethics refers to the rules of conduct we live by. It involves judgment and applies to the behavior of both people and companies. Ethics is "knowing what we ought to do, and having the will to do it."[4] Ethical behavior is judged by actions. Ethical judgments may stem from individual principles, values, beliefs, and priorities, as well as from the standards embodying the values of the business itself. If ethics is to play a major role in the way a business operates and in the kinds of strategies that are formulated and implemented, managers and employees must be clear about and adhere to corporate values and standards. These commitments are part of the choices falling into the macro-level strategy (*S1*) category of the ESC grid. They drive attitudes within the business as a whole.

Perhaps the most difficult aspect of being ethical lies in defining what is right and wrong. Adding to this difficulty is the fact that ethical guidelines vary by culture. What is considered ethical in one culture may not be in another. Varying ethical dimensions are becoming more important and more complex as global hospitality markets are developed and as guests continue to reflect a broader and broader variety of cultures and customs. Given this situation, determining absolute ethical standards covering all hospitality marketing situations is difficult, if not impossible. That is one reason that *situational ethics* is often invoked. It takes such factors as culture, mores, customs, and beliefs surrounding a specific hospitality strategy or decision into account.

Although ethics can vary by culture, some widely accepted ethical standards do exist irrespective of the culture. For example, it is widely deemed unethical to lie, cheat, or steal; to intentionally misrepresent a service or product, to use false, misleading, or deceptive advertising; or to cut corners on health and safety standards. When selecting marketing strategies, however, sometimes managers do not know what they ought to do. This suggests a challenge to training or education. Sometimes managers know what they ought to do, but do not do it. This reflects their strength of will to act ethically. The assumption usually made in choosing strategies is that managers know what to do and do it.

When ethical dimensions arise, they often tend to fall into gray areas—borderline situations that are *somewhat* questionable or a *little* unethical—but that offer very enticing profit opportunities. In the abstract, most marketers agree that adhering to high ethical standards is desirable. But can restaurateurs and hoteliers expect their staffs to place ethics ahead of profits? In many instances, probably not. The sanctions and rewards that might prompt hospitality managers to choose ethical alternatives over more profitable unethical ones are often not in place. The pressure of bottom-line considerations, costs, profits, and sales encourages expedient rather than ethical choices. The pressures to achieve short-term goals are often in direct conflict with ethical standards.

To help hospitality managers ensure that ethical actions are taken in formulating strategies and in day-to-day hospitality marketing activities, the following guidelines are suggested.

1. Develop a clear set of ethical standards covering strategic hospitality marketing decisions.

2. Establish clear responsibility for enforcing ethical standards.

3. Implement a reward and punishment system that encourages ethical conduct.

4. Work to develop an organizational climate that reinforces ethical practices.

5. Monitor ethical issues that arise and assess how well the company handles them.

Concluding Comments

The purpose of strategy is to guide a business to the achievement of its objectives. Marketing strategies are the blueprints that direct marketing plans and operations toward the achievement of marketing objectives. To be effective, they must reflect dynamic market conditions by incorporating the necessary changes to respond to market opportunities. In reality, managers face two choices: either ignore market changes in the hope that that they pass and that things will return to normal, or make the necessary strategic marketing adjustments. This chapter focuses on thinking strategically and formulating and developing effective marketing strategies.

The strategic planning process leads hospitality managers from such broad considerations as corporate mission and objectives to the implementation of plans and measurement of results. The stages involved begin with the activities fundamental to developing an understanding and knowledge base for identifying appropriate strategic response. The first four steps are part of the marketing audit, which includes the well-known SWOT analysis. They guide managers in identifying options, establishing priorities, and choosing strategic responses.

The marketing mix, which refers to a company's total offering to the market place, provides a useful framework for understanding hospitality marketing strategies and decisions. It can be viewed from a number of organizational perspectives ranging from the overall company purview to that of a single product or service. It is rooted in systems thinking and encompasses four broad decision areas: product and service mix, pricing mix, promotion mix, and distribution mix. Regrettably, hospitality marketing decisions are often made on a piecemeal basis rather than on a systems basis, resulting in a less than optimal overall marketing mix.

In developing the marketing mix, hospitality managers must cope with a complex array of data, sort out essential details, establish patterns, and then arrive at their market offering. The ESC grid is a valuable, practical management tool for dealing with strategic situations. The core idea (the strategic success hypothesis) is that strategy must match environments and capability must match strategy. A critically important point is that, in making changes, managers can never change just one thing.

Two entirely different approaches to the development and implementation of hospitality marketing strategies can be identified. The Newtonian perspective views business environments in a rather mechanistic way based on assumptions related to stable environments. The more contemporary perspective views business environments as unpredictable, continuously changing environments encompassing random events. The Newtonian view results in a management focus on measurement, analysis, prediction, and control. The latter view emphasizes a change orientation and the need for being flexible, innovative, entrepreneurial, and comfortable in dealing with risk.

In addition to the normal economic concerns, hospitality managers will confront an increasing number of ethical considerations in matching strategies, capabilities, and environments. The pressures to achieve short-term goals are often in direct conflict with ethical standards. The ethical standards themselves may become even murkier as they encompass the ethics of different cultures and mores involved in operating in expanded global markets.

Endnotes

1. IBM 1994 Annual Report.

2. See Raymond E. Miles and Charles C. Snow, *Fit, Failure and the Hall of Fame: How Companies Succeed or Fail* (New York: Free Press, 1994) for a general discussion, and H. Igor Ansoff and Edward McDonnell, *Implanting Strategic Management*, 2d ed. (Englewood Cliffs, N.J.: Prentice Hall, 1990) for a detailed analysis.

3. Ansoff and McDonnell, p. 30.

4. Stephen S. J. Hall, *Quality Assurance in the Hospitality Industry* (Milwaukee, Wis.: Quality Press, 1990), p. 30.

Key Terms

environment-strategy-capability (ESC) grid—a planning framework that links a changing environment to the choice of strategy based on an understanding of capability.

marketing audit—a systematic, unbiased analysis of the environment and of a company's operations that helps identify market opportunities and company capabilities and deficiencies.

marketing mix—the mix of controllable varibles a company uses to create its total offering to the markets it choses to serve.

strategic planning process—a process that leads managers from a consideration of corporate mission and objectives to the implementation of plans and the measurement of results.

strategic success hypothesis—states that businesses achieve optimal performance when their strategies and internal capabilities are in line with the challenges of their external environments.

SWOT analysis—an approach to strategic planning, closely related to the ESC grid, that emphasizes strengths, weaknesses, opportunities, and threats.

Review Questions

1. What is the purpose of a hospitality marketing strategy?

2. What are the steps involved in developing and implementing a hospitality marketing strategy?

3. What is the strategic planning process? How does it help formulate the marketing strategy?

4. What are the four areas of decision-making involved in developing the marketing mix? How do these four areas relate to one another? To the overall mix?

5. What is the environment-strategy-capability grid? Why is the ESC grid a valuable tool?

6. What are strategy gaps and capability gaps? Why are they significant?

7. What is a SWOT analysis? What is the key to an effective analysis?

8. What are the two perspectives of hospitality businesses that affect how managers function and arrive at strategic decisions? In what circumstances does each perspective work best? Which perspective seems to be more appropriate in today's marketplace?

9. Should ethics play a role in selecting hospitality marketing strategies? Why or why not? Why are ethical choices sometimes difficult to make in a business environment?

Internet Sites

For more information, visit the following Internet sites. Remember that Internet addresses can change without notice.

Hilton Hotels Corporation
http://www.hilton.com

Hyatt Hotels and Resorts
http://www.hyatt.com

IBM
http://www.ibm.com

Marriott International
http://www.marriott.com

Ritz-Carlton Hotels
http://www.ritzcarlton.com

Russell Hotel (Sydney)
http://www.therocks.com.au/
accomodation/russell

Chapter 4 Outline

Turning Strategies into Plans and Budgets
Planning Levels and Tasks
    By Level of Management
    By Task
Two Basic Questions
    What Should Marketing Planning Achieve?
    How Can Marketing Planning Be Made More Effective?
Sales Forecasts and Marketing Plans
    Using Sales Forecasts
Plans and Budgets
Monitoring Plans
Marketing Planning in Action
Information in the Marketing Planning Process
Marketing Planning in Practice
    Attitude Toward Planning
    Planning Approaches: Top-Down or Bottom-Up
    Managing Marketing Planning
Concluding Comments

4

Strategic Hospitality Marketing Planning

"Perfection of means and confusion of goals seems to characterize our age."

—Albert Einstein[1]

HOSPITALITY MARKETING PLANNING concerns the planned use of marketing resources to achieve established goals. This activity encompasses both the process of planning, including the search for strategy, and the development and implementation of the plans themselves. Planning involves a logical sequence of tasks for setting marketing objectives and formulating the means to achieve them.

This chapter examines the ways in which management understands and uses marketing planning. Because we do not aim to develop hospitality marketing planners, our discussion will not focus on the technology of marketing planning, the statistical and analytical techniques of gathering and using information, or the detailed activities of each step in the marketing planning process. Instead, we will highlight how the creative insights of managers translate into specific initiatives and will examine what is involved in managing the planning process. We will indicate the importance and benefits of effective planning.

Developing marketing strategies and turning these strategies into documented marketing plans and budgets are closely related activities. Three questions are central to both: Where are we now? Where do we want to be? How do we get there? Answering these questions usually involves two phases of work. The first concerns trying to understand the hospitality business situation and searching for strategies that are likely to succeed. The second concerns turning these ideas into documented plans and budgets and putting them into effect. The second phase (covering the last five steps in Exhibit 1) will be the focus of this chapter.

Turning Strategies into Plans and Budgets

In the first of these last five steps, senior managers must establish the working assumptions that will help them prepare detailed hospitality marketing plans and budgets. These assumptions are normally estimates of such factors as overall demand, likely price changes, labor market conditions, the nature and timing of competitive moves, inflation, exchange rates, and other economic conditions. They consist of reasonable assessments of the future business climates on which plans are grounded.

Exhibit 1   Strategic Planning Process

Marketing Audit

1. Corporate Objectives, Mission
2. Situation Analysis
   Environment
   Strategy
   Capability
3. Strengths, Weaknesses, Opportunities and Threats (SWOT) Analysis
4. Strategic Issues Identified

Choosing a Strategy

5. Options, Priorities

Building Marketing Plans and Budgets

6. Working Assumptions
7. Marketing Objectives, Mix
8. Estimated Outcomes
9. Functional, Project Plans, Budgets
10. Implementation and Measurement

Working from these assumptions, the next step centers on developing specific marketing objectives and setting out an appropriate marketing mix to achieve them. These objectives may concern such areas as guest satisfaction levels, occupancy rates, covers, market share, growth rates, business from new markets, new product/service concepts, gross and net margins, return on assets, new locations, staff numbers, turnover, and profits. Setting out the marketing mix will lead to a detailed specification of the products/services to be offered, pricing policies and tactics, delivery and other networks to be used, and the mix of communication activities that will lead guests to learn of the business. It is helpful to specify objectives and mix decisions for each major customer group or target market as well as for the business as a whole.

Personal as well as managerial judgment is always involved in setting objectives and choosing a marketing mix. In addition to purely economic concerns, political, ethical, and human dimensions affect the choices made. Managers must judge whether targets should be set high or low to maximize marketing effort. If objectives are set too high, they might be perceived as impossible to reach and become a deterrent. If they are set too low, they will require too little effort. Setting objectives is even more complex when incentive programs are tied to performance by specifying targets for a range of objectives.

Once objectives have been set and initial choices of marketing mix components identified, it is then important to ask whether the choices made in the mix will lead to meeting the objectives. While this may seem an obvious and implicit step in the choice of mix, it is often important to focus directly on the link between action and effect—to ask, for example, what the link is between an advertising budget of a specific size and expected sales results. Using the best available data, managers in this step evaluate the proposed mix and estimate the likely results. Sometimes it becomes clear that the mix needs to be changed in some way—perhaps by increasing prices, dropping a service element to reduce costs, or shifting from media expenditure to direct sales activity. Thinking about objectives, choosing a mix, and estimating outcomes are all interrelated steps in developing a detailed marketing plan.

At this point in the cycle, plans and budgets are prepared for specific markets, market segments, functional areas, and market offerings. Managers must translate objectives into detailed goals, specify the means to achieve them, and indicate who is responsible for reaching them. Resources, especially finances and staff, must be allocated and the timing of each step must be determined.

The final step, implementation and measurement, is most crucial. At this point, all the creative thinking and careful analysis translates into marketing action. In many cases, actions will challenge the status quo and generate problems that can test a manager's commitment to planned initiatives. It is crucial to measure the results achieved, for only with adequate feedback can managers learn from experience and respond logically to the unexpected. Measurement processes must be specified as part of the planning cycle.

Marketing planning involves much more than simply inserting numbers into a predetermined plan, as too many hospitality managers seem to believe. It encompasses the careful but creative analysis of markets, options, and capabilities. It translates strategic concepts into blueprints for future action. It requires skill, knowledge, resources, and time, as well as preparedness for an uncertain future.

Marketing plans warrant special consideration because they drive all other company plans, including financial plans. While marketing plans cannot ensure successful operations, they impart a disciplined and organized approach to hospitality marketing.

Planning Levels and Tasks

By Level of Management

Planning may occur at corporate, strategic business unit (SBU), divisional, departmental, or functional levels. Large, diversified hospitality enterprises such as Disney, Hilton, McDonald's, PepsiCo, and Marriott may establish formal, structured systems for corporate planning. They may also develop plans for each of their SBUs, such as hotels, motels, restaurants, and resorts. Each division, moreover, will have its own plans for different entities, from buffet-style to gourmet restaurants. Each entity may in turn develop its own specific marketing plan. In addition, each hospitality marketing activity, such as advertising, personal selling, merchandising, and promotion, will have its own plan. Plans may be developed at any level to address the needs of specific markets or units, or to tackle specific strategic issues. Although all plans should support one another as part of the total hospitality marketing system, it is not unusual to find that they do not.

Exhibit 2   Strategic versus Operational Planning

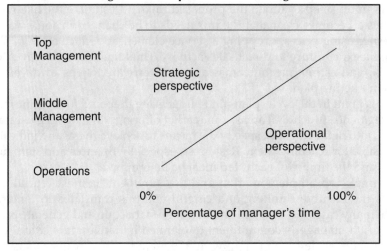

By Task

Plans must be developed for the performance of major marketing tasks. Included are plans for the performance of the normal strategic and operating marketing activities. They are part of the usual planning cycle. For example, there are advertising, personal selling, direct mail, and pricing plans. Plans are drawn up to extend markets, such as increasing convention and business sales. Managers need project plans to deal with new tasks like the opening of a new leisure property, adding facilities to an existing hotel, developing new restaurants and menus, establishing different strategic initiatives, setting up networks, and so on. Meeting competitive challenges can call for the development of plans, as can the initiative to implement changes that cannot wait for the next planning cycle. Planned approaches to the performance of marketing tasks increase the payoff from hospitality marketing efforts.

Strategic Planning. In the past decade, strategic planning has received increasing attention. This type of planning concerns a hospitality organization's primary mission and objectives and affects the scope and direction of company efforts. It has a long-term focus on turning visions and ideas into goals and objectives. Examples include strategic plans to franchise, to engage in strategic alliances, or to participate in worldwide reservations systems. Strategic planning is directed toward innovation and change and occurs at the highest organizational levels. Exhibit 2 illustrates the management levels involved in strategic and operational planning.

Strategic plans constrain and shape other plans and provide the basic framework for hospitality marketing operations. They point toward new markets, new methods of operation, and new products or services. In addition, they identify needed resources and skills, alerting management to take the steps to develop them.

A long-range perspective and vision are essential to strategic marketing planning. Reward systems must therefore reflect contributions to long-run survival as well as short-term profitability. In fact, the marketing perspective that focuses on ever-changing consumer needs encourages a strategic perspective. Long-term investments will capitalize on future market opportunities.

Strategic plans involve the greatest risk. They are more comprehensive than other plans, and are often difficult and costly to alter. They are made at the highest management levels and may not involve broad participation in the planning process. Sometimes, strategic hospitality marketing plans are made by a single person, such as the owner or the general manager.

We offer the following suggestions for more effective strategic hospitality marketing plans.

- Customize strategic plans to fit the company and its markets, guests, products, services, capabilities, management philosophy, and management style.

- Introduce strategic marketing changes gradually and gain the confidence and commitment of marketing personnel by helping them feel comfortable and secure with the changes.

- Include influential personnel in strategic planning, not just those with formal organizational titles.

- Where strategic planners other than senior managers are involved, make sure they understand important assumptions and constraints so that the plans are realistic.

- Expect resistance from some in authoritative positions and strive to gain their cooperation.

- Be as involved as possible, monitor the process and plans carefully, make adjustments, and fine tune.

Operational Planning. In contrast to strategic planning, operational marketing planning deals with short-range plans for existing activities in existing markets by focusing on current guests and available facilities. Examples include a twelve-month operating plan for a specific property (covering marketing, finance, human resources, and operations), plans prepared by the manager of a restaurant within a hotel complex, merchandising plans for specific foods and beverages, plans for a new menu, plans to supplement the personal amenities of rooms, or plans to add new wines and beverages. These plans have shorter time frames (one week to one year), involve smaller investments, and can usually be readily altered or reversed. They are more tactical in nature. Sound operational plans can have a great impact on sales, profits, and market share.

Short-term operational plans and long-term strategic plans are, of course, intertwined. The longer-run strategic plans shape, bound, and direct short-term plans. However, since short-term plans affect profits and market share, they affect a company's long-term direction. This is one reason many hospitality marketers tend to pay more attention to short-run concerns than they do to longer-range activities. In addition, short-run plans are often more attractive to time-pressed managers because they tend to be more concrete and immediate and to address practical issues.

Project Planning. Hospitality organizations may have a number of different projects at any given time. Project planning refers to the development of detailed action plans that are outside of the normal scope of operations but correspond to the organization's directions and methods. For example, a hotel chain may have a plan to incorporate health clubs into its facilities, or a restaurant may be considering the addition of Sunday buffet brunches to the normal menu. Each of these efforts must be planned in detail, although they are beyond normal operations and may not be implemented at all. Plans may be developed by project teams that include people from various functional areas and departments.

Contingency Planning. Because marketers cannot foresee all future developments, contingency plans are important. Strategic plans in particular face uncertainties that arise as unexpected developments occur. Contingency plans are an approach to the question, "What would we do if ...?" They are plans that anticipate various possible conditions. For example, suppose a hotelier is considering expanding into an area that has no serious competition. He might ask himself what he would do if a major competitor planned to move into the area. What advertising and pricing strategies would he adopt? How would he alter operations or stimulate guest loyalty? How would he react to a competitor's marketing strategies? By thinking through these possibilities and planning for contingencies, the hotelier is better prepared to meet them.

Strategic Issue Planning. A continuing appraisal of changing market circumstances will often identify strategic issues that demand an immediate response—that is, issues calling for strategic planning that cannot wait until strategic planning comes up again in the normal planning cycle. Examples of such issues might include a politically attractive tax package on hotels or restaurants introduced during an election campaign, the emergence of a major new competitor (perhaps sparking a price war), the opportunity to enter into an attractive strategic alliance, or a major disaster that can affect the business. Strategic issue planning addresses such concerns and helps management develop planned responses.

Zero-Based Planning. Hospitality plans are usually developed on the basis of past operations and existing situations. Sometimes, however, hospitality organizations can benefit by starting with a clean slate and developing plans from scratch. With zero-based planning, nothing is assumed. Rather, managers assess and justify all components of the plan on their merits, not on past practice. Projected costs and revenues for each element of the plan must be substantiated on merit. Although tradeoffs may occur among plans competing for scarce marketing resources such as advertising, personal selling, and promotion, this approach to planning offers great latitude. It challenges all proposals because nothing is built in or taken for granted. It prevents managers from becoming complacent and stimulates them to think about opportunities and goals that might not otherwise be explored. Nevertheless, zero-based planning is time-consuming and somewhat unrealistic, because it ignores the fact that some factors may indeed be unchangeable in the short run.

Two Basic Questions

In approaching planning, hospitality marketers should ask two basic questions:

1. What is the marketing planning process expected to achieve?
2. How can the marketing planning process become more effective?

What Should Marketing Planning Achieve?

Although the marketing planning process varies among hospitality organizations, an effective marketing planning process might achieve the following:

- Help design an organization's future and indicate how it might be realized. It should stimulate managers to become future oriented and think about opportunities and ways of improving a property.
- Develop a realistic, feasible marketing plan that can be readily implemented.
- Provide marketers with the mindset, information, and tools to carry out their responsibilities more effectively.
- Guide and assist the implementation of hospitality marketing strategies and programs.
- Provide an early warning system for potential problems by indicating deviations of performance from plans.
- Give the organization the means to deal more effectively with continuously changing environments.
- Offset tendencies for marketing units to optimize their own operations at the expense of others.
- Coordinate and harness marketing activities to achieve greater impact.
- Promote realistic budgeting as resources are used according to market opportunities.
- Designate marketing responsibilities throughout the enterprise.
- Communicate objectives, strategies, and approaches throughout the enterprise.
- Gain the commitment and dedication of the staff to achieve marketing goals.
- Realize an acceptable rate of return. Marketing planning must be able to justify itself.
- Develop useful information for dealing with all stakeholders, particularly lenders.
- Encourage an ongoing review system whereby marketing strategies and actions are evaluated and adjusted.

How Can Marketing Planning Be Made More Effective?

Numerous pitfalls regularly detract from the effectiveness of hospitality marketing planning. The following list describes how to avoid the most common of these dangers and, in so doing, how to enhance the effectiveness of the marketing planning process.

- Avoid confusing analysis and unnecessarily sophisticated quantitative techniques. Do not generate large amounts of market information that will not be used later. Consider pragmatic, realistic concerns. Do not pay attention to techniques at the cost of implementation. Plans do not pay off; implementation does.

- Do not confuse arithmetic manipulations of last year's plans, such as increasing or decreasing each of the categories by a certain percentage, with effective planning.

- Do not base marketing plans on straight-line projections or on the premise that past trends will continue over long periods.

- Develop good databases. Keep good records and have pertinent information readily accessible in a format that lends itself to marketing planning.

- Develop forms that marketing planners can readily use. Seek suggestions from those using the forms and data. Set up systems to get required information as conveniently as possible.

- Provide the resources necessary to support effective marketing planning. Realize that planning involves time and money. It should not be only an occasional activity.

- Make strategic changes and develop realistic plans and programs to support them, keeping in mind that they may be challenged.

- Gain the commitment and cooperation of those affected by the planning process.

- When possible, request the support of a "planning champion" (ideally a senior manager who is enthusiastic about the need for planning) who will approve plans and assist with implementation.

- Do not replace implementation and action with regular desire to defer decisions until more information can be gathered.

- Treat planning as a valuable aspect of hospitality marketing and not merely an annual ritual that results in unimportant reports.

- Guard against the power politics and vested interests that distort the logic and reality of carefully developed hospitality plans. Biases can play havoc with effective plans.

- Do not confuse the development of plans with the implementation of actual marketing programs. Distinguish between marketing failures due to poor planning and those caused by ineffective implementation. Fair or good plans with fine implementation are preferable to fine plans with only fair or poor implementation. The goal, of course, is to couple fine plans with fine implementation.

- Do not sacrifice long-term goals for short-term payoffs. Keep the company on track. Developing and maintaining loyal customers requires focused marketing efforts.

- Regularly review plans and the planning process with an eye to improvement. Planning, like all other important marketing activities, must be managed.

- Keep in mind that plans must be changed when basic conditions change. While plans need to be stable, they must also be flexible enough to reflect fundamental market changes.

- Relate marketing plans to the capacity, scope, image, reputation, resources, risk profile, and capabilities of a specific business. Dreaming and thinking big must not negate the pragmatics.

- Ensure that the specific responsibilities for implementation and follow-up are carried out.

- It is not enough to have a plan in mind. Written plans give visibility to ideas and foster communications.

Marketing planning confronts a variety of behavioral obstacles. Gaining the commitments necessary to effective implementation can be difficult and resistance may be encountered along the way. As we noted, some people may view planning as a meaningless ritual. The uncertainties inherent in planning make others uncomfortable. Some dislike the risks and probabilities of planning. Still others view planning as an activity that can potentially challenge their vested interests. Clearly, hospitality marketers face many pitfalls and complex activities in the planning process. The individuals involved in the planning process make a real difference. They govern effective implementation, which in turn governs the planning payoff.

Sales Forecasts and Marketing Plans

Sales forecasts and marketing plans are closely related. This section examines how sales forecasts are used in marketing planning because all marketing plans, whether implicitly or explicitly, involve sales forecasts.

Marketing plans deal with the future. They either refer directly to expected sales (revenues) or implicitly assume them. Marketing plans are developed with a certain level of sales in mind. Three related terms are useful in this regard: market potential, sales potential, and sales forecast.

Market potential refers to the upper limit of industry demand in a certain market segment over a specific time period. Hotels, for example, may be concerned with the maximum demand for rooms in a specific locale over the next quarter. To take another example, a city that is planning for the next Olympics will want to estimate the potential demand for hotel rooms and to communicate this to existing owners and possible developers.

Sales potential refers to the market share a given hotel or restaurant may gain in a certain time period if it exerts a maximum effort. This is the maximum market share a company can achieve and may possibly cost more to reach than it is worth.

Companies rarely, if ever, have the market potential as their sales potential—competitors will always gain some of the market.

Sales forecasts concern the actual sales that a hospitality enterprise estimates in a specific market over a particular time period (a month, a quarter, or a year), given its specific situation and proposed commitment of marketing resources. They are made for a variety of categories, such as market segments, geographic destinations, different groups of guests, age and income classes, average achieved room rate, average check, and food and beverage items. Seasonal trends are identified and forecasts can be altered accordingly. Sales forecasts are very important to marketing plans. The more accurate and specific the forecasts, the better the marketing planning.

Exhibit 3 shows the sales forecasting/marketing planning relationship. It indicates that market opportunities are inherent in changing environments. Marketing managers are challenged to estimate market potential (the upper limit for the industry) and then the sales potential (the upper limit for the company). They can then develop sales forecasts for the next month, quarter, or year. The sales forecasts in turn guide marketing plans, which also affect sales estimates. When sales forecasts indicate great market potential in the business and convention markets, for example, hospitality marketing plans can exploit that potential. Conversely, when marketing plans are implemented, they can increase or decrease perceived opportunities and sales. If advertising and sales expenditures are cut back beyond required budgets to achieve certain sales levels, for example, then expected sales will be affected.

Operationally, the most useful forecasts are those that are most specific. They are the forecasts that deal not just with the sale of food and beverages, but specify the kinds of food and types of beverages. However, such forecasts are also the most likely to contain the largest errors. While it is difficult to forecast overall sales (revenues), it is even more difficult to forecast sales for narrow market segments, small classes of guests, and very specific product and service categories. Despite such difficulties, sales forecasts go with the hospitality marketing territory. Managers do not have the choice of whether to forecast, but only how to do so, be it implicitly or explicitly.

Using Sales Forecasts

Hospitality enterprises often base their forecasts on the previous year's sales with some adjustments, such as adding five percent to sales revenues. This is a common approach because it is so convenient and simple. However, it can be totally misleading. The form in Exhibit 4 illustrates this procedure for a 200-room hotel with just under 80 percent room occupancy. Assume that management forecasts a five percent increase in total revenue next year. How should this be allocated across markets, rooms, and rates? Clearly, this issue raises some very important questions for management that must be answered before the naive forecast can be accepted.

Using this simple but flawed procedure, which at least pays some attention to different market segments, is better than not forecasting at all. It does, after all, raise some important questions for managers to consider. It can be risky, however, to infer that this year's sales are just an extension of last year's performance. The

Exhibit 3   Sales Forecasting and Marketing Planning Relationship

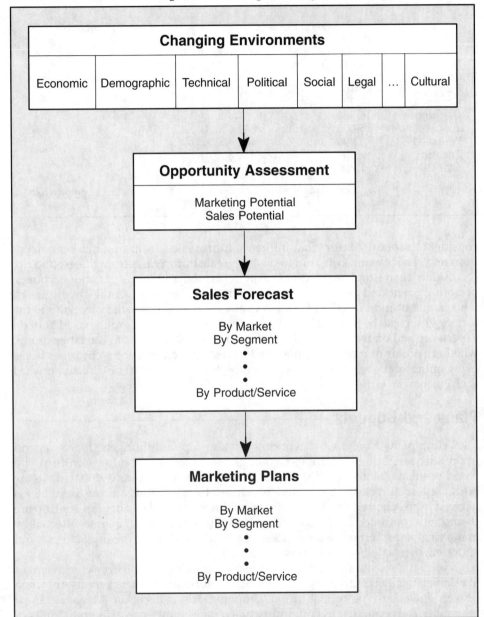

future need not mirror the past, and straight-line projections can be very misleading. This notion is particularly dangerous when market conditions turn abruptly, as they did in the early 1990s when many hotels in America and Asia headed sharply downward after growing steadily for several years. Instead, it is much better to

Exhibit 4   Forecasting Room Sales Revenue by Market Segment

	2000 Results			2001 Forecast		
Market	Room nights	Average rate ($)	Revenue	Room nights	Average rate ($)	Revenue
Rack	20,160	180	$3,628,800			
Corporate	17,280	140	2,419,200			
Convention	5,780	130	751,400			
Tour	5,660	150	849,000			
Weekend	2,890	160	462,400			
Theatre	2,805	160	448,800			
Other	1,880	140	263,200			
TOTAL	56,455	156.28	$8,822,800			$9,263,940

consider the specific factors that influence future sales, including market perceptions and capacity concerns, and to develop realistic forecasts from the ground up.

Rather than simply extend past experience, think in terms of major accounts, of both current and potential guests. Distinguish between off-the-street guests, who cannot be individually identified in advance, and those who can. Sales to the former group can be forecast by market segment or customer group based both on experience and on the level of planned marketing effort. Sales to the latter group, whether regular or new users, may be forecast on a customer-by-customer basis, using both experience and an assessment of the sales effort to be directed toward each customer.

Plans and Budgets

Marketing plans have a close working relationship with budgets. Plans depend upon adequate budgets for effective implementation, and budgets, in turn, are based on plans. Moreover, just as plans and forecasts are directly related, so are budgets and forecasts. Estimated revenue—the first line on any budget—is derived from sales forecasts. Thus, budgets (the major tool of financial control) are themselves controlled by sales forecasts. Sales forecasts are, of course, affected by marketing plans. If the resources necessary to implement marketing plans are not allocated, then sales forecasts must be altered.

Hotel and restaurant managers often pay attention to industry-wide averages in establishing their marketing budgets. Such information can be very useful when broken down by type of institution, property size, or location. Managers must remember, however, that overall industry averages lump many different kinds of properties and situations together that may bear little resemblance to any particular property. In establishing budgets, every hospitality enterprise must consider its unique situation, paying attention to market conditions, competition, people, approaches, strategies, and plans. In other words, marketing budgets should relate to marketing tasks, plans, and programs, regardless of industry averages.

In establishing budgets for hospitality businesses, the categories of revenues and expenses included will depend upon the needs of the organization. Included may be proposed expenditures for such marketing activities as direct mail brochures, sales personnel, merchandising, promotions, newspaper, TV, and radio advertising, trade shows, and so on. When appropriate budget categories have been established, management can budget expenditures, monitor them by comparing actual and budgeted expenses, and allocate expenditures to various activities or units. For example, expenses for advertising, selling, promotion, entertainment, or travel could be allocated to a restaurant, bar, health club, or other unit. In this way, management can determine the profitability of various departments and units.

Marketing budgets should be somewhat flexible in order to reflect changes in marketing plans and programs. Adequate resources are necessary for success. Difficulties arise when hospitality enterprises increase the scope and level of their marketing plans without adjusting their budgets accordingly. For example, a manager may plan to offset low weekend occupancy rates by lowering room prices and adding theater packages. Suppose, however, that to control costs, the manager does not allocate additional advertising funds to cultivate demand. A potentially good strategy could fail. In this case, advertising costs are controlled to the detriment of room occupancy. Pressure to cut budgets understandably arises during difficult periods. However, short-term goals of reduced expenses may be achieved at the cost of developing and maintaining loyal guests.

Monitoring Plans

Because hospitality markets are continuously changing, plans must be monitored and updated. Planning forms that list information about objectives, planning activities, target dates, and budgets give management the opportunity to monitor plans, conduct audits, and generally assess how well a company is doing. Managers can then determine any needed adjustments and examine if short-range, intermediate, and long-range plans mesh, and whether the marketing plans of various units coordinate with each other and with enterprise objectives.

Monitoring plans involves comparing actual results with planned or expected results. Expected results are the standard or yardstick that specifically indicate what the plans are designed to do. These planning yardsticks may be stated in terms of profits, margins, market share, average check, table turnover, average room revenue, return on investment, and other measures. When actual results are compared with plans, variations can be noted and the reasons for them assessed. Necessary adjustments can be made to the standards, the marketing plans, or both. Deviations may suggest a reassessment of basic objectives and strategies or just minor modifications in tactics. Adjustments are especially important when there are large discrepancies between plans and reality.

Some adjustments result from the dynamics of marketplaces. Decreasing demand for hotel rooms in the 1990s, for example, greatly affected the occupancy rates of luxury hotels, necessitating adjustments. Similarly, changes in the American tax code that cut allowances for business expenditures on meals and entertainment

Exhibit 5   From Marketing Situations to Actions

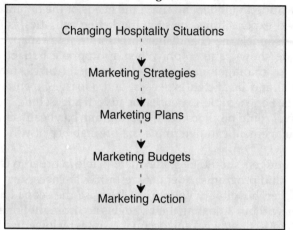

significantly affected revenues at many pricier restaurants. Shifts in laws regarding smoking, in guest attitudes toward meat, high-cholesterol foods, and alcoholic beverages, and in guest preferences toward shorter but more frequent vacations mean that hospitality enterprises are often faced with making changes to their operating and strategic marketing plans.

Marketing plans should be monitored regularly. Whether it is done on a daily, weekly, monthly, quarterly, or annual basis depends on particular circumstances. It is not unusual for restaurants to evaluate receipts daily to see if they meet expectations, or to verify that what guests are eating and drinking corresponds to expectations. Managers regularly monitor monthly, quarterly, and year-end sales and revenues to determine their targets and whether or not plans should be changed. Although marketing plans do not change with each shift of the wind, they should be altered when fundamental changes occur or when important considerations differ from initial assumptions.

Marketing Planning in Action

Marketing planning works. Planned activities have proved to be more effective than unplanned ones. Planning enhances efficiency and effectiveness and permits organized, coordinated marketing thrusts.

Plans specify the results expected from marketing strategies. They indicate whether or not a different image, an increase in sales, improved market share, a higher return on investment, or an improved competitive posture should be expected. They also specify the resources needed to implement strategies, indicate the sequence of marketing activities necessary to carry out plans, and facilitate the assessment and control of marketing activities to achieve specified goals. Exhibit 5 summarizes the relationship between marketing situations, strategies, plans, budgets, and actions. It highlights the flow of activities involved in the progression of

Exhibit 6   Marketing Planning Questions

Marketing Planning Questions	Marketing Planning Role	Marketing Planning Achievements
Why?	Identifies the planning goals: market share, profit, image, guest satisfaction, sales.	Specifies the purposes of each marketing strategy and action.
How?	Develops programs for each unit; indicates the use of marketing resources.	Develops the marketing mix and allocates resources to marketing.
What?	Establishes goals for each program and control point.	Permits measures of performance in specific time periods.
Who?	Identifies responsibilities.	Specifies accountable units and persons.
When?	Plans the time sequence.	Establishes time lines for all activities.
Where?	Deals with location and distribution/ networking plans.	Specifies where activities will take place.

marketing planning from assessment and analysis to the development and monitoring of plans.

During the planning process, hospitality managers seek answers to common questions: Why? How? What? Who? When? Where? As hospitality marketers answer these questions in detail, they generate critical planning information. Such information is relevant to the development and implementation of meaningful, practical marketing plans. Exhibit 6 highlights what these questions mean to hospitality planning.

Information in the Marketing Planning Process

In our initial outline of the steps involved in planning (Exhibit 1), we showed that planning follows a progression from gathering and analyzing marketing information, to making marketing assessments, developing actual marketing plans and programs, implementing them, monitoring results, and finally, making necessary adjustments. Exhibit 7 provides a more detailed outline of the hospitality marketing planning process, identifying many of the specific steps needed at each stage of the

Exhibit 7   Detailed Marketing Planning Process

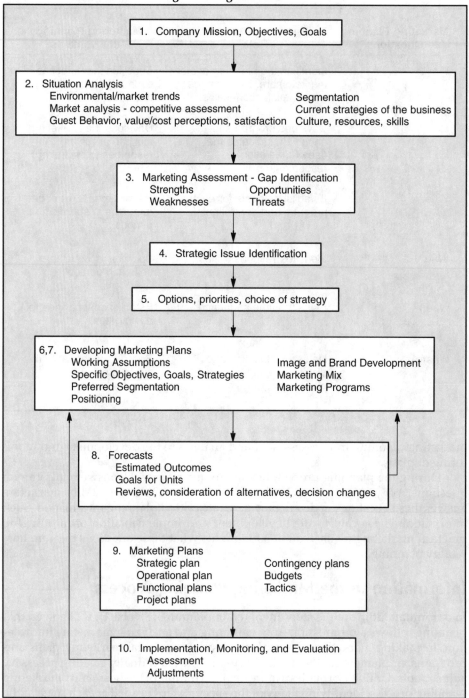

process. It also highlights both the overall flow of the analysis and the presence of feedback from forecasts to the development of plans (sometimes the forecasts point to a need to change the plan if objectives are to be satisfied), and from measurement to plans, where management adjusts plans in the light of experience.

Pertinent and timely information is the basis for planning activities. Market intelligence derived from research into various market segments, guest wants and needs, guest behavior, competitive analysis, market trends, and emerging market opportunities is coupled with internal data about operations, costs, sales, and revenues to allow management to create informed plans. For example, if we intended to purchase and operate a resort hotel, we would consider economic, political, demographic, guest, and market information and direct specific attention to data about past and projected costs and revenues.

A realistic assessment of the situation based on an environment-strategy-capability evaluation that points to gaps between strategy and environment, and between strategy and capability (leading to an identification of SWOT—strengths, weaknesses, opportunities, and threats) is also valuable and can be compared with similar data from competitors. Two useful kinds of comparisons result from a detailed SWOT analysis: comparisons with immediate and direct competitors and comparisons with the best in the industry—the benchmarks. Both areas of comparison provide information and ideas for improvements.

Important information can be gained from detailed analysis of internal statistics about past and future marketing operations and trends. Revenue data should be tracked, and guest behavior and reactions should be analyzed. Other sources of information include published data and personal observations of competitors' properties. Such an analysis will help identify profitable market opportunities, competitor soft spots, overlooked market segments, and marketing strategies. Keep the guest's viewpoint in mind at all times.

Some hospitality enterprises gather and summarize employee opinions about company strengths and weakness and compare the results with those of competitors. The hospitality offerings of a particular enterprise, like physical property, food and beverage, guest services, room amenities, and recreational facilities, are evaluated and compared with those of competitors and improvements can be recommended.

Exhibit 8 offers a hypothetical example of a competitive analysis. This simple format provides a ready indication of how the Central Hotel measures up to competitors. In actual practice, marketers would use an extended list of relevant attributes, including all the features of the competing properties that influence guest decisions. Central Hotel's rank in the competitive hierarchy, its advantages, and its potential for improvement can then be determined. The benchmark group indicates the performance of industry leaders and provides role models to emulate or at least to furnish ideas for improvement.

In our example, Central Hotel lacks a business center and a health club, is probably due for refurbishment, and has a significantly lower occupancy. Such knowledge suggests opportunities for change. Introducing these facilities and beginning a refurbishment might provide guests with better service and value. On the other hand, management is aware that the hotel has certain location, price, and meeting room advantages over its competitors.

Exhibit 8   Competitive Analysis for the Central Hotel

Hotel	Rooms	Staff	Years since refurbishment	Facilities*	Occupancy (%)	Price range (singles)
Oriental	600	270	5	BC	70	$ 84
Capital	160	45	15		65	56–64
Railway	400	225	2	BC	75	88–104
Central	300	175	7		60	81–90
BENCHMARK						
Criterion	480	430	10	BC,HC	85	104–130
Harveys	250	120	4	HC	72	90–120
Rubicon	200	125	3	BC	75	96–104

*Note: BC refers to Business Center, HC to Health Club

Exhibit 9 summarizes the kinds of market information various hotels actually use in planning. Derived from interviews with hotel managers, we intend this information to be indicative and suggestive, rather than all-inclusive. Each category can be broken down further and analyzed in more detail to generate necessary information.

Marketing Planning in Practice

Until now, we have discussed the theory of hospitality planning. What happens in the real world? In general, the procedures, outputs, and approaches to planning overlap considerably among larger hotels in global markets. While the sequence of activities as well as the organization and presentation of planning data may differ among hospitality enterprises, most hospitality plans are similar to the basic structure set out in Exhibit 1.

Several observations result from an analysis of actual hotel marketing planning processes. First, a great amount of detailed data is essential to meaningful planning, as is pertinent and timely information. Second, detailed analysis will bridge the transition from marketing data to market intelligence. Only information that can be readily used for planning purposes is valuable to management. Third, effective hospitality marketing deals with the impact of both internal and external factors. Fourth, hospitality planning requires commitments of crucial resources, including time, people, and money. Fifth, merely going through planning exercises and blindly participating in annual planning rituals is a wasteful, meaningless activity. Management is more interested in the results of marketing planning than in routinely developed plans.

Exhibit 9 Kinds of Planning Information Used by Hotels

SITUATION ANALYSIS

Economic, Social, Political and Technological Change
Global
National
Regional
Local

Market Conditions
Room supply
Room demand
Competitive hotels
Occupancy
Rates
Market share
Guest origin
Seasonality

MARKET SEGMENTS, GUEST BEHAVIOR

Demographics—location (international, regional, local), age, etc.
Guest profiles, preferences
Benefits sought
Competitor's guests
Corporate guests—frequency, preferences
Conventions, business seminars
Transients
Group travel, tours
Airline staff, government, other special categories

GUEST SATISFACTION, VALUE/COST MEASURES

Surveys of guests, agents, and opinion leaders/influentials
Guest satisfaction cards
Incidence of repeat visits
Service staff perceptions
Service encounter analysis
Product cost data
Identification of high yield segments

COMPETITIVE ANALYSIS (For each major competitor, by segment)

CULTURE, RESOURCES, AND SKILLS

Identification of major competitive assets
Prevailing culture
Barriers to change
Facilities design, management systems, data bases
Level of skills, staff development and training
Barriers to effective service delivery

(continued)

Exhibit 9   *(continued)*

PRODUCT/SERVICE EVALUATION

        Strategies
        Issues
        Specialist areas—concierge floor, butlers, clubs
        Facilities—business center, health, sports etc
        Services offered
        Competitors
        Development plans

COMMUNICATION MIX

        Personal selling
                Sales organization
                Sales teams
                Sales contacts
                Sales support
        Communications
                TV, newspaper, magazines
                Direct mail
                Media plans
                Trade shows
                Public relations
                Merchandising

PRICING MIX

        Policies
        Rates
        Packages
        Discounts
        Alliances
        Frequent guest programs

DISTRIBUTION NETWORKS

        Alliances
        Travel agents
        Partners

PROFIT CENTER REVIEWS
    Restaurants
        Revenues
        Menus
        Room service
        Poolside service
        Expansion and contraction
        Seating
        Trends
        New concepts

Exhibit 9 *(continued)*

Beverage service
 Revenues
 Bars
 Happy hour
 Mini-bars
 Poolside service
 Room service
 Clubs

Rooms available
 Room inventory
 Types of rooms
 Rooms added
 Rooms deleted
 Refurbishing of rooms
 Occupancy rates
 Revenues

Other facilities—utilization and revenues
 Business center
 Sports and health facilities

Attitude Toward Planning

Many hospitality enterprises neglect both formal and informal marketing planning. Despite the fact that it often takes three to five years to develop markets, the industry seems more attuned to short-term sales efforts and daily operations than to intermediate and long-term marketing efforts. Neglecting marketing planning activities directly affects long-term sales and profits. Despite this fact, many hospitality firms do not even develop annual operating plans. Although marketing plans are becoming commonplace in larger hospitality enterprises, they are still seldom used by medium-sized and smaller businesses.

The reason for this neglect of planning among smaller hospitality providers is twofold: many believe they have little or no time for planning, and they simply feel more comfortable participating in daily operations than they do in planning. These providers are really saying that they feel the payoff from time spent on current operations exceeds that from planning. Although some profess the importance of marketing planning, most smaller hospitality enterprises do not appreciate the benefits that derive from effective hospitality marketing planning (such as increased productivity and profit).

While smaller companies may have little need for sophisticated plans and procedures, they are often the ones that could benefit most from planning. Even when the marketing planner is the owner/operator of a business, plans—however informal—are beneficial. Costly errors could result without proper planning. Moreover, written plans make thoughts and ideas visible and promote better communication among members of the marketing team.

Planning Approaches: Top-Down or Bottom-Up

Should marketing plans develop from the top down or from the bottom up? The choice of a top-down or bottom-up approach depends greatly on the character and style of the managers involved. Top-down marketing plans are devised by a centralized group and then communicated to various levels throughout the organization for implementation. Bottom-up approaches engage operating personnel in developing plans for their units. These plans are then compiled and coordinated into an overall marketing plan.

Effective marketing planning in the hospitality industry requires the contributions of those on the firing line—those who are actually delivering services. Plans should be sensitive to the concerns of the actual "doers" as well as those of the upper echelons of management. Managers must remember that payoffs depend on attitude and commitment. They do not simply flow automatically from competent planning.

Managing Marketing Planning

Top management's attitude makes a big difference in how plans are developed and implemented. Research suggests four main factors must be considered for effective management of the planning process.[2]

1. *Techniques and systems.* Provide the techniques and systems to develop credible operational marketing plans. In other words, make sure the systems are in place to make plans.

2. *Behavioral issues.* These include management attitudes toward and perceptions of planning, commitment, training, and participation.

3. *Organizational issues.* Offer the necessary support and reinforcement to planning within the organization. A lack of organizational support, particularly among top executives, will undermine otherwise effective planning preparations.

4. *Consistency among all of the above.* These factors should work together and support each other, synthesize, and eliminate cross-currents and conflicts. Planning suffers when these integral components work at cross-purposes.

Concluding Comments

Through planning, hospitality marketers can effectively achieve their objectives, coordinate marketing actions, and develop a focused marketing thrust. Marketers are challenged to create realistic, credible, and practical marketing plans that can be readily implemented to achieve specified goals. Ultimately, plans should provide the capability to better serve guests at a profit.

In reality, however, marketing planning is often considered a bothersome ritual. Companies produce extensive plans that are quickly forgotten until annual planning time returns. Although such plans reflect the expenditure of considerable effort, they are a waste of time and resources. Effective planning is a matter of realism. Choices must be made and efforts must be focused. The efficacy of hospitality marketing planning is directly related to the careful selection of realistic goals, the development of focused, practical strategies and decisions, and the logical implementation of activities. Successful planners will also pay special attention to hospitality environments and see things through the eyes of guests.

Marketing planning is not a matter of planning for planning's sake, nor should it be seen merely as an opportunity to display one's skills. It should result in plans that people accept, believe in, and use in everyday operations. Marketing planning is really anticipatory decision making, for it logically and systematically orders marketing resources and activities by getting hospitality managers to think in terms of missions, opportunities, and objectives. Effective hospitality marketing planning will help:

- Establish objectives.

- Formulate strategies.

- Encourage a logical and organized approach.

- Identify market opportunities.

- Identify differential advantage.

- Allocate and organize marketing resources.

- Insure coordinated, integrated programs.

- Generate successful marketing efforts.

Whether it relates to taking over an ongoing operation, starting a new enterprise, or reinventing and repositioning existing companies, marketing planning is fundamental to designing an effective hospitality marketing mix. It touches almost every aspect of hospitality management, including budgets, the allocation and control of marketing resources, and marketing strategies and tactics. Furthermore, it concerns old and new opportunities, as well as long-term, intermediate, and short-term situations.

Marketing planning provides the road maps—the plans that guide marketing decisions and actions. Plans direct hospitality operations by helping companies allocate resources and achieve their objectives effectively. They help to achieve the teamwork necessary to realize common marketing goals. When plans are realistic, feasible, and pertinent, they are easily implemented. As Mr. Ricardo Castaneda, General Manager of Thailand's five-star Melia Hua Hin Hotel, cautioned so insightfully, "Marketing plans can be well-developed, comprehensive, and logical. They can be beautiful. Nothing happens, however, until the plans are implemented, until they are put into effect. The planning payoff is in the implementation."[3]

Endnotes

1. Albert Einstein, *Out of My Later Years* (New York: Philosophical Library, 1950).

2. Nigel F. Piercy and William D. Giles, "Managing the Marketing Planning Process: The Search for Continuous Competitive Renewal," in Sidney J. Levy, George R. Frederichs,

and Howard L. Gordon, eds., *The Dartnell Marketing Manager's Handbook* (Chicago: Dartnell, 1994), pp. 683–684.

3. Personal interview, May 1994, Hua Hin, Thailand.

Key Terms

contingency planning—the process of developing plans that prepare managers with alternatives should unexpected threats or opportunities occur.

market potential—an estimate of the maximum possible sales for an entire industry during a time period.

operational planning—the process of developing weekly, monthly, quarterly, and yearly plans that deal with current operations.

project planning—the process of developing plans that deal with specific projects such as creating and marketing new products.

sales forecast—an estimate of dollar or unit sales for a specified future time period under a proposed marketing plan or program.

sales potential—the portion of the market potential that a particular business can reasonably expect to achieve.

strategic issue planning—the identification of strategic issues that might well demand immediate responses and the development of plans to deal with them outside the normal planning cycle.

strategic planning—consideration of decision alternatives in light of their probable consequences over time. Distinguishing characteristics include an external orientation, a process for formulating strategies, analysis of strategic situations, and commitment to action.

zero-based planning—the development of plans that starts with a clean slate, taking nothing for granted and assuming everything can be changed.

Review Questions

1. At what level of management does marketing planning occur?

2. Why must plans be developed for major marketing tasks? What are some types of plans?

3. Why do strategic plans involve the greatest risk? How can that risk be minimized?

4. What is operational planning? How does it differ from strategic planning? Of the two, which is more often neglected? Why?

5. What are the benefits of an effective marketing planning process? What are the costs of an ineffective process?

6. What are some of the most common pitfalls of marketing planning? How can they be avoided?

7. When is marketing planning a time-consuming but largely useless activity? How can this situation be avoided?

8. What is involved in monitoring marketing plans? Why is it important to monitor such plans?

9. How are sales forecasts and marketing plans related? Budgets and marketing plans?

10. Why do many hospitality businesses neglect marketing planning?

Internet Sites

For more information, visit the following Internet sites. Remember that Internet addresses can change without notice.

Hilton Hotels Corporation
http://www.hilton.com

Marriott International
http://www.marriott.com

McDonald's Corporation
http://www.mcdonalds.com

PepsiCo
http://www.pepsico.com

Walt Disney Corporation
http://www.disney.com

Part II

Guests: The Focus of Hospitality Marketing

Chapter 5 Outline

Models of Guest Behavior
Purchase Stimuli
    Guest Behavior as Information Processing
    Guest Drives and Motives
    Motivation: Behavior Primacy
    Motivation: Need Primacy
    Motives of Non-Guests
The Guest Search Process
Purchase Decisions
    Preference Models
    Perceptions and Images
    Self-Image
    Guest Attitudes
Purchase Outputs
    Guest Behavior and Learning
    Cognitive Dissonance
External Forces
    Cultures and Subcultures
    Reference Groups
    Social Class
Applying Guest Behavior Models
Concluding Comments

5

Individual Guest Behavior

"The consumer consumes not things but expected benefits."
—Theodore Levitt

Gᴇᴏʀɢᴇ Lᴇᴇ is the general manager of a well-established, upscale resort property in southern California. One day while sitting in his office overlooking the Pacific Ocean, George reflected on the themes of several presentations he heard while at a recent international hospitality management conference in Istanbul. Speaker after speaker emphasized the importance of understanding guests, and both determining and catering to their wants, needs, and motives. This philosophy would be the key to hospitality success in the twenty-first century. As George contemplated the wide variety of guests his resort hosted, he thought about their needs and motives. How could he characterize the essence of these needs and motives and use this knowledge to better manage the property?

George's concerns are shared by all hospitality providers who must predict guest reactions to their services well before guests have actually experienced them. For these reasons, the cornerstone of successful hospitality marketing is knowledge of guests. When guest needs are recognized and understood, hospitality managers can respond appropriately and increase the effectiveness of marketing operations.

Hospitality services represent different things to different guests and even to the same guests at different times. While dining out is primarily a means of satisfying hunger for some, for others it represents a business opportunity, a pleasurable social experience, or social status.

Guests are tugged and pulled by numerous complex factors when they make hospitality purchases. These influences include their wants, needs, drives, attitudes, opinions, perceptions, social class, education, self-image, and peer or reference groups. The last three decades have produced many important concepts and models of buyer behavior. Although these models were largely developed in relation to product marketing, they can be effectively adapted for and applied to hospitality. This chapter examines models from such varied disciplines as economics, sociology, psychology, and anthropology in order to more clearly understand buyer behavior in the hospitality industry.

While it is never easy to anticipate and understand guest reactions, these behavioral models translate into practical solutions for marketing challenges in the hospitality industry. As a result, hospitality management will be richly rewarded with more effective marketing decisions.

Exhibit 1   General Components of Consumer Behavior Models

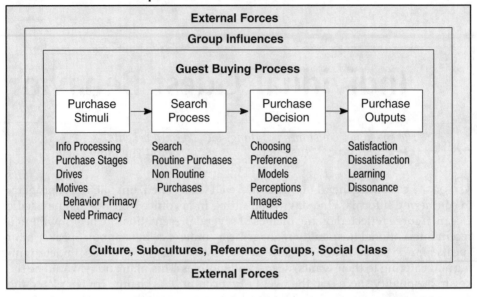

Models of Guest Behavior

In one chapter, we can address buyer behavior in only a limited way. Therefore, we have selected carefully from among the most pertinent topics for hospitality marketing and treat them briefly. Readers wishing to pursue the subject will find that extensive literature and specialized journals are readily available.

Several widely accepted models of consumer behavior apply to hospitality situations. While they may vary in emphasis, detail, and orientation, four basic components underlie most of them: external and internal purchase stimuli, the search process, the decision process, and the resulting outputs (see Exhibit 1). This chapter is organized around each of these major components.

Exhibit 1 details the specific elements discussed under each topic, as well as the four external factors covered: culture, subcultures, reference groups, and social class. Many of the topics are difficult to pigeon-hole because they pertain to more than one component. For example, attitude and perception may affect purchase stimuli, the search process, and the purchase decision. We have exercised authors' prerogatives in choosing where to put them in order to facilitate our discussion.

External stimuli include activities like advertising, merchandising, personal selling, public relations, and peer recommendations. They relate to such internal stimuli as guest wants, needs, motives, perceptions, images, thoughts, feelings, preferences, experiences, and responses. Both external and internal stimuli contribute to the search and purchase decision process.

The search process itself may be short and routine or lengthy and complicated. The search may be completed, postponed, or continued. If it continues, the

Exhibit 2   Stages of Activities in Guest Purchase Behavior

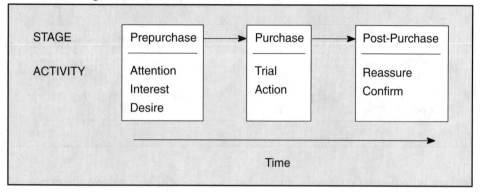

resulting information and experiences will shape attitudes and observations and may stimulate future purchases.

The actual act of buying is but one stage in the process. Guests must evaluate alternatives and make a purchase decision. They may postpone a decision in order to seek more information or end the search process altogether. Note also that purchasers may not be the actual consumers, but may make purchases for them.

Outputs of the buyer-behavior process are the actual purchase and use of hospitality services. The experiences and opinions resulting from encounters between guests and service providers contribute to these outputs. Guests are satisfied if their expectations are met or exceeded. On the other hand, they may be disappointed or dissatisfied if their expectations are not met. In addition, experiences with hospitality offerings feed back into the search process and influence future purchase decisions.

Purchase Stimuli

Guest Behavior as Information Processing

Individual guests process various kinds of information as they carry out their buying activities. Guest behavior may be viewed as information processing. Exhibit 2 illustrates the three stages of the purchase decision: prepurchase, purchase, and post-purchase. Information may be processed at any of these stages.

During the prepurchase phase, potential guests are seekers and users of information. Information helps them clarify their wants and needs, search for satisfying alternatives, and assess their choices. At this stage, information attracts and informs guests and creates desire. For example, a pizza chain might entice guests with television and newspaper ads that include tempting pictures of different pizzas, special coupons, and prices.

In the purchase phase, marketing efforts aim to influence guest purchase decisions. Advertising, personal selling, and various other merchandising and promotional efforts create desire and motivate guests to try products. Many fast-food operations, for example, offer coupons, discounts, and specials to entice guests. As

Exhibit 3   Drives, Motives, and Purchase Behavior

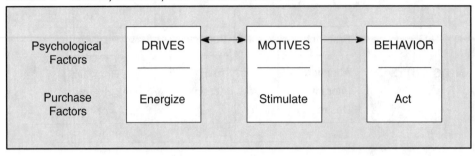

the purchase phase progresses, guests can make, postpone, or reject their choices. Guests who reject a hospitality alternative return to the prepurchase phase and seek other options.

Once the purchase is made, the post-purchase phase begins. Guest reactions may be total satisfaction, partial satisfaction, or dissatisfaction. How an enterprise reacts during this phase can engender guest loyalty and help overcome any unsatisfactory experiences. The famous Cloister resort at Sea Island, Georgia, sends guests an informative in-house publication to follow up on guest activities and show how guests enjoy their lifestyles. Pizza Hut's policy of providing a free lunch if food is not delivered within a specified period is designed both to prevent slow service and to overcome customer dissatisfaction should slow service occur. In a similar vein, a well-handled complaint is an important post-purchase activity. Efforts in the post-purchase phase can pave the way for future sales.

Guest Drives and Motives

Drives (or needs) and **motives** are basic elements of guest behavior. They are closely related terms and, in practice, are often not clearly distinguished. Drives are the objects, conditions, or activities toward which motives are directed. Drives are goals that dispose people to take some action, and as such, they energize or trigger motives. Motives inspire people to act. A drive may be the reason a guest is motivated to dine at a certain restaurant or stay at a particular hotel. Exhibit 3 depicts the interrelationships between drives and motives. This section examines how drives and motives influence individual guest behavior.

Drives vary in type, and hospitality products and services may appeal to any or all of them. There are *visceral drives, activity drives, aesthetic drives,* and *emotional drives.* Visceral drives include hunger, smell, taste, and thirst. Activity drives include exercise, rest, and environmental change. Aesthetic drives encompass ambience, design, fashion, style, color, and music. Emotional drives include love, fear, joy, empathy, rage, and disgust.

Guest motives stimulate individuals to act. They explain guest behavior. Although motives are complex and difficult to determine, they are often simplistically classified as either emotional or rational, with the implication being that people acting on the basis of emotional motives have not logically evaluated a situation. Instead, this reasoning holds that they have succumbed to ego-boosting forces such as status, style, self-image, or reputation. In truth, however, emotionally-stimulated decisions can be quite rational. Eating, for example, is not simply a rational response to hunger. Consumers may logically decide that it is in their best interest to eat in a sensible manner. In other situations, however, people may eat foods they would not otherwise consume as a response to stress, pleasure, or simply a lack of time or available alternatives. While these choices may be emotional, they are not necessarily irrational.

Many motives may contribute to a single hospitality purchase which, in turn, can satisfy more than one need. One guest's dining experience may appeal to hunger, aesthetic desires, and prestige, while different guests may exhibit the same purchase behavior based on quite different motives. For example, different guests may select the same resort, but for different reasons. Some will come for the golf facilities, others for the food, others for the beaches, others for the conference facilities, and others for the reputation. Similarly, various guests may choose a particular restaurant for different reasons, such as ambience, status and prestige, an exceptional wine cellar, a convenient location, or special services. Moreover, guests with identical motives can make entirely different decisions. People who are interested in enjoying the finest Italian or Cantonese dishes or who wish to experience truly exceptional service may choose entirely different restaurants based on their own opinions.

Motivation: Behavior Primacy

Behavior primacy and need primacy are two theoretical models that help us understand guest motivation. The theory of **behavior primacy** holds that human behavior results from interactions with various environments. Guests change their behavior to cope with environmental shifts. For example, as tax policies change regarding deductible business expenses, so do sales at luxury restaurants and conference resorts. Similarly, hospitality decisions often reflect changes in environments. When a company covers business expenditures only for food and not for alcoholic beverages, expenses for entertaining customers may be included in one total meal charge without a breakout for beverages. As another example, a client company with a policy of paying for employee lodging at conferences but not for spouses' lodging may prompt a hotel to quote the same room rate for single and double occupancy, so that spouses can come at no additional charge. Reduced airline fares for those staying over a Saturday night have caused many conferences and meetings to take place over a weekend.

According to the behavior primacy theory, the environmental forces shaping guest reactions must be considered in order to understand and predict guest behavior. This entails watching recent demographic, economic, social, political, legal, technological, and international developments. Given a growing proportion of elderly in our society, for example, hospitality providers might offer lighter meals, smaller portions, baked instead of fried foods, menus printed in larger type, and seniors' clubs and discounts. Many hospitality corporations, such as Marriott and Hilton, have already responded to this growing demographic sector by offering special programs to seniors. Marriott has also entered the nursing home field.

Exhibit 4   Maslow's Hierarchy of Needs

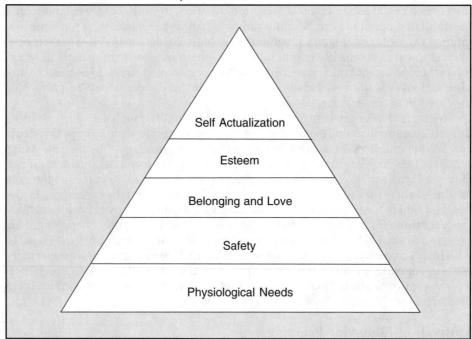

Motivation: Need Primacy

The **need primacy** model holds that all human behavior is motivated by needs for such things as food, safety, and self-esteem. Needs generate tensions that guests seek to reduce—sometimes by purchasing and consuming hospitality products or services.

Although the terms *needs* and *wants* are often used interchangeably, it is useful to distinguish between them. A need is something that a person requires to satisfy emotional or rational goals. Wants result when people recognize that a certain product or service will satisfy their needs. To illustrate, a guest may be hungry and *need* a meal. While the guest may *want* to dine in a world-class gourmet restaurant, is this what the guest needs? Who decides what specific guests really want or need? For various reasons (for example, to entertain VIPs), a certain guest may actually need a luxurious suite at New York's Hotel Pierre. Other guests without such specific requirements may only need a room at the Motel 6. By the same token, does a hotel beauty shop fulfill the wants or the needs of a guest? Does a guest really need a facial or a hair cut? Ultimately, the guests themselves are in the best position to determine their wants and needs.

Maslow's Hierarchy of Needs. Maslow's **hierarchy of needs**, also known as a hierarchy of motives, is one of the most widely-referenced need-primacy theories (see Exhibit 4). Needs at the bottom of the hierarchy (or pyramid, as it is usually depicted) dominate those above them. At the base of the pyramid are the most potent needs of all, the physiological needs for food, clothing, water, air, and sex.

When these physiological needs are largely satisfied, other needs begin to dominate—the need for safety, order, and stability. Hospitality providers have a particular ability to meet safety needs. A *Wall Street Journal* survey reported that "Hotel security is the prime concern for pleasure travelers...Eighty percent of 850 respondents said the safety of a hotel and destination was critical to enjoying a trip."[1] A spokesperson for Howard Johnson's noted, "If [security] is not the top priority in guest surveys, it's the second."[2] Hotels and motels often rely on sophisticated card-locking systems to improve security and generate a greater sense of guest safety. Hilton has highlighted its state-of-the-art guestroom locking systems in advertisements.

As the need for safety is satisfied, people begin to search for belonging and love in the form of acceptance as a member of a group or organization. Family relationships help satisfy this need, as do memberships in exclusive clubs.

Needs for esteem become increasingly important as people find belonging and love. Guests not only desire to be part of a group, but to be esteemed within that group. They search for outward signs of respect, prestige, and success. Many prestigious organizations, restaurants, and hotels appeal to this need and price their offerings accordingly. The $1.25 drink of Perrier water at a local restaurant may cost $4.95 in a prestigious Beverly Hills restaurant.

At the top of Maslow's pyramid lies the need for self-actualization, or developing one's self and capabilities to the fullest extent. In order to satisfy this need, one must do what one is best suited for, in the best possible manner. Thus, a vintner might develop herself to the fullest extent possible, become one of the most knowledgeable wine authorities around, cultivate a most discerning palate, write research papers, and be respected and envied by colleagues. Self-actualization may culminate in outstanding achievements that are recognized by various symbols such as honorary doctorates and scientific prizes.

Maslow's hierarchy does not rigidly adhere to a prescribed order. Several needs may contribute to a single situation. Guests may patronize a certain restaurant to satisfy biological needs such as hunger and thirst as well as a need for belonging and esteem. The way in which a door attendant, maître d', or server handles guest service will determine whether guests' needs for belonging and esteem are met. Different guests may satisfy the same need in different ways. For some guests, the need for love and esteem is satisfied by membership in a particular club. For others, this same club provides an opportunity for making business contacts or realizing social and political aspirations.

Although guest motives are difficult to identify and measure, marketing researchers use such techniques as the following to clarify them.

- *Observation.* Watch for guest reactions as they assess and use hospitality services. Note the questions they ask, and think about and try to interpret their motives.

- *Self-reports.* Ask guests why they make various purchases. Assume that guests know why and are willing to tell.

Exhibit 5   Guest Search Process

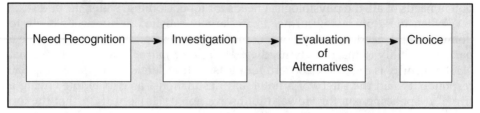

- *Focus group interviews.* Assemble a group of guests and ask them to share comments and insights about their motives for making hospitality choices.

- *Psychological Tests.* Use various psychological tests and techniques, as well as disguised stimuli, to get consumers to indicate their true motives.

Motives of Non-Guests

It is sometimes important to understand the motives and behavior of those who choose *not* to use hospitality services. When Florida's travel industry realized a slump in 1994, industry members and governmental officials were not sure why. To understand the problem, tourism officials conducted a marketing research study of tourists who chose not to visit Florida. When marketers understand the motives of non-guests, they are in a better position to develop strategies and programs that are effective in overcoming important objections. They are better able to transform non-guests into guests, thus increasing the market. Second, they can make meaningful changes in their offerings and communicate them to the market. This will result in serving guests more effectively, and will help stem the flow of guests to the status of non-guests.

The Guest Search Process

During the search process, guests investigate and assess hospitality alternatives under the influence of marketing efforts. This interactive process is depicted in Exhibit 5. It consists of four stages: need recognition, investigation, evaluation of alternatives and expectations, and choice.

Guests investigate hospitality products and services in order to satisfy needs. Their search may be routine, nonroutine (exceptional), or mixed. As Exhibit 6 shows, routine hospitality purchases anchor one end of the spectrum and nonroutine purchase anchor the other. Hospitality purchases that are a mixture of both types occupy the middle of the spectrum.

Routine hospitality purchases require very simple and short guest searches. These purchase decisions require relatively little time or effort, reflecting low personal involvement. Price and convenience are often more important considerations than ambience and prestige. Examples of routine hospitality purchases include going to the usual places for a fast breakfast, stopping at a hamburger spot for a brief snack, or hanging out at a local bar or fast-food place. Such searches border on the habitual.

Exhibit 6   Hospitality Purchase Search Spectrum

Kind of Purchase	Routine hospitality purchases	Mixed hospitality purchases	Nonroutine hospitality purchases
Degree of Involvement	Low personal involvement	Mixed involvement	High personal involvement
Restaurant Examples	Fast food	Dinner with friends	Anniversary dinner

In contrast, nonroutine hospitality purchases are anything but habitual. They are special and have high personal involvement. Service quality, reputation, and ambience are critical. These purchases may entail long searches involving considerable time and effort. Such purchases indicate personal commitments and reflect upon the self-image, attitudes, beliefs, and status of the guest. Examples of nonroutine hospitality searches include selecting a honeymoon site or that special restaurant for an anniversary celebration.

Most hospitality purchases are a varying mixture of both routine and nonroutine elements. There is often some personal involvement as well as some routine in selecting a restaurant for dinner with friends, arranging a golf outing at a popular local course, planning a conference at a nearby motel, or booking a weekend at a bed and breakfast.

Guests tend to be personally involved in many hospitality situations. They have direct experience with service providers and usually consume service on the spot. The impact is immediate and personal as guest and server interact. As a result, guests assess hospitality providers instantly and form opinions about them. These reactions influence future guest behavior.

With so many types of service encounters, hospitality businesses have numerous opportunities to satisfy guests and create a loyal customer base. Staff members should be trained and encouraged to capitalize on these opportunities. On the other side of the coin, however, there are also numerous opportunities to create dissatisfied customers. One unfortunate guest experience will override numerous pleasant ones. And while one dissatisfied guest invariably influences many others, the truly satisfied guests tend to share their opinions with fewer people.

Purchase Decisions

Guest behavior is goal-oriented and purposeful. Guests make hospitality decisions to further their own best interests and achieve their objectives. They freely choose from among a broad range of food, beverage, and lodging alternatives. Their experiences, as well as those of family, friends, and peers, provide information that establishes the criteria against which they evaluate alternative hospitality offerings. Through this evaluative process, guests arrive at preferences and make their purchase decisions.

For guests, the most economical or utilitarian choice is not always the most logical or fitting. Emotional or aesthetic factors may be even more important than practical considerations. An emotionally-based decision may be the best choice for a particular guest. A guest may deem that a glass of wine, when served in the Polo Lounge of the Beverly Hills Hotel amid Hollywood celebrities, is worth more than the same glass of wine available at a fraction of the price in a local pizzeria.

Hospitality marketers must strive to understand guest purchase reactions for two important reasons. First, this knowledge will help marketers design hospitality offerings that are more attuned to guest expectations. Second, it helps marketers favorably influence guest reactions toward their hospitality offerings. While personal selling, advertising, public relations, and merchandising techniques are significant means of influencing guests before, during, and after their purchases, nevertheless, guests will freely assess their options and select those offerings they deem best.

Preference Models

Knowledge of guest preferences gives hospitality providers opportunities to differentiate their offerings, develop effective and appealing marketing programs, and cultivate satisfied, loyal guests. **Non-compensatory** and **value expectancy preference models** help us conceptualize these preferences and understand the role of preferences in choosing specific hotels, motels, or restaurants.

Assume a guest is evaluating possible lodging facilities at a vacation site. The guest has gathered information from the tourist bureau and is considering three options in order to select the best one. She rates all three properties according to the attributes she deems important, like restaurants, golf courses, tennis courts, swimming pools, children's activities, location, parking, and room size. Each property has both desirable and undesirable features, and no single property is the best in all categories. She rates each attribute on a scale from 1 to 5, with 5 representing the highest rating and 1 indicating that the attribute is not available.

In a non-compensatory model, one or more factors are critical to the guest. Assume an Olympic-size pool and a children's game room are absolutely essential to this guest. A high rating for one or more non-critical attributes will not compensate for a low rating on any one critical attribute. For example, as our hypothetical guest compares various properties, a high score for a restaurant would not offset the lack of an Olympic-size pool or a children's game room. Those properties without the required pool and game room would be eliminated.

The value expectancy model specifies attributes and rates the properties as before. In this case, however, attributes are weighted according to their relative importance. With this model, the swimming pool and the children's game room would be weighted more heavily than the other attributes, but the lack of either would not by itself disqualify a property. A property's overall score is the sum of the weight assigned to each attribute multiplied by its rating. According to the value expectancy model, the property with the highest score would be chosen.

Perceptions and Images

No hospitality can be extended until guests actually choose and receive services. Hospitality does not really exist in the abstract. It exists only when it is experienced by guests. Guest perceptions and images give hospitality offerings their value and meaning.

Perceptions are subjective mental impressions of people, objects, and situations, such as hotels, restaurants, menus, staff, and advertising. Sometimes inanimate objects take on personalities or images in the mind of the guest—one hotel may be seen as informal and friendly, while another is seen as formal and distant. Certain wines, liqueurs, cheeses, and ice creams also take on personalities. Guest perceptions have a tremendous effect upon hospitality choices.

Guest perceptions depend upon stimuli such as design, location, and color, as well as personal factors such as moods, experiences, values, desires, and needs. Different guests will not perceive the same object or situation in exactly the same way. Moreover, perceptions of hospitality offerings may well differ from reality. Guest *perceptions* of reality, however, are at least as important to hospitality marketing as actual reality. Guests base their actions on what they believe. If they believe one wine, restaurant, or hotel is superior to another, the objective truth of their perceptions is irrelevant to their purchasing decisions.

Guest perceptions and the images they conjure of a hospitality enterprise can be so potent that they can make or break a business. Consider the situation of one London restaurant, the Green Champagne and Oyster Bar and Grill. Located near Parliament, the restaurant had an upper-class image that the government's socialist members could not risk being associated with—especially when unemployment was high. When the restaurant was renamed Shepherd's, business increased. As one socialist Member of Parliament explained, "Shepherd's is just the kind of thing for us, because people could think you are going in for shepherd's pie."[3]

A Midwestern American restaurant had a more dire situation. When a shipment of meat caused minor food-induced illnesses for a few guests, the problem was immediately and quietly addressed to the satisfaction of all concerned, including the guests and the local government. Nevertheless, an investigative reporter of a local TV station learned of the situation and publicized it weeks after the event. Articles soon appeared in the local papers. Although the local health department assured the public that the danger was past, the damage had been done. The restaurant now had a reputation for serving unsafe food. Sales fell precipitously at all of the chain's local units. Only after months of concerted merchandising, promotion, and advertising did business bounce back.

Self-Image

Self-perceptions or self-images are basic human attributes. Guests seek both to achieve and to bolster a favorable self-image and tend to base their hospitality choices on this desire. How guests are greeted by the maître d', where they are seated in a restaurant, and how they are attended by the staff will affect and reflect their self-image. Some guests request particular tables at fashionable restaurants

Exhibit 7   Hospitality Marketing and Self-Images

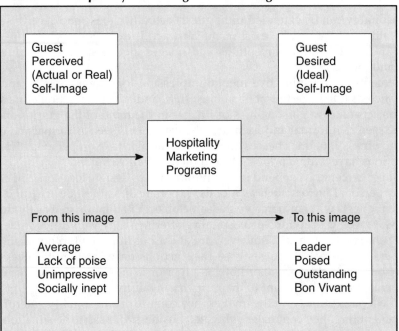

and become upset if seated elsewhere. Where one is seated in a room or at a table indicates the guest's position in the pecking order.

There are two distinct kinds of self-images—the actual or real self-image and ideal or desired self-image. Hospitality marketers may find information about actual versus desired self-images important to their efforts. For example, guests are more likely to purchase something that they believe will move them toward a desired self-image. As Exhibit 7 indicates, the degree to which hospitality offerings meet a guest's desired self-image determines guest reactions. While it is not easy to determine guest self-images, various psychological techniques help marketing researchers do so.

Guest Attitudes

Guest attitudes often determine purchase actions. Favorable attitudes tend to lead to purchases, while unfavorable attitudes do not. Three interrelated factors contribute to guest attitudes: cognition, evaluation, and action. The cognitive component (the basis for both evaluation and action) refers to information such as that concerning hospitality institutions and their offerings. The evaluative component deals with guest opinions and their intensity about such situations and offerings. The action component refers to guest preferences and intentions to purchase.

Knowing about hospitality offerings (cognition), liking them (evaluation), and actually making the purchase (action) are vastly different issues. Because it is difficult to isolate and individually measure these three components, marketers approach guest attitudes as an overall concept and assume that positive guest attitudes lead to more purchases than negative attitudes. Marketers are challenged both to prevent and to transform unfavorable attitudes through training, advertising, selling, merchandising, and complaint handling programs.

Guest attitudes are often inferred from their responses to various stimuli. Questionnaires and other devices provide information about guest attitudes. Negative or sour employees engender negative guest reactions. As Byron Langton, CEO of Holiday Inn Worldwide, says, "A smile costs nothing, [but it is important] to make a particular person feel he or she is the one person you want to see at that moment of time."[4] The Ritz-Carlton directs employees to "Smile. We are on stage." Nevertheless, we have all encountered employees who were ill-suited to guest-contact positions.

A server's attitude had a most unfortunate effect in the following situation. Two dinner guests were seated in a unit of a well-known national restaurant chain next to a table occupied by people who were finishing their dessert and coffee. The server arrived without greeting the new guests, was actually very sullen, seemed annoyed, and carried out her order-taking duties in a most perfunctory manner. Guests at both tables remarked on how unhappy the waitress looked, and that she made the guests feel that they were imposing on her. One guest commented, "She has an attitude." Another reported, "She never smiled once during the whole meal—we won't be back!"

Guest attitudes perform or affect four important functions: adjustment, expression of values, knowledge, and ego-defense.[5] Adjustment occurs when guests modify their purchasing behavior to maximize their pleasure and minimize their pain. Guests who have certain strong values may express them in their purchase choices, for example, by choosing the most economical or ecologically-friendly hospitality alternative or by selecting a very expensive hotel that they believe shows their discerning tastes. Through attitudes such as these, guests project their values and commitments.

Guests may also select hospitality services based on their knowledge of foods, foreign customs, hotels, or travel destinations. For these guests, their knowledge adds meaning to their hospitality experiences. For example, a guest who has been to China and has studied that country's cuisine and customs may have a heightened sense of enjoyment while dining in a Chinese restaurant.

Ego-defense occurs when attitudes attempt to cover up deficiencies or weaknesses. For example, guests who loudly insist on special treatment while treating hospitality providers as inferiors have a strong need to defend their egos. Ego-defensive attitudes are extremely difficult to change, particularly when a guest attempts to conceal a deficiency, such as ignorance about wines. For example, uninformed guests who attempt to contradict an expert wine steward upon receiving their order may become ego-defensive. In such instances, the wine steward would only make the situation worse by arguing with the guest. The wine steward may win the argument but lose the guest. It is better to prevent ego-defensive situations from arising in the first place, rather than try to change attitudes after they do.

Rather than incite a disagreement, a sensitive wine steward might follow the example of a colleague we encountered in a splendid Houston restaurant. This wine steward was familiar with one of the guests and commented favorably on the wine selection. Continuing, however, he described the virtues of another selection that was relatively new to the restaurant, but was both a superior wine and far less expensive. By tactfully suggesting alternatives, the wine steward favorably influenced the attitudes of guests, added to their dining enjoyment, and made them feel as if they received superior service and value due to his knowledge.

Truly negative attitudes are difficult to change. The first and most important task for hospitality providers is to determine why guests hold such attitudes. Because negative attitudes are rooted in experiences, both actual and vicarious, actions can be taken to change these experiences. Competent restaurateurs and hoteliers often meet complaints or mistakes with complimentary meals, beverages, or lodging so that guests can experience very positive results first-hand. This paves the way for marketing activities to reinforce positive guest experiences.

Purchase Outputs

After purchasing hospitality offerings, guests evaluate them. The purchasing process generates individual service encounters and experiences that guests label as satisfying or unsatisfying. Both expectations and desires affect guest satisfaction. Guests are not satisfied when offerings meet expectations but not desires.[6] As they have these hospitality experiences, guests learn, judge future alternatives, develop expectations, and make choices. Past experiences determine future purchase actions.

Guest satisfaction with past and current hospitality offerings increases the probability of future purchases and creates guest loyalty. Conversely, unfavorable experiences and dissatisfaction decrease the probability of future purchases and lead the guest to reassess hospitality providers.

Hospitality providers hope that guests will feel they have received full value for their money and that guests will become loyal repeat purchasers. Furthermore, they hope guests will inform their friends and associates of their satisfaction and influence them to also become loyal customers.

Guest Behavior and Learning

Guests continuously learn from their hospitality exposures and experiences. Learning may occur directly, through trial and error, or indirectly, by observation and talking with others. Attitudes that affect purchase preferences are learned from childhood on.

Contemporary learning theory falls into two categories—behaviorist and cognitive. Behaviorist theories are further subdivided into stimulus-response and operant conditioning theories.

Of the two types of behaviorist learning theories, **stimulus-response theory** proposes that people are conditioned by various stimuli to respond in a desired manner. Guests are viewed as passive beings who are shaped, influenced, and conditioned through the constant repetition of marketing messages and actions.

In contrast, **operant conditioning theory** assumes that guests act in a voluntary and goal-directed manner. They interact with and manipulate their environments. Guests respond and react to environmental cues. Their reactions to hospitality offerings stimulate learning and result in choices.

When specific hospitality behavior is positively reinforced, guests tend to build habitual responses. When it is not reinforced, guests will try different approaches until their actions bring more positive results. When a response is not reinforced over time, learned habits may cease. Much of guest behavior can be characterized as operant behavior, with positive reinforcement generating loyal and repeat guests.

Cognitive learning theory focuses on perception, thought, reason, and memory and stresses human symbolic processes (that is, the way people perceive objects and situations and associate symbols and meaning with them). Guests do not simply respond to stimuli, but act on their beliefs, express their opinions and attitudes, and strive to achieve their goals. The theory assumes that current guest behavior is shaped and influenced by past behavior, and that recent events have a greater impact than do earlier ones.

Cognitive Dissonance

The theory of **cognitive dissonance** further broadens our understanding of guest behavior. According to this theory, people experience discomfort when they have logically inconsistent thoughts about an object or event. In hospitality, for example, dissonance sometimes arises in the form of post-purchase conflict. An eagerly-anticipated meal at a chosen restaurant may have been disappointing, or an expensive weekend at a world-class hotel was unsatisfactory. Given the innumerable hospitality options available to guests, moreover, many guests will naturally wonder if they made the right choice. They must somehow deal with the tension these questions create. Guests often try to regain a psychological balance by selectively seeking supporting information, or by distorting contradictory information. Guests reduce the internal post-purchase conflict by making cognitive adjustments such as changing their attitudes, rationalizing their decision, ignoring information, or viewing situations selectively.

When tremendous disparities between expectation and performance result in extreme dissatisfaction, however, no amount of optimism or rationalization is likely to overcome the negative reaction. In these cases, guests are likely to make other choices.

External Forces

As seen in Exhibit 1, many external forces influence individual guest behavior and reactions to hospitality offerings. We could address such factors as technology, economics, politics, international developments, and social and legal considerations. For our purposes here, we shall limit our discussion to four important general topics found in discussions of consumer behavior that are particularly relevant for hospitality marketers: cultures, subcultures, reference groups, and social classes.

Cultures and Subcultures

Culture refers to the totality of values that characterize a society, those factors that exert the broadest influence on guest behavior. It establishes gender roles, age norms, standards of hygiene and dress, responses to work, leisure, and play, and food and beverage preferences. Culture dictates customs, celebrations, lifestyles, family arrangements, and gift-giving. As we develop a global economy, hospitality enterprises are challenged to respond appropriately to diverse cultural considerations.

Hospitality providers must pay careful attention to the dietary requirements and customs of diverse religions and nationalities. For example, McDonald's uses meat that adheres to Muslim requirements in Saudi Arabia, has deleted beef from its menu in India, has opened a kosher restaurant in Israel, and offers beer and wine in some countries. Burger King offers durian milk shakes in Southeast Asia (durian is a fruit with a pungent, overwhelming odor that Westerners often find distasteful). Cultural celebrations and religious traditions such as weddings, christenings, anniversaries, birthdays, and holy periods create a demand for hospitality services.

Like so many other countries, the United States is facing radical cultural transitions. In addition to a growing acceptance of alternative lifestyles which include divorced and single-parent families and homosexuality, the United States has changed demographically with a more visible population of senior citizens, professionally-employed women, and citizens of African, Asian, and Hispanic extraction. Common "American" foods such as bagels, pizza, tacos, salsa, pasta, yogurt, and sushi now reflect this cultural smorgasbord.

Regardless of important steps toward multicultural assimilation, acute cultural differences can strongly affect hospitality enterprises, as a recent example shows. A wealthy Arab sheik who was visiting a prestigious Beverly Hills hotel considered the service of a dining-room waiter too slow and inattentive for his position and taste. As was customary in his homeland, the sheik insisted that his aide strike the waiter. When the aide tried to explain that such behavior is not appropriate in the United States, the sheik himself arose and slapped the waiter's face. The waiter immediately complained to the union steward, who in turn threatened management with a walkout unless the sheik was removed from the hotel. The hotel dealt with the situation by finding suitable accommodations at another luxury establishment nearby.

Subcultures, which may be grouped by geography, religion, ethnicity, race, age, education, nationality, occupation, or other traits, also affect guest reactions and purchase behavior. Even within the United States, we recognize that Midwesterners differ culturally from Northeasterners, and that these differences are stratified even further by a wide variety of ethnic, racial, and religious groups. Similarly, although Indonesia is one country, it has over 300 different ethnic groups with a variety of customs, mores, practices, and languages.

Hospitality marketers often develop special programs and strategies that appeal to important subcultures—in the United States, for example, Hispanics, African and Asian Americans, senior citizens, singles, children, teenagers, or many others. Each subculture itself, however, may not be homogeneous in its purchasing reactions and decisions. Although Mexicans, Puerto Ricans, Cubans, and Spaniards are all considered Hispanics, they have very different cultural orientations and may prefer different products. Seniors are both rich and poor, healthy and infirm, staid and adventurous.

Regardless of important differences within a subculture, various subcultures usually share certain homogeneous tendencies. Important values and beliefs can cut across subcultural boundaries. Whether they are white or black, Muslim, Jewish, Catholic, or Protestant, middle-class guests with similar levels of education, occupation, and income may have similar hospitality preferences. Japanese guests, regardless of age, income, social class, or profession, may share many significant food and beverage preferences. The great degree of homogeneous wants and needs within heterogeneous subcultures challenges hospitality providers both to appeal to similarities and address important differences.

Reference Groups

Reference groups include families, friends, co-workers, members of clubs, and social classes that serve as standards of comparison as guests develop their attitudes, values, and purchase behavior. These groups influence guest behavior through both contact and aspiration. Personal contact, such as recommendations made by friends, may influence choices. Guests also make choices based on their aspiration to be like people they admire and respect. For instance, some people are encouraged to follow the example of celebrities who frequent New York's Russian Tea Room or who take ski vacations in Vail.

Reference groups may be primary or secondary. Primary reference groups are those small, intimate groups in which members interact personally and communicate face-to-face. The primary reference group leader's approval of hospitality offerings can benefit hospitality providers. Secondary reference groups include larger social organizations, professional associations, interest clubs, and religious groups. Although they are less personal, they also influence guests.

Social Class

Although income is an important determinant of purchase behavior, it alone does not decide guest lifestyles or purchase selections. Social class is also a major factor. **Social class** refers to the capacity of social position to shape and determine a particular way of life for various segments of society. While income plays a role, family background, occupation, education, race, ethnicity, and even one's address are important components of social class.

Social class explains why two families of the same size and income, one headed by a husband and wife who are tradespeople and the other by a husband and wife who are professionals, are likely to exhibit significantly different aspirations and purchase behavior. This by no means implies that one family is superior to the other. It merely means that they exhibit different ways of living—different preferences and expenditure patterns. The lifestyles of the upper social classes are more likely to emphasize graceful living, the arts, literature, and other cultural activities, while those of the lower social classes may be more oriented to acquiring material goods, working with their hands, and enjoying certain kinds of sporting

Exhibit 8   Social Classes and Their Orientations

Social Class	Lifestyle Orientation	Purchasing Tendencies
Upper class	Good taste Graceful living Good things in life Individual expression Interest in arts and culture	Quality merchandise Expensive hobby and recreation equipment Art Books Travel
Middle class	Respectability Conformity Propriety	Items in fashion Items related to self-presentation Nice clothing, neighborhood, and home Items for children

Working class	Fun oriented
	Parochial
	Unsophisticated taste
	Focus on possessions, not
	  ideas
		Newest appliances
		Sporting events
		Hunting, boating, fishing, and
		  bowling equipment
		Newest and biggest items

Lower class	Close family relationships Chauvinistically loyal Not interested in world affairs Neighborhood oriented Immediate gratification	Status symbols Products enhancing self-esteem Pseudosymbols of prosperity, such as used Cadillac Readily available products

Source: This material was prepared for a special research project by Dr. Richard Coleman.

activities. The upper classes have been described as being more interested in wine, and the lower classes in beer.

One study of modern social classes concluded that society in the United States is composed of four classes: upper, middle, working, and lower. The study estimated that one-sixth of all Americans are in the upper class, about one-third compose the middle class, another third are members of the working class, and a sixth are in the lower class.[7] Exhibit 8 summarizes the lifestyle orientations and purchase behavior of each of these classes.

As this figure shows, the upper class lives gracefully and enjoy the good things in life. The middle class focuses on respectability, conformity, and propriety. The working class is less sophisticated in its tastes, focuses on possessions, and is more parochial and fun-oriented. The lower class exhibits the closest family relationships, is more neighborhood-oriented, favors immediate gratification, and is less interested in world affairs.

Education and initiative generally spur people up the social ladder. Nevertheless, neither the proportion of the population in each class nor the values of each class are expected to change much in the foreseeable future. A family in one class is likely to retain that class's values even as family income and status increase. Income does not automatically boost a family to a higher social class, although people may well be able to afford the trappings associated with it.

Some theories of consumer behavior contend that tastes and preferences trickle down from the upper to the lower classes. If the upper classes prefer a vacation destination, hotel, or restaurant, the middle classes will subsequently emulate them, later followed by the lower classes. By the time this process is in place, however, the upper classes will be interested in something different.

Social class can be a useful construct to explain the hospitality choices of some guests. Understanding different social classes can also help hospitality providers target markets, develop a property's image, and create marketing programs. How can we classify guests according to their respective social classes with any accuracy? We have already noted that income, although heavily relied upon as an indicator of class, can be misleading. Since social distinctions are often difficult to measure, hospitality marketers might set out to acquire a good knowledge of their community and to identify the leaders of various nonprofit, charitable, and cultural organizations, as well as members of prestigious clubs and social and professional organizations.

Applying Guest Behavior Models

How can we apply guest behavior concepts and models to practical hospitality situations? How can they help us understand individual guests and improve hospitality operations? They can furnish insights and information and indicate ways of changing operations and services. Returning to the example of George Lee, whom we discussed in our introduction to this chapter, let us see how behavioral concepts and models can help.

Assume that, as George pondered the broad range of guest wants, needs, motives, and purchase behaviors he encountered in hospitality marketing, he thought of many specific situations.

1. The resort recently hosted a large fiftieth wedding anniversary celebration with guests from around the country. They were highly complimentary about the facilities, floral arrangements, food, and music.

2. A leading Japanese industrialist and his key executives reacted adversely to a waiter's allegedly disrespectful behavior. They visited his office about it.

3. A local politician's aide called to reserve rooms for a friend's family over the extremely tight Thanksgiving weekend.

4. He just received a letter booking facilities for a company's annual board meeting.

5. An irate guest complained because room service did not meet his expectations nor did it match the reputation and image of the resort.

6. He met a couple and their four children in the lobby as they were investigating a possible family reunion at the special weekend rates.

Exhibit 9   Sample Classification of Hospitality Situations

George Lee's Observations	Purchase Stimuli	Search Process	Purchase Decision	Purchase Outputs	External Factors
Specific Situations	13, 14, 15, 17	3, 6, 7, 8, 12	4, 5, 8, 10, 11 12, 16	1, 2, 5, 11	9

7. The CEO of a large international company has occupied the presidential suite for a week and is considering holding a board meeting at the resort.

8. The State Department has contacted him about arranging accommodations and security for the royal family of a Middle Eastern country.

9. A local resident threatens to picket and lead a boycott unless he receives a satisfactory response to his concerns about waste and environmental issues.

10. The guest database indicates that less than 20 percent of all guests are using the health club since the $10 daily charge was initiated six months ago.

11. Beverage purchases from in-room bars do not cover costs. He wondered what purpose they served.

12. The director of the local chamber of commerce phoned to inform him that the chamber will decide within the next two weeks whether to hold their annual Christmas meeting at the hotel.

13. A local TV news personality has asked to do a report on the outstanding service award the hotel recently received.

14. Some services such as room service, valet parking, and valet laundry and cleaning are scarcely used, although requests for irons and ironing boards, baby sitters, and children's games are increasing.

15. Business guests frequently request access to fax, computer, printer, and copying services.

16. He just signed a contract for a large convention to be held in two years.

17. He just learned the hotel has received a Five Diamond Award for excellence.

As George considered these specific situations, he wondered how best to classify and report this information so it would be useful to management. His first task was to group the factors and variables of particular hospitality situations according to a behavior model. Using the model in Exhibit 9, George categorized each of the 17 buying situations as a purchase stimuli, part of the search process, a purchase decision, a purchase output, or an external factor. Sometimes George classified a particular situation under two categories. Although someone else might arrive at slightly different results, the process of classifying these factors gives hospitality marketers added insight into particular situations. Each situation can therefore be better understood in its particular context.

Having created this chart, George can analyze each situation further and determine the most critical factors. By creating a diagram, he can consider how these factors relate to one another, which factors govern others, and how management can deal with them. Consider situation number 10 regarding health club services at the resort. In this instance, George could collect information about users and non-users, the impact of pricing, what competitors offer, and so on. He could then consider each of these individual factors within the context of our behavioral model, grouping each according to purchase stimuli, the search, the decision, and outputs. This process would allow George to assess consumer perceptions of the health club services and facilities, consumer reactions to pricing, the consumer search and decision process, and the results of their purchases. This approach usually suggests ways to improve guest services and use hospitality resources more effectively. In George's case, following this model would better position him to make decisions about the health club, its services, and prices, and to improve marketing programs within the resort.

Hospitality marketers who follow George's example will have a better understanding of the various factors contributing to the hospitality purchase situation and how they function. This procedure will also indicate existing hospitality gaps and will highlight the means by which current hospitality offerings can be improved. In addition, this model can identify future market opportunities, for the very process of working through the model will inevitably yield insight into practical and profitable courses of action.

Concluding Comments

Knowledge of guest behavior, particularly understanding their wants and needs, is the cornerstone of hospitality marketing. The concepts and models of consumer behavior presented in this chapter help us understand guest purchasing decisions.

Although accepted models of consumer behavior vary, most comprise four basic components: external and internal purchase stimuli, the search process, the decision process, and the resulting outputs. The consideration of purchase stimuli highlights the perception of guest behavior as information processing during the prepurchase, purchase, and post-purchase phases. It deals with guest drives and motives. Drives refer to the objects or conditions toward which motives are directed, while motives stimulate guests to act. Drives may be classified as visceral, activity, aesthetic, or emotional. Motives may be of either the behavior primacy or need primacy categories.

Behavior primacy theories explain human behavior in terms of guests interacting with various environments—social, psychological, and physical. Need primacy theories explain human behavior in terms of guests acting to satisfy their needs. A widely referenced need primacy theory is Maslow's hierarchy of needs. While guest motives are hard to determine, various marketing research techniques can help management do so.

In their search process, guests investigate and assess hospitality purchase alternatives. The search process encompasses need recognition, investigation, evaluation of alternatives and expectations, and choice. The search may be routine or nonroutine, short or lengthy, and entail high or low personal involvement. In making their decisions, guests tend to be goal oriented and purposeful even when decisions are emotionally rather than rationally based. Guest perceptions and images, especially self-images, are important purchase considerations.

Purchase decisions are often conditioned by attitudes; favorable attitudes are more likely to result in purchases than unfavorable ones. Attitudes encompass cognitive, evaluative, and action components. They perform four important functions: adjustment, value expression, knowledge, and ego defense. While attitudes are difficult to determine and measure absolutely, they are often inferred from various stimuli such as questionnaire information and observations.

As a result of their service encounters and the information guests gather, learning occurs, resulting in guest expectations, choices, and future actions. When guests are satisfied, the probability of future purchases and the development of guest loyalty increases. Unfortunately, disappointed guests tend to share their disappointments with others more so than satisfied guests do.

Contemporary learning theory may be behaviorist or cognitive. Behaviorist theories are subdivided into stimulus-response and operant-conditioning theories. Stimulus-response theories explain that stimuli condition people to respond in a desired manner. Operant-conditioning theories hold that guests operate in a voluntary and goal-directed manner. Cognitive learning theory focuses on the way people perceive objects and situations and associate meaning with symbols. It deals with such important considerations as perception, thought, reason, and memory and is concerned with the effects of past behavior in shaping current guest behavior.

Among the external forces influencing guest behavior are cultures, subcultures, reference groups, and social class. Culture deals with the overall values that characterize a society—those exerting the broadest influences on guest behavior. Subcultures focus the broad influences according to such factors as geography, religion, ethnicity, race, age, sex, education, nationality, and profession. Reference groups refer to groups that serve as standards for guest attitudes, values, and purchases—groups that influence guest behavior through either contact or aspiration. Social class is concerned with the capacity of social position to shape and determine a way of life for various segments of society. Income alone, while important, does not explain significantly different aspirations and purchase behavior of various guests.

Behavioral concepts and models give hospitality managers an opportunity to improve their understanding of the factors that govern guest purchase behavior. They can suggest how existing hospitality offerings can be improved so that they better satisfy guest wants, needs, and expectations.

Endnotes

1. *The Wall Street Journal,* 4 Jan. 1994, B1.

2. "Hotel Safety: Out in the Open," *The New York Times,* 4 Sept. 1994, XX4.

3. "Appraising Caine, the Businessman," *The New York Times,* 7 April 1996, F6.

4. "Holiday Inn 1—Reposition, Segmentation Source," *Sky,* Nov. 1994, p. 56.

5. Daniel Katz, "The Functional Approach to the Study of Attitudes," *Public Opinion Quarterly,* Summer 1960, pp. 163–164.

6. Richard A. Spreg, Scott B. Mackenzie, and Richard M. Olshavsky, "A Re-examination of the Determinents of Consumer Satisfaction," *Journal of Marketing,* July 1996, pp. 15–32.

7. Richard P. Coleman, unpublished research study.

Key Terms

behavior primacy—a theory of human motivation that explains that behavior results from interactions with various environments.

cognitive dissonance—a theory dealing with the discomfort that people feel when they encounter logically inconsistent thoughts about a situation and their resulting actions.

cognitive learning theory—a theory of learning that focuses on the way people perceive objects and situations and associate meaning with them; assumes that people act on their beliefs.

culture—the totality of values that characterizes a society.

drives—the objects, conditions, or activities toward which motives are directed.

hierarchy of needs—a theory of human motivation that deals with the potency of various needs or motives.

motives—the stimuli for human behavior; explanations for why people act as they do.

need primacy—a theory of human motivation that holds that behavior is motivated by needs.

non-compensatory preference model—purchase model in which the lack of critical attributes in purchase alternatives is not offset or compensated for by the presence of other desirable attributes.

operant conditioning theory—a behaviorist theory of learning that explains that guests act in a voluntary and goal-directed manner as they interact with and manipulate their environment.

preference models—models that deal with consumer evaluations of purchase alternatives based on the purchase attributes they desire.

reference groups—groups that influence consumers through contact and aspiration.

social class—characterization of the outlook and way of life of groups in a society according to their social position.

stimulus-response theory—a behaviorist theory of learning that proposes that people are conditioned by various stimuli to respond in a desired manner.

subculture—the culture of a segment of a society such as religious, ethnic, or age segments.

value expectancy preference model—purchase model in which the attributes of various purchase alternatives are weighted according to their relative importance.

Review Questions

1. Why is guest behavior viewed as information processing?

2. What are the three stages of the purchase decision? What happens in each stage?

3. What are drives and motives? How are they related? How do they influence individual guest behavior?

4. How do behavior primacy and need primacy theories differ?

5. What are four stages of the guest search process?

6. How do preference models, perceptions and images, self-image, and attitude all affect the purchase decisions of guests?

7. How does cognitive dissonance affect guest behavior?

8. What is the contemporary learning theory?

9. What external forces influence guest behavior and reactions to hospitality offerings? How does each influence guest behavior?

10. How can guest behavior models be used to improve hospitality operations?

Internet Sites

For more information, visit the following Internet sites. Remember that Internet addresses can change without notice.

Cloister Resort
http://www.cloister.com

Marriott International
http://www.marriott.com

Hilton Hotels Corporation
http://www.hilton.com

Pizza Hut
http://www.pizzahut.com

Holiday Inns Worldwide
http://www.holiday-inn.com

Ritz-Carlton Hotels
http://www.ritzcarlton.com

Howard Johnson
http://www.hojo.com

Chapter 6 Outline

6

Business Guest Behavior

"We're not the ones who determine the value of our product. It's the customer who does."

—Richard E. Hecker, Former President of DuPont

This chapter considers the hospitality purchasing decisions of businesses, non-profit institutions, and governmental agencies. We refer to these buyers as **corporate customers**, although their purchases are more than strictly corporate.

Corporate purchasing adds dimensions to buying decisions that typically are not present in individual buying decisions. This is because the motivation to buy and the considerations governing purchase choices reflect not only the individual needs, perceptions, and biases of the decision-maker, but also (and more importantly) the needs and operating methods of the organization itself. The decision-making process will often be more complex, reflect a wider range of considerations, involve a number of different people, require more justification, take longer to make, and take effect over a longer period of time.

Business guests are very important to hotels, resorts, and restaurants. Frequently, those actually using the hospitality services are not the ones who purchased them. For example, convention organizers contract for large, short-term hospitality commitments that are actually used by the attendees. These organizers are strongly influenced by the nature of the convention (business, scientific, professional, etc.) and work within closely defined budgets to meet client-specified objectives and needs. In contrast, tour wholesalers seek longer-term contracts with hospitality providers and consider not only costs, but also how hospitality services can add value to the tour packages being created. Airlines seek special deals for air crew accommodation, and while they are very cost conscious, they are also aware of the need to provide acceptable standards of living for crews. And governments, as very important customers, often look for large numbers of rooms across a range of prices to accommodate staff from the most senior to the very junior.

In each of these situations, the decision processes involve people acting on behalf of an organization and a host of guests, negotiating purchases of hospitality services from one or more suppliers. Understanding the nature of the activities involved and translating these insights into an effective marketing response are essential skills of the hospitality marketer and the subject of this chapter.

A Case History

The following interview with a director of travel services, responsible for the travel arrangements of about 5,000 staff members at all levels in a large insurance company, illustrates several general points. As you read it, try to develop your own list of the factors that you think differentiate the corporate customer from the household or individual customer. If you were the sales manager of a major hotel hoping to win the business of this insurance company, which of the factors would you have to build into your sales approach? Which might require some change in the way your hotel operates? Effective marketing often begins with careful listening to what the customer is saying.

Q. Do you have a policy regarding the selection of hotels?

A. Yes, the Managing Director decided that we should have a preferred hotel in each city. Despite the recession, we were in the middle of starting to expand, and so we were very busy running people around opening up offices in different cities. This was about three years ago maybe. I already had had some dealings with different chains, and so the Managing Director said we will pick a reputable chain so that we had a hotel in each city. That was the way the company was going to go; but a few years ago, when we first started to go international, there were hardly any big hotel chains in Sydney. There were only the Hilton and the Sheraton with local offices and they have a phone number where you can ring up and book all over the world. So, we were using the Hilton and the Sheraton chain for most of the overseas hotels. But then in these last couple of years we've got Marriott coming in as well as Nikko.

Q. There are quite a few hotel chains now and a few new stand-alones, like the Park Lane, or Grand, it's called now. So did you, having gone with the Sheraton and the Hilton, now change to one of their rivals?

A. Yes, we asked Sheraton and then the Hilton and the Park Lane. When they were building the Park Lane, they had established a sales office and the sales people came in to see me once or twice. They said, "We are building this big hotel," and I said, "When you are ready, come back and see me." So, when they were ready, they came back and because they were new in the country and because they were stand-alone, I said, "You have a very tough chance to compete with a big chain like the Hilton and the Sheraton." Not long after, my company put in place a very strict policy that we would have a nominated hotel in each city. So, when we negotiated the rates with a particular hotel, we said, "We'll give you all the business, if you review and give us a really good rate." The first priority was location!

Q. So, location, closely followed by rate?

A. Yes.

Q. And these are five-star properties generally?

A. Yes. We have a view that if it's good enough for the general staff, then it's good enough for the senior executives!

Q. So when you decided to switch from the Hilton or the Sheraton, can you say why you changed?

A. Yes, well, for the Sheraton Wentworth, we were using them in the old days and I think if you are looking at it from a marketing point of view, the problem was then that their marketing and sales people moved around a lot. And at that time they suffered because their own internal staffing was being restructured and we were getting a lot of different new rates and nobody knew who was looking after which account.

Q. So no follow through and you had a feeling that you had been left in the wilderness?

A. Yes. And there was another reason, too. Because they were having all these internal problems, they double booked! They double booked us for a big conference! We have a big annual conference that we had already paid a deposit for. It was 450 rooms for the weekend, plus a big conference space.

Q. That sounds like the entire hotel!

A. Yes. They had also double booked the ballroom and the banqueting hall with company "A" and both of us were longstanding accounts. Company "A" wasn't going to budge for the ballroom. We needed the ballroom and the next room together. Somebody made a very bad decision in there and they gave us back the deposit. The conference was supposed to be September and they didn't let us know that they had made that blunder until early August.

Q. And for that number of people, you can't just find somewhere else just like that?

A. Well, Hilton came in to help us out and so we were really inclined to use the Hilton at that stage to give them the business. At the time when we started to use the Hilton, the Park Lane also came on the market and their location was almost the same. And the Park Lane was very smart, very central, and very new, a really grand hotel. They were coming with a rate $10 better than the Hilton to get the business, so that was the difference.

Q. So over a large number of room nights that's pretty substantial?

A. Yes, in the next year we had 1,500 room nights at the Park Lane.

Q. So the decision to switch to the Park Lane really came down to the rate, apart from the fact that it was such a nice property?

A. Nice property and rate. Sheraton didn't have the regular staff, regular sales people that knew the account. There were some new people there who came in and gave us a rate that was $20 more expensive than the Park Lane—and it's a much older hotel.

Q. So the Park Lane, apart from being the new kid on the block, tried really hard to look after you?

A. Yes. And some of the big hotels just refused to budge on their rates right in the recession. They said, "Oh well, maybe we'll have half your business for your senior executives."

Q. And you don't make a differentiation?

A.   Yes, as I was saying, what was good enough for the lower and middle managers should be good enough for the senior managers. We made an agreement with the Park Lane that we would give them 100 percent of our business and that they would give us a very good rate across the board so that everybody would stay in the hotel, but the agreement is that they will upgrade our senior people or the executives from overseas who like to be in a room that they would normally sell for $280! It's just the top level, the 20 percent at the top level and then the others go into the really standard rooms, the ones that they would normally book the tourist groups into and all that. So this way the company is happy and they are happy.

Q.   What other aspects of the service there are important? Is it things like business services?

A.   No, because none of our executives use the business services.

Q.   Because they have their office nearby?

A.   Well from our company point of view, yes, except on the odd occasion when we are opening up other offices. When we go to a city to open up another office, we need the en-suite boardroom for interviewing staff. Only in the very early stages, mind you, when we have one or two managers going down on a one or two week basis, you know, staffing the office. But it's a very short period and…once the office has got a decent setup we don't really need those in hotel business facilities.

Q.   Is there a particular service or feature of the operations that appealed to you about the hotel you converted to? Is there any one thing or more than one apart from the fact that it was a brand new property and they were giving you this good rate?

A.   Service! They are very enthusiastic. The staff are always very enthusiastic. Our people, they tend to complain if there is even a five minute wait.

Q.   They are demanding?

A.   They are demanding! They don't have to pay for it, but they are always demanding! I wonder if they are just as demanding when they go on their own holidays!…because it's the business style, they have to be more demanding! If they have been held up a little bit at reception when they are checking in—and because the particular hotel knows the account, they know our staff and they know we are such a big account with them—maybe they work extra hard, the service is really good.

Q.   Do you survey your staff about their requirements when they are staying in hotels on business and whether they like where they go?

A.   Yes. There are a few of them who will talk to me a lot. They will let me know if they had a bad stay.

Q.   But do you actually survey all these people to ask how is this, did it measure up, is it what you want?

A.   No. Only the policy makers, like the Executive Director and the Managing Director.

How do corporate customers differ from individual guests? Some of the ways that can be seen in the above interview are:

- The size and growth rate of the organization

- The kind of business and the extent to which travel is part of that business

- The location of headquarters

- The criteria used to select suppliers

- The extent of loyalty to existing suppliers

- The impact of a "critical incident" in opening up a sale

- The people involved in making a decision—their roles in the organization, their hopes and fears, the information on which they rely, and the speed with which they act

- The importance of personal networks and the role of the sales representative

- The stages in the decision process or in the negotiations that take place

- Distinction between repeat buying and a new purchase

- A tension between a desire for something new or novel and a predictable, well understood provision of service

- Interaction between senior managers and the people making the purchasing decisions

Clearly, there are significant differences in the needs that have to be satisfied, in the way the decision is worked out, in the nature of the buyer-seller relationship, and in the number and roles of the different people who seem to have a say. Each of the factors we identified from the interview point to important marketing issues. For example, high growth companies may be better prospects than those in decline; those with headquarters located near a hotel may be better prospects; minimizing or exploiting critical incidents may be an important element in successful marketing. Clearly, if we are to put together an overall marketing strategy or design a sales or promotional program that will work with the corporate market, we need first to understand how the business market makes purchase decisions.

Size and Composition of the Corporate Market ──────────

Determining the size of the corporate market for hospitality services is difficult. The American Hotel & Motel Association estimates that 26 percent of lodging travelers are attending a conference/group meeting and 30 percent are transient business travelers. Although these categories do not correspond directly to our definition of the corporate market, they clearly indicate the importance of corporate guests to the hospitality market.

An analysis of the amount spent by various groups on hospitality indicates quite different patterns of demand. The government sector use of hotels is probably very different from that of the banking sector. The transport industry sectors together account for over 10 percent of sales and have distinctive sets of requirements. The long-distance trucking market will have different needs than airlines have. Wholesale and retail trade account for nearly $1 in every $5, a situation that emphasizes the importance of these sectors.

These patterns will, of course, differ dramatically between large urban hotels (where the business guest is probably the most important source of sales) and small bed and breakfast properties or guest houses located in the country, catering to the weekend trade (for which the corporate sector would play a trivial role). At the individual property level, we need to think not only in terms of the current mix of guests and current sales, but also of potential sales and of what would be an optimal mix. For example, in downtown Sydney among the major hotels, the proportion of corporate guests ranges from 20 to 70 percent. The 70 percent figure is associated with hotels that specialize in meeting the specific needs of business guests and have carefully designed function rooms that facilitate effective corporate meetings.

The current importance of the corporate market for a specific hospitality service provider can be determined by assessing guests who have been served over a period such as a year. Registration data and internal data banks can generate the information needed, classified by type of corporate customer. For restaurants, it may be a little more difficult, but creative analysis of reservations, corporate credit card information, and spot samplings of guests has proven useful. Such data not only provides a guide to the current importance of certain business segments, but also can be used to spot trends over time. It indicates whether the size of certain business guest segments is increasing or decreasing, perhaps changing in a way that reflects changing local or general economic conditions or shifts in other factors such as gender or location. While keeping track of this kind of information may seem bothersome, the resulting records provide valuable insights over time into trends and corporate market changes.

Derived Demand

In corporate markets, unlike individual or household markets, demand levels are driven by demand in downstream markets. That is, the size of the business traveler market depends directly on the demand for the goods and services offered by the companies concerned. If the demand for company products and services declines, then the company's demand for hospitality services will also decline.

For example, the volume of business that airlines do with hospitality organizations depends on their own volume. The demand for flights and air freight establishes the need for crew accommodations. Demand for hospitality services in the incentive market reflects the volume of business of those using incentive travel as a motivational device. The business volume of brokerage houses affects their use of hotel and restaurant facilities, which became particularly clear to many operators of upmarket restaurants and hotels that suffered a jolt from the 1987 U.S. stock market crash.

As corporate customers begin cutting costs in response to declining demand, they reduce the amount of face-to-face contact with their customers, minimize

Exhibit 1   Buyer Decision Process

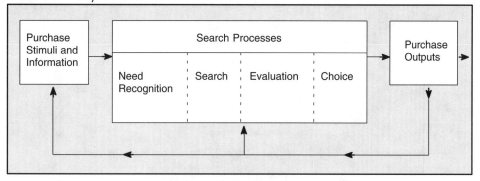

overnight stays, and rely much more on the telephone and fax for communication. A characteristic of derived demand is that it tends to fluctuate quite widely, reflecting the swings in business markets.

How Corporate Purchasing Decisions Are Made

At a very general level, business decision-making is similar to the decision-making of individual guests acting on their own behalf. Both are purposeful, goal-directed processes; both combine rational analysis with emotional feelings (although we suspect that the rational element is a little more pronounced in the corporate situation); both involve searches for information and carry risks of being wrong; and both involve learning. But the similarity stops there.

In contrast to individual purchasers, corporate customers have different needs to satisfy, different ways of making decisions, different buyer-seller relationships, and more complex decision processes due to the greater number and variety of people involved. Corporate decisions to purchase hospitality services are influenced by many factors, including the size, type, location, and growth rate of the business and the extent to which travel is part of that business. Other factors include the corporation's criteria in supplier selection, as well as its loyalty to certain suppliers, personal networks (both within the organization and between the organization and its suppliers and their sales representatives), and the stages in the corporation's decision and negotiation processes. This is only a partial list of influential factors. Hospitality marketers must consider all relevant issues in order to satisfy the needs of corporate customers. To determine whether a factor is relevant, consider whether that factor would make a difference in your marketing effort. If it could make a difference, it is important to consider.

Let us try to sort out these impressions and put together a comprehensive picture or model of the forces at work. Once we have constructed such a model, we can use it to identify what we need to know about corporate guests in order to lay a foundation for effective marketing. In so doing, we shall keep the test suggested above firmly in mind, namely: would knowing about the factor make a difference in the way we go about marketing to a specific corporate guest? Exhibit 1 sums up

Exhibit 2   Understanding the Corporate Guest

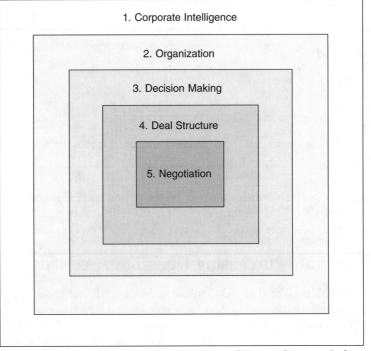

Adapted from B. P. Shapiro and T. V. Bonoma, "How to Segment Industrial Markets," *Harvard Business Review,* May-June 1984, p. 104.

the general flow of the decision process and can be used for both corporate and individual guests.

Now let's look behind the flow of the decision process and identify the specific factors that are likely to influence the corporate customer at each stage. Exhibit 2 summarizes how we suggest you look at corporate guests. The work involved in understanding and winning the business of corporate decision-makers is rather like peeling an onion—it involves working through several layers of analysis before we can begin to plan the negotiation in detail.

The outermost layer, and the one most easily assessed, is concerned with corporate intelligence. Here we collect data on the industry involved, its dynamics, possible futures, the business itself, its size, location, accessibility, profitability, growth, and so on. This kind of information helps identify enterprises, both public and private, that are in an expansive or growth mode, those with real short-term growth prospects. Such organizations are likely to be above average users of hospitality services.

The second layer digs a little deeper into the strategies management is pursuing and into the kind of organization that we may be dealing with. Some of this data will be available from the company's own reports, as well as from the trade or financial press and personal or sales contacts. Strategy can be important for such purposes as distinguishing firms that emphasize cost leadership from those seeking to win market success through the effective differentiation of their products. It can distinguish expansion-minded firms from those with a strong focus on stability and the status quo, companies building on innovations from those simply strengthening existing product lines, companies seeking merger or acquisition possibilities from those seeking to stand alone, and firms choosing to remain local or national from those seeking international markets. All of these orientations influence the extent to which hospitality services may be needed, the level and kind of expenditures that might be involved, and the benefits that managers are looking for when they purchase hospitality services. For example, such strategic options mentioned above will influence the frequency and extent of meetings, the importance of putting deals together in a congenial atmosphere, and the frequency of interstate, national, or international travel.

The way that an enterprise is organized also makes a difference. Is it centralized or decentralized? Where are real decision-makers located? How sophisticated is their purchasing office? Are hospitality services treated separately or included with other purchased inputs? Does the business buy through an in-house agency? Is the company a big spender on travel? What are the spending patterns? How experienced are they at buying hospitality services? Have policies been put in place regarding the purchase of hospitality services? Are their decisions significantly influenced by consultants or other advisers? These are examples of the kinds of pertinent organization questions that can be raised.

In a sense, the first two layers provide essential background information that help us to understand the motivations that lie behind the purchase decision and to assess the extent of any future prospects.

This leads us to the third layer, which focuses directly on the decision itself and the way in which it is likely to be made. There are three key dimensions that need to be examined closely:

1. The type of decision that is to be made

2. The stages of the decision process

3. The people who are likely to be involved at each point

Understanding the interaction of these three dimensions lies at the center of effective marketing and sales planning for the corporate sector. Let's take each dimension in turn.

As for the type of decision being made, there are three possibilities: a **straight rebuy**, a **modified rebuy**, and a **new task**.[1] The first of these, as the name suggests, is simply a repeat of an earlier purchase decision. The second refers to a purchase decision that involves some significant changes to an earlier decision, while leaving the essential structure of the decision intact. The third refers to a decision that has not been made before, where managers may lack experience or direct knowledge of the options involved and have to feel their way.

The new task is the most difficult and complex. More people are involved in new task buying decisions than in the other two kinds. In new task purchases, the information needs are high, experience is low, and evaluation of the alternatives is critical. It is at this point that sellers are given their best opportunity to be heard and to display their creative selling ability in satisfying the buyer's needs.

Straight rebuys, in contrast, are routine purchases with minimal information needs and no real consideration of alternatives. They are at the other extreme of the purchasing spectrum from new tasks. Buying decisions are often made directly and routinely in line with established policy. Such is the case with the purchase of travel services. It usually involves going back to previous suppliers whose service has been known to be acceptable. Under these circumstances, it is difficult for a supplier that has not dealt with the firm before to get onto that short list and gain the attention of buyers who themselves are faced with time pressures.

Modified rebuys fall between straight rebuys and new tasks in terms of the time required, the information needed, and the options considered. In this situation, management will usually have well-defined criteria in mind, but may be unsure which suppliers will be the most suitable.

The second dimension focuses on buying as a *process* rather than as an event. The stages in the corporate buying process are:

- Recognition of a problem
- Determination of what is needed
- Specification of the possible solutions
- Search for suppliers
- Gathering of proposals
- Evaluation and selection of a supplier
- Implementation of the choice
- Evaluation and feedback

These steps are very similar to those that a rational guest would go through in making purchases. From our present point of view, however, the importance of understanding the stages turns on developing sales efforts that are carefully tailored to meet the requirements of each stage. Thus, in the early stages, where a problem or buying situation is emerging, sales emphasis may be given to communications that show corporate buyers how a hospitality provider's services will help handle the situation, implanting an idea of "what could be" in the minds of key decision-makers. As the buying process moves through successive stages, more and more detail is needed and the role of personal selling becomes critical. When the decision process reaches the point where the decision to purchase is made, people in both organizations work directly with each other, and the quality of service plays an extremely important role. It is ultimately reflected in the evaluation that the company makes of hospitality providers. This, in turn, will be reflected in any subsequent purchase or recommendation.

Keep in mind that the concept of benefit is a driving force, both in the decision to buy and in the way that hospitality offers are put together. Benefit emerges early in the process with recognition of a problem or need—what are the benefits that we are offering to corporations and decision-makers? Benefits may be related to the needs of the organization, or to the individuals who are involved in the purchasing decision, or to both. They may be simple or complex; immediate or long term; tied to a one-time transaction or to a sustained relationship. Benefits sought may be easily quantified and dollar driven or impossible to quantify, being linked with such issues as status, image, power, or other intangibles. Whatever the nature of the implicit or explicit benefits business customers have in mind, hospitality providers must think in terms of the customer's world. Do not assume that what matters to the hospitality provider matters just as much to customers. In the corporate setting, this search for understanding is often far more complex than it is in the world of marketing to individual guests or household consumers.

The third dimension—identifying the people involved in the purchase decisions—is closely linked with the first two dimensions, particularly regarding the stages of the decision process. One of the most difficult problems in marketing hospitality services to corporate buyers is determining who in an organization is actually going to buy the product. We are interested not only in who actually buys, but also in who influences the buying decision, who determines the specification of the service that will be provided, who actually makes the final decision, and who places the order. Typically, several people are involved. Even in a small company, where the owner or manager makes the decisions, there is usually consultation with employees or staff before the final decision.

A useful concept is that of a **buying center**. A buying center can be defined as all the individuals or groups who are involved in the decision to buy hospitality services. It includes people who play one or more of the following roles:

- *Buyers:* those who select the final supplier, negotiate the deal, arrange the terms of sale, and process the actual order. Sometimes this might be done centrally in a purchasing office, but in the case of hospitality services, it is often done by secretaries or managers appointed specifically to cope with travel requirements.

- *Influencers:* those who set the specifications and influence buying decisions as a result of their position, political power, or technical expertise. In hospitality decisions, influencers may also include agents or consultants who can play a critical role in determining the outcome of a purchase.

- *Initiators:* those who trigger the decision to buy hospitality services. They may emerge at any level in an enterprise with a good idea that translates into the purchase of hospitality services.

- *Deciders:* those who have authority to approve the final buying decision that the buyer has organized, regarding the supplier and the kind of services that will be purchased. In the case of hospitality services, these are often senior managers.

- *Users:* those who actually use the service that has been purchased.

- *Gatekeepers:* those who control the flow of information within the organization and between the hospitality service provider and the buying organization. These people may be consultants, agents, secretaries, receptionists, or technical personnel.

The interaction of these roles is illustrated in Exhibit 3.

Exhibit 3   Interacting Roles

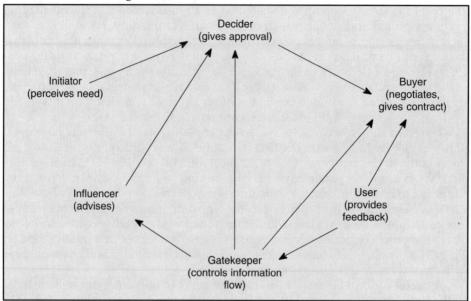

Adapted from B. P. Shapiro and T. V. Bonoma, "How to Segment Industrial Markets," *Harvard Business Review,* May-June 1984, p. 104.

Often, several people in an organization will play the same role, or there may be one person who fills many roles. A secretary, for example, may be a user, an influencer, and a gatekeeper in the purchase of hospitality services.

The size and composition of the buying center will vary considerably. Even within a given organization, the size and makeup of a buying center will often depend on the nature, complexity, and extent of the deal involved—that is, on whether it is a straight or modified rebuy or a new task.

Since business purchasing decisions involve people, their interactions in the purchasing process will concern such factors as: power (who has it?), perceptions (what do I know about the issues involved?), expectations (what do I want to happen?), role orientation (what am I doing here and what is expected of me?), perceptions of risk (what happens if things go wrong down the track?), motivation (why should I bother anyway?), information needs (what do I need to know to contribute to the decision?), education and training (have I the skills needed to make this decision?), habits of information search (who do I know that might be able to help?), and patterns of behaving in a buying situation (do I take the first option that looks OK or consider carefully a number of defined alternatives?).

The variety of people involved in hospitality buying situations and the wide differences that exist between companies present real sales challenges. As salespeople contact various people trying to determine who is involved with purchase decisions and who does what, it is easy to call on the wrong executives. Even when salespeople know who the decision-makers are in a particular situation, these decision-makers may be very difficult to reach. Despite such barriers, it is true that the more that sales representatives know about a prospect and the better they understand purchaser needs, interests, and decision processes, the more likely they are to make a sale.

The fourth layer of our "corporate onion" concerns the structure of the deal itself. This includes such matters as the size, specifications, performance criteria, price sensitivity, timing and urgency, and the period of the contract. In addition, it is important to pay attention to the politics of a particular deal and to see it as occurring in a network of relationships that the potential client has with others. There are many political concerns, such as: Will success in dealing with this client exclude us from dealing with others in the same industry? Will it lead to success with other network members? Will it add to the status of our property? Will it detract from our property? Will it result in a favorable or unfavorable price image? All of these affect the overall attractiveness of the proposed deal. Other important questions include: What will it cost us to deliver on our offer? What is the profit potential, both short term and long term? What kind of supporting facilities or resources would be needed from us?

In evaluating a deal, it is important to identify the competitors. Knowing what the deal involves, hospitality providers and their sales representatives can focus directly on their most likely competitors. They can establish the competitive edge to best each of them.

The fifth and final layer of our onion deals with negotiation or sales strategy. The questions center on how we will handle the situation. Included are such critical questions as timing, the people involved, the choice of locations, service expectations, delivery and payment schedules, a careful choice of an initial price point, the service mix, an analysis of the dependency of the parties on each other, an identification of the areas where conflict is likely to arise, the maneuvers necessary in an extended negotiation. This layer encompasses dealing with all of the essential elements of the final agreement. The responses will reflect company expectations about how the sale or deal will evolve, unfold, and conclude.

Such considerations are summarized in Exhibit 4, which you can use as a checklist of factors that might be considered under each of the five headings. In making this kind of analysis, we suggest the use of a worksheet such as that shown in Exhibit 5. We have listed each general factor down the side and asked you to summarize the issues that emerge with respect to each, together with an assessment of their likely impact on sales, advertising, or marketing planning.

As an example of how all this works, Exhibit 6 shows an analysis of the insurance company interview that began this chapter. You can see how the worksheet helps to sort out the important information, put it in perspective, and identify issues that would be important in creating a marketing plan for this customer.

The Meetings Market

One of the most important examples of corporate decision-making is to be found in the purchase of hospitality services for meetings and conventions. For many major hotels and resorts, this business accounts for 20 percent or more of their total

Exhibit 4   The Corporate Guest: Some Factors That Can Make a Difference

1. **Corporate intelligence**

   Industry—life cycle, prospects
   Growth of firm
   Size
   Profitability
   Location, spread of offices
   Ownership
   Competitors

2. **Organization**

   Strategy choices
   Culture/orientation
   Sophistication
   Structure of the organization
        centralized/decentralized buying of service
        buying center—sophistication?
        MIS etc. support
   Linkages—formal, informal
   Amount spent on hospitality—spending patterns, experience with industry,
     perceptions
   Travel needs
   Policy regarding travel, etc
   Significant influentials—agents, consultants, etc.

3. **Decision-making**

   Types—new task, modified rebuy, straight rebuy
   Stages—benefits sought, etc
   People involved—buying center, roles, power, risk perception, motivation,
     information needs, education or training, buying processes

4. **Deal structure**

   Size, performance criteria, price sensitivity
   Timing, urgency
   Length
   Politics—network, exclusion, status
   Attractiveness—what will it cost, short-term and long-term profit potential,
     support needed
   Who are the competitors?

5. **Negotiation or sales strategy**

   Dependency—how important to win?
   Staffing
   How do we play it?
   Conflict possibilities
   Maneuver/tactical issues
   Agreement

Exhibit 5   Planning for the Corporate Guest

Factor	Issues	Impact
Corporate Intelligence		
Organization		
Decision-Making Type Stages People		
Deal Structure		
Negotiation or Sales Strategy		

business. It is a very important part of the total corporate market, and is also a good example of the decision processes that we have been talking about.

Where does the meetings market business come from? How do the people involved reach their decisions to buy? Turning these questions around, how can hospitality marketers succeed in this market?

Like most corporate markets, the meetings market is very much influenced by economic conditions. Consider the effects of the economic downturns during the late 1980s and early 1990s that were felt in many countries. The result was a marked decline in the number of meetings, and those that did occur strongly emphasized obtaining value for the money spent. When the economies turned around, however, hotels reported a rise in their meetings business, although the nature of this business was not quite the same. The technology of communications changed, as did the needs for face-to-face meetings. Meetings now tend to be more focused, to involve more working sessions, and to exploit the distinctive or special characteristics of a property. Meeting planners are also more careful about costs.

Exhibit 6   Analysis of the Insurance Company Case

Factor	Issues	Impact
1. Corporate intelligence	Recently privatized Expanding Profitable Sydney based	Decision process changed Heavy user Price sensitivity Location

2. Organization	Multi-state, expansion strategy
	Sophisticated
	Centralized decision making
	Links with other public sector business?
	Policy requirements:
	    Reputable chain
	    5 Star quality
	    For all staff
	    International links
		Meetings business important
		Sales strategy
		Link with senior executives?
		Possible extension business
		
		Fit with our hotel chain?

3. Decision-making		
Type	Modified re-buy	Role of sales staff? Information needs met?

Stages	Benefits
	    Local booking
	    Status/reputation
	    Location
	    5 star quality
	Service requirements
	    New
	    Room size
	Stability in sales/account reps
	Booking etc. systems
	Deliver on promises
	Less interest in business services
		Staff awareness of account importance
		How to communicate reputation?
		Do we have locational edge?
		How are these defined by client?
		Does design, layout matter as well?
		Appoint account manager?
		Quality control at client level?
		Choose service offer carefully

People	Trust, relationship with sales staff
	Role of Director of Travel Services
	    Professional
	    Low loyalty
	    Information base
	Survey of staff experience with hotel
		Choice of sales contact staff
		Level of contact—use senior management initially?
		How to build loyalty?
		Can we link information systems?
		Ask for quick feedback to us and act on what we hear?
		Estimated sales volume

4. Deal structure	All the business in a city Negotiated rates Upgrades for senior staff Annual review?	Cost of the business? Flow on effects? Choice of negotiator Clipping service? Competitive information system?
5. Negotiation or sales strategy	Timing Information about competitive situation Crisis response	Awareness of an opportunity Plan the negotiation How important is this prospect?

Exhibit 7   Meeting Characteristics

	Sales Meetings	Management Meetings	Training Seminars	Professional/ Technical Association Seminars	Incentive Trips
Average Number of Attendees	73	52	79	116	84
Average Duration (Days)	2.9	2.5	2.7	2.5	4.5
Lead Time to Contact Signing (Months)	4.8	5.2	6.4	8.9	7.8
Average Number of Hotel Rooms	73.4	54.3	61.3	113.5	79.4

Source: "State of the Industry," *Successful Meetings,* July 1993.

The emphasis on value for money has helped many regional or second tier markets that offer good facilities at lesser prices. With occupancy down, lead times in arranging meetings have also shortened. Such changes point to a market that is buying with care and whose needs and expectations must be carefully considered.

An important sub-category of the meetings market is incentive travel. This was strongly affected by the recession in the early 1990s. Typically, today's incentive travel package involves both meetings (for networking) and activities (for fun), with a little more emphasis on the networking side than has been the case in the past. This shift is driven both by productivity concerns and an awareness of shifts in the tax treatment of incentive expenditures.

The results of relevant studies on the meetings market can furnish management with useful insights. For example, *Successful Meetings* magazine sponsored a survey of meeting planners a few years ago in both the corporate and associations markets. To qualify, association planners had to plan meetings with an attendance of 100 or more, and corporate planners had to plan at least four meetings annually. Some of the major findings of the study are shown in Exhibit 7.

In assessing this exhibit, keep in mind the sample selection criteria that were used. The planners responding were from the larger associations and larger and more active companies. You will want to add to these figures your impression of the "smaller meetings" market, which is increasingly important to many hotels. Companies often want to meet at short notice, away from the distractions of their businesses,

Exhibit 8   Where Meetings Are Held

Type of Facility	Association Planners (%)	Corporate Planners (%)
Airport Hotels	12.2	13.8
Conference Hotels	3.8	7.0
Convention Centers	4.9	3.9
Cruise Ships	0.6	0.9
Mid-Town Hotels	44.2	37.4
Resort Hotels	16.0	16.6
Suburban Hotels	18.3	20.6

Source: "State of the Industry," *Successful Meetings*, July 1993.

to consider strategy and policy choices or to train staff in small groups. Associations may need to provide special interest forums that attract limited audiences. In terms of Exhibit 7, these meetings represent an additional source of business.

With these qualifications in mind, Exhibit 7 suggests that the average length of incentive trips is considerably greater than that for other forms of meetings, lead times are a little longer, and the average number of hotel rooms needed a little higher. Management meetings are smaller, shorter, involve less lead time, and are largely residential. Training seminars are organized well in advance, but may use fewer hotel rooms, as some participants will choose to come from home each day or stay with friends.

What factors do meeting planners consider in a choice of venue? The survey showed that perceived service and availability of rooms are most important, with room rates and security also rating highly. Within the meetings planner group, it is often useful to distinguish between association and corporate planners. While the differences between association and corporate planners are in a sense predictable, they are also important in influencing the attractiveness of these two markets and the way in which they should be approached. For association planners, square footage for exhibits and meetings and rooms within a three-mile radius are three areas that have much greater influence than is the case with corporate planners. Association planners attach less weight to sporting facilities, travel time, and travel costs. For incentive planners, the key factors are quality and availability of facilities, service and friendliness, climate, image of the site, and the activities available.

The kinds of location that are chosen by the two groups of planners are similar. Exhibit 8 shows that both groups prefer midtown hotels. Corporate planners show a slight preference for suburban locations and for conference centers, while association planners are a little more likely to choose a convention center. The pattern changes, however, for incentive planners, where over 75 percent of locations are classified as resorts.

What happens when budgets are cut? The differences between the two groups of planners are marked, with corporate planners reducing the number of meetings and association planners reducing the number and cost of catered events.

Key issues for the hotel marketer that emerge from this process include how to:

- Get on the short list of potentially acceptable locations.

- Understand as early as possible the benefits that the planners and clients are looking for and how to relate to these in a convincing manner.

- Decide whether the hotel really wants the business.

- Price the deal.

- Influence the planners, consultants, and decision makers involved favorably.

- Organize the response to the client to ensure that needs are fully understood and met.

Concluding Comments

Are corporate guests really different from individual guests? The answer is both yes and no. The underlying logic is essentially the same—beginning with a need that has to be met and going on to a realization of the benefits sought, a search for alternatives, evaluation of the options found, choice or decision, and finishing with an assessment of the outcomes that resulted. In both cases, more than one person is often involved, the process takes time, is perceived as risky in monetary or social terms, and leads to flow-on effects as guests talk about their experience.

Corporate guests, however, are buying for an organization, not for themselves. In corporate purchases, the interplay between individual and corporate needs, risk perceptions, options or choices, information flows, and assessments is central. Corporate purchasing is often presumed to be a rational process, making it different from that of individual guests. While this is partially true, the case study we examined points to the importance of feelings or emotion, as well as rational calculations, in arriving at corporate purchasing choices. The balance between rational and emotional factors will change as the negotiations proceed. This is particularly important in establishing good personal relationships based on a mutual understanding of each other's needs and goals, a process that lies at the very heart of personal selling, and the subsequent delivery of promised service.

The corporate market is an important one for most hospitality providers. A clear understanding of the needs of prospective guests and a willingness to go the extra mile in meeting them is essential for success.

Endnotes

1. Patrick J. Robinson, Charles, W. Faris, and Yoram Wind, *Industrial Buying and Creative Marketing* (Boston: Allyn & Bacon, 1967), pp. 183-210.

Key Terms

buying center—all the individuals or groups that are involved in a decision to buy hospitality services.

corporate customers—businesses, nonprofit institutions, and governmental agencies.

modified rebuy—a purchase decision that involves significant changes to an earlier decision, while leaving the essential structure of the earlier decision intact.

new task—a purchase decision that has not been made before.

straight rebuy—a repeat of an earlier purchase decision.

Review Questions

1. What are corporate customers? How do they differ from individual customers? How are they similar?

2. What factors influence corporate purchasing?

3. What are the five layers of the "corporate onion"? Why is each layer significant?

4. What is a straight rebuy? Modified rebuy? New task? Which is the most difficult and which is routine?

5. What are the stages in the corporate buying process?

6. What is a buying center? What six roles are included?

Internet Sites

For more information, visit the following Internet sites. Remember that Internet addresses can change without notice.

American Hotel & Motel Association
http://www.ahma.com

ITT Sheraton
http://www.sheraton.com

Hilton Hotels Corporation
http://www.hilton.com

Nikko Hotels International
http://www.nikkohotels.com

Chapter 7 Outline

Demographic Information
Data About Hospitality Markets
Demographic Shifts
    Births
    Life Expectancy
    Immigration
    Population Projections
    Where Will Guests Live?
    World Population
Income and Wealth
    Family Income
    Household Income
    Per Capita and Discretionary Income
    Wealth and Affluence
    Mature Guests
    Expenditures on Hospitality Offerings
Guest Lifestyles
    Guest Orientations
    Changing Values
    Future Lifestyles
Concluding Comments

7

Guests of Tomorrow

"It is the common wonder of all men, how among so many millions of faces there should be none alike."

—Sir Thomas Brown

Hospitality marketers are involved with managing a company's future. This critical and demanding task is rooted in such marketing considerations as: What will the guests of tomorrow be like? How will they differ from today's guests? What hospitality offerings will they want? What kind of service will they expect? How will they react to advertising, merchandising, and personal selling? These are neither trivial nor simple questions.

If we could see clearly into the future, we would be able to manage hospitality marketing activities much more effectively and be better able to meet guest desires and increase profits. Of course, we can't see into the future with certainty. When hoteliers and restaurateurs make decisions (whether those decisions concern major renovations or simply changing a wine list), they must make assumptions about the likely desires and responses of future guests. Risks are involved.

Fortunately, we can gain important insights into the *likely* responses of future guests from readily available information that helps us identify, and assess the opportunities and risks inherent in, emerging hospitality markets. This chapter indicates how hospitality managers can gain information about three important dimensions of markets: people, money, and the willingness to buy. It focuses on identifying demographic trends and analyzing and interpreting available data in order to make informed predictions and better business decisions. Although far from being comprehensive, the chapter illustrates some of the kinds of information that are readily available about future hospitality guests.

Unless otherwise indicated, the statistics throughout this chapter are drawn from *The Statistical Abstract of the United States*, an annual publication of the U.S. Census Bureau. Similar data sources exist in many countries.

Demographic Information

Demography is the study of the size, composition, and distribution of human populations. Demographic information is probably the most important determinant of future hospitality developments. Demography reflects the interplay of three basic factors: births, deaths, and immigration/emigration. Demographic factors are central to targeting markets, formulating marketing plans and strategies, developing effective hospitality offerings, and establishing a competitive advantage. Neglecting such factors can result in missed opportunities and unrecognized shifts in demand.

Pertinent and timely demographic information is the basic building block for most critical hospitality marketing activities, including:

- Strategic planning

- Environmental scanning

- Market opportunity analysis

- New service and product offerings

- Market segmentation

- Location analysis

- Pricing decisions

- Positioning

- Distribution channel selection

- Market communications

With the aid of micro computing, CD-ROMs, digital mapping, and so forth, today's hospitality marketers have easy access to more demographic data than ever before. The U.S. Census Bureau and its counterparts in other countries provide a continuing stream of data relevant to the hospitality industry and the composition of its markets. Today, there is no reason other than management ineptitude for being demographically uninformed.

Despite this fact, demographic information remains among the hospitality industry's least used and most underappreciated assets. For example, it took far too long for many well-established restaurant chains to follow their guests from the cities to the growing suburbs and malls, although demographic trends indicated they should. Similarly, hotel and restaurant policies, strategies, physical designs, and amenities have long neglected the particular needs and desires of seniors, widows, female business travelers, and families, although demographic trends predicted the increasing presence of these groups in the hospitality market. Careful analysis of pertinent demographic information helps hospitality marketers better understand their guests and meet guest needs.

Data About Hospitality Markets

Hospitality markets may be defined as people with the money and the willingness to purchase hospitality offerings. Demographic information is useful in defining these markets because, as populations age and as migration and household patterns shift, hospitality wants and needs change and market opportunities rise and fall. The fortunes of the hospitality industry are directly related to demographics.

Information is available about each of the three market elements (that is, people, money, and willingness to purchase), although the amount and quality of the information regarding each element varies. By far the most and best information concerns demographic changes. With regard to data about money—income (salaries and wages) and wealth (total assets)—neither the quantity nor quality of data matches that of the people dimension. Nonetheless, valuable information about both income and wealth is available. In the United States, such agencies as the Census Bureau, the Bureau of Labor Statistics, and the Office of Management and the Budget collect and publish pertinent data about income and wealth. Similar data are available worldwide, particularly in highly industrialized countries. Information about consumer willingness to purchase is neither as accessible nor as concrete as that pertaining to demographic and income trends, but lifestyle analysis does offer practical insight into the willingness to buy and future guest purchase reactions. Lifestyle tendencies can be inferred from both demographic trends and relevant research.

Our analysis of demographic data will focus on U.S. developments, with a few references to other countries. Space does not allow us to look at demographic trends throughout the world. However, parallel analysis can be made for most countries using data published by those countries and by such bodies as the World Bank, the United Nations, and the Organization for Economic Development.

Demographic Shifts

Within the last three decades, U.S. population patterns have changed radically, veering in new and often unanticipated directions. Some age categories are realizing the most marked demographic changes in U.S. history. According to the most recent (1990) census of the U.S. population:

- The United States has about 4.7 percent of the world's population.

- The United States is now a slow-growth nation with a population of over one-quarter of a billion.

- Between 1980 and 1990, the U.S. population's growth rate was only 9.8 percent.

- Immigration accounts for one-third of U.S. population growth.

- The U.S. population continues to move to the southern and western parts of the country.

- Minorities constitute one-quarter of the population.

- The population has never been as old before.

- Only 56 percent of households are maintained by married couples.

- One-quarter of all households consist of a single adult.

Information about such trends can help management with such decisions as where to locate, the kinds of services and food and beverage offerings to have, the communications media to use, and the promotional appeals to adopt.

The following sections examine recent demographic data relevant to the hospitality industry in the United States and worldwide, including statistics regarding births, immigration, and population growth.

Exhibit 1   Projected Fertility Rates

Year	Total Fertility Rate
1996	2,059
2010	2,108

Source: *Statistical Abstract of the United States* (Washington, D.C.: Bureau of the Census, 1997).

Births

Population growth in the United States signals potential markets for hospitality products and services. The two drivers of population growth are births and immigration. Births represent population growth from within a country. In the United States, approximately two-thirds of the population growth between 1980 and 1990 was attributable to births. U.S. birth rates are expected to remain relatively low; the number of live births is not expected to exceed the replacement rate of 2.1 children per woman of childbearing age. Other industrialized nations are also realizing lower birth rates, in contrast to the relatively high birth rates of underdeveloped economies. An indicator of the number of future births is the total fertility rate, which measures the number of children per 1,000 women over their lifetime. Exhibit 1 presents Census estimates of U.S. fertility rates for 1996 and 2010.

Lower birth rates and smaller families in industrialized nations can be largely explained by economic and social factors such as increasing numbers of women who work outside the home, the rising costs of child rearing, employment opportunities, low wages, and general economic difficulties. Today, married households have an average of two children, compared with four in the 1950s and 1960s. In addition, many women now opt to start families at a later age, have fewer children, or forego having children altogether. In 1975, 4.8 percent of married women between the ages of 18 and 34 expected to have no children, while 12.1 percent expected to have four or more. By 1992, the number expecting no children had risen to 9.3 percent, while the number expecting four or more had fallen to 8.8 percent.

Exhibit 2 presents statistics regarding births and fertility rates from 1930 to 1995. The total number of births during this period peaked at 4.3 million in 1957 (during the "baby boom" years), while 1973 marked a low point of only 3.1 million. In 1989 and 1990, births were higher than they had been since 1964. The number of live births created a so-called "echo baby boom." Births to unmarried women in all age categories have risen sharply and in 1994 constituted about 32.6 percent of all births in the United States. As all these children grow, the need will increase for education, heath care services, recreation facilities, and products in this emerging market. Hospitality establishments will reflect the new demand for a family-oriented focus and child-related services. Certain hospitality providers have already responded to the call. Las Vegas has worked hard to change its image from an adult gambling and entertainment center to a family vacation destination.

Exhibit 2   Annual Births and Total Fertility Rate (TFR) in the United States, 1930–1995

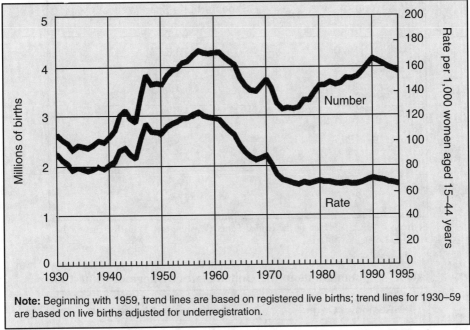

Note: Beginning with 1959, trend lines are based on registered live births; trend lines for 1930–59 are based on live births adjusted for underregistration.

Source: National Center for Health Statistics, *Monthly Vital Statistics Report*, 10 June 1997, p. 3.

Similarly, Radisson has introduced family-focused programs that offer free breakfasts, discounts on extra rooms, and a "family approved" designation for those properties that offer children's menus, a pool, child-care services, and other family-centered amenities. Other hotels, such as Holiday Inn, Howard Johnson, and Marriott, offer similarly targeted programs.[1]

Life Expectancy

Because seniors will constitute an increasing proportion of the population, they will have even greater impact on hospitality opportunities and offerings. In this regard, it is important to consider statistics regarding life expectancy. Some experts estimate that 85 years is about the maximum age that the average person can reach; others feel that an average of 85 will never be achieved; yet others argue that the limit will be 100. Regardless of disagreements over exact figures, the average life expectancy is increasing. In the United States, life expectancy has sharply increased from an average of 47 years in 1900 to about 76 years today. Exhibit 3 shows the continuing increase in life expectancy. By 2010, people are expected to have a projected life expectancy of nearly 78 years.

Females live an average of seven years longer than males, and the median age of first marriage for men is about two years more than it is for women. If we couple life expectancy and marriage data, the fact emerges that, on the average, married

Exhibit 3   Life Expectancy at Birth

Year of Birth	Expected Life Span (Years)
1960	69.7
1970	70.8
1975	72.6
1980	73.7
1985	74.7
1990	75.4
1995	75.8
Projections	
2000	76.4
2010	77.4

Source: *Statistical Abstract of the United States* (Washington, D.C.: Bureau of the Census, 1997).

Exhibit 4   Immigrants to the United States by Region, 1980–1990

Region of Origin	Percentage of Immigrants
Europe	10
Asia	43
Latin America	43
Africa	3

Source: U.S. Immigration and Naturalization Service, *Statistical Yearbook* (annual).

women are expected to outlive their spouses by about nine years. The hospitality industry will confront expanding market opportunities among the growing body of older women living a significant part of their lives as singles, whether widowed or not, with many of them relatively affluent.

Immigration

While birth rates indicate population growth from within a country, immigration represents growth from without. Immigration now accounts for over 30 percent of U.S. population growth and expectations are that it will continue to increase. Both legal and illegal immigration to the United States have resulted in profound market changes.

Since the 1970s and 1980s, the dominant immigrant groups have shifted from Europeans to Asians and Latin Americans, as shown in Exhibit 4. These new immigrant groups have in turn settled in specific regions of the United States, greatly

Exhibit 5   U.S. Population Growth Estimates: 1900–2020

Year	Number (in thousands)	Additions by Decade (in millions)
1900	75,994	
1930	122,775	
		9
1940	131,669	
		19
1950	150,697	
		29
1960	179,323	
		24
1970	203,302	
		23
1980	226,542	
		22
1990	248,718	
		26
2000	274,634	
		23
2010	297,716	
		25
2020	322,742	

Source: *Statistical Abstract of the United States* (Washington, D.C.: Bureau of the Census, 1997).

influencing local hospitality offerings. Pizza and tacos have replaced burgers and roast beef as the most popular foods in the United States. Other international cultures are increasingly represented in food choices such as bagels, croissants, shish kabob, sushi, and a greater variety of international beers, wines, cheeses, fruits, and vegetables. Many immigrants have been successful in opening restaurants, working in the hospitality industry, and supplying hospitality products.

Multicultural influences are also witnessed in changing styles of furniture, clothing, music, art, and customs. The preferences and lifestyles of U.S. consumers in turn shape those of consumers globally. Consumer tastes around the world are growing more alike and coexisting with important national and cultural differences.

Population Projections

Rapid population growth in the past, coupled with economic advancement, meant prosperity for hospitality enterprises. The expanding populations of the 1950s, 1960s, and 1970s supported many hospitality providers who made money in spite of their inefficiency. Hospitality failures multiplied, however, during the slower population growth years of the late 1980s and the 1990s.

Exhibit 5 presents realized population totals from 1900 to 1990 and projections to the year 2020. The population grew by over 22 million in the 1980s and is expected to grow by 26 million in the 1990s, resulting in a total population of nearly

Exhibit 6   Percentage Distribution of the U.S. Population: 1970–2000

Age	1970	1980	1990	2000
Under 5	8.4	7.1	7.5	6.3
5–14	20.2	15.5	14.2	14.2
15–19	9.4	9.3	7.2	7.1
20–24	7.9	9.4	7.7	6.3
25–34	12.3	16.4	17.4	13.4
35–44	11.3	11.4	15.1	16.4
45–54	11.3	10.1	10.0	13.8
55–64	9.4	9.6	8.5	9.0
65–74	5.9	6.8	7.2	7.2
75+	3.9	4.4	5.2	6.3

Source: *Statistical Abstract of the United States* (Washington, D.C.: Bureau of the Census, 1997).

275 million by the year 2000. The U.S. population is expected to increase beyond the year 2000, but at a slower rate. Most growth over the next century is expected to occur within the first 50 years and then virtually stop as zero population growth is approximated.

The proportionate changes in the actual and projected composition of the U.S. population, as shown in Exhibit 6, reveal how population dynamics shape markets. These statistics demonstrate the aging of the U.S. population. In 1970, the median age was 30.6 years. By the year 2000, it will have shifted markedly to 36.3 years. While the percentage of the population between ages 15 and 24 will decline, the percentage that is 35 to 54 and over 74 will increase significantly. Notably, income is highest among those between ages 45 and 54, an age segment that is very important to hospitality businesses.

Choice Hotels has responded to the needs of an aging and graying market by promoting new "senior-friendly" room designs and special discount rates. These decisions resulted from interviews with seniors, comments on guest cards, and information gathered from the American Association of Retired Persons (AARP). Rodeway similarly conducted research about mature travelers and redesigned their rooms accordingly.

Hospitality enterprises will have to develop marketing plans and strategies geared to lower population growth and keener global competition. Inefficient restaurateurs and hoteliers will no longer be propped up by a rapidly growing population.

Where Will Guests Live?

The maxim that the three most important factors in success of hospitality businesses are "location, location, location" is still valid. Good locations, where guests want to be, afford tremendous advantages. Conversely, poor locations can

Exhibit 7   Where Do Americans Live?

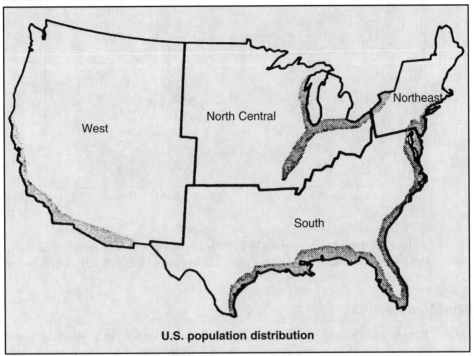

U.S. population distribution

sabotage otherwise feasible hospitality ventures. Knowing where guests live and will want to live is an important step toward success in the hospitality industry.

In the United States, over half of the population lives near a body of water. Americans seem to prefer the coasts and waterways to the plains; the West and South to the North; the mountain and southern states to the north-central plains; and urban areas to rural ones. The shaded areas in Exhibit 7 highlight where the greatest concentrations of Americans live. Americans tend to congregate along a few rather narrow strips.

The United States will continue to be an urban culture with population concentrations in established metropolitan areas and their sprawling suburbs. The more affluent will continue to move to the suburbs and to smaller towns or rural locales near larger cities ("ruralia"). Areas that combine the benefits of both rural and urban living will continue to develop. So-called "megalopolises" or sprawling urban areas will be extended, as is already the case in cities like New York, Washington, Miami, and Los Angeles.

Since hospitality product and service offerings are truly local, geographic concerns affect the hospitality businesses in many ways, such as food preferences. For example, Philadelphians prefer pepper pot soup, while Miami favors chicken broth. The South leads the nation in the consumption of iced tea, while herbal teas are preferred in the West. Southerners like Russian and Thousand Island salad dressings, while Midwesterners prefer Italian. Inhabitants of the mountain states

Exhibit 8   World Population Figures and Projections: 1970–2020

Year	Total (in millions)
1970	3,698
1980	4,458
1985	4,855
1990	5,282
1995	5,691
2000	6,090
2010	6,858
2020	7,593

Source: *Statistical Abstract of the United States* (Washington, D.C.: Bureau of the Census, 1997).

consume almost a third more cookies than those in the rest of the country.[2] Clearly, Americans have a mosaic of food tastes and where people live can tell us quite a bit about their purchase preferences.

World Population

Exhibit 8 highlights world population data and projections from 1970 to 2020. By 2020, it is projected that world population will increase to 7.6 billion, more than doubling the 1970 population. About three-fourths of the world's population lives in developing nations. That proportion is projected to increase to over four-fifths in 2020. The ten countries with the largest populations are:

China . . . . 1.22 billion
India . . . . 968 million
United States . . . . 268 million
Indonesia . . . . 210 million
Brazil . . . . 165 million
Russia . . . . 148 million
Pakistan . . . . 132 million
Japan . . . . 126 million
Bangladesh . . . . 125 million
Nigeria . . . . 107 million

As mentioned earlier, it is not possible in a chapter such as this to include detailed data about guests from various countries around the world. However, most countries publish relevant demographic information paralleling the U.S. data we've been discussing. Exhibit 9 presents a guide to many international statistical abstracts. In addition, a wealth of data is available in the International Population Reports of the U.S. Census Bureau and the publications of the United Nations, the World Bank, and the Organization for Economic Development.

Exhibit 9   International Sources for Statistical Abstracts

This bibliography presents recent statistical abstracts for Mexico, Russia, and member nations of the Organization for Economic Cooperation and Development. All sources contain statistical tables on a variety of subjects for the individual countries. Many of the following publications provide text in English as well as in the national language(s). For further information on these publications, contact the named statistical agency which is responsible for editing the publication.

Australia

Australian Bureau of Statistics, Canberra
Yearbook Australia. Annual. 1997 767 pp. (In English.)

Austria

Osterreichisches Statistisches Zentralamt, P.O. Box 9000, A-1033 Vienna
Statistisches Jahrbuch for die Republik Osterreich. Annual. 1996 612 pp. (In German.)

Belgium

Institut National de Statistique, 44 rue de Louvain, 1000 Brussels
Annuaire statistique de la Belgique. Annual. 1994 822 pp. (In French and Dutch.)

Canada

Statistics Canada, Ottawa, Ontario, KIA OT6
*Canada Yearbook: A review of economic, social and political developments in Canada.*1997 515 pp. Irregular. (In English and French.)

Croatia

Republika Hrvatska, Republicki Zavod Za Statistiku
Statisticki Ijetopis 1995 644 pp. (In English and Serbo-Croatian.)

Czech Republic

Czech Statistical Office, Sokolovska 142, 186 04 Praha 8
Statisticka Rocenka Ceske Rpubliky 1996 707 pp. (In English and Czech.)

Denmark

Danmarks Statistik, Postboks 2550 Sejrogade 11, DK 2100, Copenhagen
Statistical Yearbook. 1995. Annual. 559 pp. (In Danish with English translations of table headings.)

Finland

Central Statistical Office of Finland, Box 504 SF-00101 Helsinki
Statistical Yearbook of Finland. Annual. 1996 661 pp. (In English, Finnish, and Swedish.)

France

Institut National de la Statistique et des Etudes Economiques, Paris 18, Bld. Adolphe Pinard, 75675 Paris (Cedex 14)
Annuaire Statistique de la France. Annual. 1997 1002 pp. (In French.)

Greece

National Statistical Office, 14-16 Lycourgou St., 101-66 Athens
Concise Statistical Yearbook 1995 254 pp. (In English.)
Statistical Yearbook of Greece. Annual. 1994–1995 528 pp. (plus 7 pages of diagrams). (In English and Greek.)

Iceland

Hagstofa Islands/Statistical Bureau, Hverfisgata 8-10, Reykjavik.
Statistical Abstract of Iceland. 1994. Irregular. 303 pp. (In English and Icelandic.)

(continued)

Exhibit 9   *(continued)*

Ireland

Central Statistics Office, Earlsfort
Terrace, Dublin 2
Statistical Abstract. Annual. 1996
411 pp. (In English.)

Italy

ISTAT (Istituto Centrale di Statistica),
Via Cesare Balbo 16, 00100 Rome
Annuario Statistico Italiano.
Annual. 1996 679 pp. (In
Italian.)

Japan

Statistics Bureau, Management &
Coordination Agency, 19-1
Wakamatsucho, Shinjuku Tokyo 162
Japan Statistical Yearbook.
Annual. 1997 914 pp. (In
English and Japanese.)

Luxembourg

STATEC (Service Central de la
Statistique et des Etudes), P.O. Box
304, L-2013, Luxembourg
Annuaire Statistique. Annual.
1996. (In French.)

Mexico

Instituto Nacional de Estadistica
Geografia e Informatica, Avda.
Insurgentes Sur No. 795-PH Col.
Napoles, Del. Benito Juarez 03810
Mexico, D.F.
*Anuario estadistico de los Estados
Unidos Mexicanos.* Annual.
1993 610 pp. Also on disc.
(In Spanish.) *Agenda
Estadistica 1994* 186 pp.

Netherlands

Centraal Bureau voor de Statistiek.
428 Prinses Beatrixlaan P.O. Box
959, 2270 AZ Voorburg
Statistisch Yearbook 1996. 599 pp.
(In Dutch.)

New Zealand

Department of Statistics, Wellington
New Zealand Official Yearbook.
Annual. 1996 592 pp. (In
English.)

Norway

Central Bureau of Statistics, Skipper-
gate 15, P.B. 8131 Dep. N-Oslo 1
Statistical Yearbook. Annual. 1996
445 pp. (In English and
Norwegian.)

Portugal

INE (Instituto Nacional de Estatis-
tica), Avenida Antonio Jose de
Almeida, P-1078 Lisbon Codex
Anuario Estatistico: de Portugal.
1995 339 pp. (In Portugese.)

Russia

State Committee of Statistics of
Russia, Moscow
*Russian Federation in the Year
1993. Statistical Yearbook.* 1993
383 pp. (In Russian.)

Slovakia

Statistical Office of the Slovak Republic, Mileticova 3, 824 67 Bratislava
Statisticka Rocenka Slovensak
1996. 681 pp. (In English and
Slovak)

Slovenia

Statistical Office of the Republic of
Slovenia, Vozarski Pot 12, 61000
Ljubljana
*Statisticni Letopis Republike Sloe-
venije* 1996. 619 pp. (In
Slovenian.)

Spain

INE (Instituto Nacional de Estadistica),
Paseo de la Castellana, 183,
Madrid 16
Anuario Estadistico de Espana.
Annual. 1995 878 pp. (In
Spanish.)
Anuario Estadistico. 1988. (Edicion
Manual.) 976 pp.

Sweden

Statistics Sweden, S-11581
Stockholm
*Statistical Yearbook of
Sweden.* Annual. 1997 566 pp.
(In English and Swedish.)

Exhibit 9 *(continued)*

Switzerland	**United Kingdom**
Bundesamt fur Statistik, Hallwylstrasse 15, CH-3003, Bern	Central Statistical Office, Great George Street, London SW1P 3AQ
Statistisches Jahrbuch der Schweiz. Annual. 1997 464 pp. (In French and German.)	*Annual Abstract of Statistics.* Annual. 1991 349 pp. (In English.)
Turkey	**West Germany**
State Institute of Statistics, Prime Ministry, 114 Necatibey Caddesi, Bakanliklar, Yenisehir, Ankara	Statistische Bundesamt, Postfach 5528, 6200 Wiesbaden
Statistical Yearbook of Turkey. 1996 690 pp. (In English and Turkish.)	*Statistisches Jahrbuch fur die Bundesrepublic Deutschland.* Annual. 1996 755 pp. (In German.)
Turkey in Statistics 1994 150 pp. (In English and Turkish.)	*Statistisches Jahrbuch fur das Ausland. 1996.* 399 pp.

Source: *Statistical Abstract of the United States* (Washington, D.C.: Bureau of the Census, 1997).

Income and Wealth

The second factor in our definition of hospitality markets is money, which includes income and wealth. Income data are not as readily available as population data and government agencies do not publish income projections on a regular basis. Still, an investigation of available data can yield valuable insights into likely trends and tendencies, and hence into profitable market opportunities.

Americans realized unprecedented growth in their incomes and living standards from the 1960s to the 1980s. While **real income** (that is, income adjusted for inflation) and living standards have not stopped increasing, their rates of growth have slowed and the former rates are not likely to be repeated in the foreseeable future. Nevertheless, an increasing proportion of future guests will be able to afford the luxurious lifestyle previously available to only a privileged few. An era of more democratic affluence is emerging. In the future, hospitality providers in the United States will be challenged to serve the growing number of affluent and aging families and households. Various non-hospitality businesses have recognized the opportunities these groups provide and have adjusted their operations accordingly. For example, the venerable U.S. Trust now offers the private banking services and special privileges once reserved for only the very wealthy to a far greater number of customers—particularly those who earn at least $75,000 per year and have at least a million dollars in assets.

Family Income

Slower economic growth has caused many people to question the American Dream, with its promise of an ever-better lifestyle.

Many American families, particularly those in the middle class, believe they have lost ground economically and are worse off than their parents were at similar

Exhibit 10   Median Family Income: 1970–1995

Year	Current Dollars	1995 Dollars
1970	$ 9,867	$ 36,410
1980	21,023	38,930
1985	27,735	39,283
1990	35,353	41,223
1995	40,611	40,611

Source: *Statistical Abstract of the United States* (Washington, D.C.: Bureau of the Census, 1997).

Exhibit 11   Family Income Distribution in Constant (1995) Dollars: 1970–1995

	Percent Distribution							Median
Year	Under $10,000	$10,000–$14,999	$15,000–$24,999	$25,000–$34,999	$35,000–$49,999	$50,000–$74,999	$75,000 and over	Income (dollars)
1970	7.7	6.7	15.4	18.0	24.5	19.0	8.8	$36,410
1980	7.3	6.7	15.2	14.9	21.9	21.3	12.8	$38,930
1985	8.3	6.4	14.7	14.6	19.8	20.8	15.5	$39,283
1990	7.7	6.1	13.7	14.2	19.4	21.0	18.0	$41,223
1995	7.5	6.5	14.4	14.1	18.5	20.4	18.6	$40,611

Source: *Statistical Abstract of the United States* (Washington, D.C.: Bureau of the Census, 1997).

stages of their lives. Income data, however, do not support this conclusion. Although American middle-class families and households have not fared as well as they did in the upbeat years of the 1960s and 1970s, nor as well as the top five percent of families and households, the median family income in 1995 ($40,611) was about $4,200 higher (in 1995 dollars) than the real median family income in 1970. Exhibit 10 shows the median family income in current and real dollars for selected years from 1970 to 1995. In real terms, the median family income grew about 11.5 percent.

Exhibit 11 presents the distribution of families according to income level in constant (1995) dollars for the period 1970–1995. Throughout these years, the proportion of families earning under $15,000 remained about the same. The

Exhibit 12   Share of Aggregate Family Income: 1970–1995

Year	Bottom 20% of Families	Middle 60% of Families	Top 20% of Families
1970	5.4%	53.6%	40.9%
1980	5.3%	53.6%	41.1%
1990	4.6%	51.2%	44.3%
1995	4.4%	49.1%	46.5%

Source: *Statistical Abstract of the United States* (Washington, D.C.: Bureau of the Census, 1997).

proportion of families in both the $25,000–$34,999 and $35,000–$49,999 brackets decreased steadily. In contrast, the proportion of families earning $50,000 or more per year increased substantially. In fact, the proportion of families earning $75,000 and over more than doubled in these years.

The term "middle class" is a somewhat arbitrary definition. Does it comprise, for example, the middle 20 percent of households? 40 percent? 60 percent? As Exhibit 12 shows, trends emerge when families are grouped according to the lowest 20 percent, the middle 60 percent, and the top 20 percent of income. Between 1970 and 1995, the top 20 percent of families gained ground.

Such growing affluence bodes well for the hospitality industry, as it indicates possible support for the expansion of hospitality market opportunities. Although middle class incomes will not rise as rapidly as they have in the past, the wealthier families and households, which earn the top one to five percent of incomes, will fare very well.

Despite the doubts of younger consumers, the American Dream survives. Consumer expectations about the future, while tempered, continue to rise.

Household Income

Households are often used as the unit for demographic analysis. Generally, the more workers in a household, the higher the total income. Households with three or more wage earners are more likely to earn $50,000 or more, although two-earner households enjoy a higher individual income. In 1995, about 32 percent of U.S. households had incomes of $50,000 or more. This figure includes more than 500,000 households without any wage earners whatsoever.

From 1970 to 1995, the real median household income grew (in 1995 dollars) from $32,229 to $34,076 (see Exhibit 13). Exhibit 14 presents the proportionate distribution of household income from 1970 to 1995 according to income categories in constant (1995) dollars. The under-$10,000 category decreased slightly, while the $10,000 to $14,999 range increased. The $25,000 to $34,999 and the $35,000 to $49,999 income ranges also decreased. In contrast, the proportion of households earning $50,000 and over rose from 24 percent to 32 percent of all households. The proportion of households earning $75,000 doubled to just under 15 percent of all households.

Exhibit 13   Median Household Income: 1970–1995

Year	Current Dollars	1995 Dollars
1970	$ 8,374	$ 32,229
1980	17,710	32,795
1985	23,618	33,452
1990	29,943	34,914
1995	34,076	34,076

Source: *Statistical Abstract of the United States* (Washington, D.C.: Bureau of the Census, 1997).

Exhibit 14   Household Income Distribution in Constant (1995) Dollars: 1970–1995

	Percent Distribution							Median
Year	Under $10,000	$10,000– $14,999	$15,000– $24,999	$25,000– $34,999	$35,000– $49,999	$50,000– $74,999	$75,000 and over	Income (dollars)
1970	14.3	8.0	15.8	16.9	21.3	16.3	7.5	$32,229
1980	13.3	8.7	16.5	14.6	19.3	17.4	10.3	$32,795
1990	12.5	8.1	15.5	14.4	17.7	17.6	14.2	$34,914
1995	12.3	8.7	15.9	14.2	16.9	17.1	14.8	$34,076

Source: *Statistical Abstract of the United States* (Washington, D.C.: Bureau of the Census, 1997).

Per Capita and Discretionary Income

As Exhibit 15 shows, real per capita income grew by 47 percent between 1970 and 1995. Interestingly, per capita income is highest in two-earner households. Hospitality providers are very interested in the proportion of per capita income that is **discretionary income**. According to a joint publication of the Census Bureau and the Conference Board, discretionary income is "the amount of money which would permit a family to maintain a living standard comfortably higher than the average for similar families."[3] Households with the most discretionary income are composed of those aged 50 to 59, followed by those aged 45 to 49.

On a per capita basis, households composed of people over age 60 had significantly higher discretionary incomes. As household incomes increase, discretionary income and per capita discretionary income increase. Households earning $75,000

Exhibit 15   Per Capita Income: 1970–1995

Year	Current Dollars	Constant (1995) Dollars
1970	$ 3,177	$11,723
1980	7,787	14,420
1985	11,013	15,598
1990	14,387	16,776
1995	17,227	17,227

Source: *Statistical Abstract of the United States* (Washington, D.C.: Bureau of the Census, 1997).

and over account for about one-half of aggregate discretionary income. Households earning $100,000 and over average $47,320 of aggregate discretionary income, or $14,163 per capita.

An analysis of the proportion of discretionary income by household income levels indicates, as might be expected, that households earning less than $25,000 annually have a very small proportion of discretionary income. In contrast, almost 80 percent of households earning $50,000 and over have discretionary income. The aggregate amount of discretionary income was estimated at $319 billion, yielding an average of $12,232 per household and $4,633 per capita.

Among the findings of the joint Census Bureau/Conference Board research are:[4]

- Homes with annual earnings of $40,000 and over (about one-quarter of the population) constitute over two-thirds of discretionary income homes.

- Householders between ages 35 and 60 accounted for over half of all discretionary income.

- Householders age 65 and over accounted for 16 percent of all discretionary income.

- After age 55, average discretionary income begins to decline but per capita discretionary income continues to increase.

- Households composed of people under age 30 have relatively little discretionary income.

- Two or more earner households accounted for almost 65 percent of discretionary income.

- Over half of the households headed by the holder of a college degree had discretionary income.

Wealth and Affluence

Affluent families are often composed of a large proportion of people in their peak earning years—usually between ages 35 and 54. Data indicate that almost two-thirds of the heads of these families have graduated from college. In addition,

Exhibit 16   Estimated Percentage of the Nation's Wealth Held by the Richest One Percent of Americans: 1770s–1980s

Year	Percentage of Wealth
1770s	14.6
1860s	27.0
1920s	35.4–42.6
1930s	32.1–35.1
1940s	26.1–28.7
1950s	27.8–30.1
1960s	30.0–33.2
1970s	17.6–28.0
1980s	19.8–36.3

Based on *The New York Times,* 16 August 1992, p. E3.

affluent families have fewer dependent children, more wage earners, live primarily in the suburbs of large cities, and almost always own their homes. Ninety percent of households in the top 20 percent income bracket are families, and 80 percent are married couple households. Non-family households make up only ten percent of this group.

Affluence is variously defined. By some measurements, the affluent comprise the top 20 or the top five percent of income and wealth. Other definitions of affluence are an annual income level of $75,000 to $100,000, specified ranges above mean or median incomes, or a predetermined amount of net worth or investable assets.

In 1990, families in the top five percent income bracket earned over $102,358, with an average income of almost $150,000. Between 1977 and 1989, families with incomes in the top one percent income bracket accounted for about 70 percent of the increase in average family income, and those in the highest 20 percent income bracket accounted for all of it. From 1980 to 1988, the percentage of families earning more than $100,000 (in 1988 dollars) doubled from 1.6 to 3.2 percent.

Exhibit 16 shows the wealth of the richest one percent of Americans from the 1770s through the 1980s. Wealth is highly concentrated among those who are the very richest. This is supported by data on mean net worth of families. The net worth of the 20 percent of families with incomes of $50,000 and over in 1989 was nearly four times greater than that of the 23 percent of families in the $30,000–$49,999 range. Other data show that married-couple households are much wealthier than singles, and that households in the top 20 percent income bracket have 44 percent of the net worth. In 1989, the median net worth of U.S. households was $183,700, 43 percent of which was the family home.

An estimated 3,683,000 households, or 3.9 percent of all households, had a net worth of more than $1,000,000 in 1992.[5] There are estimates that in 1996 over 20 million households had incomes of over $75,000 and a net worth of $300,000 or

Exhibit 17   Householder Age and Median Income: 1995

Age of Householder	Median Income (in dollars)
15–24	$20,979
25–34	34,701
35–44	43,465
45–54	48,058
55–64	38,077
65 and over	19,096

Source: *Statistical Abstract of the United States* (Washington, D.C.: Bureau of the Census, 1997).

more. The number of U.S. billionaires grew from 21 in 1982 to 71 in 1991. And of special importance to hospitality businesses is the fact that a large proportion of the U.S. population is approaching both the highest income-earning and net worth accumulating years—between ages 45 to 64. This segment portends an expanding and very attractive hospitality market.

Mature Guests

A common misconception about elder guests is that they are poor. In terms of income, this segment has fared better than the population at large over the last two decades. The median income of senior (age 65 and over) households grew 21 percent in real dollars from 1980 to 1990, compared to six percent for all households. These are the so-called "retirement winners," although some elderly, such as those depending entirely on social security, have been left behind.

The definition of income as "regularly received income," which precludes retirees, ignores noncash benefits and such assets as wealth. Exhibit 17 shows the 1995 real median household income by age of the householder. As expected, income steeply declines in households headed by people age 55 and over. These statistics reflect an increasing number of voluntary and involuntary retirees and the large number of elderly people, particularly women, who live alone.

As the population ages, the opportunity for wealth accumulation increases until retirement. Median net worth goes up with age until around age 65 to 70, as indicated in Exhibit 18. Not only do older people continue to enjoy above average wealth, but they have also outgrown the many financial obligations confronting younger families such as buying and furnishing homes and educating their children.

Expenditures on Hospitality Offerings

Detailed data on expenditures by American consumers are published by the United States Bureau of Labor Statistics. Some of this information relates to the hospitality industry, including data about expenditures on recreation, travel, and

Exhibit 18   Median Family Net Worth by Age of Family Head: 1995

Age of Head of Family	Median Net Worth (in dollars)
Under 35	$ 11,400
35–44	8,500
45–54	90,500
55–64	110,800
65–74	104,100
75 and over	95,000

Source: *Statistical Abstract of the United States* (Washington, D.C.: Bureau of the Census, 1997).

food and beverages consumed away from home. Of particular interest to many hospitality providers are data on travel and tourism expenditures.

Hospitality marketers have a variety of data available to help them understand current trends and developments in the travel market that affect the demand for food and lodging. The Travel Industry Association of America (TIA) distributes the publications and data of the U.S. Travel and Tourism Administration (USTTA). It regularly publishes pertinent and timely statistics on travel, including studies concerning the overall economic impact of travel: the annual *National Travel Survey*, which tracks consumer travel plans (from 1979 on); *Travelscope*, the report of a monthly survey of trip and traveler characteristics; and the annual *Outlook for Travel and Tourism*.

International travel has grown tremendously since the 1960s. Travel to the United States has grown in each decade since the 1970s, reaching more than 40 million in 1990. Conservative estimates project about 67 million yearly arrivals in the United States by the year 2000.[6]

Around the world, international travel is affected by economic and political factors such as inflation, unemployment, business conditions, exchange rates, political stability, and terrorism. Spending by international consumers greatly affects the demand for hospitality products and services. Travel and tourism are expected to continue growing, extending the market opportunities for hospitality businesses.

Guest Lifestyles

Lifestyles are the third set of factors in identifying future market opportunities.[7] Tomorrow's guests will have different expectations, behave in a different manner, and enjoy different lifestyles than their counterparts of the 1970s, 1980s, and 1990s. These guests are likely to be less fettered socially and economically, more independent and secure within themselves, better informed, and more discerning and

Exhibit 19　Changing Consumer Orientations

Traditional Guests	Future Guests
Quantity	Quality
Materialism	Spirituality, humanism
Price, cost	Value
Uninformed	Information-seeking
Insecure and sheltered	Worldly wise, confident
Acquiescent	Discerning and demanding
Self reliance	Societal net
Women at home	Working women
Postpone purchases, save	Credit; spend and enjoy
Economic constraints	Time constraints
Utility	Aesthetics, image
Plebeian tastes	Cosmopolitan tastes
Earn a living	Self-fulfillment
Defined gender roles	Blurred gender roles
Acceptable style	Multiple styles
Group mores	Independent choice
Local and regional	Global
Passive	Active
Stable	Impermanence, seeking the new

culturally aware than ever. They will be more likely to challenge accepted ideas and practices and make their feelings and opinions known.

Hospitality markets will certainly be greatly affected by these future changes. They will become more segmented and fragmented. They will also reflect greater individualization and customization of hospitality services to better fit the lifestyle wants and needs of market niches and individual guests. A variety of published research studies address how various groups of guests will live. This section focuses on the behavioral trends shaping lifestyles, some emerging guest orientations, and the basic themes that emerge throughout guests' lives.

Guest Orientations

Future guests will have different orientations and outlooks from their predecessors, as depicted in Exhibit 19. In contrast to past guests, who lived to work and amass material possessions, future guests will work to live and will place a greater emphasis on the overall quality of life. Family and social contributions will be increasingly central to their lives.

Future guests will be more sophisticated, cultured, and informed than their often provincial forerunners. Living in an age of information and technological innovation, these guests will have convenient and immediate access to information.

Travel and communication technologies such as television and the Internet will expose them to other cultures and will keep them informed of world events. Future guests will also have more global perspectives and tastes and will purchase hospitality products and services from around the world.

The worldly guests of the future will be knowledgeable, secure, and confident. They will be more discerning and demanding than ever and will have higher expectations of hospitality products and services. Product durability, service, reliability, and value will assume a greater importance relative to price and cost. Guests will also be more concerned with aesthetic considerations such as design, color, and taste as they make their hospitality choices. The constant demand for something new and different will challenge hospitality providers to be creative and innovative.

Future guests, in their hospitality desires and expectations, will reflect many social changes. The ever-increasing numbers of women who work outside the home will drive hospitality providers to consider this segment's impact upon consumer choices, entertainment, travel, and child-care options. In addition, clearly defined guest roles based on gender or marital status will continue to blur. Many different lifestyles will be increasingly tolerated and accepted, and guests will be at greater liberty to live as they please.

In the past, guests were frugal and postponed purchases until they could afford them. In contrast, current guests are among the "now generation," buying things now on credit and paying for them later. This trend will be reinforced in the future. And while future guests may not be as limited economically as guests of the past, they will face time constraints as a limit to their consumption. They may not have the time to consume what their resources may afford. Competition among hospitality providers for guests' time will grow ever keener.

Changing Values

America is often described as a society of the middle class. However, the middle-class values of the past have given way to an increasingly heterogeneous and fragmented array of values and lifestyles. We are all familiar with the catchy labels, such as Yuppie (young urban professional), Dink (dual income, no kids), and Generation X, attached to some of these ways of life. Guest values and lifestyles indicate who guests are and reveal insights into their behavior, yielding clues about the kinds of purchases that they are likely to make with regard to cars, homes, clothing, and hospitality products and services. Lifestyles are a means of identifying and segmenting groups of guests.

One of the widely referenced topologies of lifestyles and value shifts of American consumers is know by the acronym VALS (which stands for *values and life styles*). VALS was developed by the Stanford Research Institute. The initial research identified the values and lifestyles of three main population groups: survivors and sustainers (12 percent), outer-directeds (71 percent), and inner-directeds (17 percent). These groups were further segmented according to their attitudes, opinions, activities and interests.[8]

Currently, attention is being directed at the lifestyles of Generation X—those people born between 1965 and 1974. They have been identified as having different psychological and sociological outlooks than the cohort of a generation ago, and this offers clues about marketing to them. They are said to have been raised on television, are familiar with the creation of advertising images, and are more suspicious of marketing hype. Generation Xers are familiar with such household activities as comparison shopping and bargain hunting, and resent being patronized and manipulated. They are often overeducated and underemployed and are characterized as being more concerned with product utility, functionality, value, and usefulness—with getting value for their money—than with fanciful images and hype. Members of Generation X respond to "campaigns that depict the lifestyles of a group that has come of age in the wake of the better-off baby-boom generation."[9]

Future Lifestyles

Purchase and census data yield consumer profiles that provide greater insight than ever into guest lifestyles. These consumer profiles help companies target their marketing efforts. For example, such data indicate that Volvo owners are likely to own a VCR, belong to a health club, play golf or tennis, take cruises, and ski. Consumers of Peter Pan Peanut Butter are heavy video renters, go to theme parks, and are below average television viewers but above average radio listeners. Those who drink Coors Light beer are more likely to belong to a health club, buy rock music, travel by plane, rent videos, give parties, and participate in sports.[10] Hospitality providers can develop similar profiles that will help them gear hospitality offerings more precisely to the desires of their particular guests.

The rest of this chapter lists some of the major themes that run throughout both existing and emerging lifestyles that will shape future guest attitudes and hospitality behavior. Hospitality businesses must try to anticipate the implications of such lifestyle orientations for company offerings and operations.

Think about the implications of these themes for future hospitality offerings and develop your own list of potential opportunities for hospitality businesses that are of interest. Among the future lifestyle themes are the following.

My Life My Way. Future guests will be more inclined to live their lives as they see fit and less interested than previous age cohorts were in what others think of them and their lifestyles. They will exhibit a more individualistic philosophy of life and a greater sense of self-assurance, which may on the surface seem somewhat selfish. However, it need not indicate a disregard for others or for important societal and ecological issues. The *my life my way* orientation focuses on self-fulfillment and suggests a need for flexibility on the part of hospitality companies. For example, rigid hotel and restaurant dress codes of the past, such as requiring ties, jackets, and evening wear, may have to give way to some of the informal lifestyles and clothing preferences of future guests. Guests will feel less inhibited and will demand special services and accommodations that are in line with their desires. More attention will be directed to individuality as compared to the mass in dealing with markets. It will be more a matter of accommodating and catering to individual guests than making them conform to company approaches.

Psychological Self-Enhancement. Future guests will be concerned with improving their psychological well-being and self-esteem. They will be motivated to acquire self-enhancing products, services, and symbols. Hospitality providers can cater to this self-enhancement orientation just as other enterprises have with their status automobiles, designer clothing, exclusive clubs, prestige credit cards, and self-improvement books, courses, and tapes. Some hospitality providers have capitalized on such opportunities with prestigious hotels and restaurants, concierge floors, dining clubs, wine-tasting sessions, and "members-only" appeals.

Physical Self-Enhancement. This theme complements the enhancement of the psychological self ("healthy body, healthy mind"). Guests are becoming ever more health-conscious and concerned with both their actual well-being and their physical appearance. Both will be underscored by our society's continuing quest for youthfulness. This is evidenced by a wide variety of products and services, such as vitamins, cosmetics, plastic surgery, and health foods. Hospitality opportunities include health clubs, spas, trainers, beauty salons, healthy food offerings, and even the alliance of resorts with medical and nutrition clinics.

Rising Tastes and Cosmopolitanism. As the most educated, traveled, and affluent consumers in our history, future guests are more likely to enjoy cosmopolitan style and tastes. They will be exposed to cultural activities, foods, beverages, and lifestyles from around the world. Increasing emphasis will be placed on art, music, ballet, museums, and the theater. Future guests will be more conscious of aesthetics, good design, and good taste. This orientation will be reflected in their choices of hotels, restaurants, and hospitality activities, as well as their homes, furnishings, and wardrobes. They will seek to experience "the better things in life." Hotels and tour operators will increasingly develop packages for guests encompassing theater, dance, museum, opera, and other cultural offerings.

Independence and Interdependence. These seemingly conflicting lifestyle themes will influence the lives and purchases of future guests. On the one hand, future guests (as we have noted) will be more willing to express themselves, be more certain of their choices, and less fettered socially and economically—they will be more independent. At the same time, however, they will recognize the interdependence of people and nations in our modern, global, high-tech society—in other words, their dependence on others. This will highlight the need for good citizenship and cooperative approaches for the greater good. Maintaining a healthy hospitality environment requires such elements as clean air, water, and food and safe transport that are dependent on cooperative efforts among businesses and nations. The reality of interdependence among nations will assume heightened importance in hospitality markets. The recent examples of smoke from fires in neighboring Indonesia negatively affecting tourism in Singapore and of the fires in Mexico affecting the environment in Texas are examples. In the future, nations will become ever more sensitive to the effects of their decisions and actions on neighboring states and to the need for cooperative efforts leading to actions that benefit all.

Impermanence and Change. The guests of tomorrow will be relentless in their pursuit of that which is new—new restaurants, resorts, food, clothing, recreation, entertainment, and living environments. They will seek change, and hospitality offerings will be less permanent than ever. Future guests will exhibit a voracious appetite for new hospitality experiences, actively seeking and expecting innovations, thereby heralding new opportunities for creative firms. Increasingly, hospitality managers will be challenged to develop innovative offerings, and more resources will be dedicated to developing and promoting new products and services accordingly.

Conservation. The above-mentioned emphasis on newness and change will be tempered somewhat by a countering need for conservation. Future guests, while seeking new offerings, will also be more keenly attuned to conserving resources. The current approaches of hotels that encourage guests to conserve energy and water by controlling temperatures, turning off lights, and limiting the amount of water for showers and bath will be extended. New approaches will emerge, such as hotels encouraging guests to reuse towels, seeking guest permission to reduce the daily change of linen during longer stays, and restaurant efforts to reduce waste. Through such efforts as the "green movement," heightened guest awareness will lead to a future atmosphere that is much more conservation friendly, permitting the efforts of hospitality managers to both control costs and conserve scarce resources.

Convenience and Instantaneity. Future guests will expect convenient, readily available, user-friendly hospitality products and services. They will expect hospitality offerings to be available when and where they want them, 24 hours a day, seven days a week. Instantaneity refers to the "now syndrome"—to guest quests for instant gratification. An idea of the impact of this trend on the hospitality industry and its market potential can be seen by considering the host of products and services that cater to convenience and instantaneity such as fax machines, VCRs, copiers, computers, direct-dial telephones, rental cars, videos, pre-prepared and delivered foods, microwave ovens, automated global reservations, and all-night diners. Future guests will be even more impatient, demanding instant availability of personalized and customized hospitality products and services tailored to their individual needs. Increasingly, convenience and availability will be the hallmarks of successful hospitality providers.

Product and Service Dominance. In the future, consumers will be increasingly dominated by and dependent upon products and services not under their control. We all know how much our lives are disrupted and disturbed when automobiles, telephones, computers, fax machines, or air conditioners break down. Under such conditions, product quality and durability will assume far greater importance. And as machines become more and more dominant in providing hospitality services, future guests may be made to feel that they are little more than a number and that they are dominated by machines. Hospitality businesses will face the challenge of providing smoothly functioning mechanized services coupled with what will become increasingly important—the personal, human touch.

Work as a Means. Future guests will see work as a means to a better life, rather than an end in itself. In contrast to an earlier generation that lived to work, they will work to live. Although future guests will spend less time on the job and have more discretionary time (that is, time beyond that needed to take care of their basic needs), this does not mean that they will have more time with nothing to do. While hospitality products and services can help them enjoy life, the fact is that future guests will confront wider and more attractive assortments of hospitality offerings competing for their discretionary time. One result will be that, in addition to money, time will become a severe constraint limiting guest consumption of hospitality offerings. Those hospitality products and services that extend guest time, whether through mechanization, automation, and efficiency or through the availability of various guests services, will be in demand.

Risk Avoidance and Security. As future guests encounter an increasingly complex and sometimes hostile society confronted with crises such as crime, drugs, disease, pollution, unemployment, and technological threats, they will attempt to avoid risks and seek greater security. Attacks on tourists have a tremendously negative effect on hospitality providers. They will challenge hospitality companies to create secure and attractive environments that protect guests and their property. Many products and services now in use makes guests feel safer, including key cards, room safes, surveillance cameras, security guards, and insurance. Cruise operators have started offering tours to islands that they develop and control so that they can guarantee safe and enjoyable environments for guests. Security and the perception of security will assume increasing importance among guests of tomorrow.

Privacy and Retreat. As a reaction to increasingly complex, intrusive, and hostile environments, future guests will seek privacy and tranquility. They will build "privacy fences" around their homes and into the design of their work spaces. Psychological privacy fences may include taking more frequent vacations to visit retreats, vacation cottages, farms, and time shares, as well as spending time in psychological counseling, the pursuit of hobbies, and other "escape" measures. In a world where people are constantly barraged by beepers, fax machines, cellular phones, radio and television, junk mail, phone solicitations, clogged highways, and noise pollution, future guests will seek to limit some of the annoying intrusions into their lives. Hospitality providers will have the opportunity to provide privacy amid relaxing and enjoyable environments that let guests unwind. Providers will also need to consider means of maintaining guest privacy, of keeping personal information personal, and of controlling the accumulation and sale of personal guest data. Many protective measures are already in place, including unlisted phone numbers, special access codes and combinations, one-way mirrors, and surveillance cameras. Protective laws will join these options.

Experience Extension. As guests increasingly desire to live life to the fullest, they will want a wide variety of experiences, both actual and vicarious. Hospitality experiences appeal to guest desires to extend their taste of life's offerings through travel and association with different cultures, customs, foods, and beverages. Technology, particularly that which overcomes human limitations, will be particularly valued for its ability to heighten sensory experience. Examples of such technology include interactive television, video phones, and virtual reality. In the future, guests will be able to experience the sensation of golfing on the great golf courses of the world, climbing the highest mountains, or surfing the world's oceans—all from the comfort of their hotel or living rooms.

Life Space Enhancement. Life space enhancement is related to experience extension. Future guests will continue to expand their life spaces by leading much of their lives beyond the boundaries of their immediate locales, residences, and work places. Besides homes and offices, life spaces include commuter trains, automobiles, social clubs, restaurants, gyms, airplanes, malls, recreational facilities, churches, educational institutions, and so on. A major part of life space enhancement for future guests will be furnished by hospitality facilities, which will make conveniently available many services, facilities, and experiences formerly available only to members of special clubs or in the homes of the very wealthy.

Information Society and Overload. Living in an even more highly developed information society, future guests will be swamped with information. Sales and advertising messages will confront them at a quickening pace. Guests will cope by using various screening strategies and devices, deflecting undesired information via computer programs, and even seeking the protection of the law. Contacting future hospitality markets and getting guests to respond favorably to direct promotions will become even more challenging for hospitality marketers.

Leisure and Recreation. Leisure and recreation will be very important to the guests of the future. Leisure time and recreation will assume much of the same cachet and status as money. Many future guests will trade opportunities to make additional money for increasing amounts of leisure time, and will be able to participate in an ever-expanding variety of leisure and recreational activities. They will enjoy shorter and more frequent vacations and breaks from the routines of work and life. Leisure and recreation markets will be enhanced by shorter work weeks, increased life expectancy, longer retirements, and increasing affluence. Hospitality providers will have many opportunities to respond creatively and profitably to the markets such trends portend.

Mobility. In the past, people did not stray too far from their place of birth, often literally spending their lives in one locale. Lifestyles reflected this stability and family support. In contrast, in the United States today, almost one-fifth of the population (mostly young people) changes residences each year. Today, jobs and lives are pursued far from home base and entire neighborhoods are composed of transplanted citizens. Also, people are more mobile and think nothing of driving hundreds of miles, or flying to another country for a weekend.

In the future, guests will be increasingly mobile geographically, professionally, physically, and socially. Future guests will have smaller families and be more portable—the children will travel with them. Guests may pursue several careers over a lifetime and reside in numerous locales. Physical mobility will be aided by health services and technology supports for people with physical disabilities. Education and achievement will open ever wider paths to social and professional advancement. Society will become increasingly sensitive to opportunities for the advancement of those from other nations who will comprise a growing portion of the hospitality sector. Social mobility will become less a matter of who you are and more a matter of what you can accomplish and have done.

Value and Rising Expectations. As future guests increasingly become citizens of the world and welcome the products and services of the world into their homes, they will become even more value-conscious. They will expect to lead more rewarding and fulfilling lives. They will expect tomorrow to be better than today. They will have a wider array of choices from products and services from around the globe to satisfy their wants and needs. Future hospitality providers can respond by embracing value-enhancing approaches when considering altering their offerings. They can ensure that they are furnishing better guest values, rather than merely focusing on controlling costs and raising prices.

Concluding Comments

Hospitality managers too often ignore important trends in the marketplace. Admittedly, detecting them and trying to discern the possible implications for a business is a very challenging task. No one can foresee the future and determine for sure what the emerging hospitality opportunities will be. Nor can they identify with certainty which of the current profitable endeavors will decline. Since demographics drives markets, however, hospitality managers can develop a good feel for some of the important likely emerging dimensions of future markets by carefully assessing people trends.

This chapter is concerned with future market trends and their impact on hospitality. It illustrates how hospitality managers can gain information about three important dimensions of markets, namely, people, money, and the willingness to buy. Such demographic thrusts in the United States as the aging and graying of the population, lower birth rates, population movements to the West and South, the increasing proportion of working women, growing numbers of legal and illegal immigrants, marriage and divorce rates, which have all been well established over the past three decades, are explored. Several other demographic trends that are not quite so clear, but will affect future hospitality offerings and operations, are considered.

The addition of some 22–23 million people to the U.S. economy in each decade since the 1970s helped foster the expansion of hospitality markets. In the future, however, population growth is expected to slow. Thus, over the long run, hospitality businesses will be challenged to adapt their marketing strategies and plans to a slower population-growth focus.

The importance of mature consumers—the 65 and over market—to the hospitality industry will increase. So will the very important 35–54 age segment that comprises a vast, expanding, relatively affluent market. Hospitality marketers will confront a substantial middle-age market with resources and an increasing life expectancy.

Data concerning individual, family, and household income and wealth indicate that affluence is not increasing as rapidly as it did during the "golden age" of the 1960s. Real median family and household income has grown, and so has per capita income. Discretionary income and wealth are concentrated in households at the top of the income ladder. American consumers continue to be spenders, not savers. Generally, data relevant to income augur well for expanding hospitality market opportunities.

Anticipating the willingness of guests to purchase by considering their lifestyles and values deals with non-quantitative but nevertheless important guest information. Indications are that the lifestyles and values of future guests will differ markedly from those of the past. Included are such considerations as the enhancement of physical and psychological self, cosmopolitanism, impermanence, instantaneity, work orientations, product dominance, attitudes to leisure and recreation, mobility, and life space enlargement.

In assessing guests of tomorrow and evaluating future opportunities, hospitality managers must consider the market implications of demographic and related trends. All too often, hospitality managers fail to treat demographic, income, and lifestyle data as the important assets that they are. Currently, such data are among the most underutilized assets in the hospitality marketing arsenal.

Endnotes

1. *New York Times,* 19 May 1996, p. XX4.

2. Florence Fabricant, "The Geography of Taste," *The New York Times Magazine,* 10 March 1996, pp. 40–41.

3. Fabian Linden, Gordon W. Green, Jr., and John F. Coder, *A Marketer's Guide to Discretionary Income* (New York: Bureau of the Census and Consumer Research Center, The Conference Board, 1989).

4. Linden, Green, and Coder.

5. *The New York Times,* 21 March 1993, p. F6.

6. *The Economic Review of Travel in America,* 1995 ed. (Washington, D.C.: U.S. Travel Data Center and Travel Industry Association of America, 1995), pp. 47–50.

7. This section is based on William Lazer, *Handbook of Demographics* (New York: Lexington Books, 1994), chapter 10.

8. Rebecca Durto, "VALS the Second Time," *American Demographics,* July 1991, p. 6.

9. *The New York Times,* 17 April 1994, p. F5.

10. *The Wall Street Journal,* 18 March 1991, p. B1

Key Terms

demography—the study of the size, composition, and distribution of human populations.

discretionary income—the amount of money which would permit a family to maintain a living standard comfortably higher than the average for similar families.

real income—income adjusted for inflation.

⁇ Review Questions ————————————————————

1. What is demography and why is it relevant to managers of hospitality businesses?

2. What are some of the ways that recent birth rates and the ever-lengthening life expectancy may affect hospitality offerings?

3. What impact does immigration have on hospitality offerings?

4. What kinds of information are available concerning the income and wealth of potential hospitality markets in the United States? What do trends in this information suggest with regard to the demand for various hospitality offerings?

5. What is the relationship between per capita income and discretionary income? Why is this relationship relevant to hospitality providers?

6. What trends related to the wealth and affluence of the U.S. population seem to suggest excellent opportunities for providers of hospitality products and services?

7. What types of data are available that detail expenditures by American consumers on hospitality products and services?

8. How are the values and lifestyles of future guests likely to differ from those of past guests? Why will these differences significantly affect hospitality providers? How will hospitality products and services need to change to meet the needs of future guests?

🖳 Internet Sites ————————————————————

For more information, visit the following Internet sites. Remember that Internet addresses can change without notice.

National Center for Health Statistics
http://www.cdc.gov/nchswww/default.htm

Organization for Economic Cooperation and Development
http://www.oecd.org

Travel Industry of America (TIA)
http://www.tia.org

Travelscope
http://www.travelscope.com

United Nations Statistics Division
http://www.un.org/Depts/unsd

U.S. Bureau of Labor Statistics
http://stats.bls.gov

U.S. Census Bureau
http://www.census.gov

VALS—Values and Lifestyles (SRI)
http://future.sri.com/vals/valsindex.html

World Health Organization Statistical Information System
http://www.who.int/whosis

For an extensive list of international statistical sites with links, see:
http://stats.bls.gov/oreother.htm

Chapter 8 Outline

Market Segmentation
Segmentation: A Strategic Commitment
    Choosing Guests: Some Examples of the Strategic Challenge
    Not All Guests Are Equal
Ways of Segmenting Markets
    Geographic and Demographic Factors
    Behavioral Factors
    Psychographic Factors
    Benefit Factors
Criteria for Effective Segmentation
    Segmentation and Marketing Strategy
Concluding Comments

8

Segmenting and Targeting Markets

"Marketing must invent complete products and drive them to commanding positions in defensible market segments."
—William H. Davidow[1]

As THE MARKETING MANAGER of a major hotel in downtown San Francisco, you stand in the lobby late one mid-week afternoon and attempt to pick out typical guests. Are they like the harried executive who has just pushed his way into the lobby and strides purposefully toward the elevators? Perhaps they are more like the smartly dressed couple with their designer luggage. Then again, perhaps they are like the small group of Japanese visitors clustered around a tour leader. As you continue to observe the crowd, you note two teenagers who just arrived and have gone to the front desk to collect their room keys, a gray-haired couple talking with their family near the entrance to the lobby bar, and the aircrew waiting for their bus to the airport. Perhaps all of these people are typical guests. What matters to management is that diverse guests, with obvious differences in needs and interests, have been drawn to the same hotel.

Market Segmentation

Hospitality markets present a diversity of demand patterns. Catering to diverse groups of guests introduces marketing complexity. **Market segmentation** reduces this complexity by providing a clearer picture of the similarity of needs and interests of groups of prospective guests. In contrast to market aggregation, where markets are treated as a whole and without regard to internal diversity, market segmentation is a process whereby managers divide a varied market into distinctive and relatively homogeneous subgroups or segments. Segments may be based on guest wants, needs, motives, attitudes, behaviors, or a host of other factors. Having identified them, management can then select a segment or a specific market niche as a target market and create specific offerings and marketing programs for that segment. By adopting a segmentation approach and focusing on various segments, hospitality managers choose a "rifle" strategy rather than a scattered "shotgun" approach to markets.

Management's guiding principle in segmenting markets is to make the segments as homogeneous as possible (intra segment homogeneity) and the differences between segments as great as possible (inter segment heterogeneity). With

181

effective segmentation, services and facilities can be designed according to the needs of each segment. Resources can be allocated to the most significant segments, and databases can be structured to provide a continually updated picture of segment needs and behavior. As a result, hospitality providers have a better chance of successfully differentiating their offerings and satisfying guests.

Consider, for example, the many hospitality companies that market their properties under a variety of names, each specifically addressing a different market segment. Holiday Inn Worldwide (now Hospitality Inns) developed Holiday Inn Express, Holiday Inn Select, Holiday Inn Sunspree Resort, Holiday Inn Garden Court, and Holiday Inn Hotel and Suites, in addition to the original Holiday Inn.[2] Developing a number of different brands to appeal to diverse market segments helps hospitality marketers capitalize on the diversity of both properties and guests, and provides profitable opportunities for growth.

Market segmentation, which focuses on the needs and interests of various kinds of guests, is a guest-oriented process. Managers consider important differences among segments, the competitive ability of their hotel or restaurant to meet the needs of each segment, and the associated costs and potential profits. In light of such factors, management chooses those market segments it deems most important. Some may target the elderly or the young, business guests or families, individual travelers or groups, luxury or economy segments, and so on.

By tailoring their market offerings to particular segments, hospitality providers can better satisfy guest needs and use marketing resources more efficiently. A small hotel, resort, or restaurant with limited resources, potentially overwhelmed by the total market, may choose to specialize in a small market niche or just one or two market segments, gaining economies from specialization in services offered and from the concentration of advertising, sales, and promotion. Even larger firms (which usually have more choices) that have more of an aggregate marketing strategy are able to benefit from market segmentation.

Market segmentation can be a mixed blessing, for costs and risks may be associated with segmentation decisions. Extending specialized offerings to different groups of guests, rather than dealing with the overall market, can involve additional costs. Segmentation may require more extensive menus with enhanced choices, rooms that are unique in design and furnishings, and duplicated or enhanced facilities. Advertising and selling costs may rise in order to reach different markets. Inventories may also increase as a more diverse set of demands necessitates a wider range of items.

In addition to costs, poorly chosen segments can leave a property vulnerable to changing market conditions. For example, a business built on tourism in the Middle East can be deeply affected by an unexpected surge in terrorist activity. Similarly, hotels and restaurants geared to tourism from specific countries can feel the pinch of declining currency values.

When the benefits of segmentation outweigh costs and risks, segmentation strategies are attractive. Even market segments that do not seem to fit carefully planned segmentation strategies may be dealt with profitably over time. Rather than completely ignoring them, managers can emphasize priority segments first

Consider the effective segmentation strategy developed by Frank Banks, the General Manager of New York's highly successful Rihga Royal Hotel:

"We had to segment the market. If we tried to make the hotel upscale-upscale, there was not enough business at those high rates to fill us up. If we wanted to take it down low, then we could fill it up but we wouldn't generate enough revenue to pay the mortgage. What we had to do was segment the market and come up with different products for those segments. The 50 Pinnacle Suites on the top floors, targeted to the upper market tier, have more amenities such as chauffeur-driven limousines, cellular phones, private phone lines, suite faxes, etc. The mid-tier Imperial Suites, from the middle of the hotel to the 43rd floor, appeal to an upscale business market; while they have fewer amenities than the Pinnacle Suites, they have pagers, faxes, and CD and stereo tape players, among other amenities.... Royal Suites are the standard accommodation marketed to the corporate market on a contract basis at a fixed rate."

(designing their offerings accordingly) and then, over a period of time, shift their focus to segments not being served.

Segmentation: A Strategic Commitment

In planning for the future, the choice of customers is one of the most important decisions hospitality managers can make. A hospitality provider who serves many different kinds of guests requires great flexibility in hospitality offerings and marketing activities and runs the risk of failing to serve any particular guest segment very well. Hospitality managers must therefore carefully consider the types of guests they are best suited to serve and how they can meet those guests' distinctive needs. Providers who serve specific groups of guests may offer more tailored benefits and thereby increase guest satisfaction.

Although this strategy makes a great deal of sense, it is often neglected. Many managers in large hospitality businesses argue that they will serve anyone who comes through the door willing to pay the going rate. While this position is certainly reasonable and hospitality providers may be legally bound to serve all customers, not all guests are equally profitable. Some guests use hotel facilities extensively, while others spend little time at the property except to sleep. Some guests are repeat visitors, while others are visiting the hotel for the first and possibly only time. Guests with modest incomes who make considerable demands on hotel staff and facilities, such as families with active young children, may be unprofitable.

It is important to choose guests wisely and focus marketing activities on particular guest segments. This helps establish sustainable competitive advantage. Although it is difficult to estimate costs and returns of different segments, it is possible to estimate guest yields. Because all guests are not equal, profits will improve if managers adjust the mix of guests toward the high-yield end without sacrificing occupancy levels. Market segmentation, which recognizes diversity while targeting high-yield guest segments, offers a conceptual framework for hospitality success.

Choosing Guests: Some Examples of the Strategic Challenge

To achieve a strong position in a particular market segment, a business must be committed to the interests of the segment. The following examples illustrate the importance of carefully conceived strategic commitments to specific market segments. Each case provides distinctive guest interests and involves critical strategic decisions. The market segments we shall consider are:

- Businesspeople/customers in a convenience zone
- The gay market
- Single older women
- The religious market

In each case, consider the consequences if the segment accounted for five percent, 30 percent, or 70 percent of the turnover. What changes would be needed in order to first gain and then maintain a level of commitment? Consider how, in the long term, the choice of a segment might influence refurbishment, room design, restaurant options, athletic facilities, price structures, strategic alliances, or promotions. Could a major part of the business be built around just one of these segments?

Convenience Zone Marketing. A **convenience zone** is an area surrounding a property where the convenience of the location gives the property a competitive edge, particularly for the business or corporate market. As Scatchard has emphasized in a detailed discussion of this important issue, a convenience zone should be identified early in a hotel's development.[3] Because travel costs and competition determine the convenience zone, a hotel's management must effectively exploit its natural advantage in order to succeed. An initial means of determining this zone is to plot the location of the hotel and its nearest competitors on a detailed map.

As an example, consider the situation faced by one of three hotels offering similar facilities, each located on the fringe of a major industrial park. Management should mark the three hotels on a detailed map and then draw lines identifying the zone for each hotel where that hotel is the closest choice in time or distance for every business in the zone. This involves judgment, and care is needed to take freeways, one-way streets, traffic flows, parking, and other natural or artificial features into account. The result is a convenience zone for the hotel—a market where the hotel has an immediate edge over its competitors and in which, other things being equal, it should have a major share of the business. For another kind of business in the same area with a different competitor group, the convenience zone would probably be quite different. For example, the convenience zone for a bistro or bar would differ from a zone appropriate to overnight accommodation.

Identifying potential competitors is an essential first step in convenience zone marketing. To identify competitors, put yourself in the shoes of a potential customer from the community. The businesses this customer may consider as alternatives will depend on the services offered and customer needs. Also consider how convenient your business is for potential customers. Examine, for example, the availability of parking and public transportation, the structure of one-way streets, and traffic patterns.

Community involvement is an important means of developing the convenience zone market. Lists of the businesses or offices located within the relatively compact convenience zone can serve as the starting point for personal sales calls and promotional offers aimed at guests from within the zone. Managers can demonstrate their commitment to the community by participating in local events, by joining community groups such as the Rotary or Lions clubs, and by working with local schools. Educational institutions in particular can be major sources of long-stay guests, but may also have special requirements regarding transportation, work facilities, and equipment.

In developing this market, it is important to maintain records of guest usage in order to distinguish between promotions that are working and those that are not, and to identify repeat customers and their needs. Such records will guide salespeople in planning call patterns and will help define the boundaries of the convenience zone more effectively.

The Gay Market. America's estimated 15 to 25 million gay men and women constitute a potentially profitable market segment. They are much more likely to buy up-market products and services than the general population.[4] Those in this market are likely to be better educated, have incomes significantly above the national average, are much more likely to travel (39 percent will vacation five times or more in three years), and dine out an average of eleven times each month. Though the market is more affluent than the general population, spending patterns differ among income segments. In the higher income groups, there is a tendency to spend more on luxury or time-saving goods and services.

The gay market may have both seasonal and longer-term trend components. Seasonality occurs when communities have yearly celebrations that attract gays, such as the Sydney Mardi Gras or various New York and San Francisco celebrations. Long-term trends are reflected in the strong demand for hospitality services by this segment of the population.

Homosexuals can be directly accessed by means of mailing lists, the Internet, or advertising in publications directed at a gay audience. Homosexuals are often loyal to advertisers who are not afraid to publicly cater to their needs.

Single Older Women. In a segmentation report, *The Successful Hotel Marketer* identified single older women as a rapidly growing portion of the leisure market.[5] The report noted that this segment includes unmarried middle-aged professional women and senior women who have outlived their male counterparts. Older women who purchase hospitality services and products in the 1990s are often retired members of the work force, as well as aging homemakers. They are financially savvy and well-informed. They are more educated, better traveled, and in better physical and financial condition than they were a decade ago. They also have the time to seek hospitality values and capitalize on them.

Hospitality marketers can appeal to the older female market without losing their existing share of more youthful segments, but they must first dispel some common stereo types. Today's seniors are not sedentary and helpless. Older women share the attitude of the younger leisure customers in seeing themselves as energetic travelers, not tired grannies. "They see themselves as active, not sedentary, and capable, not helpless," says Barry Smith, senior vice president of marketing for Choice Hotels International. "The reality is the 50-plus set takes more trips, spends more nights away from home, and buys more travel products than any other group."[6]

Advertising strategies in this market segment should emphasize discounts, value, and convenience. The older generation aims for value, not brand loyalty. Advertisements should be positioned so that they will be seen by older consumers, but should not necessarily be targeted exclusively toward them. General news and business magazines that do not address a specific senior market are good sites for advertising.

In the senior female market, lower interest rates could reduce the demand for travel and hospitality products because retirees are among those most affected by dwindling investment interest yields. Decreasing discretionary income can also change single older women's travel patterns. This segment may respond to such unfavorable changes with shorter and less frequent trips, off-season travel, increased use of economy properties, and by seeking specials and discounts.

The Religious Market. The religious conference market offers tremendous opportunities for the hospitality industry. Statistics from the Religious Conference Management Association (RCMA) suggest that religious conferences can attract from 2,000 to more than 50,000 attendees.[7] The average conference attendee spends over $100 per day on food, lodging, sightseeing, and gifts. In addition, religious conferences are long, typically lasting up to 14 days. They are often booked during soft periods, including holiday weekends. Since the conferences are family oriented, mom or dad might bring the kids, adding to expenditures on gifts, meals, and entertainment.

DeWayne Woodring of the RCMA cites the following "Ten Commandments" for attracting the religious market:[8]

1. Don't underestimate the religious market.

2. Religion is recession-proof. Religious meetings have their best attendance during the bleakest times.

3. Don't assume religious meeting attendees are cheap.

4. Be prepared for long stays.

5. Conference attendees aren't rowdy and keep their rooms tidy, so don't worry about typical conference problems.

6. Be competitive. Attendees seek value.

7. Work closely with religious meeting planners. They will look to you for help and guidance.

8. Meet their needs and give them value.

Exhibit 1   Sydney Hotel Example: Ability to Cater to Guest Needs by Market Segment

Segment	(Not At All)		(Moderately)			(Very Well)	
1. Seniors	1	2	3	4	5	6	7
2. Families	1	2	3	4	5	6	7
3. Japanese Tour Groups	1	2	3	4	5	6	7
4. Yuppies	1	2	3	4	5	6	7
5. Backpackers	1	2	3	4	5	6	7
6. Japanese FIT	1	2	3	4	5	6	7
7. Achievers	1	2	3	4	5	6	7
8. Executives	1	2	3	4	5	6	7
9. Frequent Visitors	1	2	3	4	5	6	7
10. European Tourists	1	2	3	4	5	6	7
11. Middle-Aged Conservatives	1	2	3	4	5	6	7
12. Wealthy	1	2	3	4	5	6	7
13. Status Seekers	1	2	3	4	5	6	7
14. Management Seminar	1	2	3	4	5	6	7
15. Disabled	1	2	3	4	5	6	7
16. Health Conscious	1	2	3	4	5	6	7
17. Single Women	1	2	3	4	5	6	7
18. Tour Wholesalers	1	2	3	4	5	6	7

9. Shower attendees with service. Make them feel welcome. Your attitude is crucial.

10. Remember that religious groups are loyal. They are more likely to return when satisfied.

Not All Guests Are Equal

So far, our discussion of segmentation strategy has focused on guests, their needs, and the importance of responding to particular segments in a way that leads to a distinctive competitive advantage that maximizes profits. In practice, management often begins to think about segmentation by looking carefully at the current guest mix and then explores opportunities for more carefully focused marketing efforts within the present context.

An easy way to identify important market segments for a particular property is to simply draw up a list of currently or potentially represented segments. Exhibit 1 presents an example of such a list for a hotel in Sydney. The hotel's managers were asked to rate the hotel's ability to cater to particular market segments on a scale of one (not at all) to seven (very well). A rating of four indicates that the hotel could meet guest needs moderately well.

In addition to creating such lists and rating systems, managers can ask important questions about each market segment. The following sample questions illustrate a number of the possibilities.

1. What proportion of room nights does this segment presently account for compared with competing hotels?

    - Higher than most competing hotels

    - About the same as competitors

    - A smaller proportion than competing hotels

2. How well does the hotel now cater to the needs of each group?

    - Not at all.

    - Moderately well.

    - Very well. This segment is a specialty.

3. How does each segment rate in terms of profit contribution relative to average guests? (Consider the amounts spent by guests and the costs incurred to serve their needs. Are their needs costly or difficult to satisfy? Do they spend relatively little at the hotel?)

    - More profitable than average guests

    - About the same

    - Less profitable than average guests

4. What is the relative importance of this group over the last year?

    - Growing in importance

    - About the same

    - Declining in importance

In our Sydney hotel case, we asked question two of 133 staff ranging from senior managers to supervisors. The results of our inquiry are shown in Exhibit 2. The staff clearly believes that the property caters best to Japanese tour groups and independent travelers (a specialty area), as well as executives and frequent visitors. This is not a property that attracts yuppies, status seekers, the health-conscious, or the disabled.

Some interesting patterns emerge when we examine the perceptions of different management levels. Not surprisingly, those who worked more closely with guests saw the property's potential a little differently. While the segments are ranked similarly among each of the management groups, supervisors are less convinced of the hotel's ability to cater to some important groups. For example, supervisors saw tour wholesalers as more of a problem segment. These management perceptions should be compared to available guest data, including computerized information and opinion polls. The point is that such an approach encourages management to think about segmentation strategy in terms of guest needs and hotel capabilities.

Exhibit 2   Sydney Hotel Example: Percent of Positive Responses to Question 2

Segment	All Managers (%)	Senior Managers (%)	Supervisors (%)
1. Seniors	21	20	22
2. Families	19	11	22
3. Japanese Tour Groups	71	86	65
4. Yuppies	18	11	20
5. Backpackers	6	8	5
6. Japanese FIT	53	71	44
7. Achievers	24	23	24
8. Executives	55	60	52
9. Frequent Visitors	66	68	65
10. European Tourists	45	57	39
11. Middle-Aged Conservatives	38	46	35
12. Wealthy	38	40	38
13. Status Seekers	16	17	16
14. Management Seminars	32	37	29
15. Disabled	21	17	22
16. Health Conscious	14	11	16
17. Single Women	19	26	16
18. Tour Wholesalers	54	73	46

Ways of Segmenting Markets

The hospitality market is generally divided into broad categories such as lodging, food and beverage, products, or services. Sometimes we narrow the field further with references to more specific markets, such as hotels, resorts, particular locations, or guest nationality. While such categories are good starting points, they are too broad to be truly useful in developing market segmentation strategies. We usually want to move beyond roughly defined categories and identify more precisely the specific market(s) that interest us. The more precise our specifications, the more accurately we can tailor hospitality offerings, strategies, and programs for specific market segments and niches.

How then do we identify the factors that will form a base for segmentation? The most effective process is both creative and pragmatic. First, we must creatively explore segmentation options—preferably those that cannot be easily duplicated by competitors. Segmentation helps define markets so that a particular hospitality business gains differential competitive advantage, but if every hotel defines its markets in the same way, then the competition is likely to be "head-on." Success is far more likely if one hotel identifies a distinctive market segment and serves its needs with flair and insight. Measurement techniques and calculated choices add a pragmatic note to this creative process. Market segments must be large enough to be worth pursuing and accessible enough to be reached with available resources. In the end, market segments must result in measurable profits.

Systematic methods guide creativity and further help to identify possible segmentation variables. A market can be examined from the following three perspectives:[9]

1. Customer groups

2. Customer functions, needs, or benefits

3. Products or services

In a hospitality setting, the first perspective concerns guests, especially *who* they are. The second perspective focuses on *why* and *how* they might buy. The third dimension examines the product or service—the *what, when,* and *where* of hospitality purchases. Exhibit 3 presents some segmentation possibilities. In this exhibit, we distinguish between individual and corporate guests and suggest segmentation variables for each type of guest according to the above three perspectives.

Market segments constructed at this level of detail reveal myriad possibilities to the observant manager. Following this model, we might consider a market segment of retirees (customer group) who seek familiar comforts at a reasonable price (customer needs) in a suburban motel with an in-house restaurant (product form). Another segment might consist of Japanese tour groups (customer group) who wish to stay in a five-star hotel with harbor views (product form) where Japanese is spoken and Japanese food is available (customer needs).

As these examples indicate, buying behavior is rarely linked to a single variable. Thus, effective segmentation usually involves several factors simultaneously—linking who, what, when, where, why, and how. And a market segment might be described according to several factors. Instead of a market segment of married couples, we might further define this segment according to age, occupation, income, children, lifestyle, and ZIP code. Different factors are nonetheless often closely related. Typically, such related variables include education and income, age and family income, household income and the number of workers, and stage in the family life cycle and assets. Lifestyles are closely related to such factors as education, occupation, and social class.

Above all, remember that the overriding goal of segmentation is to identify target markets that are large and profitable enough to cultivate and that permit an enterprise to establish a defensible competitive edge. The strategic significance of segmentation decisions demands that managers take time to think through the process, seek relevant data from multiple sources, carefully screen segmentation options, and identify potentially successful markets. Although it can be tempting and convenient to work with market segments that are already well-defined and targeted by competitors, we should never neglect the search for segments nor settle for superficial segmentation strategies. Doing so can lead us to miss profitable market opportunities and keep us from developing differential advantages and important competitive edges.

Exhibit 3   Some Segmentation Options

Segmentation Base	Consumer Markets	Industrial and Corporate Markets
Who?	Geography	Industry, SIC Code
	Country	Growth
	Location	Profitability
	Language	Turbulence
	Urban/Rural	Competitiveness
	Climate	Size
	Demography	Location
	Age	Ownership
	Sex	Local
	Education	Multinational
	Family Life Cycle	Sector
	Occupation	Private
	Religion	Public
	Ethnicity	Markets Served
	Income	Corporate Culture
	Social Class	Conservative
	Behavior	Spending
	Usage	Market Oriented
	Travel Patterns	Sales Oriented
	Media Consumption	Past Oriented
	Interests	Future Oriented
	Sports	Usage Patterns
	Hobbies	Network Linkages
		Corporate Life Cycle
Why, How?	Psychographics	Decision Type
	Personality	Rebuy
	Lifestyle	Partial Rebuy
	Benefits Sought	New Buy
	Appearance	Stages Involved
	Reliability	Roles Played
	Responsiveness	Benefits Sought
	Assurance	Facilities
	Empathy	Location
	Decision Process	Type of Use
	Stages	Price Sensitivity
	Information needs	Use of Consultants
	Influentials	Capacity Utilization
	Price Sensitivity	Contractual Period
	Image Perceptions	

(continued)

Exhibit 3   *(continued)*

Segmentation Base	Consumer Markets	Industrial and Corporate Markets
What, When, Where	Type of Facility	Type of Facility
	Hotel	Rooms
	Resort	Communication
	Size	Links
	Room Type	Timing
	Timing	Urgency
	Duration of Stay	Access
	Reservation	Location
	No Reservation	Support Facilities
	Access	Transportation
	Airport	Entertainment
	Connections	Sports
	Networks	Adventure
	Location	Flexibility
	Urban	
	Rural	

There are four specific sets of segmentation factors that are of particular importance in hospitality marketing:

- Geographic and demographic factors
- Behavioral factors
- Psychographic factors
- Benefit factors

Let's explore each of these in more detail.

Geographic and Demographic Factors

Geographic and demographic factors are among the basic variables used in segmenting household, individual, and corporate markets. Hospitality companies regularly segment their markets according to location and serve guests from the immediate vicinity, city, or state (an example of convenience zone marketing). Local businesses are important sources of guests and sometimes hospitality providers will specialize in addressing the needs of a particular industry. For example, a property located in the middle of a financial district will be drawn to the financial or insurance sector. It will work hard to build links with key decision makers and provide the specialized services that are sought by managers in such firms. Still other providers may specialize in meeting the needs of tourists and business groups from different regions. Some locations in Florida, for example, cater to French Canadians, others to guests from Germany. Japanese business groups are the targets of many hospitality enterprises in Malaysia, Thailand, and Hawaii, especially those that have relatively inexpensive and easily accessible golf courses.

Demographic variables such as age, sex, income, education, profession, and stage in the family life cycle are among the most widely used bases for segmentation. Consumer needs are often directly related to such observable and measurable variables. This information can be stored for future analysis and helps with such hospitality marketing activities as assessing the size of potential markets, selecting target market segments, and monitoring progress in market penetration. Kontiki Tours, for example, is a South Pacific tourist organization that caters to those age 35 and under. Numerous tours cater to such segments as senior citizens, singles, affinity groups, and religious organizations.

Behavioral Factors

Behavioral factors emerge from patterns of hospitality service usage. Loyal guests can be distinguished from transients, frequent from non-frequent users, those who use health clubs from those who do not, and so on. Behavioral segmentation offers the distinct advantage of allowing data to be accessed from the property's guest database. In this way, direct observation of behavior can be incorporated with discrete questioning of guests.

Frequent users of a hospitality service are not always the preferred segment. While they may be unwilling to change hospitality providers, they may not be a particularly profitable segment. In contrast, light users who have little knowledge of a particular hospitality service or who feel awkward in unfamiliar situations sometimes constitute much more attractive and profitable segments.

In a corporate setting, behavioral segmentation helps to distinguish different categories of corporate business, including business travel, meetings, and conventions. Hospitality providers may wish to focus on firms or managers who have recently switched contract business from one hotel to another. These customers may still be dissatisfied with the current facilities, service, or price and may well be tempted by a new property or a fresh deal.

Behavioral segmentation may appear to be straightforward and quite simple in the corporate market, but that is not so. Corporate managers responsible for choosing hospitality services may have their own set of behavioral concerns and may operate within highly variable corporate cultures. These corporate cultures may range from the very permissive to the highly conservative. Effective behavioral segmentation in the corporate market means understanding both individual and corporate behavior in choosing corporate clients and the marketing methods for dealing with them.

Psychographic Factors

The psychographic approach to segmentation groups people with similar lifestyles, interests, attitudes, opinions, or preferences. A hotel or restaurant may try to reach health-conscious, socially and environmentally responsible guests or those seeking outdoor adventure and challenge.

Several research studies have identified various consumer lifestyle categories that are relevant to the hospitality industry. While there are many ways of

Exhibit 4   VALS Topology and Lifestyles

Topology	Lifestyle Orientations
Actualizers	Upscale, independent, intellectual
Strugglers	Nostalgic, downscale, mostly elderly women
Fulfilleds	Principle-oriented
Believers	Principle-oriented
Achievers	Status-oriented
Strivers	Status-oriented
Experiencers	Action-oriented
Makers	Action-oriented

Source: Rebecca Durto, "VALS the Second Time," *American Demographics,* July 1991, p. 6.

achieving a pyschographic segmentation, two or three will serve to illustrate the kinds of consumer groupings that emerge. One segments consumers into such categories as the following:[10]

- *Cocooning*: The tendency to surround oneself with security and luxury and to withdraw from contact with the external world.

- *Fantasy*: The tendency to escape from reality (Disneyland, for example, appeals to this category).

- *Egonomics*: The desire to have one's ego satisfied through high-status hospitality products and services.

- *Small Indulgence*: The desire to please oneself as a reward without being too expensive—flowers or an expensive or handmade chocolate on the pillow are examples of a hotel response to this need.

- *Down Aging*: The desire to be seen as younger than you really are. This links to the way hotels treat their guests and especially to the attitudes of staff in daily contact with guests.

A widely referenced lifestyle research study is known as VALS (*values and life styles*). The initial study segmented American consumers into three groups: survivors and sustainers (12 percent of the population), outer-directeds (71 percent), and inner-directeds (17 percent). A follow-up study identified eight segments and their lifestyle orientations (see Exhibit 4). An Australian study using the VALS methodology identified ten lifestyle groups, three of which are described briefly in Exhibit 5.

The findings of such research can give managers important clues about how to market to their respective guest segments more effectively. Each segment will approach the purchase of hospitality services rather differently. To reach them on their own terms, it is important first to understand their viewpoints, to consider if your message will be understood and accepted, and to design service concepts that are likely to be valued.

Exhibit 5   Descriptions of Three Sample Lifestyle Groups

Visible Achievers: Highly career- and success-oriented. They enjoy higher incomes than others and retain traditional values about home, work, and society. Many have achieved success without a college education. They seek recognition, financial rewards, stimulating employment, and visible signs of the good life—travel, sport, club memberships, and assets. Eleven percent of the population.

Socially Aware: People in the socially aware segment see themselves as socially responsible, community-minded, socially active, progressive, and essentially middle-class. They enjoy persuading others to agree with their opinions, and are likely to be involved in green movements. They are least likely to oppose a woman's right to work outside the home. They support freedom of choice and believe religion should not be taught in state schools. Seven percent of the population.

Traditional Family Life: Although their families have often left the nest, this group retains a strong commitment to traditional family roles and values. Many are grandparents and value the links of an extended family. Most are retired. Many are religious and feel that God has an important place in their lives. Nineteen percent of the population.

Source: Gary C. Morgan, "Understanding Investor Behaviour," Personal Investment Money Show, March 1989, Sydney. Quoted in W. J. Stanton, K. E. Miller, and R. A. Layton, *Fundamentals of Marketing*, Third Edition (Sydney: McGraw-Hill, 1994), p. 102.

Benefit Factors

Market segmentation on the basis of guest benefits is consistent with the logic of adopting a guest orientation to hospitality. Guests do not really purchase products and services—rather, they purchase the perceived benefits from using those products and services. From the point of view of hospitality providers, it is the marketing of benefits that is important. Three ways of thinking about perceived benefits for the purposes of segmentation have been identified:[11] (1) push versus pull, (2) high value versus low price, and (3) critical success factors.

Push versus pull focuses on the way that hospitality providers reach guests and deliver benefits. Under the push strategy, guests are reached through various intermediaries such as travel agents or tour operators who push specific hospitality offerings to guests. Intermediaries are, of course, offered incentives to do so. By contrast, in the pull strategy, hospitality providers contact guests directly via promotional efforts such as advertising or direct mail and get guests to contact sources such as tour operators or travels agents to purchase the offerings. In this manner, guests pull hospitality products through the channel. In terms of benefits offered to guests, the adoption of a pull strategy tends to be closer to the self-service end of the market.

Benefit segmentation on the basis of high value versus low price distinguishes those guests who seek luxury and excellent service from those who concentrate on getting low prices. Critical success factors emphasize the product or service attributes that are critical for particular guests. For example, communication network access through computers, faxes, and mobile telephones may be important to some corporate guests, while others may desire peace and quiet or predictable accommodation from a known hotel chain.

The first step in benefit segmentation is to identify the range of hospitality benefits that actual and potential guests may seek. Although brainstorming by management may produce a list of benefits, normally managers must look beyond their preconceived ideas and ask the guests themselves. Learning what guests want and assessing the size of market segments may entail sophisticated market research techniques, such as focus groups, supported by multivariate statistical procedures.

While benefit segmentation may be demanding in practice, the idea is straight forward. Suppose we are considering benefit segments for an ocean cruise ship. The benefits may include recreation, the opportunity to meet new people and make friends, education, visits to exotic destinations, sumptuous dining, and relaxation. One or more of these benefits may be important to prospective groups of passengers. Their decision to take the cruise will hinge upon their perception of how well the cruise will meet their needs. In turn, their perceptions will depend upon the product and services themselves, costs, and the messages that are sent and received. To develop effective marketing programs, managers would like to know how passengers rate each benefit and the tradeoffs they are willing to make.

Criteria for Effective Segmentation

As we noted earlier, segmentation is both an art and a science. Creativity plays an important role in identifying possible segmentation variables and in designing strategies to capitalize on emerging opportunities. Practical, scientific approaches are used to gather segmentation information from company records or market research, to assess segmentation options, to select those segments that offer the best prospects, and to develop hospitality marketing strategies for cultivating chosen segments. Central to this process is the question of whether a particular segmentation structure will deliver a strategic advantage to the hospitality provider.

The following seven criteria aid in the choice of market segmentation options and help identify strategically feasible segments:

1. *Sales and Profit Potential.* Assess whether the segment is big enough to justify specific attention. The ultimate test is not just the segment's size, but its profitability. Estimate dollar sales and profitability in order to rank segment alternatives by long-term profit potential. Consider the number of potential customers or guests, growth prospects, the costs of meeting service expectations, and the actual and potential profit. Profitability is affected by density. Although a segment may be large, the density of the guests who interest us may be insufficient, resulting in a segment that is very costly to reach. Concentrated, high-density markets can result in relatively low marketing costs. Also, consider the likelihood of the segment remaining viable. Some segments, particularly lifestyle segments, can disappear or be altered radically as a result of rapidly changing social structures and lifestyles.

2. *Similarities and Differences Among Segments.* Ideally, the guests grouped together within a segment should exhibit similar behavior and needs. Just as knowledge of similarities will help construct market offerings to meet certain

needs, knowledge of differences among segments will justify unique treatment of each segment.

3. *Accessibility.* This criterion focuses on identifying and reaching segments and the associated costs. Segmentation is not feasible when members of a particular segment cannot be identified or when the segment is too difficult or too costly to reach. As media options become increasingly customized and specialized, such as those available on the Internet, media access may become less of an issue. Consequently, a wider range of new segmentation options may become viable.

4. *Responsiveness.* The more responsive a segment is, the more desirable the segment. But managers must also consider the interplay among segments because the benefits available to one segment may discourage another. For example, a resort with a strong offering to the family market may inadvertently turn business guests away.

5. *Capabilities.* Is the business able to serve the identified segments effectively? If certain services or locations are critical factors, can the property meet these requirements?

6. *Identifiable Competitive Advantage.* Does the business have a competitive advantage in the segment? Managers must carefully examine all of the major competitors serving their segment—both actual and potential. If a company does not have a real competitive advantage, then the attractiveness of the segment should be questioned. Potential guests will wonder why they should choose one competitor over another.

7. *Defensibility.* Is the business able to keep competitors from successfully entering the market? This can depend on having a service or product that can be copyrighted or patented or that may be too difficult or costly to imitate, or can stem from a variety of advantages such as a particular location, established contacts with a marketing network of agents and other referrers, reservation systems, or the quality of the staff. Such factors can build barriers to competitive entry and justify a segmentation strategy.

Segmentation and Marketing Strategy

Hospitality marketers use three closely related strategic ideas—segmentation, differentiation, and positioning. Nearly every facet of hospitality marketing is inspired and directed by their interaction. Markets are often initially treated as aggregates with competing firms offering similar products and services to prospective customers. But it is not long before each competitor tries to differentiate its offerings from those of other firms. If successful, the process of differentiation reveals distinct market segments. Larger market segments attract additional competitors, leading to even more differentiation. For example, Marriott has segmented the market for its eight hotel brands by price and the orientation of guests in target markets as is indicated in Exhibit 6. Its portfolio of hotels covers market segments from economy travelers to discerning and demanding guests at the upper levels.

Exhibit 6   Segmentation of Market by Marriott

Marriott Brand	Price Segment	Target Market—Guest Appeal
Ritz-Carlton	$175–$300	Luxury, personalized service, unique experiences, top level executive, successful entrepreneurs, upper classes.
Renaissance Hotels and Resorts	$90–$235	Discerning business and leisure travelers who seek value and pay attention to their surroundings and services.
Marriott Hotels Resorts and Suites	$90–$235	Guests who seek consistent quality associated with Marriott hospitality.
Residence Inn	$85–$110	Guests seeking a residence type hotel—longer stays.
Courtyard	$75–$105	Affordable accommodation for the "Road Warrier."
Springhill Suites	$75–$95	Business and leisure guests seeking more space at affordable prices along with amenities.
Towerplace Suites	$55–$70	Suites at moderate rates for stays of 3 to 4 weeks.
Fairfield Inn	$45–$65	Economy for "upper tier economy travelers" both business and leisure.

Based on "Marriott Outfits an Old Chain for New Market," *The Wall Street Journal,* 13 Oct. 1998, B 14.

Positioning within each major segment is one of the keys to successful hospitality marketing. Positioning refers to the careful choice of differentiation factors within a segment. The factors that matter in this process are those that produce a strong perception of competitive advantage in the mind of guests in the segment(s) of interest. Positioning involves both intangibles, such as quality service, and tangibles, such as design features. Whatever the basis for positioning, it aims to shape current and future guest perceptions of the business and its offerings, leading ultimately to favorable purchase decisions.

Perhaps the most important point to note is that positioning is something that happens in the mind of the guest or prospective guest. It results from their perceptions of the actions taken by the hotel or business, how it performs relative to other competing businesses, from their understanding of the vision (or lack of it) that inspires management. While positioning is something that management can initiate and results from the segmentation and differentiation choices made by management, it is real only if guests accept the proposition that management has in mind.

Effective positioning will meet four criteria:[12]

- *Salience:* The positioning will involve attributes that really matter to the guest. For example, positioning a hotel on the basis of height is unlikely to be successful.

- *Strength:* The positioning must turn on an attribute that is perceived to be a real strength of the restaurant or hotel. If service quality is the basis, guests must perceive this service quality.

- *Competitive advantage:* There is no point to positioning on attributes that are common to other competing properties.

- *Communication:* It must be possible to communicate the positioning in a way that is simple, clear, and understandable to the guests that are to be reached. Otherwise, it will be difficult to motivate guests.

The importance of positioning can be seen from the experience of hospitality firms that have achieved outstanding success—for example, the magic of Disney, Q,S,C and V for McDonald's, and the specific appeal of each of the Marriott brand concepts. Positioning is central to the success of a market-driven hospitality enterprise. It rests on a careful definition of the benefits to be offered to each of the target market segments, an understanding of the segments and their specific needs, an awareness of competition in each segment and a precise identification of the ways in which your business is different, and finally, a clear statement of the perceptions you would like guests to carry in their mind.

Concluding Comments

Catering to diverse groups of guests introduces complexity in making marketing decisions. Segmentation, which is the process of dividing a varied market into distinctive and relatively homogeneous segments, helps reduces this complexity. It permits management to target specific market segments and create specific offerings and programs to serve them.

Market segmentation is a guest-oriented process. The guiding principle of segmentation is to develop intra segment homogeneity and inter segment heterogeneity. By so doing, management can concentrate on the needs of the most profitable market segments and develop offerings that not only satisfy those segments, but also help differentiate a company from its competitors. However, segmentation can also increase costs and risks by adding to the number of guest offerings, in contrast with a "one size fits all" approach. Market segments must be large enough to be profitable and also be accessible to a company given its resources and capabilities.

The choice of target markets is one of the most critical marketing decisions. Hospitality managers must consider carefully the types of guest that the business can best serve. Not all guests are equally profitable, and some may actually be too costly to serve. Focusing on profitable market segments is important. Estimating the costs and returns of various market segments is difficult, but getting hospitality managers to think in these terms is beneficial and, despite difficulties, estimates can be derived.

Myriad bases exist for effective segmentation. Included are such distinguishing guest characteristics as age, sex, income, geographic location, lifestyle, religion, sexual orientation, and behavioral, attitudinal, and expectation factors. The more precise the segmentation, the more accurately offerings can be tailored and the greater the likelihood of success. Four specific sets of segmentation factors are particularly relevant in hospitality marketing: geographic and demographic factors, behavioral factors, psychographic factors, and benefit factors.

Managers often begin to think about segmentation by looking at their current mix of guests and then considering the kinds of market opportunities that exist. Then they may explore the business's ability to compete in the different segments. They may consider market segments from three perspectives: customer groups, customer functions, and the products or services. The first deals with who the customers are. The second with why and how they might buy. The third examines the actual offerings—the what, when, and where.

Effective segmentation involves more than just manipulating data—it involves management judgment and creativity. Management faces the decision of whether the segments selected will yield strategic advantage. Criteria for developing effective market segments include such considerations as: sales and profit potential, segment similarities and differences, segment accessibility, responsiveness, capabilities, competitive advantage, and defensibility. Segmentation is closely related to both differentiation and positioning, and together these three activities affect nearly every aspect of hospitality marketing. Criteria for positioning include salience, strengths, competitive advantage, and communication.

Endnotes

1. William H. Davidow, *Marketing High Technology: An Insider's View* (New York: Free Press, 1986), p. 13.

2. *The Wall Street Journal*, 17 April 1996, pp. B1, 2.

3. Bill Scatchard, *Upsetting the Applecart: A Common Sense Approach to Successful Hotel Operations for the 90's* (Tampa, Fla.: First Effort Books, 1992), pp. 36ff.

4. Unless otherwise indicated, all statistics in this section are taken from "Emerging Market Report," *The Successful Hotel Marketer*, February 1993.

5. *The Successful Hotel Marketer*, March 1993, pp. 1, 3.

6. *The Successful Hotel Marketer*, March 1993, p. 1.

7. Cited in *The Successful Hotel Marketer*, August 1993, p. 7.

8. Quoted from *The Successful Hotel Marketer*, August 1993.

9. Derek F. Abell, *Defining the Business: the Strategy Point of Strategic Planning* (Englewood Cliffs, N.J.: Prentice-Hall, 1980).

10. Faith Popcorn, *The Popcorn Report* (New York: Doubleday, 1991), pp. 27–85.

11. Derek F. Abell, *Managing With Dual Strategies: Mastering the Present, Preempting the Future* (New York: Free Press, 1993) pp. 58–59.

12. David Arnold, *The Handbook of Brand Management* (Reading, Mass.: Addison-Wesley, 1992), p. 93.

Key Terms

convenience zone—an area surrounding a property where the convenience of location gives the property a competitive edge.

market segmentation—a process whereby managers divide a varied market into distinctive and relatively homogeneous subgroups or segments.

positioning—the careful choice of differentiation factors so as to produce a strong perception of competitive advantage in the mind of guests in the segment(s) of interest.

Review Questions

1. What are some other examples of hospitality companies that, like Hospitality Inns, have developed specific property concepts addressing different market segments?

2. What benefits can segmentation bring to the operation of a hospitality business? What costs are involved? Can you find examples of benefits and costs?

3 Why is the choice of segments best thought of as a strategic commitment?

4. Consider the four examples of strategic segmentation. Could a major part of a hospitality business be built around just one of these four segments?

5. What steps would you take to identify key segments for a resort that sought your advice on the matter?

6. Choose a hospitality business that you are familiar with and identify possible segmentation variables under each of the three perspectives—customer groups; customer functions, needs, and benefits; and product/service.

7. What is meant by the phrase "segmentation is both an art and a science"?

Internet Sites

For more information, visit the following Internet sites. Remember that Internet addresses can change without notice.

Hotel Marketing Newsletter
http://www.hotelmarketing.com

Marriott International
http://www.marriott.com

McDonald's Corporation
http://www.mcdonalds.com

Meetings.net
http://www.meetingsnet.com

Religious Conference Management
Association (RCMA)
http://www.meetingsnet.com/
rcm.com

Rihga Royal Hotel New York
http://ny.rihga.com

VALS—Values and Lifestyles (SRI)
http://future.sri.com/vals/
valsindex.html

Walt Disney Corporation
http://www.disney.com

Part III

Managing the Hospitality Marketing Mix

Chapter 9 Outline

The Need for Marketing Information
    Some Applications
    Experience as Information
Obtaining Marketing Information Through Research
    Customers and Competitors
    Marketing Intelligence
The Hospitality Marketing Research Process
    Problem Definition
    Formulation of Hypotheses
    Research Design and Analysis
Using Marketing Research Approaches
    Questionnaires, Surveys, and Interviews
    Sampling
    Focus Groups
    Validity and Reliability
Marketing Information and Problem-Solving
    Problems of Fact
    Problems of Value
    Marketing Information Sources
    Marketing Information Categories
Developing Hospitality Marketing Information Systems
    Desirable Characteristics
Sales Forecasting
Concluding Comments

9

Marketing Data and Information Systems

"The essence of knowledge is, having it, to apply it."

—Confucius

THE EXECUTIVES of a well-known international restaurant chain were assembled for a weekend retreat designed to reengineer the company. One of them, who had been with the company about a year after spending several years with a major manufacturer of food products, emphasized that the chain lacked basic marketing data. She went on to suggest that concerted efforts be made to gather and use marketing information to much better advantage. She emphasized the value of guest surveys to determine attitudes and opinions, experiments to determine appropriate menu items, and guest focus groups to obtain suggestions for improvement. She also stressed the importance of developing a guest database and using cost and revenue data in appropriate formats to guide marketing decisions. In each instance, she indicated what some competitors were doing and pointed out the benefits they were realizing. She concluded with a strong statement about functioning in an information society and the need for management to recognize marketing information as the valuable asset that it is. The result was a transformation in both the effectiveness of company decisions and the insight with which the decisions were made.

Marketing information is a key to corporate survival because it affects profitable decisions. It helps hospitality businesses keep in close touch with guests and better meet their needs and expectations. The more that businesses know about their guests, the better products and services they can provide, thereby increasing the likelihood of creating loyal guests and increasing revenues and profits. Informative guest profiles can help service personnel in their continuing quest to serve guests better. And technology has increased information-gathering capabilities as well as potential uses.

Information technology has a great effect on hospitality marketing methods, approaches, and operations. Its impact is felt in such activities as reservations, check-in and check-out, guest databases, food and beverage options, guest communications, telephone and message systems, menu engineering, cost analysis, security, promotions, merchandising, and sales. It is pervasive, influencing virtually every hospitality marketing activity. Despite the impact of technology, marketing's effectiveness comes not just from computers and databases, but from

205

using marketing information strategically—making skillful, insightful use of marketing intelligence.

Marketing research is defined as the "function that links consumer, customer, and publics to the marketer through information—information used to identify and define marketing opportunities and problems, generate, refine, and evaluate marketing actions, monitor marketing performance, …[and] improve understanding of marketing as a process."[1] Information-gathering approaches take many different forms and employ an endless variety of techniques, instruments, and measurement methods.

This chapter examines the need for marketing information and describes the collection, analysis, and various uses of marketing information. It takes a close look at marketing research approaches and techniques, the nature of hospitality marketing problems, problem-solving measures, characteristics of hospitality marketing information systems, and the role of sales forecasting.

The Need for Marketing Information

In this information age, marketers are involved with the information superhighway, cyberspace, computer networks, webs, telecommunications, desktop publishing, on-line databases, e-mail, faxes, and virtual reality. The information revolution is affecting the timeliness and pertinence of marketing data inherent in every hospitality business. Yet, marketing information is rarely accepted for what it is—among the most valuable of all hospitality assets. It offers insights for extending markets, creating new hospitality opportunities, developing new hospitality offerings, and differentiating companies from their rivals.

Every hospitality provider needs an information system to gather, evaluate, and disseminate pertinent and timely marketing information, whether formal or informal. An information system is "a collection of interrelated and interdependent subsystems dependent on a data base that supports the managerial decision-making process, helps monitor and control operations, and is responsive to the dynamic needs of the firm."[2] Systems vary in their complexity from those dealing mainly with internal accounting data to those using sophisticated marketing research techniques and quantitative models. Large hotel and restaurant chains have formal systems that often rely on sophisticated research approaches and techniques. Smaller hospitality enterprises often rely more on informal approaches reflecting personal assessments, judgments, feelings, estimates, and opinions. Most hospitality marketing information systems are an amalgamation of both the formal and informal, although the industry trend is moving in the direction of formal systems.

Some Applications

Hotels and motels interested in gathering guest information often ask guests to rate the quality of their services from check-in to check-out on a scale ranging from excellent to poor. Sometimes, they place postcard questionnaires in each room asking about guest experiences. In some chains, the completed postcards are mailed to headquarters where the information is noted. Guests receive a letter of thanks and, if there is a complaint, an explanation from a top executive of what's being done to handle the situation. The cards are then sent back to the respective properties for their action.

Likewise, many restaurants have questionnaires on their tables seeking guest comments on the quality of the food, prices, service, and physical surroundings, along with space for suggestions for improvement. Others have their servers distribute similar questionnaires to guests on a regular basis. Guests who complete the questionnaires are sometimes eligible for a prize—dinner for two, cocktails, or a bottle of wine, for example.

The owner of two Atlanta restaurants gathers information about competitors and generates new ideas by giving his managers a food allowance so that they will dine out and bring back reactions and ideas.[3] Singapore Airlines regularly asks its passengers to complete detailed questionnaires regarding the quality of various passenger services such as baggage handling, check-in, in-flight services (including food and beverage service), and entertainment offerings. The information obtained furnishes clues about ways of increasing guest satisfaction.

Hotels are actively developing guest databases. Rihga Royal Hotel, a deluxe suite hotel in New York City, used internal data to develop a research database and create profiles of its guests. Then, using Dallas as a test city, researchers overlaid guest profiles on area codes and credit cards to identify residents who travel to New York as potential guests. The prospects received a letter with a special offer to induce them to stay at the Rihga Royal. Similar profiles were developed for San Francisco, Los Angeles, Chicago, and certain cities abroad.[4] The famous Peninsula Hotel in Hong Kong tracks guest orders and notes specific guest diets, food and beverage preferences, and special dates such as anniversaries and birthdays. Las Vegas hotels track the moves of guests in their casinos through the guest cards they issue. Guests insert cards into machines to play games and their winnings and losses are recorded, leaving a paper trail. These databases give hospitality businesses opportunities to extend superior services, create loyal guests, and raise guest expectations beyond the level of their competitors.

Fast-food chains use computers to track customers and their eating habits, as well as to eliminate bottlenecks in taking orders. Boston Market gathers information from its customers at the point of the transaction through questions on touch screens. The screens ask a few direct questions and guests respond by holding their hands on a replica of a thermometer that permits them to indicate their degree of satisfaction. Its restaurants can track the sales of every menu item on an hourly basis and determine what items to prepare and when. Taco Bell is using an interactive computer program that allows customers to place their orders directly; the computer not only handles the necessary ordering processes, but stores, classifies, and summarizes data about guest preferences and choices. Management can then analyze and use this guest information in making decisions about offerings at various stores. The program, which also features commercials, generates information and gives consumers something to do while they are waiting. Restaurants use POS (point of sale) or ECR (electronic cash register) systems to furnish information about menu items, prices, guests served, payment method, beverages and deserts sold, and other information useful for marketing decisions.

Servers in some restaurants use handheld computers to record orders that are automatically transferred to the kitchen. Using this information, the Chili's chain has developed an extensive database of over two million guests that is updated daily, providing information about guest habits and preferences that is invaluable for menu decisions.[5]

These examples illustrate the kinds of valuable information that can be gathered readily. Many of the most-used approaches do not involve sophisticated statistical or mathematical research techniques, are relatively low in cost, and can make a big difference on the bottom line.

Experience as Information

Seasoned hospitality executives internalize a vast array of marketing information from their own experiences. They develop a "gut feel" for hospitality markets, and their intuition and feelings are often right on target. However, following one's reactions and instincts without adequate marketing research confirmation can be misleading and costly. Consider the following actual situations.

A successful restaurateur walked through the food court of a very large mall observing the array of fast-food establishments. He stopped abruptly and asked his companion, "Where is the baked potato with the toppings?" He pointed to a location and exclaimed, "It should be right there." He went on to explain the profit potential of such a venture. But how could he be so sure? He hadn't done any formal marketing research—he just reacted intuitively and instinctively. Yet, less than a year later a baked-potato outlet was initiated and, eight years later, was continuing to enjoy great success. The restaurateur had gathered useful marketing research information, but had done so informally, based on his experiences and insights; he automatically used this knowledge in reaching decisions.

In contrast, another very successful entrepreneur, who thrived on making decisions based on his feelings, was most impressed with the taste of some hickory-smoked chicken and ribs at a local restaurant. Following his instincts, he pursued discussions with the owner of the restaurant and wound up purchasing a major interest in it. Then he established another outlet and investigated plans to franchise the concept. The result was not successful, culminating in a substantial loss and the closing of both restaurants.

An analysis of what went wrong indicated that marketing research could have uncovered a number of concerns—questionable market potential, poor location, ineffective market positioning, keen competition, low profit margins, very competitive prices, poor cultivation of the takeout market, and the need for advertising and coupons. In this case, personal opinion and an emphasis on internal operations were no match for marketing considerations.

Obtaining Marketing Information Through Research

Information about markets, guests, and competition is a critical need for effective hospitality marketing management. **Hospitality marketing research**—the systematic gathering, recording, and analyzing of data about problems relating to the marketing of hospitality goods and services—fulfills that need.

While hospitality's use of marketing research is relatively recent, the benefits the industry has derived assure widespread application in the future. In assessing the industry's opportunities for carrying out marketing research, one industry expert notes:

> The guest is *in* the hotel (restaurant). He or she made a reservation (or walked in), registered, provided credit evidence, is beginning to accrue charges, and will eventually settle the bill and check out. The idea is to use all these processes to obtain the marketing data needed and to do so in a way that creates the smallest amount of inconvenience to the guest. The high technology of today provides the mechanical tools necessary to do the job. It is simply a matter of forethought, redesign, and reeducation for the employees.[6]

Marketing research provides practical, problem-solving information. It is not an academic exercise. It helps managers deal with the uncertainties of the marketplace by providing facts, improving judgment and decisions, and adding information to intuition and "gut feel." Marketing research helps monitor market trends, solve today's problems, and develop perspectives of the future. It keeps a firm fix on guest wants and needs, helping hospitality providers stay in touch with their markets. It enhances but does not replace judgment.

Large hotels, restaurants, and food service operations, particularly chains, are among the most likely users of marketing research on a regular basis. Marriott, for example, has its own marketing research department and also purchases research from marketing research suppliers. Marriott used marketing research when it initiated its Courtyard Hotels. Hyatt Hotels used marketing research before introducing rooms with work stations, fax machines, and computer hookups to aid business guests.[7] And Sheraton Chicago advertises its Hotel and Towers Cityfront Center using the headline, "Introducing the Result of 600 Hours of Market Research."

By putting market research at the fingertips of district managers, restaurant chains like McDonald's and its rivals have provided new tools to subdivide urban markets further. Marketing research indicated new ways of increasing McDonald's market share by opening stores about half the size of typical stores in smaller towns, using satellite sites like Wal-Mart stores and Chicago's Union Station, and locating at other nontraditional sites, including the MGM Grand Hotel in Las Vegas, Mobil gas stations, and the Manchester, New Hampshire, airport.[8]

Restaurant chains also use test markets to try out new concepts. They regularly use focus groups (groups of present or potential guests who are asked to offer their opinions and observations about the business as well as guest preferences) and have developed sophisticated information systems with extensive databases. They also buy marketing research data from services that track consumers, like CREST—Consumer Reports in Eating Share Trends—and publications of GRD Enterprises that track fast-food businesses. Many hotels use *Lodging Outlook* published by Smith Travel Research.

Larry Reinstein, the vice president of Souper Salad Restaurants, says, "The biggest lesson we've learned is that knowing your market is at least as important as knowing your business."[9] Yet it is apparent that many hospitality executives, who are steeped in operations, often tend to place greater value on financial and

Exhibit 1   Hypothetical Competitive Analysis—Excelsior Hotel

Competing Hotel	Rack Rate Double	Rooms	Estimated Occupancy	Facilities							
				Restaurants & Lounges	Banquet Capacity	Health Club	Pool	Valet Parking	Location	Room Service
Spartan	$80–90	80	80%	1R, 1L	600	Yes	No	Yes	Downtown	No
Premiere	$75–85	130	45%	2R, 1L	1,000	No	Yes	No	Airport	No
American	$70–85	250	63%	1R, 1L	800	No	Yes	No	Off Highway	No
Excelsior	$80–95	110	55%	2R, 1L	900	Yes	No	Yes	Downtown	Yes

operating data than they do on marketing data; they do not appreciate the benefits of using marketing information.

Customers and Competitors

Marketing research embraces a variety of diverse and useful information—sales trends; occupancy and utilization rates; average room rates; realized revenue; market share; analysis of competitors and their strategies; market segmentation; market positioning; images; market trends; guest expectations, attitudes, and perceptions; the evaluation of advertising, sales, and merchandising effectiveness; guest complaints; forecasts of demand; guest histories; and more.

Hospitality companies have better opportunities to gather and use relevant consumer information than do many other businesses, because hospitality, by its very nature, involves direct contact with customers—the guests. Reservations, registration, credit cards, billings, menu selections, service choices, and frequent-user programs are examples of kinds of personal contacts that furnish the opportunities. Also useful are regular in-house questionnaires, as well as the published information of both private and government data suppliers.

In gathering information about competitors, hospitality marketing researchers do not confront the severe problems of secrecy and legal or other constraints that often exist in other industries. Competitive hospitality establishments are open to the public, so researchers can readily develop a feel for how well their companies are doing relative to competitors. It is easy to sample competitors' food, beverage, and lodging offerings, to review their menus and wine lists, and to assess their facilities, guestrooms, and services.

Hospitality marketers can evaluate their competitors' strengths and weaknesses. What do competitors do well, and what do they do poorly? Doing a competitive analysis of physical properties is straightforward. This is illustrated in Exhibit 1, which summarizes the attributes of local hotels competing with the

Exhibit 2   From Data to Marketing Intelligence

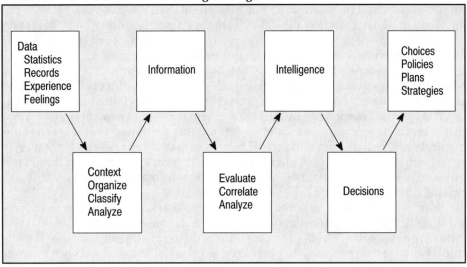

Excelsior. The information can be prepared from such readily accessible sources as published data, telephone calls, and Chamber of Commerce and association resources such as those of AAA. While assessments of physical properties are helpful, competitive assessments of threats and opportunities involve more than bricks and mortar. They involve assessing marketing effectiveness, including the degree of guest satisfaction with hospitality offerings and services.

Assessing how competitors seem to be doing is facilitated by the incredible amount of marketing data that can be obtained. The research challenge is (1) to determine clearly what information to seek, (2) to establish whether the information exists, and (3) if it does exist, to determine who has it. Then management must decide what the information is worth—what the company is willing to pay for it. The actual value of marketing information depends on the difference that the information would make; the difficulty is that the real difference is known only after the fact. If management would make the same decision with the information as it would without it, the information is worthless. If, on the other hand, having the information available would lead to significant increases in profits or cost savings, gathering it is worthwhile. Management would opt to proceed with data collection and analysis. With marketing research decisions, management confronts the usual situation of having to take a risk and decide beforehand whether to incur the costs of the research. Thus management judgment comes into play.

Marketing Intelligence

Exhibit 2 distinguishes among hospitality data, information, and intelligence, and indicates what is involved in moving from data to marketing intelligence. Data systems by themselves do not automatically yield either information or intelligence. When businesses gather data about occupancy rates, menu items selected, room revenues, profitability of different market segments, or competitors, the results may indeed be interesting, but they are not what we mean by marketing information. Rather, **marketing data** are the raw inputs from which marketing information may be drawn. When data are organized, classified, analyzed, and put into an appropriate context, they result in **marketing information**.

In a like manner, information is not intelligence. Information furnishes the raw materials for generating marketing intelligence. When information is properly analyzed, evaluated, correlated, and geared to handle hospitality marketing situations, it becomes **marketing intelligence**. Intelligence is information in a format that is useful in managing operations—formulating plans and policies, determining strategies, and making decisions. The goal of marketing research is not merely to generate data, but to provide intelligence. Of course, more hospitality enterprises have marketing data than have marketing information, and fewer still possess marketing intelligence.

Having drawn this important distinction, we acknowledge that marketers speak about marketing information when they really mean marketing intelligence. While we acknowledge this practice and use the terms interchangeably for this study, we want to emphasize that management is usually concerned with generating marketing intelligence.

The Hospitality Marketing Research Process

Marketing research, as the major tool for generating hospitality marketing information, may be thought of as a process—the process of generating, collecting, and analyzing hospitality marketing information. The general outlines of the marketing research process are sketched in Exhibit 3.

A detailed description of the research process is beyond the scope of this chapter. The process is summarized in the following discussion of major stages.

Problem Definition

The marketing research process begins with the consideration of one or more problems. Examples include such situations as a decline in market share, falling profits, increasing guest complaints, a decline in the effectiveness of advertising or merchandising efforts, guest resistance to prices, and a decline in repeat business. Business problems also include untapped opportunities. Market opportunities represent problems to be solved, situations to be handled. Pertinent and timely marketing information can deal effectively with opportunities as they arise, as well as help head off crises before they develop into problems. The most important hospitality problems are generally those dealing with future opportunities.

The first phase in dealing with such situations is to identify and define, in researchable terms, the problems involved. Problem definition is the most important stage of the whole research process. It guides and circumscribes the rest of the activities. The adage that a marketing problem well-defined is half solved has some validity. However, defining hospitality problems in researchable terms can prove to be very challenging, and the problem-definition phase is not scientific. It involves gathering background information from external and internal sources to

Exhibit 3   Outline of Marketing Research Process

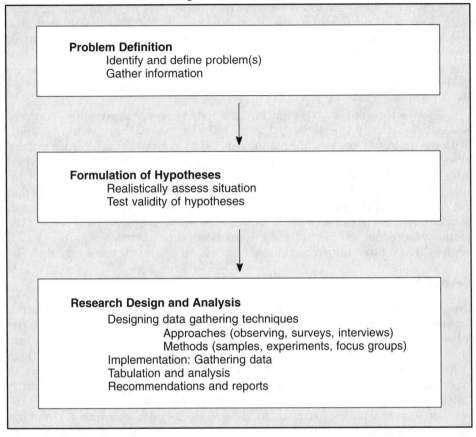

Problem Definition
   Identify and define problem(s)
   Gather information

Formulation of Hypotheses
   Realistically assess situation
   Test validity of hypotheses

Research Design and Analysis
   Designing data gathering techniques
         Approaches (observing, surveys, interviews)
         Methods (samples, experiments, focus groups)
   Implementation: Gathering data
   Tabulation and analysis
   Recommendations and reports

get a feel for the dimensions of the real problem. And different managers confronting the same hospitality situation may well perceive quite different problems. Problem definition is a subjective phase of scientific marketing research.

Short-circuiting problem definition and information-gathering can be disastrous. Unless problems are clearly defined beforehand, data will be gathered about the wrong, or nonexistent, problems. The time spent on defining market research problems is time well spent.

Formulation of Hypotheses

When hospitality problems are clearly defined, management can determine how they might be approached and solved. Researchers formulate hypotheses—likely solutions about ways of dealing with defined problems. When hypotheses are formulated, the information needed to test them, to verify or negate their validity, can be detailed. In such a way, hypotheses indicate how to deal with problems.

For example, if a hotel or restaurant is suffering from loss of market share, its market researchers may question guests, gather information about competitors and suppliers, look at external and internal data, consider trends, and develop a feel for what is going on. Based on what they learn, they might hypothesize that their service does not measure up to guest expectations, that they have targeted the wrong market segment, and that their advertising is not effective. Then they might hypothesize further that guest services have to be altered along certain lines, or that advertising has to be refocused on different target markets. They can specify the information necessary to test their hypotheses to see if the tentative solutions are valid.

Before setting out to gather any information, however, the situation should be assessed realistically. Questions such as the following should be raised: What information is desired? Does the information exist? If so, who has it? Is it readily obtainable? What are the costs and time involved in doing so? What published information and records exist that might be helpful? If the data desired are not available, or if the costs are too high, or if the time required to gather the data means that the window of opportunity to deal with the problem effectively will have passed, then basic decisions must be made. Should the research be dropped? Should the problem be redefined? Should the information be restructured within practical bounds? The information to be gathered must meet pragmatic requirements.

Research Design and Analysis

Once the preceding activities are completed, questions about research design arise. Researchers need to decide how to go about gathering the data—which basic research approaches (observing, asking questions, conducting polls, and/or using published sources) to use. They also need to make choices concerning methods (random sample, nonrandom sample, experiment, focus group, scales, types of questions) and techniques to be used in gathering and analyzing data (research instruments, quota sample, convenience sample, systematic sample, mailed questionnaire, interval scales, Latin square design, open-ended questions). When the preceding considerations have been addressed and decisions made, programs can be put into place to identify information sources, complete research instruments, and carry out the marketing research.

Hospitality marketers should bear in mind that many practical pitfalls may be encountered in carrying out marketing research projects. Inadequate attention to the sampling process, to the careful design of research instruments, and to the manner in which the research is actually carried out can result in biased and flawed data. Where data are flawed, the conclusions reached from the data analysis will be of questionable value. Inappropriate measurement techniques, incomplete interviews, and interviewer bias are more common than is recognized. They result in misleading conclusions and recommendations and poor hospitality marketing decisions.

In marketing research, it is important not only to gather the right data, but also to conduct the right analysis. The analysis must be done very carefully to yield unbiased results so that the proper conclusions and logical inferences can be drawn. Faulty analysis, of course, negates the value of good data. Planning for data analysis should take place early in the research process, at the time that the kinds of data to be gathered and research instruments are being considered. The analysis being planned has an impact on the questions asked, questionnaire construction and layout, computer programs, and the reports generated.

To interpret research data properly, the assumptions underlying various statistical techniques, research instruments, and measurement approaches must be kept in mind. It is easy to attach numbers to various scales that measure attitudes, preferences, opinions, and the like. But what do they mean? In analyzing and interpreting data, researchers must keep the assumptions and limitations clearly in mind. Although such considerations are well beyond the scope of this chapter, we caution you to be concerned with the limitations of research data.

Marketing research findings and conclusions are the basis of recommendations and reports. When the appropriate decision-makers receive the recommendations and reports, they can deal with the problems that started and guided the research process.

Using Marketing Research Approaches

Questionnaires, Surveys, and Interviews

Hospitality businesses rely heavily on guest questionnaires and surveys to gather information. Guests are asked to fill out questionnaires left in hotel rooms or on restaurant tables. Questionnaires are seen as easy and inexpensive ways of gathering guest data, but constructing questionnaires properly is not as easy as most people believe. Evaluations of some of the questionnaires used by hospitality businesses have noted such errors as faulty wording, misleading and biased questions, inadequate guest choices, dubious methods of soliciting guest cooperation, lack of attention to the characteristics of respondents, and neglect of important questions. The lack of well-constructed questionnaires in so many situations suggests questionable research results.

Exhibit 4 presents some practical guidelines for questionnaire construction. The guidelines begin by emphasizing that the issues being researched must be clearly defined. For example, in asking questions about food and beverage service, the specific service aspects being addressed must be clearly stated so that respondents understand what aspects they are being asked about. If respondents have not used various restaurants, bars, or room service, comments about such services may not be relevant. The exhibit also includes some guidelines regarding different types of questions—open-ended, yes/no, and multiple choice; some "dos and don'ts" when interacting with respondents; and some suggestions about questionnaire design, wording, readability, layout, and general considerations. When these guidelines are followed, many common errors may be prevented and questionnaires improved. At the very least, the importance of properly constructed questionnaires is underscored.

Questionnaires are used in various survey approaches. Exhibit 5 compares three of the most common: mail surveys, telephone interviews, and personal interviews. They are compared on the bases of the type of data they yield, speed of data collection, expenses, interview bias, and nonresponse problems.

Personal interviews provide the greatest degree of flexibility and, since they often permit probing questions, can provide in-depth data that may not be

Exhibit 4   Guidelines for Questionnaire Construction

1. **The Issue**
   Clearly understand the issue yourself.
   Fully define the issue.
   Be as precise as possible.
   Make sure the issue is meaningful to respondents.

2. **Types of Questions**
   Open-ended Questions
   > Try to convert the item into a limited question.
   > If used, indicate the number of ideas expected (use a probe).
   > Try to use precoded response sheets.

   Yes-No Questions
   > Do not imply alternatives.
   > State the negative alternative in detail ("or not" is too vague).
   > Leave room for "No opinion" and "Don't know."
   > Are choices mutually exclusive?
   > Is some middle ground provided?
   > Try to learn intensity of response as well as direction.

   Multiple-choice Questions
   > Do not overlook any alternative.
   > If you restrict choices, be aware you are doing so.
   > Choices should be mutually exclusive.
   > Issues in each item should be clear.
   > Do you want one choice or more than one?
   > Provide for "No opinion" and "Don't know."

3. **Interaction with Respondents**
   Avoid talking down to respondents.
   Use good but not stilted grammar.
   Do not use slang or falksy language.
   Avoid double meanings and double negatives.

4. **Questionnaire Design**
   Wording
   > Use as few words as possible.
   > Use simple wording.
   > Use words with only one pronunciation.
   > Use familiar, frequently used words.
   > Be aware of local meanings of words.

   Readability
   > Avoid misplaced emphasis.
   > Simplify punctuation.

   Layout
   > Arrange in logical order.
   > Place difficult questions near the end.
   > Group related questions.
   > Group questions with similar formats.
   > Ask sensitive questions as late as possible.

   Overall Considerations
   > Keep the questionnaire as short as possible.
   > Give clear instructions.
   > Be aware of tabulation methods when constructing questionnaire.

Exhibit 5   Comparison of Major Survey Methods

Factors to Consider	Mail Survey	Telephone Interview	Personal Interview
Type of data	Encourages respondents to be more candid aboutsensitive issues; eliminates certain types of questions, such as those needing probes	Provides immediate feed back; works well if interview is less than five minutes long	Provides large amounts of data; particularly good for aided recall
Speed of data collection	Likely to be very slow; little control over return of questionnaires	Fastest, most controllable survey method	Controllable, fast collection but has time-consuming arrangements and execution
Expense	Low cost per survey mailed but generally high cost per survey completed	Low cost per survey completed	Usually most cost method because of travel time and expenses
Interviewer bias	None, since respondents use own words	Depends on control over interview situation	Greatest potential for interview bias
Nonresponse problem	Usually high percentage of nonrespondents	Usually low percentage of nonrespondents	Generally few problems with nonrespondents
Other	Respondents can answer at leisure and can consider responses; only those interested in the subject may reply	Wide sample of rerespondents; no need for field staff; callbacks simple and economical	Respondents are known; most flexible means of data collection; dangers of bias and cheating

obtained by mail or telephone. However, they are often the most costly and time-consuming, and they involve considerable training.

Mail questionnaires are less costly than personal interviews, can deal with sensitive issues, and can encourage candid responses. But they tend to have high nonresponse rates, and high costs per completed survey. Response rates of only five to ten percent are not unusual.

Telephone interviews give immediate feedback, are low in cost, fast, controllable, and simple. They can be automated with a tape recording guiding respondents who answer questions by pushing the appropriate touch-tone buttons. However, they are not feasible for interviews that are extensive and involve a considerable amount of time, or that require considerable probing.

Sampling

Marketing research gathers information from *samples*—groups or segments that are representative of larger entities. Guests' attitudes, interests, preferences, and opinions are among the major subjects sampled by research. Samples may be of many varieties; some are scientifically designed and selected at random, and others are *convenience samples*, comprising guests who happen to be on the premises. In conducting marketing research, three questions arise: Who is to be surveyed (identification of the sampling unit)? How will participants be selected (sampling technique)? How many are to be sampled (sample size)? The answers affect research costs as well as the quality of the results.

Identification of the sampling unit involves identifying that part of the whole universe of guests that the researchers are interested in (the *sampling frame*). The universe might be all foreign guests, all business guests, all guests over 18, all married guests, or the competitors' customers.

The sampling technique used may be random or nonrandom. **Random samples**, also called **probability samples**, are samples in which each unit of the population has a known chance (probability), usually thought of as an equal chance, of being selected in the sample. For random samples, the risks of sampling error and measures of reliability can be calculated. But random samples can be more difficult to select and more costly to implement than nonrandom samples.

Nonrandom (or **nonprobability**) **samples** are samples that involve researcher discretion and judgment in choosing sample members. Calculations of sampling error and reliability cannot be made. Yet carefully designed nonrandom samples can yield valuable information. Exhibit 6 describes various kinds of random and nonrandom samples.

The remaining sampling decision concerns the size of the sample. There is usually a compromise between larger samples and cost. For random samples, it is possible to calculate the reduction in sampling error associated with samples of different size. In other words, the sample size necessary to meet a specific, allowable sampling error can be determined. Generally, the larger the random sample, the more reliable the results, although the reliability does not increase proportionately with the increased sample size. Doubling the sample size does not double the reliability, and, as the sample size increases, so do costs. It is a matter of balancing the desired levels of precision with costs.

Focus Groups

Focus groups are a commonly used approach to get information about guests' attitudes, opinions, perceptions, and preferences concerning various proposed decisions or actions. A focus group may comprise perhaps eight, ten, or twelve "typical" guests who are selected by researchers as the kinds of guests likely to frequent a hotel or restaurant. In return for their cooperation and participation, they are usually offered an incentive such as a meal at an outstanding restaurant, a free hotel weekend, donations in their names to favorite charities, or a gift. When the group is assembled, a skilled moderator leads the discussion regarding the issues under consideration.

Exhibit 6   Descriptions of Random and Nonrandom Samples

Probability and Nonprobability Samples	
Type of Sample	**Description**
Probability Samples	
Simple random sample	Each population member is assigned a unique number, and the sample is selected by means of a random-number table, each member has a known, equal chance of being selected.
Stratified random sample	Total population is divided into mutually exclusive, exhaustive subsets (*strata*), and simple random samples of members in each subset are selected.
Cluster random sample	Total population is divided into mutually exclusive, exhaustive subsets (*clusters*), and a simple random sample of entire subsets is selected.
Systematic random sample	Every *n*th element in the total population is designated for inclusion, after a random start.
Nonprobability samples	
Purposive (judgment) sample	Sample units are selected on a basis of expert judgment.
Quota sample	Important characteristics of population and proportions of population with these characteristics are identified.
Convenience sample	Most accessible population units are selected.

For example, the group discussion might focus on such issues as layout alternatives for hotel rooms, new amenities being considered for hotel bathrooms, the kinds of exercise equipment being considered for a new health center, a new menu, or new food and beverage offerings. The skilled moderator establishes rapport with group members and primes them to participate actively and share their feelings freely. Moderators ask questions, direct and channel the discussion, and probe to determine true reactions and meanings.

Focus group sessions are often audio- or videotaped. Observers from the hospitality company sometimes sit behind one-way mirrors to observe the session. The insights gained from the focus group members are analyzed for their meaning and implications. However, since the findings are qualitative in nature, and judgment is involved in analyzing them, the conclusions reached, and implications developed by different researchers, may vary.[10]

Validity and Reliability

In using various marketing research approaches, hospitality managers are concerned with the value of results. Validity and reliability are two concepts used to estimate how good the results are. Marketing research carried out properly in terms of research design, sampling, instruments used, data gathered, and analysis yields results that are both reliable and valid.

Validity is the degree to which research actually measures what it is supposed to measure. There are various types of validity: face validity, construct validity, and internal validity. If we are measuring room profitability, face validity deals with whether the research actually measures profitability, or whether some aspects such as cost/revenue relationships have been ignored. Construct validity deals with the construct that is being measured. It asks what is actually being measured, and if that is what is supposed to be measured. For example, if researchers are seeking to determine guest motives, do their constructs really measure motives or something from which motives can be inferred? Internal validity measures freedom from bias. Are the findings free of biases from interviewers, samples, respondents, and questionnaires?

Reliability is tested by the reproducibility of a study. If we were to repeat the study in the same way, would we get the same results? If so, the research is reliable. When research results are reliable, sample findings can be used to draw conclusions about the whole population.

Research results may have reliability without validity. That is, repeated studies could yield the same results but they could lack face, construct, or internal validity; they may not measure what they are supposed to measure. However, research cannot have validity without reliability. If the research is not reproducible and cannot be applied to the whole population, it does not measure what it is supposed to.

Marketing Information and Problem-Solving ——————

Marketing research is problem-driven—it gathers information to help management deal with problems. Generally, hospitality problems can be categorized as problems of fact or problems of value. The distinctions between them are summarized in Exhibit 7.

Problems of Fact

Problems of fact are generally dealt with more readily than problems of value, for they are more definite, concrete, and measurable. They lend themselves more readily to quantitative approaches and, sometimes, optimum solutions. Included are such factual problems as establishing the cost per square foot of hotel space and the revenue necessary to be profitable, or determining average expenditures for food and beverages by different types of guests for various restaurants, regions, and hotels. Two managers dealing with the same factual problem should arrive at essentially the same decision.

Problems of Value

Problems of value, on the other hand, are concerned with what decision-makers *ought to do* or *should do*. Problems of value are based on judgment, not facts. Here are some examples:

Exhibit 7   Problems of Fact and Problems of Value

	Characteristics	Examples

Factual Problems
"The facts are"
	• Definite
	• Impersonal
	• Different Managers =
	  Same Decision
	• Best Approach
	  (Maximize)
		Deciding On:
		• Conference Capacity
		• Meal Costs
		• Occupancy Rates
		• Market Share
		• Parking Capacity

Value Problems
"What should we do?"
	• Judgments
	• Assessments
	• Appraisals
	• Opinions
	• Estimates
	• Different Managers =
	  Different Decisions
	• Satisfactory Approach
	  (Satisfice)
		Deciding On:
		• Market Potential
		• Competitive Appraisal
		• Advertising Budget
		• Locations
		• Menu Choices
		• Amenity Offerings
		• Additional Services

- How much should be spent on advertising?
- What items should be added to and deleted from menus?
- What new services should be offered to guests?
- What prices should be charged for various offerings?
- What strategies should be adopted to meet competitors?

The choices made depend on the values and judgment of individual decision-makers. Two hospitality executives facing the same value problem, therefore, may arrive at entirely different solutions. Moreover, they may both have appropriate responses that will prove to be effective. Value problems lend themselves to satis-factory rather than optimal solutions; that is, executives may seek to *satisfice* (arrive at a satisfactory solution) rather than to *optimize* (arrive at the best possible solution). In pricing menu items, for example, two restaurateurs may decide on different prices for the same items, with both approaches yielding good results. Both recognize that the prices they set are not going to achieve the theoretical opti-mum, but will achieve satisfactory results. Executive assessments of future envi-ronments, sales forecasts, and strategic marketing plans involve values.

Marketing Information Sources

The diversity of hospitality marketing information sources, formats, and uses, both internal and external, is extensive. There are information sources for decisions about market potential for new hospitality services; the allocation of resources among advertising, personal selling, and merchandising; the addition and deletion

Exhibit 8   Hypothetical Operating Summary and Breakdown—Host Hotels

Operating Summary—May 199X

Hotel Revenues	$630,000
Costs	$490,000
Gross Margin	$140,000

Operating Summary Breakdown by Hotel—May 199X

	A	B	C
Revenue	$110,000	$300,000	$220,000
Costs	$60,000	$270,000	$160,000
Gross Margin	$50,000	$30,000	$60,000

of menu items; and the consideration of new properties, new markets, and price changes. There are a vast range of marketing information sources available, including invoices, annual reports, accounts receivable, census data, sales records, customer research, and cost and profitability analyses.

Hospitality marketers often require information in different formats, and over different time intervals, than do other hospitality company executives such as controllers or financial analysts. Too often, data exist in a format that is useful for accounting purposes, but not for marketing purposes.

For example, suppose that Host Hotels owns three properties, A, B, and C. From an overall accounting perspective, the operating summary presented in Exhibit 8 is useful, but a breakdown by hotel yields additional useful information. It is evident that while Hotel A generates the least revenue, it also has a very high gross margin. Hotel B, by contrast, generates high revenue but relatively low margins. Hotel C has the highest gross margin, but on revenue that is two times that of Hotel A. A breakdown facilitating an investigation of the costs incurred by each hotel, and how and why B generates such high revenues, could provide useful insights. For example, B could be spending a disproportionately high amount on generating more sales. By contrast, A might not be spending enough on marketing and its revenues may be suffering as a result.

Marketers might want data classified according to the types of guests, whether business, group, individual, or convention; the geographic area; price category; and the profitability of each market segment. They might want to massage data and organize them according to functions, products, or market segments, using various schemes of allocating costs and expenditures, thereby facilitating more extensive analysis than that of the usual financial statements.

Marketing Information Categories

When we normally think of gathering marketing information, the tendency is to think in terms of getting all the facts. However, much of the information that is important is not factual, but consists of attitudes, opinions, interests, and perceptions. Some information is primary information, while much of it is secondary information. Information may be internal or external, past or future, qualitative or quantitative, descriptive or explanatory, and may be the result of inferences or deductions. The categories are not mutually exclusive; for example, descriptive data may be secondary external data about the past. Let us briefly consider each category.

Primary and Secondary Information. Primary information is marketing information generated for the purpose of solving some specific problem at hand. Examples are conducting surveys, experiments, or focus group sessions to generate the specific information needed to determine new offerings, services, advertising themes, or pricing strategies. When companies gather primary information, they can control and tailor the research to their specific requirements.

Secondary information, by contrast, is information that has been gathered for some other purpose than the company problems at hand, but is nevertheless useful in dealing with them. It is usually external information. Secondary information is readily available, for the volume and quality of secondary data have multiplied greatly in recent years. Examples include the vast array of census information in addition to information published by the Travel Industry Association of America, the American Hotel & Motel Association, the National Restaurant Association, and numerous other agencies and associations. Companies like PKF Consulting, Smith Travel Research, and Arthur Andersen publish data annually about hospitality and financial trends. PricewaterhouseCoopers publishes a quarterly journal, *Hospitality Directions*, with forecasts and analyses of the hospitality industry. Some secondary data about such factors as occupancy rates, average daily rate, and average daily rooms sold provide benchmarks that properties can use to assess how well they are doing in comparison with others in the industry.

Hospitality marketers are too often unaware of the kind and amount of pertinent secondary data available. Secondary data save time and money. However, since they are gathered for purposes other than particular company situations, the data may not exist in the desired format, or may be too general to handle company-specific situations. Caution, therefore, must be exercised in interpreting and applying the results of secondary research. Researchers must pay close attention to how terms like income, household, families, attitudes, values, and sales are defined for purposes of the research.

External and Internal Information. Most secondary information is external information gathered from sources outside the company—suppliers; local, state, national, and international government agencies and associations; competitors; and distribution channels. Widely used information about changing

Exhibit 9   Use of Internal Data: Analysis of Market Share

July 1, 199X					
Competing Hotels	**Number of Rooms**	**Rooms Sold**	**Percent Occupancy**	**Proportionate Market Share**	**Realized Market Share**
Spartan	100	80	80.0	10.0%	14.0%
Premiere	300	130	43.3	30.0%	22.8%
American	400	250	62.5	40.0%	43.9%
Excelsior	200	110	55.0	20.0%	19.3%
Total	1000	570	57.00	100.0%	100.0%

environments—whether economic, social, political, cultural, technological, legal, or international—is secondary information published by a variety of sources. Companies like Marriott, McDonald's, Holiday Inn, Hyatt, Burger King, and Pizza Hut continuously use information about emerging environments to develop a broad picture of future business climates. This helps with their assessments of future markets and with their sales forecasts.

Internal information comes from the company itself, and is generally much easier to assemble, summarize, and use than external information. However, it can also be more costly. We have noted that hospitality companies have better opportunities for gathering pertinent and timely internal information than various other businesses because of their continuing interactions with guests. Regardless, hospitality providers do not seem to know as much as they could, or should, about actual and potential guests.

A guideline in gathering information is to determine the marketing information management seeks and what the company is willing to pay for it—what it is worth. In other words, assess the feasibility of doing the research first. Most hospitality businesses have such information about their operations as average room rate, average check, average number of covers, and frequently ordered menu items. Further, they can develop databases using information from frequent guest programs, guest registrations, guest check-outs, surveys of guest attitudes and preferences, facilities usage, and guest behavior and choices. Such sources are underutilized.

Internal information can be used for a variety of marketing purposes. Exhibits 9 and 10 illustrate the use of internal analysis regarding market share and revenue per room. Exhibit 9 presents a hypothetical example illustrating market share analysis for the Excelsior Hotel and its competitors: Spartan, Premiere, and American. The hotels are listed along with the number of rooms each has and the number of

Exhibit 10   Use of Internal Data: Analysis of Revenue per Room

July 1, 199X					
Competing Hotels	Number of Rooms	Rooms Sold	Average Room Rate	Total Revenue	Revenue per Room
Spartan	100	80	$70.00	$5,600	$56.00
Premiere	300	130	$65.00	$8,450	$28.17
American	400	250	$60.00	$15,000	$37.50
Excelsior	200	110	$75.00	$8,250	$41.25
Total	1000	570	$65.49	$37,300	$37.30

rooms sold on July 1. The occupancy percentage for each is calculated by dividing the number of rooms sold by the number available. The proportionate market share is calculated by dividing the number of rooms each hotel has by the total number of rooms. The actual market share realized is derived by dividing the actual number of rooms each hotel sold by the total number of rooms sold. Spartan and American exceed their proportionate share while Premiere fared poorly and Excelsior was slightly under.

Exhibit 10 presents the analysis of revenue per room using the same four hypothetical hotels. In this analysis, the average room rate is calculated and is multiplied by the number of rooms actually sold to derive the total revenue. To calculate the revenue per room, total revenue is divided by total number of rooms available in each hotel. The Spartan Hotel had a very favorable revenue per room of $56 versus the poor Premiere performance of $28.17.

Internal data can be used to compile occupancy and revenue performance by different guest sectors. This is illustrated in Exhibit 11. Such a breakdown shows management where to direct its marketing effort. The exhibit shows that military and government business is not nearly as profitable as transient business, and conferences do not contribute proportionately to the bottom line. The business segment seems to be very profitable; marketing efforts to increase the number of business guests and to develop methods of catering to them could pay off handsomely.

The preceding examples are but three of many market analyses that hospitality businesses can perform using internal data. They show that market analysis does not have to be costly or time-consuming and that sophisticated statistical techniques are not required to provide useful management information.

Descriptive, Explanatory, Qualitative, and Quantitative Information. Descriptive information is information about the past—it describes what has actually happened. Examples include descriptions of the profiles of guests, reports on the sales revenue of food and beverage items, occupancy rates, realized market share, gross

Exhibit 11   Revenue, Occupancy, and Profitability by Market Segment

Market Segment	Revenue		Occupancy	Profit
	($000)	%	%	%
Business	300	15	20	27
Conferences	500	25	15	12
Transient	800	40	35	41
Tour	250	12.5	20	13
Government/Military	150	7.5	15	7
Total	$2,000	100%	100%	100%

margins and profits per room, the profitability analysis of market segments, and guest assessments. It is factual, describing what is occurring or what has occurred. In contrast, explanatory information sets out to explain not just *what* is so, but *why* it is so. Research information may tell management why pricing policies fail or succeed, or why certain menu designs are more effective than others.

Future information is speculative and involves assumptions, conjectures, judgments, informed opinions, and uncertainties. It deals with "future facts," with likely occurrences, and with probability estimates that are integral to hospitality marketing forecasts, plans, and strategies. Descriptive information often forms the basis for future information.

Marketing researchers rely on measurements. They often prefer quantitative approaches and information to the qualitative counterparts. **Quantitative information** is measurable and has an aura of objectivity—of being scientific and precise; it is often referred to as "hard" data, as compared with **qualitative information**, which is deemed subjective and "soft." Both can be pertinent and valuable, and it is erroneous to believe that quantitative marketing information is, per se, superior to qualitative information, or vice versa. Qualitative information, such as that pertaining to guest attitudes, motives, opinions, preferences, and perceptions, can be among the most valuable of all in solving hospitality problems.

While almost anything can be measured, the important question is what do the resulting data really mean. All measurement is subject to limitations associated with the techniques, instruments, and processes used to gather data, as well as the methods of analysis—the quantitative techniques applied. Regrettably, such limitations are too often ignored, resulting in the misinterpretation and misuse of quantitative data. This is particularly true when such quantitative methods as sampling, scaling, and experimental designs are applied. When interpreting data, managers often forget that they are dealing with samples; ignoring limitations, they draw inferences that become misleading conclusions.

Inferences and Deductions. Inference proceeds from the specific to the general. When researchers gather primary data, they draw inferences from specific samples and conclusions about the population being studied. For example, when random samples of hotel guests are surveyed, sample results are used to draw inferences about a whole class of guests, the population. If a random sample indicates that 78 percent of the guests have a favorable attitude toward a property's offerings, inferences will be made about the attitudes of guests at large. Inferential reasoning is basic to scientific marketing research.

Deduction proceeds from the general to the specific. That is, marketing researchers use general tendencies, such as averages and rules of thumb, to deduce information. Suppose that a hospitality manager notices that whenever direct mail brochures are sent to households with incomes above $100,000, the average inquiry rate is about 12 to 15 percent. However, for households with incomes of $50,000 to $100,000 the rate seems to be around three to four percent. These generalizations may be used to deduce information about expected inquiries from a direct mail brochure that is going to be sent to households in a new market that the company is entering.

Developing Hospitality Marketing Information Systems

A hospitality marketing information system is a *system* designed to gather, process, and make available pertinent and timely marketing information to hospitality managers in a format that permits them to function more effectively. The systems concept stresses the interrelationships and total integration of all system components. Rather than focusing on a sequence of individual, self-contained components, attention is directed to the interaction of all system parts. Integrated information systems create synergies that allow the system to be more than the sum of its parts.

Desirable Characteristics

The dual purposes of operations and strategy must be kept in mind when developing effective hospitality marketing information systems. Conflicting information objectives may exist because market information is developed for both short- and long-range situations. Hospitality managers must deal with present and future marketing situations. They are concerned with immediate sales and profits, as well as long-range opportunities and future images. Thus, marketing information systems must provide an appropriate mix of data. Although there are no hard and fast rules, some experienced observers suggest a mix of information somewhere in the range of 35 percent for current purposes and 65 percent for longer-range uses.

Beyond the appropriate mix, an effective hospitality marketing information system should, of course, meet the information needs of those involved in carrying out marketing hospitality responsibilities, gathering and furnishing information as conveniently and as efficiently as possible. It should also:

- Provide marketing information in a format that is convenient and relevant for users.

- Provide up-to-date, accurate, reliable, timely, and pertinent marketing information.

- Direct marketing information to those who need it, in time for them to act.

- Provide marketing information that permits the company to capitalize on its potential.

- Furnish information about market trends and likely future developments.

- Provide marketing information that encourages changes in both outlook and operations.

- Minimize the investment of money, time, and other resources in providing needed marketing information.

Realistically, compromises will have to be made. It may be too costly to gather the desired information. The desired information may not even be available. It may not be possible to obtain up-to-date industry data or government statistics for the time periods desired. And sometimes the categories used are not broken down the way a researcher might like to have them. For example, while the census may report on households with incomes of $75,000 and over, a luxury hotel might want to know about households in the ranges of $100,000 to $150,000, $150,000 to $200,000, and so on. Priorities will have to be established, and choices will have to be made.

Designing a hospitality marketing information system to meet the preceding requirements is by no means easy. Consideration must be given to both internal and external information sources, the information to be generated, the applications, and the anticipated results. Sometimes it is useful to start with the desired results and work back to the information required and their sources.

The general thought process flows from information sources to information that can be generated to applications and then to results. In this way, practical information systems can be developed that meet company needs and embody desired characteristics.

Sales Forecasting

Sales forecasting provides critical hospitality marketing information.[11] Sales forecasts are important ingredients of such pivotal marketing tasks as strategic planning, the deployment of marketing resources, and the control of marketing efforts. Sales forecasters analyze past sales data, searching for patterns that can be used to predict future sales. For example, the data charted in Exhibit 12 of past sales of the AAA Hotel contains trend, seasonal, and cyclical data patterns that can help with sales forecasts.

Trends simply represent the sales pattern over several years—the long-run general sales thrust. Various techniques, such as linear regression, may be used to determine the long-run patterns, which can then be used to forecast future sales. Seasonal patterns deal with short-run phenomena, such as monthly or quarterly sales that fluctuate in a regular pattern. For example, sales in Florida resort hotels and restaurants have a seasonal spurt in January, February, March, and April. Then

Exhibit 12   Illustration of Underlying Patterns of Data for a Hypothetical AAA Hotel

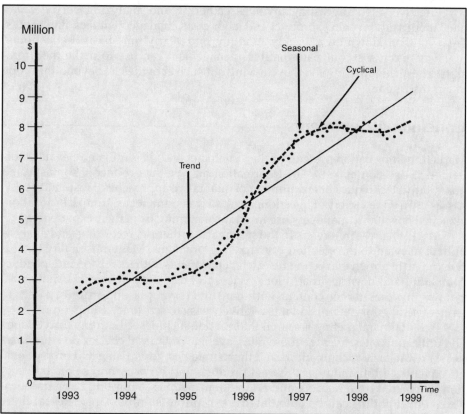

Adapted from Raymond S. Schmidgall, *Hospitality Industry Managerial Accounting,* Fourth Ed. (Lansing, Mich.: Educational Institute of the American Hotel & Motel Association, 1997), p. 373.

they drop off and may be the lowest in August and September. When seasonal patterns are identified, they can be used to forecast sales by month and quarter.

Cyclical patterns are longer-range in nature, with cycles occurring over many years. They are often portrayed as movements about a trend line, as is the case in Exhibit 12. An example is the wave-like movements pertaining to the periods of contraction and expansion of the business cycle. Cyclical patterns are more difficult to measure and predict than the patterns related to seasonality and trends. Nevertheless, hospitality executives take these patterns into consideration when evaluating marketing results. For example, flat sales during a business recession are evaluated differently from those occurring during a period of business expansion.

Various sales forecasting techniques can be used to determine existing sales patterns as well as to actually make sales predictions. A scheme classifying some of the more common sales forecasting methods used in hospitality is shown in

Exhibit 13 along with a very brief description of the methods. It includes both quantitative and qualitative methods, and scientific and judgmental techniques.

Effective sales forecasting involves gathering and analyzing very detailed data about sales revenues, product and labor costs, management fees, and profits, breaking them down on a weekly, monthly, and yearly time basis. By so doing, researchers can seek out patterns that management can use to make their forecasts. The techniques involved in carrying out such activities lie beyond the scope of our discussions.

Concluding Comments

Marketing information systems gather, evaluate, and disseminate relevant information to decision makers. The information may be the product of sophisticated quantitative techniques or any number of qualitative approaches. Hospitality businesses use a wide variety of questionnaires, surveys, and focus groups. In addition, seasoned hospitality managers use intuition stemming from their experiences.

Marketing research refers to the systematic gathering, recording, and analysis of data relevant to the solution of marketing problems. Many hospitality institutions have their own marketing research departments. Others rely on independent companies and agencies that offer services to hospitality businesses. Since hospitality involves direct contact with consumers, ample opportunity exists to gather useful information, and it is relatively easy to scrutinize competitors.

Hospitality marketing research information includes sales trends, occupancy and utilization rates, average room rates, average restaurant checks, revenue, market share, analysis of competitors and their strategies, advertising and promotional effectiveness, profitability of different products and services, and so on. Information is gathered from random and nonrandom samples. Sampling error and measures of reliability can be calculated for random samples only. Researchers determine sample size and deal with the validity and reliability of research results. Although managers generally refer to marketing information, what they are interested in is market *intelligence*.

The research process involves problem definition, formulation of hypotheses, and research design and analysis. The basic research challenge is first to determine what information to seek, then establish whether the information exists and, if it does, who has it and what the company is willing to pay for it. Information is valuable if it makes a difference in the decisions being made.

Problems may be either problems of fact or problems of value. Problems of fact are more definite, concrete, and measurable and lend themselves to optimal solutions. Problems of value are based on management judgment and lend themselves to satisfactory rather than optimal solutions.

A wide variety of internal, external, primary, and secondary hospitality marketing information sources exist to help managers solve problems. Although secondary information may not always be available in the format that marketing decision makers require, hospitality managers should become familiar with published information sources; these sources can often be useful, and the costs are modest compared with those of generating primary data.

Exhibit 13   Sales Forecasting Methods

Approaches				Brief Description
				Ad hoc, judgmental or intuitive methods
Sales Forecasting Methods	Quantitative Methods	Casual Methods	**Regression Analysis**	Independent variables are related to the dependent variable using least squares: $y = A + Bx_1 + Cx_2$. Approaches include simple linear regression, multiple linear regression, and nonlinear regression.
			Econometrics	A system of interdependent regression equations describing one or more economic sectors.
		Time Series	**Naive**	Simple rules such as forecast equals last period's actual activity.
			Smoothing	Based on average past values of a time series (moving average) or weighting more recent past values of a time series (exponential smoothing).
			Decomposition	A time series that is broken down into trend, cyclical, seasonality, and randomness.
	Qualitative Methods		**Survey Research**	Gathering information from potential customers regarding a "new" product or service.
			Experiments	Gathering information from potential guests by conducting experiments.
			Juries or Executive Opinion	Top executives or authorities jointly prepare forecasts.
			Salesforce Estimates	A bottom-up approach to aggregating unit managers' forecasts.
			Delphi Method	A formal process conducted with a group of experts to achieve consensus on future events as they affect the company's markets.

Adapted from Raymond S. Schmidgall, *Hospitality Industry Managerial Accounting,* Fourth Ed. (Lansing, Mich.: Educational Institute of the American Hotel & Motel Association, 1997), p. 374.

Marketing researchers rely on measurements and generally prefer quantitative to qualitative data. Both are useful, however, and it is wrong to assume that quantitative data are somehow inherently superior. Qualitative data about guest preferences, attitudes, and opinions may yield the most important information of all. In interpreting measurements, the assumptions and limitations of quantitative techniques used must be kept clearly in mind.

Sales forecasting provides critical hospitality information for budgetary, planning, and strategic purposes. Many techniques are available to assist with generating forecasts, including the analysis of cyclical and seasonal factors. Sales forecasting uses both scientific and judgmental approaches. Some techniques are intuitive and others are mathematically and statistically sophisticated. Since managers must make sales forecasts, they must choose which forecasting techniques to use.

Endnotes

1. Peter D. Bennett, *Dictionary of Marketing Terms*, Second Ed. (Chicago: American Marketing Association, 1995), p. 169.

2. Michael L. Kasavana, *Hotel Information Systems* (Boston: CBI, 1978).

3. *The Wall Street Journal,* 5 March 1995, p. A1.

4. As reported by Frank Banks, General Manager, Rihga Royal Hotel, New York, in a personal interview during August 1994.

5. *The Wall Street Journal,* 25 October 1995, p. B1.

6. A. Neal Geller, *Executive Information Needs in Hotel Companies* (New York: Peat, Marwick, Mitchell & Co., 1984), p. 7.

7. *The Wall Street Journal,* 1 February 1994, p. B1.

8. *The New York Times,* 9 January 1994, p. F5.

9. "How to Tackle Expansion," *Restaurant Magazine,* March 1988, p. 65.

10. Joe L. Welch, "Focus Groups for Restaurant Research," *Cornell Hotel and Restaurant Administration Quarterly,* August 1985, pp. 75–85.

11. This section is based on Raymond S. Schmidgall, *Hospitality Industry Managerial Accounting,* Fourth Ed. (Lansing, Mich.: Educational Institute of the American Hotel & Motel Association, 1997) pp. 372–374.

Key Terms

deduction—a conclusion reached by the process of reasoning from the general to the specific.

focus group—a commonly used approach in which researchers select and convene a group of "typical" guests in order to gather information about guests' attitudes, opinions, perceptions, and preferences concerning proposed decisions or actions.

hospitality marketing research—the systematic gathering, recording, and analyzing of data about problems relating to the marketing of hospitality goods and services.

inference—a conclusion about a general unit or group drawn from a specific sample.

marketing data—the raw inputs from which marketing information may be drawn.

marketing information—data that has been organized, classified, analyzed, and put into an appropriate context for marketing use.

marketing intelligence—information that has been properly analyzed, evaluated, correlated, and geared to handle hospitality marketing situations; marketing information in a format that is useful in managing operations—formulating plans and policies, determining strategies, and making decisions.

nonrandom (nonprobability) sample—a sample that involves researcher discretion and judgment in choosing sample members. Calculations of sampling error and reliability cannot be made.

primary information—marketing information generated for the purpose of solving some specific problem at hand.

quantitative information—information that is measurable and has an aura of objectivity, of being scientific and precise; it is often referred to as "hard" data.

qualitative information—non-measurable information that is often deemed subjective and "soft."

random (probability) sample—a sample in which each unit of the population has a known chance (probability), usually thought of as an equal chance, of being selected in the sample. The risks of sampling error and measures of reliability can be calculated.

reliability—the degree to which a research approach consistently produces the same results.

research instrument—any of the wide variety of tools and techniques researchers use to gather information.

secondary information—marketing information gathered for some other purpose than company problems at hand, but nevertheless useful in dealing with them.

validity—the degree to which a research approach actually measures what it is supposed to measure.

Review Questions

1. Why do hospitality companies need marketing information, and why are they in a better position than other businesses to obtain certain types of information?

2. What is marketing intelligence, and how does it differ from marketing information and marketing data?

3. What three stages summarize the hospitality marketing research process?

4. What are some of the problems that have been noted in evaluating questionnaires used by hospitality companies?

5. What research approach provides the greatest degree of flexibility and can gather in-depth data that may not be obtained by mail or telephone?

6. What are the advantages and disadvantages of mail questionnaires? Of telephone interviews?

7. How does validity differ from reliability in marketing research?

8. How do problems of value differ from problems of fact? Of what significance is this difference?

9. What are the main categories of marketing information, and what types of information might they comprise?

10. What is a hospitality marketing information system, and what are its major elements and desirable characteristics?

11. Sales forecasts provide market researchers with what types of information? For what purposes?

Internet Sites

For more information, visit the following Internet sites. Remember that Internet addresses can change without notice.

American Hotel & Motel Association
http://www.ahma.com

Educational Institute of the American Hotel & Motel Association
http://www.ei-ahma.org

National Restaurant Association
http://www.restaurant.org

PKF Consulting
http://www.delve.com/PKF/pkf.html

Arthur Andersen
http://www.arthurandersen.com

PKF Worldwide
http://www.PKF.com

PricewaterhouseCoopers
http://www.pwcglobal.com

Smith Travel Research
http://www.str-online.com

Chapter 10 Outline

What Is a Hospitality Product?
    Hospitality Product Complexity
    Hospitality Product Decisions
Designing the Hospitality Product Offer
    Elements of the Product Offer
    Levels of Product Elements
    Modifying the Product Elements
Analytical Tools for Product Decision-Making
    Blueprinting
    Value Chain Analysis
    Customer Value Analysis
    Product Life Cycle Analysis
Brands in the Product Decision
Concluding Comments

10

Product/Service Mix: The Offer

"You can have the best product in the world, but if you can't sell it—you've still got it!"

—Diamond Jim Brady, 1901[1]

HOSPITALITY PRODUCTS (which always include services) are the bundles of tangibles and intangibles that hospitality businesses offer to satisfy the needs of their targeted guests. The economic value of hospitality products is derived from the products' capacity to satisfy the needs and desires of prospective buyers or users. This central idea, which guides our thinking about the development or modification of hospitality products, is a major theme of this chapter.

There are two general approaches to the development of new or improved hospitality products. The first begins with a careful analysis of the needs, interests, and preferences of potential guests and seeks ways of building products that will meet guest needs better than anything else being offered, at prices that guests will pay and that yield satisfactory profits. The second begins at the other end of the spectrum, with an idea for a product that is attractive to management. Potential markets are then identified where the new products are likely to have a strong competitive appeal.

Both approaches have had success, but the first, and the one we advocate, has been more effective. Many times, hospitality managers have developed and put on the market hospitality products they thought were attractive that then failed because they did not meet guest needs. There have been over-priced and unwanted luxury offerings; guestrooms that did not meet the needs of business or family travelers; the lack of desired guest facilities and services like health clubs, parking, and leisure activities; poor locations; and ineffective implementation of otherwise sound concepts that failed because guests (the most important component) were neglected from the beginning. Starting with an open mind and a clear insight into guest needs and preferences helps avoid many problems.

What Is a Hospitality Product?

When we refer to hospitality *products*, the term includes services. The hospitality product offer encompasses both the product and service elements that hospitality businesses offer to guests. Service is a critical defining component of hospitality products. When we wish to focus on the service components alone, we use the term **service offer.**

Products are often best thought of as bundles of benefits. While this perception is important, it is not the whole story. Hospitality products (as with most service industry products) are bridge builders; they link the needs, interests, and capabilities of businesses to the needs, interests, and preferences of guests. Just as bridges need to be anchored at both ends, hospitality products must faithfully reflect both guest needs and the hospitality business's objectives and capabilities. Let's look at some examples of hospitality products.

The Delano Hotel, Miami Beach: A Family Resort.[2] New York hotelier Ian Schrager, involved with the hospitality industry for over 25 years, has successfully anticipated the mood of the times and developed hospitality products to capitalize on them. Examples include Studio 54, which catered to the disco fever of the 1970s; boutique hotels like the Paramount and Royalton in New York in the 1980s; and his latest 1990s venture, the Delano at Miami's South Beach. Schrager saw an opportunity for a family resort at reasonable prices—but with cutting edge style—in Miami, one of America's most energized cities. Responding to this opportunity, he created a unique environment: a 238-room hotel reflecting a new simplicity, but featuring fun and surprise.

Built in 1947, the Delano maintains much of its yesteryear charm: a curved driveway, a large open verandah, bellhops attired in white shorts and matching blazers, a dark and restful lobby, a mixed collection of art and furniture, and generous armchairs and plump sofas creating areas of comfort and intimacy. The emphasis is on shapes and finishes from leather to canvas, silk to velvet, and all natural materials. The designer, Philippe Starck, explained the ambience as "less to see, more to feel."

By contrast, the rooms (suites and duplex townhouses) are eye-poppingly bright and crisp—models of "monastic modernism." The bathrooms, however, feature freestanding Victorian-style baths, custom-made enamel sinks set in marble-topped tables, and wooden ladders as towel rails. The Delano is a self-contained resort for the whole family, including a large pool; a garden dotted with an oversized chess set; a women's bathhouse, featuring spa, aromatherapy, and relaxation facilities; a gym; a supervised children's play area; a dollar movie theater; and numerous eating areas. Schrager's vision for the 1990s, via Starck, was "a new generation of resort where you can have your style and siblings, too."

Observatory Hotel, Sydney, Australia: Hotel Packages.[3] The Observatory Hotel is a leading five-star hotel in Sydney. It is located on a quiet street in a historic precinct a short distance from the center of the city and near the old Sydney Observatory. The following is an excerpt from an interview with the Director of Marketing (at that time) of the Observatory Hotel.

Q: Do you have a whole range of packages, like weekend specials, theater packages, and so on?

A: Yes. In designing our packages, I had a long chat to Reservations about it and asked them what were the most popular ones. They said what people ask for mainly is the standard package, overnight accommodation, parking, and breakfast. The next most common one is with the bottle of champagne. So, you go from the Weekend Affair, which is the standard, to the Champagne Celebration, to specialty packages. We have a Romantic Rendezvous package which involves a three-course candlelit dinner, bath oil, roses, a massage, and so on. We even have an Astrology package. We also have a clairvoyant—two, actually.

Q: No one else would have that, I guess. That's really clever!

A: Well, it involves two readings with a clairvoyant. I call the package "See the Stars," and I'm just putting it together now. In summer, I have a city resort package with tennis lessons—the hotel lends itself to that.

Q: Do you have any theater packages?

A: Yes, "Phantom of the Opera" and "Miss Saigon." We don't do a lot of those.

Q: When you set the theater packages up, do you go and see a particular specialist organization or deal directly with the theater?

A: There is a particular company you have to contact regarding these kinds of tickets. You have to maintain a good relationship. The company is called Showbiz. I don't deal with a particular person, just whoever is on the line. There are a few special agencies that do it, actually. They handle the bookings and they negotiate with the hotels, but what you do is pre-buy those tickets. And, what has unfortunately happened to most hotels in Sydney is that they have been left with so many tickets that they can't sell because people have lost interest in Phantom now! You have to book in advance. We booked at the beginning of last year until the end of this year and in the last couple of months interest has waned. No one wants to go anymore. The market is mainly local.

As we think about these two examples, it is evident that the hospitality product is more complex than might first appear. The hospitality products developed in these examples are illustrative of the kinds of product decisions that hospitality managers must handle with insight and skill.

Hospitality Product Complexity

Hospitality products are complex because of both the intangible and tangible elements involved and the fact that they usually do not stand alone. Rather, they must be viewed as part of a hospitality company's product portfolio designed to meet the needs of a number of different market segments through a range of diverse product offers. For example, a new hotel may be one of a chain of properties, operating internationally under one or more advertised brand names, each directed toward different market segments. A restaurant may be one of a number of company restaurants geared to several different markets, either in a single property, such as a hotel, or in a variety of locations. A single menu presents a variety of offers that appeal to different guests.

As we look more closely, there are products within products, different kinds of suites and rooms in the same hotel, different kinds of restaurants in one location or property, special dishes adding accents to a menu, and a variety of services offered within packages. Often, the product requires the use of external specialists—a parking firm to manage the hotel parking lot, childcare specialists to manage the childcare facility, theater owners to cooperate in providing guests with attractive packages, or wine wholesalers to construct and deliver an attractive wine list. A diversity and hierarchy of products within hospitality product portfolios exists that must be managed.

As if all this were not enough, hospitality products involve the interaction of staff and guests in a variety of settings, systems, and facilities. Such interactions—which greatly affect guest responses to hospitality products—are not easily controlled. Facilities or settings are not always exactly right, systems may not always cope well with guest situations, and staff members are not always up to the tasks and demands and may not respond appropriately. In addition to all this, guests are often unpredictable.

The point is that hospitality product decision-making is complex. Hospitality products are the result of interactions taking place in guests' minds, involving both tangible and intangible elements as well as settings, systems, and staff members. Hospitality managers, in creating new products or modifying existing ones, have to keep such complexities in mind.

Understandably, the temptation to oversimplify product situations can be enticing, but the perils of oversimplification should not be minimized. This chapter suggests some of the tools that can be used to keep hospitality product decisions focused on creating value for guests and profits for businesses, while also keeping product and development activities well within reasonable limits of complexity for hospitality managers.

Hospitality Product Decisions

Hospitality product decisions go to the very heart of the business. In approaching them, managers must be mentally flexible and willing to challenge assumptions on which past product decisions were based. They need to recognize market changes that have occurred and adopt a creative problem-solving posture. Flexibility and creativity are integral components of effective hospitality product development processes.[4]

Product decisions involve both strategic (longer term) and operational (shorter term) considerations. Look at our examples: for the Delano Hotel, design considerations played a strategic role in structuring the product and will influence the operational choices open to management for many years; for the Observatory Hotel, shorter-term operational issues were relatively more important in designing a weekend package that achieved a profitable mix of guests within the next planning or budget period. Packages can easily be redesigned and have only a limited lifetime. However, choices made in package design may also have longer-term effects on the image or positioning of the hotel. For example, packages directed to tourists in a predominantly business traveler hotel could attract a mix of guests that are at variance with the longer-term objectives of the business.

Strategic versus operational concerns involve mastering the present while "preempting" the future (that is, limiting options of competitors and creating

Exhibit 1 The Service Iceberg

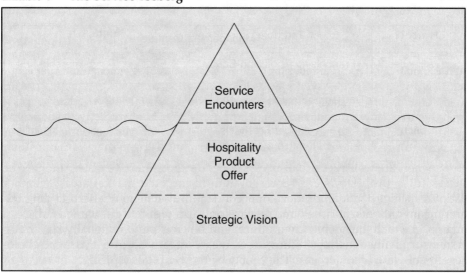

capabilities to manage future developments).[5] A view of this dilemma is illustrated in Exhibit 1. The part of the "service iceberg" that guests see and managers tend to worry most about is the tip—the service encounters ("moments of truth") that guests experience. This is where careful planning is translated into perceived value. Hidden from view is the thinking leading to the hospitality product offer, where management makes sure that each service encounter is part of an overall plan to meet the needs of each target market and is supported by the necessary systems, staffing, and facilities. Equally hidden is the strategic vision that provides the inspiration and focus needed to give meaning and purpose to the hospitality product and thus to the business as a whole. Change in any one of these three levels without a matching change in another level affects the balance of the iceberg—icebergs have been known to tip over!

In managing hospitality products, management must cope with the tension between strategic and operational concerns, carefully evaluate the hospitality product in terms of its ability to meet customer needs, assess competitive challenges, and satisfy business objectives. Meeting and satisfying customer needs involves recognizing the many guests comprising target markets. Confronting a competitive challenge means building a distinctive advantage into the hospitality product offer, giving your preferred guests a real reason to choose your offer over all others. Satisfying business objectives requires that the hospitality product offer capitalize on company strengths.

Designing the Hospitality Product Offer ─────────

Let us define more precisely what we mean by a hospitality product offer. A hospitality business may approach the development of a product offer from three

Exhibit 2   Service Offer Elements—Delano Hotel

Elements	Tangible	Intangible
Explicit	• Room design • Children's facilities • Garden chess	• Style—monastic modernism
Implicit	• High standard of meals • Comfortable meeting areas	• Meeting families with similar interests

different perspectives. First, developing a product offer involves specifying the product ingredients, facilities, and services to be provided to guests. Second, it is a process in which the hospitality products and services are provided by staff using systems in defined settings. Third, from the guest perspective, it is a bundle of benefits or desired outcomes. The first sees the hospitality product in terms of inputs, the second as a process, and the third in terms of perceived outputs. All three points of view are important.

From an input perspective, the hospitality product centers on a package or bundle of services and related facilities that will be provided for guests. This is the service component of the product offer. In this regard, four levels of abstraction (discussed later in this section) have been identified in defining a product—generic, expected, augmented, and potential.[6] Also, distinctions are drawn between tangible and intangible elements, and explicit and implicit promises (see Exhibit 2).[7] In the hospitality context, the product offer, including the service component, has been separated from the presentation mix.[8] The product offer focuses on the combination of products and services directed to the needs of targeted markets. The presentation mix refers to all those elements that are used to increase the tangibility of the hospitality product, such as the physical facilities, ambience or atmosphere, price, and employees.

The process perspective focuses on the activities involved in the delivery of each of the products offered, seeking to ensure that staff are trained and available, that the information needed to deliver the service elements is readily accessible, and that the facilities are appropriate to the task at hand.

The guest perspective focuses on the output or result that customers look for from their purchase of a service. One important approach to the specification of these benefits is embodied the SERVQUAL model, which has identified five distinct output dimensions, all of which have direct application to hospitality products.[9] They are:

1. *Tangibles*: Appearance of the physical facilities, staff, and communication materials.

2. *Reliability*: Ability to perform the promised service dependably and accurately.

3. *Responsiveness*: Willingness to help customers and provide prompt service.

4. *Assurance*: Knowledge and courtesy of staff and their ability to convey trust and confidence.

5. *Empathy*: Caring, individualized attention that is provided to customers.

Elements of the Product Offer

The **hospitality product offer** may be thought of as a package or bundle of different services, including tangible and intangible elements, explicit and implicit promises, directed toward meeting the needs of targeted markets. It is an integral part of the total offer that hospitality businesses make to prospective guests. The **total offer,** a term used interchangeably with the **market offer,** embraces all aspects of the marketing mix. In broad terms, the **marketing mix** is the means by which hospitality enterprises are linked to their target markets. By altering the ingredients of the mix, organizations can adjust to changes in the marketplace.

In considering the product offer, the tangibles—such as buildings, furniture, fittings, signage, uniforms, and so on—are often dealt with independently of the other elements of the offer. Decisions are often made without careful consideration of the target markets. It is in this sense that a systems perspective, based on service to selected markets, is of great importance. In thinking about the components of the product mix, management must not lose sight of the guests' point of view. While products are offered, guests seek benefits. Perceived cost is in the minds of the guests. Distribution concerns the choices made that affect availability (such as logistics, transportation, and delivery) and bring products to guests. Promotion is concerned with the communication choices made to gain guest attention, interest, and purchase commitment.

An important question to consider when designing a hospitality product offer is what kind of relationship you want with your guests. At one extreme is a focus on each individual transaction, with an emphasis on convenience, speed, and efficiency. Examples of businesses with this focus might include McDonald's, cafeteria services, or budget motels. At the other extreme is a focus on building deeper, long-term relationships with guests, seeking to enhance their stay through a wide range of value-added services. Here, involvement, tailoring an offer to meet individual needs, and quality service become central to management's thinking. This is demonstrated in the approach of the famous Savoy Hotel in London (see sidebar).

The actual elements that make up a hospitality product offer are limited only by the imagination of the managers concerned. Some examples that caught our attention include:

- Golf vacations. Golf is attracting increasing support from the upscale leisure segment, from international tourists (especially the Japanese), and from the meetings market.[10] Hotels often make arrangements with nearby golf courses, particularly well-known ones, securing preferred tee-off times and special packages of carts, green fees, and club storage for their guests.

- A chef for every room. The Inn at Essex near Burlington, Vermont, partnered with the New England Culinary Institute to bring the Institute into the Inn.

Savoy Hotel

The Savoy Hotel, which is almost 110 years old, "is not a hotel…[it] is an institution. Everything here is a showcase. Everyone takes their standard from us," noted Mr. Herbert Striessnig, Director and General Manager. Over a century ago, the Savoy advertised itself as "the perfection of luxury and comfort." Today it still has that very special image of being at the pinnacle among the elite hotels of the world. It continues to offer exceptional levels of outstanding pampering and catering to the individual desires of its guests.

At the Savoy, foodservers, housekeepers, and valets are still summoned by touching a button at bedside. The hotel has its own florist, ages its own meat, has its own chauffeur-driven cars to pick up guests, manufactures its own extremely comfortable beds, and still makes its own chutney. Some long-term guests have their own furnishings moved into their rooms. Departing "regulars" can have items packed and stored for them, and then unpacked and ready for them upon their return. When certain guests occupy specific rooms, they may pick the paint and wall coverings.

As guests enter hallways, housekeepers switch off vacuum cleaners and greet them, and every floor has its own attendant on duty. There are four servers to tend to a guest in the Grill Room. The Savoy accommodates guest preferences for sheets, pillows, fruit, various foods, and favorite servers. Door attendants open taxi doors and take the bags. Cars are parked for guests. Three people are employed for each room, about double the average for London hotels in the same price range. The Savoy "overservices, which is why people go there… Space, service, and style is our motto and for excellence we strive."

The Savoy has always been known for maintaining its sense of tradition, for keeping things pretty much as they are. But markets change, creating the difficult challenge of balancing shareholder demands and profits with Savoy's excellent reputation for outstanding service. Delivering unparalleled service profitably involves the difficult management tasks of increasing productivity, modernizing, and even lowering standards a bit, while still continuing as a leading outstanding luxury hotel.

To cater to the needs of contemporary guests, the Savoy, while maintaining its rich heritage and tradition, is changing. A health club was built, a new kitchen was added, bathrooms have been remodeled and modernized, heating and air conditioning have been updated, and rooms have been refurbished. Management faces the responsibility of maintaining an outstanding level of service and keeping the Savoy's image and reputation intact, and at the same time controlling costs and increasing profits.

Based on *The Wall Street Journal*, 25 Oct. 1994, pp. B1, 16.

The result? Fifteen instructors and 100 students preparing food for hotel guests in the kitchens of the Inn. The substantial additional investment in kitchen facilities was justified by the additional business generated. Package opportunities abound—including weekend getaways for "semi-serious" cooks, southern chefs, and guests who want to experience the "magic" of gourmet cooking.

- High-tech guestrooms. The corporate guest market, in need of confidentiality and speed in its communications, rates these rooms highly. It can be important for some hotels to have rooms equipped with computers, dedicated telephone lines, TV conference facilities, facsimile machines, and the like. Where guests bring their own equipment to the hotel, the ability to find plug-compatible outlets for laptop computers, an Internet connection, and room furnishings that facilitate work (desk space, lighting) are essential product offer elements.

To summarize, a guest-oriented view of the product offer is concerned with such issues as:

- *Benefits*: Tangible and intangible elements, explicit and implicit promises, generic to potential components; expectations, standards, and perceived quality.

- *Perceived costs*: Dollars, time, risks, learning, and tradeoffs.

- *Availability/delivery*: Market networks, reservation/booking systems, organization, location, logistics, delivery systems, guest/staff interactions, and settings.

- *Communication*: Personal or mass, direct or indirect, advertising, public relations, telemarketing, trade shows, exhibitions, networking, and incentives.

All of these dimension are related; decisions made in one area will have a direct or indirect impact on the others.

As we think about the hospitality product offer, the complexity of the marketing decisions involved becomes evident. Understanding the important markets and recognizing what matters to each is a good starting point for constructing a coordinated market offer. Achieving an integrated market offer not only requires each specialized area to coordinate its thinking (pricing, advertising, distribution, etc.), but also necessitates a clear management understanding of the needs, interests, preferences, and choice processes of guests in each of the key target markets. This understanding provides the thrust for a coordinated market offer that has competitive impact.

An essential element not often discussed is the importance of power—power to influence the achievement of goals that a business has set for itself. Marketing is, in one sense, about power—acting with an eye on who has the power to influence outcomes. The priorities managers allocate to each target market must reflect the realities of power. If tour wholesalers, for example, play a dominant role (as can happen in destinations dependent on a continued flow of tourists from various nations), then this market will be front and center in management's thinking and action. If political issues concerning access to markets are important, then marketing must take them into account.

Levels of Product Elements

The creativity reflected in each of these responses is an essential part of developing successful hospitality product offers. Of course, it is essential to explore options systematically so that the whole range of viable alternatives is considered. One

Exhibit 3   The Four Levels of Hospitality Product Elements

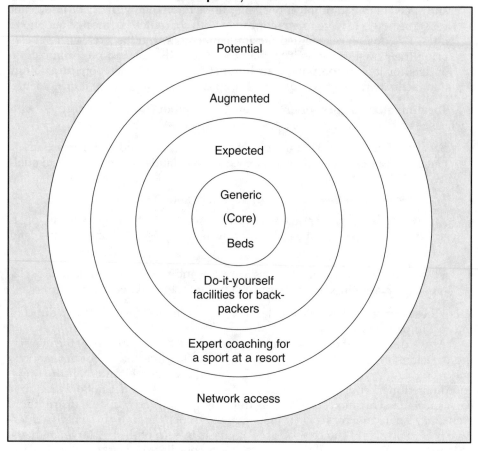

way to do this is to consider the hospitality product at the four levels of abstraction mentioned earlier (depicted in Exhibit 3). The generic level refers to the core or essential elements that must be included—the facilities and systems that every guest knows will be available such as beds, bathroom facilities, check-in procedures, and closets for hotels; tables, chairs, menus, servers, and kitchen facilities for restaurants. The components of the generic offer, however, will vary enormously—ranging from basic facilities for an overnight stay at a remote lodge in a national park to the luxury of a major five-star hotel in a destination city.

The expected product elements vary among different kinds of hotels or restaurants. They include both facilitating services (those needed for guests to use the core service) and support services (those used to increase value). Guests at a backpacker hostel will expect bunks, shared bathrooms, do-it-yourself cooking facilities, notice boards, and contact points—all for a low price. Guests at a resort property expect not only accommodations and food, but access to many forms of sports and recreation. A five-star hotel would be expected to have such services as a reservation network, rooms at a range of prices, restaurant facilities, international telephone and facsimile systems, and trained service staff.

Augmented product attributes are those that differentiate one hotel, resort, or restaurant from another in the same broad category. In selecting appropriate augmented product attributes for its mix of guests, a resort might consider golf courses, swimming pools, sailing and water skiing, health clubs, message stations, room service, restaurants, and transportation. Over time, augmented attributes tend to become increasingly standardized and, to this extent, lose some of their ability to differentiate one property from another. The augmented attributes of yesterday, such as swimming pools and exercise equipment, tend to become today's expected attributes.

Finally, there are potential attributes that might contribute to the product. They require insight into the benefits that would be valued by specific categories of guests. Over time, potential attributes often become augmented attributes. For example, such potential attributes of a few years ago as facsimile machines, beepers, and cellular phones have now become augmented attributes or even expected attributes for some properties. To an extent, the speed with which potential benefits become commonplace is a measure of how rapidly markets and technologies are changing.

Perceptions of what lies ahead for hospitality can be the stimulus for generating ideas about potential benefits. For example, consider an individual property as an integral node in a larger, total network, such as an information or distribution network. Potential benefits flowing from such a network may be identified for guests who wish to live and work in a "virtual community," where computer networking is integral to their way of life, and ideas for extending those benefits may be suggested.

Modifying the Product Elements

As markets and competitive situations change, market offers will need to be modified. Three key considerations play a major role in the task of modifying or adjusting a hospitality offer:

1. Will the modifications add value in the eyes of the guests that really matter?

2. What is the cost of making the modifications?

3. Will the results attract guests from key target markets and add to the competitive strength of the business?

Adding value involves change along one or both of two product dimensions. The first deals with the range or scope of the product offer. As we add to the bundle or package of product and service elements, we add to the scope of the offer. The second deals with guest perceptions of the quality of the hospitality offer delivered. This quality dimension depends on the ability to provide such benefits as reliability, responsiveness, assurance, and empathy, as well as benefits arising from the tangibles in the product. Perceived improvements of one or both of these dimensions will show up in higher perceived value.

Together, these two dimensions comprise the value created through additions to a hospitality product offer. Tradeoffs are possible both within and between the dimensions. Added scope may well reduce a business's ability to provide the quality desired. Similarly, an increase in quality levels may limit a business's ability to provide a wider scope. Product modifications usually offer opportunities to trade off one component against another in order to reduce overall costs or improve competitive position.

The costs of a new or modified hospitality product offer are important to both managers and guests. Managers see the direct and indirect cost consequences of making changes to a product offer. Guests see the direct and indirect costs of acquiring the benefits that management has in mind. An assessment from both points of view is needed.

From the manager's perspective, relevant cost information can, in principle, be derived from the accounting system. Value is more difficult to assess because it reflects judgments about how product modifications will affect margins and competitive advantage. It depends on careful observation, good guest research, and an information system that tracks guest needs and responses. Moreover, the costs perceived by the guests may go well beyond direct monetary price of a hospitality package or of each component, and may include the costs arising from the time needed to figure out a new or unfamiliar service or the social or psychological costs of appearing wrong or inept. While it may be difficult to put a value on such costs, nevertheless it is important to identify areas of high or low perceived cost.

Analytical Tools for Product Decision-Making

Blueprinting

It is hard to design success into hospitality offers. There are so many complexities involved with the product development process, such as predicting guest satisfaction, assessing risks and the possibility of new product failure, optimizing the use of scarce resources such as time and money, and identifying how profits might be increased. **Blueprinting** is an analytical tool that is helpful. It enables hospitality business to explore planned product offers on paper and work out many of the problems before products are marketed. It permits management to consider the product and service components in detail and to suggest ways of improving them to enhance guest satisfaction and increase productivity and profits. Blueprinting encourages creativity, helps build team commitment, and is a way of coming to terms with the inherent complexity of designing product offers.[11]

Blueprinting begins by identifying the service encounters in which typical hospitality guests participate as they move through the service process. As far as guests are concerned, this sequence of service encounters provides the visible evidence that the process is under way. As far as management is concerned, the real challenges often lie in the processes or activities that go on behind the scenes.

The sequence of service encounters will not always be the same for every guest—and the differences may point to differing sets of needs of various segments. When beginning a blueprinting exercise, it is important to achieve a balance between using too much and too little detail. Given too little detail, important points will be overlooked where service failure can occur, costs may be reduced, or profit margins may be enhanced.

An initial listing of critical service encounters identifies the visible face of the service processes inherent in the hospitality product. The next step takes us behind the external process to consider the activities necessary to ensure that each service encounter is a winner. The "six S's" of service encounters are very useful here:

1. Specification: What is to be done?

2. Staff: Who will be involved?

3. Space: Where will the encounter take place?

4. Systems: What systems will play a role?

5. Support: What supporting activities are needed?

6. Style: How will the service be provided?

In raising these questions, answers are sought from the staff directly involved and, if possible, from the guests. Managers are not always as well informed as they ought to be, and part of the benefit of blueprinting is simply to obtain agreement on what is and what ought to be happening.

Value Chain Analysis

While blueprinting looks at each major product in detail, **value chain analysis** takes a broad perspective by considering the portfolio of hospitality products in terms of its capacity to enhance competitive positions. Unlike blueprinting, where the primary focus is on the details of service provision to the guest, value chain analysis focuses on where value is created within the hospitality business and provides a way of thinking about competitors and the search for competitive advantage.[12] The central concern of value chain analysis is the search for a distinctive ability to create value for guests by offering either lower prices for a similar level of benefit or greater benefits for the same price.

Competitive advantage stems from effective differentiation and a strong relative cost position, both of which have their origin in the skills and resources in the particular set or chain of activities that a firm performs. Differentiation for a major hotel may flow from such elements as a preferred location, talented service staff, information systems, creativity and persistence in selling hotel services, or the reliable quality of services offered. Cost advantage may stem from effective cost management systems, standardization in service design, good layout of physical facilities, a team-based commitment to productivity, or network links that provide access to services of specialists at lower cost.

The key question is: Does the existing or proposed product range fully exploit the sources of competitive advantage? To answer, we need a systematic way of identifying sources of differentiation and relative cost position within the business; in short, we need value chain analysis.

A value chain divides a company into its strategically relevant activities so that the behavior of costs and the existing and potential sources of differentiation

Exhibit 4   Hospitality Value Chain

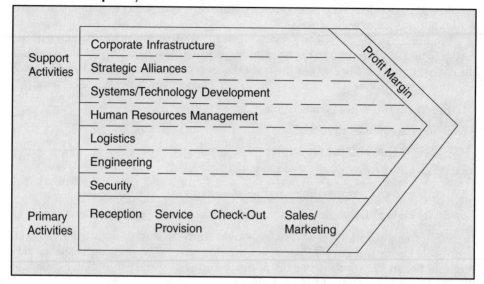

can be understood. A strategically relevant set of activities for a hotel is shown in the hospitality value chain shown in Exhibit 4. In this value chain, primary activities are those directly concerned with the marketing and delivery of hospitality products to guests. Support activities back up the primary activities by ensuring security; establishing and managing the flows of information, people, and resources; contributing innovative products, systems, and technologies; establishing and maintaining strategic alliances within tourism and hospitality networks; and providing overall strategic and operational management. Within each of these primary and support activities are the detailed activities that together build value into the hospitality services provided. The profit margin, then, is the difference between the total cost of performing the services offered by the firm and the price that guests are willing to pay for them.

The kinds of detailed activities that generate value in a major hotel are shown in Exhibit 5. The list is not comprehensive, but rather points to activities where value-adding or cost-reducing changes could be considered as part of an overall evaluation of the product offer. The hospitality products offered by a hotel draw on these activities to varying degrees. They will be successful to the extent that each product offers either a competitive edge valued by guests or a relative cost advantage, giving guests either additional benefits or lower prices.

The differentiation factors that generate uniqueness include those listed in Exhibit 6. A relative cost advantage may accrue from a similar set of factors as seen in Exhibit 7.

Customer Value Analysis

Why is it that some restaurants or hotels do better than others? Basically, guests believe that they get better value from the businesses they patronize. In making

Exhibit 5   Detailed Value Chain for Major International Hotel

Activity	Examples—Value-adding, cost-reducing options
Reception	Queue management Baggage handling Car parking Room allocation and choice—upgrade options Managing the guest mix
Service Provision	Executive/club service options Room service Housekeeping flexibility Business center In-room facilities Retailing outlets in hotel
Check-out	Express systems Baggage handling Car return Taxi, coach, airport, train links
Sales/Marketing	Personal selling Group sales Public relations Advertising—media, agency Direct mail Web site
Security	Information display/provision to guests Emergency procedures In-room security—room access limits Security in grounds, car parks
Engineering	Air-conditioning Energy management systems Elevator operations Noise levels
Logistics	Transport systems Purchasing systems Inventory management—assortment, depth
Human Resource Management	Ability to attract, retain talented staff Training, staff development Incentive/reward systems Team building
System/Technology Development	Reservation systems Customer/guest data bases Market research
Strategic Alliances	Tourism operators Retail outlets Theaters Major client loyalties Political connections
Management Infrastructure	Location Market positioning Culture Organizational design Business planning

Exhibit 6   Differentiation Factors

Policy choices: What a hotel offers and how the services are performed. This includes service design, skill and level of marketing activity, use of guest information systems, staff selection and training, team-building skills, quality of raw materials used, management of service quality, and use of new technology to expand offerings.

Linkages: Effective coordination of all activities within the hospitality firm; external linkages with suppliers, including tour operators, attraction operators, transport companies, and government agencies.

Timing: Being first to offer a service or to open at a new location often offers first-mover advantages. Being second, third, or later may enable a firm to avoid mistakes and position carefully to exploit changing tastes or unsatisfied needs.

Location: One of the most important factors in hospitality marketing.

Interrelationships: Shared facilities or resources with affiliated companies. May include sales force, computer networks, reservation systems, and joint advertising.

Learning and response: The capacity to not only learn quickly, but to respond effectively, which requires flexibility to change.

Integration: Integration into related attractions or destinations, ownership of transport links, ownership of reservations systems are examples. May also be a source of weakness.

Scale: Large scale may allow for tailoring unique responses to guest needs. Multiple locations and service diversity contribute to this.

Institutional factors: Includes such external forces as union and government relationships.

Based on Michael E. Porter, *Competitive Advantage: Creating and Sustaining Superior Performance* (New York: Free Press, 1985), pp. 124–127.

marketing decisions, therefore, hospitality managers should focus on guest value. Research tools that are beyond our scope here, such as PIMS (Profit Impact of Market Strategy), are available to help managers do so. In fact, PIMS research begins by constructing a customer value map that focuses on two important considerations: competitive advantage and value/cost ratios. The data can furnish valuable insights for product decisions.[13]

Research has clearly demonstrated the importance of relative quality and relative price in influencing profitability. High market share businesses are able to charge a higher relative price, based on higher relative quality, and achieve higher before-tax profit ratios. This reflects the following factors:

- Superior relative quality is achieved by skillful product/service design and the choice of markets.

- Superior relative quality enables a business to charge a higher relative price and gain in market share.

- Gaining market share translates into scale benefits with cost advantages.

Exhibit 7   Relative Cost Advantage Factors

Policy choices: Eliminate options or activities that do not contribute to differentiation and those for which cost exceeds buyer value; invest in technology that reduces costs; develop more effective purchasing or procurement systems; eliminate unnecessary frills.

Capacity utilization: Look for ways of stabilizing demand at high levels of capacity utilization.

Linkages: Exploit tradeoffs within service systems to reduce costs without reducing perceived value; just-in-time deliveries; coordinated service networks.

Timing: Exploit cost advantages accruing through first-mover (being first into a market with a new product) or late adopter options (gaining the advantage of learning from the mistakes of the first mover). Make full use of staff, supplier agreements. Or wait until new technology emerges, initiate system improvements. Time purchases to capture business cycle benefits.

Location: Look for labor cost reductions, lower logistic costs, tax holidays, regional incentives.

Interrelationships: Look for cost reductions through sharing facilities or resources with sister companies. May include sales force and computer networks.

Learning: Manage the learning curve to reduce costs as quickly as possible. Protect know-how to ensure that competitors miss out. Learn from competitors wherever possible. Actively experiment with new procedures or options. Measure everything.

Integration: Look for possibilities in de-integration. Could costs be reduced through buy-in of services?

Scale: Look for ways of obtaining scale benefits; emphasize activities where scale makes a difference.

Institutional factors: Look for ways around institutional barriers that may be long established and rigid.

Based on Michael E. Porter, *Competitive Advantage: Creating and Sustaining Superior Performance* (New York: Free Press, 1985), pp. 100–107.

In performing value analysis, it may be difficult to pull together the data needed and to do so as objectively as management might like. Information from guest research is an integral component because it focuses on the priorities and perceptions that guests bring to their choices. Although getting pertinent and timely data can be difficult, that is no reason to circumvent customer value analysis. In fact, the frank consideration of product positions, guest perceptions, and such factors as price and value can in and of itself be most revealing and useful.

Product Life Cycle Analysis

Product life cycle analysis is concerned with what happens to hospitality products over time, from their initial formulation to life in the marketplace. At each stage of the product's development, management has important choices to consider that affect the financial viability of the product. These choices, and the factors influencing them, tend to vary in a systematic way, responding to evolutionary change in markets, competitive pressures, and internal changes in the hospitality enterprise itself. From a strategic point of view, where long-term product innovation is essential for business survival, management choices regarding innovative ideas are of central importance.

Let's examine the life cycle for hospitality products in greater detail. The following stages may be considered in product planning.

1. Development

2. Pre-launch

3. Introduction

4. Growth

5. Maturity

6. Decline

Development. The development phase begins with a new concept or idea. This idea may come from a variety of sources—for example, staff, guests, or a careful analysis of the opportunities or threats raised by such important factors as changing market demand, the emergence of new technologies, government developmental initiatives, or competitive challenge. Whatever the source, experience suggests that successful innovations flow more readily from a large pool of ideas than from a limited or restricted pool; the more ideas that are presented, the more likely it is that a sustained flow of potential innovations will emerge. Since most ideas fail to win acceptance at the early screening stage (where commercial viability is assessed), it is critical to begin with a broad idea base.

Once an idea has passed through the initial screening, it enters a developmental stage where it is fleshed out in detail and subjected to market tests to optimize design, pricing, and other critical choices. Sometimes market testing involves extensive and sophisticated market research. The development of Courtyard by Marriott is a classic example in which sophisticated statistical analysis was used in surveys of potential guests to guide design priorities and base pricing on perceived benefit. Sometimes the process involves experimentation, as in the development or modification of menus where experiments help pinpoint guest reaction to alternative menus. The results help with estimates of demand and the effects of price alternatives.

Toward the end of this stage, a detailed business plan will usually be constructed that explores the financial consequences of the proposed development, looking at capital needs, rates of return, and risks.[14]

Pre-launch. The pre-launch phase begins when product development is completed and a firm commitment is made to proceed. This phase may not be needed for many hospitality products in which the link between commitment and action is straightforward, such as the addition of a menu item or a new service concept that is easily implemented. However, for major projects such as opening a new hotel or restaurant, a pre-launch period of two or more years can be filled with intense activity as partners are identified and sold on the concept, financing is arranged, construction is completed, the market is prepared for the new venture, and detailed operational planning is completed.

During this phase, full details of the proposed marketing strategies need to be worked out, including the choice of markets, the scope of the product offer, pricing schedules, initial selection and development of marketing distribution networks, and a preliminary outline of the promotional, selling, and advertising plans. Much will depend on the mix of markets to be served. For a convention hotel, the corporate market will play a major role; it is important to identify potential clients and, if possible, involve them in detailed facility design or specification. For international tourists, contacts with major wholesalers will play a major role and, like the convention business, require long lead times to gain commitments for the opening year. If the incentive market is important, then meeting space may not be as crucial, but creativity in the development of attractions linked to the hotel may be vital.

Once this basic planning is completed, the next few months (perhaps even 12 months before opening) will see the emphasis shift to building local contact networks and gaining opening year commitments. The visible evidence of construction at this stage helps to convert hesitant customers. Operational planning now becomes feasible as the issues become clearly defined. Operating systems need to be tested, links to major reservation networks opened, staff roles defined, training completed, advertising placed, and sales teams placed in action.

Toward the end of this stage, a "soft opening" is often possible, where guests are received so that operating procedures can be thoroughly tested. Invitations may be issued to local government, business, and tourism leaders to visit the property and see staff and facilities at work. If all goes well, the official opening follows.

Although our picture of the pre-launch procedure is geared to the opening of a new hotel, much the same story can be told for a major restaurant, resort, or other hospitality venture.

Introduction. In the introduction phase, the product offer is implemented, resources are committed, and staff are working hard to attract and satisfy guests under new, often difficult circumstances. Both guests and staff may be experiencing the product for the first time. Unanticipated operational difficulties will emerge and need to be quickly resolved. Unforeseen opportunities may arise that can often be turned to advantage. As the introduction proceeds, budgets will need to be rethought, staff skills developed still further, and systems redesigned. This is a learning phase, where experience is the teacher.

This phase may be a period of intense activity as guests try the new service and form initial opinions of quality and price. In most cases, there are competitive challenges, and guests have the option of visiting competitors. It is at this stage that the initial identification of major target markets and design of the product offer are put to the test. The product must meet the targeted guests' expectations, which are often shaped by the pre-launch and introductory advertising and promotions. The major objective in this phase is trial, followed (it is hoped) by favorable word-of-mouth publicity.

When new products are in the idea, development, and pre-launch phases—the "paper phases"—the associated costs tend to be relatively modest. Once products are launched, however, both the costs and attendant risks rise dramatically. In the introduction phase, sales are just beginning, meaning that limited revenues are generated while substantial costs are usually incurred. Up-front investment is required. Consider the hundreds of millions of dollars involved in introducing the new Las Vegas Bellagio Hotel with its casinos, restaurants, recreational, lodging, and parking facilities. Or think about the sizeable investment needed to launch a new Hard Rock Cafe. Regardless of the attention given to the development and pre-launch phases, substantial risks may be involved in putting a new hospitality product on the market.

Since new product introductions are so risky, it is very important to monitor how well new products are doing. When new product results are below expectations, the decision of whether to stay the course and incur further costs or to abandon the new product, limit losses, and move on can be a difficult one. Sometimes, managers give up too early. Other times, they stay with the new product too long. When failure occurs, the earlier in the introduction phase that it is recognized and dealt with, the better. When new products are abandoned, it is important to determine the reasons for failure and to learn from them. Sometimes, perfectly good product concepts fail because of inadequate or ineffective marketing support. Other times, the product concept itself is poor.

Apart from the need to attract prospective guests, the introduction phase is critical to the internal marketing to staff and network partners. They need to know how the product is doing, what is working and what is not, and which contributions are highly valued. Above all, it must be remembered that mistakes are not forever!

Growth. Assuming guests accept the initial product offer, the growth phase develops. This may become clear quite quickly if the concept is an immediate success and repeat business begins to build. However, it is also possible that the product offer will have a very short lifetime. Examples include various fads, some forms of ethnic and diet cuisine, and locations that are popular for a brief period and then decline rapidly. It is not always easy to decide exactly what markets are attractive (as distinct from those sought initially), and whether profitable repeat business is likely. In this regard, good guest records (addresses from a register, phone bookings for a restaurant, or car registration numbers) or simply asking guests about themselves and their expectations can help.

Assuming that repeat business is beginning to build in ways that are consistent with the initial planning, management may emphasize building longer-term relationships with key target markets, pricing to achieve penetration, strengthening distributor relationships, and the refining the product offer. Since cash flow is likely to be strongest in this phase, it may be the right time to introduce the next round of product innovation, remembering the long lead times that can occur between a new hospitality idea and its implementation.

Maturity. During the maturity phase, market growth begins to slow and a period of superficial stability begins that can sometimes continue for many years. The stability is superficial because behind-the-scenes competition is likely to be intense as prices are trimmed, margins decline, cost pressures mount, profits are squeezed, and competitors seek to define niche markets and differentiate themselves from others. While some companies will survive and remain successful by implementing a distinctive service strategy, others will fail, reflecting their complacency or lack of insight into, and willingness to do, what has to be done. Innovation and outstanding guest relations, achieved through the delivery of breakthrough service, are among the means of coping with competitive pressures in the mature phase of the life cycle.

Decline. The final phase is one of decline, and the result is either closure or rebirth of a product or a business in a new form, sometimes under completely new ownership. This is quite common in the restaurant business, where new restaurants often replace those that failed. New owners may succeed with a new concept. That was the case in South Florida where a failing family-type chain restaurant was reinvented as a successful diner, and a failed fish restaurant was transformed into a successful Greek restaurant by simply copying the offer of a nearby competitor.

This six-stage life cycle can help managers estimate sales, revenues, costs, and returns over time. A typical pattern for such flows is shown in Exhibit 8. Note the losses during the initial phases, the rise in profits during the growth phase, and the cap on sales and profits at maturity.

The product life cycle presents a general idea of what often occurs. The duration of each phase varies greatly—from many years or even decades for major hotel projects, to months or weeks for short-term packaged product concepts or menu items. Some products will compress or skip phases, moving (for example) directly from introduction to decline. The nature of market pressures exerted in each phase also varies widely. Competition may become intense during the introduction if the concept is easily matched, or may be minimal until maturity if the product is protected by location, networking, patents, or other factors that inhibit competitive matching. Managers must not consider these evolutionary patterns as foreordained. They are merely general tendencies resulting in patterns that can be useful in understanding hospitality innovations.

The lesson for management is that strategic choices must be made as markets change and companies shift their competitive positions. Choices must reflect the essential logic of the need to match strategy with environment and capability with strategy. Regardless of any caveats, the preceding patterns suggest the kinds of action that might be considered as a market evolves and product situations change.

Brands in the Product Decision

Effective brand management seeks ways of building the value of the brand name so that it will acquire a life and appeal of its own.[15] Well-known and accepted brands draw guests on the basis of the product offer that is embodied in their service strategy. For the guests, strong brands can simplify the choices that have to be made and increase the satisfaction derived from a visit. For example, a stay at the Waldorf-Astoria or the Plaza Hotel in New York is, for many people, a memorable

Exhibit 8   Hospitality Product Life Cycle Chart

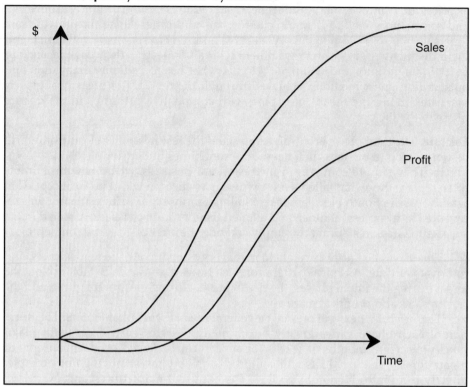

experience simply because of the power of the brand name and the reputation that goes with it. For the hospitality firm, a strong brand can bring many benefits: it increases the effectiveness of marketing programs, especially when entering new locations or offering new packages; it enhances brand loyalty, reducing the likelihood that many guests will try something different; it "buys time" to respond when competitors innovate; and it can lead to increased margins through premium pricing and reduced marketing costs. Well-accepted brands also provide an opportunity for growth through brand-extension programs, such as merchandising products that display the brand name prominently. They increase market power in dealing with travel wholesalers, incentive packagers, and other channel members and provide a competitive barrier to those firms going after the same market segments.

Many hospitality businesses have developed multiple brands for their product offers, aiming them at several different market segments. Marriott has developed Fairfield Inn for the budget market and Courtyard for the midprice segment, while Holiday Inn has introduced the Holiday Inn Crowne Plaza as its up-market brand. Whether it is better to develop distinct names or to use one common brand (e.g., Hyatt) is still an open question. The strength of a brand, however, depends on:

- Brand loyalty

- The extent of brand awareness among members of key market segments

- Perceptions of quality embodied in the brand's service strategy

- The appeal of ideas or associations linked with the brand

- The use of proprietary brand assets such as trademarks (the Golden Arches) and distribution channel linkages

Each of these factors requires continuous investment of marketing resources if brands are to be maintained as valuable assets. In this sense, expenditures on marketing are both current costs and investments in the future of the business.

Concluding Comments

In this chapter, we have highlighted the complexity of the product decision in hospitality marketing. This is an area where marketing choices must reflect the strategic vision of management, translating this into the services and facilities that will be used every day to satisfy the wants of guests attracted to the business. The product includes both tangible and intangible elements and must deliver on both explicit and implicit promises. The hospitality product is almost always in a state of change, evolving in response to the changing needs of guests. It requires detailed thought in both design and execution, a keen awareness of the ways that value is created in the eyes of the guests, an understanding of the tradeoffs that guests make in their appraisal of their experience of the business, and an appreciation of the dynamics arising from the product life cycle.

Hospitality managers must ask various kinds of questions of any proposed hospitality product. Such questions as those below focus on creating value for guests and profits for the business:

- Is there a balanced offer of benefits that works for each of the crucial market segments?

- Has the emphasis been on relationships with guests rather than transactions?

- Does the hospitality product offer fit with the other dimensions of the market mix? Price? Distribution? Promotion?

- Is due attention given to those who have market power? Are the needs of those who can influence success or failure being satisfied?

- Have the company's capabilities to develop competitive advantage been maximized?

- Is the timing right?

- Is there a clear statement of service strategy and is it widely accepted within the business? Can it be translated into a strong brand?

Marketing is always about the real world and our ability to respond to the opportunities that continually emerge. Each of the preceding questions is part of a reality check. Since product decisions are central to hospitality marketing, the above considerations will automatically lead into the other areas of the marketing mix.

Endnotes

1. Quoted by Jim Sullivan and Phil Roberts, *Service That Sells! The Art of Profitable Hospitality* (Denver: Pencom Press, 1991).

2. *Belle Design and Decoration,* December–January 1996. See also "Ian Schrager, a Hotelier for Jaded Baby Boomers," *New York Times,* 19 July 1998, pp. B1, B9.

3. Angela Clarke, personal interview, Sydney, Australia, 1995.

4. Edward De Bono, *Serious Creativity* (London: HarperCollins, 1995).

5. Derek F. Abell, *Managing With Dual Strategies: Mastering the Present: Preempting the Future* (New York: Free Press, 1993).

6. Theodore Levitt, "Marketing Success Through Differentiation—of Anything," *Harvard Business Review,* January–February 1980, p. 85.

7. Richard Normann, *Service Management: Strategy and Leadership in Service Businesses* (New York: Wiley, 1984).

8. Leo M. Renaghan, "A New Marketing Mix for the Hospitality Industry," *Cornell Hotel and Restaurant Administration Quarterly,* April 1981, pp. 31–35.

9. Valarie A. Zaithaml, A. Parasuraman, and Leonard L. Berry, *Delivering Quality Service: Balancing Customer Perceptions and Expectations* (New York: Free Press, 1990).

10. Sarah Morse and Pamela Lanier, "Golf Resorts—Driving into the '90s," *Cornell Hotel and Restaurant Administration Quarterly,* August 1992, pp. 42–48.

11. G. Lynn Shostack, "Designing Services that Deliver" *Harvard Business Review,* January–February 1984, pp. 133–139.

12. Michael E. Porter, *Competitive Advantage: Creating and Sustaining Superior Performance* (New York: Free Press, 1985).

13. Robert D. Buzzell and Bradley T. Gale, *The PIMS Principles* (New York: Free Press, 1987).

14. A good example of this analysis is provided in George R. Overstreet Jr., "Profiles in Hotel Feasibility: A Case Study of Charlottesville, Virginia," *Cornell Hotel and Restaurant Administration Quarterly,* February 1989, pp. 8–19.

15. The following section is based on the work of David A. Aaker, *Building Strong Brands* (New York: Free Press, 1996).

Key Terms

blueprinting—an analytical tool that enables a service company to explore its products on paper and work out many of the problems before public exposure.

customer value analysis—an analytical tool that can be used to improve a product offer in terms of specific products as well as an overall portfolio.

hospitality product—a package or bundle of different services, including tangible and intangible elements and explicit and implicit promises, directed toward meeting the needs of targeted markets.

hospitality product offer—synonymous with the hospitality product, looked at from the guest point of view.

marketing mix—the means by which hospitality enterprises are linked to their target markets.

market offer—another term for the marketing mix, but looked at from the guest point of view.

product life cycle analysis—an analytical planning tool for hospitality product decision-making concerned with what happens to hospitality products over time.

service offer—a package or bundle of different services designed to meet the needs of targeted markets that is an essential part of a hospitality product.

total offer—synonymous with market offer.

value chain analysis—an analytical tool for product decision-making that breaks down a hospitality business into economically significant activities and then assesses the way in which each such activity contributes to cost and value.

Review Questions

1. How do hospitality products differ from products of other industries?

2. What are the three perspectives involved in making decisions about creating or modifying a hospitality product?

3. What is a hospitality product offer and why is it important?

4. How does the four-level approach to thinking about the hospitality product assist in designing a new product or modifying an existing one? Can you find examples of each of the four levels from a hospitality business that you are familiar with?

5. What is meant by "value in the eyes of the guests"? How might this differ from value as seen by management? What elements are involved in assessing the value of product offer components?

6. What is blueprinting and how does it differ from value chain analysis?

7. For what purposes might customer value analysis and product life cycle analysis be used and how do the two types of analyses differ?

8. What is the role of the hospitality product decision in the hospitality market offer?

9. On what factors does brand strength depend?

10. In making product decisions, what environmental factors need to be considered and why is a reality check recommended?

Internet Sites

For more information, visit the following Internet sites. Remember that Internet addresses can change without notice.

Club Med
http://www.clubmed.com

Delano Hotel
http://www.newhotels.com/delano.htm

The Inn at Essex
http://www.innatessex.com

ITT Sheraton
http://www.sheraton.com

Marriott International
http://www.marriott.com

McDonald's Corp.
http://www.mcdonalds.com

New England Culinary Institute
http://www.neculinary.com

Observatory Hotel
http://www.orient-express
hotels.com/pages/obmenu.htm

Plaza Hotel
http://www.hotel-plaza.com

Qantas Airways Limited
http://www.qantas.com

Ritz-Carlton Hotels
http://www.ritzcarlton.com

Savoy Hotel
http://www.hotel-savoy.com

Taco Bell
http://www.tacobell.com

Waldorf-Astoria Hotel
http://www.waldorf-nyc.com

Chapter 11 Outline

Distribution Mix: Hospitality Networks

"No matter how you put it together, we live in a networked world."
—Novell advertisement[1]

Hotels, restaurants, and travel agencies do not operate in isolation. They require the assistance and cooperation of many independent businesses, suppliers, agencies, and specialists. The institutions that deliver actual products and services to guests are parts of the marketing network for a hospitality enterprise. These networks assemble and make available hospitality offerings that meet guest needs and desires. Each network member depends upon the performance of others. Together, they constitute the **hospitality distribution network** of a hotel, resort, or other hospitality enterprise.

Consider the coordinated effort involved in developing a weekend tour of New York for Mrs. Cooper and the members of her local bridge club. The package includes two popular Broadway plays, a New York Philharmonic concert, a tour of the city and the harbor, dinners at the famous Windows on the World and Tavern on the Green restaurants, and an after-theater dessert at Sardi's. Mrs. Cooper read about the trip in the travel section of the *New York Times* and only had to call one phone number to sign up for the discounted total package.

This chapter addresses how such offerings are arranged, who creates attractive hospitality packages, and how a variety of products and services get from providers to guests.

Logic of Distribution Networks

Distribution networks span gaps—whether they be geographic, temporal, or informational—between hospitality entities and guests. For example, networks can bring geographically distant guests closer to hospitality providers. Networks can increase guest knowledge about available hospitality alternatives. Similarly, networks facilitate the transfer of hospitality offerings to guests. By overcoming such gaps, distribution networks help provide better service to guests.

Hospitality managers are challenged to create seamlessly functioning distribution networks that make hospitality products and services accessible and attractive to guests. Three basic principles underlie successful network development. First, independent businesses are better able to serve guests through cooperation than by operating on their own. Second, by eliminating or reducing some

Exhibit 1 Communications Via Individual Efforts

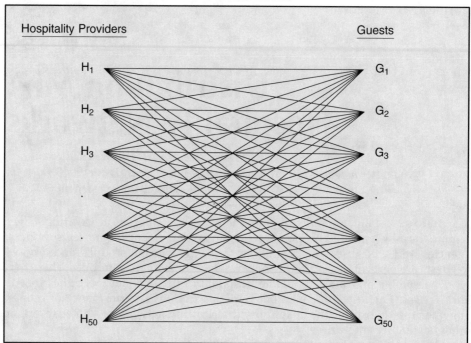

activities, productivity and efficiency may be increased. For example, costs may be reduced and outputs increased. Third, by giving up some independence and cooperating as a member of a network, each entity gains more than it would by going it alone.

The creation and management of such distribution networks are integral parts of the hospitality marketing process. To create them, managers must first identify businesses that are willing and able to distribute hospitality products and services. Once found, the terms of business must be accepted by all involved in the network.

In this chapter, we focus on the *distribution network,* a broader term and concept than the more commonly used *distribution channel* or recently used *supply chains.* We do this to emphasize the complex distribution arrangements and degree of cooperation necessary in hospitality that go well beyond most of the usual distribution decisions discussed in many marketing books.

Exhibits 1 and 2 help visualize some of the benefits associated with developing effective distribution networks. Suppose that 50 providers were each attempting to distribute their hospitality offerings or reservations services to 50 guests. The resulting net of distribution contacts would appear as indicated in Exhibit 1—very messy, with needless duplication of effort. Now suppose that some distribution intermediary, or central system, is introduced to aid in the distribution flow. The resulting net of distribution contacts is greatly simplified, as seen in Exhibit 2; this is the case when joint reservation systems or tour operators are introduced.

Exhibit 2   Communications with a Supporting Institution

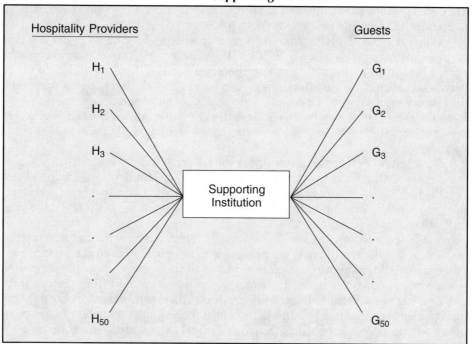

Distribution Networks

As we have already mentioned, distribution networks consist of a number of independent or related organizations that meet specified criteria working together so that the products and services of a hospitality enterprise are effectively and efficiently delivered to guests. Despite their importance, distribution networks are a neglected area of hospitality marketing. Although distribution activities lack the appeal of advertising, selling, promotion, or merchandising, they offer significant opportunities for differentiating hospitality products and services, for increasing profitability, and for outperforming competitors. Hospitality distribution activities are worthy of serious management attention.

Distribution networks consist of systems of relationships among the various independent institutions that carry out hospitality distribution functions. Networks may be highly structured, well-organized systems, such as chains, or loose coalitions and informal affiliations. Whatever the case, networks assemble and disperse hospitality products and services, bridge gaps between hospitality providers and guests, and supply guests with the hospitality offerings that meet their needs. They are referred to by such terms as affiliations, referral groups, or consortia. They offer many of the advantages of franchises but the participating businesses keep their own names. A hospitality offering such as a vacation package, for example, may require the coordinated efforts of a host of independent businesses—hotels, motels, restaurants, airlines, ships, rail and bus companies, travel agencies, rental car agencies, credit card companies, food and beverage suppliers, and laundry outlets among many others. Managers are challenged to develop each of these entities into a smoothly functioning network.

Wholesalers and retailers are the principal actors in hospitality networks, and participants may play one or both roles. **Wholesalers** assemble hospitality packages, often from many different suppliers, and make them available to other network participants. **Retailers**, including hotels, motels, bars, and restaurants, deal directly with guests. Of course, wholesalers, which include agents, may perform retailing activities when they deal directly with guests. Similarly, retailers may perform some wholesaling activities by assembling and brokering hospitality packages.

Distribution in a hospitality context differs considerably from distribution in the context of tangible manufactured products. Unlike laundry soap and breakfast cereals, hospitality products and services do not physically move from manufacturers to wholesalers to retailers and finally to consumers. In hospitality, the provider may serve as the manufacturer, wholesaler, and retailer. Furthermore, in product-based retailing, the supplier is usually separated from the customer by the retailer. In hospitality, the customer or guest is inseparable from the service provider. If not sold, moreover, hospitality products and services typically cannot be stored; an unsold hotel room, for example, cannot be stored in inventory until demand increases. Because hospitality products and services also involve a strong human element, are often produced and consumed simultaneously, and are combined with many other products (airplanes, rental cars, resorts, golf courses, etc.), they result in unique distribution situations that require variations of the usual considerations of marketing channels.

With such complexity, one wonders why managers should bother to form networks of independent businesses rather than perform all distribution activities in-house. Although it sometimes pays to bring certain activities in-house, such as reservation systems or rental car services, the costs of supporting in-house distribution activities are often prohibitive. As members of a network, specialists can spread their costs over a broad clientele, thereby reducing costs to those clients. In turn, individual enterprises can use their resources more effectively because they do not need to tie resources up in distribution activities. As part of a network, each entity can do what it does best and everyone benefits. Some of the many functions network members may perform include:

- Assisting with finances.

- Providing market access.

- Furnishing market knowledge.

- Generating low-cost sales contacts.

- Giving market coverage over a wide area.

- Furnishing low-cost distribution.

- Assembling assorted hospitality offerings.

- Offering special guest services.

Exhibit 3   Direct and Indirect Ways of Contacting Guests

Direct	Indirect
• Mail	• Franchisees
• Telephone	• Consortia
• Fliers	• Reservation Networks
• Advertisements	• Affiliates
• Coupons	• Representatives
• Lodging and Food Establishments	• Incentive Houses

Direct and Indirect Channels

Within a distribution network, hospitality providers use both direct and indirect channels to reach their guests. **Direct channels** consist of only two participants, the hospitality provider and the guest. Direct mail to potential customers is one example of a direct channel. In contrast, **indirect channels** involve **intermediaries** such as travel agencies, reservation networks, consortia, affiliates, and sales representatives. Indirect channels facilitate interactions between hospitality providers and guests and assist in various distribution activities. Exhibit 3 notes some of the more common direct and indirect ways to reach guests.

Direct channels are often enticing because they appear to be simple and manageable. To be effective, however, they require know-how and a commitment of resources, including people and finances. Because many hospitality providers do not possess the requisite assets, indirect channels are most commonly used.

Designing Distribution Networks

Designing hospitality distribution processes involve a considerable investment of time and other resources. But the payoffs from developing an effective network may include reduced costs, increased guest satisfaction, and significant competitive advantage. Even when the result of management assessments of distribution activities results in few changes, the very analysis of this critical aspect of hospitality marketing is valuable.

Exhibit 4 presents an overview of the kinds of considerations and elements management must consider in designing a hospitality distribution network. Of prime importance are the wants, needs, and expectations of guests and the market opportunities they portend. A number of company concerns are germane, such as the use of direct versus indirect channels, the degree of control desired, the resources available, market coverage, and ease of market entry. Such concerns are matched with both internal and external alternatives available in arriving at effective organizational arrangements.

Exhibit 4   Hospitality Distribution Network: Design Considerations

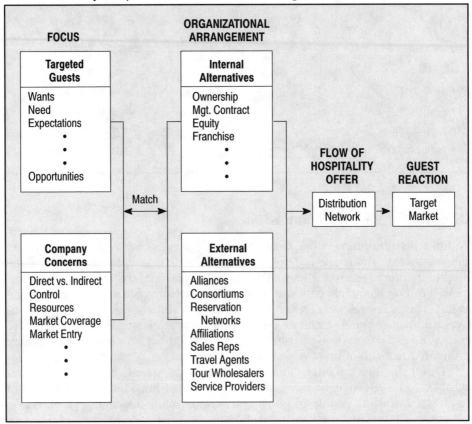

Design Steps

There are six steps in designing an effective hospitality distribution network.

1. *Determine What Guests Want.* Determine when and how guests want hospitality products and services, not just the kind they want. This involves grouping guests into market segments, selecting target segments, and focusing on how to reach them. Consider what guests are willing to pay for. If they want 24-hour availability but are not willing to pay for it, then the issue is moot. Other considerations include determining how far to decentralize services in order to reach guests, deciding upon the variety of offerings, specifying purchase size (group versus individual sales), and delineating markets.

2. *Consider Assembly and Distribution Options.* In order to relate distribution to the wants and needs of different market segments, managers can consider how hospitality products and services are usually made available and what distribution alternatives exist. Then they can investigate how to become more effective in dealing with various market segments. Can managers find service

specialists who can add value to current packages? Should they sell packages through new travel agents or other outlets, work with overseas tour wholesalers, improve access through reservation networks, or develop self-service alternatives through systems such as the Internet? These are the kinds of questions that should be raised. To succeed, managers cannot be tied to current practices, but must consider possibilities.

3. *Conceptualize the Ideal Hospitality Distribution System.* Although the ideal is not likely to be attainable, available, or cost-effective, managers should nevertheless consider their ideal distribution network. Considering the ideal can often highlight neglected areas of the distribution network and point out activities that can be improved.

4. *Evaluate Realistic Alternatives.* Network managers must focus on the realities of developing a market-driven hospitality distribution network by considering both management's objectives and company constraints as well as guest desires. Issues to evaluate include whether distribution will be direct or indirect, the types of network participants available, the networks or channels used by competitors, poorly performing network activities, and areas for improvement. Both ideal and realistic alternatives can be compared with current distribution networks. The degree to which the real situation meets the ideal determines the network's overall health. Gaps provide management with opportunities to make adjustments and changes.

5. *Design and Implement the Distribution Network.* Once gaps have been identified between the current network and the ideal, specialists must be found to join the network and overcome these gaps. New network participants can add significant value to the network, help plan future activities, and keep the network members informed of effective actions, opportunities, and threats. The distribution system should be adjusted for current realities, and decisions should result in the most practical distribution network. Sometimes, parts of the existing system may have to be scrapped or modified, and entirely new alternatives may have to be put into place.

6. *Monitor the Performance of Distribution Networks.* Distribution networks should be monitored to determine their performance levels and any needed adjustments. While networks are not as readily changed as other aspects of marketing, nevertheless they can be adjusted over time to meet changing conditions. As conditions change, the performance of network functions shifts among the members of the network. Some members may take on more responsibility while others may retrench and new members may be introduced. Hotels, for example, may assume more of the facilitating or packaging functions previously delegated to outside specialists. Conversely, functions such as food preparation and reservations, formerly performed in-house, may be contracted to outside suppliers.

Distribution Design Pitfalls

Unfortunately, hospitality marketers commonly make the mistake of letting networks evolve without a plan. Networks seem to grow like weeds, becoming messy and imbalanced. They exist for a long time and take on a life of their own. The following five pitfalls should be avoided in designing and managing hospitality distribution networks:

1. *Overemphasizing Products and Services.* The physical aspects of hospitality systems—such as air conditioning, refrigeration, heat, televisions, telephones, faxes, exercise facilities, parking, swimming pools, cleaning and laundry services, and security—easily and understandably lead to an overemphasis on hospitality products and services in network design. Managers conclude that better networks result from minimizing the costs of these features. Such a limited perspective, however, tends to ignore, to the detriment of all involved, the value-adding opportunities that arise from dealing with the needs and objectives of both guests and individual network members.

2. *Network Myopia.* Individual network members may ignore their roles as members of a larger network dedicated to satisfying guest wants and needs. They may function only for their own convenience and satisfaction, to achieve their own limited objective, rather than for those of guests and the total network. Consider the unfortunate situation that occurred at a Grand Canyon property. While guests were awakened in time to see the magnificent 5 A.M. sunrise, restaurants did not open until 6:30 A.M. Guests who wanted coffee were told that the restaurants were not open and that coffee was not available anywhere in the whole complex. Nothing was done to accommodate their needs.

3. *Physical Property Dominance.* Managers often pay attention to the flow of products and services through networks, allowing them to overshadow other important factors such as information, promotion, risk, assortment, and ownership. Networks must be understood as providing many critical benefits for both guests and network members in addition to dealing with the flow of products. For example, networks facilitate critical information flows (such as reservations and the advertising of travel packages), spread risks over a number of network members, and, as a result of cooperative efforts, extend desired services to guests very conveniently. When management focuses on physical property, some very important distribution considerations can be overlooked.

4. *Dominance of a Single Network Member.* Sometimes one or two members in a network receive a preponderance of consideration and attention. A very prestigious hotel in a consortium or a profitable restaurant within a chain may use its power for its own benefit rather than that of the overall network. This can undermine the cooperative spirit of the network, create significant problems, and work to the detriment of the whole network and other members.

5. *Static Perspective.* Distribution networks should not be perceived as static entities. They require periodic evaluation and change. Network needs change as hospitality markets change, as the dynamics of competition shift, and as new hospitality products and services appear. Distribution networks must be dynamic to effectively link hospitality providers with changing guest wants and needs.

To be managed effectively, distribution networks should be planned and evaluated regularly. The tasks of each member should be clearly specified and network members should be sufficiently motivated so that they perform to their potential. Managers should determine which network members are performing efficiently and effectively and which are not.

Hospitality providers must work hard to gain and maintain the cooperation of network members. Because network members are independent businesses, they serve several providers and have their own goals and objectives. They are not mere extensions of one hospitality provider's business. Effective network management emphasizes the complementary goals of all the participating businesses, reduces conflict to the extent possible, and develops a seamlessly functioning network.

Distribution network design has far-reaching consequences for hospitality marketing. Distribution decisions have a great impact on other hospitality marketing variables. Once put into place, networks are not readily changed. They usually remain unchanged longer than most other elements of the marketing mix, such as price, advertising, or products and services. Thus, distribution choices have longer-term effects. Network decisions, therefore, should reflect both current situations and management assessments of future needs.

Organizing Distribution Networks

Hospitality businesses may use various means to assemble and distribute their products and services. They may own network participants partially or completely, franchise, enter into management contracts, or form alliances. Each of these alternatives may, in turn, take a number of different forms. Alliances, for example, may be instituted as consortia, affiliations, reservation systems, sales representatives, tour operators, incentive houses, and travel agents. As a result, network decisions are complicated. For example, although restaurants and hotels may have familiar names such as Pizza Hut or Sheraton, most of these businesses are not owned by the respective companies identified. Instead, they may be owned by builders, developers, or franchisees. Some hospitality entities, like Marriott, may even franchise their name to other hospitality companies. Many are simply operated by management companies. To add to the complexity of network development, various formats may appear within the same company.

Exhibit 5 lists some of these alternatives along with the degree of control and resource commitment involved. As the exhibit shows, network ownership gives the greatest degree of control, but also requires the greatest commitment of resources. A hospitality enterprise such as a hamburger or pizza chain may therefore expand more rapidly through franchising because it requires a lesser commitment of resources. However, it also involves losing a degree of control over such important factors as quality control, design, layout, and market coverage. Let's look at each of these organizational alternatives.

Ownership

Ownership provides the greatest degree of control and assures quality maintenance. Because it best protects and conserves brand value and company reputation, ownership can maintain the integrity of a hospitality offering.

Exhibit 5   Distribution Network Alternatives

		Management Contract		
Alliances	Franchising	Non-Equity	Equity	Ownership

Degree of Control, Risk, and Resources Required

Least ◄──────────────────────────────────► Most

Owners are well aware that success depends upon effective distribution. To be successful, a property needs representation in targeted market areas, whether national or international, primary or secondary. But achieving effective distribution means that enterprises have to develop their reputations. Some businesses may choose to do this in local markets first and then expand regionally, nationally, or internationally. When the right market, whatever it may be for a particular business, is cultivated first, other markets may be targeted subsequently.

Sometimes it is impossible to succeed in a market segment without representation in specific locations. Meetings and conventions are often held in major markets such as Las Vegas, Orlando, New York, San Francisco, and Chicago. To compete in the convention business, hotels seeking the benefit of ownership control must be represented in these areas. Similarly, those involved with the incentive travel market may require a presence in exotic locations like Hawaii, Hong Kong, Singapore, or Bali.

The difficulties of developing distribution networks increase in direct proportion to ownership requirements. Ownership necessitates investments that often exceed company resources and capacities. It is much easier to expand a business through affiliations or franchises. Mixing ownership with other distribution formats, such as franchising, while fostering direct distribution contacts, can also present problems. The quality of products and services is often different in a mixed property, disappointing and even alienating some guests. Yet some hotels and restaurants with very demanding standards, such as Ritz-Carlton and McDonald's, have successfully maintained worldwide product uniformity.

Management Contracts

For control purposes, particularly the maintenance of quality standards, managing is the next best format to ownership. With **management contracts**, companies operate a property for a fee, which may be based on gross sales with performance-related bonuses. However, management companies are usually interested in much more than money; they often seek a physical presence in certain markets in order to establish their brand name. Hotel companies such as Westin or Peninsula may contract to run hotels in markets such as Malaysia, Japan, or the United States. In this way, they gain representation and recognition without ownership.

Sometimes management companies will assume an ownership position, although it is usually a minority one. Much depends upon the relevant tax laws, perceived future property value, risks, a company's financial position, and its basic objectives.

Problems result when products and services are not commensurate with the brand's image. Difficulties arise and guests grow dissatisfied when owners are unwilling to invest necessary funds into managed properties, resulting in run-down properties or reduced services. Even though the property is independently owned and controlled, such situations reflect unfavorably upon the brand name of the managing company.

Franchising

A powerful distribution strategy, **franchising** is one of the most widely used methods of developing hospitality distribution networks. Franchising permits another party (the franchisee) to sell products or services in the name of a specific company (the franchisor). For example, Kemmons Wilson developed the concept and name of Holiday Inn and then offered others the opportunity to use it for a fee. Companies like Holiday Inn Worldwide (now Hospitality Inn), Hospitality Franchise Systems, and McDonald's are recognized franchising leaders. Franchising allows hospitality companies with limited financial resources to increase geographic presence and add to their revenues and profits. Motels and fast-food chains have made particularly widespread use of franchising.

A licensing agreement between the franchisor and the franchisee outlines fees (often a percentage of sales), support systems, territorial rights, and other details of the business relationship. Sometimes a franchisee obtains exclusive rights to the franchisor's presence in an entire country or region. Some companies, such as Hospitality Inn and Hilton, rely heavily on franchising, while others franchise very little or not at all. The proportion of franchisees in a network varies by company. Much depends upon the company's outlook, the amount of control it desires, and whether franchisees will meet franchise standards.

Franchising has many advantages. It extends a company's reach, making its brand, products, and services available to more guests over a wider region. The more locations a company has, the greater its exposure to guests and the greater the chance to create brand loyalty over extended market areas. This in turn enhances the value of the brand name, and thus of the franchise itself. Similarly, franchising provides instant positioning in a market. The familiar brand is immediately recognized by guests who may be favorably predisposed to purchase its offerings.

Franchising eliminates many of the costs associated with ownership. Franchising provides lodging properties with a ready-made reservation network. Some franchisors have considerable sales forces that provide market exposure the franchisee could not otherwise afford. By representing many franchisees, sales teams can spread their costs. Some franchisors offer technical, operational, and financial support, including marketing, management, and training. McDonald's even has its own school—"Hamburger U." Other franchisors offer centralized commission handling for travel agents, toll-free numbers, group booking services, and one convenient sales representative for all of the property's needs.

Franchisors recognize that their ability to develop distribution networks depends upon available capital. In addition, conflicts can arise when franchisee profits are squeezed due to contractual obligations. For example, a franchisor may be the exclusive provider of a certain product for the franchisee, but the franchisee may be able to obtain a similar product, such as pizza dough or cheese, for a lower price from a competitor.[2]

A further difficulty with franchising is that the hospitality product or service may vary among franchises. Problems arise, furthermore, when a unit does not measure up to franchise standards. This often occurs when a hotel chain, such as Ramada or Radisson, takes over a property that has been operated under another name for several years. Guests may be troubled by variations within the same hotel group.

Strategic Alliances

Hospitality enterprises use many types of alliances, such as consortia, reservation networks, affiliations, and independent sales representatives to distribute their offerings. Many of these formats overlap so much that operationally they can be indistinguishable. Let us comment briefly on each of them and then consider some other important hospitality network members such as incentive organizations, travel agents, tour operators, and specialist service providers.

Consortia. A **consortium** consists of independently owned and operated properties that loosely join together to distribute and market their offerings. This distribution network combines the strengths of independent ownership with many of the advantages of chains. For example, Leading Hotels of the World and Preferred Hotels consist of independent properties aimed at a similar market. While they must meet certain requirements of the consortium, members function as independent entities and continue to exercise entrepreneurship and initiative. Consortium members may cooperate in such activities as promotions, merchandising, advertising, purchasing, and information and reservation systems.

Consortia have proven to be effective marketing networks. Combining member marketing efforts provides strength and clout while still permitting individuality and spreading the costs of advertising and reservations. However, consortia do not have the clout of formal chains.

Problems sometimes result from the variable quality and even flagrant violations of standards and policies among individual offerings and properties within a consortium. Although guests may realize that properties are not "cookie-cutter" duplicates of each other, they expect certain standards to be met. Unpleasant experiences with one member of a consortium may affect the other members. While potential members may be carefully screened, and standards can be clearly established, it is difficult to control independent members of a consortium.

Reservation Networks. Reservation networks and consortia overlap. **Reservation networks** refer to the common reservation facilities and procedures used by a number of individual properties. Fees are usually charged for each reservation. While a consortium may use a reservation network, reservation networks do not have the membership requirements, control, and various common policies of consortia.

Sophisticated reservation systems give customers around the globe convenient access to network members with one phone call. Chains like Hospitality Inn,

Sheraton, and Hilton have established their own reservation networks. For independents and small chains, however, it is more practical to become a member of a network and pay a fee per reservation.

Affiliations. **Affiliations** are voluntary links between hospitality properties and other properties for such mutually advantageous purposes as distribution and marketing. Among the common activities of affiliations are joint sales efforts, cooperative advertising campaigns, cooperative merchandising efforts, reservations, building rapid identification, entry into new markets, serving guests in markets where no properties are owned, and achieving better utilization of various facilities. Examples of affiliations include the unions of Clarion Hotels with Quality Inns and Mövenpick Hotels International with Radisson Hotels. Best Western is an affiliation of over 3,400 independent properties worldwide that operate under a common brand.

Sales Representatives. Some hotels and groups of hotels use independent sales representatives to distribute their offerings to various markets. In so doing, hotels no longer have to invest in and develop their own sales organizations, reservation networks, or marketing departments. Sales representatives permit small hotels to contact and cover markets they could not otherwise reach.

Hotels use sales representatives in many ways. They may perform the entire gamut of sales and/or marketing activities, essentially serving as the marketing department for client hotels. Hotels may use sales representatives to augment their own sales efforts in selected regions or markets. They may rely on them to perform a variety of marketing activities, including advertising, direct mail, public relations, and personal selling. Sales representatives may furnish information about hotel facilities, screen suitable hotels, serve as meeting planners, negotiate rates, and generally assist the hotel group. They represent a very flexible marketing resource that can serve in a variety of ways to meet hotel needs.

Sales representatives are usually paid on a retainer or fee basis. Fees for their services are commensurate with the functions performed and are usually paid when the group involved checks out of a hotel. By marketing a group of hotels rather than just a single hotel, sales representatives spread costs across a broader client base. Thus, they are able to offer cost-effective distribution for groups of hotels. Sales representatives can also perform marketing activities for the group that none of the hotels could justify economically on its own.

Travel Agents. Travel agents are probably the best-known hospitality network members. They are intermediaries who provide many travel services, including arranging tours, reserving hotel rooms and rental cars, obtaining visas, and furnishing information about international locales in addition to the normal booking of tickets. Travel agents usually receive a commission or set fee, paid by providers, for their services. In numbers and coverage, travel agents are the most pervasive of the distribution channel intermediaries. Operating at both wholesale and retail levels, their market includes not only individual travelers, but also groups, business travelers, and corporate and association meetings.

Since most travel agencies are small, they sometimes form alliances to give them the mass necessary to negotiate the best arrangements for their clients. Such arrangements afford access to commercial customers who frequently require travel services. Acting in consort, groups of agencies can gain significant concessions for customers.

Travel agents are information specialists. They are professionals who handle the increasingly complex travel decisions of both businesses and households. They depend upon sophisticated computer systems, such as Apollo and SABRE, for current information about airlines, hotels, and rental car agencies. As airlines change their fares and routes, and as markets become increasingly dynamic, travel agents are challenged to keep abreast of rates (a very trying and increasingly difficult task), amenities, locations, ground transportation, customs, health requirements, recreation facilities, and entertainment.

A recent study by the worldwide publication *Hotel & Travel Index* highlights the importance of travel agents in the United States.[3] The study examined the influence of U.S. travel agents on their clients' hotel selections. It found that 60 percent of domestic leisure travel clients asked for help in selecting a hotel and 23 percent of those who asked for help asked agents to name specific properties. For domestic business clients, 34 percent sought help and 42 percent asked for a specific suggestion; for international clients, 63 percent asked for help and 23 percent asked for suggestions.

Due to the travel agent's role in customer decisions, hotels that cooperate with travel agents can realize handsome dividends. By promptly paying commissions and by providing travel agency customers with special services, such as upgrades and complimentary food and beverages, hotels can increase both customer satisfaction and their chances of receiving high recommendations from travel agents. Some hotels have created the position of Director of Travel Agent Marketing supported by a Travel Agent Advisory Board. This individual ensures that travel agents are served by someone with the time and incentive to listen to their needs and to maximize their potential as network participants.

Familiarization (fam) trips sponsored by various nations and hotels offer travel agents first-hand exposure to facilities and attractions. When travel agents are impressed by their personal experience of a site, they will recommend particular hotels and locations to group and individual guests. Familiarization trips have paid handsome rewards for the economies of Singapore, Hong Kong, Bali, Hawaii, and Bangkok. The results are similar for hotels. Hilton, for example, introduced the "Hilton Fam Club" in 1992, a program that guaranteed travel agents 50 percent discounts on minimum rack rates at all Hilton properties.

Recently, travel agencies' profits, revenues, and margins have been under increasing pressure by airlines. Some airlines have capped the commissions they pay to travel agents at a dollar amount per ticket, such as $50, and/or have lowered the commission percentage. In addition, the same information technology that permits travel agents to better serve their clientele also encourages direct distribution. It enables customers to deal directly with airlines via the Internet and airlines and hotels to deal directly with customers and challenge traditional channels of distribution. For example, Delta Airlines has several offices in the Palm Beach, Boca Raton, and Fort Lauderdale area that sell tickets to the traveling public. They receive tremendous business in the winter season by offering special fares to seniors in the form of books of four to eight tickets; these sales do not require any commission to travel agents. Because of these changes, some travel agents may have difficulty staying in business while others will be forced to charge customers for formerly free services, thereby driving business away. Nevertheless, travel agents are still in a position to influence customers and pull products through the channel.

Tour Operators. Tour operators perform both wholesaling and retailing functions. As wholesalers, they purchase the accommodations and space in bulk that they then sell (retail) to their own customers. They buy space in hotels and restaurants; negotiate with airlines, bus companies, ships, and railroads; and develop and market travel packages to travel agencies and other channel members. They may deal directly with individual retailers. American Express, one of the largest and best-known tour wholesalers, performs retailing functions when it sells tour packages to individual guests; it often uses its charge card lists to contact individual guests directly.

Tour operators arrange special-interest tours for such groups as university alumni associations, professional organizations, sports teams, religious institutions, and high school groups. In making arrangements with hospitality providers, they perform wholesaling functions. They offer foreign and domestic tours for groups and usually prepare attractive and detailed brochures highlighting tour features, accommodations, sights, and meals. To reach their intended markets, they rely heavily upon direct mail. In such situations (when they deal with individual members of specific groups), they act as tour retailers.

The success of tour operators depends upon the capabilities and cooperation of network members. Tour operators may assume considerable risk when their tours do not sell well, as they may be stuck with a perishable inventory of hotel, airline, and restaurant space. In addition, tour operators often encounter cash flow problems, and the strict cancellation clauses of hospitality enterprises have left some tour members stranded—sometimes in foreign countries. There are many instances of consumers suffering from the unfulfilled promises of tour operators.

The tour operator's importance to other network members varies considerably by market. Some destinations and national sources account for a substantial part of the total wholesale business. In Australia, for example, the two largest Japanese wholesalers account for almost 40 percent of Japanese travel to Australia. The Japanese are the most important source of tourism in certain regions of Australia. One company operates exclusively in the Japanese market and has two customers who account for 70 percent of sales.[4]

Incentive Organizations. Incentive organizations are intermediaries that specialize in incentive reward travel. They cater to companies that use travel incentives as rewards for exceptional performance among salespeople, dealers, wholesalers, retailers, and employees.

Travel rewards have long been recognized as effective incentives, and companies are continually challenged to discover unique and exotic travel destinations that deliver hassle-free travel. Since conditions can change so readily in foreign travel and unforeseen problems can arise, hospitality enterprises need information and good foreign contacts to design and implement incentive packages.

Smoothly functioning distribution networks are integral to success in the incentive market—otherwise, both incentive companies and travel destinations suffer. Incentive organizations realize that they will be blamed if members of a distribution network do not perform satisfactorily, even though they are not directly involved in delivering hospitality offerings. Customers may choose different incentive houses unless each member performs as promised.

Hotels benefit greatly by being on the list of an incentive organization's preferred destinations. Business customers, however, pay for the service of incentive houses, not hotels. By consistently meeting or exceeding guest expectations, hotels will gain the approval of incentive organizations and may generate significant incentive business. Because it is both costly and time-consuming to perform the necessary activities to develop effective travel incentives, such as visiting and inspecting hotels, restaurants, vacation properties, and supporting facilities, incentive travel organizations are an enormous asset. As specialists, these organizations can spread their costs over a large client base. They can therefore make incentive travel packages not only more affordable, but also more enticing.

Specialist Service Providers. Specialist service providers include a wide variety of specialists such as advertising agencies, market research firms, government tourism offices, insurance specialists, transportation firms, attraction operators, tour guides, show business packagers, duty free shopping outlets, theaters, and cultural institutions. By using their creativity and imagination, these network participants extend the attractiveness of hospitality offerings for different market segments. For example, a show business packager in conjunction with business and government agencies in Ft. Lauderdale, Florida, has developed an annual air show in the late spring. It attracts performers and visitors from around the world, as well as more than one million guests. The cooperation of many network specialists is required for such a successful venture.

Push and Pull Strategies

Push and pull strategies increase the flow of hospitality offerings through distribution networks. With the **pull strategy**, guests are contacted directly and induced to request hospitality offerings. Hospitality providers stimulate guest demand so that guest requests "pull" offerings through the network. For example, French wineries promote their new Beaujolais wines each year with festivals and wine-tasting sessions. Their efforts create guest demand and the product is pulled through the distribution channel. As a result, hospitality businesses benefit through increased accommodation and restaurant sales. In this example, marketing activities of suppliers *outside* the hospitality network produce direct benefits for hospitality firms. Similarly, a resort may promote its offerings to a specific market segment and attract business that indirectly benefits other network participants.

Push strategies function in the opposite manner. In this case, network members are given incentives to sell a particular hospitality product or service to guests. The provider "pushes" the hospitality offering through the channel. Travel agents, for example, often receive special incentives to promote various travel packages and tours. Mexican breweries have offered Mexican restaurants monetary incentives to aggressively promote their beers. A wide variety of discounts, specials, and promotions capitalize on the push approach.

Managing Distribution Networks

Developing good working relationships within a distribution network is key to effective hospitality distribution management. Consider what each individual member receives from the network in the context of that member's perspective. What potential does the network offer for cooperation and participation? When members do not believe they are receiving a fair return for their contributions, cooperation diminishes, channel effectiveness declines, guests needs are not met, and guests become dissatisfied. The network loses distribution impact.

Network members should be chosen carefully, using a long-term perspective. Each member should understand its long-range benefits to the network. Agreements among network members should be in writing, and all network members should clearly understand the conditions and their responsibilities, as well as those of other members.

All members of a distribution network are rarely completely satisfied. The objectives of some network members may conflict with those of others. When conflicts arise, networks break down and members feel unrewarded or exploited. Compromise and negotiation can pave the way for cooperation. When conditions shift radically, network relationships must be reassessed to the satisfaction of all involved. Networks must operate on the basis of a win-win philosophy for all members and guests.

Effective management of hospitality distribution networks involves three major factors: recruiting and selecting network members, motivating them, and evaluating and adjusting operations. Recruitment is a continuous task because members drop out, markets change, and new conditions emerge. Key members of a distribution network will be enticed to join competing networks and there will always be network members, hopefully few, who do not function effectively and must be replaced. Effective network managers, therefore, should be prepared for turnover and have pre-screened alternatives available.

Network members must be continuously motivated. Those who design and implement marketing networks recognize the importance of such motivational devices as incentive trips, cash and product awards, bonuses, or performance awards. Incentives are effective means of getting network members to exert extra effort in distributing hospitality products and services. Motivational opportunities are limited only by company imagination and creativity. But motivational devices are not a substitute for effective network management. They cannot replace the personal attention necessary to gain member participation. Network managers who appreciate the efforts of network members and recognize their contributions will generate goodwill and motivate members to perform.

Networks and their members should be regularly evaluated and adjusted. Sales and profits attributable to network participants such as airlines and tour wholesalers should be determined. Hotels can monitor statistics about room sales, length of stay, and profitability. Restaurants can analyze the effectiveness of coupons, recommendations, and advertisements. Management can consider the breakeven point of business required from network members and payments made to them. Above all, guest satisfaction must be tracked. For unless guests are satisfied, hospitality entities may be better off on their own—operating without networks.

Concluding Comments

Hospitality providers require the assistance of many other independent businesses to deliver their products and services to guests. These businesses make up the distribution networks that assemble and make available hospitality offerings.

Distribution networks span gaps between hospitality businesses and their guests and facilitate the transfer of products and services between them. Cooperation among independent businesses results in better guest service, increased productivity and efficiency, and higher profits for the independent entities than they would achieve by going it alone.

Distribution networks consist of a number of independent organizations that meet specified criteria and work together so that hospitality products and services are delivered to guests efficiently and effectively. These networks may be highly structured and well organized systems, as in chains, or loose coalitions and informal arrangements. They comprise wholesalers and retailers and perform such functions as providing market access, furnishing market information, performing sales activities, assembling and packaging offerings, and performing a host of special guest services.

Hospitality providers use both direct and indirect channels to distribute their offerings. The design of effective distribution networks can involve a considerable investment of time and other resources. However, the payoffs include cost savings, increased guest satisfaction, and important competitive advantages. The steps in designing effective distribution networks include: determining guest wants and needs, considering distribution alternatives, conceiving the ideal network, evaluating realistic options, designing and implementing the network, and monitoring and adjusting the network as needed.

The organizational arrangements that hospitality businesses may use vary from complete to partial ownership, management contracts, franchising, and a variety of alliance and affiliation formats. Managers must carefully consider the benefits and drawbacks of each feasible alternative. The use of sales representatives, incentive organizations, travel agents, tour operators, and various providers of specialized services as distribution network members can extend the options and increase potential markets and profitability. The choice made depends on company resources, the degree of control desired, and the risk that the businesses are willing to take.

Developing and maintaining good working relationships among network members is critical to achieving effective distribution. Considerations should be given to what each member receives from the network. Network members should be chosen carefully with a long-term perspective in mind. However, conflicts are bound to arise, dissatisfied members will emerge, and compromises and negotiations will be necessary. Achieving seamless distribution requires good recruiting, selection, and motivation of network members, along with constant evaluation and adjustment.

Endnotes

1. *The New York Times Magazine*, 28 Sept. 1997, p. 11.

2. See Jeffrey L. Bradach, *Franchise Organization* (Boston: Harvard Business School, 1998) for extensive references to restaurant franchises and their management problems, particularly in systems where there is a mix of ownership.

3. Melinda Bush, "The Travel Agency Market is Key," *HSMAI Marketing Review*, Winter 1994, p. 11.

4. "Dependence and Uncertainty in Buyer-Supplier Relationships in a Cross-National Service Industry: The Case of Inter-Firm Relationships in Australia's Inbound Japanese Travel Market," Master of Commerce (Hons) thesis, Roger StG, March, University of New South Wales, 1995.

Key Terms

affiliations—voluntary links between hospitality properties and other businesses for mutual advantage in activities such as distribution and marketing.

consortium—a group of independently owned and operated hospitality properties that agree to form a loose coalition to distribute and market their offerings.

direct channel—a communications medium involving direct contact between the hospitality provider and the guest.

franchising—an agreement by an owner to allow the use of a name or business format by another business for the purpose of selling the product or service carrying that name or using that business format.

hospitality distribution network—a number of independent or related organizations, each with specific skills, that agree to work together to assemble and deliver hospitality products and services to guests in selected markets.

incentive organizations—intermediaries that specialize in incentive reward travel.

indirect channel—a communications medium between hospitality providers and guests involving intermediaries, such as travel agencies, reservation networks, consortia, affiliates, and sales representatives.

intermediaries—independent business concerns that operate as links between suppliers and guests, rendering services that add value to the guest, and who may or may not take title to the hospitality products involved.

management contract—an agreement in which one company agrees to operate a hospitality property for a fee, which may be based on gross sales with performance-related bonuses.

pull strategy—a marketing strategy in which guests are contacted directly and persuaded to request hospitality offerings.

push strategy—a marketing strategy in which network members are given incentives to sell a particular hospitality product or service to prospective guests.

reservation network—common reservation facilities and procedures used by a number of individual properties.

retailer—a seller of hospitality goods and services who deals directly with guests.

specialist service provider—a wide variety of specialists such as advertising agencies, market research specialists, government tourism offices, insurance specialists, tour guides, duty free shopping outlets, attractions, theaters, etc.

tour operators—organizations that plan, assemble, and market travel packages at both the wholesale and retail level, often purchasing accommodation and hospitality services in bulk.

wholesaler—assembles hospitality products, often from many different suppliers, and makes them available to other network participants.

Review Questions

1. Why do independent hospitality firms choose to be part of a hospitality distribution network?

2. Construct an example of a hospitality distribution network that involves a local hospitality business. Has this network changed over time? What factors might influence the structure and functions of a hospitality distribution network? Can you identify firms that play the role of wholesaler? Of retailer? What might the ideal hospitality distribution network for this business look like? Was the network planned or did it just evolve?

3. Under what circumstances would each of the following be part of a hospitality distribution network: airline; tourist attraction; theme park; government tourism agency; coach company; duty free shop; shopping mall?

4. What kinds of business might become part of a hospitality distribution network created by a cruise ship company? A major, up-market city restaurant? A tropical island resort?

5. What factors might be important to management of a hospitality business in choosing between building its own sales force and making use of independent sales representatives?

6. What are the advantages and disadvantages of franchising?

7. The power or influence that some members of a hospitality distribution network may be able to exercise is sometimes raised as a problem. In what way might this become a concern for an individual business that is part of such a network? Does this have wider social ramifications?

8. In what ways can travel agents be said to be information specialists?

Internet Sites

For more information, visit the following Internet sites. Remember that Internet addresses can change without notice.

American Express/Business Services
http://www.americanexpress.com/travelservices

Apollo
http://www.apollo.com

Best Western
http://www.bestwestern.com

Clarion Hotels
http://www.clarionhotel.com

Delta Airlines
http://www.delta-air.com

easySABRE
http://www.easysabre.com

Hamburger U
http://www.mcdonalds.com/careers/hambuniv/index.html

Hilton Hotels Corporation
http://www.hilton.com

Holiday Inn Worldwide
http://www.holiday-inn.com

Hotel & Travel Index
http://www.travel.net

ITT Sheraton
http://www.sheraton.com

Leading Hotels of the World
http://lhw.com

McDonald's Corporation
http://www.mcdonalds.com

Mövenpick Hotels & Resorts
http://www.movenpick-hotels.com

Pizza Hut
http://www.pizzahut.com

The Preferred Hotels of the World
http://www.preferredhotels.com

Quality Inns
http://www.qualityinn.com

Radisson Hotels Worldwide
http://www.radisson.com

Ritz-Carlton Hotels
http://www.ritzcarlton.com

Chapter 12 Outline

Pricing: Part of the Marketing Mix
    Example 1: Price Alone Is Not the Answer
    Example 2: Perceived Value Drives Price
    Example 3: Price Matters, but So Does Guest Loyalty
    Example 4: Pricing for a Specific Market Segment
Pricing and Guest Value Perceptions
Pricing: Six Basic Questions
    Creative Pricing
The Economics of Pricing
    Markets, Costs, and Volume
Psychological Factors and Guest Expectations
    Reference Pricing
    Competitive Pricing
The Unique Challenge of Pricing for Services
An Overall Pricing Policy
    Pricing Objectives
    Pricing Strategies
    Pricing Programs
    Pricing Tactics
Restaurant Pricing
Hotel Pricing
Concluding Comments

12

Pricing Mix: Strategies and Tactics

"The secret to success in the lodging business will be to provide guests with higher quality and better value at reasonable prices. Those who improve their price-value perception will tap into a nearly inexhaustible supply of new guests."

—Robert C. Hazard, Jr.[1]

PRICES HAVE a more direct and immediate impact on sales, profits, and guest reactions than any other hospitality marketing variable. They are visible, generate direct guest response, and can be adjusted readily to meet new situations. When used properly, pricing can be a most effective and versatile hospitality marketing tool. When applied inappropriately, pricing can result in adverse guest reactions and negate the favorable effects of other marketing variables.

Pricing issues can arise in many different ways and reflect quite different points of view. There are any number of hospitality managers who believe that pricing decisions are among the most important decisions they will make. Some argue that cost is the major determinant of prices. Others point to the effects of competitors' pricing or the hospitality benefits and values perceived by guests. Sometimes managers focus on long-term effects of pricing, while at other times they emphasize short-term goals and negotiated prices. These disparate perceptions of pricing may all be appropriate at different points in time.

In this chapter, we explore the many ways in which pricing issues can arise in the practice of hospitality marketing. We discuss some concepts and approaches that are essential in trying to resolve these issues in a rational manner and arrive at effective pricing decisions.

Pricing: Part of the Marketing Mix

While pricing is just one aspect of the marketing mix, it plays many different roles. Prices influence guests in their perceptions and purchase reactions; affect image, expectations, and guest satisfaction; and are important considerations in positioning. Significantly, guests use prices as indicators of value and proudly refer to getting a "bargain" or "their money's worth" and purchasing on sale. Value reflects the relationship between what guests give up (including the prices they pay) and what they receive. Prices actually paid represent guest perceptions of value received (benefits through products and services) for what they exchange, in terms of both money and such factors as time, inconvenience, and effort expended.

Prices, therefore, are the result of decisions on the part of both guests and hospitality providers. While providers may set prices, guests' reactions determine the prices actually paid, for they may choose to buy or not. The amount of control that providers exercise on prices varies depending on such factors as the degree of differentiation, competition, and guest response.

We approach pricing from the perspective of hospitality managers assigning prices to services and products to achieve company objectives. Prices may be used to establish and maintain specific images—from the luxury and prestige of a five-star hotel to the practicality of economy-priced lodging. They can be the means of signaling price leadership, increasing sales, extending market share, improving profits and return on investment, and creating new and loyal customers. Thus, price should not be thought of in isolation, but rather must be seen in the context of the total hospitality offer being made to specific market segments. Before we examine the pricing process, let us look at a few examples of how pricing has been used and misused.

Example 1: Price Alone Is Not the Answer

Two South Florida restaurants of similar size were located within a block of each other on the same side of a busy street. They catered to the same breakfast and lunch markets, and both featured bagels and deli foods. The first restaurant had been in business two years and was extremely successful; there was always a line of people waiting to get in. The second restaurant had been in business less than a year. It had superior facilities and opened offering a lower price for its breakfast specials, served three eggs to the competitor's two, and featured handmade bagels. However, it did not attract many guests. As a result, it reduced its prices further in the form of Sunday specials for their "regulars." That did not work. Although it had a much nicer environment and equally good food, the restaurant closed within a few months.

In this situation, management did not understand pricing's role on the total marketing mix, let alone appreciate the affect of pricing on guest behavior. Guest wants and needs were not brought into the pricing equation, although the competitor's prices were considered. Other aspects of the marketing mix were mishandled, for service was sadly lacking, communications with potential guests were inadequate, and even information about the relatively low price did not reach the market.

Example 2: Perceived Value Drives Price

Price is not always the dominant factor in choosing a hotel. Paul Iacovino, at the time a hotel executive at the Regent Hotel in Sydney, noted that astute customers will look at the total cost of achieving the purpose of a visit and will agree that sometimes it is wise to spend a little more to make a visit more productive.

> We are not selling price here, we are selling service. We're selling productivity, the idea that guests will be productive when they stay with us because of the services we provide. It may be something mundane, like

providing transportation to their first appointment in the morning. Or it might be something more significant, like providing breakfast.

An early check-in is a big deal here because we have international travelers who arrive at 6 A.M. at the airport. We can attract them at their high rate and sometimes offer pre-registration so they get here in the morning and they have their room available and that's a big deal!

Service is the first thing guests will come to. So they ask: "Do you have 24-hour room service?" "Can I get early check-in if I'm coming internationally?" "Can I get my blouse and skirt pressed or can I get my shoes shined?" In other words, we have to tell guests why it's worth $250 a night to stay with us—and why it's worth it here more than anywhere else. I want them to leave here saying, "I've really got value out of my $250 room, even though it might have been cheaper to stay at the XYZ Hotel down the street." Service issues are what count.[2]

Example 3: Price Matters, but So Does Guest Loyalty

In a leading five-star hotel not far away from the hotel discussed in the previous quote, a manager explained that consumers choices of hotels "will often get down to rates. It's so price driven." Hotels are in the position where "there is another hotel in this city, just around the corner, which offers a similar product and works to undercut prices...and the corporate market is also very rate driven." He points out, however, that customer loyalty is also important. "In the corporate market, there are more (hotel) programs in place that sustain and support customer loyalty because its such an important market...and that's another reason why they [corporate consumers] are harder to swing." As the manager emphasized, in spite of the importance of prices, other factors operate to incur and maintain guest loyalty.

Example 4: Pricing for a Specific Market Segment

Turning to a quite different market, we see pricing decisions from another perspective—that of a manager trying to put together a competitively superior package of services for a specific market segment. Janet McGarry of Youth Hostel Australia (YHA) Travel has a clear view of the prices that will work in her market—the youthful backpacker—and negotiates with prospective suppliers to control costs.

A lot of the smaller companies trying to reach our market will approach YHA and ask us to promote their products through our hostels. My basic position is that I cannot assist them with their promotion unless they are offering something specific to our members.

For instance, I had an outdoor operator planning to operate a coach trip between Sydney and Byron Bay. He wanted his brochures and posters splashed all over our hostels. Well, that's all very nice, but I can't do that unless he's going to do something for our members. When he called today, I suggested that he offer YHA members a special discount. He hadn't thought of offering discounts, but he agreed. He'll give a 10 percent discount to YHA members! It's worth it for him to get the exposure.

Each of these examples deals with a pricing challenge—whether it be the integration of menu pricing with a total service offer or a focus on competition as a major force driving prices. Of course, pricing issues extend well beyond these situations as we shall see in the materials that follow.

Pricing and Guest Value Perceptions

Prices are sometimes seen merely as numbers indicating what guests must pay to purchase items offered. But that is an inadequate and misleading perspective. Prices are not merely the reflection of costs, but are declarations of guest values. As a result, establishing appropriate hospitality prices involves a complex set of activities. The challenge for managers is to see that their prices reflect the value guests feel they receive.

Difficulties arise when hospitality enterprises charge prices that are substantially higher or lower than what guests believe the value is. When guests feel that prices exceed value, they will not purchase. When guests perceive value that far exceeds prices, sales increase, but hospitality enterprises forego fine profit opportunities. Yet in both cases, prices may well be in line with costs.

In developing **value-based pricing**, hospitality managers face the task of determining how much value guests will assign to the benefit packages the company offers. That is no easy task. Individual guests will assign varying degrees of value to products and services and to the tradeoffs and compromises involved in obtaining them. Value is subjective, and the values assigned to the same attributes by different guests vary. Thus measuring and quantifying them in order to assign prices can be complicated. Management's objective should be to increase perceived value to get guests to believe that enhanced value differentiates a property's offerings from those of its competitors.

Competitive advantage flows from furnishing superior value in guests' eyes. Superior value stems from offering guests the same benefits for lower prices, providing added benefits for the same price, or giving added benefits with values exceeding additional prices charged. Since it is relatively easy to gather information about competitors' prices, both published and actual, managers can make direct comparisons.

Prices higher than those of much of the competition may signal superior services and products. The all-suites Rihga Royal Hotel in New York has successfully used a premium pricing strategy by pricing at rates just below those of the top of the line—but well above mid-level hotels—and emphasizing their differentiated, unique business amenities such as individual faxes, cellular phones, private phone numbers, and limousine service. The result is an extremely high occupancy rate.

Similarly, prices lower than those of the competition may be interpreted as reflecting lesser quality and appeal to a much different market segment. Examples are Motel 6, Budgetel, and Super 8, where guest expectations are far lower, and the lack of amenities and extra services is expected—guests are just buying "the basics."

Pricing: Six Basic Questions

Answers to six basic questions can provide hospitality managers with useful information in meeting price challenges and establishing prices for their offerings. They are:

1. What should be the balance between costs, the competition, and customers in arriving at a price?

2. Will the deal be a once-only transaction or the beginning of a relationship with potential long-term benefits?

3. Is the price to be a fixed number (or schedule) or something that will be negotiated, bargained for, and possibly changed over time?

4. Are we dealing with a single customer, guest, or buyer, or with a group of people?

5. Which parties to the deal have sufficient power to influence the outcome of a negotiation and what is the source of this power?

6. Does the price in question require pricing a single, specific service or does it involve a full schedule of prices—perhaps for a range of rooms or services or for a complete menu?

The first two questions set the stage for a pricing decision. While costs, competitors, and customer needs are each important factors, it is essential to blend all three factors together in reaching a decision. And we need to decide whether the price relates to a once-only deal, with no long-term consequences, or should be thought of as the first (and often critical) step in establishing a long-term, mutually profitable relationship.

The third question asks about the process by which a price will be decided. Is it something we decide and the guest accepts or rejects? Is it something we negotiate or bargain over? Quite often, it is the latter with which we must cope. For example, when a guest asks for a discount or special price at the time of check-in, management may or may not be directly involved and the negotiation may or may not be productive. Almost certainly, the process of bargaining will take time and effort. If a relationship is involved, the costs of a poor negotiation may have consequences for an extended period of time. Examples of this kind of situation arise in dealing with the incentive or frequent traveler markets.

The fourth and fifth questions focus on who is likely to be involved and how much "clout" they can bring to the negotiation. In dealing with tour wholesalers, for example, a hotel manager may feel herself to be in a difficult position if the wholesaler is able to control a large slice of a profitable market. This may happen in dealing with large foreign wholesalers who control the flow of tourists from their country and who negotiate hard for the best possible deals. The youth hostel manager profiled earlier provides another example of market power at work in influencing prices.

The last question deals with the complexity of the choice that has to be made. While the decision may simply be one of choosing a price for a specific transaction, quite often the issue is one of deciding on an entire rate structure. In dealing with wholesalers, for example, it may be necessary to think through the entire rate structure that will be used, relating it to room types and the kind of guests that the wholesaler may be able to provide. You may need to decide what characteristics will distinguish different categories of rooms—those with a harbor view and those that look across city roofs, those that have single occupancy and those with double occupancy, smoke-free or in general use. Complicating these decisions still further are the current rack rates and the discount structure to be used (such as corporate, super saver, government, airline crew, weekend, special interest group, or local business rates).

In most practical pricing situations, it is important at the outset to think through the interplay of the factors that emerge in answering the above questions. Usually one or two factors will be most important, but all must be kept in mind and in balance.

The prices set must cover costs and guests must perceive value that is at least as good as or better than that available from competitors. Typically, costs come down when relationships endure, because marketing economies result from maintaining ongoing relationships rather than always trying to find and negotiate with new guests.

Finally, it is essential to strike a balance in the rate structure, whether for rooms or menus, between that which benefits a particular department or function of a hospitality company and that which benefits the entire operation. The pricing options selected directly affect the ability of staff to sell more rooms, services, and menu items, or to build guest loyalties. This in turn directly influences the entire business's ability to improve performance and achieve its goals.

How profitable are specific hospitality offerings and guests? Determining the costs of delivering services to each guest or guest category is often difficult, if not impossible. Identifying precisely what guests "consume" each time they work out in a health club cannot be done. Guests use whatever facilities and services they wish at a particular period, and of course may vary their workout routines. Establishing whether a guest is profitable or not is difficult. The basic management pricing decision is to see that the incremental cost associated with an additional guest or service is covered so that the enterprise is better off with the guests or service than without them. In the long run, of course, it is important to cover all costs and make a profit.

Creative Pricing

Managers often think of price as something that is determined and then remains constant for a period of time. All too often, price is seen as a constant that is set mechanistically rather than as a significant variable in an overall marketing mix. In dynamic market environments, however, pricing can have a profound effect on the bottom line. Pricing decisions should be seen as a means of marketing hospitality more effectively. Creative pricing helps hospitality managers achieve their objectives.

There are many hospitality examples of creative pricing, where price is used as a flexible marketing factor. Basic variations include maintaining the same price but giving guests smaller portions, lowering the price while reducing unrequired services and portions, keeping prices steady while increasing quantities or quality, and combining goods and services at a single price that is less than the total price of the individual items.

Hospitality managers often adopt such pricing approaches as the following:

- Varying prices among different guest segments
- Varying prices during off-peak hours
- Varying prices according to the season
- Varying prices to direct guest decisions
- Providing various kinds of discounts—senior citizen, frequent customer, seasonal, weekend, etc.
- Offering various kinds of coupons
- Offering free merchandise
- Offering free products such as hors d'oeuvres, beverages, use of facilities

Pricing can help direct guests to act in a manner that the hospitality business prefers. Many hotels in the United States, Europe, and Asia set prices of individual breakfast entrées high enough to encourage guests to select the whole breakfast buffet. Some restaurants lower the prices of their dinners during the early evening hours to attract early diners and maximize their facilities. Bars and restaurants offer "two-fers" (two for the price of one) to attract guests during off-peak hours.

The Economics of Pricing

A common hospitality business perception is that higher prices translate into larger profits. However, that may not be the case. Profit depends on the effects of price increases on patronage, which economists refer to as **elasticity**. Elasticity measures the responsiveness of demand to price and can be a useful guide to pricing, even if it is only approximated.

Generally, higher prices result in reduced demand. When a price increase (say, five percent) results in a proportionately larger decrease in demand (say, eight percent), demand is said to be elastic. Conversely, when a price increase results in a less than proportionate decrease in demand, demand is said to be inelastic.

Elasticity is roughly calculated (because the data are usually hard to get) by the following equation:

$$\text{Elasticity} = \frac{\text{Percent change in demand}}{\text{Percent change in price}}$$

By convention, we ignore the negative sign. When the ratio is greater than one, demand is elastic; when the ratio is less than one, demand is inelastic. Suppose a hotel raises its average room rate by five percent and room sales fall by ten percent. The equation would look like this:

$$\text{Elasticity} = \frac{-.10}{.05} = 2.0$$

Since the price elasticity ratio is greater than one, demand at this hotel would be elastic. Generally speaking, when demand is elastic, total revenue *decreases* when prices are raised.

A careful study of sales and price data for a whole hotel, or for specific room categories, can lead to an estimate of elasticities that can then be used to provide useful insights into pricing. Of course, demand in some market segments—such as business guests and travelers who seek quality of experience or exclusivity—is relatively inelastic. The demand curve of such guests are relatively price insensitive. Management can use such information in making decisions about increasing or lowering prices.

Markets, Costs, and Volume

In setting prices, management should consider the economic impact of three important variables: markets, costs, and volume. A careful assessment of the relevant markets will tell us something about the relationship between price and volume (elasticity) and may indicate a ceiling for prices—the highest prices that guests will pay. Costs establish the floor, the level below which prices cannot fall if costs are to be covered over the long run. Volume has an impact on costs by affecting the amount of fixed costs that are allocated to each hotel room, seat, service, or other unit of capacity. As volume increases, the fixed costs allocated to each unit decrease and average total costs per unit decline. Thus, increases in volume lead to decreases in average costs per unit, and the prices charged can be lowered accordingly.

This is an important relationship in the hospitality industry. To succeed in the long run, of course, hotels and restaurants must generate enough volume to cover their total costs. In the short run, however, they may be willing to set unit prices below the total cost per unit, as long as those prices cover their variable costs and make at least some contribution to fixed costs. In the short run, as long as variable costs are more than covered, the company is better off making the sale. A small profit margin is better than none at all.

In applying this marginal approach to pricing, hotels and restaurants face quite different cost mixes. In the hotel industry, fixed costs tend to be relatively high, while variable costs are relatively low. In the restaurant industry, it is just the reverse. The relatively low variable costs of hotels give managers greater leeway to offer larger discounts than restaurant managers normally can. Hospitality managers, in determining their prices, can benefit from thinking in terms of the make-up of cost structures on prices and prices on volume.

The concept of covering total costs is often illustrated using a **breakeven chart** (see Exhibit 1). In this chart, the horizontal axis measures volume (rooms sold, occupancy, covers, seats, or other measures of capacity used) and the vertical axis measures dollars of cost or revenue. In Exhibit 1, the fixed costs line reflects the fact that fixed costs remain the same as volume increases. (This is usually just an approximation. Some costs will jump in a step-like fashion at certain points as volume increases. Costs can jump as extra facilities have to be brought into use to meet demand.) Fixed costs must be paid regardless of volume.

The variable cost line shows the costs that vary directly with the volume of business (that is, the incremental cost of serving each customer). In a restaurant, these costs will include the costs of the food, beverages, and utilities. It might not include wages if they have to be met irrespective of the actual demand. It is sometimes difficult to decide which costs are fixed and which are variable. This does not

Exhibit 1 Breakeven Analysis Chart

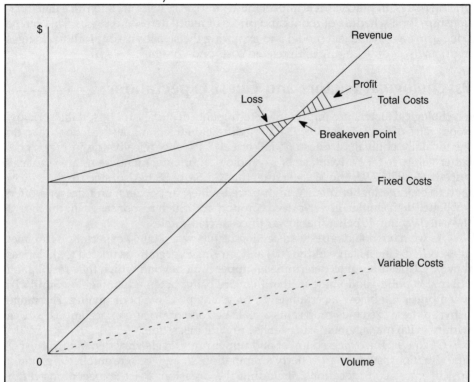

negate the value of breakeven analysis, but it does require that managers think very carefully about what they are trying to achieve by their pricing decisions.

The total costs line combines the fixed and variable costs. The revenue line charts sales revenue. The point where the revenue line crosses the total costs line is known as the breakeven point. It shows the amount of revenue and sales volume necessary to cover total costs.

A key consideration for hoteliers is whether it is possible to realign or shift rates within a pricing structure to lift the overall average room rate. In making such a determination, such questions as the following arise:

- Is the gap between single and double occupancy too large?

- Have we struck the right balance between rack and corporate rates?

- Are our corporate and promotional rates doing their job—that is, are they effective at bringing large groups into the hotel?

- Do we need to make changes between weekend and weekday rates?

By considering the mix of guests and their price sensitivities, "run of the house" pricing can often achieve a higher overall average rate.

The economics of pricing plays a major role in thinking through hospitality pricing issues. In practice, it is important to build cost, volume, and price data relationships for a schedule of rooms and prices or menu items and prices. This can be done using a spreadsheet model and exploring the sensitivity of profit to changes in pricing schedules, along with related costs and volumes.

Psychological Factors and Guest Expectations

Psychological factors are important determinants of successful hospitality pricing. Room rates of $149.95 or $199.95 have a different effect on guest reactions than do the virtually equivalent rates of $150 or $200. Psychologically, the former signal better value. To take advantage of psychological pricing, menu items are regularly priced at $5.95, $7.99, and $29.95 rather than $6, $8, or $30. Also, since higher prices tend to connote higher quality, high-priced wines, appetizers, and desserts often sell better than similar, lower-priced counterparts. Such responses fly in the face of the usual economic belief that lower prices increase sales.

As we have noted, guest satisfaction results when guest expectations are met or exceeded. Guests have individual and varying expectations related to the prices they pay. Guests seem to determine an upper limit beyond which they feel that an offering is not a good value or that they are being taken advantage of. Similarly, when prices fall below a certain level, they may perceive poor quality. The range between these extremes represents a realistic zone of pricing expectations, a zone within which management can exercise pricing discretion.

Of course, the expected lower and upper price levels vary depending on specific situations, such as a property's reputation, image, geographic setting, and a host of guest considerations, including the occasion. Price expectations differ between the coffee shop and the dining room, room service and the self-service breakfast bar, the luxury hotel and the economy motel, the hotel room in London and one in rural America, and the dinner dance on New Year's Eve compared with other evenings. Although the actual cost of the same bottle of beer may be identical for both the local bar and the famed Polo Lounge of the Beverly Hills Hotel, consumer price expectations are not. In setting prices, managers must consider not only economic aspects but also such psychological factors.

Reference Pricing

Because guests receive psychological value from getting discounts, some hotels set their rack rates high so that they can offer substantial discounts to guests. However, this practice may lead guests to believe that hotel rooms are priced too high. To get value, they may tend to expect, and even demand, discounts.

Businesses want to price their offerings so that they get the highest possible price from each customer. Guests, on the other hand, want to get a good deal. The theory of **reference pricing** explains that guests have two prices in mind: the price being asked, such as the rack rate or the published list price, and a reference price, or benchmark, against which guests assess whether they are getting "a good deal." But how are reference prices established? Consumers might use the lowest price they have seen for similar offerings, prices they saw in advertisements and promotions, past discounts they have received, rates paid when attending conferences, information from friends, or any number of past experiences.[3] Currently some companies, such as Wal-Mart, are adopting a pricing strategy of "everyday low pricing," thereby giving guests a general reference point.

One important purpose of brands is to insulate the company from price pressures, permitting it to maintain a price edge. Yet, even when guests are brand-loyal, they may still seek bargains. Guests need to be able to justify or rationalize the higher prices they pay for branded offerings and such offerings must provide an acceptable rationale for guests. Guests must be able to reconcile the fact that the same bottle of wine they can purchase at a supermarket will cost three or four times more in a famous restaurant.

Sometimes premium offerings are used for reference pricing purposes. Similar rooms in a hotel that are priced at a much higher rate, or similar wines that are high priced, provide reference prices, making lower-priced or mid-range offerings acceptable to guests. Reference prices can help trade guests up to a higher-priced suite or room. Suppose that suites are priced at rates significantly higher than those for luxury rooms and that many suites are available. A guest has reserved and is registering for a luxury room at $249 per night. The desk clerk notes that although suites are regularly $395, she can let the guest have the suite for just an additional $35. The guest has reference prices, perceives the suite to be a real bargain, and is more likely to accept the offer and trade up. Moreover, whenever guests accept a hospitality business's "everyday low price" philosophy, they actually give the business credibility and in so doing give management price discretion. In bestowing their acceptance of the philosophy, guests establish a general reference point for company prices and management may have opportunities to actually increase their prices.

Discounted prices may take many forms including coupons, off-price promotions, rebates and allowances, "two-for-the-price-of-one" deals, or any of a number of variations. When managers use them, they can depreciate the value of their own brands. This counters the ability of well-known brands like Hyatt, Hilton, and Ritz-Carlton to command premium prices from guests.

When guests are being charged what they perceive as high prices, they may react negatively, particularly when they are surprised by the difference between the price paid and the services offered. Consider the following actual situation. A couple decided to celebrate Valentine's Day by having dinner at a well-known restaurant that they visited on a regular basis. When they were seated, they were surprised by a special Valentine's Day menu. The usual à la carte prices were increased by one-third to one-half and a special wine list, consisting of the normal wines at much higher prices, was in use. The restaurant also offered a very pricey set dinner. The guests were irritated, feeling that they were "being taken." Although their food was fine, their evening was needlessly spoiled. One year later they had yet to return to the restaurant, and their story of being gouged had been repeated numerous times to their friends. The restaurant's pricing strategy surely boosted Valentine's Day profits, but perhaps at a longer-range cost.

It is helpful for hospitality managers to try to determine well ahead of time what guests feel they should pay for a product or service. Insights into guest expectations about prices can help managers establish prices that are more in line with expectations. Guests expect to pay more for a glass of imported wine than a domestic wine that may even be superior. It is one thing to price a serving of *sherbet* but quite another to price *sorbet*. Just as trendy—and pricey—cuisines come and go over time, guest expectations and market conditions change. The $45 five-star Singapore hotel room of the early 1980s was in the $200 to $300 range in the early 1990s; in the late 1990s, poor economic conditions have seen the price fall again to low levels.

Competitive Pricing

The hospitality industry is very competitive. Thus, it is wise to assess the likely reactions of competitors' prices and planned changes. It is possible to readily assemble pertinent pricing information on which to make judgments. The following is a partial list of the kinds of information that can prove useful:

- Advertised prices
- Published price lists
- Competitors' prices
- Competitors' promotional campaigns
- Assessment of competitors' costs
- Competitors' published financial reports
- Competitors' past reactions to price changes
- Competitors' financial conditions
- Competitors' facilities and capacity
- Competitors' position in the industry
- Competitors' occupancy rates

The Unique Challenge of Pricing for Services ─────────

Setting prices for hospitality services differs significantly from setting prices for products. Among the differences are:

- Services are intangible and are usually "consumed" when they are purchased. They cannot be inventoried for sale at a later date. If they are not sold, revenues are lost forever.

- Guests seem to take quality service for granted, unlike quality products, and have a difficult time putting monetary values on them. Often, guests use price as a guide to determining quality.

- Most services do not lend themselves to mass production, and an increase in volume does not automatically lead to lower costs. Many services require some customization.

- Nearly all hospitality services require guests to come to the provider's place of business; they are not transportable.

- It is difficult to estimate the actual costs of providing services to a specific guest. Services delivered to different guests at different times, by different people, vary in cost. In addition to difficulties in determining the amount of labor involved, there are problems in estimating the cost of equipment and facilities used, as well as overhead burdens.

- Guests' demands for services fluctuate widely; everyone wants them at certain times, and then there is little demand for them after-hours.

It is abundantly clear from the points discussed above that although pricing hospitality offerings is a critical marketing decision, it is not a science. Trying to set the best price involves management assessments of very complex factors such as guest needs, perceptions and behavior, competitor's strategies and reactions, and cost and demand structures. Thus it is very important for hospitality managers to develop a good understanding of pricing fundamentals along with a good grasp of specific situations. The pricing decisions they reach can have tremendous impact on other aspects of the marketing mix and indeed on the whole business.

An Overall Pricing Policy

Up to this point, we have been discussing the ideas that need to be taken into account when analyzing pricing situations. Now we move to an important next step: establishing an overall pricing policy. It is unrealistic and unwise for managers to tackle each pricing challenge as a stand-alone problem. Rather, managers need to establish basic policies that can be used to determine how specific pricing problems will be resolved.

In designing pricing policies, management can apply strategic thinking and approaches to pricing considerations. To illustrate, we shall briefly discuss four main pricing concerns:

- Pricing objectives
- Pricing strategies
- Pricing programs
- Pricing tactics

Pricing Objectives

Pricing objectives specify what management wants to accomplish through pricing. It is not merely a matter of wanting to sell more or attract additional guests. Such an objective is much too general to direct pricing actions. The primary pricing objectives of most hospitality enterprises are financial—targets for gross and net profits, fixed and variable costs, return on investment, internal rate of return, cash flow, and price stability. While such considerations are essential to growth and survival, they should not become the sole or overarching pricing objectives. Since they are all intertwined with marketing, a critical focus must be on pricing as a marketing tool

Exhibit 2   Hospitality Pricing Objectives

- Increase market share by *x* percent
- Realize a specific profit level
- Achieve a specified rate of return
- Maintain an exclusive image
- Appeal to new market segments
- Use facilities in off-hours and seasons
- Exercise price leadership
- Give guests superior value
- Gain competitive advantage
- Discourage competition
- Convince guests to try new/additional items
- Increase sales of specific items
- Increase sales of complementary items
- Meet competitors' prices
- Increase volume to spread overhead
- Generate guest loyalty

to influence guests to behave in desired ways. Examples of hospitality pricing objectives are shown in Exhibit 2.

Several objectives can be pursued at the same time. A company might seek to exercise price leadership, discourage competitors from entering the market, and provide guests with superior value—all with the same pricing decision. Conversely, some objectives may conflict, such as maintaining an exclusive image and being the lowest price provider.

Where possible, pricing objectives should be quantified so that we can determine whether the pricing actions are having the desired effect. Marketing research techniques can be very helpful in providing appropriate measurements and information. Sometimes this is straightforward, as with market share and profitability data. Sometimes pricing objectives present more difficult challenges. Determining whether competition has been discouraged as a result of a pricing practice, or whether guest perceptions and images have changed, is more difficult. The goal, where possible, is to state pricing objectives so that results can be ascertained.

The test of pricing programs is not merely cost considerations and desired financial margins, but guest reactions, for they translate into profits. Albert Kelly, managing director of the Hyatt Regency Grand Cypress Hotel in Orlando, Florida, has noted the misplaced emphasis of hoteliers and restaurateurs on raising prices and reducing costs when faced with declining profits. When costs are reduced, "the product [offered] will be of lesser quality, and the sales figures will reflect customer displeasure." Given declining sales, "the solution is to adjust prices upward in order to produce the desired margins."[4] But higher prices only result in further sales reductions and hence reduced profits. In neither situation is the solution appropriate; guest reactions play a vital role.

Too often, hospitality prices are determined on a piecemeal or arbitrary basis. When setting or changing prices, management should have specific objectives clearly in mind, along with measurable means of indicating how well the pricing decision is working. It is important to follow up and see if a price change is accomplishing what it is supposed to do.

A local restaurateur who had a regular dinner clientele decided to introduce a frequent-guest card. Each time a guest paid for a meal, the card was punched. Ten punches earned the diner a free meal. In essence, this meant a price reduction for regulars. No advertising was done except for notices placed on the tables. In a few months, the offer was dropped. When asked why, the restaurateur replied that the only thing the program accomplished was to give some of the regular guests free meals. It did not bring in new guests. The frequent user card was, in reality, a price reduction that had not been thought through or implemented well. Management apparently saw it as a means of generating new customers, yet did not consider guest needs or use any promotion (other than placing notices on the tables) to advise potential customers of the new policy.

Contrast this with the actions of a large restaurant and bar in South Florida that wanted to increase both the number of guests and repeat purchases during off-hours. They offered coupons for reduced prices in a local newspaper, with the amount of the price reductions pegged to the time when guests were seated; the lowest prices were offered at the earliest dinner hours. Guest checks were delivered along with coupons covering price reductions for future dinners. The result was that long lines often developed during early hours, and the place was relatively busy even in the summer off-season.

All price changes should be well thought through. To increase sales, it is not enough merely to state that prices are being reduced. Management must make sure that the objectives of price changes are clearly stated, that the results are monitored, and that the effects of pricing actions are evaluated.

Pricing can be used to bring demand into line with supply. It can help level out the peaks and valleys in demand by encouraging consumption during slack periods and acting as a damper to purchases during peak times. Many hotels have facilities such as golf courses, swimming pools, and health clubs that are not used to capacity at certain times of the day, week, or year. By setting prices that are attractive to local residents when guests are less likely to use them, the hotels can generate additional revenue and spread fixed costs. A well-known resort in Tucson, Arizona, encouraged local patronage and increased their sales by issuing VIP cards to local residents offering a 25 percent discount. The variety of pricing approaches used to smooth out demand and increase profit is limited only by management's ingenuity.

It is worth noting that management judgment plays an important role in pricing. It is not possible to put all of the relevant information into computers and have them generate the most desirable prices. On the other hand, pricing is not just a matter of managing solely on "gut feelings" (though such feelings may well play a role). Price makers must learn to operate with imperfect information under uncertain conditions, all the while exercising sound judgment.

Pricing Strategies

We can think of **pricing strategies** as assertions of how prices will be used to achieve marketing objectives. They provide the general guidelines for an enterprise's pricing decisions over a time period. The choice of strategy brings in a longer-range operating perspective of perhaps three to five years and serves to coordinate and organize pricing activities. Pricing strategies tend to be based either on costs or markets. Exhibit 3 presents brief descriptions of various pricing strategies.

The cost emphasis often results in prices being set by formula. Fixed and variable costs per unit are determined, and a mark-up is added. In the restaurant industry, wines may be priced at a certain percentage over cost and meals at a given multiple of food costs. An alternative cost-based formula is the general rule of thumb in the hotel industry that room rates should reflect about $1 for each $1,000 it costs to construct the room. If rooms cost $100,000 to build, the room rate is calculated at $100.

In establishing these relatively simple rules for determining prices, a number of assumptions have to be made about the behavior of costs and the willingness of guests to pay the resulting prices. These assumptions may not hold. For example, in many hotels built over the last few years, construction costs have increased faster than the capacity or willingness of guests to pay, with some rooms costing in excess of $500,000. Meeting these costs and the costs of providing the service that guests expect leads to long-term loss situations. (It is sometimes said that the third or fourth owner of a hotel is the one that begins to make money.)

Cost-oriented pricing strategies are among the most commonly used, with cost-plus pricing being the most popular technique. Here, costs are established for a unit such as a room, a meal, or the use of a facility based on some method of allocating relevant costs and then adding a predetermined profit margin. Although the technique is easy to use, guest values and considerations are ignored. Thus, cost-oriented pricing may produce results that are frequently unrelated to what guests are willing to pay. It limits the creative use of price as a management tool.

Cost-based pricing leads to a very frequent pricing error made by hospitality companies, that is, setting prices high enough *to make sure* all costs are covered. In so doing, important demand factors are ignored, for costs replace guest reactions as the over-riding pricing guidelines. When such cost-based prices deter guests from purchasing, profit targets are not met, and total costs are in fact *not* covered.

Where properties have excess capacity, management may be tempted to ignore fixed costs in setting prices. They may reason that it is better to make sales at prices that cover total variable costs (and perhaps a little more) than not to make sales at all. As we noted earlier, in the short run, companies can be profitable with prices that do not cover total costs; indeed, this may be a perfectly valid short-term promotional tactic. In the long run, however, hospitality managers must see to it that prices cover the total costs.

Exhibit 3   Pricing Strategies

Cost-Oriented Pricing Strategies

Cost-Plus Pricing

Is easy to understand and apply and gives the perception that prices cover all costs. Estimates are made of both variable and fixed costs per unit. Then a markup, expressed as a percentage of either costs or the sales price, is added to costs to determine the price. Where costs are fully allocated, this is also referred to as full-cost pricing.

Marginal Cost Pricing

A short-term strategy in response to excess capacity. It involves setting low prices that do not cover total costs but do cover variable costs and make some contribution to fixed costs. The justification is that, when excess capacity exists, some contribution to fixed costs is better than none at all.

Rate of Return Pricing

Is designed to yield a predetermined rate of return on investments. Estimates are made of variable and fixed costs. Management then sets a predetermined rate of return and sales are estimated. The rate of return is multiplied by the amount of capital invested in a product or service, and the result is divided by estimated sales. This gives a return per unit, which is added to the costs to determine the price. The "$1 per $1,000" rule (which specifies that room rates should reflect about $1 for each $1,000 it costs to construct the room) uses this approach, based on specific assumptions about cost structures and rates of return.

Market-Oriented Pricing Strategies

Bundle Pricing

Charging a lower price for a combined bundle of products than would be charged if each of the items were purchased separately. Bundle pricing is often used to encourage guests to purchase a total package which gives them good value. For example, prices of breakfast buffets encourage guests to order the buffet rather than purchase juice, coffee, and eggs for about the same price.

Complementary Pricing

Where products are used together, one may be priced relatively low to encourage purchase of the other, which bears a premium price. Las Vegas hotels set relatively low prices on rooms, restaurants, and beverages so that guests will participate in their more profitable gaming activities. In many bars and some restaurants, salty snacks are offered free while the thirst-quenching beverages bear premium prices.

Going-Rate Pricing

Setting prices on the basis of the average going rate of major competitors. This keeps prices in line by charging what the competition does.

Loss-Leader Pricing

Low prices are set, sometimes even below cost, for certain products to attract guests. The theory is that once guests are attracted, they will purchase profitable items.

Market Pricing

Charging as high a price as the market will bear. Prices may not reflect costs, and in rare cases may not even cover costs. It is simply getting the most you can.

(continued)

Exhibit 3   *(continued)*

Market Segment Pricing

Charging different prices to different segments of the market, usually on the basis of discounts from list (rack) prices using such criteria as volume, position in the channel, buying power, and cost of doing business.

Penetration Pricing

Setting a relatively low price in relationship to what customers are paying and the average price charged by major competitors in order to reach or develop new markets.

Price Leadership

A leading firm in the industry changes prices up or down and other companies follow. Thus, competitive pricing is essentially eliminated and prices are stable, since the leader establishes the price for all.

Segmental Pricing

Setting different prices for various market segments based on the estimates of value that each segment receives.

Skimming Pricing

Charging a relatively high price in relationship to what customers are paying and the average prices of major competitors, hence "skimming the cream off the top of the market." It attempts to reach customers willing to buy at a high price before marketing to more price-sensitive customers.

Stay-Out Pricing

Prices set so low that they discourage new competitors from entering the market.

Tailored Pricing

Managers reverse the normal procedure for setting prices. They work back from an established price to determine what the actual components of their offering will be. Prices that guests will pay are first determined (based on research, past experience, etc.) and then the products and services offered are tailored to match those prices. Fixed-price dinners at gourmet restaurants, travel tours, and holiday "getaway" packages are among the offerings geared to certain price points.

Yield Management

Changing the discounts offered depending on fluctuating demand and advance bookings. Guests are offered the same hotel rooms for different prices depending on when the reservation is booked. Computers are used to change prices daily and hourly depending on whether demand is strong or weak.

Costs are often seen as being the sole or main price-determining factor. However, costs themselves, as we have seen, may be dependent on price. When prices are charged that significantly increase volume, then overhead costs per unit are reduced, and prices in turn can be lowered while profit margins actually increase. If the costs of staffing room service or a 24-hour coffee shop are spread over a large volume, the per-guest costs are relatively low. But if only one or two guests are served, the overhead cost per guest may even become prohibitive.

By contrast, market-oriented pricing strategies focus on guest demand and competitors' prices—on what the market will pay. This may take many forms, such as meeting competitors' prices, charging what the market will bear, and gearing prices to customary price levels. Marketing research and competitive pricing analysis can be very helpful in formulating effective market-oriented pricing strategies. Guests and their reactions must be taken into account for market factors are critical determinants of pricing effectiveness.

Pricing Programs

Once pricing strategies have been selected, managers develop **pricing programs** for implementation—the plans and procedures to put them into place. This involves pricing specific hospitality products and services in accordance with company policies and strategies. It means dealing with basic pricing issues, with the specifics of responding to various situations such as how prices will vary among different markets, different categories of guests, conditions of shortages or excess of supply, seasonal demand, and special holidays and events. Pricing programs deal with such questions as:

- What is the rack or standard price?
- What discounts should be offered?
- How will prices vary among different markets?
- Should prices reflect different market conditions?
- How often should prices be changed?
- What impact should timing have on pricing?
- What should prices be for various facilities and services?
- Should prices be unbundled for different parts of a service package?
- What prices should be charged to non-guests?
- Should each item cover costs or produce a profit?

For ease of administration, having one standard price, with no variations or discounts, is the ideal. However, such an arrangement makes little sense in light of the dynamics and competition of hospitality markets. It does not use price as a variable to increase profits and market share. Where menus are set according to a standard, and where guests value some items more highly than the standard suggests, restaurants lose the opportunity of charging higher prices and increasing profits. The lack of flexibility in using standard prices is problematic. It can also be a problem for national chains where regional situations vary; if prices are nationally standardized, optimization opportunities may be lost.

Recognizing the inherent opportunities in pricing flexibility, hotel chains and restaurants have launched a variety of creative discount plans. Operations actually increase profits by offering guests special discounts, resulting in increased volume and increased use of facilities. Restaurants often use such approaches as theater packages, fixed-price dinners, and after-concert meals to vary prices and increase

---

Yield Management Pricing

Mr. Harris Rosen, a very successful independent hotel owner, recently opened the 24-floor Omni Rosen Hotel in Orlando, Florida; his other properties include Quality Inns, Comfort Inns, Clarion, Plaza, Omni, and Rodeway. While the average occupancy rate in Orlando did not exceed 78.8 percent in the last decade, Mr. Rosen's hotels, now totaling 1,334 rooms, averaged 96 percent. He continuously fills his hotels through a yield-management pricing strategy. By openly cutting prices daily on rooms that might not be sold, Mr. Rosen is able to lure travelers to fill them.

Many hotel operators feel that such a policy will tarnish their image and, as a result, they wind up with empty rooms rather than reduce the price. By so doing they maintain their average daily rates, but profits may suffer. Rosen's approach is to try to fill every room every night, explaining that he has trouble sleeping until he knows that every room is filled.

Prices charged are determined by occupancy level, time of day, and Rosen's feelings. When rooms are not moving and vacancies seem likely, signs outside some of the properties begin flashing "$29.95!" He has great pricing discretion because debt is kept low relative to property value, and there is no need for high prices to cover interest charges. Each morning he tracks such data as the previous day's occupancy, average rate, food and beverage revenues, and today's room rates. Every night he checks to see if his hotels are sold out. If they are not, he asks why.

Based on *The New York Times*, Nov. 1995, pp. C1,8.

---

volume and revenue. Unlimited possibilities exist for price variations via creative pricing plans.

Creative, flexible pricing approaches lend themselves well to the hospitality industry. Tables at a restaurant or rooms at a hotel cannot be inventoried indefinitely. If they go unsold, profit opportunities are lost. Thus, varying prices in order to sell them by responding to different demand situations can increase profits. The drawbacks are that this can lead to price confusion by guests, and can increase guest discount expectations and administrative problems.

Designing and implementing a pricing program requires detailed analysis of costs and market data along the lines explored earlier in our discussion of breakeven analysis. Sometimes it is argued that the data available are so unreliable that making detailed calculations is not worthwhile. Although it may be true that data are often incomplete or even questionable, the very act of producing a breakeven model is beneficial. It forces managers to focus clearly on costs (measured and unmeasured), on market or demand conditions, and on pricing alternatives. The process of working through breakeven analysis, usually using a spreadsheet, makes it feasible to test assumptions and identify those factors that are crucial in determining profitability, explore the results of alternative pricing or service options, and find those combinations that seem most attractive. It is this kind of approach that gives managers real insight into the structure of pricing programs.

Pricing Tactics

Once pricing policies, strategies, and programs are determined, they may remain in place over a relatively long time. By contrast, specific **pricing tactics** change from day to day to address changing circumstances. Pricing tactics concern the mechanics of pricing and may take many creative forms. They vary depending on how routine pricing tasks are and the frequency and speed with which decisions must be made. Some popular tactics include:

- Ongoing discount programs (seniors, motor-club members, families)
- Holiday promotions
- Special-event pricing
- Package promotions (dinner/theater/room packages, travel packages)
- Meeting competitors' prices

Pricing tactics are used to change prices as market conditions rise and fall, as competitors alter their prices, as costs change, and as governmental requirements shift. Specific prices can be readily (tactically) adjusted, although the basic pricing strategy and program remain in place. For example, suppose a restaurant, through a special buy of food or beverages, realizes lower costs on selected items. It can unexpectedly lower its prices, thereby challenging its competitors who face the choice of lowering price levels or risking loss of market share.

Although prices are flexible and can be changed readily, this does not mean managers should make arbitrary and capricious price changes. Guests expect some price stability and consistency; otherwise, they can become confused about the value of products and services, and their confidence in making purchase decisions may be reduced. This is particularly so when prices increase, because guests need to be able to justify paying more. If the price of coffee or of labor increases, guests have a rationale for expecting to see some price increases.

Sometimes, pricing tactics verge on the unethical as they confuse and take advantage of guests. One New York delicatessen put a large sign in its front window with huge letters visible from across the street advertising a breakfast special—bagel, cream cheese, and coffee for 99 cents—a veritable bargain! However, when people sat down and pointed to the sign, the waitress explained, "That's for take-out only." Sure enough, at the bottom of the sign, in exceedingly small print, was "Take-out, Monday-Friday only." Why not post the restrictions in the same giant letters as the rest of the sign? Perhaps there are enough visitors to New York to keep attracting and disappointing a constant stream of new guests. Regardless, this illustrates questionable pricing tactics.

Restaurant Pricing

Restaurants operate in a price-sensitive environment. Small increases in prices can mean relatively substantial increases in profits. Restaurants also have unique opportunities to differentiate their operations and offerings and, in so doing, to gain some discretion over prices. They can vary menus, ambience, and the quality of their service, food, and beverages. To the extent that they develop meaningful differentiation for guests, they can increase management discretion in setting prices.

In competing directly with hotel restaurants, free-standing restaurants are sometimes at a cost disadvantage where hotels charge their restaurants minimal or no rent. On the other hand, hotel restaurants must remain open for the convenience of guests, even when business is slow, and perhaps offer room service, which can be unprofitable.

Many restaurants use price as a means of attracting customers. They often use "penetration" pricing to gain access to new markets. They may offer reduced prices, specials, coupons, "two-fers," and similar deals to generate awareness, attract customers, and increase market share. Once markets are penetrated successfully, restaurants may choose to raise prices, although there is always the possibility of encountering adverse consumer reaction. Relying on low prices to penetrate markets can backfire when strong competitors meet initial price reductions head on and all operations lose revenue without gaining market share. Responding to competitors' price decreases or increases should not be done haphazardly. It is not a matter of automatically meeting competitors' discounts, as often happens. Rather, each situation should be analyzed carefully in terms of market and guest reactions, and company and competitors' cost structures.

Sometimes restaurants use price appeals to generate volume for their own house brands or to move special products. They may price their private label wines below others of equal quality, thereby enticing guests to select the house brand. Or they may develop gourmet products such as salad dressings and cheese spreads under their own labels and charge premium prices.

Restaurants are under pressure to control costs and maintain profits, while the prices of labor and food rise continuously. The tendency is to pass on price increases to guests, although guests may become wary of such attempts. (The hostess at a popular family-style restaurant was proudly greeting guests with the news that they had new menus. She was stopped short when someone in line asked loudly, "What's the matter, did you raise the prices again?") Pressures to hold prices arise from the fact that guests have many dining options to pursue should one establishment's prices seem too high. Lower-priced restaurants, supermarkets, take-out restaurants, and fast-food chains are all vying for diners' dollars. If prices are perceived as being too high, guests will simply choose to eat somewhere else.

Sometimes restaurants hold or even lower prices in the face of rising costs. Fast-food restaurants such as Wendy's, White Castle, and McDonald's are examples. They can use breakeven analysis to assess the impact of price decreases and determine the volume necessary to make up for lost revenue due to the price decreases.

Guest reactions to price changes can be swift and effective. Restaurants may have relatively little leeway in raising prices for they can quickly encounter guest resistance. Instead, they often have to engineer menus creatively to maintain or lower costs and try to maintain prices in the face of rising costs of labor and other inputs. They may add new items, adopt new ways of preparing existing menu selections, or find ways to increase productivity to maintain prices. Sometimes they face well-established price ranges and price points. For example, in some locales, dinners at mid-priced restaurants will not sell at prices above $15.95, so entrées range from $10.95 to $15.95. In other family restaurants, complete dinners—from soup to dessert—are expected in the range of $6.95 to $9.95.

A small segment of the restaurant industry is price insensitive. In some upscale restaurants, prices may appear to be very high, yet guests may not be at all concerned. They may be very wealthy or have unrestricted expense accounts. Some outstanding gourmet restaurants have month-long waiting lists despite extraordinarily high prices.

A variety of elements contribute to guests' willingness to purchase at any given restaurant: the uniqueness of the menu, the quality of the food and service, the reputation of the chef, the maître d', the ambience, the image, or any of a host of other considerations. Ambience can be a very important influence in restaurant pricing policies. A meeting place for movie star and entertainment industry moguls, the famed Polo Lounge of the Beverly Hills Hotel can command relatively high prices for its food and beverages because people go there to be seen.

Hotel Pricing

Hotels generally adhere to a strategy of setting relatively high rack rates—high standard prices—and then offering guests substantial discounts from them. However, hotels also offer negotiated, corporate rates, and government rates that are significantly lower than rack rates. Such rates are generally based on a guaranteed number of room nights during a specified period and give businesses and government guests stable rates for planning purposes.

Some hotels may charge whatever the market will bear and "skim the cream" off the top of the market. Discounts are avoided, and high prices are used to enhance the hotel's image and reputation as they appeal to an upscale market. The message to guests is that the property is worth the price. Some premium-priced hotels have successfully created the image that they are the epitome of luxury, offering the finest in products and services. Of course, they do not give discounts. They have successfully used price to differentiate the property and make their unique services more tangible. Indeed, offering discounts and lowering prices would only work to such hotels' disadvantage. Guest feelings on the matter, however, may be quite different from that of management. When that happens and guests perceive that a hotel is overpriced, a difficult marketing barrier results.

Hotels have relatively high fixed costs per room, and conversely relatively low variable costs. Variable costs are estimated to run from 15 to 25 percent of total costs. This means that relatively small increases in volume can have a significant impact on profits. As a result, hotels work hard to generate volume and often willingly offer discounts to do so.

Hotels also consider the effect of pricing decisions on complementary products and services. They have the choice of a variety of pricing alternatives. For example, price discounts can be used to build a base of loyal guests who will in turn generate demand for food, beverages, and various facilities. By establishing relatively low prices for rooms and meals, Las Vegas hotels have significantly increased the demand for their very profitable gaming operations. Alternatively,

Pricing Errors

The following are some of the more common pricing errors made by hospitality enterprises. They are based on information we gathered in interviews with hospitality managers and our research into the industry.

- Basing prices on costs while neglecting marketplace forces.

- Increasing prices as costs rise, without considering other marketing factors and alternatives.

- Holding the line on prices as market conditions change, rather than adapting prices to new situations.

- Making pricing decisions piecemeal rather than as an integrated part of the whole marketing mix.

- Treating pricing as a financial rather than a marketing decision.

- Neglecting to relate price to guest perceptions of value.

- Using formulaic approaches to setting prices.

- Basing prices on management intuition and judgment.

- Unrealistically assessing acceptable consumer options regarding alternative offerings.

- Overestimating consumer reactions to company offerings.

hotels may choose to raise prices for their rooms, while keeping a lid on prices for food and beverages.

Since hotel management is often evaluated on the basis of occupancy rates, there is a great incentive to set prices that will increase occupancy. However, lowering room prices is often met by quick responses from competitors who match discounts. When this occurs, market shares may remain about the same with occupancy rates unchanged, and all involved losing revenue.

Guests often find hotel pricing practices very confusing. There is a lack of price clarity, and guests are left to wonder: What does the rack rate really mean? What are the actual prices? What should guests expect to pay? At the same time, guests are becoming more value conscious and can readily check competitors' prices. They can ask for and receive discounts, inquire about special prices given to the associations they belong to, and book through discount brokers. Guests are becoming much more sophisticated in dealing with lodging prices.

Sometimes perverse logic comes into play when establishing hotel pricing. When occupancy rates go down, some hotel managers reason that since their overhead costs per room are increasing, they have to raise their prices. Higher prices, however, tend to lower occupancy even more, further increasing overhead costs per room. Such ill-advised responses to market changes can be limited with the help of an established pricing strategy and policy.

Hotel prices in many situations have been raised at a much higher rate than inflation, sometimes perhaps unreasonably. In several popular destinations, too many hotels targeted the luxury market, which they thought would be price insensitive. However, hotel capacity was overbuilt and there were simply not enough upscale guests to fill the available rooms. Excess capacity leads to price reductions and bargains for guests. In other destinations, a recent downturn in tourism has forced luxury hotels in Hong Kong, Singapore, Malaysia, Indonesia, and Thailand to lower prices drastically.

Concluding Comments

It is important to develop an integrated pricing approach. Pricing decisions should not be made in isolation, for not only are they part of the whole marketing mix, but individual prices are part of a total pricing system. Managers should consider the four stages that we have discussed—pricing objectives, pricing strategies, pricing programs, and pricing tactics. When they do so, pricing is treated as the important contributor to hospitality marketing that it is.

Pricing involves both internal and external considerations. Consideration of internal factors alone will not do. As we have seen, while internal factors such as objectives, strategies, and costs affect prices, so do external factors such as demand, competition, guest perceptions, and government actions.

Research and pertinent data can foster effective pricing strategies and practices. However, research alone will not suffice. Determining the "best" price is not merely the result of analyzing data and applying formulas. Creative skills are required to assess guest perceptions, evaluate future demand, and determine competitors' likely strategies. Pricing involves management's "gut feel" for specific situations, and their experiences and personal insights. Two experienced hospitality marketing managers, confronting essentially the same situation, may arrive at different pricing decisions, and both may be workable.

Pricing decisions should be consistent with other aspects of the hospitality marketing mix. They should complement and support promotional, sales, advertising, merchandising, and other marketing strategies and programs. The lack of consistency and coordination between pricing and other marketing actions detracts greatly from marketing effectiveness. Special price discounts and reductions can support sales and promotional events. Trade discounts can motivate travel agents and other members of the distribution channel.

Price should result from an enterprise's overall marketing strategy. Such strategies as target marketing, niching, differentiation, and segmentation all have important implications for pricing decisions. The pricing policies, strategies, and tactics adopted should, in turn, support the totality of hospitality marketing efforts.

Endnotes

1. Robert C. Hazard, Jr. "Bracing for Changes Ahead in the Hotel Industry," *Business Travel News*, 13 May 1985, p. 26.

2. Personal interview, April 1994.

3. *The Wall Street Journal*, 23 April 1996, "Brand Managers Get Old-Time Religion," p. A23.

4. Albert J. Kelly, "Band-Aids Are No Remedy for Bottom-Line Diseases," *Hotel & Motel Management*, 7 April 1986, p. 102b.

Key Terms

breakeven chart—a chart showing revenue and costs as a function of volume.

elasticity—a measure of the responsiveness of demand to changes in price.

pricing objectives—the results management wishes to achieve through pricing.

pricing programs—plans and procedures to implement pricing strategies.

pricing strategy—a pattern or plan that integrates pricing decisions into the overall framework of marketing goals, strategies, and actions.

pricing tactics—day-to-day pricing changes to meet changing circumstances.

reference pricing—a theory which suggests that guests have two prices in mind: the asking price and a reference or benchmark price that is used to assess whether the guest is getting a good deal.

value based pricing—pricing that is based on the value guests assign to the benefit packages the company offers.

Review Questions

1. Under what circumstances would the value a guest perceives be less than price paid for a purchase from the Ritz-Carlton, a budget motel, or a McDonald's Restaurant? When would value be greater than price paid?

2. Two guests each paid $250 for an identical room at a major city hotel. One complained about the price paid as being too high. What might be the basis for the complaint?

3. Consider the situation of a major hotel, a resort, or a family restaurant. Can you identify market segments for which demand for the services of each business would be price elastic? Price inelastic?

4. How might a hotel's pricing objectives influence promotional strategies?

5. What marketing conditions might lead the management of a hotel to set "meeting competition" as a pricing objective?

6. In a breakeven chart, is the total fixed cost line always horizontal? Is the total variable cost line always straight?

7. How do differences in cost structures between a hotel and a restaurant affect management thinking about prices?

Internet Sites

For more information, visit the following Internet sites. Remember that Internet addresses can change without notice.

Budgetel
http://www.budgetel.com

Clarion Hotels
http://www.clarionhotel.com

Hilton Hotels Corp.
http://www.hilton.com

Hyatt Hotels and Resorts
http://www.hyatt.com

McDonald's Corp.
http://www.mcdonalds.com

Motel 6
http://www.motel6.com

Omni Hotels
http://www.omnihotels.com

Rihga Royal Hotel New York
http://ny.rihga.com/

Ritz-Carlton Hotels
http://www.ritzcarlton.com

Super 8
http://www.super8.com

Wendy's
http://www.wendys.com

White Castle
http://www.whitecastle.com

Youth Hostel Australia (YHA) Travel
http://www.yha.org.au/

Chapter 13 Outline

Communications in Hospitality Marketing
    The Communications Mix
Effective Market Communications
    Planning Communications
    Guest Involvement
    Implementation Guidelines
Communications Channels
    Interpersonal Channels
    Mass Communication Channels
    Channel Effectiveness
    Channel Strategies
Hospitality Advertising
    Advertising Objectives
    Advertising Challenges
    Advertising Budgets
    Media Selection
    Positioning
    Advertising Themes and Messages
    Reach and Frequency
    Scheduling
Public Relations
    Public Relations' Role and Objective
    Developing PR Programs
    Publicity
Concluding Comments

13

Communications Mix: Advertising and Public Relations

"When business is good, it pays to advertise. When business is bad, you've got to advertise."

—Anonymous

Every day, thousands of hotels and restaurants advertise using television, radio, magazines, newspapers, billboards, and so forth to reach current and potential guests. Many employ public relations programs that generate positive media coverage, increased awareness of their offerings, and invaluable goodwill.

Advertising and public relations are two major parts of the hospitality industry's total communications mix. They share so much in common that it is often hard to draw meaningful distinctions between them. Public relations efforts are frequently used to support advertising initiatives, and conversely advertising efforts are frequently used to support public relations initiatives. Both are used to influence large numbers of guests via mass media and both tailor their messages carefully to communicate with target audiences.

In this chapter, we shall first discuss communications in general, considering communication models, elements of communication systems, and communication objectives. Then we shall turn our attention to advertising and public relations.

Communications in Hospitality Marketing

Marketing communications deals with the important tasks of delivering effective information and ideas to markets and obtaining the audience feedback necessary to develop them. Exhibit 1 presents a basic model of the hospitality communications process. It depicts communication as a two-way process of presenting information to target markets and obtaining information from them. The communicator, or message sender (hospitality provider), is the source that develops message approaches and content. The message is then encoded—that is, put into "symbols" such as words (headlines, text, etc.) and illustrations—and conveyed to target markets through communications channels. Message recipients (current and potential guests) decode the messages and choose either to ignore or accept them.

When decoding messages, guests may interpret them in ways never intended by the source. Too often, cultural and language differences between marketers

Exhibit 1   Hospitality Marketing Communications Process

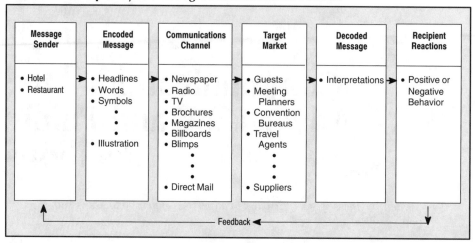

Message Sender	Encoded Message	Communications Channel	Target Market	Decoded Message	Recipient Reactions

• Hotel
• Restaurant
	• Headlines
	• Words
	• Symbols
	•
	•
	•
	• Illustration
		• Newspaper
		• Radio
		• TV
		• Brochures
		• Magazines
		• Billboards
		• Blimps
		•
		•
		•
		• Direct Mail
			• Guests
			• Meeting
			  Planners
			• Convention
			  Bureaus
			• Travel
			  Agents
			•
			•
			•
			• Suppliers
				• Interpretations	• Positive or
					  Negative
					  Behavior

Feedback ◄

and their audiences result in messages that fail to communicate accurately. Colors, numbers, symbols, and brand names can have significantly different meanings to different people, leading to unexpected reactions and responses. Interference may arise at any point in the process to disrupt and distort communications and their effects.

Receiver perceptions of both the message sender and the message medium are important communications ingredients. A message from an industry leader like Hyatt or Ritz-Carlton will have greater credibility than the same message from a little-known or unreliable lodging provider. Similarly, a message in *Time* or *Newsweek* will generally be more believable than the same message delivered in a supermarket tabloid. When receivers of communications hold favorable attitudes toward both the source and the medium, we say that **congruity** exists, which compounds communication's effectiveness. Conversely, when there is incongruity—when unfavorable attitudes exist about the source or medium—communication is impeded.

Consider one message presented by Marriott for its Stratford Court, a seniors living facility. The advertisement featured a picture of J. W. Marriott, Chairman of the Board of Marriott Corporation, with a headline saying, "When I put my name on a senior living community, it's going to feel like home…like family." By featuring himself in the advertisement, Mr. Marriott is not only helping readers put a friendly face to an already well-known brand name, he is also using his reputation to support and legitimize the advertisement's claims. As a result, a sympathetic and trustworthy source backs up the ad's statements and generates trust. Because the advertisement appears in a medium that is presumably trusted by the potential seniors audience, congruity exists.

The Communications Mix

The **communications mix** refers to the unique blend of media and messages that flow between hospitality providers and their target markets. The communications

Exhibit 2   Hospitality Communications Mix

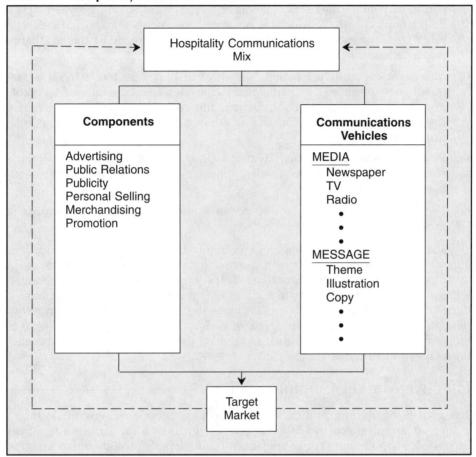

mix directly affects guest perceptions and behavior. As it focuses on answering the question, "How will our hospitality offerings benefit you?" it can increase the appeal of hospitality offerings, shape guest expectations, and guide their purchase actions. The communications mix is enhanced by market research, which gathers information about guests and suggests approaches and messages that guests will likely find appealing.

Exhibit 2 depicts the hospitality communications mix, delineating the major components and communications vehicles. Although the components are defined essentially as follows, nevertheless, they do overlap.

- *Advertising*: Any form of mass communication that is paid for by a hospitality provider. The advertiser controls the choice of media and message.

- *Public relations*: Mass communication designed to create or maintain a favorable image of the organization among its various constituents.

- *Publicity*: The principal tool of public relations, which, unlike advertising, is considered "free"; the result of media attention created by the provider's public relations efforts. The focus is on interviews, news releases, articles, and other "free" forms of communication not paid for directly by the hospitality organization.

- *Merchandising*: In-house activities such as displays, posters, wine lists, frequent guest programs, and similar activities designed to stimulate favorable images, increase customer satisfaction, and encourage purchases. Merchandising supplements and works as an adjunct to advertising and public relations efforts.

- *Promotion*: A supporting activity that includes such things as displays, trade shows, some advertising materials, contests, trade promotions, coupons, samples, and premiums.

- *Personal selling*: Direct person-to-person communication for the purpose of making a sale.

Marketers face the challenge of combining these various communications ingredients into an effective, coordinated mix that will inform and persuade target markets. Doing so involves establishing clear communications objectives, budgeting expenditures for each of the major components, and deciding how to combine them and their specific ingredients to achieve the most effective communications possible using the given resources. The variety of communications objectives ranges from increasing sales, profits, and market share to repositioning and changing images and attitudes.

Effective Market Communications

The goal in combining and coordinating communications ingredients into a unique communications mix is to achieve the greatest impact for the resources expended. The following communications fundamentals provide broad practical guidelines for doing so:

- Communicate in terms of guest interests rather than provider interests. See your message through guests' eyes and speak their language.

- Communicate in terms of benefits, not selling points. Guests are not interested in the fact that $4 million was spent to refurbish a property. They want to know what benefits the refurbishing will bring them.

- Anticipate guest questions, objections, and doubts, and set out to answer them. By so doing, you help guests overcome barriers to positive action.

- Encourage guests to act: ask them to send in a coupon, call, fill in a form, enter a drawing, etc. Involve them in the communications process.

- Match the appropriate media to your specific guest segments. For example, if you wish to attract late-night concert and theater-goers to your new piano bar, it may make sense to advertise in the arts section of the newspaper or in programs of concerts and plays.

- Follow up to assess effectiveness and learn how to improve future communications efforts.

Planning Communications

Advertising and public relations should not be the result of haphazard or spur-of-the-moment decisions. They should be planned carefully. Too often hospitality marketers attempt to implement decisions with little or no strategic planning. Such providers may operate on the premise that if they simply increase advertising expenditures, enhanced sales and profits will follow. Therefore, they buy advertising in local newspapers and on radio and TV stations suggested by media salespeople. Yet unplanned and untargeted communications frequently waste resources. By using market research information and carrying out the following sequence of activities, hospitality providers can plan their communications efforts more effectively.

- State the situation (problems and issues).
- State communications objectives, both long and short term.
- Determine target markets.
- Specify the communications action—strategies, media, messages, and presentation details.
- Set communications budgets.
- Gather guest information.
- Implement communications program.
- Evaluate the results.
- Make adjustments to future communications programs.

The actions are self-explanatory, use a common sense approach, and yet are often short-circuited. Hospitality managers are more prone to act, to do something like advertise, rather than take the time and expend the effort to think through their communications activities.

Guest Involvement

Different guest segments will interpret and respond to the same message differently, based on many factors such as their culture, socioeconomic position, family status (couples and singles, children and no children), age, and sex. Obviously, it is to the marketer's benefit to communicate in ways that appeal to guests and enhance the message's effectiveness. Because an ad's effectiveness depends on guest appeal, there is significant value in gathering guest information before developing and implementing communications programs.

Guests often hesitate to express their true feelings. When asked if a meal or a room was to their liking, they often say, "Everything was fine," even when it wasn't. They do not wish to hurt people's feelings, they want to be liked, and they do not want to be seen as complainers.

When guests *do* provide feedback—whether through guest comment cards, guest surveys, a suggestion box, personal contact, or comments to staff—it is essential that their input truly be heard. Listening carefully to guests to determine the real meaning of what they are saying is essential to effective communications. Too often marketers merely listen to what they wish to hear, screening out and ignoring negative comments that could be helpful. That was the case when the cashier at a fine restaurant asked a guest who was leaving, "How was your dinner?" He replied, "Not too good." Yet the cashier's automatic response was "I'm sorry"—and that was that! She missed a splendid opportunity to gather valuable information, establish communications, and turn around a dissatisfied guest.

At another restaurant, a regular customer was asked by the owner, "How were the spareribs?" The owner expected to hear a compliment, but the guest responded, "As a matter of fact, they were very tough." The owner was offended and became defensive, replying, "Well, the quality of the spareribs is good. They probably just weren't cooked long enough." Communication did not occur in this exchange. The restaurateur approached the situation in defense of the quality of the ribs he purchased, which was not the guest's concern. The guest was concerned with his enjoyment of the spareribs—or lack thereof. Had the restaurateur actually listened to the customer's complaint, he could have received valuable guest information enabling him to prevent the problem from happening again. More effective communication would also have made the guest feel that his problem had been taken seriously and that some satisfactory conclusion had been reached.

Implementation Guidelines

To help carry out a communications plan and improve market communications, hospitality marketers can employ the useful who, what, where, when, how, and why equation. Answering such questions as the following will be helpful:

1. Purpose: Why are we communicating this message? Or
2. Goals and Objectives: What do we hope to achieve?
3. Target Market: Who are the recipients?
4. Theme and Content: What message do we want to convey?
5. Format: How should the message be presented?
6. Media: Where should the communications appear?
7. Frequency and Continuity: When should the communications appear?
8. Decoding: How might guests interpret (or misinterpret) the messages?
9. Results: How effective were the communications?

Communications Channels ───────────────────────────

Communications channels are the means by which hospitality providers convey messages to guests and potential guests. They may be classified as either interpersonal or mass channels.

Interpersonal Channels

Interpersonal channels provide direct contact between the source and the audience, whether groups or individuals. We distinguish among three types of interpersonal channels: advocacy channels, expert channels, and word-of-mouth channels.

Advocacy channels, such as sales reps, have a direct, vested interest in conveying a message. Sales reps have many advantages as face-to-face communicators, but they also face a major limitation: as an advocacy channel, their communications may lack the credibility of unsolicited word-of-mouth comments by guests. After all, it is their job to paint a glowing picture of their offerings.

Expert channels represent a step up in credibility and effectiveness. While such expert spokespeople as business, media, and sports figures are paid for their endorsements, their reputations inspire a sense of familiarity and respect that salaried staff cannot command. What they say must be true, the audience believes, because this person is putting her or his name on the line. The downside is that such setbacks as public scandals and sagging careers can turn a once-effective spokesperson into a liability or a less-than-effective representative of the organization.

Word-of-mouth channels generally are recognized as among the most effective form of communication in the hospitality industry. In some cases, positive word-of-mouth recommendations from influential family members, friends, and club members are deemed to be many many times more persuasive than any other form of communication. In fact, many successful restaurants rely totally on the word of mouth of their guests. Thus, it is surprising that so few hospitality providers have set up programs to capitalize on positive word-of-mouth endorsements in an organized manner.

The downside of word-of-mouth channels is that negative word of mouth can take a costly toll on restaurants and hotels. A common saying is that one dissatisfied guest influences ten others, who each in turn influence another ten, and so on. Overcoming negatives can be expensive and time consuming. Unfortunately, guests are much quicker to share negative experiences than they are to share favorable ones.

Mass Communication Channels

Mass communication channels represent those media that reach a large audience simultaneously. They include, but are not limited to, newspapers; radio; broadcast, cable, and satellite television; direct mail; magazines; billboards; and the Internet. While they are capable of reaching many actual and potential guests, they also reach many people who will not become customers, resulting in wasted coverage. However, since they have the power to reach millions of people at one time, they can, nevertheless, be relatively cost effective.

By presenting the same message at one time to a large audience, mass communication channels gain maximum impact for their advertising dollars and are capable of generating heightened interest. An intriguing advertising slogan or image can work its way into popular culture, be a topic of conversation, and even become newsworthy, taking on a life of its own.

Exhibit 3 Comparison of Interpersonal and Mass Communication Channels

Characteristic	Interpersonal Channels	Mass Channels
Communication context	Face-to-face, direct	Interposed, indirect
Communicator's control over situation	High	Low
Amount of feedback	Much	Little
Speed of feedback	Immediate, direct	Delayed, indirect
Size of audience	Small (personal)	Large (interpersonal)
Message flow	Two ways	One way
Ability to overcome receiver's selective process	High	Low
Speed in reaching large audiences	Relatively slow	Relatively fast
Most efficient use	Attitude formation and change	Information transmittal

At the same time, mass communication messages cannot be aimed, directed, tailored, and adapted to specific audiences to the extent that interpersonal messages can. Every viewer of a cruise ship commercial will get the same message whether they are a frequent guest of the cruise line or have vowed never to leave dry land.

Hospitality providers use multiple channels to communicate with target markets. The challenge is to develop the most effective blend of mass and interpersonal communications. Exhibit 3 highlights a comparison of interpersonal and mass communications channels according to several important characteristics. Exhibit 4 compares advertising, personal selling, sales promotion, and public relations. They are assessed according to such important factors as target, message, cost, sponsor, flexibility, feedback, and degree of control. Such considerations can help management determine the best mass/interpersonal channel mix and the best blend of specific channels to accomplish stated objectives.

Channel Effectiveness

There has been a considerable amount of research into the effectiveness of various communications channels. Among some of the general findings of interest to hospitality marketers are:

- Different channels serve different functions and offer different kinds of information to guests.

- All channels are not equally effective during all stages of the purchase decision.

Exhibit 4   Characteristics of Marketing Communication Elements

Factor	Advertising	Personal Selling	Sales Promotion	Public Relations
Targets	Groups (mass)	Individuals	Groups, but not always mass groups	Groups (mass)
		Specific	Uniform	Uniform
			Moderate cost per contact	No media cost, moderate costs for press releases and materials
			Identified	Not identified
			Moderate	Little
			Less precise but faster than personal selling	Neither precise nor fast
			High	Low

...lative effect, increasing the likelihood

...g to the degree of attitudinal and behav-
...ests.

...nels are usually more persuasive than

- Mass ... terms of cost per person reached and for repeating information.

Channel Strategies

Two widely used communication strategies are *push* and *pull*. **Push strategies** rely heavily on the aggressive use of communications to push hospitality products and services through channels to the marketplace. The belief is that aggressive promotion will help hospitality providers increase revenue and profits. Economic incentives, such as price discounts, are important ingredients of push strategies.

Beer and wine distributors often push their products through channels by giving hotels, bars, and restaurants special prices and deals, which can then be passed along to guests as daily specials or recommendations by the waitstaff. Hotels and restaurants aggressively advertise reduced room rates, weekend specials, early bird dinners, holiday rates, the free use of health clubs, tennis courts, and club rooms.

A **pull strategy**, by contrast, is used to create guest demand and get guests to ask for certain brands or products, thereby pulling them through the channels to the markets. For example, if liquor manufacturers and distributors can encourage guests—through advertising, merchandising, etc.—to demand brandy sours or Beefeater martinis, hospitality providers will stock and sell these products. Similarly, the milk, beef, pork, and poultry industries advertise their products to consumers hoping they will request them at hotels and restaurants, thereby pulling the products through the channels.

Push strategies benefit from personal marketing: a server or host who informs guests that something is a good deal or a good product. Pull strategies tend to rely on mass communications that can generate mass interest. Subsequently, they are most effective in situations where personal contact is minimal, such as fast-food operations or where the operation itself is a "newsworthy" destination, such as hotels near popular theme parks. Pull strategies can be bolstered by in-house promotions—contests, coupons, discounts, toys, and a host of merchandising activities.

Hospitality Advertising

Advertising is what most of us think of when we think of mass market communications. It may be defined as mass communications paid for by a sponsor. The sponsor develops and controls advertising and can reach vast audiences relatively inexpensively. When done effectively, advertising can be instrumental in differentiating hospitality properties, highlighting guest benefits, and generating sales.

Advertising may be directed to various audiences: actual and potential guests, competitors, the trade, shareholders, and employees. It is used for such purposes as generating and maintaining awareness of hotels and restaurants; drawing attention to new hospitality approaches, products, and services; influencing guest perceptions and preferences; differentiating offerings; and increasing market leverage. Advertising's ultimate purpose is profitable sales.

It is really not important that guests find an advertisement's approach, theme, illustration, layout, or copy entertaining or clever. What is important is whether an ad achieves its purpose—ultimately, does it sell? Advertising's role is sometimes summed up by the acronym *AIDA*: get *attention*, generate *interest*, create *desire*, and stimulate purchase *action*. In other words, advertising is used to inform, persuade, and influence guests to buy.

Sometimes advertising has the goal of selling customers directly and immediately. Guests are actively solicited and given discounts to buy a certain brand of pizza or hamburger, or to spend a weekend at a specific hotel or resort. Most advertising, however, is designed to sell indirectly, by supporting various hospitality activities over time. Advertising does this by providing information, generating favorable images, differentiating and positioning hospitality offerings, stimulating guest interest, and encouraging buying. In addition, after-sale advertising supports and reinforces purchase decisions already made by guests, reassuring them that they made a wise choice. (Such reinforcement can be valuable for generating repeat purchases and positive word of mouth.)

One of the most successful hospitality advertising campaigns is the "Tom Bodett for Motel 6" radio campaign. It has gained great visibility, recognition, and success over an extended period of time. And it is no accident that it has been so successful, for the campaign was carefully planned and based on research into consumer behavior. The theme and messages were thoughtfully developed, with little left to chance.[1] Tom Bodett, an author and radio personality known for telling stories with quiet and homespun humor, serves as a very believable spokesperson/ user of Motel 6. His emphasis on Motel 6 as "a smart choice" and his unforgettable tagline, "We'll leave the light on for you," welcomed guests and reinforced the impact of the advertising program.

It is one thing to advertise extensively; any organization with a sufficiently large budget can accomplish that much. It is quite another thing to advertise effectively. Whether advertising is effective depends entirely on guests' reactions. Moreover, advertisers should remember that guests are constantly being bombarded by staggering numbers of advertisements. Estimates are that the average American is subjected to 3,000 advertising messages a day and about 38,000 TV commercials a year.[2] Guests become selective in determining what advertisements "get through" to them, which ones they actually hear or see, let alone respond to favorably. The overwhelming tendency is to tune out and disregard most advertisements. Thus stereotyped, contrived, and "me too" advertisements tend to fare poorly. Creativity is a major ingredient of successful advertising. Effective advertising involves approaching advertising decisions in a creative and enticing manner.

Advertising Objectives

Hospitality advertising has a host of varied objectives including:

- Differentiating hospitality properties, products, and services from those of competitors
- Promising and delivering benefits that meet or exceed guest wants and needs
- Relating to guests and making hospitality services more tangible
- Providing guests with desired visual images of the hospitality providers and offerings
- Supporting guests' purchase decisions
- Generating interest on the part of potential guests
- Creating positive influences on employees
- Positioning hospitality providers and offerings appropriately
- Generating sales
- Gaining and maintaining market share

The objectives of specific advertisements may be related to the purchase-decision stages of guests. Research suggests that guests advance through various stages in purchasing products and services. A seven-step sequence has been identified, according to which the guest purchase stages are:[3]

1. Complete unawareness
2. Mere awareness of the existence of a product or service
3. Knowledge of what the product or service offers
4. Favorable attitudes toward the product or service
5. Preference over other alternatives
6. Desire to buy
7. Actual purchase

Different advertising strategies are used to address the specific needs of guests at every stage of their purchase decision.

Advertising Challenges

Hospitality advertisers span a spectrum from very large organizations, with seemingly unlimited budgets, to independent restaurants and motor inns, whose advertising budget may be only a few hundred dollars. The majority of hospitality businesses have limited budgets and are in the position of having to stretch scarce advertising dollars to cover what advertising they do.

Some hospitality providers assume that larger advertising budgets would solve many of their marketing problems. Advertising can indeed help capitalize on an organization's strengths, bolster positive guest reactions, and extend markets, sales, and profits. But advertising, no matter how extensive, cannot overcome the inadequacies of inferior offerings. It is not a remedy for poor service, bad locations, inadequate facilities, unacceptable rooms, inappropriate menus, high prices, and unfavorable guest experiences. It cannot overcome the lack of planning.

In addition to budgetary constraints, hospitality operations face the challenge of selling many products and services that are, to a large extent, intangible. Comfortable rooms, fine lobbies, and attentive service cannot be savored by the senses the way that physical products can. Therefore, we say that hospitality marketing is "intangible dominant," contrasted with "tangible dominant" product marketing. Hospitality products and services must be experienced to be appreciated.

To compound the problem, hospitality advertisements themselves are built on intangibles: words, concepts, themes, and images—all abstractions that further increase the industry's intangibility. In a sense, hospitality advertisements are intangible promises made to guests about intangible services. They represent such intangible promises as the pleasure of relaxing at a luxury hotel on the beach, the romance of a week-long cruise, or the glamour of lingering over an expensive dinner at a world-class restaurant. Hospitality advertisers face the challenge of making these intangibles real to guests through carefully combined headlines, advertising copy, images, and symbols.

For an example of how one chain met this challenge, consider Helmsley Hotels' series of advertisements with the theme, "What's the matter with this picture?" The campaign featured pictures of hotel rooms with beds missing a pillow, rooms where the drapes did not close properly, and restaurant tables that were set incorrectly. Several ads also featured Leona Helmsley saying, "I think that hangers should come out of the closet without a struggle," or, "I can't get dressed without a full-length mirror. Can you?" In this manner, the advertisements translated abstract hospitality services into tangible symbols dealing with guest services and benefits.

Advertising Budgets

How much should be spent on advertising? While there is no easy answer to that question, hospitality businesses can take logical approaches to determining advertising budgets. The amount required depends on such factors as the type of property, marketing objectives, target markets, competition, economic conditions, profitability, and opportunities for cooperative and reciprocal advertising.

Hospitality businesses may use several budgeting approaches. Most common is a subjective approach, wherein management uses its discretion to determine the amount of the advertising budget. The amount specified may be the result of intuition or personal judgment, or may simply be a matter of whatever funds are available or can be justified. Sometimes ratios or fixed guidelines are used, where advertising may represent a certain percentage of the overall budget or a specific dollar amount. Advertisers may match a predetermined percentage of competitors' budgets. They may allocate a percentage of actual or anticipated sales or profits. Or, they may use a ratio of advertising to industry sales. While such methods are straightforward and automatic, they do not consider hospitality company situations and requirements. The consequence can be spending too few or too many dollars on advertising based on current market conditions. Setting advertising budgets by ratios means that advertising is the result of sales (such as a percent of sales) rather than the engine and stimulus of sales.

The Objective and Task Method. The most logical approach to determining advertising appropriations is the **objective and task method**. The approach is to think first about advertising objectives, and then consider the advertising tasks necessary to achieve them. Once objectives are clearly defined, and the tasks necessary to achieve them are detailed, then the required advertising expenditures can be specified. If required expenditures exceed advertising budgets, both the advertising objectives and tasks can be reconsidered and possibly altered. Alternatively, additional advertising resources may be allocated.

For example, suppose a restaurant's objective is to broaden its image from that of a bar and luncheon spot to include family dining. The tasks necessary to accomplish that objective—developing new menus, informing guests, and enticing families to try it—can be identified. Appropriate markets, messages, and media can then be determined. Next, estimates of the necessary advertising budget can be made. If the budget is insufficient, management may decide to limit the scope and tasks or increase the budget. Problems arise when insufficient budgets are matched with over-ambitious objectives. Although it is unreasonable to expect to reach advertising goals with inadequate budgets, in practice that is all too often the case.

Cost Guidelines. Cost-effectiveness is often used as a guideline in both setting advertising budgets and assessing effectiveness. Three common measures employed are cost per thousand (CPM), cost per inquiry (CPI), and cost per conversion (CPC).

Cost per thousand calculates the cost of reaching one thousand buyers. The formula for determining it is:

$$\text{CPM} \ = \ \frac{\text{Cost of advertisement} \times 1{,}000}{\text{Circulation}}$$

Cost per inquiry considers the number of inquiries generated by an advertisement and the cost of the advertising.

$$\text{CPI} \ = \ \frac{\text{Cost of advertisement}}{\text{Inquiries generated}}$$

Inquiries, of course, do not always result in sales. The cost per conversion looks at the total number of conversions—actual inquiries that become guests—and relates them to the cost of the advertisement.

$$\text{CPC} \ = \ \frac{\text{Cost of advertisement}}{\text{Number of conversions}}$$

While these measures provide some indication of the effectiveness of advertising expenditures, they ignore many important issues. The lowest cost per thousand, for instance, may not yield the lowest cost per inquiry or the lowest cost per conversion. Moreover, where advertising is not very effective, the measures do not indicate what the difficulties may be—approaches, messages, or media.

Thresholds. In setting advertising budgets, it can sometimes be beneficial to think in terms of **thresholds**. For advertising to have any noticeable impact, a threshold, or critical mass of at least a certain level, of expenditure may be required. For example, creating guest awareness may require a certain level of media coverage; spending less than that amount will do little or nothing, resulting in wasted resources. Spending one half of the advertising dollars deemed necessary may not achieve one half of the awareness. In fact, it may hardly raise awareness at all. But with enough money to carry out the awareness program and cross the threshold level, considerable impact may be realized. Indeed, once the threshold has been reached, additional advertising expenditures may yield splendid results, up to a certain limit. Once that limit is reached, however, returns will taper off, sometimes very sharply.

Determining thresholds is a difficult challenge, although companies have conducted experiments to do so. It is a matter of determining the sensitivity of sales to increases in advertising. The very act of thinking about thresholds and monitoring advertising budgets accordingly is beneficial. It keeps management focus on gaining returns for dollars spent and raises the question of whether doing a little advertising is any better than doing none at all.

Stretching Advertising Dollars. Many options are available to increase the impact of limited advertising budgets. For example, hospitality marketers may consider using advertising agencies. Various types of agencies are available, ranging from those offering a complete range of services to very specialized agencies that may focus exclusively on certain activities such as radio promotions or trade magazine advertising. Advertising agencies have experience and talents that can be helpful in performing such tasks as developing advertising campaigns, selecting media, and assessing results. Use of an agency eliminates the workspace and salary burdens of retaining an in-house staff.

Hospitality marketers also may choose to participate in cooperative advertising. Cooperative advertising involves advertising with other advertisers, and it may take the form of horizontal or vertical cooperation. **Horizontal cooperation** refers to the pooling of advertising resources by similar businesses, such as motels or fast-food restaurants, to achieve joint objectives. For example, several downtown hotels may get together and advertise cooperatively to attract large conferences or sporting events. Independent hotels have grouped together, as The Preferred Hotels of the World and The Best Small Hotels, and they advertise cooperatively.

Vertical cooperation involves advertising sponsored by several different kinds of hospitality businesses, for their mutual benefit. Hotels, airlines, and rental car agencies may advertise cooperatively and engage in premium programs targeted to their common guests. Costs are shared, and the combined budget permits a greater range of alternatives than that available to any of the individual advertisers. Such advertising may also result in a joint identification among cooperating brands, increasing sales and profits for all. Among the disadvantages are: inflexibility, lack of control, and differences in company desires and objectives. Rarely do all participants realize equal benefits.

Reciprocal advertising, also known as "trade-out" or "due bill" advertising, refers to such actions as the exchange of hotel rooms, meals, health club facilities, meeting rooms, or other hospitality services for advertising. This enables hospitality providers to extend their limited advertising budgets without additional expenditures. Moreover, an additional return may be received because participants who occupy otherwise unused hotel rooms will likely spend money on other hotel services. Also, those visiting a property as part of a reciprocal arrangement may well recommend the property to their associates.

Media Selection

Media are the channels, vehicles, or outlets used to communicate with markets. Media selection has direct impact on both the believability and acceptance of advertising. Hospitality businesses may receive assistance in developing and targeting their advertising from the media used, whether print or broadcast.

There are a wide variety of print and broadcast media. Print media include national, regional, city, and community newspapers; general and special-interest magazines; and literally thousands of trade publications. Broadcast media include radio and television, which is playing a more significant role and includes local, national, cable, and public channels. The availability of electronic media embodied in computer networks is expanding alternatives to include hospitality-specific, Internet-based marketing efforts. Other media used by hospitality businesses include movie theaters, sports arenas, display cards, outdoor billboards, buses,

and park benches. Choosing from the vast array of media possibilities means paying careful attention to advertising's purpose and target markets.

Hospitality advertising is directed to broad national and international audiences, as well as to specialized segments and niches. **Narrowcasting** (advertising
directed to more specific target markets through such media as selected direct mail
or a country western or classical music radio station) makes it possible to communicate more effectively with smaller markets. In making media choices, attention
must be given to both the ability to reach target markets and the cost of doing so.
Knowledge of how guests choose a hospitality property can help determine which
media to use. While it may be less costly, per subscriber, to advertise in newspapers, it may be more effective to reach certain groups through trade journals or
business directories, which have a higher per reader cost.

Print and broadcast media often provide valuable demographic information
about their audiences. The data can be analyzed, competitors' media selections
assessed, and informed choices made. Before committing their advertising budget,
hospitality marketers should consider which media:

- Reach the largest number of actual and potential guests at the lowest cost
- Communicate effectively
- Communicate directly with targeted guests
- Best fit the positioning and image requirements
- Are affordable
- Give flexibility to meet changes
- Effectively deliver the advertisement and its message
- Can achieve stated objectives within budget limits
- Have guest acceptability

Candid answers to such pertinent questions as these, and consideration of the
characteristics of media such as those given in Exhibit 5, enable hospitality marketers to develop valuable action guidelines.

Positioning

Positioning refers to creating an image in the minds of guests that reflects the
desirable characteristics and features of a hospitality operation and its offerings.
When the appropriate image is created, hospitality providers are better positioned
to appeal to guests, and advertising their distinguishing features positions them in
a unique slot in the marketplace. The benefits advertised by the luxurious Beverly
Hills Hotel or Hotel Bel-Air contrasts markedly with those of Motel 6, as do their
images, positioning them for different segments of the market. When hospitality
businesses are positioned appropriately, they can communicate their desired messages more readily to targeted markets.

Positioning provides a basic setting for advertising messages. It targets likely
guests and presents advertisers with opportunities to feature benefits that meet
guest needs and desires. The management challenge is to control positioning,
rather than let it develop haphazardly or at random. In consciously setting out to

Exhibit 5   Intermedia Comparisons

Characteristic	Broadcast Media		Print Media		Other		
	Radio	TV	Magazine	Newspaper	Direct Mail	Outdoor	Specialty
Exposure (reaches large audiences)	X	X	X	X		X	
Selectivity (easy-to-reach targets)	X	X	X	X	X		X
Low production costs	X			X	X	X	X
Low cost per audience member	X	X		X		X	
Flexible closing dates	X			X	X		
Long-lasting message			X	X	X		X
Appeals to more than one sense		X					
Prestige		X	X				
Suitable for lengthy, complex message			X	X	X		
Good reproduction quality	X	X	X		X	X	X
Message must stand alone (no editorial matter to attract)	X	X			X	X	X
Usually has full attention of audience		X	X	X	X		X
Little regulation			X	X	X		X
Data available about audience			X	X	X		
Data available about exposure			X	X	X		
Flexible format	X		X	X	X		X
Attended to at convenience of audience		X	X	X	X		X
Often many competing advertisers	X	X	X	X			

select a position in the market, hospitality marketers can use advertising to achieve, or hold, that position. For example, Burger King's advertising has emphasized the flavor of their flame-broiled hamburgers, Wendy's has advertised the freshness of their hamburgers, and Arby's has stressed the fact their roast beef sandwiches are not hamburgers at all. Although such differentiating images sometimes exist only in customers' minds, such perceptions are nevertheless important purchasing considerations.

Best Western International, Inc., whose properties now include resort hotels, convention hotels, business hotels, and ski lodges, at one time faced image and positioning problems. Guests perceived Best Western as a roadside chain. To change that image and position, Best Western chose an advertising campaign based on its name, with the theme "Your Best Bet's a Best Western." Specific advertisements suggested that Best Western offered the best night's sleep, the best place to cool off, and so on. The result was a 21 percent increase in calls to their reservation center.[4]

By determining the benefits that are important to various target market segments, hospitality providers can position themselves to address those benefits with the support of creative advertising. Properly planned and executed positioning can enhance advertising's effectiveness. Conversely, when providers are not positioned properly, advertising may be wasteful and ineffective.

Repositioning is an option when market conditions change due to such factors as intense competition, overcrowded market segments, the emergence of new profitable niches, the consolidation of properties, or even because previous positioning actions have failed. Repositioning involves removing the image associated with the previous position, and then using advertising to develop a new position. Ramada was involved in repositioning some of its properties when it moved upward with its Ramada Renaissance properties. Marriott did the opposite, repositioning some properties downward with its Marriott Courtyard motels.

In Boca Raton, Florida, a restaurateur purchased a unit of the Wags chain that had fallen out of favor. Largely a breakfast and lunch spot, it was repositioned as a popular-priced diner, featuring Greek food, for the whole family. The restaurant enjoyed incredible business, both in and out of season, with lines forming for dinner at 5 P.M.

Advertising Themes and Messages

Advertising themes help focus advertising messages. Themes are the concepts or organizing thoughts that clarify messages. To develop appropriate themes before preparing messages, advertisers might investigate such questions as:

- What makes their hospitality products and services unique?
- Which products and services are relevant to what target markets?
- What specific benefits do guests derive?
- How can such benefits be improved and made tangible?

Answers to such questions suggest advertising themes and keep advertising focused on target markets and desired positioning. For example, the Hotel Okura in Tokyo ran a series of advertisements appealing to business executives; the advertisements detailed the specifics of the hotel's Jet Lag Plan. The Four Seasons Hotels, in line with its theme of luxury, value, and service in targeting business executives, detailed such services as cleaning clothing overnight, breakfast even before 5:30 A.M., complimentary shoe polishing, and replacement of shoe laces. Hilton Hotels and Resorts has developed advertisements emphasizing the joy of family vacations and the fact that "kids stay free." Through the selection of appropriate themes, these hotels were able to focus their advertising messages and illustrations.

Messages are a controlling factor in advertising's impact. Effective messages will highlight guest benefits, bring the advertiser's strengths into focus, and inform and persuade guests. Although advertising messages may focus on selling directly, most set out to create favorable selling environments, support various marketing activities, and pave the way for future sales efforts.

Hospitality advertising messages sometimes suffer from a "spray approach." They lack focus, presenting a broad array of ideas and topics in the hope of having some relevance, for some guests, some of the time. Effective messages, however, are focused—tailored for specific target markets. The idea is to hit the target with a sharpshooter's bullet rather than spray buckshot in the hopes of hitting something.

Effective advertising messages are rooted in marketing research information. For example, one lodging chain emphasized money-back guarantees and free upgrades in their advertising. However, surveys and focus groups revealed that was not what guests wanted. Instead, guests wanted free newspapers, free phone calls, quick repairs, and in-room coffee makers. When the chain learned that, they changed their advertising accordingly, emphasizing free local newspapers and telephone calls, and in-room coffee and tea.[5]

Different advertising messages have appeal for various market segments. For example, research indicates that the typical 55-and-over hotel guest is financially savvy, shops for value, and switches when service declines. To appeal to them, themes and messages might feature discounts, value, and convenience.[6] Since the meeting and convention planners market is concerned with both costs and services, the Ritz-Carlton Hotel's advertising theme directed to them has long nurtured both its image as a host to the luxury class with its superior services and its special meeting packages at very competitive prices.[7]

Hilton Hotels, in the early 1990s, confronted the problem of declining income because of slow growth and decreasing occupancy rates. Research indicated that guests perceived that Hilton's services were declining. Although Hilton did not believe service truly had declined, it was nevertheless faced with overcoming an important emotional barrier. Therefore, it developed messages based on the theme "So Nice to Come Home To," aimed at capitalizing on the value of the Hilton brand name and an implied level of quality service.[8]

The essential steps for developing an effective advertising message include:

- Doing the research and gathering information about intended receivers before preparing messages.

- Designing and delivering messages that will appeal to the intended receivers.

- Making sure that words, symbols, illustrations, and other signals communicate accurately to all audiences.

- Designing messages that address market wants and needs and suggesting how the hospitality provider will fulfill them.

To check whether appropriate advertising messages have been developed, hospitality marketers can see if:

- The themes and approaches are on target for intended market segments and niches.

- The promises made are in line with what actually can be delivered.

- The identifying information—addresses, directions, toll-free numbers, etc.— is included.

- The reasons given for buying match desired guest benefits.

- Methods for evaluating messages are provided.

- Regular reviews and adjustments are made.

Reach and Frequency

The **reach** of advertising media refers to the number of people or households exposed to an advertising message at least once. Newspaper, television, and magazines have wide reach, for they expose their advertisements to masses of people. However, not all of those reached will be potential guests. Direct mail, by contrast, has narrower reach because it is delivered to a smaller audience; however, it may actually blanket a target market. When the communications reach is too broad, people who are not actual or potential guests are included in the message and waste occurs. When it is too narrow, potential guests may be missed. Generally, as reach increases so do advertising costs. The management challenge is to get a good match between media reach and target-market coverage.

Frequency refers to the number of times that the average person in a target market is exposed to an advertisement over a specified time period. It usually takes several exposures to get messages across to guests. Sometimes just getting attention requires a relatively large number of advertisements within a short time. While repetition helps in conveying advertising messages, gaining acceptance, and stimulating retention, *excessive* repetition is self-defeating. Advertisements wear out. When guests see the same advertisement too often, they may not only may tune it out—they may become annoyed. On the other hand, when guests are not exposed to an advertising message often enough, impact is diminished.

Continuity can enhance the value of an advertising campaign by helping get ideas across to guests. When advertising campaigns span an extended period, variations of the same theme, illustrations, and copy can be helpful, even entertaining. Thus, repetition helps get through to guests, while variation helps overcome the "wear out" factor.

Given limited advertising budgets, decisions must be made about reach versus frequency; authorities disagree which is more important. Regardless, selecting media with the appropriate reach and determining the appropriate frequency present continuing management challenges. Sophisticated advertisers with large budgets may use statistical techniques and mathematical models to help them make such decisions. Even so, deciding how often to run ads, over what intervals of time, is a subjective judgment.

Scheduling

Advertisers naturally want to schedule advertisements at times when they will be most effective. Sometimes advertising is scheduled to coincide with holidays, using appropriate seasonal messages. Other times, advertisements may be developed and scheduled to coincide with school breaks, winter or summer activities, or traditionally slow periods. Hotels often advertise special weekend rates and off-season discounts, while restaurants advertise early-bird or "sunset" dinner specials.

Three general scheduling patterns are commonly used: continuity, pulsing, and ad hoc. **Continuity scheduling** refers to scheduling advertising in a regular pattern over time. For example, some restaurants advertise in newspapers every Thursday and Sunday. Others have a daily TV or radio advertisement.

Planet Hollywood

Planet Hollywood is a successful chain of theme restaurants launched by Robert Earl and Keith Barish. Earl studied restaurant and hotel management at the University of Surrey and gained extensive hospitality experience. Barish is a movie producer with celebrity contacts. Coming from a successful career with Hard Rock Cafes, Earl recognized the power of publicity in launching restaurants and used it as a core ingredient of Planet Hollywood's marketing strategy. Earl and Barish developed the approach of bringing in celebrity investors as partners in individual restaurants—including Whoopie Goldberg, Sylvester Stallone, Roseanne Arnold, and Arnold Schwarzenegger. With stars appearing at restaurant openings, launchings automatically become public relations events, from which both the stars and the restaurants benefit. In Phoenix, for example, a crowd of some 5,000 people assembled in the bleachers outside the restaurant; when Arnold Schwarzenegger tossed out baseball caps bearing the Planet Hollywood logo, bedlam ensued.*

Planet Hollywood hosts screenings and parties for the stars. Restaurants promote the movies of supporting celebrities, TV monitors play movie previews, and movie memorabilia lines the walls—attracting celebrities and guests alike, particularly tourists who hope to see movie stars. Apparel sales in the average restaurant now make up about one-third of the annual $15 million sales and range from $3.50 souvenir pins to $325 leather jackets.

* *The Wall Street Journal*, 21 June 1994, pp. A1, 6.

Pulsing refers to an advertising spurt or emphasis on an irregular schedule over a specified period. If the winter months are particularly cold and snowy in the northern United States, Florida and Arizona resorts may decide to deliver an advertising pulse in the media of northern-tier states.

Ad hoc scheduling refers to scheduling advertisements when management thinks advertising is needed or whenever it can be afforded. Ad hoc decisions preclude planning and borders on being haphazard. Even so, the approach is a prevalent one.

Public Relations

Public relations (PR) is concerned with planning and executing communication and action programs to earn public understanding, acceptance, and goodwill. It involves a three-step process:

1. Evaluating public attitudes, opinions, and perceptions.

2. Assessing the policies, programs, and procedures of the hospitality provider in light of those attitudes, opinions, and perceptions revealed in step one.

3. Developing communications that address the public's concerns while delivering positive messages on behalf of the hospitality provider.

Public Relations' Role and Objective

Public relations approaches and methods are similar to those used by advertising. Like advertising, PR directly affects guest perceptions and influences company operations and revenues. However, while advertising is ultimately concerned with increasing sales, a key objective of PR is to enhance organizational and individual images mainly among outside audiences. PR is concerned with the total image of hospitality businesses as perceived by their many publics, including guests, shareholders, governments, suppliers, and other stakeholders. It both informs publics and obtains feedback about what they think so that improvements can be made.

PR is that part of the communications mix that is concerned with company acceptability—with what a hospitality provider is and what its services can and should do. It seeks to establish mutual understanding between a hospitality supplier and its many publics by using communications to influence public opinion. Maintaining good media relations is one of the most essential ingredients of effective PR.

Hotels and restaurants do not face a choice of whether they should or should not communicate with their publics. Their only choice is what kind of PR a property will enjoy: good, mediocre, or poor. Hospitality providers are in continuous and direct communication with the public. In hospitality, PR is everyone's business—from switchboard operators and waitstaff to bellstaff and top executives.

The basic components of PR are events and activities that are new and newsworthy. This has long been recognized by the Las Vegas hotels that rely on media events such as pre-opening press releases, celebrity parties, widely publicized grand openings, and gala celebrations. Often, however, what hospitality properties deem newsworthy the media do not. The fact that a restaurant has been refurbished or its theme changed is of particular interest to the property, its management, and staff, but it may not interest the media and their audiences. An effective PR program would develop activities to capture media interest and gain positive exposure for the property's improved facility and decor.

Developing PR Programs

PR programs succeed when they capture the personal interest of guests to whom they are directed and gain acceptance for the perspectives they present. To ensure successful PR programs, consider the RACE formula:[9]

R	=	Research
A	=	Action
C	=	Communication
E	=	Evaluation

Successful PR, like advertising, should be planned and integrated into the total marketing plan, geared to target market segments, designed to achieve specified objectives, and monitored to see how it is doing and how it can be improved. The effectiveness of PR plans depends on those who implement them. Sometimes the use of professional, in-house PR staff can pay off handsomely. This is particularly true when problems of community impact arise. Such potentially negative news as citations for health violations, food poisoning, fires, lawsuits, accidents, and strikes need to be handled quickly and effectively. Although most hospitality properties find it impractical to establish their own public relations departments, this does not mean that PR approaches cannot be implemented by available staff.

The communications channels and tools used by PR to reach different groups of guests vary. What is appropriate for reaching mature consumers may not be so for the younger set. Research can help determine the appropriate channels and approaches. Sometimes indirect approaches are employed to reach targeted guests, such as directing communications to opinion leaders, who, in turn, will communicate authoritatively with the desired publics.

News conferences, special events, news releases, community service, and charitable works are among the variety of ways that hospitality providers seek to furnish favorable information to their publics. Communities, governments, and various businesses plan around special events such as Carnival; the Chinese New Year; music, theater, and dance festivals; the Olympics; and the Super Bowl. Hospitality businesses are direct beneficiaries of such PR efforts.

The government of Singapore has used PR programs most successfully to create and develop the country's image as an exotic and desirable travel destination. Television and print media PR programs were used in targeted countries such as the United States. Media representatives were invited on all-expense-paid inspection trips, and then wrote articles in their home newspapers and developed TV programs featuring the attractions of Singapore. In conjunction with the campaign, the government developed policies and programs that supported tourism and encouraged the development of world-class luxury hotels and restaurants, Singapore Airlines (one of the world's finest airlines), modern shopping centers, and recreation and leisure attractions. Supported by continuing PR programs, the efforts of a small city-state of about 3.1 million people have paid off handsomely, contributing to Singapore's economic well-being in a major way.

Publicity

Publicity is a principal tool of PR. It refers to the unpaid mention of hospitality properties and their offerings, activities, and personnel by the media. It supports advertising and other hospitality marketing activities.

Publicity can be among the most effective promotional tools for many hospitality enterprises. The idea is to have an existing PR strategy in place that enables a property to seize the moment, make the most of unexpected opportunities, and respond quickly to unanticipated setbacks. For example, the choice of a hotel or resort for a visit by royalty or other celebrity generates valuable publicity opportunities. Similarly, favorable restaurant reviews are widely used for publicity purposes, as are restaurant openings or the hiring of a highly respected chef. Newspaper stories about properties can have great immediate and long term impact.

Publicists are PR specialists who plan and manage the publicity efforts of company activities. Publicists are trained to have a "nose for the news," the ability to identify those particular news angles that will be deemed "newsworthy" by the media, as well as of interest to their respective audiences. By presenting or "packaging" these angles for the media, publicists obtain media coverage and garner attention for their hospitality operations. Some larger hospitality businesses use services that track the results of publicity releases, indicating which ones have been used and by which media. This information can be valuable for fine-tuning and improving PR effectiveness and capitalizing on desirable images.

In seeking publicity, publicists must first arouse the interest of intermediaries such as reporters, editors, journalists, and publishers. These intermediaries serve as publicity gatekeepers, deciding which events are newsworthy—that is, which will be featured and which will not. Despite insiders' feelings, not every new hospitality property or offering makes for a newsworthy event in the eyes of the media. It takes news or information that goes beyond the merely self-serving or self-promotional and highlights benefits for the community or the general public.

Publicity can enhance the credibility of a company's offering or advertising message in the minds of audiences. What the news media report is more believable than an organization's own advertising message. On the other hand, negative publicity can create perplexing marketing problems. Unfavorable publicity, whether it is fair or not, can be devastating. Restaurateurs are well aware that news reports of health code violations, even after they have already been corrected, can have an immediate and sustained negative impact on revenues. People love to discuss bad news, and unfavorable publicity receives far greater attention, makes the rounds much faster, and tends to be longer lasting than favorable publicity.

Concluding Comments

This chapter deals with the important flow of communications via advertising and public relations messages from hospitality businesses to their markets. Hospitality managers face the choice of how, not whether, to communicate with guests. The quality of communications greatly affects the profitability of their operations.

Advertising and public relations messages shape guest perceptions and behavior and, as a result, affect purchase decisions. Advertising refers to mass communications paid for and controlled by hospitality businesses. Public relations, which may be thought of as "free advertising," is controlled by the media and not by the business (although the business can attempt to guide it). Public relations uses publicity as its major tool.

The objective is to develop a communications mix that gets the greatest impact for the resources used. Hospitality managers can use answers to the who, what, when, where, how and why questions about their advertising and public relations to design effective communications programs.

In communicating with guests, hospitality marketers may use three types of interpersonal channels—advocacy, expert, and word-of-mouth. They can choose from a wide assortment of media alternatives such as newspapers, magazines, billboards, cable and satellite TV, direct mail, the Internet, blimps, and a host of other promotional vehicles. In deciding which channels and media to use, managers can first detail the communications tasks to be achieved and then align them with the attributes of various channels and media.

Hospitality advertising can be directed to achieve a variety of objectives. Ultimately, all of them have their roots in making profitable sales through informing and persuading guests. Generally hospitality advertisers find themselves in the position of trying to accomplish their communications goals with too few dollars. They are faced with stretching their budgets to do as well as they can under difficult circumstances. This calls for greater scrutiny of advertising activities than usually occurs. Careful selection of media and messages can significantly increase the communications impact. Well-designed public relations campaigns can pay off handsomely. Paying attention to advertising and public relations is well worth the effort.

Endnotes

1. Mark W. Cunningham and Chekitan Dev, "Strategic Marketing: A Lodging 'End-Run,'" *Cornell Hotel and Restaurant Administration Quarterly*, August 1992, pp. 36–43.

2. Michko Kakutani, "Bananas For Rent," *The New York Times Magazine*, November 1997, p. 32.

3. Robert J. Lavidge and Gary Steiner, "A Model of Predictive Measurements of Advertising Effectiveness," *Journal of Marketing*, October 1961, pp. 59–62.

4. *The Successful Hotel Marketer*, June 1993, p. 5.

5. *The Successful Hotel Marketer*, April 1993, p. 4.

6. *The Successful Hotel Marketer*, March 1993, p. 12.

7. *The Wall Street Journal*, 28 March 1994, p. B1.

8. *The Successful Hotel Marketer*, May 1993, p. 4.

9. Steuart Henderson Britt and Norman Guess, eds., *Marketing Manager's Handbook*, Second Revised Edition (Chicago: Dartnell, 1983), p. 1113.

Key Terms

ad hoc scheduling—scheduling advertising whenever management thinks it is necessary.

advocacy channels—channels such as sales representatives that have a direct vested interest in conveying a message.

communications mix—a hospitality provider's blend of media and messages used to communicate with target markets.

congruity—said to occur when message receivers hold favorable opinions of both the message's source and medium.

continuity scheduling—scheduling advertising in a regular pattern over time.

expert channels—experts who are paid to serve as spokespeople for companies and their products and services.

frequency—the number of times an average person in a target market is exposed to an advertisement over a period of time.

horizontal cooperation—the pooling of advertising resources by similar businesses to achieve joint objectives.

narrowcasting—directing advertising to very specific target markets or niches.

objective and task method—establishing advertising budgets on the basis of the advertising objectives and tasks required to achieve them.

positioning—creating an image in the minds of guests reflecting the desirable characteristics of a hospitality business and its offerings.

pull strategies—communications designed to encourage end users to ask for specific products and services, thereby "pulling" those products and services through market distribution channels.

pulsing—an advertising spurt or an irregular scheduling of advertising in a time period.

push strategies—communications, such as aggressive promotions, designed to encourage the purchase of specific products and services, thereby "pushing" those products and services into market distribution channels.

reach—the number of people or households exposed to an advertisement at least once.

reciprocal advertising—the exchange of hospitality products or services for advertising; also known as *trade out* or *due bill* advertising.

thresholds—the upper and lower limits that define a zone of effectiveness for money spent on advertising.

vertical cooperation—the pooling of advertising resources by different kinds of hospitality businesses for their mutual benefit.

word-of-mouth channels—influential people such as family members, friends, and club members who furnish persuasive messages about businesses and their offerings.

Review Questions

1. What is congruity? What role does it play in hospitality marketing?

2. What are the elements of the communications mix? How do they relate to one another?

3. What general guidelines can marketers follow to help develop effective market communications?

4. What type of interpersonal communications channel typically has the greatest credibility? The least? Why?

5. What advantages do mass communications channels have over interpersonal channels? How are interpersonal channels superior?

6. What sorts of objectives can advertising be designed to achieve? How might these objectives relate to the purchase-decision stages of guests?

7. What are some approaches to establishing advertising budgets? How can advertising budgets be "stretched"?

8. What is positioning? How does it affect advertising messages?

9. How is public relations similar to advertising? What are some important differences?

10. How does carefully planned publicity help a hospitality business shape guest and community perceptions about the business? Why is this important?

Internet Sites

For more information, visit the following Internet sites. Remember that Internet addresses can change without notice.

Arby's
http://www.arbys.com

Best Western
http://www.bestwestern.com

Bel-Aire Hotel
http://www.bel-airehotel.com

Burger King
http://www.burgerking.com

Helmsley Hotels
http://www.helmsleyhotels.com

Hilton Hotels Corporation
hhtp://www.hilton.com

Hyatt Hotels and Resorts
http://www.hyatt.com

Marriott International
http://www.marriott.com

Motel 6
http://www.motel6.com

Ramada
http://www.ramada.com

Ritz-Carlton Hotels
http://www.ritzcarlton.com

The Preferred Hotels of the World
http://www.preferredhotels.com

Wendy's
http://www.wendys.com

Chapter 14 Outline

Personal Selling
    Personal Selling and Related Terms
    Personal Selling and Marketing
    Sales Fundamentals
    Organizational Structures
    Use of Independent Representatives
    Organizing the Sales Force
    Size of the Sales Force
    Sales Force Effectiveness
    Coordinating Sales and Operations
    Sales Techniques
Merchandising
    Merchandising Decisions
    Merchandising Guidelines
    A Case in Point
Promotion
    Types of Promotions
    Targeting Promotions
    Natural and Created Promotions
    Execution
    Problems
Concluding Comments

14

Communications Mix: Selling, Merchandising, and Promotion

"Everybody lives by selling something."
—Robert Louis Stevenson

FROM A BUSINESS PERSPECTIVE, nothing really happens until a sale is made. Sales generate revenues, while other hospitality activities incur costs. Statements like these remind us of the pivotal role of selling; hospitality marketing activities are geared toward either making or supporting sales. In this chapter, we discuss selling in the hospitality context and then deal with two related communications activities, merchandising and promotion.

Personal Selling

Personal selling, which involves direct contact between a sales person and a customer, has a major advantage over other communications activities. When in direct contact with customers, sales personnel receive immediate feedback and have the opportunity to adjust instantly to specific situations. The ability to engage in direct dialogue makes personal selling one of the most effective forms of business communication. Sales messages and presentations can be specially tailored to appeal to different customers or to satisfy specific requirements of particular sales. They can be adjusted immediately to achieve the desired response.

Personal selling, like advertising, targets guests, creates images, highlights benefits, and differentiates offerings. It may be carefully planned and organized, as in the case of formal presentations to conference planners, or it may be done informally by employees in their normal service encounters with guests.

While the focus of all hospitality organizations may be the same—serving guests and generating revenues and profits—their sales activities vary widely. They may include short- and long-term sales activities, so-called **missionary selling** (activities designed to cultivate new customers and eventual sales rather than immediate sales) and **maintenance selling** (designed to maintain current customers), and internal and external sales duties. Depending on the operation, sales reps may be responsible for such duties as:

• Calling on current customers

- Contacting new prospects
- Gathering information
- Supplying information
- Handling complaints
- Conducting demonstrations
- Providing customer services
- Maintaining relations
- Preparing reports
- Making the sale

Personal Selling and Related Terms

Personal selling, while related to sales management and salesmanship, is different from them.

Sales management involves two main sets of responsibilities, sales administration and sales force management. These tasks require a variety of skills. Sales administration refers to such responsibilities as determining sales objectives, establishing territories, allocating sales representatives, setting quotas, assessing performance, conducting sales research, and developing reports. Such tasks reflect more of the nonpersonnel components and deal with gathering and using information. Sales force management, by contrast, concerns people-centered activities that directly and immediately affect the quality of sales efforts. It involves direct relationships with sales personnel, such as selecting, recruiting, training, organizing, directing, motivating, and controlling the sales force.

Salesmanship comprises a variety of topics that deal with enhancing the sales abilities of personnel. It concerns concepts and techniques regarding the face-to-face hospitality provider/guest encounters that communicate information directly and influence buying decisions. It deals with methods of making the sale.

Personal selling is a broader but overlapping concept that encompasses more than salesmanship. It also covers the means that sales people use to implement hospitality marketing programs such as presentations, samples, testimonials, and the use of audio and visual aids to market hospitality properties to prospective customers.

Personal Selling and Marketing

Personal selling is among the most effective of all market communications methods because sales reps communicate directly with customers. They have the opportunity to tailor their sales approaches and interactions to specific guests. Personal selling involves both verbal and nonverbal communications, including handshakes, facial expressions, gestures, and eye contact.

Personal selling accounts for a significant proportion of all hospitality marketing efforts, particularly among hotels, and it is likely to become increasingly important. However, a greater emphasis on personal selling does not mean that hospitality offerings will be pushed more aggressively to guests, or that guests will be seen only as sales targets. Good sales reps will continue to think in terms of providing hospitality benefits for guests and helping guests make the hospitality purchases that they deem beneficial.

The success of hospitality sales programs starts at the very top, with the general manager of a hotel or the owner/operator of a restaurant. In small properties, owner/operators may well be responsible for the bulk of marketing communications, including personal selling. They may make sales calls, particularly on important customers. This may also be the case among larger hotels, where GMs may assist their sales reps in dealings with particularly important accounts.

Personal selling is especially suited to larger hotels and restaurants. The reasons for this are highlighted in Exhibit 1, which briefly summarizes some of the characteristics of the marketing mix components that make personal selling particularly valuable in hospitality marketing.

Sales Fundamentals

Sales reps must clearly understand exactly what—and to whom—they are selling. It is too often forgotten that guests do not buy a property's features per se—they purchase benefits. An often-mentioned example points out that, although cosmetic companies manufacture lipsticks, powders, and facial creams, what retailers really sell their customers is hope. When hospitality providers furnish health clubs, guests do not buy the use of lockers, steam rooms, weight rooms, exercise equipment, and pools. Rather, they purchase the image of well-toned bodies, improved health, a sense of well-being, and personal attractiveness.

Effective sales staff match particular benefits derived from property features with specific guest needs and desires. By carefully gathering information about guests and keeping in close touch with markets, sales reps can identify important sales features matching guest interests. This facilitates presenting an operation in the best possible light and suggests opportunities for differentiating its offerings from those of its competitors.

Two common errors of hospitality sales presentations are (1) misunderstanding guest wants and needs, and (2) focusing on features rather than on guest benefits. This was highlighted when one of the authors returned to a Singapore hotel he often visited. Several staff members proudly told him about the complete renovation of the suites on his floor, mentioning the new carpeting, bathroom fixtures, showers, wallpaper, paint, furniture, and furnishings. Although there were numerous opportunities to do so, not one staff member translated these features into guest benefits.

Sales reps must remember that different guests may have vastly different needs. Bar and dining facilities may signal different desires for young single guests than they do for mature couples. This was highlighted in a Mexican restaurant and bar that wanted to appeal to two entirely different market segments, seniors in the early evening and the younger set later on. However, at the early dinner hour they made the mistake of playing loud, bass-heavy rock music. The senior guests requested that it be turned off or, at least, turned down. The music did not offer a guest benefit but was actually an irritant.

Exhibit 1   Conditions Affecting Relevance of Personal Selling

---

PERSONAL SELLING IS ESPECIALLY VALUABLE WHEN:

The Service/Product

- Customers receive application assistance, as with reservations and confirmations.
- Machines such as computers, telephones, and faxes are involved.
- Personal demonstrations, directions, and information are required.
- There is a major commitment on the purchaser's part.
- Intangibles are involved.

Pricing

- Prices are negotiated, not fixed.
- Different price lists exist for different market segments.
- Margins are adequate to support sales expenses.
- Specific situations must be considered.
- Competition is keen.
- Excess capacity exists.

Distribution

- Distribution channels are short and direct.
- Channel intermediaries require training and assistance.
- Intermediaries influence a large market segment.

Communication

- Advertising media do not reach all intended markets.
- Advertising cannot adequately provide the required information.
- The size and dispersion of markets makes advertising too expensive.
- Promotional budgets are small, and sales per customer are high.
- Personal selling is perceived as part of the offering.
- Gatekeepers such as travel agents must be convinced.

Adapted from William Lazer and James D. Culley, *Marketing Management* (New York: Houghton Mifflin Co., 1983), p. 752.

Organizational Structures

Hospitality sales organizations vary greatly depending on the size of properties, nature of the markets, company philosophies, and people involved. Chains often operate regional sales offices in large cities, sometimes worldwide. Sheraton, for

Exhibit 2   Sales Organization—Large Property

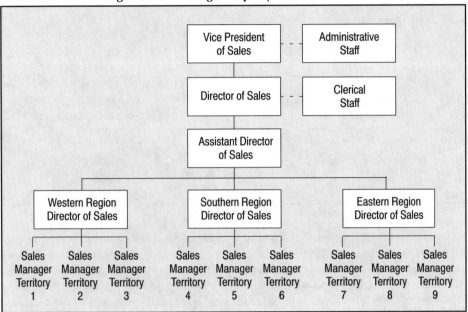

instance, has regional offices in such cities as London, Tokyo, Paris, Toronto, Brussels, and Melbourne. They not only promote and publicize a property, but also gather information about business opportunities, develop sales leads, and do the actual selling. Staff members may include area sales directors, senior account executives, account executives, research directors, office managers, and clerical personnel. A sales organization chart for a large property is shown in Exhibit 2.

By contrast, in very small properties, the owner or general manager, along with support staff, may assume the total sales function. In mid-sized properties, there may be a director of sales over individual sales managers, who in turn oversee sales reps and assistants. This is shown in Exhibit 3. The director of sales performs administrative, sales, and supervisory functions. Responsibilities may include setting sales objectives and targets, training and evaluating sales people, supervising the sales office and support people, evaluating sales programs, managing and assisting sales managers, calling on key accounts, developing sales plans and strategies, and preparing sales reports. Sales managers may be responsible for assigning accounts and territories; supervising, directing, and controlling sales personnel; assisting sales reps; and handling some additional sales tasks.

Use of Independent Representatives

Individual hotels may desire sales representation in various cities where it is not financially feasible to set up their own sales outlets. In such instances, they may use independent representatives to perform specified sales activities. Given the variety of sales services available, individual hotels can purchase packages of sales services

Exhibit 3   Sales Organization—Mid-Sized Property

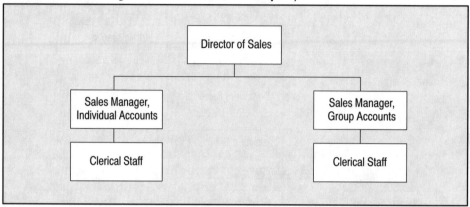

suited to their needs, ranging from taking over the total selling function to providing very specialized and limited sales support. Independent reps may serve as out-of-town business contacts for several noncompeting properties, thereby spreading the costs of doing business among them. They can provide individual properties with the regional representation that chains enjoy, at more reasonable cost than any of the hotels could realize on their own.

Organizing the Sales Force

The effectiveness of a sales force is influenced both by how it is organized and by how the sales resources are allocated. The purposes driving sales organizations include minimizing travel time and expenses, balancing workloads, relating company resources to market potential, maximizing sales results, providing customers with quality service, and fostering ease of administration. Ideally, territories or customer units should be organized to give each rep the same sales responsibilities and opportunities. In practice, however, that is not possible, and sales potentials vary among reps.

In the hospitality industry, sales reps and their activities are usually organized by either customers or territories. Hotels that organize their sales staffs by customers often group them according to three classes: group, transient, and catering. Group sales deal with customers who purchase multiple rooms or blocks of rooms at one time such as tour companies and large businesses. Group sales reps may also be involved with selling function space such as meeting rooms and ballrooms. Where markets are large enough, sales personnel may be specialized and deal exclusively with specific markets—cruises, conferences, bus tours, or sports teams.

Transient sales reps deal with customers who purchase rooms on an individual basis. This may include dealing with individual guests, their travel agents, executive secretaries, travel departments, and others involved with satisfying individual guest needs. Catering sales people handle such activities as social events, weddings, seminars, and meetings, which may require several sleeping rooms but not large numbers of them. They are mainly involved in selling function rooms and food and beverages.

Organizing sales people by territory is common. Not only are many countries already divided into logical regional territories, but large metropolitan areas may be further subdivided. Greater Los Angeles may include the sales territories of Beverly Hills, Hollywood, Century City, Burbank, Venice, Santa Monica, and Malibu. Sales reps may be given exclusive sales responsibility for one or more territories. In that manner, clear lines of authority are drawn, travel time and expenses may be controlled, and the reps may get to know their customers and prospects well enough to understand and cater to their specific needs. Territorial organization helps eliminate the customer complaint of being contacted by several sales reps from the same hotel, each selling part of the hospitality offerings.

A common sales problem occurs when large customers centralize purchases. Where this occurs, one customer in a territory may purchase for the whole company, regardless of the kind of hospitality product or the specific location of the property. These customers do not wish to deal with several sales people from the same company, regardless of how the sales responsibilities are organized internally. The result is often the development of "national accounts," which are assigned to a specific sales person and cut across territory and customer allocation. Internal arrangements can be made to deal fairly with the territorial and product sales reps so affected, especially with regard to compensation.

Meeting Customer Needs. Balancing hospitality offerings with the sales needs of different customers can sometimes result in perplexing occurrences. Consider the situation where a small yearly conference was held at an independent hotel. The two-day conference operated on a stringent budget, was more of a community activity, and was not particularly profitable. However, it was the main event of a social and educational organization in the community, which the hotel was pleased to support. The organization regularly booked a modest number of sleeping rooms and a small conference facility at the hotel, one year in advance.

In the meantime, a large international business organization, which had been contacted several times by the property's catering sales reps seeking business, phoned about a booking. It expressed interest in exploring a contract covering several one-week seminars to be held at the hotel. The dates of the first seminar, however, conflicted with the dates that the smaller organization had already booked for its conference. Both groups wanted the use of a specific meeting room. Moreover, the number of sleeping rooms available for the company seminar was a few short of what was needed.

The conference committee was contacted about the possibility of moving their two-day meeting, either one week forward or one week back, for a price concession. They refused. The catering sales rep, however, continued negotiating with both sides and introduced an attractive solution. He got the conference committee to release the required number of rooms by offering to house displaced conferees at a nearby luxury property, at a very low rate, supplying bus service for them, and providing a free cocktail party to all conference attendees. These extra sales efforts resulted in satisfying the needs of both groups, set up a very profitable sale, and generated loyal customers on both sides.

Exhibit 4   Size of Sales Force—Market Potential Method

Estimated sales potential (basis for estimated revenues)	$400,000
Estimated revenues	$250,000
Less: Costs of support	$110,000
Less: Expected profits	$50,000
Equals: Maximum investment for sales force	$90,000

Size of the Sales Force

The size of the sales force depends on such factors as the tasks to be performed, the number of potential customers, the size of the territory, and the number of sales calls to be made.

Customers often complain about inadequate coverage and lack of service. Inadequate sales coverage may reflect a sales force that is too small, one that is inefficiently deployed, or both. Similarly, unnecessary customer contacts and coverage of unlikely prospects decrease sales productivity and increase personal selling costs. When adding, eliminating, or realigning sales reps, attention must be focused not just on costs, as is often the case, but also on revenues. Research indicates that smaller, less profitable customers too often receive more calls and attention than their potential warrants. Conversely, the most profitable customers, current and potential, receive less coverage than they should.

The appropriate sales call frequency can be determined by considering the actual and prospective sales opportunities that various customers represent. The greater the perceived potential, the more frequent the calls. Thus, sales profitability and effectiveness can often be increased by adjusting sales efforts to bring them in line with actual sales potential. Three widely used approaches are **market potential, ratio of sales to calls**, and **return on assets managed**.

Market Potential. The first step in using market potential to determine the size of the sales force is to estimate or forecast the sales potential for a control unit, such as a group of customers or a territory. Then, estimated revenues that the control unit would yield are calculated. The costs of supporting a sales rep are determined, as are desired or expected profits. The estimated costs and profits are subtracted from the revenues. The remainder is the most that can be invested in a sales rep's salary and related sales expenses while still maintaining profitability. The figure so calculated serves as a criterion for determining whether additions or subtractions should be made to the sales force. This is shown in Exhibit 4.

Ratio of Sales to Calls. This method of determining the size of the sales force involves judgments about the number of calls that should be made on different

Exhibit 5   Size of Sales Force—Ratio of Sales to Calls Method

Customer	Number of Accounts	Number of Calls	Sales Coverage
Group	90	5	450
Conferences	120	4	480
Transient	500	2	1000
Catering	75	3	225
Cruises	60	4	240
Total Sales Coverage			2395

- Management's Estimated Calls Per Sales Rep = 600

- Number of Reps Needed $= \dfrac{2395}{600} = 4$

classes of customers. The approach first classifies customers according to criteria such as actual or potential sales volume, profitability, or, as seen in Exhibit 5, type of account. Then the number of sales calls per account that each type of customer receives is specified. The number of accounts is multiplied by the stated number of calls to determine the sales coverage required. Management then uses relevant data and its judgment to estimate the average number of calls that a sales rep can make. By dividing total sales coverage by the average number of calls per sales person, the required number of sales reps is established. At this juncture, experience and judgment take over to determine the actual size of the sales force.

Return on Assets Managed (ROAM). Calculating the return on assets managed can furnish useful guidelines, especially when decisions are being made about market expansion or contraction or reallocation of the current sales force.

In using the ROAM approach, managers consider the investments necessary for ongoing support of sales operations in the markets under consideration. Clearly, some markets require a more substantial investment than others. For example, the transportation, travel, telephone, fax, and sales support costs involved in maintaining sales reps in Los Angeles or New York can be much different than those for Lansing, Michigan, or Des Moines, Iowa.

The return on assets managed for each territory (or control unit) can be calculated by determining the ratio of estimated profits to estimated total investments. It requires a list of all the anticipated necessary investments, along with management's estimates of profits for each territory—whether that is a set of customers or a geographic area. Then, ratios of estimated profits to investments can be calculated using the formula:

$$ROAM = \frac{\text{Estimated profits}}{\text{Estimated investment}}$$

Suppose that the total investment to support a sales person is estimated to be $100,000. Suppose further that the estimated profits for territories A, B, and C are $300,000, $160,000, and $75,000, respectively. If we had only one sales person, we would cover territory A. We would think about hiring a second person to cover territory B, but territory C would not be covered unless we could improve the profit potential.

ROAM indicates how the sales force might best be deployed to ensure that the most profitable territories, related to investment, are covered. In addition, it indicates the size of the sales force that would be most cost effective.

Sales Force Effectiveness

Simply budgeting the necessary funds to hire a sales force is no guarantee that it will perform effectively. Sales performance is directly related to the efficacy of such sales management functions as recruiting, selecting, training, motivating, compensating, and controlling sales personnel. Regrettably, they are too often given short shrift in the hospitality marketing program.

Recruiting, Selecting, and Training. Recruiting, selecting, and training are particularly critical factors of sales success. Recruiting and selecting determine the competency of people available to carry out the important sales tasks. Individual sales personnel vary markedly in their dedication and productivity; generally, a small proportion of the sales reps account for an unduly large proportion of sales. Hiring the right sales reps is indeed important.

The hotel sales department is prone to high turnover. This makes recruiting and training unduly costly, increases the costs of supporting sales personnel, and usually results in dissatisfied customers and lost sales. When high turnover rates exist, the reasons for them should be investigated immediately and the existing problems dealt with. An effective recruiting and selecting program can help keep this problem under control.

Sales training is often considered a one-time activity. In reality, it is an ongoing function, necessary on a regular basis for both new and experienced hospitality personnel. Yet many hospitality businesses, particularly smaller ones, view sales training as being too costly for them. What they fail to consider are the real costs of *not* training. Informal, on-the-job training based on trial and error can be both ineffective and costly in terms of lost customers and sales opportunities. Consider the following situation.

Two guests were regular diners at a family restaurant. A new waitress was on the job without having received any training. She did not know the menu and could not respond to such questions as, "Has the fish been frozen?", "Can the dish be prepared without butter?", "Can we have the sauce on the side?", "Is it possible to get a baked potato?" and so on. Each time she was questioned, she had to find someone else to ask about food preparation. The order took an inordinately long time to place. When the meal arrived, it was all mixed up. The disgruntled guests ate some of it, though they were heard to state loudly, "It'll be a long time before we come back to this place." Hence, the "savings"—and the very real costs—of not training.

Motivation, Incentives, and Compensation. Maintaining an effective, highly-motivated sales force can pay off handsomely and continuously. Motivation is achieved through incentives, both internal and external. Internal incentives are those that personally encourage individual sales reps, such as group recognition, a feeling of accomplishment, the fear of others' disapproval and group rejection, and the desire to succeed. Many employees are motivated by continuing their education or earning certification and official industry recognition, thereby realizing a sense of achievement.

External incentives include such motivational devices as sales quotas, compensation plans, contests, invitations to special meetings, merchandise, and travel awards. Hotels and restaurants may post pictures to recognize the "Employee of the Month" and encourage accomplishment with special parking spaces, awards, and prizes. One such prize for an "Outstanding Employee" might be a complimentary champagne dinner in the hotel's dining room.

Sales compensation plans usually include incentive components, such as commissions on business generated, linking compensation to sales performance. (Operations people, by contrast, generally receive a salary, which may be supplemented by a bonus based on how well a property is doing or on guest ratings.) Sales quotas are widely used to motivate sales personnel. Quotas reflect customer, product, or territory sales volume expected for a designated period, such as a quarter or year. When sales people exceed their quotas, they earn additional compensation. Since quotas become benchmarks for measuring how well individual sales reps are doing, members of the sales force should have input in setting them. Quotas should be fair and reasonable—high enough to motivate but not so high as to be unattainable and discouraging.

Sales compensation plans include three components: expense allowances, fringe benefits, and direct income. **Expense allowances** are designed to reimburse sales persons for costs incurred in performing their sales duties. **Fringe benefits** are those extras that provide sales reps with some security and generate good morale, loyalty, and job satisfaction. They may include pension plans, extended vacation allowances, flexible work schedules, and so forth. The **direct income** component may be based on straight salary, straight commission, salary and commission, salary and bonus, or commission and bonus.

Straight salary gives an assured regular income and controls sales costs. It compensates sales people for the control that management will exercise over them and their time. It contributes to a management feeling of being free to direct and assign sales people. But salaries reward time, not results; they do not stimulate outstanding sales effort.

Straight commission, by contrast, provides strong incentives and encourages aggressive sales efforts. It can result in neglect of important nonselling customer service activities. Sales reps on straight commission may resist management attempts to direct the use of their time or control their activities. They tend to feel that their time is their own.

Compensation plans combining elements of both salary and commission are by far the most commonly used. As for the appropriate balance between the two, the more effective sales reps prefer plans with higher commissions and less salary. The less-effective ones generally prefer a greater salary component.

Bonuses may be used to recognize exceptional sales performance. However, a potential problem with bonuses concerns management's determination of what is exceptional, which creates questions of fairness among sales reps. Since bonuses are usually given yearly, management is able to retain and use the capital for bonuses for extended periods before actually having to pay it out.

The starting point in selecting a sales compensation plan is to decide what management wants sales reps to accomplish. If the goal is to obtain volume, then total sales may be used as a compensation base. If a property is realizing excessive cancellations, then compensation may be based on actual payments received. If management is trying to control expenses or achieve price reductions, the payment basis may be gross margins. Compensation rates can vary according to the desired types of business, customers, or products being sold. Regardless of the compensation scheme used, hospitality enterprises must pay the going rate to attract the number and quality of sales people required.

A controversial question about sales compensation is whether a ceiling should be placed on the amount that can be earned. Conflict arises when extraordinarily large commissions result from unusual "windfall" circumstances that are not at all related to the sales effort expended. For example, when a large government department took the initiative and contacted a Washington hotel about a conference it was running that needed many hundreds of rooms for several days, a windfall ensued for the sales rep covering the Washington area.

Coordinating Sales and Operations

Achieving the greatest market impact requires close coordination between sales and operations. Operations personnel must become aware of the important sales roles that they also perform. Too often, a "territorial perspective" is adopted, with each functional group taking care of its own activities and disregarding others'. This results in neglected guests and lost sales opportunities. A recent restaurant situation underscores this point.

Two regular restaurant customers, a husband and wife, included oatmeal in their breakfast order. When it arrived, it was undercooked and soupy. They summoned the waitress, explained the situation, and indicated that they wanted to change their cereal order. The waitress exclaimed loudly, "Well, don't blame me, I didn't make it! I only serve it. That's the way they made it this morning." The waitress offered no apology or expression of concern and did not seem to think that she, as part of the restaurant, shared the responsibility for what had occurred. She did not seem to recognize that her actions affected sales. Her response bordered on making the guests feel that they were to blame. The guests themselves were heard to comment that they did not have to return to that restaurant.

Similarly, hotel reservationists do not merely take orders; they are an important part of the sales team. They communicate with guests, actual and potential, about the hotel and its offerings. Though they are part of operations, they need sales skills to carry out their activities effectively. Recognizing this, some hotels have designed sales training programs to teach reservationists how to handle and sell prospective customers. The result has been more satisfied guests as well as increased revenues.[1]

Conflicts too often exist between sales and other departments so that interdepartmental roadblocks spring up. Sales reps are characterized as spenders who have the pleasure of entertaining customers on company expense accounts. They make promises to guests that are difficult or even impossible for operations to keep. Moreover, they do not have to become directly involved with the myriad problems inherent in actually providing guest services once sales are made. That burden falls to operations.

Good communication between operations and sales is essential to effective hospitality sales programs. Sales and operations should work at understanding each other's perspectives and viewpoints, and recognize that they are both part of the same hospitality system, with the same objective: satisfying guests at a profit. Sales must recognize that without operations sales are impossible; operations must appreciate that nothing really happens until sales are made.

Usually when guests request something out of the ordinary, sales and operations react quite differently. Sales has the tendency to say yes in order to please customers, without regard to how difficult it will be for operations to deliver. Operations, on the other hand, has a tendency to stick to its standard operating methods and say no to requests that fall outside the normal routines. Some flexibility is required, but with an eye fixed clearly on "the possible."

At an international resort hotel, a guest who was an accomplished pianist asked to be allowed to play the hotel piano whenever it was convenient for the hotel to permit it. The front desk manager, the food and beverage manager, an on-duty assistant manager, and a guest relations person all deemed the request impossible. The reasons varied from "The hotel does not own the piano" to "Only the owner, who is on vacation, can grant permission." The real reason, it turned out, was that someone would have to unlock the door to the bar where the piano was located, turn on the air conditioning, and, afterward, lock the place up each time the piano was used. It was just too much trouble for the staff.

When the hotel's executive vice president, who was directly involved with group sales and who knew that a positive recommendation would mean future business, was asked by the seminar coordinator whether the use of the piano could be arranged, he responded immediately: "I don't see why not." He then told the food and beverage manager and the front desk personnel to accommodate the guest, which was done immediately.

What is often required in selling hospitality effectively is a willingness on the part of all staff members to go out of their way to accommodate guests. They must be willing to do a little more, to extend the services offered, and to use facilities in a slightly different way that satisfies guests. It is that extra effort to accommodate guests that distinguishes one property from another and gives an edge in competing for future sales. Both operations and sales staffs should be trained and empowered to make such reasonable accommodations.

Sometimes, of course, sales people do act unreasonably by promising too much to make a sale. Effective sales performance is built on a clear understanding of the quality of hospitality that can be delivered, and not promising more. The focus of both sales and operating personnel should be to meet guest needs to the extent possible. Where there is uncertainty regarding customer requests, *sales must defer to operations*. Where sales promises exceed performance, guests may be lost. Where hospitality delivered exceeds promises, satisfied and loyal guests may be created.

Sales Techniques

A good grasp of personal selling strategies is appropriate for those in hospitality marketing. Extensive sales literature is readily available. In a book of this nature, however, we can comment only very briefly on techniques. We have selected two important sales activities for consideration—prospecting and closing.

Prospecting. **Prospecting** means searching for new customers. It involves calling on people who are not currently customers but have the potential to become customers. This is much more challenging and demanding than calling on current customers. Prospecting involves a different level of selling because new prospects may not even be aware of a company's hospitality offerings. Prospects lack experience with the company; they must be informed and convinced. Their positive experiences with competitors must be overcome by emphasizing the superior benefits of the unfamiliar hotel or restaurant.

Before calling on new customers, sales persons should *qualify* them. That is, prospects should be clearly identified to determine whether they are really potential customers who can benefit from a property's features. For example, convention planners who commit to facilities three to five years ahead of time are hardly potential customers for hotels seeking to boost near-term occupancy rates. Local branch managers of national companies are not in a position to commit to facilities for national sales conferences.

Prospecting involves taking direct aim at competitors' customers and realistically expecting them to take aim at yours. The process includes identifying competitors' customers, assessing the benefits that competitors are providing, realistically delineating the superiority of your property's features, and expressing those features in terms of prospect benefits. Trying to sell property features that do not translate into superior prospect benefits is not realistic.

Sometimes sales reps make *cold calls*—that is, they call on customers without any advance notice or appointment. They just drop in on the person in charge of hotel reservations or conference planning. The sales rep hopes to meet them, establish personal contact, and perhaps cultivate rapport. Often a cold call by telephone leads to a follow-up personal contact. While cold calls can prove to be a waste of time, and may even be somewhat uncomfortable, they can also furnish valuable information for future calls. Frequently, a sales person will drop by to deliver a small, useful gift such as a golf umbrella or a meeting planning kit just to establish the initial contact, and set a follow-up call for a later date.

Closing. When making sales presentations, sales reps gather guest information as well as present the features and benefits of their offerings. Sometimes, as a result of the guest information gathered, they can perceive new needs that have not been discussed and mention new features and benefits. Sales reps focus on getting customer agreement, obtaining customer commitment, and getting the order. In **closing**, they ask customers "to sign on the dotted line." While sales reps seek closure, customers may offer resistance, seek to postpone purchase decisions, or reject offerings. Sales reps use many well-known closing techniques to overcome such barriers, counter resistance, and close the sale. Sometimes they can get prospects to visit facilities and experience the hospitality firsthand—sample the food, stay in the rooms, or visit the health club—before trying to close. This can give guests concrete experiences to refer to when evaluating several possible providers. Above all, effective sales people stay focused on closing the sale.

A common mistake is not asking for the order soon enough. Far too many sales people keep on selling well after prospects have already been convinced. In so doing, they waste time and increase the odds of losing a sale. Learning to close effectively pays handsome sales dividends. But it must also be understood that experienced, knowledgeable hospitality prospects are informed negotiators and do not commit to purchases before they are satisfied and are ready to do so.

Merchandising

Merchandising focuses on marketing hospitality products and services to guests once they are on the premises. It overlaps promotion and deals with those in-house marketing activities—other than personal selling, advertising, and public relations—that are used to stimulate guest purchases. Among the commonly used merchandising activities are:

- Service directories in guestrooms
- Display cards
- Posters
- Tent cards on tables
- In-house video channels
- Giveaways such as calendars, key chains, and paperweights

Many of the actions employed to get guests onto the premises can go on to enhance in-house merchandising.

Merchandising activities are directed at guests wherever they may be on a property—in their rooms, lobbies, elevators, restaurants, health clubs, concierge desks, lounges, salons, gift stores, or golf and tennis courses. Hotels use signs in the lobby, information pieces handed out at check-in, promotional flyers in the rooms, in-house TV commercials, elevator posters, as well as information furnished by desk clerks, bellstaff, telephone operators, and concierges. Hotel merchandising concentrates on selling items other than the basic room or meal such as wines, desserts, special foods, clothing, accessories, mementos, and entertainment. The objective is to generate additional experiences that are enjoyable for the guest and

---

Merchandising of Gambling Casinos

In 1993, 92 million Americans visited casinos—more than attended all major league baseball games combined. Gaming revenues totaled $30 billion, with an estimated $330 billion spent on all types of wagering. Partly because of the proliferation of state approved lotteries (undertaken with the rationalization of providing more funds for education, or senior citizens, without raising taxes), gaming has been transformed from its former status of a sin into an acceptable entertainment form.

Las Vegas casinos know they are in the entertainment business. They merchandise gaming by creating extravaganzas. They have giveaways, free food and drinks, special drawings, coupons, free shows, contests, low hotel and meal rates, and an array of other attractions to generate casino excitement. They feature shows with world-renowned entertainers and the most incredible sight and sound effects, as well as special events like world championship boxing matches. All of these things are used to merchandise casino games.

Harrah's in Las Vegas merchandise The Pit, six blackjack tables marked by helium balloons, by having the dealers act as entertainers—they joke, joust guests with collapsible swords, ring bells, and whack bettors with rubber hammers—it's party time! A year after adopting this approach, revenues were up more than 50 percent, and on Saturday nights guests may be five deep waiting for seats. The same approach is being franchised at other Harrah's casinos.

Las Vegas merchandising takes on grand proportions. Steve Wynn's Las Vegas Mirage Hotel, with its tropical theme, has an erupting volcano outside, while inside the lush atrium setting are trees, a waterfall, and boulevard. The casino itself is wrapped around the tropical setting, and includes such attractions at the famous white tigers and a marine life exhibit. Circus Circus features free circus acts, such as trapeze performances and clowns, in its casino area. The Luxor, a 30-story glass-encased pyramid, has guests travel from the registration desk by boat along the "River Nile." They also use elevators that climb at a 39 degree angle, offer a laser light show in the central atrium, and offer adventures into the past, present, and future. Treasure Island, a takeoff on the classic Robert Louis Stevenson story, has a Buccaneer Bay theme park, designed like the 18th century port, with an hourly battle between the pirates and British Officers on its two 90-foot frigates. Other casinos and themes include Bellagio, which is being designed like the famous Italian locale, and New York, New York. All casinos provide merchandising opportunities to generate excitement, attract and entertain guests, and get them to continue coming back.

Based on Gerri Hirshey, "Gambling Nation," *The New York Times Magazine*, 17 July 1994, pp. 34–44, 50, 53.

---

increase sales and profits for the property. Hospitality merchandising opportunities are limited only by the imagination and creativity of the staff.

When used wisely, merchandising can be very effective, but it can also be a double-edged sword. Displays may announce the availability of pizza and other foods through room service, dessert carts and trays may tempt guests, and special arrays of wines, beers, and cheeses may all increase sales. However, the array of merchandising notices, brochures, displays, and actual items can occupy so much of the table, desk, and bureau space in a hotel that they become annoying to guests.

Sometimes good merchandising opportunities are neglected or are approached from the perspective of serving the company rather than the guest. Wine lists are a case in point. Too often they are developed solely to increase profits rather than to provide guests with choices that would increase their dining pleasure, at prices they are willing to pay. In fact, the important task of developing a wine list is often relegated to a wine distributor, who creates lists built around wines the distributor is selling, not wines that guests may want. Some wine stewards then neglect their opportunities to serve guests and merchandise wines effectively, choosing instead to exhibit an attitude of superiority.

Merchandising Decisions

Hotels have the basic task of selling their rooms, and in so doing, maximizing room revenues. An ever-present decision is what rooms to sell, and when. Should the hotel book a large block of rooms at a low conference rate two or three years in advance, or should it hold on to them in hope of getting a higher rate and take the chance of not selling them at all? Making such decisions under uncertain market conditions involves balancing perceived risk with perceived payoffs.

Merchandising may be used to upgrade guests to higher-priced rooms. This need not be an unpleasant or overbearing experience for guests, although that is sometimes the case, as the following situation illustrates. While driving through the Smokey Mountains of Tennessee during a spring Saturday evening, one of the authors and his wife stopped at a roadside motel in popular Gatlinburg to inquire about vacancies. Rooms usually ranged from $35 to $50. The desk clerk informed us that there were not many rooms available in town, that it was Saturday night, and it was getting late. He said that he did have a suite available "for $135." Surprised and annoyed, the offer was refused and a drive to another motel less than a mile down the road got a room for $45. The attempt to upgrade—and gouge—failed. To date, whenever the author is in the area, he recalls the event and avoids that particular motel. However, both authors have also been upgraded, skillfully, many times by reservations people, merchandising superior accommodations to the ones reserved, at reasonable prices. The result is additional hotel revenue and increased guest satisfaction.

Merchandising activities can make a big difference and should be tracked and evaluated on the basis of costs and revenues to see what their effect is on profits. Attention should be given to determining why certain merchandising approaches worked well and why others failed. This information can help establish practical guidelines for future merchandising efforts. We know that some restaurants have successfully used merchandising to enlarge the size of a check, increase the number of customers, increase business during off hours and seasons, and increase the sales of alcoholic beverages, desserts, and featured items. The result is direct additions to the bottom line—profits.

Merchandising Guidelines

The basic tenet of merchandising, as in all marketing endeavors, is to consider guest wants and needs and develop activities from the perspective of guests. The offerings involved should be readily and conveniently available, when and where guests want them, at prices guests are willing to pay—and they should meet or exceed guest expectations.

In our information society, guests are well-informed, readily aware of prices and value, have many hospitality choices available, and do not like to feel that hospitality businesses are taking advantage of them. When guests are charged extraordinarily high prices for the snacks and beverages being merchandised in-room, they often resist; they know that the exact items are readily available in nearby markets at significantly lower prices. The result is not merely rejection of the offer but the creation of guest resentment.

Practical guidelines for improving hospitality merchandising include:

- State the purpose of merchandising efforts and make sure that the staff involved understand it.

- Base merchandising activities on serving guests better.

- Make sure merchandising activities are compatible with and reinforce marketing programs.

- See that merchandising vehicles communicate effectively with guests.

- Check for such qualities as clarity, simplicity, timeliness, practicality, and visibility of communications.

- Develop informed, supportive employees who are knowledgeable about merchandising programs.

A Case in Point

Some interesting merchandising situations occurred at a large international business congress held in a five-star hotel in Istanbul, Turkey. As is common in many countries, guests were instructed to drink bottled water. It was available in very small bottles from the in-room refrigerators and room service. The price, however, was about five times that of the same brand sold in stores a few blocks away, for bottles four times the size. The result was that hundreds of guests brought bottled water into their hotel rooms daily. The adjacent retailers were delighted at the situation, and were all set up to capitalize on the bonanza.

The hotel also merchandised its continental breakfasts by providing conference guests and their families with reduced-price coupons at registration. The breakfasts, however, were only served in a single designated hotel location and consisted of a nondescript "orange-flavored drink," bread, rolls, butter, jam, and tea or coffee. The normal continental breakfast, offered in the restaurant, consisted of fresh orange juice; a variety of croissants, sweet rolls, and attractive local breads; cheeses, spreads, cold meats, and jams; and beverages. In addition, the reduced price offered to conferees proved to be substantially higher than prices in nearby restaurants. The hotel merchandising activities not only generated ill will, but resulted in many attendees eating all their meals outside of the hotel.

The hotel also merchandised tea, coffee, and alcoholic and fruit beverages through tent cards and drink menus on tables throughout their large lobby lounges and bars. The prices, however, particularly for alcoholic beverages, were astonishingly high by any standards. The result was lots of sitters and very few drinkers at the lobby tables.

Merchandising may supplement other components of the marketing mix, but it cannot make up for deficient products/services or pricing policies. While hotels and restaurants have continuing streams of opportunities to merchandise their offerings, such activities, like other communication, should be carefully planned. When carried out properly, they are both excellent sources of additional profits and ways of creating guest satisfaction.

Promotion

Promotion carries a variety of meanings. It overlaps many other kinds of marketing communications, especially advertising and merchandising. Here, however, we limit our discussion of **promotion** to sales promotion activities—activities designed to generate hospitality sales in the short run. In that sense, promotions are used for such specific sales purposes as:

- Generating new business

- Stimulating sales during slow periods or off seasons

- Creating guest awareness

- Encouraging guests to try hospitality products and services

- Winning customers from competitors

- Countering competitors' actions

Promotions include direct mailings, contests, brochures, special events, coupons, and reduced prices. When competitive conditions intensify, hospitality marketers may turn to these approaches to increase the number of guests, enhance revenues, and generate profits. The challenge is to design promotions that will enhance current sales and profits without detracting from either in the short or long run.[2]

Promotion plays a most important role in the success of certain hospitality enterprises. Many celebrities own restaurants and use their celebrity status to promote them. The renowned actor Michael Caine, who owns a half interest in five London restaurants, recognized that promotion can make a difference because the hospitality business is like show business. "It's the contact with people," Caine says. "Owning a restaurant is like going back into the theater. You think of it in terms of opening a play or stage show: 'Will anyone come? Will it get good reviews?'"[3] Knowing that guests visit his restaurants to see celebrities, Caine makes frequent appearances.

Promotions, as supplements to advertising and personal selling, sometimes take on a life of their own and have a great effect on sales and profits. That was the case with McDonald's extremely successful 1997–1998 Beanie Babies program. The collectors' frenzy generated such strong demand for the small stuffed animals that customers bought food just to get the Beanie Babies. The promotion sold out, and McDonald's strong 1998 second quarter earnings were largely attributed to the promotion.[4] Similarly, Burger King ran a very successful in-store toy promotion in

1995 associated with the Walt Disney film *Toy Story.* The company bought 35 million toy premiums and 15 million hand puppets patterned after the characters in the movie and included them with kids' meals. The giveaways drew children and families to Burger King restaurants, and the results far exceeded expectations.[5]

Even though they are short term in nature and focused on immediate sales, promotions may have long-running results. Sometimes promotions attract guests who become regular customers. Examples are the Hilton Honors program and the Holiday Inn Priority frequent-traveler program, which improve current sales and help keep customers loyal.

Types of Promotions

Hospitality sales promotions are classified as either in-house or outside promotions.[6] In-house promotions parallel and supplement in-house personal sales activities. Included are premiums, games, contests, coupons, special occasion clubs, gift certificates, and the gamut of special events like food festivals and art exhibits.

Outside promotions include the use of sales materials and promotional pieces such as fliers, letters, postcards, and newsletters. Many national chain restaurants regularly mail fliers containing discount coupons. Some reproduce, post, and distribute favorable reviews to potential guests. A Florida restaurant located near a courthouse distributes promotional fliers daily, with breakfast and lunch coupons, to people selected for jury duty. Although jurors only serve for a few days at a time, others take their place daily, and a continuing promotional opportunity exists.

Sales promotions that contact guests directly are becoming increasingly important in hospitality marketing as a practical and cost-effective way to reach targeted customers. Direct mail may be used to perform the whole sales job or for introductory purposes, as well as to follow up and support personal sales presentations. It has great flexibility and can be tailored to meet the needs of specific market segments. While planning and carefully crafting messages are important, developing and maintaining up-to-date mailing lists are absolutely critical. Mailing lists are the lifeblood of all direct-mail promotions.

The test of promotional efforts, as with other forms of market communication, is whether target markets are being reached with the desired impact. Are the promotions stimulating favorable guest responses? Are they generating additional revenue, bolstering images, and generating favorable publicity? While promotions may certainly be significant contributors to successful hospitality marketing programs, regrettably they are sometimes considered to be a convenient way of disposing of leftover items that markets already have rejected. Such offerings may be priced attractively (often at a loss) and promoted to guests just to get rid of them. But to really do their job, promotions require more than just attractive prices; they must have guest appeal.

Targeting Promotions

When promotions are targeted to specific market segments, their impact is increased. The well-known five-star and five-diamond Boca Hotel and Club in Boca Raton, Florida, targeted promotions to local secretaries who handled hotel bookings for their companies. Secretaries were entertained at a special lunch given in their honor and were given gifts as expressions of appreciation for their efforts. This promotion generated loyalty and repeat business.

Promotions may also be targeted to those who are not yet loyal or regular customers. To attract new customers in specific market segments, hospitality promotions use such themes as:

- "Kids stay free"

- "Buy one dinner and get one free"

- Low weekend rates

- Special golf and tennis tours

For example, both Hilton and Marriott developed promotional campaigns for infrequent guests, offering them lower room rates and special vacation pricing.

Natural and Created Promotions

There are two basic types of hospitality promotions: natural and created. **Natural promotions** are those that stem from events that many people in a society normally celebrate or recognize. In the United States, examples include Independence Day, Halloween, Easter, Secretaries Day, and Mother's Day. Such events lend themselves naturally to special hospitality promotions like brunches, dinners, travel packages, and weekend events. Think of green beer promotions during St. Patrick's Day or the couples' specials featured on Valentine's Day.

Created promotions are those events developed for the specific purpose of generating commercial opportunities. Disney theme parks capitalize on many created promotional events with their host of daily celebrations featuring Mickey Mouse and other well-known Disney characters. Hotels and restaurants create such events as wine and cheese festivals; French, Italian, or German food nights; seafood buffets; arts and crafts celebrations. They also participate in performing arts festivals, summer music concerts, and art exhibits—all resulting in commercial opportunities.

The kind and number of hospitality promotions are limited only by management's creativity and imagination. Many are simply variations on a theme, while others are truly innovative and unique. Regardless, promotional objectives must be clearly understood, keeping guest needs and expectations well in mind. Promotions, which all too frequently are mounted on the spur of the moment, should actually be planned carefully and coordinated with ongoing marketing activities.

With hospitality marketing taking on more of a global dimension, one caution must be kept in mind. Cultural factors are becoming a more important consideration in planning promotions. The approaches that work so well in one culture may not transfer smoothly or effectively to another. Different cultures may respond in diverse ways to the same promotional stimuli. Words, phrases, illustrations, colors, and themes that work well in one country's promotions may, in fact, generate negative reactions and even rejection in another locale.

Execution

As with all marketing communications, execution is critical to effective promotions. Promotions require a clear and concise message that can be conveyed effectively to guests in terms of a hospitality product or service tie-in. Successful promotions create an atmosphere of excitement and anticipation and give guests special reasons to expect very satisfying experiences. If disappointment ensues—if delivery does not match promotional promises—considerable damage can result. Since it is more difficult to counter promotional disappointments than it is to build consumer expectations, meeting or exceeding promotional promises is important.

Effective execution includes planning to ensure that all of the required systems are in place and all necessary inventories are on hand. Having designed a promotion of German beers only to find that stocks are inadequate serves to crush guest expectations and create ill will. It is better to err on the side of having too much on hand than to try to save money and risk ineffective execution and guests' ill will.

Also, effective execution requires the willing participation of dedicated staff members. Getting the entire staff to appreciate, accept, and participate in promotions requires effort, but it pays off. When staff members are involved directly in the design and development of promotions, the results are valuable ideas, enthusiasm, and feelings of proprietary interest, belonging, and commitment—highly important ingredients for successful promotions.

Problems

Promotions can backfire if they do not generate enough additional business to offset costs. This occurred when a restaurant used an in-house table display offering coupons promoting "Buy one meal and get another of the same value free." The promotion merely reached those who were already regular dinner guests willing to pay the normal price. As a result, it lowered the price for regular guests, thereby reducing revenues and profits. Perhaps that would have been an acceptable strategy if the restaurant were using the promotion to thank loyal guests with reduced prices. However, the restaurant was actually trying to attract new guests by offering discounts. From that perspective, it failed.

Problems arise regularly with promotions offering guests something additional, like frequent-guest programs. Once they are instituted, it becomes very difficult to withdraw them, as the airlines learned when they attempted to terminate their frequent-flyer programs which resulted in hostile consumer reactions and the possibility of lawsuits. Similarly, restaurants that offer guests substantial price reductions in the form of coupons or early dining discounts may encounter guest resistance when they try to eliminate such programs. Guests can readily become conditioned to expect giveaways as a matter of course and refuse to buy without them. That was the case with one family restaurant that offered a promotional coupon for "Buy one dinner and get the other at half price" during the early dining hours. When the coupons stopped, so did much of the patronage, and the restaurant soon had to be sold.

Like other forms of market communication, promotions should be evaluated to determine whether guests are satisfied with them and the extent to which they meet company goals. The evaluation can help establish the agenda for future promotional opportunities—indicating how to improve promotions and providing practical management guidelines for what and what not to do.

Concluding Comments

Personal selling has a major advantage over other communications methods. It can receive immediate feedback and adjust sales approaches and messages accordingly, thereby enhancing communication effectiveness. Personal selling is related to, but different from, salesmanship and sales management. While the objective of personal selling activities is the same for different hospitality businesses, the activities involved may vary. Two common errors of personal sales presentations are lack of understanding guest wants and needs and focusing on features rather than guest benefits.

Hospitality sales organizations vary by property size, markets, company philosophy, and people involved. Large companies may have regional sales offices, while in small companies, the owner or GM may assume the total sales function. Mid-sized companies may have a director of sales managing several sales managers. Hotels may use independent sales representatives to perform all or part of the selling function.

Sales activities may be organized by customers or territories. Hotels often organize activities using three customer categories: group sales, transient sales, and catering sales. Organizing sales by geographic territories, both on a national and global basis, is very common. To determine the size of the sales force needed, such tools as market potential, ratio of sales to calls, and return on assets managed (ROAM) may be used.

The quality and effectiveness of a sales force is related to the performance of sales management activities like recruiting, selecting, training, motivating, compensating, and controlling sales personnel. Compensation, which can be particularly important, encompasses three components: expense allowances, fringe benefits, and direct income. The management challenge is to design a combination that leads to optimum sales results.

Sales reps are not the only ones that perform sales functions. Operating personnel must recognize their important sales roles. Coordinating operations and sales efforts is particularly important in delivering quality hospitality service.

Merchandising and promotion overlap, and it can sometimes be difficult to distinguish among them. Merchandising deals with marketing products and services to guests once they are on the premises. It includes such activities as display cards, tent cards, posters, in-house TV channels and various giveaways. When used effectively, merchandising can add significantly to hospitality sales and profits, but this requires effective planning and implementation.

Promotion is another term used in a variety of senses. We focused on sales promotion activities, those designed to generate short-run sales. They are used for such purposes as stimulating sales during slow periods, getting guests to try offerings, or to counter competitors' actions. The management challenge is to enhance current sales and profits without detracting from long-run marketing effectiveness.

Endnotes

1. *Successful Hotel Marketer,* December 1993, p. 6.

2. Paul Frumkin, "Independents Boost Promotion Strategies," *Nation's Restaurant News,* 20 October 1986, p. 97.

3. "Appraising Caine, the Businessman," *The New York Times,* 7 April 1996, pp. F1, 6.

4. *The Wall Street Journal,* 21 July 1998, p. A3.

5. *The Wall Street Journal,* 16 February 1996, p. A4.

6. Adapted from James R. Abbey, *Hospitality Sales and Advertising,* Third Edition (Lansing, Mich.: Educational Institute of the American Hotel & Motel Association, 1998), pp. 271–279.

Key Terms

closing—sales techniques that focus on gaining the customer's final commitment to the sale.

created promotions—promotions based on events that are created for commercial opportunities.

direct income—the monetary component of sales compensation that may be computed on the basis of salary, commission, or a combination of both.

expense allowances—that part of sales compensation designed to reimburse sales persons for costs incurred in performing their duties.

fringe benefits—the compensation benefits, such as medical, pension and vacation benefits, designed to increase loyalty and performance.

maintenance selling—sales activities designed to maintain current customers.

market potential—a method of determining the size of the sales force by calculating the amount that can be spent on a sales force while still covering costs and achieving desired profit.

merchandising—activities that market hospitality products and services to guests once they are on the premises.

missionary selling—sales activities directed at cultivating new customers and eventual sales, rather than making immediate sales.

natural promotions—promotions stemming from events that societies normally celebrate, such as Christmas or Mother's Day.

personal selling—the direct contact of a sales person with businesses or guests to sell hospitality products and services.

promotion—as used in this chapter, sales activities such as contests, direct mailings, and coupons that are designed to generate hospitality sales in the short run.

prospecting—those sales activities designed to generate new customers by focusing efforts on people who have the potential to become customers but who are not.

ratio of sales to calls—a method of determining the size of the sales force based on judgments about the number of sales calls that should made to classes of customers.

return on assets managed—a method of determining the size of the sales force based on calculations of the return on assets managed.

Review Questions

1. What approaches may be used to determine the size of a sales force?

2. If you were hired as a consultant to organize the sales force for a large hotel, what alternatives would you consider? What factors would influence your decision?

3. Under what conditions would you advise a hospitality business to engage in merchandising activities?

4. What guidelines would you suggest to a large restaurant chain considering a sales promotion campaign? What common problems might the chain face?

5. What sorts of difficulties often exist in hospitality businesses between operations and sales? How can these difficulties be addressed?

6. What are the differences between personal selling, sales management, and salesmanship?

7. Under what conditions would you recommend the use of independent sales reps?

8. What sales compensation alternatives can hospitality businesses use? Under what conditions would you apply each alternative?

Internet Sites

For more information, visit the following Internet sites. Remember that Internet addresses can change without notice.

Burger King
http://www.burgerking.com

Holiday Inn Worldwide
http://www.holiday-inn.com

Hyatt Hotels and Resorts
http://www.hyatt.com

ITT Sheraton
http://www.sheraton.com

Lodging Outlook
http://www.str-online.com/products/outlook.html

Marriott International
http://www.marriott.com

McDonald's Corporation
http://www.mcdonalds.com

MGM Grand Casino
http://www.mgmgrand.com

Walt Disney Corporation
http://www.disney.com

Part IV

Achieving Hospitality Marketing Leadership

Chapter 15 Outline

Moments of Truth
Quality in Service Delivery
Service Diversity
Service Systems
Pitfalls in the Management of a Service System
Managing Service Quality: The Baldrige Award
Service Standards of Leading Providers
    Know the Guest
    Design Customer-Pleasing Services
    Manage Guest Expectations
    Guest Satisfaction Is Everyone's Business
    Commit Resources to the Creation of Satisfied Guests
    Set High Standards
Achieving Breakthrough Performance
Concluding Comments

15

The Service Challenge: Managing Moments of Truth

"…the goal of achieving quality is…doing everything on time, every time, and all the time."

—TQM The Ritz-Carlton Way

AMONG HOSPITALITY BUSINESSES, quality means superior service. Service, in turn, is directly related to performance. Regrettably, if only one person or department fails—be it the host or hostess, a food server, the chef, reservations, the front desk, housekeeping, or security—the guest's perception of service quality will be negatively affected regardless of any fine performances by the rest of the service team. The totality of service performance—the whole service offering—comprises quality service.

Despite the importance of service, hospitality businesses generally seem more inclined to invest in upgrading such areas as the physical plant and equipment, improving data systems, and upgrading technical expertise than they are in investing in people. Yet people are the key to quality service performance.

Moments of Truth

Moments of truth occur whenever hospitality providers and guests interact, when the hospitality services extended by a provider are delivered to guests. It refers to that defining moment when guests actually experience hospitality services. As a result of their experiences, guests form perceptions and opinions of hospitality organizations. Consider the moments of truth reflected in the following situation.

> It was just after 10 A.M. when we walked into the hotel restaurant and were led to our table, passing the breakfast buffet on the way, and seated with the breakfast menus. The staff was having a meeting and it was a few minutes before anything happened, so we decided to make our way over to the buffet for a cold breakfast—all that we really wanted, apart from a cup of coffee.
>
> As we walked across the room, one of the serving staff met us and told us that the buffet was finished; it closed at 10 o'clock and had to be removed. We retreated to our table and looked again at the options on the menu. It was going to cost a lot more to order from the menu, so we settled for a simple choice: baked goods and coffee.

371

I expected to receive a small basket with a selection of croissants, muffins, and danish. Instead, we were asked what items we wanted. I settled for a croissant. A few minutes later, while the buffet was being removed, the server returned bearing a small plate with one croissant.

Somewhat uncharitably, I wondered whether the croissant had come from the buffet via the kitchen—and whether allowing us five minutes at the buffet would have made that much difference to their schedule or the quality of the food. Couldn't the staff meeting have been delayed just a little to allow us to get the buffet? Couldn't the situation have been handled with better results for all participants?

This service encounter is an example of a moment of truth. It was a point where the guest entered the encounter with expectations shaped by the reputation of the hotel and was disappointed. On such occasions, it is inevitable that the guest's disappointment will spill over into other aspects of a visit. To recover and win the guest back, the hotel has to work that much harder. Every moment of truth—whether good or bad—has a cumulative impact on guest perceptions, influencing the degree of satisfaction felt and thus the perceived quality of the hospitality experience.

Quality in Service Delivery

Before we look closely at the details of effective service, we need to consider the importance of quality in hospitality services. Although all hotels or restaurants may offer guests essentially the same kinds of services, the quality of service extended and guest perceptions of services received may differ markedly. The manner in which essentially the same services are carried out makes a real difference. Implementing quality service depends on people paying attention to relatively small details that culminate in great differences.

Superior service is the key to superior marketing performance; it is a distinguishing characteristic of the most profitable hospitality enterprises. Despite the widespread lip service given to the importance of service quality in hospitality, however, surveys and guest complaints indicate that service quality might actually be deteriorating. Since even *good* service is not all that common, excellent service providers establish an important edge in the marketplace. Excellent service means more than just satisfying guests. It means continuously exceeding their expectations.

At the world-class Regent Hotel in Hong Kong, a guest placed an inexpensive wristwatch and a ring in a tissue and left it in an ashtray. The guest went out for the evening, the room was made up, and the housekeeper discarded the tissue. The next morning the guest remembered the watch and ring, could not locate them, and deduced what had happened. The guest reported the incident to an assistant manager, stating that both items were inexpensive and did not much matter, but should they happen to show up, the hotel would know whose they were. The guest then went on with her sightseeing and forgot the situation. The Regent, however, did not forget.

Hotel staff first checked lost and found. Then they went through part of the preceding day's trash that was still in the hotel and on a truck. When nothing was

Exhibit 1   Service at Raffles Hotel Singapore

"IT'S A SCANDAL!" EXCLAIMED MRS CHEE,
AS SHE SET TO WITH NEEDLE AND THREAD.

Not one to be swayed by the vagaries of fashion, the trend for designer jeans with lacerated legs was lost on the hotel housekeeper. The fact that the young man in suite 360 had paid an inordinate amount of money to become the proud owner of these Italian trousers in just such a torn state, was of little consequence. A couple of hours of delicate darning and the ghastly gaps gaped no more. Thus rendered rather more pristine and pressed to perfection, the de-holed denims were ready to be returned. Mrs Chee presented the neatly wrapped package in person to the style conscious guest. As he held up her handiwork, his wide eyes and stunned silence were all the praise she needed. She left him, her bosom swelled with pride. Extraordinary endeavours have always been a part of the rich tapestry of Raffles, the grand old dame of the East. The perfect place to stay, to dine, to shop, or simply to sip on a sling. Raffles Hotel, 1 Beach Road. Singapore 189673. Tel: (65) 337 1886. Fax: (65) 339 7650. Telex No. RS 39028 RHSIN.

A RAFFLES INTERNATIONAL HOTEL

found, they checked the trash that had already been loaded aboard a barge. When the guest returned to the hotel late that afternoon, an assistant manager presented her with the ring and the watch. When told how they were found, she was flabbergasted.

On a more humorous note, the world-famous Raffles Hotel in Singapore, widely recognized for the quality of its guest orientation and services, ran the advertisement shown in Exhibit 1. The ad emphasizes the hotel staff's caring attention to deail, albeit in this instance leading to an unexpected (and rather amusing) result.

Exceptional service requires three ingredients: explicit leadership commitment, dedicated management to sustain it, and the devotion of support and contact staff. Developing and maintaining hospitality service quality is directly linked to leadership. The service ethic flows from the top down. It requires continuous training and attention. Not only is outstanding guest service extremely hard to attain; once achieved, it is also exceptionally difficult to sustain. Therein lies an ongoing and critical hospitality marketing challenge.

In the hospitality industry, many factors tend to reduce service quality. Guests can be difficult to deal with, overbearing, demanding, insulting, and rude. Service situations can become fatiguing and overwhelming. And since hospitality jobs often lack status, employees may feel unappreciated, disregarded, unrewarded, and demoralized. These emotions can certainly affect employees' interactions with guests. While service providers may be on the job physically, they can become machine-like and automated, depersonalizing services and routinizing contact with guests. When that happens, an unhealthy orientation evolves that affects job performance and guest services, and usually requires retraining to rectify.

The best response to such service pitfalls is dedication to the development and maintenance of an overriding service culture that instills the desire to "be the best we can be." This culture must permeate the whole organization—its values, mission, goals, personnel, and operations. It requires the development of a team spirit that embraces a pride and loyalty that underlie, nurture, and support quality service.

Service Diversity

What is considered outstanding hospitality depends on the markets being served. Consider the myriad markets that comprise the hospitality industry, such as:

- Vacation travel—Club Med

- Luxury hotels—Ritz-Carlton, Peninsula, Okura

- Mid-class hotels—Sheraton, Marriott, Hilton

- Casino properties—Circus Circus, Mirage, Caesar's Palace

- Top restaurants—Trois Gros (France), Level 41 (Sydney)

- Backpacker establishments—Youth hostels

- Boutique Hotels—Russell (Sydney), Royalton (New York), Halkin (London)

- Cruise ships—Royal Viking, P&O

- Family restaurants—McDonald's, KFC, Burger King

- Motels—Best Western, Holiday Inn, Travelodge

Each market segment comes with unique expectations and demands. In some cases, hospitality businesses may provide a limited menu of services to a clearly defined market—and do it very well. Other restaurants and hotels may appeal to a wide range of guests, offering a broad menu of services. International hotels, for example, may cater to families, business travelers, upscale guests, incentive groups, and conferences. Regardless of the diversity of services offered and markets targeted, achieving outstanding quality within any category requires commitment and specialized attention.

In developing outstanding service quality, management must keep two factors clearly in mind. The first is the number of distinct guest groups whose diverse needs have to be managed. The second is the number of distinct services or service systems that must be provided. Where specialization in both guests and services provided is possible, the definition of outstanding quality is relatively straightforward and easily communicated to all staff. In addition, guests' expectations are more easily managed through effective marketing of the specific service concept. For example, if the Star-Lite Motel advertises a location close to an interstate exit, uncluttered rooms, and an easy walk to the town's only diner, guests will probably not expect much more than that. As long as the advertised amenities are provided, guests tend to be satisfied.

However, if the very same property had tried to market itself as "fulfilling your every dream of pampered luxury amid elegant surroundings," the managers likely would end up disappointing the majority of guests they attracted. That is the essence of how marketing can drive guest expectations. The critical issues faced are likely to center on ensuring conformity to clear standards in providing services and continually measuring guest satisfaction to make sure that the service provided matches guest expectations and needs.

Where more than one basic kind of service or service system is provided, the management task becomes more complex. In most larger hotels, for example, there are at least two major service systems involved in the delivery of quality service to guests: the restaurant (food and beverage) service system and the accommodation service system. The mix of guests can be managed through effective marketing and the delivery of services through successfully selecting, training, and empowering employees and making sure the necessary systems are in place.

When guests include many different market segments, each with distinctive needs and expectations, the complexity of hospitality service management is greatly increased. How can managers deal with it? One approach is simply to ignore it and adopt a one-size-fits-all philosophy. That is often a solution of many public sector service providers, and it usually leads to high levels of dissatisfaction. An exception arises when the services are priced very low, as is the case with hostel accommodations. In most cases, however, the one-size-fits-all solution is an unsatisfactory compromise. Exhibit 2 shows low and high diversity examples of single- and multiple-service systems.

Where many different markets are served through a variety of different service systems—for example, where major hotels cater to individuals, tour groups, international guests, and corporate and conference travelers—complexity increases. In most cases, such hotels have large conference facilities; function facilities including ballrooms, restaurants, and meeting rooms; a business center; health, recreation, and exercise facilities; and a variety of food and beverage facilities. Hospitality managers are challenged to manage not only the individual systems as such, but also the interfaces among the systems, such as between conference and regular guests.

No matter how simple or complex an organization's service systems may be, each involves guests, staff, activities, and facilities in the delivery of service

Exhibit 2   The Diversity Challenge

Customer Diversity	Single Service System	Multiple Service Systems
Low Diversity	• Club Med • Backpacker • Boutique - Regents Court • McDonald's • Trois Gros Restaurant • BeauRivage • Travelodge Motels	• Ritz-Carlton • Las Vegas Casino
	ISSUE: Conformity, Satisfaction	ISSUE: Capacity, Utilization
High Diversity	• "One size fits all" • State University • Public transport system	• Sheraton • Hyatt • Shangri-La • Marriott brand options • Holiday Inn brand options
	ISSUE: Compromise, Averaging	ISSUE: Interference, Complexity

concepts. Each generates streams of moments of truth that, for guests, add up to their perception of service quality.

Service Systems

Four key elements make up a **service system** as diagrammed in Exhibit 3:

• The guests—their needs, interests, and behavior

• The product offer—the benefits to be provided

• The support service systems—which guarantee that benefits reach guests in a cost-efficient manner

• The delivery systems—through which guests and service providers come together

Each of these components identifies an important feature of the service system. Guests are the obvious starting point, for here each market segment will have its own needs, attitudes, beliefs, expectations, and behavior that must be catered to in the development of the product offer, the support systems, and the way service delivery is accomplished. The sidebar on Club Conrad presents an example of one

Exhibit 3   The Elements of a Service System

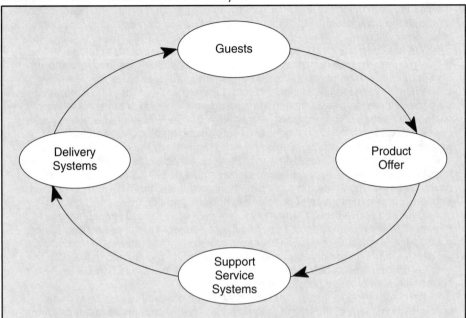

Club Conrad—Managing Quality Service

In the following interview, Keith Lamb, casino marketing executive at the Conrad Jupiter Casino on Australia's Gold Coast, outlines some significant challenges his organization has discovered in managing quality service, along with the steps they have taken to meet them.

I look after the gaming segment of the market, predominantly the top end of that market. Our private VIP room is called Club Conrad, and I am responsible for attracting people to the room. We are looking for individuals who would be coming to the Gold Coast for a weekend or a couple of days and have about $5,000 (AUS) or more in entertainment funds with them. Because they have a certain level of disposable income, they tend to be older business people. They have worked very hard at being successful, and when they come here they like to play hard. We have to make their time away from work as enjoyable as possible. It's my job to be the middle man between the client base and the casino.

When guests are playing in Club Conrad, their drinks are complimentary and the service levels are higher than they are on the main floor because we have a greater concentration of staff to patrons. It's like the first-class section of an airplane. We also have a buffet every evening, so guests can stay in the room and have their refreshments provided while they are there.

Club guests are very special clients to us because they bring in relatively large amounts of money to play with. And, because they are a special segment of the

(continued)

market, they are being targeted not only by us but by competition. We need to compete with the other casinos, in addition to promoting our own operation as being a good destination.

We hold onto our club guests by giving complimentary benefits to some of our bigger players, things like drinks, show tickets, accommodations, or even airfares. So the more a person plays, the more benefits they are going to earn.

When it comes to our premier players, I know them and they know me. A large percentage of these people have been coming here ever since there have been casinos in Australia. To keep them interested and attract more guests at this premier level, we run a number of special events, including blackjack and baccarat tournaments. For a relatively small entry fee, people have the opportunity to win a large amount of money. We also try to make it as attractive as possible for people to travel to one of these events, offering special airline deals, accommodations, etc. It costs the casino money to run the tournament, obviously, but it is worth the expense to get an influx of quite a lot of people who normally wouldn't visit us.

Over and above these tournaments, we have what we call Premium Player Events. These are built around a specific event happening in or around the casino, such as the Formula One Grand Prix or a major horse race, and we will provide VIP facilities at that event and invite people at our expense to come along to watch the event. About six weeks before the event, we send out invitations. I follow up by telephone with a lot of these people personally.

I'm not alone in regard to that kind of personal contact. Our staff are part of our public relations, part of the image of the casino. They know service is not just a matter of standing at the table and pulling cards from the shoe. The impression that clients get from us can be the lasting impression they go away with. So, it's very important that they are part of the whole service side of the business. There's been a lot more emphasis put on that over the last few years and that's probably a result of competition. In addition to providing training specific to each person's job, each of the major casinos operates a training department where staff learn to successfully handle difficult situations by observing other people.

Repeat business relies very much on service. I think that's right across the board—whether it be in restaurants, hotels, or casinos, service levels have improved dramatically in the last decade. Improvements have been driven by the changing marketplace. People's expectations are much higher than they used to be.

We have a casino marketing department, and a lot of our advertising is done to create front-of-mind awareness about our casino. Although I personally don't feel there are too many premium players out there who aren't aware of us, we are constantly giving people front-of-mind awareness that we are here. We hope that name recognition will lead them to come here rather than go somewhere else.

casino's response to its various guest segments. The club focuses special attention on the "high rollers" whose spending power is a major factor in the operation's success. Other segments—for example, the family on a fun night out—will have a very different set of needs and priorities and will need a service system of its own. These two segments will differ in the games they prefer, the amounts of money they are willing to spend, their preferences for food and drink, and the facilities they expect. Understanding guests translates into a specification of the product offer—the guest benefits that will be provided.

Exhibit 4   The Elements and Linkages of a Service System

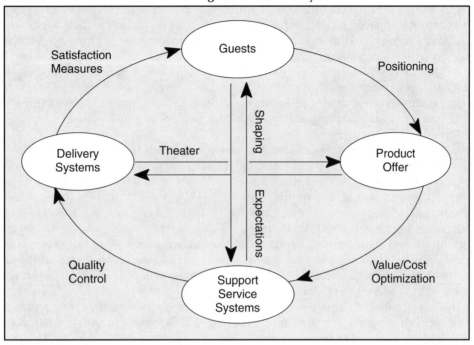

Next, attention must turn to the design of the **support service systems** that must be in place if the product offer is to work. These systems include information, planning, coordination, marketing and sales, human resource management, quality control, engineering, and security. In particular, the processes that lead to an effective integration of different systems across segments and service areas need careful and sustained thought and attention.

The fourth major element is the **delivery system** itself. Here issues of capacity management, particularly at peak periods, become important. How long are the waiting times? How will queuing be managed? Is it obvious to guests what they have to do? Does the design of the facility work effectively? How will quality be managed? These are the kinds of questions that arise as we begin to think about service delivery.

These four elements are linked by six critical processes, all of which contribute to the success or failure of the service system. The six processes are shown in Exhibit 4, which is an extended version of Exhibit 3. Each of these processes involves conscious management decisions.

Positioning is concerned with the design of the product offer, ensuring that the needs and priorities of each segment are carefully considered with an eye on what competitors are doing. The positioning that matters is something that happens in the minds of guests and prospective guests.

Value/cost optimization is concerned with those aspects of the system where there are significant possibilities for reducing cost, increasing perceived value, or both. This can be done through careful use of standardization or customization in the design of the product offer. There will always be elements of a hospitality offer that can be standardized without loss of value to guests (a buffet service, for example) or customized to link the offer directly to them (a manager's efforts to personalize relationships with important guests).

Quality control issues are an important link between support service systems and delivery systems. Attention must be paid to communication, internal marketing, human resource management (rewards, supervision, training, development, and peer group interaction), and searching for ways to enhance guest perceptions of quality.

The link between support service systems and guests highlights the processes involved in shaping guest expectations of the hospitality service experience. These processes include such marketing activities as research, advertising, sales, merchandising, promotion, and public relations. Knowing guests enables an organization to shape guest expectations accordingly; both are critical steps in achieving perceived high levels of service delivery.

In the service encounter, several elements come together in one (or more) crucial contact situations. It is here that staff and guests interact in the most direct manner and where moments of truth are created and managed, for better or worse. Here support service systems and delivery systems combine to create a level of guest service that, if properly executed, will positively differentiate an operation from its competitors. The element of theater can contribute to differentiation in important ways. It may be as simple as the style a server uses to toss a salad, the patter of the courtesy van driver on the way to the airport, or the calm assurance of a security officer. Or it may be as complex as operating a casino's outdoor laser light extravaganza or successfully hosting a major trade show. Often, the element of theater is remembered when all else is forgotten.

Finally, we come to the measurement of guest satisfaction. A variety of techniques may be used to gather guest input, including questionnaires, focus groups, hotlines, and established complaint procedures.

Each of these four elements and six processes is present in every service system. While it is important to consider each of them individually, they present two major management challenges: (1) seeing how they can be combined into a high-performance system that delivers consistent, high-quality service and (2) dealing with the critical coordination issues that arise when many service systems must operate concurrently and interact smoothly.

To achieve coordination, management may design systems with a great deal of slack or underused capacity. This was an option selected by many businesses in the past. It assured the necessary capacity to cope with issues and emergencies arising at the interface between operating systems. But it is a costly approach; underused staff and capital resources can become expensive.

These, then, are the keys to developing service quality in the hospitality industry:

- Develop and clearly state an explicit guest service mission. This means that the company sees service as a pivotal component of success—as a superior way of challenging competitors, as a most important continuing activity, as the very foundation of hospitality marketing.

- Adhere to high guest service expectations. Service excellence is a prime target, something to strive for—ever changing but never reached. In striving for the ultimate in guest services, hospitality businesses should recognize that it is always possible to do better, to continuously improve.

- Strive to do it right the first time. By fulfilling obligations and responsibilities, rather than presenting reasons for falling short when guests are disappointed, hospitality businesses signal service quality commitments and generate guest loyalty.

- Earn guest trust. Do the right thing the right way at the right time, and you will create an atmosphere of integrity that earns the respect of guests and the envy of competitors.

- Be proud. Outstanding hospitality service is commensurate with the degree of pride that staff have in their organization. When employees are proud, they will put forth that extra effort so they don't let their colleagues down. Excellent service instills pride, which in turn engenders excellent service.

- Maintain the personal touch. Outstanding service is built on communicating and working harmoniously with all staff. Those at the top should pitch in and be approachable.

- Recognize outstanding service. It is important for management to bestow deserved recognition on those who have earned it. By so doing, achievement takes on personal meaning, pride grows, staff gain goals to work for, and outstanding contributors feel appreciated.

Pitfalls in the Management of a Service System

Research has identified a number of potential pitfalls for managers seeking to raise perceived service quality flowing from the operation of a service system.[1] One study highlighted the following list of problem areas resulting from managers, staff, and guests interacting with each other in the daily operation of a service system:[2]

- Culture, climate, and mission problems
- Quality of work life problems
- Employee cynicism
- Executive credibility problems
- Organizational arthritis
- Middle management inertia
- Conflicted value systems
- Game playing
- Headquarters/field conflict

Culture, climate, and mission problems. If service is to be the cornerstone of the company mission, then it must become integral to the corporate culture. Difficulties arise when systems or procedures compete, when priorities change, or when employees receive differing signals about the importance of service. The service priority is also minimized when staff are more concerned with protecting their own turf or are intent only on meeting the minimum performance requirements for their position. This can be particularly troublesome when the business is under real pressure to contain costs in difficult economic circumstances.

Quality of work life problems. Quality of work life is very important. Disgruntled staff are unlikely to go out of their way to please guests. Managers must learn to listen to their staff and understand what it is really like to deliver the kind of service they envisage. When work force cynicism sets in, even new programs fail to stir the kind of excitement that they used to. Quality of work life is affected by burnout, playing favorites with insider groups, and failing to recognize and reward true excellence. Under such circumstances, executive credibility erodes; without credibility, leadership cannot be exercised; and without leadership, a service vision cannot be implemented.

Employee cynicism. When employees are cynical (whether it's warranted or not), their attitudes are directly affected. This carries over into their service encounters with guests and can have negative affects. Dealing immediately with cynical employees is important before the attitude and its implications spread to other employees.

Executive credibility problems. Trust between executive and service employees is an integral component in delivering quality service. Executive credibility is earned; executives' deeds must match their words. When executives are not deemed credible, employees are unlikely to create the kind of organization and environment that excellent hospitality service requires.

Organizational arthritis. Problems are compounded by organizational arthritis—rigidity and a lack of flexibility that afflict hierarchical, rule-driven organizations that become unresponsive to changing circumstances. This occurs particularly among hospitality businesses where guest service ranks lower in the scheme of things than does simply carrying out the necessary tasks.

Middle management inertia. Not infrequently, senior managers overestimate the willingness of middle managers to get behind a new project or program. Typically, it works like this: When a senior manager has an exciting idea, he or she sells it to upper staff members, each of whom is half as excited about the idea as the boss. They in turn sell the idea to their staffs, who are only half as excited as their bosses, and so on. By the time the compelling idea is to be implemented, it is a mere ripple in the life of the organization—unless it can be amplified to the point where everyone really gets behind it.[3]

Conflicted value systems. The values of the particular hospitality enterprise matter greatly. How is excellence in service really regarded? Is it rewarded and cherished, or taken for granted? The mission of many a service business refers in glowing terms to the importance of guests, but in practice, when guest priorities conflict with short-term business pressures, they lose. A company's true values are always apparent to service staff and these value send important signals that affect staff willingness and ability to deliver on service promises.

Game playing. Game playing arises when managers and employees play politics with regard to resources, people, and communications. For example, staff members fighting the demand to improve service levels may contend that increasing service quality requires more money and people. This can often bring service improvements to a dead halt. One study uncovered the story of a hotel where the staff wanted to offer guests fresh orange juice but were unable to get the food and beverage managers to deliver, so they played games. They told guests that fresh orange juice was available, hoping that guest requests would pressure managers to deliver on the promise. Instead, the result was an increase in guest complaints and exasperation on the part of service providers.[4]

Headquarters/field conflict. Finally, there is the problem of tension that too often arises between the head office and other locations. Since hospitality encounters and the delivery of service occur in a local setting, service expectations are often culturally or locally determined. Local management may be quite right in pointing out that a national or global standard or procedure makes no sense locally.

Managing Service Quality: The Baldrige Award ————————

An objective approach to assessing service excellence is provided by the criteria embodied in the Malcolm Baldrige National Quality Award. The United States Congress established the award in 1987 to recognize U.S. companies for their achievements in quality and business performance, and to raise awareness of the importance of excellent quality in a competitive marketplace. The award's criteria are now accepted in the United States and around the world as the standard for performance excellence. (To date, the Ritz-Carlton Hotel Company, which earned the Baldrige Award in 1992, is the only hospitality organization to be so recognized.)

We can learn a lot about the delivery and assessment of service quality by studying the kind of information that is gathered and the factors that are assessed by the award committee. As seen in Exhibit 5, the committee's board of examiners uses seven criteria, together with the relative weights, to make their judgments. These criteria are relevant in auditing the quality of hospitality management. The assessment calls for consideration of the company's approach, how it is implemented in each part of the company, and the results achieved.

The criteria include guest focus and satisfaction. They cover an understanding of near-term and long-term guest expectations and desires, an evaluation of a company's skill in managing guest relationships, the extent of its commitment to its guests, how service commitments are evaluated and improved, how guest satisfaction and future intentions are measured, and how guest approval compares with that achieved by competitors.

Leadership looks at the involvement of senior executives in establishing a culture that values quality excellence, considers the extent to which a guest focus is integrated into daily activities, and concludes with a review of public responsibility and corporate citizenship. Questions about information and analysis focus on identifying those areas requiring more attention and those that can be used as internal

Exhibit 5   The Seven Criteria for the Malcolm Baldrige National Quality Award

Category	Points
Leadership	110
Strategic Planning	80
Customer and market focus	80
Information and analysis	80
Human resource development and management	100
Process management	100
Business results	450
TOTAL	**1000**

benchmarks. Strategic planning considers the short- and long-term planning processes for achieving and maintaining leadership in guest satisfaction. Human resource development and management deals with one of the most challenging aspects of service management: the management of those involved with delivering guest services. It begins with planning; looks at ways in which the company enables staff to contribute effectively to quality goals; explores employee education and examines training and employee performance, recognition, promotion, compensation, reward, and feedback mechanisms; and assesses employee well-being and satisfaction.

Attention is also given to process management—from design through service delivery, including support services such as accounting, information systems, engineering, and security. The award criteria conclude with a careful and detailed assessment of business results, for the ultimate test of the design and delivery of a high quality service system is to be found in the business outcomes achieved by management. It is for this reason that business results are given the highest weight.

Service Standards of Leading Providers

Service policies are interrelated and need to be considered as a whole rather than as a number of separate components. Excellent service means creating a service culture that systematically builds long-term guest satisfaction. Staff should be committed to exceeding guest expectations, and hospitality managers must commit the resources necessary to support desired service outcomes. Established standards must be in place to measure achievement.

Six characteristics (see Exhibit 6) are shared by nearly all leading service providers.[5] Such firms:

1. Are obsessive about knowing what customers really want.

2. Design their services to maximize customer satisfaction.

Exhibit 6   Six Characteristics of Leading Service Providers

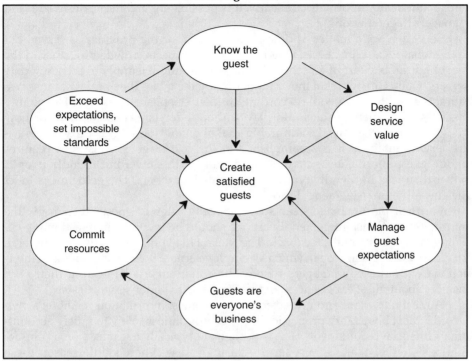

3. Create and manage customer expectations.

4. Make customer satisfaction the business of every employee at all levels.

5. Put resources behind their commitment to the customer.

6. Set "impossibly high" standards and strive to achieve them.

Let's consider each of the six characteristics.

Know the Guest

Hospitality businesses often make inadequate attempts to really know their guests. Traditions in the industry implicitly prescribe what are *believed* to be guest needs, which are reflected in such areas as facility design, room layout, menus, training, and the variety of service specifications. However, most of us in our roles as guests are conscious of areas where we wish management had paid more attention to our real interests and less to the usual industry practices.

In room design, for example, guests can be frustrated by little things like shower stalls without soap holders, towel racks that are out of reach, chairs that are too low for desk work, the lack of full-length mirrors, closets that are not deep enough for suits, inadequate lighting, no makeup mirrors, hangers that cannot be detached, and the lack of places to drip-dry clothing. In the restaurant, guests regularly confront menus that are long on flowery descriptions but short on nutritional and dietary information. Clearly, it is possible for architects, designers, and managers to get it wrong!

Service is not a matter of doing what is best for the provider or server, but doing what is best for guests. One regularly sees guests crowded together in the most undesirable part of an otherwise empty restaurant, simply to accommodate servers. Guests are told that they cannot occupy the tables they prefer because restaurants want to seat people according to their established systems. Hospitality businesses put their systems into play without adequate consideration for how guests feel. For example, the admirable goal of giving speedy service can depreciate service quality if it is accomplished at the cost of guest hassles or requires undue guest effort. Guests may prefer dealing with slower but friendly people, rather than fast, unfriendly types who operate like robots. The guideline is to let the guests, not management, decide.

For their part, managers can strive to really listen to guests, then apply the information and insight gained. Everyone should be involved in questioning, listening, and sharing guest feedback. The Melia Hua Hin Hotel, a five-star hotel in Thailand, keeps a daily log in which all employees note their discussions and interactions with guests; managers review the comments daily, adding their own insights about guest experiences, and use the data to better serve guests.

A most important and neglected source of guest information is a hotel's own records. Most hospitality properties keep records almost solely to satisfy accounting or financial requirements. As such, they are typically organized on a transaction basis rather than a guest-service basis. And yet there's little reason these records cannot be sorted according to relevant guest factors such as type of guest (business, group, family, etc.), whether the guest is a repeat visitor, place of residence, length of stay, dollars spent, how the property choice came about, credit cards used, and the mix of services used. Using such information, a detailed picture of the guests being attracted to a hotel can be developed. While it is more difficult to build such databases for restaurants, many restaurants assemble basic data by putting one or two classification items on their discount coupons, by getting guests to fill in forms for their complimentary birthday and anniversary offerings, or by analyzing information from sales receipts. With the right records in place, restaurants can experiment with new menu design, services, and other items to expand markets and quickly adapt to changing guest trends.

Design Customer-Pleasing Services

Leading hospitality providers base the design and specification of hospitality services on their customer knowledge. At the strategic level, a concern for core guest needs led Harry Sebel of the Sebel Town House in Sydney, Australia, to travel the world, talking to prospective guests and studying hotel and room designs to discover the kind of room that appealed to the high-profile guests he sought to attract. Similarly, Frank Banks of Rihga Royal Hotel in New York City focused on pleasing business executives when he outfitted his Pinnacle Suites with fax machines, multiple telephone lines, pagers, and cellular phones, and offered complimentary limousine service to Wall Street and the local airports, along with a host of other amenities for business guests.

In designing an effective service system, managers must keep both the individual components of the system and the whole system in mind. What goes on in the back of the house—in the kitchen, in housekeeping, or in reservations—affects the front of the house. It is particularly important to pay specific attention to those parts of the system that guests encounter. This means paying attention to each service component and asking, Is it guest friendly? How can it be improved? What are the possible service failure points?

Manage Guest Expectations

Managing the expectations and desires that guests bring to a hospitality business is often overlooked in achieving outstanding service and pursuing such marketing goals as increasing market share, sales, and profits or positioning. Most hotels and restaurants use various forms of advertising and personal selling to communicate with agents, wholesalers, major clients, and everyday guests. Their choice of media and the tone and content of what is communicated, directly or indirectly, shape guest expectations, as do the physical property itself (through layout and appearance) and the attitudes and appearance of staff who deal with guests. Guest experiences at each service encounter throughout a visit contribute to the cumulative impression of hospitality expectations, desires, and attitudes. At the end of a visit, an assessment of expectations and experiences, whether made explicitly or implicitly, will drive decisions about return visits and referrals.

Club Med, a recognized hospitality leader, has effectively managed expectations. For years, its advertising has been carefully directed toward young adults—often single—who share similar lifestyle interests. It creates expectations for them that highlights the informality, carefree relaxation, and fun group activities of each resort. Guests come prepared for a stress-free experience and leave with their desires and expectations exceeded by their experiences. As a result, guests are a major source of referrals for future Club Med customers.

Skillful management of guest expectations is a key to service excellence. This in turn rests on identifying core guest market segments, understanding what they desire from a hospitality experience, specifying corresponding services, delivering appropriate services, and reaching out to each segment with consistent messages that under-promise and over-deliver.

Guest Satisfaction Is Everyone's Business

A characteristic of leading service firms is that everyone is deeply and personally committed to guest satisfaction. This sense of commitment goes far beyond the staff that deal directly with guests and includes all support staff and managers. The commitment even reaches beyond the formal boundaries of a company to include partner organizations and strategic alliances, as well as the variety of agencies and networks involved in marketing hospitality.

Leading firms display a sense of service commitment that flows from the top of the organization, where values are defined and displayed. Paul Kirwin, vice president of operations for Country Inns & Suites by Carlson, summarizes his company's philosophy:[6]

> The first and most important task is to ensure a corporate commitment to absolute guest satisfaction. Your organization must have a culture that says satisfying customers is "job number one." Our mission statement and our service pledge to guests both reflect our commitment to providing a quality product and guest satisfaction. Successful companies ensure their commitment to satisfaction is more than mere words on paper. How do they do it?
>
> *Focus on employees.* Focusing on employees is the most important element. Concerted effort must be placed on selecting friendly, outgoing individuals—those who project enthusiasm, fun, and happiness. We have learned that the sort of attitude and motivation we look for cannot be developed in training sessions. Therefore we hire according to guidelines we call "PICI." We look for Passionate, Intelligent, Compassionate, and Intense employees. With those attributes, we know our staff will deliver quality service.
>
> *Offer training and staff recognition.* Training programs aimed at coaching employees on the skills of handling guest complaints and providing value-added service are essential to developing an effective staff. Country Inns' "Honor the Promise" and Radisson's "Yes I Can" are two examples of quality training programs that help teach employees how to work with guests.
>
> *Empower.* Many hospitality enterprises fall short in empowerment. Somehow attitudes, policies, and procedures have developed reflecting distrust in employees' ability to handle problem situations with guests properly. They advocate getting a manager who will decide what to do rather than train staff members to do what it takes within reason to satisfy guests. The message to employees is that resolving complaints and being committed to satisfying guests isn't their responsibility; the manager will decide what should be done to help guests. A true commitment to guest satisfaction by all employees means that they must have the power to meet guest needs and problems.

All members of a hospitality organization must feel that they are important, that they belong, and that their efforts are appreciated. Those at the very top must demonstrate that they understand the value of each person's contribution and that they too are part of the service team. To foster such understanding, Hyatt once a year has their executives trade places for a day with those on the front line and serve as bellstaff, waitstaff, front desk clerks, housekeepers, and so on. This enhances understanding and appreciation of service staff contributions and the situations they confront. Managers can encourage teamwork by mixing with all groups, communicating well, being approachable, and recognizing and appreciating the contributions of all team members. Each hospitality area must develop a sense of contributing to the level of service quality and the creation of satisfied guests.

The involvement of all hospitality staff in guest satisfaction reduces the chance that functional areas will define their contribution in narrow, non-guest-related terms, such as cutting costs, reducing cycle time, minimizing handling, and decreasing the number of sales contacts. Because it can be difficult to measure service quality and establish cause-and-effect relationships, managers often focus on measurable items such as costs, sales, number of guests, revenue per available room, sales per check, turnover, and short-term profitability. When such measurements become the focus, however, it is likely that service quality is neglected—a first step on the path to indifferent service performance.

Commit Resources to the Creation of Satisfied Guests

Excellent service firms focus their resources on activities that generate guest satisfaction. This may range from the direct allocation of funds for guest service budgets (perhaps as part of the marketing budget) to committing resources to the redesign of systems and facilities that clearly will enhance service delivery. For example, Swissair, which places punctuality high in its understanding of passenger needs, instructs pilots to use high-speed cruise—significantly increasing fuel costs—when flights are delayed beyond a certain point; savings are made up in other service areas that passengers do not deem so critical.[7] Focusing resources on activities related to customer priorities becomes even more critical when the economic climate is difficult, as was the case in the U.S. hotel industry in the late 1980s and early 1990s. When economic conditions are favorable and business is good, the unfortunate tendency is to slack off and customer satisfaction is neglected.

Establishing a guest service budget sends a message to all staff that spending money to satisfy guests is acceptable behavior. This enables staff to deal directly with guest complaints and make necessary on-the-spot adjustments. Since no system is perfect, things will go wrong. However, with guest service budgets in place, both the staff and guests are likely to feel that satisfaction is indeed central to management's thinking.

Set High Standards

Outstanding service providers insist on meeting what appear to be impossibly high standards that stretch their organizations and motivate employees to perform beyond their expectations. This has implications for both measuring and assessing performance. Swissair, for example, surveys 7,000 of its passengers each quarter to rate the airline on numerous points. The company achieves a very high 70 percent response rate because passengers know that the survey matters. And Swissair sets its sights high, for management insists that a minimum of 97 percent of the respondents rate performance as good or excellent. This attitude extends to individual elements of service provision, such as check-in, boarding, in-flight service, deplaning, and baggage handling. Where aspects of performance fall below specified standards, managers are expected to act swiftly to bring them up to par.[8]

Similar approaches have been adopted by other well-known hospitality business. Forte PLC, known throughout Great Britain for its outstanding guest satisfaction ratings, pays careful attention to service quality ratings in its hotels and restaurants. In explaining how the company accomplished this goal, Chairman Rocco Forte stated: "We have concentrated on three principal areas: ensuring that our products are leading in the increasingly competitive markets in which they operate, winning market share by enhancing our sales and marketing activities, and improving margins by reducing costs."[9]

The popular practice of benchmarking, which refers to using the best service standards in the industry as reference points, can be helpful. In this way, the best levels of performance become the standards for assessing company service delivery levels. The idea is to either improve and develop world-class service levels in-house or outsource those activities that do not measure up. The result is that each major element of service is at least competitive with, if not superior to, the best.

Looking back over the policies and actions of several service leaders, a common theme emerges—namely, that of purposely remaining close to guests. This does not mean being close to every guest. Rather, it means focusing on the significant core groups, those specific groups of guests that are most important to please. For some hotels, convention attendees are the critical group, so facilities and services can be tailored to meet their particular needs and desires. For other hotels, the core groups may be business executives, overseas tour groups, families with children, public sector employees, or senior citizens, and hotel services can be planned accordingly.

Hospitality businesses cannot be outstanding in meeting the needs of every guest group. Group requirements vary and even conflict. What works for families in restaurants or hotels may not work for senior executives or convention groups. The essence of marketing strategy is choice—choice of guests, image, market position, and the elements of the marketing mix. These choices can be translated into service needs and priorities, and, hence, into the six service steps just discussed. When the steps are properly carried out, they become a self-sustaining loop that embodies moments of truth and spells out what is meant by the comment, "Service is the centerpiece of hospitality."

Achieving Breakthrough Performance

While well-managed, successful service firms accept and implement the six steps just discussed, the truly outstanding firms—those that are the best of the best—go even further in their service philosophies and operations and achieve *breakthrough service*. They leverage investments in staff, space, and systems to achieve elevated levels of customer satisfaction and profitability. They are:

> firms that seem to gain momentum, almost as if they are propelled by an additional force not available to their competitors. Firms that seem to have broken through some sort of figurative "sound barrier"; that have passed through the turbulence that precedes the barrier into the relatively quiet, smooth zone beyond, in which a management action produces exaggerated results, results that often exceed reasonable expectations. Firms that alter the very basis of competition in their industries.[10]

Such firms consider the interactions among policies and see how they can be implemented to achieve synergy, generating additional momentum to propel them forward and distinguish them from other excellent companies.

Exhibit 7   The Traditional Model

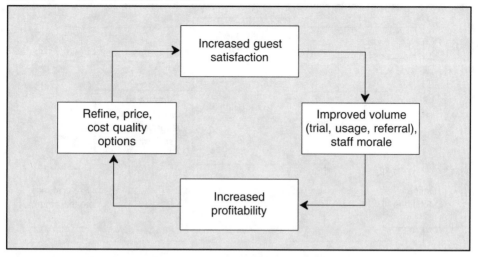

An important part of their success is based on their deep understanding of the dynamic interaction between the key management variables that define the performance of a service system. The more traditional companies view their essential or core sets of variables and their interactions as shown in Exhibit 7.

Hospitality managers who see their world in more traditional terms tend to address a decrease in profitability by reevaluating pricing, cost structures, services offered, and quality—in effect, emphasizing resources expended. They assess service operations in terms of balancing profitability and guest satisfaction. Thus, price increases or cost reductions are evaluated in terms of their impact on perceived quality, with the recognition that when quality diminishes so might the flow of satisfied guests, resulting in reduced revenues and profits. They may make tradeoffs that culminate in higher prices and margins that may reduce sales while increasing overall profitability. Or they may improve quality which will increase costs but also result in higher levels of guest satisfaction, thereby actually increasing sales, improving overall profitability, and generating loyal guests.

Breakthrough companies not only consider such interactions, they also develop a richer model of key managerial variables and the way they interact to drive profit performance and guest satisfaction. A few possibilities are illustrated in Exhibit 8.

The more traditional hospitality companies tend to focus management thinking on price, cost, and quality decisions, and are primarily influenced by profit and volume considerations (the cycle labeled B). Breakthrough companies start with a sharpening of management's focus on understanding the real needs and priorities of core guest groups, rather than the needs managers believe are important (the cycle labeled A). They carefully monitor changes in priorities of core guest groups over time. They work hard at being outstanding in meeting core group needs and at the same time satisfying other guests as best they can.

Exhibit 8   The Breakthrough Model

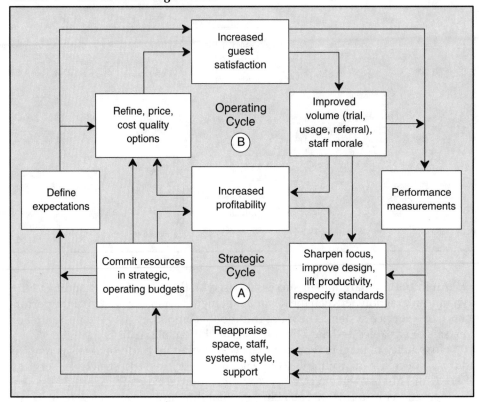

By carefully targeting guests, designing services that reflect guest needs and desires, and establishing high standards, breakthrough businesses enhance profits. Managers reappraise operations and rethink resource allocation for space, facilities, staff, rewards, staff development, and technology. They reassess company philosophy, culture, strategy, policy, and style. And the decisions made are reflected in the budgeting process to provide the resources necessary to support operating activities. In this manner, the effects of changes in pricing, cost, and quality and their impact on guest satisfaction can be tracked. This, in turn, leads directly to the cycle of enhanced guest satisfaction and profit performance we considered earlier.

A key difference between breakthrough and other companies is that attention is directed to strategic considerations as the driving concern, rather than operational or short-term activities. The long-term perspective is kept clearly in mind and is not sacrificed for short-term gains. Experience indicates that, in service enterprises, inspired strategic thinking, coupled with informed operating choices, ultimately results in increased profitability.

Assuming that expectations have been managed well, the decisions regarding price, cost, and quality will reflect real guest needs and increase guest satisfaction.

By getting it right, restaurateurs and hoteliers can expect to increase guest values and satisfaction, generate additional sales and market share, and increase profits. Enhanced profits permit additional investments in properties, operating systems, market communications, and staff. This allows successful hospitality businesses to differentiate themselves even further from their less profitable competitors.

Finally, the two outside loops in Exhibit 8 need special comment. Keeping service systems closely focused on the needs of key target markets necessitates continuous measurement of attitudes, beliefs, expectations, desires, and behavior of actual and prospective guests. Otherwise, hospitality providers are simply guessing. There are two primary sources of data. First, guest feedback is critical to choosing target markets, designing and improving services, establishing relevant standards, and implementing operating systems. Second, sales feedback will provide valuable information about repeat and new business, the incidence and nature of referrals, and the profitability of guests and various offerings.

The second loop in Exhibit 8 is concerned with shaping guest satisfaction through communications and the design of operating systems. The way staff respond to guests, the atmosphere created by skillful space management and design, and the responsiveness of computers and other technology systems all play a role in shaping the expectations that guests bring to the service. They need to be managed with this in mind.

Outstanding performance in the management of service systems is not accidental. It arises from detailed insights into, and feel for, the interaction of all the variables we have explored. It requires dedication and commitment. For ultimately, all the planning and thought involved in designing hospitality systems will be tested in the day-to-day world of service encounters—the critical moments of truth.

Concluding Comments

This chapter is concerned with the challenges that arise as management seeks to deliver the quality of service it believes to be appropriate to the markets sought and the prices charged. Hospitality businesses can fail not only through poor choice of strategy, but also from poor implementation of an otherwise sound strategy. In this chapter, we have sought to show how the choice of strategy for a hospitality business (often focused on a choice of target markets and a product concept) interacts with choices made in the design of support systems and in delivery of service to determine overall success or failure. The common element to all of these choices is people—a commitment to leadership, dedicated management at all levels, and the devotion of support and contact staff.

Taken together, the choice of target markets and the products and services to be offered, the design of support systems, and the ways in which service is to be delivered can be thought of as a service system. In many hospitality businesses, a number of such service systems will need to be designed and operated at the same time, serving different kinds of guests, each with distinctive needs. Where this happens, there is a diversity challenge that management must meet as well. Each of these service systems interacts with all the others, creating complex situations at the interface between each that demand skillful management if service disasters are to be avoided.

Many pitfalls lie in wait for managers looking for quality outcomes from the service systems they are responsible for. These include problems arising from an inappropriate corporate culture, poor quality of work life, employee cynicism, low levels of executive credibility, rigid organizational structures, middle management inertia, conflicted value systems, game playing, and poor communication between corporate levels, teams, and groups. Knowing that these kinds of problems can and do arise is an important first step toward making sure they do not occur, or if they do, reaching an effective resolution.

Success in the hospitality business turns on much more than thinking about just one or two aspects of a service system. A brilliant choice of market niche can be undone through poor delivery of service. An outstanding operational concept may fail through inappropriate choice of markets. All of the elements needed for outstanding success in service delivery are brought together in the criteria for the Malcolm Baldrige National Quality Award. While the recognition of excellence flowing from the Award is something to aspire to, the detailed criteria provide a framework that managers can use to assess both their own levels of quality in service delivery and those achieved by competitors.

The experience of outstanding service businesses translates these general ideas into specific prescriptions for success. Each of the elements of a service system is designed and operated to "impossibly high" standards. This leads to the concept of "breakthrough" companies, where operational and strategic management is of a high order, informed by a rich flow of data, and focused on achieving economic success through breakthrough service. This is the challenge that hospitality firms face in the opening years of the next millenium.

Endnotes

1. This concept owes much to the work of Richard Normann, *Service Management: Strategy and Leadership in Service Businesses* (New York: Wiley, 1984) and to James L. Heskett, W. Earl Sasser, Jr., and Christopher W. L. Hart, *Service Breakthroughs: Changing the Rules of the Game* (New York: Free Press, 1990).

2. Karl Albrecht, *At America's Service* (Homewood, Ill.: Dow-Jones Irwin, 1988), pp. 62 ff.

3. Albrecht, p. 71.

4. Albrecht, p. 72.

5. Albrecht, p. 157 and Lilind M. Lele, *The Customer Is Key* (New York: Wiley, 1987), p. 51.

6. Paul Kirwin, "Increasing Sales and Profts through Guest Satisfaction," *Cornell HRA Quarterly,* October 1992, p. 38.

7. Lele, p. 71.

8. Lele, p. 71.

9. Mike Sheridan, "Checking in at Forte," *Sky,* March 1994, p. 62.

10. Heskett et al., pp. 1–2. See also James L. Heskett, W. Earl Sasser, Jr., and Leonard A. Schlesinger, *The Service Profit Chain* (New York: Free Press, 1997).

🔑 Key Terms

delivery systems—staff, locations, and facilities where service is delivered to guests.

moments of truth—the moments when hospitality services are actually provided to guests; the interactions between service providers and guests that influence guest perceptions and opinions of the service provider.

service system—a system with four components: guests, product offer, support system, and delivery system.

service diversity—the number of distinct services or service systems that must be managed.

support service systems—include information, planning, coordination, marketing and sales, human resource management, quality control, engineering, and safety.

❓ Review Questions

1. What are moments of truth? Why are they of critical importance to hospitality businesses?

2. What are the three ingredients of exceptional service? What sorts of factors tend to reduce service quality in the hospitality industry?

3. When developing outstanding service quality, what two factors must management keep in mind? How does the number of distinct guest groups and distinct services affect the quality service challenge?

4. What are the four key elements of a service system? How are these elements linked by critical processes?

5. What general problems has research identified that interfere with attempts to raise service quality? How can these problems be addressed?

6. What is the Malcolm Baldrige National Quality Award? What are the seven selection criteria for the award? How might studying these criteria help a hospitality organization improve its service quality?

7. What characteristics are shared by almost all leading service providers? How do these characteristics apply to hospitality organizations?

8. What is breakthrough service? What are the traits of firms that provide breakthrough service?

💻 Internet Sites

For more information, visit the following Internet sites. Remember that Internet addresses can change without notice.

Club Med
http://www.clubmed.com

Country Inns & Suites
http://www.countryinns.com

Hyatt Hotels and Resorts
http://www.hyatt.com

Malcolm Baldrige National Quality
Award
http://www.quality.nist.gov

Marriott International
http://www.marriott.com

Melia Hua Hin Hotel
http://www.tiscoverasia.com/
meliasgle

McDonald's Corp.
http://www.mcdonalds.com

Radisson Hotels Worldwide
http://www.radisson.com

Regent Hong Kong
http://www.rih.com/locations/Hong
Kong/index.html

Rihga Royal Hotel New York
http://ny.rihga.com

Ritz-Carlton Hotels
http://www.ritzcarlton.com

Sebel Town House
http://www.oztravel.com.au/
travel_mall/hotels/
Sebel_Town_HousElizabe.html

Swissair
http://www.swissair.com

Chapter 16 Outline

Entrepreneurship
     An Entrepreneur's Orientation
     Entrepreneurial Behavior
The Entrepreneurial Process in Hospitality
     The Assessment Process
     Entrepreneurial Approaches
     Traits of Successful Entrepreneurial Ventures
Creativity
     Promoting Creative Thinking
     Creativity in Hospitality
     Barriers to Creativity
     Lessons from Research
Innovation
     Three Types of Innovations
     The Innovation Process
     Factors Affecting Success and Failure
     Leadership and "Followership"
Concluding Comments

16

Energizing Hospitality Marketing: Entrepreneurship, Creativity, and Innovation

"We can only continue to offer a good life for all of our people through entrepreneurship and innovation ... Without a climate of enthusiasm, new enterprises and new ideas are likely to be stillborn."
—Arnold Toynbee[1]

"Imagination is more important than knowledge."
—Albert Einstein[2]

Entrepreneurship, with its emphasis on creativity and innovation, is now a more important business force than ever. Entrepreneurs have long been a driving force in the hospitality industry. Today, Hilton, McDonald's, Holiday Inn, and KFC are all internationally recognized brands. They are the brainchildren of entrepreneurs Barron Hilton, Ray Kroc, Kemmons Wilson, and Harland Sanders, respectively. Such world-famous hotels as the Okura in Tokyo, the Ritz in Paris, the Savoy in London, and the Waldorf-Astoria in New York City were begun and developed by enterprising hoteliers. J. W. Marriott, the founder of the Marriott enterprises, began with a root-beer stand in Washington, D.C., in 1927. This nine-seat stand has grown into a global lodging and management services hospitality company, employing over 200,000 people.

Successful hospitality entrepreneurs invariably have an instinctive feel for markets. They are attuned to guest needs, are sensitive to opportunities for new and creative innovations, and appreciate the important role of marketing in the success of hospitality offerings. In turn, effective hospitality marketing thrives on entrepreneurial approaches. Hospitality marketing and entrepreneurship are so closely intertwined that it is often hard to distinguish where one ends and the other begins.

Since entrepreneurship, creativity, and innovation have extensive bodies of literature, we can deal with these topics only briefly. We shall refer to some of the basic ideas and concepts that are particularly relevant to hospitality marketing. Exhibit 1 highlights our approach to these important areas.

Successful hospitality entrepreneurs by and large seem to have an appreciation of the importance of marketing. They seem to be attuned to potential profitable market opportunities for new and creative approaches. They are willing to

Exhibit 1   Relationship of Entrepreneurship, Creativity, and Innovation

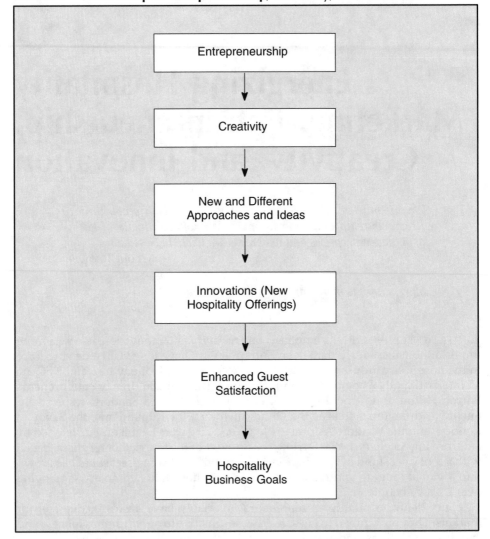

innovate and take risks. In reality, successful hospitality marketing and entrepreneurship go hand in hand.

This chapter deals with entrepreneurship, creativity, and innovation. We begin by considering the entrepreneur's role in hospitality, the entrepreneurial process, and the characteristics and approaches of successful entrepreneurs. Then we turn to a consideration of creativity as a process, the stimuli and barriers involved, and the ways of fostering creativity in hospitality organizations. We conclude by considering the types of innovation, alternative innovation strategies, and factors responsible for the success and failure of hospitality innovations.

Entrepreneurship

McDonald's founder Ray Kroc is recognized as one of the greatest entrepreneurs of all time. He developed a thriving global hospitality enterprise, inspired the fast-food industry, and was instrumental in making his hospitality offerings—hamburgers, milk shakes, and fries—an integral part of the American culture. He stimulated the growth of franchising in the industry, and his ideas influenced lifestyles and eating habits around the world. Entrepreneurs like Ray Kroc are responsible for bringing the all-encompassing fast-food industry to its present state of development.

Entrepreneurship involves creating something new, be it new methods, approaches, products, services, or combinations of resources. Entrepreneurs seek to change things. They sense and respond to shifts in the existing marketplace. They develop untapped markets. They take risks. They either do something different or do the same thing in a new and superior way.

Entrepreneurs stand behind the growth of most successful hospitality enterprises. They created such hospitality innovations as motels, franchising, drive-in restaurants, and fast foods. Daniel Forge, owner of the BeauRivage restaurant profiled in the sidebar, sensed that the trend toward eating healthier, lighter food would grow. He seized the opportunity, capitalized on an innovative concept, and set about creating not only a successful restaurant, but a new restaurant category.

An Entrepreneur's Orientation

Entrepreneurs are achievement oriented, focusing on accomplishments, bottom-line results, and getting the job done. They are not as concerned with organizational hierarchies, job titles, or filling out the appropriate forms. Their motivation lies not merely in money, although they may become very wealthy, but in autonomy and independence, being their own boss, and gaining peer recognition. They do things their way.

From a management perspective, entrepreneurial behavior is a valuable resource, a force that translates perceptions of hospitality opportunities into successful enterprises. Entrepreneurship can flourish at all management levels. It can be evidenced in ongoing ventures as well as new ones, in local and global hospitality companies, in large and small companies. However, the entrepreneurial spirit tends to thrive better in smaller businesses because the bureaucratic approaches of larger organizations tend to stifle entrepreneurial energy and drive.

Entrepreneurial Behavior

The widely accepted characterization of entrepreneurship as "creative destruction" emphasizes the entrepreneur's innovative and iconoclastic bents.[3] In a sense, entrepreneurs destroy what exists—but in a creative way that leads to improvements. It is behavior that goes against the grain of vested interests, challenges the accepted wisdom, and seeks the new and different. As a result, entrepreneurs may be seen as outsiders who challenge those seeking to protect their current positions and the status quo.

Profile—BeauRivage Mediterranean Restaurant

Daniel and Luciana Forge own and operate the BeauRivage Mediterranean Restaurant in Malibu, California, a premier Mediterranean restaurant on the West Coast. They nurtured it from an idea into the successful, award-winning restaurant that it is today. Daniel explains, "Fifteen years ago, when I first proposed the concept, there was no Mediterranean restaurant category. It seems that I was actually the first one to think of it. I remember simply thinking, 'I am French, and my wife, Luciana, is Italian, so let's put the two together and make this a Mediterranean restaurant.'"

They purchased the property in Malibu with a cafe on it, intending to tear the building down and construct a new restaurant. Because of strict Malibu zoning laws, however, they left the original cafe standing and built around it. Daniel brought extensive hotel and restaurant experience, both in the United States and abroad, to the venture, having served in capacities from busboy to maître d'. Luciana, a professional opera singer and an artist, developed the restaurant's distinctive ambience through her own interior decorating, painted murals, and hand-painted vests worn by the waitstaff.

BeauRivage, which opened for business in 1982, today comprises several charming rooms, each with its own distinctive Mediterranean character and a view of the ocean. Daniel explained, "I felt strongly that Mediterranean food would be well received. It is very healthy food. Look at the Mediterranean people: they dance, they sing, they eat, and they live to be 106." Luciana added, "The place just seems to generate good feelings among our guests. The atmosphere is warm, comfortable, gracious, and friendly. It is rustic, yet elegant. It is not pretentious. It is genuine and has a good feeling about it that guests like and enjoy. It exudes hospitality."

Daniel emphasized, "We pay a lot of attention to treating the customer right and go out of our way to cater to guests, to run the restaurant to satisfy them. We strive to make guests feel as if they are guests in our home. Our philosophy is to use only the best ingredients; we do not compromise freshness and quality; we pay attention to food preparation and prepare healthy and tasteful food; we stay close to our guests and cater to their tastes and needs; and we have a well-trained staff to run the show."

The restaurant caters to a variety of market segments: weddings, private parties, anniversaries, receptions, birthdays, small banquets, business conferences, and individual diners. "Our repeat business is high—well over 50 percent—with several customers dining here more than once a week."

Source: a personal interview in September 1995.

Definitions of entrepreneurship highlight a variety of distinguishing traits, including:

- Sensitivity to trends and the new business opportunities they portend.

- Knowledge of available resources that can be harnessed, including financial and people skills.

- An emphasis on growth and expansion.

- A willingness to take business risks.

Entrepreneurial behavior stands in direct opposition to bureaucratic behavior. Successful entrepreneurs seem to be especially attuned to changes in the marketplace and have the ability to move fast in responding to them. Bureaucrats, on the other hand, are too often attuned to keeping things the way they are.

Many successful hospitality entrepreneurs have confronted personal adversity. They were fired, could not get a job, suffered discrimination, or were displaced by company takeovers and cutbacks. Some report that they started their own businesses because they felt their talents and ideas were not appreciated by their employers and wanted the opportunity to put them into effect. Others ran into conflicts with their bosses or just wanted to control their own destiny. Out of necessity, they became entrepreneurs, innovators, creators, and risk takers. In our interviews with successful entrepreneurs, one explained that if he had not been fired, he would probably still be "slugging it out in a factory." Another immigrated to the United States, needed work to support his family, started in the hospitality industry as a busboy, rapidly worked his way up, then left to start his own restaurants.

The Entrepreneurial Process in Hospitality

In hospitality, the process of entrepreneurship involves two sets of activities: those concerned with assessing the overall viability of a hospitality venture and those related to moving from the stage of ideas and concepts to developing actual hospitality offerings.

The Assessment Process

The assessment process deals with realistic evaluations of factors in four main areas: the hospitality venture itself, the people involved, the environmental variables, and strategic considerations. By grouping all of the information available according to these four factors and evaluating them in both quantitative and qualitative terms, a realistic appraisal of a hospitality venture can be achieved.

1. *The venture itself.* Entrepreneurs must decide whether the venture is worth the investment. They must determine whether the idea, product/service, or approach will likely be successful. Included are assessments of such factors as markets, competition, risks, and potential payoffs, as well as the finances, knowledge, and skills required to make it work. In making their assessments, entrepreneurs may think in terms of the concept itself, spin-offs, sources of new ideas, and, importantly, growth potential. Some ventures may be franchised while others cannot.

2. *The people involved.* Given a good concept, it is the people involved and how they carry out their duties that, to a large extent, can make or break a hospitality venture. People truly make the difference. Management must detail carefully the tasks that people are to perform and the education, training, and capabilities necessary for success. These requirements then must be related to the people resources available—that is, will it be possible to find or develop people with the specific skills and experience needed? The major investor of a well-known successful restaurant chain reported that the rate of expansion is limited by the lack of competent store managers.

The most critical people involved are the entrepreneurs themselves. One venture capitalist has remarked, "I often bet on the entrepreneur rather than the venture as such. A top-notch entrepreneur with just a fair venture is worth the risk. An incompetent entrepreneur with a top-notch idea is not."

3. *The environmental variables.* Environmental variables set the boundaries for business opportunities. When ventures are in line with such factors as economic, cultural, demographic, governmental, technological, social, political, and legal developments, the chances for success are greatly enhanced. For example, hospitality entrepreneurs have capitalized on such trends as healthier eating, the increasing number of senior citizens, the Internet, the desire to eat and run, reliance on automobiles, and the needs of two-income families. Careful consideration of whether external factors support a proposed hospitality opportunity is important. It is a lot easier to operate within a supportive external environment than it is to go against the tide. Even good fortune can play an important role. For example, an entrepreneur took over quite an ordinary bar and restaurant that was barely making it because it was located in an area that he felt would be developed. A condominium developer finally succeeded in getting the zoning changed to permit the construction of a large number of apartments. The result has been a very profitable venture, due mainly to external forces.

4. *Strategic considerations.* Successful entrepreneurs seem to be good strategists, managing such important aspects as direction, timing, magnitude, and use of resources. They sense what ventures fit their values, goals, and methods of operations—the opportunities that tie in with their overall abilities and talents. They recognize the benefits inherent in leveraging resources and capabilities, know how to assemble the required assets and skills, and are able to develop the team needed to capitalize on perceived opportunities.

Entrepreneurial Approaches

Since entrepreneurs set out to do things differently, flexibility, adaptability, and a commitment to continuous renewal are desirable traits. Entrepreneurs may seize the initiative by being the originators of ideas, or they may capitalize on existing concepts by giving them a different twist. They may be major financial risk takers, arranging the necessary backing to support their ventures. Or they may deal with venture capitalists who provide capital, often when other financial institutions will not. Venture capitalists, however, take part ownership—and some control—of the company.

Successful hospitality entrepreneurs recognize people's talents and skills, appreciate the need for the division of labor and the use of specialists, and understand the group effort required. They are also well aware of the need to create lean organizations, reduce management layers, develop teams, and organize core groups of workers. They are able to serve in many different capacities—workers, managers, and leaders—as needs arise. Hospitality entrepreneurs tend to do what is necessary; they are visionaries and leaders who are willing to get their hands dirty.

There seem to be two types of entrepreneur in hospitality: *doers* and *thinkers*. Doers follow their intuition, beliefs, rules of thumb, and personal guidelines. They assess situations, often quite subjectively and informally, decide on a course of action, and pursue it. They may act very quickly. Having acted, they watch what develops, make adjustments, and then act again. Their orientation is action first, then evaluation, then response. This process characterizes the actions of the bulk of hospitality entrepreneurs, particularly those operating on a smaller scale. Of course, some act when they should not, misread the results, or choose the wrong response, which results in failed businesses. However, chances are they will not be out of business for long. Entrepreneurial doers will likely launch a new venture soon, setting the whole process in motion again.

By contrast, thinkers first develop a vision or idea, which they set out to explore. In so doing, they arrive at a concept. The concept is then translated into operational terms and dimensions that can be considered further. As a result of such deliberations, thinkers may rule out a situation or choose to go ahead. If they decide to go ahead, they may develop a detailed plan that can be translated into specific programs of action. Sometimes a trial launch is used to gain information and round off the rough edges before introducing a full-blown program. Sometimes operations are launched and then, depending on the results, are rethought, reevaluated, and adjusted. The pattern is think first, act, rethink, adjust, and so on.

The result of both entrepreneurial approaches is the same: the creation of new hospitality ventures or ideas. But both approaches do not lead equally to success. In our keenly competitive hospitality environment, the thinker approach is probably wiser, as long as it is coupled with timely action. Thinking alone does not produce entrepreneurial results. Conversely, action without thought too often ends in failure and wasted resources. The very high proportion of first-year restaurant failures among independents, which has been estimated at over 50 percent, attests to this.

However, the two approaches are not mutually exclusive. It is not a matter of choosing one and ignoring the other. Doers certainly think about entrepreneurial opportunities as they size them up. They internalize their experiences, develop their own procedural guidelines, and employ them to arrive at decisions. Similarly, thinkers, once they have assessed a situation, are prone to act—sometimes quite quickly. Achieving the proper balance of thought and action is invaluable in initiating successful hospitality entrepreneurial ventures.

Traits of Successful Entrepreneurial Ventures

A considerable body of research is emerging on successful entrepreneurial ventures in hospitality and other businesses. Such ventures typically:

- Are fairly small, adaptable, and flexible.

- Have the ability to change direction rapidly.

- Benefit from the synergistic effects of one opportunity leading to others in a continuing stream.

- Have a culture that encourages individual initiative.

- Are highly sensitive to new opportunities resulting from changing factors such as environments, markets, technology, and customers.

- Maintain close contact with the marketplace.

- Are willing to act and accept risks.

- Use the capital, resources, knowledge, and capabilities of others.

- View failures as temporary setbacks and learning opportunities on the road to success.

- Are open to new ideas, methods, and approaches.

- Anticipate and create change.

- Decentralize operations when the organization becomes large.

As for hospitality entrepreneurs themselves, hard work, long hours, determination to succeed, and dedication are among their essential characteristics. The successful ones seem to be obsessed with their ventures and have a strong belief that they will succeed. Their intense personal commitment drives them to be successful.

Creativity

When we think of creativity, we tend to think of musicians, artists, dancers, actors, or scientists. In business, we often associate creativity with people whose ideas lead to new products that tap a previously unknown market, technological advances such as satellites and microchips, or brilliant and effective advertising campaigns. But it is not only the few geniuses with earthshaking ideas who qualify as creative. Everyone has creative ability to a greater or lesser extent, and this ability can be harnessed. That is the very idea behind company programs like Singapore Airlines' "Staff Ideas in Action" program. Developed to encourage creative and innovative thinking among staff, it recognizes creativity as a valuable and renewable asset.

Creativity is a habit of mind that incorporates a search for ideas and the use of imagination, seeking the new or novel while revamping the current. It is often associated with such terms as *breakthroughs, surprises,* and *leaps of logic.* To be creative is to be on the cutting edge of knowledge, generating fresh ideas, and developing new alternatives.

Creative hospitality ideas need not be earthshaking to be effective and profitable. Hospitality innovations tend to be mainly variations or adjustments to what already exists. It is more a matter of creating *pan* pizza, *rotisserie* chicken, *fat-free* desserts, and chicken *nuggets* than inventing an absolutely new food. Creativity in hospitality is mainly a search for those minor modifications that nevertheless make a big difference to guests and the bottom line.

Consider the long-held perceptions of coffee. For decades, coffee was perceived and marketed as a mature commodity, regardless of whether the brand was A&P, Kroger, Maxwell House, or Hills Bros. Narrow margins, coupons, and price discounts were firmly in place. Then Starbucks creatively developed attractive coffee bars that served gourmet coffees with exotic names, exuding an image of quality and status while charging premium prices. A profitable billion-dollar industry was created, serving a new niche carved out of very traditional markets.

Sometimes creativity results from luck. Just by chance, a person may be exposed to an idea from a different country or industry or may try a unique combination of elements that happen to work well together. Many restaurateurs have been asked by guests to begin retail sales of their home-made salad dressing or barbecue sauce, actions that eventually developed into businesses in their own right.

While serendipitous creativity certainly occurs, we will focus on more directed approaches to harnessing creativity. We will consider creativity as a manageable resource involved with the process of striving for improvement.

Promoting Creative Thinking

Hospitality management needs to promote creative thinking among the whole staff. To consider how this might be done, we will consider creative thought processes, barriers to creativity, and some pertinent research findings.

Creative people have a mental openness among them and tend to exhibit less respect for precedent than most. They are willing to spend time thinking, to seemingly do nothing, to fantasize and dream, to let the mind wander. They expand their knowledge and experiences using ideas, suggestions, and approaches from a broad variety of sources. For this reason, some businesses believe it is worthwhile for their executives to interact with professionally creative people such as musicians, dancers, and artists. The assumption is that such associations will extend sensitivity, perceptions, and thinking, giving executives increased flexibility of thought, fresh perspectives of their businesses, and new insights into market opportunities.

Managers may use two kinds of thought processes: convergent and divergent thinking. In **convergent thinking**, new experiences and ideas are filtered through existing precepts, beliefs, and biases. They are shaped and adjusted to meet preconceived notions. This is depicted in Exhibit 2.

Divergent thinking has the reverse effect. It requires an openness of mind and exposure. Managers start with current ideas, concepts, and approaches. As a result of new experiences and ideas, however, original models are extended and new insights are gleaned. Thus, new information alters approaches and concepts— managers begin to think in different contexts and dimensions. They become more creative and less confined by our preconceived ideas. This is depicted in Exhibit 3.

Research indicates that creative people tend to think divergently. They gather new perspectives, insights, and understanding from their exposure to new ideas and are open to exploring alternative ways and methods. The process extends and replaces their preconceived ideas, broadening their perceptions.

Creativity in Hospitality

In hospitality, creativity tends to be problem driven. When hospitality marketers attempt to solve problems, a stimulus is generated to become more creative.

For example, cruise ship operators are well aware that their guests enjoy the Caribbean for their beaches, water recreation, warm weather, and shopping. At the same time, guests do not like the less-than-hospitable conditions sometimes

Exhibit 2   Convergent Thinking

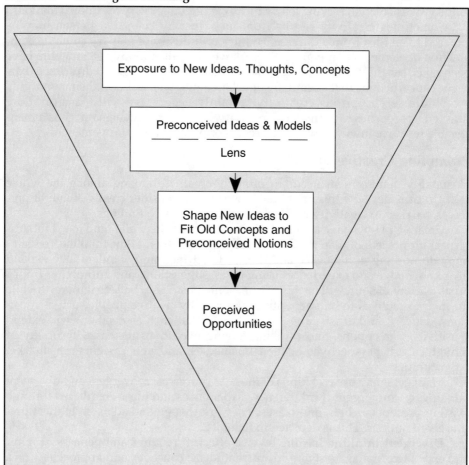

encountered while visiting ports of call. Some cruise lines have adopted a creative solution: They purchase or rent their own private dream islands and beaches, offering guests clean, hospitable surroundings in a controlled Caribbean paradise. In addition to overseeing the infrastructure of the island, the companies are in complete control of food and beverage sales and merchandising. Indeed, it was reported that Disney, a company built on its creative output, is developing such an island in conjunction with its future Disney Cruise Line. A Disney spokesman noted, "Given our creative capability ... our private island won't be like anybody else's."[4]

In 1994, with tourism down, hotels on the island of Maui, Hawaii, were challenged to be creative in identifying new market opportunities. They found a lucrative one in weddings. They learned that Americans who were marrying for the second time and Asian couples composed significant segments of their new target market. Maui hotels capitalized on this newly discovered opportunity by

Exhibit 3   Divergent Thinking

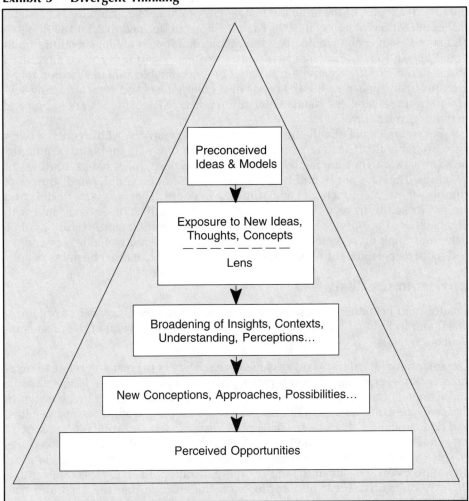

promoting their ability to offer beautiful surroundings and ocean views, while handling all of the myriad details for successful wedding celebrations. By quickly adapting their facilities and procedures to meet market needs, the island's hotels have made it possible for couples to get a marriage license, have their ceremony, and hold a hotel reception—all on the same day. At the Westin Maui, the wedding coordinator, known as the "Director of Romance," can even suggest creative ways to propose.[5] The Grand Wailea Resort, with its Seaside Chapel featuring three $100,000 Italian chandeliers, has hosted as many as seven weddings in a single day.

Creative hospitality approaches need not be complicated, time consuming, or involve considerable investments to be profitable. Consider the actions of Mama Giovanni's, an intimate, mid-priced, family-run Italian restaurant in Boca Raton,

Florida. Because of their largely Jewish clientele, business always suffered during the first two nights of the annual Passover celebration, when traditional Passover dishes are served at home. In 1996, Mama Giovanni decided that for the first two nights of Passover she would abandon the normal Italian menu, substitute traditional Jewish foods, and have two dinner sittings. The dinners were advertised and sold out. A little creativity translated an unprofitable annual situation into a very profitable one, meeting the needs of regular guests and even attracting several first-time customers. Mama Giovanni reports, "My customers are happy and that makes me happy."

Several personal qualities are associated with creativity. At the core is a tolerance of ambiguity. Creative people are willing to live with ambiguous, unstructured situations. They are not bound by existing actions, roles, habits, routines, or activities. They are not bound by their functional responsibilities and sources of stimuli—they have functional and stimulus freedom. They are very flexible and are not locked in by as many common restrictions such as those associated with organizational position. They are willing to delay gratification, readily assume risks, and think divergently. Creative people tend to be motivated less by money and more by personal fulfillment and peer recognition than other business people.

Barriers to Creativity

Creativity in hospitality marketing may be hampered by a number of organizational and individual barriers. We shall briefly mention several of the most common ones.

Organizational Barriers. Many organizational barriers to creativity relate to management style, especially the ways managers work with their staffs. Blame, threats, and demands can stifle creativity. When bosses pull rank, do not involve staff in decisions affecting them, fail to seek and value employee opinions and insights, and do not offer feedback—especially positive feedback—creativity is hampered.

Traditions, "accepted" modes of behavior, and standard operating procedures can also hinder creativity. Hierarchical rigidity acts as a major damper; good ideas do not necessarily reside at the top of an organization. Even success can stand in the way of creative ideas and approaches; the attitude that the tried and true should dominate can be very difficult to change.

To harness the creative capabilities of individuals requires a supportive working environment: one that encourages and rewards experimentation, that expects challenges to current approaches and operations, and that stimulates implementing new ideas and taking reasonable risks.

Quite often, when creative approaches to problems and situations are suggested, people with vested interest in the current approach try to squelch or at least delay them. The following is a partial list of negative reactions to creative marketing suggestions that we have encountered.

- It is not in the budget.
- We tried that before.
- Now is not the time.

- Has anyone else ever tried that?
- It is too hard to administer.
- That takes too much work.
- That approach is too academic.
- Let's wait and see.
- Let's look at it at some future time.
- We can't afford that yet.
- Let's form a committee.

None of these organizational barriers stands up to real scrutiny. Each response is an attempt to sidetrack creative approaches and continue with business as usual. All are designed to protect personal interests rather than work for the future good of the organization. Whenever such reactions are encountered, hospitality marketers should immediately be on their guard. They are signals that creative approaches are being blocked.

Individual Barriers. Individual barriers to creativity include thought patterns and conditioning that cause people to ignore creative opportunities that run counter to current beliefs. In hospitality marketing, relying too heavily on personal experiences and knowledge enmeshes people in the past and limits them to their own exposure. Similarly, assumptions that stem from the accepted wisdom or are based on the judgment of recognized authorities can relegate some very creative ideas to the trash can.

Executive egos often interfere with the adoption of creative marketing approaches. Staff quickly learn the approaches, ideas, and words that bosses deem unacceptable. As one hospitality manager reported, "I know what should be done, but if I tell the boss, he'll just get angry with me." Another said, "My boss thinks he is the fountain of all worthwhile ideas." Individual creativity is thereby hampered and restrained.

Sometimes, very profitable creative approaches and concepts are ignored because people fear failure. They have been so conditioned by past management reactions that they are afraid to take reasonable risks. Since there are always risks inherent in new approaches and ideas, individuals should be encouraged to accept reasonable risks. A successful entrepreneur reported that he hoped the new manager he just hired would make a decision that "will cost me some money." He explained that when the new manager sees there are no repercussions, other than being expected to learn from his actions, "he will become a better manager and make money for the firm."

We should note that creative management is much different from managing creativity. Creative managers apply concepts and approaches in a creative fashion in developing their marketing programs and approaches. Managing *creativity*, however, refers to facilitating, stimulating, and motivating people in a manner that encourages and harnesses their creative capabilities. In hospitality, we are concerned with both creative hospitality management and managing hospitality creativity.

Lessons from Research

Research into creativity has investigated highly creative individuals in an attempt to find common elements among them. This research has identified some qualities that hospitality managers can use to stimulate creative approaches. For example, one researcher has recently found that creativity seems to be influenced by the culture that surrounds a person. Common factors include supportive and encouraging parents and teachers, and opportunities to gain knowledge and understanding in addition to a formal education. Sometimes, special projects that were undertaken stimulated a flow of creativity and revealed talent that became the life work of a person. The needs of a specific field or changes that were occurring have sometimes attracted talented people who, because of their unusual abilities, became leaders in their fields. While chance and talent play important roles, dedication and perseverance were found to be of major importance. Knowing and being comfortable with a field such as a business or profession contributes to the flow of creative ideas. So does support of one's peers. Creative people are motivated by the intrinsic rewards that come from being the first to accomplish something or lead the way in carrying out a project.[6]

We have reviewed the extensive literature dealing with creativity, asking, "What is known about creativity that is pertinent to hospitality marketing?" The following generalizations seem to be germane.

- Pressures to conform or to pursue "rational" or "normal" actions tend to suppress individual creativity.

- Creativity is associated with such activities as relaxation, dreaming, playing, and falling asleep rather than with exerting more effort.

- Naivete and innocence, fresh questions, and different people and approaches tend to enhance creativity.

- Creativity is associated with clearing the mind and overcoming the commonly accepted wisdom. The addition of more details and information about current practices does not seem to enhance creativity.

- Creativity is enhanced by expanding knowledge and broadening experiences through exposure to other ideas, disciplines, industries, companies, and people.

- Groups and group interactions can stimulate creativity. Creativity is enhanced by bouncing ideas off of others and gaining the reactions of different members of a group.

- Business environments where rules and procedures dominate tend to dampen creative approaches.

Hospitality marketers should remember four facts about creativity. First, creativity can be learned. We will not all become creative geniuses, of course, but we can all learn to become more creative—to make the most of our creative abilities. Second, hospitality businesses can develop cultures that encourage and stimulate creativity. This requires conscious management efforts to remove creativity-inhibiting barriers and to adopt those approaches that encourage creativity. Third, creativity is a valuable, renewable resource for hospitality marketing that is an important asset to be managed and harnessed. A wide variety of techniques have been used successfully to stimulate creativity including brainstorming, free association, reasoning by analogy, drawings, dreams, and meditation. Fourth, in hospitality, relatively simple and inexpensive creative approaches can pay off handsomely. Small differences can yield significant results.

For example, for several years, golf has been attracting increasing support from the upscale leisure segment, including international tourists and the meetings and convention market. Hotels that do not have their own golf courses are forced to compete with those that do. As a creative solution, some have been very successful in making arrangements with nearby golf courses, particularly well-known ones. They secure preferred tee times and special packages of carts, green fees, and club storage for guests.

Innovation

We turn now to a brief discussion of innovation as an important focus of both hospitality marketers and entrepreneurs. Innovation has been characterized as the lifeblood of companies, the means of renewal, the core of the marketing challenge, and the continuing source of growth and profit. But what is innovation? Does it refer to the use of new technologies such as computers, faxes, and satellite teleconferencing? Does it include minor changes in presentation, style, packaging, and delivery methods? Is something innovative if it is simply new to a particular market segment?

Hospitality innovations can, but need not, incorporate advanced technologies or involve an entirely new concept. Innovations deal with different dimensions of newness, including the application of new knowledge or technology, new investments or resources, and the use of new approaches and methods. When existing hospitality institutions reposition, modify, adapt, or target their offerings to different market segments, innovation is involved. Simple adaptations or minor adjustments are often enough to replace existing offerings, achieve differentiation, garner new customers, and have great market impact.

Marketers distinguish between innovations and inventions. Inventions embody new ideas and concepts that may or may not be accepted by the market. In fact, the bulk of them will be rejected. When guests accept inventions in the sense of being willing to pay for them—that is, when inventions meet the test of the marketplace—we deem them to be innovations.

Consider the situation confronting the chief financial officer of a restaurant company that was merged into a larger company. Suddenly out of a job, he decided to open a buffet restaurant in 1983. He was successful and opened another restaurant, then another, and kept expanding. In less than a decade, he had launched 140 Old Country Buffet Restaurants and had revenues of $247 million. He used the concept of all-you-can-eat for a set price, which was not new. However, instead of the usual buffet line where guests can only go as fast as the person ahead of them, he brought innovation to Old Country Buffets by implementing a scatter-buffet table arrangement. Eight different tables contained different foods. There were individual tables with salads, soups, vegetables, hot items, and desserts. As a result, not only were guests moved faster, but more guests were accommodated. When he converted a conventional buffet restaurant, sales jumped as much as 20 percent.[7] This simple variation on the well-established set-price buffet was a profitable innovation that changed a segment of the industry.

A similar recent innovation is the concept of fusion—blending different ethnic cuisines, such as Italian, Mexican, and Asian. Examples are Southwestern lasagna and egg rolls, pizza burritos, Thai jungle salsa, and moo shu pork pizza. The combinations, which at the outset may seem unlikely, have surfaced in some upscale restaurants, gaining guest attention. These multi-cuisine offerings mirror the diversity of our society and are designed to capitalize on higher-than-average sales increases in ethnic foods. As innovations, they offer restaurant guests fascinating choices.[8]

Three Types of Innovations

We may distinguish among three main types of hospitality innovations based on the degree of change required in guest behavior. Innovations may be fundamental, functional, or adaptive.

Fundamental innovations are those that require considerable habit changes before guests will comfortably use and enjoy them. They sometimes require large investments in research and development and may take a long time to develop and emerge as commercially viable products or services. They may revolutionize and improve our lives, create whole new industries, and alter lifestyles in a major way. Examples include satellites, automobiles, television, VCRs, computers, xerography, fax machines, frozen foods, microwave ovens, vacuum packaging, and air conditioning.

Fundamental innovations in hospitality are relatively few. Motels were fundamental innovations that altered auto travel and lodging methods. Similarly, fast-food chains and drive-through operations have had a major impact on eating habits and, in turn, used many other innovations associated with refrigeration, food preparation, and packaging. More recent fundamental innovations include hotel-based business centers, voice-mail systems and teleconferencing.

Functional innovations are those that perform functions that were done before but in a somewhat different way. They require some change in guest habit patterns, but not a great deal. An example is the use of key cards instead of keys to enhance security. This requires that guests change their door-opening habits. Similarly, pay-per-view movies require guests to use television sets in a different manner, as does the use of home computers to learn about travel destinations, book hotels, and reserve airline tickets.

Most hospitality innovations are **adaptive innovations**. They are new product/service offerings that involve minor modifications of what already exists, necessitating few, if any, changes in guest habits. Included are the development of new menus, new services, theme bars and restaurants, new beverages, and the myriad innovations geared to merchandising guest purchases.

Steve Nikolakakos, a restaurant entrepreneur, provides an interesting example of applying adaptive innovations to a small hospitality business. He started as a busboy, worked his way up, and eventually purchased his own coffee shop, Gracie's Corner in New York City. When a new espresso bar moved into the area and began extending its offerings, he responded. He invested in a large, copper espresso machine and has been busy ever since. Nikolakakos explains, "You have to keep offering new things. You see what the guy on the next corner is doing and you learn how to be better. That's how my coffee shop survives. I'm always looking. I tell people, 'If you see anything you like at these other coffee bars—let me know.'" He has already extended his menu to include brick-oven pizza, pasta, organic fruit juices, and frozen yogurt.[9]

An important marketing consideration is that, as we move up the innovation ladder from adaptations to functional changes and then to fundamental innovations, the changes required in guest reactions and habits increase. Making guests comfortable with new amenities, procedures, and technologies requires support from marketing programs and trained staff. Guests need information and assistance that will reorient them and show them how to use the innovations. For example, when an East Coast resort hotel first made the switch from keys to key cards, many guests were frustrated and befuddled. They could not get into their rooms and had to seek assistance from the front desk; bellstaff had to show them how to use the cards. Sometimes the cards did not work. The required support systems to help guests feel comfortable with a functional innovation were not in place.

The Innovation Process

There is a creative process—formal or informal—that underlies the development of all innovations. The general stages involved are indicated in Exhibit 4. They need not be followed in the designated order, and entrepreneurs may skip some of them entirely, perform several concurrently, or treat some in a perfunctory manner.

We can see how this process may be applied to the addition of an on-premises beer-brewing facility to an existing tavern. Suppose the owner has gathered information about the success, acceptance, and operation of in-house breweries. He has a vision and explores the idea of expanding his existing tavern to accommodate the brewery. And he goes on to develop an entirely new concept built around the sporting events of local college and professional sports teams.

He visits various sports bars in several cities, meets with owners of microbreweries, and talks with equipment suppliers, his employees, and guests to gather background information. As a result, he expands and clarifies his original vision, explores various ideas, and begins to evaluate the viability very seriously. He considers markets, guest behavior, competition, technology, government regulations, and a host of other external factors. He pays special attention to the financials—estimating costs and revenues based on optimistic, pessimistic, and average scenarios.

As a result, he has developed a model in his mind and sets the ideas down on paper. He involves his staff in developing a mock-up of the facility. They develop flow charts of the activities involved, rough design layouts, and financial flow charts. Since things seem positive, he decides to develop a pilot and try limited

Exhibit 4   Creative Innovation Process

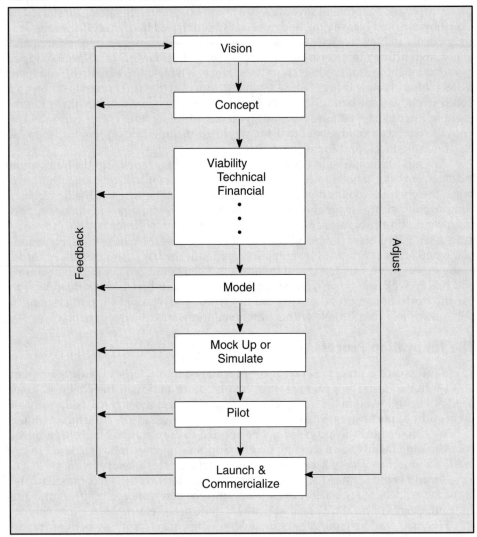

brewing. He adds big-screen televisions purchased on a contingency basis. He tries out the food operations on a small scale just to make sure the operations will work as anticipated, all the while learning what adjustments to make. Seeing how it actually works helps determine what might be required in the way of skills, staff, equipment, and procedures.

Since the pilot results are promising, a full-scale launch is begun. As experience is gathered, further adaptations are made. The entrepreneur then has the opportunity to decide whether to use the knowledge and expertise gained to establish other ventures of this nature, to franchise the operation, or to continue as is.

Factors Affecting Success and Failure

Why do some hospitality inventions meet with great success while others fail dismally? What factors make for success or failure? As a result of our research and experiences, we have drawn some conclusions for hospitality businesses.

Innovations should be approached with a mind-set that we can never understand everything about any situation, regardless of how much we think we know. There are always new insights to be gained. Any hospitality offering can be improved; there is no single, immutable way. Moreover, nothing is as it appears to be, for when we dip below the surface and investigate, new dimensions will be revealed. Alternatives always exist and innovators need an open mind for receptivity to new ideas. While successful innovations may appear to result from inspiration, hard work and dedication are the keystones. Remember Thomas Edison's oft-quoted statement that genius is one percent inspiration and 99 percent perspiration.

Several important factors contribute to the success of innovations. Hospitality inventions are more likely to be successful when they:

- Fit the needs and desires of the marketplace.

- Are superior to existing offerings, particularly where technology is involved.

- Have the support of top management and are backed by the efforts of the whole organization.

- Adopt and use new and more effective processes and procedures.

- Operate in a favorable competitive environment.

- Apply new ideas, fanciful thoughts, different approaches, and do not automatically reject challenges to the existing wisdom.

- Realize that some failures will occur as new things are tried, but so will learning and insight.

When inventions result in better value for guests, the likelihood of acceptance is increased. When they result in higher prices, require widespread changes in guest behavior, or have little advantage over current offerings, guest resistance will increase. The hospitality inventions most likely to succeed (to become innovations) are those that offer guests genuine benefits.

A large proportion of all hospitality inventions fail, and the resulting impact may vary from insignificant to disastrous. When major investments are involved, and returns do not live up to expectations, there can be major consequences. That was the case with EuroDisney, the Disney theme park located in France that encountered early losses in the hundreds of millions of dollars. Some hard decisions and restructuring were required. By contrast, the fact that a new dinner item added to a local restaurant's menu did not attract the expected guests is of relatively minor consequence; immediate changes can be made.

The following are some of the most common reasons for the failure of hospitality inventions:

- *Inadequate market analysis.* This is the result of a lack of understanding of guest needs and motives, overstatement of market potential, misjudgment of what the market wants, and neglect of demographic, economic, social, political, and other environmental factors.

- *Product/service deficiencies.* These lead to quality and performance that do not measure up to guest expectations. This is especially so when innovations offer guests little advantage over current offerings.

- *Inadequate marketing programs.* Hospitality enterprises sometimes neglect to support their inventions with the necessary marketing efforts. Included are inadequate sales and advertising programs, as well as a lack of staff training.

- *Higher costs than anticipated.* The tendency is to underestimate costs, particularly for fundamental and functional innovations. When this occurs, prices must be increased, which may lower sales, resulting in higher per-unit overhead costs that can lead to price increases, and so on.

- *Underestimating the competition.* The speed and impact of competitors' reactions to an innovation are commonly misjudged. Realistic assessments of the quality of competitive responses and competitors' ability to improve on an innovation are critical factors.

- *Poor timing.* A frequent error is to introduce a product or service too late, well after competitors are entrenched, the window of opportunity is essentially shut, and the market is overcrowded. On the other hand, failure also occurs when offerings are introduced too early, before the market is ready.

- *Technical and delivery problems.* If hospitality enterprises cannot produce and deliver the products in the quality and quantities necessary, on time, and in the manner that suits guests, the likelihood of success wanes.

Leadership and "Followership"

Innovation leaders are recognized for being on the cutting edge. They blaze the trails that others follow. Hospitality enterprises may choose to employ one of two basic innovation strategies: leadership or "followership."

Acceptance of a leadership strategy may require substantial investment in research and development, as well as good marketing capabilities and technical expertise. Being first on the market with products and services—while potentially profitable from both a financial and an image-building perspective—also involves investments and risks. Some failures must be expected. However, acceptable failure rates and loss limits can be put into effect. Extremely low failure rates may indicate timidity in accepting risks associated with new offerings, as well as an accompanying loss of opportunities and profits. Excessively high failure rates, on the other hand, may indicate an overly speculative posture, inadequate assessment procedures, and the misuse of resources. Although leaders should expect some losses, developing a good success rate is important.

Being a market follower is in some ways a less risky strategy. When guest reactions to a leader's innovation indicate real growth opportunities, then followers attempt to act quickly, offer similar items, and capture a share of the market. They may be able to modify and improve on the initial innovation, as well as avoid some of the mistakes made by the leader. Followers may also avoid or reduce much of the expense associated with developing and testing new offerings, a savings that may be reflected in lower prices. However, followers also run a great risk—the risk of entering markets too late and not being able to establish market position. They can be closed out of opportunities. The effectiveness of a follower strategy depends on the ability to respond quickly and effectively.

There is more to implementing a follower strategy than simply imitating the leaders. Companies must decide which followership posture to adopt. Will they be early followers, late followers, or laggards? The specific posture adopted governs how soon after an innovation appears that a company will enter markets. In turn, pricing and other marketing strategies are affected.

A continuing consideration in assuring the success of an innovation is determining who will function as the innovation captain. What person or unit will perform that critical role of nurturing, guiding, and managing an innovation? The answer depends on the particular enterprise. In any event, *hospitality marketing has significant responsibilities regarding innovations*: keeping the focus on actual and potential guest wants and needs, delineating market segments, monitoring competitive forces, and developing better offerings and the supporting marketing programs to appeal to guests. Of course, the innovation process involves more than just the marketing function. The potential contributions of many others must be recognized and harnessed. Finance, food and beverage, housekeeping, catering, servers, and front desk personnel are all involved. They can offer different, valuable perspectives and support activities for innovations.

Concluding Comments

This chapter deals with three related areas that are integral to successful hospitality marketing: entrepreneurship, creativity, and innovation. Entrepreneurs change things; they are creative and innovative. Creativity leads to innovations that enhance guest satisfaction.

Entrepreneurs have long been a driving force in the hospitality industry. They are involved with creating new approaches, methods, and product offerings. Entrepreneurial behavior has been characterized as creative destruction, sensitivity to business opportunities, ability to harness resources, and a willingness to take risks—all with an emphasis on growth. Entrepreneurs are more concerned with getting things done than with the status and symbols of organizational positions so dear to bureaucrats. While entrepreneurs may indeed become wealthy, money is not the main drive. They are more interested in autonomy, independence, peer recognition, and being their own boss.

In hospitality, the entrepreneurial process involves two sets of activities: assessing the viability of ventures and moving from concepts to market offerings. Hospitality entrepreneurs may be generally characterized as doers or thinkers. Doers tend to follow their feelings, act quickly, see what develops, adjust, and act again. Thinkers tend to think first, then act, rethink, and adjust. The result is the same for both—creating new hospitality ideas, ventures, or offerings—and the approaches are not mutually exclusive.

Creativity is a mental attitude that involves the search for new or novel ideas. Creativity in hospitality tends to be problem driven. Creative solutions need not be earthshaking to be effective and profitable. Most tend to be minor variations or adjustments to current practices. Since everyone is creative, hospitality managers are challenged to develop a work environment that promotes creative thinking on the part of all staff members.

Creative people tend to think divergently, expanding their horizons and insights as a result of being exposed to new concepts and experiences. Both organizational and individual barriers exist that hamper creativity. Organizational barriers arise in the form of pressure to conform to or pursue "accepted" approaches and practices. Individual barriers involve thought patterns and conditioning that cause people to avoid "the new," thereby ignoring creative opportunities.

Innovations deal with different dimensions of newness, from major technological breakthroughs to very minor modifications. They may be fundamental, functional, or adaptive, depending upon the degree of change required in guest behavior to use them. Most hospitality innovations are adaptive, requiring little change in guest behavior.

The stages in the overall creative process that underlie innovation, from the initial idea or concept to the actual launch and commercialization of the resulting offering, can be identified. In specific situations, the steps involved may not be performed in sequence, and some may be skipped or combined. Choices can be made between leadership and followership strategies and the implications they entail. Innovation in hospitality settings can be managed more effectively by focusing on the innovation process and making sure that the support systems are in place.

Innovations must be seen as learning processes. We try, see what happens, learn from the errors and failures, arrive at dead ends, and realize false starts. They are all part of the innovation process. The final innovation—the offering that will actually appear on the market—may differ markedly from the original concept. Also, the original innovation often leads to secondary innovations, as new opportunities and approaches are revealed.

The innovation process is aided by committed, visionary leadership. Patience may be required, not only in developing innovations, but in making the necessary modifications. Resources, particularly money and people, are required up front, as are flexible time horizons and plans.

Endnotes

1. Arnold Toynbee, as quoted in *The Royal Bank Letter*, December 1987, Royal Bank of Canada.

2. "What Life Means to Einstein: An Interview by George Sylvester Viereck," *The Saturday Evening Post*, 26 October 1929.

3. J. A. Schumpeter, *Capitalism, Socialism, and Democracy* (New York: Harper, 1950), chapter 7.

4. *The Wall Street Journal*, 16 February 1996, p. B1.

5. *The Wall Street Journal*, 19 July 1994, p. B1.

6. Mihaly Csikszentmihalyi, *Creativity: Flow and the Psychology of Discovery and Invention* (New York: HarperCollins, 1996).

7. "The Best Small Companies In America," *Forbes*, 7 November 1994, p. 224.

8. "Marketers Whip Up Weird Ethnic Blends," *The Wall Street Journal*, 8 November 1994, p. B1

9. John Tierney, "The Big City," *The New York Times Magazine*, 5 June 1994, p. 26.

Key Terms

adaptive innovations—new products or services that are minor modifications of existing offerings and that require few if any changes in guest habits.

convergent thinking—thinking that filters new ideas and experiences through existing precepts and beliefs.

divergent thinking—thinking that alters current ideas and concepts on the basis of new information and insights.

functional innovations—innovations that perform similar functions to those performed by other products and services in a different way and that require some change in guest habits.

fundamental innovations—innovations that require considerable habit change by guests before guests can use and enjoy them.

Review Questions

1. What are the distinguishing traits of entrepreneurs? What are the traits of successful entrepreneurial ventures?

2. How do the entrepreneurial approaches of doers and thinkers differ?

3. How do convergent and divergent thinking differ? Which holds the greatest promise for creativity? Why?

4. What are two fundamental types of barriers to creativity? What are some examples of each type? How can these barriers be overcome?

5. What research generalizations about creativity are applicable to hospitality?

6. What are fundamental, functional, and adaptive innovations? Identify examples in hospitality.

7. What difference does it make to hospitality marketing whether an innovation is fundamental or adaptive?

8. From a marketing perspective, what is the difference between an invention and an innovation?

9. What factors contribute to the success or failure of hospitality inventions and innovations?

10. What is the effect on hospitality marketing if a company adopts a leadership or a followership strategy?

Internet Sites

For more information, visit the following Internet sites. Remember that Internet addresses can change without notice.

BeauRivage
http://www.palmcrest.com

Disney Cruise Lines
http://www.disney.com/Disney
Cruise/index.html

Grand Wailei Resort
http://www.grandwailei.com

Hilton Hotels Corp.
http://www.hilton.com

Holiday Inn Worldwide
http://wwwholiday-inn.com

KFC
http://www.kfc.com

Kroger
http://www.kroger.com

Marriott International
http://www.marriott.com

Maxwell House
http://www.kraftfoods.com

McDonald's Corp.
http://mcdonalds.com

Okura Hotel
http://www.travelweb.com/okura/
tokyo

Old Country Buffet
http://www.buffet.com

Ritz-Carlton Hotels
http://www.ritzcarlton.com

Savoy Hotel
http:www.hotel-savoy.com

Singapore Airlines
http://www.singaporeair.com

Waldorf-Astoria Hotel
http://www.waldorf-nyc.com

Walt Disney Corporation
http://www.disney.com

Westin Maui
http://www.westinmaui.com

Chapter 17 Outline

Developing a Future Orientation
    Keeping the Future in Mind
    A Changing Mind-set
    Changing Hospitality Marketing Emphasis
Serving Future Guests
    The Personal Touch
    The Internet
    Mini-Mass and Niches
    Understanding Guests
Managing the Hospitality Marketing Mix
    Market Information
    Product/Service Offer
    Distribution
    Advertising and Promotion
    Pricing
Achieving Future Hospitality Leadership
    Changing the Leadership Paradigm
    Future Marketing Management Orientations
    Hospitality Organization
    Decision Making and Problem Solving
Future Hospitality Marketing Developments
    Global Hospitality Marketing
    Relationship and Network Marketing
    Entrepreneurship
    Social Focus
Future Developments for Restaurants and Food Service
Future Developments in the Lodging Sector
    In-Room Technology
    Communications
    Changing Guest Needs
Concluding Comments

17

Hospitality Marketing: Future Perspectives

"Managers have no choice but to anticipate the future, to attempt to mold it, and to balance short-range and long-range goals."

—Peter F. Drucker[1]

"Either you shape the future, or the future shapes you."

—Adage

J. W. MARRIOTT, chairman and president of Marriott Hotels, Resorts, and Suites, indirectly underscored the importance of keeping the future in sight in marketing when he said, "Marketing is really about managing change."[2] Managing change requires a future perspective. As marketing competence becomes a more important determinant of hospitality success, so will future thinking. This means two things. First, the assessment of likely future marketing developments will assume increasing significance for hospitality managers. Second, hands-on industry experiences and being steeped in hotel and restaurant operations—previous requisites to promotion and success—will be less highly valued in the future. As hospitality becomes ever more marketing driven, and hence driven by change, past orientations become outmoded, and future orientations become ever more important.

Hospitality marketers will be challenged to keep their eyes on rapid changes as guest wants and needs veer in new directions, business environments become less stable, trends become less predictable, and decision-making time shortens. Hospitality managers will be forced to pay closer attention to new developments, their implications, and the necessary adjustments that will have to be instituted in response.

In this chapter, we investigate future hospitality management challenges, likely hospitality marketing developments, and general approaches for dealing with them. We focus directly on how hospitality marketers can develop a future orientation and put it to work. We will organize ideas about the future according to four major parts: developing a modern marketing perspective, serving guests, managing the hospitality marketing mix, and achieving hospitality leadership. The chapter concludes with observations on specific trends and developments in the lodging and food service sectors.

Developing a Future Orientation ———————————————————

In less than 20 years, hospitality marketing has progressed from a synonym for sales to a focal point for hospitality operations. And it will play a pivotal role in the future as an overarching corporate philosophy, as serving guests becomes an even more predominant hospitality business theme. Marketing thought, approaches, and activities will pervade all hospitality activities. Marketing will not operate as a separate, stand-alone function. Rather, hospitality marketing will be integrated more effectively with other management areas. The barriers stemming from functional authority and departmental boundaries will be traversed, and hospitality marketing information and communications will be improved. As a result, marketing perspectives will pervade hospitality businesses and more attention will be directed to the effective implementation of marketing programs.

As hospitality marketing's role is broadened, and its activities transcend the formal boundaries of the marketing department, marketing will become a more important part of top management's purview. The emphasis will be on more effective marketing performance rather than the place of marketing in the organization chart. Recognition will grow that everyone is involved with marketing to a some degree.

In addition, the future will see an increasing industry-wide need for talented hospitality marketing people, both generalists and specialists. Specialists will support generalists and marketing managers in such areas as personal selling, advertising, marketing research, strategic marketing planning, merchandising, and public relations, as well as in sub-specialties such as focus group research, direct mail advertising, guest databases, and modeling.

Keeping the Future in Mind

Who is in charge of our future? Who is responsible for monitoring demographic, economic, sociological, and technological trends, discerning their implications, and assessing possible company opportunities? When the response is "everyone," as is often the case, in essence, no one is really in charge. The result is that important marketing responsibilities that can greatly affect operations are neglected. Certainly, hospitality marketers are charged with the task of keeping a continuing focus on future market opportunities. But dealing with the future is never easy. After all, who can foresee and foretell what will happen? The one certainty is that today's predictions will ultimately prove wrong. It is merely a matter of how wrong, how far off target they will be. Regardless, hospitality marketers have no real alternative. They must try to peer around the corner, look ahead, and develop glimpses of the future.

Intel, the leading manufacturer of computer chips, which produces chips for 85 percent of the world's computers, is concerned with perspectives of the future. It has a Director of Business Development whose job is to look over the horizon. His main responsibilities are to envisage the future, to encourage creative minds to develop innovations, to harness the ideas of creative entrepreneurs who are developing cutting-edge concepts, and to find ways to make personal computers ever more indispensable. And when a good idea is identified, then Intel's capabilities are marshaled to make it happen.[3]

Hospitality providers already have some insights about future developments. For example, they know that future hospitality marketing approaches, strategies, and operations will not be completely different from those of today; they will be logical outgrowths of current practices. They also know that some important changes will occur. Marketing in the future, as a mixture of both sameness and difference, will challenge managers to deal with likely deviations from their perceptions. But the very act of trying to predict them, regardless of inaccuracies, will furnish valuable marketing insights.

It is not difficult to identify some of the basic factors that will shape future markets and point out trends. But in trying to discern the future, we cannot simply rely on straight-line projections. For example, the trend toward eating more fish and poultry, as compared with beef, is also balanced by the great success of steak houses such as the Ruth's Chris, Outback, and Morton's chains. The emphasis on low-fat yogurt and fat-free desserts is countered by the success and profitability of fat-laden Ben and Jerry's and Häagen-Dazs ice creams. The growth of ethnic foods in the United States—including Thai, Vietnamese, Indian, and Mediterranean, in addition to such standbys as Chinese, Mexican, and Italian—has occurred in the midst of a growing market for regional American cuisine.

Information about basic trends can provide a good foundation for discerning likely general market developments. However, detailed forecasts for specific hospitality products and services require more focused research and directed investigations. The more specific the focus, the greater is the possibility of predictions missing their mark, sometimes by a wide margin. For example, restaurant chains will have more confidence in forecasting guest purchases of fish and steak for the next quarter than they will have in forecasting purchases of specific kinds of fish or cuts of steak.

When dealing with the future, hospitality marketers should keep three points in mind. First, expect the unexpected. This can help limit surprises. Second, remember that every trend seems to contain the seeds of a counter trend. This means that trends have the potential to shift gears and even reverse themselves. They may not develop as expected, can break sharply from the past, and place a premium on the ability to adjust and adapt to other developments. Third, recognize that competent and informed hospitality marketers may hold vastly different views of the future. Viewing exactly the same landscape, they may arrive at incompatible assessments of future business opportunities.

A Changing Mind-set

Charles Kettering's observation that "we should all be concerned with the future because we shall have to spend the rest of our lives there"[4] is rich with meaning for hospitality businesses. But it flies in the face of current practices. Hospitality marketers are more oriented to the past and present than they are to the future. They are more concerned with current operating situations and direct too much attention to recent sales, costs, and profits—to what is and has been. Ideally, hospitality executives should have as good a feel for future developments as they have of the past, but people being what they are, that is not the case. They need to shift focus from an emphasis on day-to-day internal considerations to developing greater concern with emerging business environments, emerging markets, and new opportunities.

When managers make hospitality decisions today, they are betting on their assessments of the future. Since uncertainty cannot be eliminated, managers must develop a mind-set for dealing with it. They cannot merely rely on hard data and facts. They must go beyond them and develop knowledge and insights about the future. Such thinking is based on opinions, probabilities, feelings, intuition, and informed guesses, in addition to facts.

When considering likely future developments, marketers must guard against the tendency to look through the distorted lens of the past. Considering the future in terms of past precepts and experiences can lead to gross distortions. Instead, management must develop a mind-set that focuses realistically on what might be, rather than what was. This implies anticipating, challenging the status quo, and acting rather than reacting. It involves dealing rationally with the knowable future and factoring future "facts" into current marketing decisions and actions. While that is not easy to do, the payoffs can be great.

Changing Hospitality Marketing Emphasis

In the future, hospitality marketing managers will emphasize a different array of activities and decisions than they have in the past. They will direct more attention to:

- Scanning hospitality environments.

- Discerning market trends and tendencies.

- Developing and assessing future market scenarios.

- Delineating emerging market opportunities.

- Developing contingency marketing plans and responses.

- Adjusting market offerings.

Service will become an even greater defining element of hospitality than it is today. The prior watchword of successful hospitality properties—*location, location, location*—is rapidly being joined by *service, service, service*. Service will be seen as an all-encompassing determinant of future guest value, the critical factor in creating differential advantage and in gaining a competitive edge.

The future hospitality marketing emphasis will include:

- Greater appreciation of the importance of marketing to the success of total hospitality operations.

- Acceptance of hospitality marketing as a responsibility of top-level executives.

- More pertinent and timely marketing information about guest habits, actions, attitudes, opinions, and expectations.

- More precise delineation of hospitality market segments and niches and clearer specification of company opportunities.

- Greater emphasis on differentiating hospitality products and service offerings.

- The addition of marketing specialists to hospitality marketing staffs.

- Improved correspondence between hospitality offerings and guest expectations, resulting in enhanced guest fulfillment.

- Acceptance of marketing as a change agent—the means of altering hospitality products and services, challenging competition, and achieving goals.

- Attention to programs for motivating and supporting the staff who carry out marketing activities.

- Greater emphasis on harnessing the innovative and creative abilities of staff members.

- Establishment of strategic alliances and other cooperative arrangements that organize independent businesses to develop seamless marketing and maximize resources.

- Continuing emphasis on global hospitality markets and marketing programs.

Serving Future Guests

As a result of technological developments such as databases, smart cards, and various computer-based applications, hospitality businesses will be in closer contact with guests. They will be able to conduct continuing dialogues with guests, especially important ones, interact with them, and collect information on a real-time basis. Hospitality businesses will be able to keep track of who is buying what, build a one-to-one relationship, run a continuing guest profit and loss statement on them, customize offerings, and offer benefits and value so that guests will remain loyal. Attention will be directed at creating a meaningful guest experience at the point of provider/guest interactions. The hospitality marketing job will be seen not merely as marketing to guests, but as effectively managing long-term relationships with them.

As more intense competition becomes the hallmark of the hospitality industry, guest expectation levels will rise. This will challenge hospitality providers to offer better and better values. To do so, it will be even more important to maintain close contact with guests to understand and satisfy their expectations.

Hospitality marketers will need to become more attuned to the necessity of maintaining and reducing costs while increasing productivity to enhance guest values. This will mean continually striving for improvements, seeking diligently for ways to serve guests better and to accomplish more with less.

The Personal Touch

Personal service is crucial to hospitality success. Despite this fact, the hospitality industry is becoming more impersonal as machines and self-service take over. The do-it-yourself trend is becoming entrenched, replacing certain personal services in an effort to reduce costs and increase efficiency.

Some guests are happy to make their own hotel and airline reservations through computers and interactive screens, check in at hotel kiosks, and check out automatically through their in-room television set. Automatic check-in and check-out will likely become a future industry standard. And guests will be able to automate concierge services by using touch-screen monitors to obtain information about such things as restaurants, concerts, plays, tours, and sights.[5]

While technology will supplement the human element in extending hospitality services, guests will still expect to deal with people. The management challenge will be to determine the right mix of technology and humans to best meet guest needs. This will involve experimentation and adjustments, with staff members performing certain activities in conjunction with various machines at different stages of the service chain. The resulting reduction of guest encounters will make the remaining guest interactions even more important. There will be fewer opportunities for personal service to right the wrong of unmet guest expectations.

The Internet

Part of the future impact of technology on hospitality businesses will center on the Internet. The Internet is a two-way communications medium that will foster greater interaction with guests and make available pertinent real-time guest information. It will change the very nature of the relationship between hospitality providers and their guests. Many consumers now use it to enhance their travel and recreational activities. Travel sites have proven to be popular Internet destinations. Travel information, tickets, hotel reservations, and arrangements for golf, tennis, and various entertainment activities lend themselves to the Internet's interactive, multimedia environment. It gives consumers in-depth information about trips and facilities, permitting them to experience properties before making their decisions. They can pull up maps of cities, sample area attractions, take virtual tours of hotel properties, and exchange thoughts with other travelers about destinations around the globe.[6]

A major future benefit of the increasing use of the Internet will be the availability of lower hospitality prices for a larger number of guests. The continuing growth of personal computers will result in more direct marketing by providers to guests; the reduction of unused capacity, which will increase opportunities to apply yield management pricing; and the development of better guest data bases. Since unused hotel rooms, airline seats, and cruise cabins are perishable, the Internet will be used increasingly to sell capacity that would otherwise remain unused.

Mini-Mass and Niches

Future hospitality marketing efforts will shift from the mass marketing approaches and emphases of yesteryear to mini-mass, niche, and individual guest emphases. Markets will be more fragmented, with market offerings and marketing programs tailored for specific groups of guests. The one-size-fits-all approach of the past will give way to customizing and tailoring hospitality offerings to meet more precisely the needs of guests in niche markets. Doing so will require pertinent, timely guest information and heightened sensitivity to and understanding of the guest preferences of different cultures, social classes, age groups, lifestyles, and similar demographic segments. The challenge will be to develop tailored offerings without incurring a high price tag. It is a matter of achieving the productivity associated with standardized hospitality offerings while delivering a level of guest satisfaction associated with individualization.

Relatively small hospitality markets that were formerly unprofitable will evolve into attractive opportunities as they are aggregated across country boundaries or other market sectors. This trend will be heightened as incomes rise around the world, signaling profitable global market niches. The result will be a counter-emphasis to culturally tailored offerings in the form of truly global hospitality offerings—nationless hospitality products and services. Hospitality offerings will mesh, resulting in greater homogenization of hospitality products, services, and properties among countries around the world. While global hospitality consumers, with similar, well-recognized wants and needs, will be in place, at the same time, market diversity will continue to be recognized.

Understanding Guests

Future guests will be more informed, sophisticated, demanding, and better traveled than past counterparts. Vast amounts of information about hospitality alternatives will be readily available. Guests will be able to better assess the array of hospitality offerings and to judge which choices are best for them.

Hospitality providers, in turn, will need to explain and justify the benefits and value of their offerings as compared with those of their competitors. As a result of computers and databases, hospitality providers will have improved knowledge about actual and potential guests, how they purchase and use hospitality products and services, and what can be done to serve them more effectively. These providers will have the information to segment markets more precisely, resulting in micro-market segmentation, along with the ability to combine many small segments across various market sectors, thereby identifying profitable market opportunities. Future hospitality success will not be as intimately related to cost cutting as it will be to harnessing the creative and innovative talents of people to come up with fresh offerings that better satisfy guests.

In understanding future hospitality guests, it is worth noting that an increasing proportion of them will always be *transitioning*. That is, they will be in the process of becoming "something else": marrying, divorcing, moving back with parents, changing jobs, being laid off, embarking on new careers, returning to school, starting a family, adjusting to widowhood, establishing a home, and retiring. As transitioning occurs on a more massive scale, future guests may be harder to categorize—and determining guest wants and needs, never an easy task, may become even more complicated. A larger segment of hospitality guests will become "moving targets," increasingly difficult to identify, understand, and service.

The Senior Segment. The U.S. population, like that of most industrialized countries, is aging and the future population will never again, within the next century, be as young as it is now. And like today's senior, those of the future will see themselves as being far younger than their chronological age. They will be healthier, more active, and expect more from life than did their predecessors. Tomorrow's seniors will be more devoted to health and fitness and will expect restaurants and hotels to support their lifestyles. Many will assume second and third careers, and they will comprise an increasingly fine labor pool for hospitality businesses, bringing maturity, people skills, knowledge, and experience to their jobs.

We shall see growing numbers of mature guests with financial resources. The growth of the 45 to 55 age group (the age when most guests realize their highest incomes) and the 55 to 65 group (who are relatively well off compared with other age groups) will be increasingly felt. The groups have grown up eating out, and are fine restaurant customers. But, they will also have higher expectations and be more sophisticated and cosmopolitan in their food tastes. For many of them, a scarcity of time, rather than money, will be a major factor governing their consumption of hospitality products and services.

Guests 65 and over defy the oft-held caricature of being poor and disabled. By and large, they are relatively well off and active and represent a large and growing market. They are unusually well-informed and have had broad exposure because of their travels and hospitality experiences. They have the flexibility of time and money to take advantage of special offerings such as early bird dinners, off-day prices, and off-season travel. As a senior explained, "For us, every day is Saturday and Sunday."

As guests age, many develop health problems and become intensely concerned with meal contents, sodium, fat, and sugar, as well as how their food is prepared. Is the fish broiled in butter? Do the noodles contain eggs? What is the fat and cholesterol content of various dishes? A large proportion of those over 80 (the "older olders") have physical limitations and a consequent need for special services such as wheelchairs, easy access, and home delivery.

What are older guests really like? How can restaurants cater to them? Research suggests that older consumers:

- Have stronger preferences for healthier foods such as salads, vegetables, and non-fried foods like chicken, turkey, and fish.

- Seek nutritious foods.

- Prefer casual, lower priced, but full-service restaurants.

- Want menus with information about nutrients and ingredients.

- Desire food that supports a high quality of life for seniors.

- Want restaurants to work with nutritionists to develop acceptable items.

- Want easy access, good lighting, noise reduction, chairs supporting their backs, and appropriate table heights.

Hospitality businesses will be redesigned to meet the needs of the aging population sectors of most industrialized countries around the globe. Publications and easily accessed data banks will be available to inform the elderly which lodging establishments and restaurants cater to them. Hotels may be age-rated, with the ratings based on such considerations as ease of access, special food preparation, physical therapy, heating pads, in-room refrigerators, whirlpools, and bed covers.[7]

In marketing future travel and tourism to older members of the population, research suggests that the following ideas will be helpful:

- Intergenerational touring in which grandparents travel with their grandchildren

- Family reunions and affinity groups that get together on a regular basis

- Tourism emphasizing broadening guest interests such as eco-tourism, educational and cultural tours, archeological digs, or trips with musicians, writers, and dancers, and those dealing with various social projects

- Special tours, such as around-the-world journeys, anniversary trips, and those surrounding various religious and holiday celebrations

- Mini-tours of three or four days that cover special places and events: for example, gaming in the Grand Bahamas, color tours of New England, theater weekends in London, or a Broadway tour of New York

Post Baby Boomers. Post baby boomers—those born between 1965 and 1976—will be used to and will expect convenience and ready accessibility. To appeal to the post baby boomers, hospitality offerings might use family activities and themes, represent themselves as affordable luxuries, offer discount packages, offer child care and activities for children, and furnish guarantees. Advertising and promotional messages could feature security, safety, family values, and community involvement. Distribution methods will include a greater emphasis on computers and communications technology such as the fax, Internet, and CD-ROM, as well as remote access computer-based self-service.

Managing the Hospitality Marketing Mix

In this section, we consider some of the likely future developments that will affect various components of the marketing mix.

Market Information

The effects of computers and information technologies on the hospitality marketing mix will be continuous and substantial. Hospitality marketers will have more pertinent and timely information, from both internal and external sources, to help them with their marketing mix decisions. There will be increased demand for marketing people who can gather, organize, and interpret vast arrays of data, discern company implications, develop meaningful marketing plans and strategies, and effectively communicate to the appropriate management levels. The future need will not merely be to generate more data, but to create the kind of knowledge and intelligence that leads to profitable ideas.

Improved software and the instant availability of pertinent information on a real-time basis, as well as through virtual reality, will mean enhanced decision-making capability. This will facilitate faster management response time, more accurate planning, and improved reactions to market changes. Hospitality businesses will have the knowledge to tailor their facilities, products, and services to guest needs.

Computer networks will make it easier to bridge some of the existing gaps between guests and hospitality providers. Guests will have information about properties available on their home computers and be able to compare values, make more rational choices, and enhance their satisfaction. They will be able to make reservations directly. As marketers are able to identify and target markets more precisely, advertising and promotional materials will be delivered directly to guests at their convenience, at the time and in the format that they desire.

Product/Service Offer

Guests will see a greater variety of hospitality offerings that more closely match their needs, expectations, and desires, and will have more knowledge than ever on which to base their decisions.

The emergence of **smart products** containing microchips will benefit hospitality providers and guests alike. Hotels and restaurants will be able to use products that recognize speech, follow directions, have long-lasting memories, and perform boring and menial tasks. These smart products will give management unparalleled opportunities to reduce costs, add convenience, and make offerings available whenever guests want them. They will enhance guest use and enjoyment. Included may be new security approaches; smart cleaning and cooking appliances; products that close and open rooms, call for assistance, and can change the shape and environment of a room to better suit guest requirements. Although the technology is currently prohibitively expensive to implement on a large scale, the capability already exists for guests to carry small electronic sensors that "remember" their individual preferences, track them from place to place, and thereby offer untold opportunities to cater to them by incorporating their personal tastes into every aspect of hospitality. (The multi-million dollar private home of Bill Gates, chairman and cofounder of Microsoft Corporation, was among the first to put this technology to use. There, wall-mounted screens display artwork according to the occupant's preferences; preferred temperature settings are "remembered" and established when the occupant enters a room; and telephone calls ring automatically only on the phone extension nearest the homeowner.) Smart products will be vehicles for sustaining mutually beneficial, long-term relationships, enhancing a provider's capacity to develop loyal guests.

Part of the drive to serve guests better will be reflected in paying more attention to guest safety and security. This will address both psychological and physical concerns. Creating an atmosphere of guest safety and security, which involves both providing the appropriate symbols and images and actually delivering safety and security, will take on increasing importance. Management's understanding and offerings will reflect guests' desire to escape society's deficiencies—crime, violence, unsafe food, polluted air and water, and such environmental threats such as earthquakes and fires. Future guests will value safe and secure hospitality environments globally. Hotels and restaurants will seek out new technologies to improve their ability to provide such environments.

The time between conceiving hospitality concepts and translating them into offerings will be shortened. Competition will also be keener, as competitors move rapidly to counter innovations. As a result, the time span in which to reap the benefits of new offerings will be shortened considerably, and the payoff period of investments reduced. Hospitality businesses will need to be ever quicker to sense new opportunities and capitalize on them. They will focus on the capacity to get out of certain products or markets and move rapidly on to new opportunities.

To outperform the competition consistently, hospitality companies will have to be "offering obsessed." Everyone involved will have to strive not just to achieve good offerings, but to cultivate the attitude—and achieve the realization—that their hospitality products and services are clearly superior. An obsession with excellence and value will be the hallmark of those companies on hospitality's future leading edge.

Distribution

The future will see the continuation of scrambled hospitality distribution patterns, with companies often bypassing the traditional channels used to market their offerings. Such trends as that of restaurant chains to set up in malls, airports, mass retailing enterprises, universities, and other non-traditional outlets will be reinforced. Restaurants will be more actively involved with take-out and home delivery, and supermarkets will intensify competition by featuring a more complete array of prepared foods, meals, and in-house restaurants.

The **codistribution** of previously unlikely service combinations will also become more common. For example, there will be more outpatient medical services in hospitality settings, such as physical examinations and medical tests offered in resort hotels, plastic surgery done in vacation resorts, education classes combined with global travel, vacation day-care programs offered by hotels, and senior day-care services offered by food and lodging establishments.

Home computers, the Internet, and telemarketing will be used increasingly to distribute information about and sell hospitality offerings. The use of three-dimensional images will commonly be employed to help guests select hotels, restaurants, vacation destinations, and resort areas. Focused contact with guests via direct advertising tailored to their needs will enhance the convenience and effectiveness of the distribution of hospitality offerings. Various cooperative arrangements among independent hospitality businesses and agencies, such as strategic alliances, will be put in place to provide seamless distribution of hospitality products and services.

Advertising and Promotion

Given the intensity of future competition and the growing number and variety of hospitality offerings, hospitality marketers will pay increasing attention to differentiating their offerings, selecting target markets carefully, and focusing on market segments and niches. As they do, advertising and promotional budgets and programs will receive greater emphasis. Hospitality businesses will have more and different advertising channels to reach potential guests. The media used and the messages conveyed will be more tailored and focused to targeted guests. The result will be reduced waste and increased effectiveness.

Such developments as software programs, guest databases, interactive TV, and desktop publishing—currently in use on a limited basis—will become prevalent and are indicative of the kinds of technological developments that will facilitate direct marketing to targeted guests. Both printed and electronic direct marketing pieces, including audio and video promotions, will result in dedicated advertising and promotion. The use of fax, e-mail, and computer messages will multiply.

One warning: As hospitality communications and promotions multiply, and as competition for guest attention increases, guests may suffer from communications overload. To the extent that this occurs, advertising and promotional efforts will lose some of their effectiveness.

Pricing

Hospitality marketers will direct more attention to *managing* prices, rather than just mechanistically setting prices. Future pricing will be accepted as the important marketing variable that it is, directly affecting sales and profits. They will have more timely and complete financial information than ever on which to base their pricing decisions. Relevant cost and profit data will be available in convenient formats useful to marketers. Such data may be classified by type of guests, market offerings, geographic regions, and basic marketing activities (as opposed to merely accounting for transactions). The information may be available on a real-time basis.

Armed with such information, hospitality marketers will be able to use flexible pricing approaches to capitalize on market shifts and developments. Hotels will be able to unload excess inventories of rooms on short notice using their up-to-date, computerized information. Guests will be able to make reservations at bargain rates directly through computerized reservations systems. Restaurants will be able to calculate guest acceptance and profitability of menu choices as food and labor costs vary, so that marketing efforts can be directed accordingly.

In the future, hospitality marketing managers will have the capability to match prices more precisely with changing guest demand, keep track of changing total and variable costs, and monitor and set prices to maximize profits.

Achieving Future Hospitality Leadership

Why do some hospitality companies continue as successful hospitality leaders, while others that were once so successful encounter difficult times? An answer is suggested by Charles Darwin's observation that it is not the strongest of the species that survives, but the most adaptable. So it is with hospitality businesses. Successful companies seem to have the ability to respond effectively to the unexpected, to adapt to unanticipated market changes. Unsuccessful businesses do not seem to do so. Rather, they tend to rely on the successful methods of the past, which have lost pace with emerging business developments and changing market opportunities.

The ability to deal with the unexpected, which is already an invaluable marketing asset, will become even more so in the future. The inability to do so may rapidly transform today's winners into tomorrow's losers. This is evidenced in many marketing areas. For example, Wal-Mart has used information and flexibility to adjust so readily to new market opportunities that it challenged and surpassed its much feared and larger competitor Kmart, which was not able to make the transition. Similarly, in creating Infinity and Lexus, Nissan and Toyota adjusted to the changing desires of luxury auto buyers to challenge Mercedes' well-established market position.

Future hospitality leaders will not be able to thrive by maintaining the status quo. Success will not be merely a matter of rolling with the punches and doing a little fine-tuning. Companies will have to keep on top of changing trends, understand their implications, and be prepared to shift basic operations and radically alter approaches that have proven successful in the past. Management must learn to be comfortable handling unexpected occurrences and dealing with less-structured situations. That is a tall order, but it is the necessary leadership posture for a dynamic future.

At the same time, it will also be important to articulate pervasive, fundamental company values. Values give meaning to a company and its operations, guide employees in the means used to carry out their duties, and provide guidelines for dealing with guests. Other than the primary value of being guest oriented, two sets of competing values will shape future hospitality marketing operations. First are those that center on the company and its concern for efficiency, controlling costs, earning profits, and getting a fair return on investments. Second are those that focus on contributing to the well-being of society. This might include such responsibilities as creating jobs, protecting environments, feeding the hungry, and developing employees to their fullest extent. In this regard, future hospitality marketing actions will confront a number of value-laden situations, including nutrition, health considerations, waste disposal, air and water pollution, and energy consumption.

Changing the Leadership Paradigm

Future marketing leadership approaches will be quite different as hospitality markets become less stable, orderly, structured, and predictable. The past guidelines of "measure, analyze, predict, and control" will have to be modified. The emergence of disorderly, unstable, and even chaotic business conditions will force changes in leadership orientations. Hospitality marketing will focus more on accepting disorder and learning to deal with it as normal. This suggests the need for new management guidelines, for it will not be possible to manage effectively using the approaches of past marketing eras.

Consider the following general marketing management guidelines for dealing with the new hospitality environment. First, establish the core boundaries for marketing action by clearly specifying company values, mission, goals, and culture. In dealing with turbulent environments, this provides managers with needed direction.

Second, train employees and empower them to take initiative, accept reasonable risks, and act on market opportunities presented. Companies can encourage and reward entrepreneurial initiatives and actions.

Third, recognize that marketing systems are nonlinear. This means that returns are not necessarily proportional to efforts or investments; small improvements and differences can result in disproportionately large payoffs. Conversely, their neglect can result in disproportionately large losses. Future hospitality marketers may well seek small changes on a continuous basis.

Fourth, recognize that similar situations in different circumstances—whether time periods, personnel involved, companies, or countries—are not the same. A new service or product introduced in very similar but different hospitality settings may require vastly different marketing approaches. Marketing programs and strategies that are effective in certain settings may not be universally applicable.

Future Marketing Management Orientations

How will the future orientations of hospitality marketing managers change as compared with those of the present? We shall comment on four developments: proactive marketing, just-in-time marketing, value-based marketing, and leading-edge marketing.[8] They tend to complement one another and result in more productive and efficient marketing among hospitality businesses.

Proactive hospitality marketing emphasizes the tendency to introduce changes, to develop companies along new paths before competition and changing conditions force them. It sees marketing as a change mechanism, a means for dealing with dynamic conditions.

Just-in-time hospitality marketing, which depends on having real-time information available, synchronizes hospitality marketing activities with guest requirements and market reactions. It emphasizes having hospitality products, services, and supporting marketing programs available at the very time when guests need them, thereby reducing costs and increasing satisfaction.

Value-based hospitality marketing focuses on the use of marketing resources to increase guest value. Increasing guest value will be a critical guideline for all hospitality marketing action. Hospitality marketers will develop offerings that better meet guest needs, do so at lower prices, and focus on quality service.

Leading-edge hospitality marketing stretches the limits of a company's marketing technology and capabilities, leveraging it to better satisfy changing guest wants and needs. This implies being on the forefront of innovations and making company offerings and marketing approaches obsolete before competitors do. The focus is on new ideas, creative changes, and regrouping and reorganizing for new situations.

Hospitality Organization

Tomorrow's leading hospitality providers will continuously rethink and reengineer their organizations and methods of operation. They will strive constantly for improvement, knowing that the ultimate organizational format cannot be realized; it is a matter of striving but never arriving. The process implies continuous organizational adaptation and adjustment. This will involve greater attention to the interaction between hospitality marketing and other hospitality activities, such as front desk operations, housekeeping, security, menu planning, room design, engineering, lobby arrangements, and food and beverage offerings. Marketing's overarching dimensions will affect all organizational units and activities.

As information technology fosters improved communications, it facilitates decentralization. It fosters the development of hospitality organizations as learning organizations, using their knowledge to adapt, grow, improve, and renew themselves. Organizations will feel continuing pressure to downsize, reduce layering, become more entrepreneurial, empower employees, and seek increasing efficiency. Such tendencies will encourage innovative responses to guest problems and desires.

In their quest to serve guests more effectively, hospitality organizations will become increasingly intertwined with other businesses, both within and outside the hospitality industry. Flexible, boundary-spanning organizational formats will become more prevalent. Network marketing will combine independent hospitality entities into a more effective total marketing system of affiliates or associates. This will maintain the capabilities of each of the individual businesses while promoting the overall efficiency of a total hospitality system. Networks will promote "one-stop hospitality shopping" by aggregating the services of independent restaurants, hotels, travel agents, airlines, auto rental agencies, entertainment enterprises, and others into convenient packages at substantial savings for guests.

Although the hospitality industry currently comprises mainly small organizations, the future will see increasing development of formal chains, less-formal associations, and cooperative arrangements. There will be fewer small operators functioning as true independent businesses and more functioning as part of interdependent larger organizations, formal and informal. Closer contractual relationships and informal cooperation will evolve as suppliers and hospitality providers collaborate to devise ways of serving guests better. Some suppliers will develop dedicated facilities oriented to the needs of specific important customers to ensure their demands are met on time.

Cooperation among independent hospitality providers will achieve economies of scale in such marketing activities as advertising, communications, marketing research, merchandising, selling, distribution, promotion, and purchasing. The ability of smaller entities to deal with large customers will be enhanced. The organizational downside is the possibility of incurring the inefficiencies and separation from guests so often engendered by the bureaucracies of large-scale organizations.

The future will see a bimodal distribution among hospitality organizations. That is, businesses at both ends of the size spectrum will have the best opportunities of prospering. Medium-sized businesses may lack the flexibility of small companies and be unable to generate the power and efficiency of large firms.

Decision Making and Problem Solving

Exhibits 1 and 2 contrast future hospitality marketing decision-making approaches and management orientations with those of the past. In Exhibit 1, the decision approach represented by quadrant three indicates that the traditional decision emphasis focuses on using facts, data, and statistics and on solving problems. The

Exhibit 1   Hospitality Marketing Decision Approaches

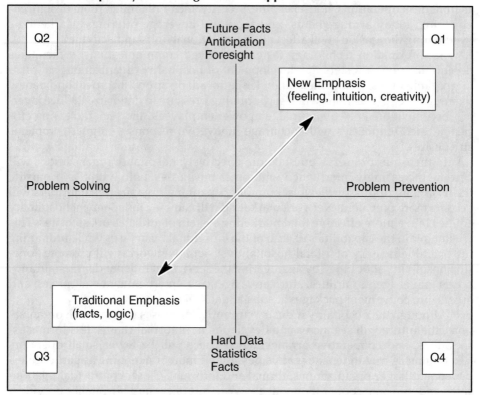

future tendency, however, as depicted in quadrant one, will be characterized more by problem *prevention* and the use of management information in the form of feelings, intuition, opinions, and judgment, as well as facts.

Exhibit 2 deals with hospitality marketing management orientations. The traditional orientation of hospitality marketers, as represented by quadrant three, has been more reactive and focused on current business situations. The future perspective (quadrant one) will emphasize being proactive and focusing on new opportunities.

Future Hospitality Marketing Developments

What will happen in the general development of hospitality marketing in the future? Although no one can tell for certain, there is every indication that four current trends will be reinforced. They are the extension of the emphasis on global hospitality marketing, a heightened focus on relationship and network marketing, a greater emphasis on entrepreneurship, and increasing concern with societal dimensions. Let us comment briefly on each.

Exhibit 2   Hospitality Marketing Management Orientations

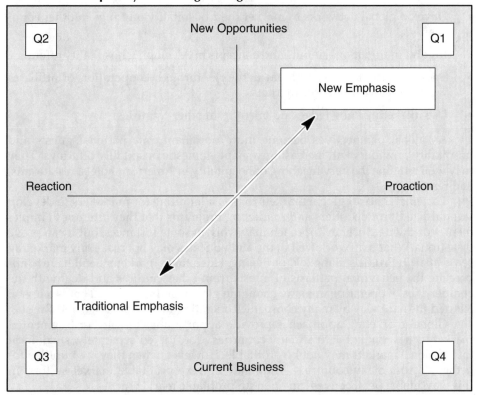

Global Hospitality Marketing

Hospitality markets are increasingly taking on a global flavor. In 1995, McDonald's international sales grew over 20 percent, totaling $14 billion and accounting for an estimated 38 percent of its units and 40 percent of its profits. Now even some of the second tier chains and smaller organizations are beginning to benefit from increasingly profitable international operations.[9]

Yet the reality is that, while market perspectives are shifting to global considerations, most hospitality enterprises do not have a global marketing agenda in place. Although future hospitality enterprises will still operate locally, they will have to think globally. International marketing opportunities will become a more important part of the core business rather than just a little add-on to domestic operations.

Globalization will continuously challenge hospitality marketers to become more sensitive to different cultures, mores, and tastes and to develop offerings and communications that will appeal to guests worldwide. Globalization implies an increase in marketing diversity and a rapid retreat from a local or ethnocentric mindset. Instead, local perspectives will broaden to geocentric (regional) and polycentric (global) orientations. Hospitality marketers will be more willing to:

- Acknowledge guest diversity and market multiculturalism.

- Develop global networks to market their hospitality offerings in other countries.

- Involve multinational inputs and concepts in developing hospitality offerings.

- Sponsor and encourage global networks through cooperation of affiliates worldwide to better serve markets.

- Use marketing knowledge and talent from other countries.

As global perspectives become more dominant, international guests and hospitality providers will increasingly shape domestic hospitality offerings. They may well redefine the very meaning of hospitality in American hotels, restaurants, and resorts.

The emergence of global markets makes it tempting for marketers to develop standardized product offers and marketing programs that they attempt to implement worldwide. Such an approach may work in some instances, but it can prove disastrous. What may work well in the United States may not make any marketing sense at all in Brussels, Bangkok, or Beijing. Hospitality marketers will have to appreciate the behavioral patterns of guests from other cultures and deal with the complexities of operating in many changing global environments. That is a lesson learned the hard way by many companies operating in Europe, Asia, and Russia.

Global marketing approaches provide opportunities to cater to fragmented market niches that cut across many countries. Considered separately, small local international markets may not be profitable. However, when they are bundled together—across many countries—they may be very profitable market sectors. In this way, global perspectives can open up profitable market niches.

A global emphasis will tend to have the following effects on hospitality marketing operations:

- The complexities of world developments will become a normal part of hospitality marketing plans and decisions, reflecting worldwide market opportunities.

- Domestic hospitality marketing operations will be evaluated in light of such international factors as exchange rates, global customs, market barriers, and the political and legal considerations of other nations.

- Global standards will be imposed on domestic operations to bring them into line with world market expectations and opportunities.

- A long-term perspective will be adopted when cultivating international markets. Such actions will be viewed much like research and development efforts needing front loading and an adequate time frame to become profitable.

- International competition will intensify, affecting smaller and regional enterprises most heavily.

- Greater emphasis will be given to developing international chains, franchises, strategic alliances, and management contracts.

Relationship and Network Marketing

Future hospitality marketing will emphasize the related thrusts of relationship marketing and network marketing. **Relationship marketing** refers to establishing long-term, close working relationships with guests and suppliers to improve hospitality marketing performance. It builds on the goals of the parties involved to achieve more effective hospitality marketing. For example, corporate contracts that guarantee a hotel a certain number of rooms a week will, in turn, facilitate hotel contracts with food and beverage suppliers that can help iron out production peaks and valleys, giving suppliers cost savings, which make it possible to grant price concessions to the hotel.

Alliances and networks combine the complementary abilities of independent hospitality providers to create organizations or systems. They serve guests better while permitting participants to realize their own objectives more effectively. They result in such joint actions as shared reservation systems and cooperative advertising, promotion, and merchandising. They can market "one-stop shopping" by combining the services of independent restaurants, hotels, travel agents, airlines, auto rental agencies, entertainment enterprises, and others into complete hospitality packages.

The emphasis on strategic alliances and networks will leverage the marketing capabilities of individual entities through the coordinated use of their joint resources. Alliances and networks can help independent businesses achieve jointly what none of them could do singly. Such arrangements will be especially suited to businesses operating in the global hospitality marketplace.

Entrepreneurship

Hospitality has always benefitted from the ideas, creativity, innovations, and initiative of entrepreneurs. The future will see a concerted emphasis on encouraging entrepreneurial approaches. Managers and employees will be empowered and motivated to become more entrepreneurial and less bureaucratic in growing hospitality businesses and dealing with guests. The tendency of large companies to "massify"—to focus on mass marketing, standardized offerings, and uniform, unwieldy systems and processes that are imposed on guests—will provide entrepreneurial opportunities for others, small businesses in particular. Openings will exist for perceptive entrepreneurs who can serve guests better, cater to various niche markets where needs are being neglected, and use their initiative, creativity, and flexibility to gain market advantage. Larger corporations, in turn, will strive to harness the entrepreneurial drive and energy of their employees and become increasingly involved with promoting intrapreneurship.

Social Focus

In the future, hospitality marketers will focus on activities extending well beyond such typical business goals as sales, revenues, and profits. They will see hospitality businesses as serving social purposes and improving the quality of life. This will stem partly from more stringent government and legal requirements and partly from a feeling of social responsibility. Hospitality businesses and managers will become quite concerned with being good corporate citizens who behave in an ethical and socially-sanctioned manner. More attention will be directed at such considerations as the role of hospitality marketing decisions and actions in increasing standards of living, overcoming poverty, providing jobs, training and educating employees, advancing ethical practices, and providing for the health, safety, and security of employees and guests. Hotels and restaurants will be challenged to deal directly with such issues as litter, waste, sewage, air pollution, water and energy conservation, and feeding the hungry. Even though all of these issues go beyond the bottom line, they will become increasingly important hospitality marketing considerations.

Future Developments for Restaurants and Food Service —

In the future, restaurant marketing will shift its focus from aggressive sales to providing guests with the products and services they want, where and how they want them, and at prices they are willing to pay.[10] The emergence of two types of food service has been predicted: the traditional and the modern.[11] The traditional follows current practices, in which food servers take orders and serve, cooks prepare the food, and customers make their selections, including entertainment such as music, games, etc. The modern reflects technological developments resulting in a variety of possible scenarios. For example, there might be devices at tables that take orders and transmit them instantaneously to a kitchen computer. Computers will control such activities as purchasing, storage, food preparation, and processing. Conventional cooking devices may be eliminated. However, regardless of such possible scenarios, the impact of external technological forces on restaurants and food service is not expected to be as great as it will be on other parts of the hospitality industry.

The significance of food in daily life will take on new dimensions as guests display growing concern for what they eat, including how food is produced, prepared, and served. Among the considerations will be the use of additives, chemicals, fertilizers, and cooking ingredients such as fat, sugar, and salt. The technologies of organic farming, bioengineering, and new means of cooking will be investigated. Guests will opt for healthier food alternatives. Restaurants will need to meet new health standards while delivering good taste.

Scientifically developed and altered foods will increase as a result of processes such as gene splicing and cloning. Guests may register initial concerns about them, leading some restaurants to make a point of marketing their "old-fashioned organic foods." Food preparation processes such as radiation and vacuum packaging will be further explored, particularly in take-out and fast-food situations. Aquaculture and hydroponics will increase the natural sources and varieties of seafood, fruits, vegetables, and grains. Foods may be grown in air. Storage technologies will enhance our ability to maintain freshness and reduce spoilage, while providing year-round economical supplies.

We are likely to learn more about nutrition and its impact on health in the next 15 to 25 years than we have in all of the past centuries. This knowledge explosion will shape guest eating habits and affect menus and kitchen operations. As knowledge grows, and as we better understand the roles that all foods can play, a more varied set of food alternatives that appeal to taste and health will greet guests. Indications are that vegetarian dishes, fish, chicken, turkey, and such currently uncommon foods as ostrich and buffalo will offer more varied and healthy diets.

Computers will keep track of personal diet profiles that can then be linked with the detailed nutritional contents of menu items, permitting guests to tailor their meal selections. Restaurant menus may be stored in guest computers and adjusted automatically to meet particular guest requirements. Restaurants will be able to download an individual guest's nutritional desires into their own computers, match them to their menus, make automatic adjustments, and print out alternative choices for guests to consider.

The family mealtime, formerly an integral part of the American home lifestyle and cultural tradition, will continue to disintegrate. Ordering meals will be facilitated by interactive TV, computers, and fax machines, coupled with a growing reliance on take-out and delivery services and eating fast food in automobiles. In essence, the home will become a proxy restaurant, furnishing meals on demand to members of the household. Increasingly, family feeding will occur outside the home.

As the function of homes keep changing, market opportunities for restaurants and hotels will be affected. Future consumers will see their homes as providing extensive recreation, leisure, and entertainment facilities. Amenities formerly available only outside the home will abound in the form of swimming pools, exercise rooms, total communications centers, computer games, and experiences of virtual reality. The world will be brought into our homes. "In-home vacations" will increase, where families and friends spend time at home, yet will still get away from it all without the need to physically travel. Hotels and restaurants will be challenged to capitalize on market opportunities these trends portend by providing lodging and restaurant-related services such as in-house catering; party, vacation, and clean-up services; and everyday meal preparation. And as more and more people work at home, new markets will emerge for meal and food service providers. Closer linkages will evolve between homes and the products and services of the hospitality industry.

Future Developments in the Lodging Sector

In-Room Technology

Almost every aspect of hotel operations will be affected by the flood of technological advances. Such developments as video cameras, monitors, sensors, and speech recognition will result in intelligent rooms that will learn guest behavior and adjust environmental settings accordingly—lights, room temperature, and ambience. Sensing materials will be embodied into such objects as coffee pots, cups, and glasses that will automatically prepare beverages and control their temperature. They will keep track of files and important documents, as well as personal items such as eye glasses, wallets, and keys. On-person computers will connect guests to virtually any electronic device. Libraries and books will be placed at guest fingertips. Consumers will be not only able to shop the stores of the world from their hotel rooms, but actually experience the contours and feel of merchandise. And it will be possible to tailor items for specific people, rooms, or settings. Vastly more efficient work areas will be available.[12] Other advances will likely include such applications as:[13]

- Robots to clean and sanitize rooms
- Linens dispensed from automated systems
- An automatic central vacuum system
- Computers that respond to guest voices and answer a wider variety of guest questions
- Continuous contact with guests via cellular phones connected to the switchboard
- Video-telephone-fax-personal computer systems
- Hookups with information networks and entertainment systems
- Nutritional analysis and computer suggestion of entrées based on guest needs
- Personal health systems connected to video-telephones for continuous monitoring of vital signs of guests and communications with medical authorities
- Guest security systems
- Video telephone system showing people at door
- Room sensors to control temperature, lighting, and air quality

Technology will continue to affect such amenities as electronic safes; minibars; automatic check-in and check-out; self-serve reservations for airlines, hotels, recreation, and entertainment; messaging systems in multiple languages; and the provision of a complete in-room office. It will lower the costs of international phone calls, making it economically feasible for hotels to extend their marketing reach to guests around the world. New toll-free numbers will permit calls from all corners of the globe.

Interactive TV (already emerging) has the potential to conveniently furnish guests with a wide variety of services and information. For example, it may be used to conduct guest surveys that can be computed and reported instantly. It can help merchandise offerings directly to guests, giving them access to shopping options inside and outside the hotel. It can inform and persuade guests about hospitality offers that are likely to appeal to them, thereby increasing sales and profits.

Communications

New communications technologies will touch every facet of hotel operations, from the way lodging operations are marketed to the manner in which guest needs are served. They will greatly improve the quality of guest experiences and may raise service standards to new levels. Telecommunications and computer technologies will especially affect how operations communicate with guests and how guests respond to those messages and make purchasing decisions.[14]

Multimedia communications will integrate a number of technologies, including television, video cameras, telephones, fax machines, and computers. Global communications capabilities will be greatly enhanced, with instant and informative audio and visual communications becoming a reality. Data—as text, audio, and video—will be delivered to personal fax, audio, and video mailboxes, in addition to today's common e-mail boxes. As a result of virtual reality, it will be possible for guests to "experience" hotels and restaurants from the convenience of their home computers before making choices. New telephone and voice messaging systems will better cater to guests' needs.

Imagine a traveler making a hotel reservation by inserting a smart card containing personal, credit, and travel information into a communications device that automatically dials a reservationist, activates a video display and telephone, and transmits the appropriate information. The traveler is then linked automatically to a hotel, and the desired room reservations are made, as are reservations at restaurants and recreational facilities. The hotel will provide the room number, key the lock to the frequent-traveler card, and send an e-mail confirmation.

In a similar vein, satellite tracking systems in automobiles will display maps that guide drivers directly to their hotel via the best routes. Convenience will be enhanced as communications technology changes hotel booking and check-in and check-out procedures. Better links between hotel and airline reservation systems could well account for a larger proportion of hotel bookings. Hotels will also be linked to global computerized reservation systems that can be accessed directly from personal computers. Guests will be able to check in directly from airport limos and vans. Guestrooms may be accessed with systems based on electronic recognition of fingerprints, voice, or other physical features.

A downside of the development of multimedia communications technology for hotels may be less need for face-to-face meetings. Sales reps may be able to handle their business from their computers, eliminating some of the need to travel and meet with customers. Video conferencing could eliminate the need for seminars and conferences. This, in turn, could reduce the demand of business guests for hotel rooms and services. At the same time, however, hotels will be able to market their facilities more effectively to their guests via these very networks. Given the human need for personal contact, the increasing use of depersonalized communications technology will open the opportunity for hospitality markets to develop creative ways of personalizing their approaches.

Changing Guest Needs

Future hotels will be geared to better fit the needs of diverse groups of guests. To do so, a broader variety of lodging alternatives will be developed. Many of them will be specifically focused on the needs of particular groups. Some will expand on the traditional hotel services offered, while others will eliminate many hotel services and facilities. Some will cater to long- and short-term guests and their needs, others to seniors, families, international travelers, and so on. And there will be hotels that cut across various market segments, catering to lodging needs in general.

The requirements of foreign and domestic business travelers, who want facilities that enable them to perform their job-related tasks at reasonable costs, will be taken into consideration in future hotel designs and operations. Some hotels will be developed without bars, restaurants, spacious lobbies, and a variety of other specialized personal services and conveniences to reduce costs and better meet specific markets. Some will focus on more work-oriented amenities, including personal computers, printers, larger desks, better lighting, in-room faxes, scanners, and copiers.

Some hotels will extend those services that appeal to traveling families, offering a variety of child-support and child-entertainment services and facilities. Others will seek to accommodate guests who are physically and health challenged and who require special assistance, services, and room designs.

Concluding Comments

Developing a future perspective is essential to managing change and capitalizing on emerging market opportunities. However, no one can foresee the future with certainty and identifying future developments is no easy task. Nevertheless, insightful managers *can* identify emerging trends, assess their implications, and arrive at valuable perspectives of the future.

In dealing with the future, three basic points should be borne in mind. First, expect the unexpected; second, remember that trends may also contain counter trends that can temper any tendencies; and third, remember that perspectives of the future may vary greatly among managers. In addition, managers must resist the temptation to view future developments through the lens of the past—to make future perspectives conform to current precepts.

Developing a future perspective involves paying more attention to such activities as scanning future environments, assessing trends and opportunities, determining future scenarios, delineating market opportunities, developing contingency plans, and adjusting market offerings. While a prior watchword in hospitality was location, location, location, in the future it will be joined by service, service, service.

In the future, managers will pay more attention to mini-mass and niche markets, and to targeting demographic segments such as the post baby boomers and the seniors markets. The hospitality marketing mix will be affected by such developments as smart products, safety and security concerns, the rapid launching of new offerings, scrambled distribution, new distribution channels, increased attention to differentiation, tailoring and focusing of communications, and improved linking of pricing strategies with market demand. Among the valued marketing leadership qualities will be the ability to adapt to unanticipated changes, to articulate core values, and to deal effectively with unstable, disorderly, and unstructured marketing situations.

Future hospitality marketers will be more proactive in their approaches. They will use just-in-time approaches, focus on value, and be concerned with leading-edge thinking. They will rethink and re-engineer hospitality organizations to better serve guests. Networks and systems will be developed overarching formal organizational boundaries, integrating and coordinating the efforts of different companies. Decision making and problem solving will shift from the current focus on hard facts and logic to include a greater emphasis on feelings, opinion, and creativity.

The heightened global marketing focus will continue to change both hospitality marketing perspectives and operations. Hospitality will not only be challenged to deal with increasing numbers of guests from other cultures, but will have to change hospitality marketing methods and approaches to conform to other operating environments. And hospitality managers will be challenged to develop relationships and networks globally, stimulate entrepreneurial behavior among employees, and encourage innovative and creative hospitality approaches. Increasingly they will be concerned with ecological and social developments.

Marketing literature contains references to likely future scenarios, sometimes in very specific terms, for both the food service and the lodging sectors. By considering these predictions, hospitality marketers can gain insights into possible developments and the kinds of turbulent changes that they may well confront in the not-too-distant future. At the very least, such scenarios underscore management's need for a vastly different mind-set to deal effectively with hospitality marketing challenges of the future.

Endnotes

1. Peter F. Drucker, *Management: Tasks, Responsibilities, Practices* (New York: Harper & Row, 1974).

2. *Marketing News*, 29 February 1988, p. 2.

3. *USA Today*, 14 March 1996, p. 4B.

4. Charles Kettering, voice record, Michigan State University Voice Library.

5. *The Wall Street Journal*, 18 June 1994, p. B1.

6. *The Wall Street Journal*, 17 June 1996, p. R6.

7. Dan Lago and James Kipp Poffley, "The Aging Population and the Hospitality Industry in 2010: Important Trends and Probable Services," *Hospitality Research Journal* 17, no. 1 (1993): 30–43.

8. William Lazer et al., *Marketing 2000 and Beyond* (Chicago: American Marketing Association, 1990), pp. 222–224.

9. "Over There," *Restaurant Business*, 1 September 1996.

10. The following section is based on John Young Wallace, "Gateway to the Millennium," *Hospitality Research Journal* 17, no. 1 (1993): 59–65.

11. Frank D. Borsenik, "Hospitality Technology in the 21st Century," *Hospitality Research Journal* 17, no. 1 (1993): 262–269.

12. Based on Elizabeth Royte, "Life as We'll Know It," *New York Times Magazine*, 28 September 1997, p. 83.

13. Borsenik.

14. Richard G. Moore and Scott Wilkinson, "Communications Technology," *Hospitality Research Journal* 17, no. 1 (1993): 140–144.

Key Terms

codistribution—coupling of hospitality products and services with others that are not normally distributed together, such as plastic surgery and vacation resorts.

just-in-time hospitality marketing—making marketing resources and programs, such as advertising and merchandising, available just at the time that they are needed.

leading-edge hospitality marketing—being on the forefront of hospitality marketing through innovation and making creative changes.

proactive hospitality marketing—the tendency to introduce changes and develop companies along new paths before market conditions force changes.

relationship marketing—marketing that establishes long-term, close working relationships with guests and suppliers.

smart products—products containing computer chips that extend product capabilities, enhance guest benefits, and increase management efficiency.

value-based hospitality marketing—a focus on the use of marketing resources to increase guest value, as opposed to increasing marketing efficiency or reducing costs.

Review Questions

1. What are future facts? Is this a conflict in terms? Why or why not?

2. Who should be in charge of the future in a hospitality organization?

3. What activities are marketers going to pay more attention to in the future than they have in the past?

4. What will future hospitality marketing emphasize?

5. How might the hospitality leadership paradigm change in the future? Why?

6. What are four likely future orientations of hospitality marketing managers? Describe each.

7. How will changing technology affect hospitality offerings and hospitality marketing? Does this have any ramifications regarding the personal touch in hospitality services?

8. How are marketing decision-making and problem-solving approaches likely to change in the future? Why might these changes be necessary?

Internet Sites

For more information, visit the following Internet sites. Remember that Internet addresses can change without notice.

Ben & Jerry's
http://www.benjerry.com

Häagen-Dazs
http://www.haagendazs.com

Hilton Hotels Corp.
http://www.hilton.com

KFC
http://www.kfc.com

Kmart
http://www.kmart.com

Marriott International
http://www.marriott.com

McDonald's Corp.
http://www.mcdonalds.com

Morton's of Chicago
http://www.mortons.com

Outback Steakhouse
http://www.outback.com

Pizza Hut
http://www.pizzahut.com

Ruth's Chris Steak House
http://www.ruthschris.com

Wal-Mart
http://www.wal-mart.com

Walt Disney Corporation
http://www.disney.com

Appendix:
Marketing Case Studies

The following cases have been developed through the involvement and support of industry leaders. The issues and problems presented in these cases illustrate the types of situations you can expect to encounter when working in hospitality marketing. The discussion questions at the end of each case direct your attention to important issues, but you needn't limit your analysis to finding the answers to these questions. Examining the cases from different perspectives can help you get more out of each case.

Here are some guidelines that might be helpful in analyzing the cases:

- Read each case study carefully, noting important information and facts.

- Construct a time line of events leading up to the situation being considered.

- Identify all of the significant characters in the case.

- Identify the problem presented by the case and define it. Is there more than one problem?

- Analyze the problem. What are its causes? Whom does it affect?

- List important factors in the case that affect your analysis (for example: type of property, location of property, time of year).

- List items you think should be addressed in developing a solution to the problem.

- Identify a solution (or solutions) to the problem. Remember that often-times the first solution that comes to mind is not the best.

- Evaluate your solution. If your solution was implemented, would it solve the problem? What would be the possible consequences? Might it cause new problems?

- Look at the case again, taking the perspective of a different character in the case. Explore the problem and your solution(s) from that character's perspective.

Studying these cases will help you learn important lessons and develop critical thinking skills that will be valuable to you in your hospitality career.

Special thanks go to A.J. Singh for his initial development work on several of the case studies in this appendix.

Departmental Conflict at the Ultra Hotel

Case Number: 370CA (3 pages)

This case pits marketing and sales against the rooms division in a battle over a sensitive hotel issue: how many rooms can marketing and sales have for group sales? To land an important piece of group business, the marketing and sales director wants more rooms than are usually allotted to group sales; the rooms director thinks the group's business is not worth inconveniencing the hotel's regular transient guests.

No Vacancy

Case Number: 370CB (3 pages)

The negotiation process is one of the most challenging aspects of hospitality sales—particularly if both sides at the negotiating table are to be satisfied. In this case, the sales manager of the Monte Sereno Hotel negotiates with Jon Stonewall, the unyielding manager of a national computer software company who wants to hold a regional meeting at the hotel. The challenge is to arrive at a win-win situation for the hotel and the client.

Don't Just Tell It—Sell It! or Needs Satisfaction Selling: Booking Business by Turning Features into Benefits

Case Number: 370CC (4 pages)

In this case, veteran salesperson Sandra Savvy shares techniques for combining courtesy and customer needs satisfaction to build business, a common sense approach often overlooked in sales. New salesperson Drew Newbie also gets some tips from Sandra on how to turn property features into guest benefits.

Selecting a Salesperson

Case Number: 370CD (10 pages)

One of the biggest challenges a small property can face is selecting the right person to fill a sales job. In this case, sales consultants ask the same interview questions of four candidates for a sales position. Which applicant should be hired?

Sales Slump in Sun City

Case Number: 370CE (3 pages)

The new GM at the 122-room Sun and Surf Inn inherits problems in building business through tour group operators and wholesalers. Hand-offs between the sales director and the front desk manager seem to drop the ball as word on current packages fails to get to the property's reservationists and the central reservations office.

Reviving Revenue Management

Case Number: 370CF (3 pages)

> After surviving the opening of a competing hotel, the GM and sales staff at the Hearthstone Suites Hotel are challenged to revive the property's revenue management program. While occupancy is at budget year-to-date, average daily rate (ADR) is down by $6.00. Also, the mix of commercial business is lower than planned (40% of guest mix instead of 50%), and the SMERF segment is higher than it should be (15% of guest mix instead of 5%).

Distributing Sales Functions Between a Hotel's Sales and Catering Departments

Case Number: 370CG (3 pages)

> Year-end projections for a 400-room first-class suburban hotel show banquet food sales will be off by $60,000 to budget and audiovisual revenues and room rental revenues will miss budget by $30,000. The director of catering learns to rely less on the hotel sales department and takes ownership of the problems.

Sales Underperforms Even While Meeting Budget

Case Number: 370CH (3 pages)

> The new general manager at a 180-room economy/business property in a booming suburb of a major city is challenged by the regional director of operations to increase the hotel's market penetration rate. The case focuses on increasing the volume of group business as well as raising the ADR for groups.

Leadership at the Hamilton: Impasse Between the General Manager and Director of Sales

Case Number: 370CI (4 pages)

> The general manager of a 500-room first-class, downtown hotel calls in a marketing consultant to shake up the sales staff. Year-to-date occupancy is down 4% with a year-end projected shortfall of $700,000 in revenue, but marketing expenses are already $55,000 over budget. The consultant's recommendations must temper the unrealistic expectations of the GM and refocus the efforts of the director of sales.

Overcoming Rate Resistance—Among the Sales Staff

Case Number: 370CJ (2 pages)

> The 263-room Park View Hotel has too much contracted business at a low rate. The director of sales works with the sales staff to replace a third of this business—about 5,000 room nights—with higher rated transient and group business. They look at what business to keep, new sources of business to replace the contract business, and scripts for the sales staff to use with current clients of the preferred group rate.

⌕ Case Study

Departmental Conflict at The Ultra Hotel

A quick glance out the lobby window revealed wind-blown gray clouds bunching up over the city. Storm's brewing out there, thought Rick Roland, the Ultra Hotel's marketing and sales director. In here, too, he thought as he walked past the lounges and restaurants on the ground floor of the 500-room, three-star convention property.

Unconsciously, Rick's pace slowed as he got closer to the meeting room where the end-of-the-month executive committee meeting was due to start. How ironic, he thought, to feel so apprehensive even though I'm almost ready to close on one of the biggest pieces of business I've landed in quite some time.

Taking a deep breath, Rick paused before entering the room. Images of the people waiting inside flashed through his mind: Fred Franklin, the general manager, a tough but fair boss who liked to give his staff members a chance to present their side of an argument; Norma Lopez, the no-nonsense controller with the laser-like focus on the bottom line; Claude van Fleet, the temperamental food and beverage director piloting a department through a terrible month; Camille Petrocelli, self-described "people person" and human resources director; and last, Jeanelle Causwell, rooms director, a fast-track performer, a favorite of Mr. Franklin's, and possibly my mortal enemy by the end of this meeting, Rick thought wryly.

Exhaling, Rick entered the meeting room. The meeting raced by for Rick until the moment he was waiting for. Mr. Franklin turned to him and said, "What have you got for us, Rick?"

"Well, gosh," Rick began, trying to inject some folksiness into a speech he had rehearsed a dozen times, "I'm about to land a nice piece of business for us. As all of you know, we've been after the ConveyorMatic meeting planner for months. The good news is, I think the guy's ready to commit in a big way. We're talking 250 rooms the second week of September, Sunday through Thursday, and—get this— it's a mandatory sales meeting for their big-spending sales staff, so filling up at least 240 of those 250 rooms is a cinch."

Seeing some nods and looks of interest, Rick went on. "Claude, you'll love this. We're getting three dinners, three lunches, three upgraded breakfasts, and two cocktail receptions with heavy hors d'oeuvres, which is big-time food and beverage sales—and that doesn't include spending in the outlets. It projects out to $130,000 in business for the hotel. Last year, we had only about $80,000 the same week."

"Excuse me, Rick, but isn't it hotel policy that you're only allotted 200 rooms for group sales?" Jeanelle said, launching her first salvo.

"Good point, Jeanelle, but if I book this group this year, they could be repeat customers every year. Plus, this guy is active in Meeting Professiopnals International, so he could give us some great referrals."

"I love it. Let's book 'em," Claude interjected, looking relieved and grateful.

"I do have to book it today, by five o'clock. That's why I want to get us all together on this," Rick explained.

"Excuse me again, Rick," Jeanelle said, "I'm sure you didn't make any promises to this group that would affect our room assignments, right?"

"Not really." Rick turned quickly to the controller. "What do you think, Norma?"

"I think we need to take a look at the numbers and make sure they're as good as you say," Norma said.

"Camille?" Rick continued eagerly.

"What?" Camille smiled, looking up from an issue of *HR Weekly*. "Oh, it sounds good; we could keep ten or fifteen people a day working for four days. Might slow down the turnover of our part-time kitchen staff."

"Rick, let's back up a minute." It was Jeanelle again, refusing to be sidetracked. "When I asked whether you'd made any promises to this group that would affect room assignments, you said 'Not really.' Could you define 'Not really' for me?"

"Well, I, uh," Rick looked down and mumbled rapidly, "I told them they could have fifty percent of their block in our new wing."

"What!" Jeanelle yelled, "You gave away my new wing! What do I tell my transient, repeat guests? My regulars stay three or four days, six times a year. You want me to tell them I'm kicking them out of the new wing? Why don't we just save time and tell them to go stay across the street from now on, because that's just what they'll do."

"But we're talking about 250 rooms!" Rick protested.

"At what rate?" Jeanelle shot back.

"Well, because of the F&B business, I gave them a discount—$79 a night."

"Wow! That's twenty percent off our regular $99 rate. Give those rooms back to me, Mr. Franklin. If we open up the corporate reservations center for discounts, I'll sell every one at $89. And I won't have to dump my best guests out of the new wing for these conveyor salesmen."

"Now, Jeanelle..." Rick pleaded.

"Now, nothing!" she snapped.

"But, Jeanelle, the F&B revenue!" Claude said, dreaming of making up last month's budget shortfall. "You know as well as I do that transient guests don't eat at the hotel. This group will mean big bucks in F&B."

"Mr. Franklin, you're the general manager; it's your call," Rick said resignedly. Jeanelle and Claude nodded in agreement. The staff leaned back, waiting for the GM's decision.

Discussion Questions

1. What reasons might the GM have for deciding to turn down the business? What conflicts on the executive committee would have to be resolved if the GM decides to turn down the business?

2. What reasons might the GM have for deciding to take the business? What conflicts on the executive committee would have to be resolved if the GM decides to take the business?

Case Number: 370CA

This case was developed in cooperation with Bill Flor and Randy Kinder, authors of *No Vacancy: A Tried & True Guide to Get More Rooms Business!*; The No Vacancy Company; Jacksonville, Florida; toll free 1-888-976-7653.

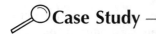 **Case Study**

No Vacancy

Jon Stonewall is a regional manager for IntelTech, a Seattle-based company that produces computer software. He is responsible for planning the annual meeting of his account representatives in District 12, which encompasses the entire Pacific Northwest. The meeting, normally just an opportunity for education and socializing, will be especially important this year because the company is introducing several several new products. After reviewing several several locations, Jon decided to have the meeting in Sacramento and asked his secretary Chris to gather information and solicit bids from at least five Sacramento hotels. Jon is a hard-nosed businessperson who likes to get what he wants. To waste as little time as possible, he systematically examined his choices and narrowed the selection down to two. Now it was time to make a deal.

Jon was in his office when he received a call from Julia Chavez, the sales manager of the Monte Sereno Hotel in Sacramento. She began the conversation by introducing herself and her property, a mid-range hotel with 248 rooms, 8,000 square feet of meeting space, and a 5,200-square-foot ballroom that could be divided into four equal sections.

"We're so pleased you've selected the Monte Sereno as a possible site for your next meeting," Julia continued. "I've spoken at length with your secretary and wanted to speak with you personally to be sure we understand your needs. Do you have a moment to talk?"

Jon was at the start of a busy day and was a little annoyed at the interruption, but brusquely told her to go on. Concerned by his tone, Julia thanked him for his time and proceeded cautiously.

"I understand your group will arrive Sunday afternoon and leave Thursday. You'd like 48 rooms, single occupancy, and an opening-night reception with heavy hors d'oeuvres. Is that correct?"

"Yes," Jon grunted.

"Chris told me that you'll begin each morning with a continental breakfast at 8:00 a.m., followed by a general session at 8:30. The general session meeting room is to be arranged classroom-style, with a luncheon in a separate room beginning at noon. From 1:00 to 5:00 p.m., your account reps will break into groups of 10 to 15 and require separate meeting spaces."

"That's right," Jon replied, "except that everyone will be on their own at lunch time."

Julia had carefully considered this sales opportunity, weighed the options, and decided on an appropriate rate before making the call to Jon. She had taken into account the property's sales history, which showed a 92 percent occupancy rate on the particular days IntelTech had in mind. She was concerned because this meeting would use only 20 percent of the hotel's rooms while using 65 percent of the hotel's meeting space. From her standpoint, it wasn't a great piece of business. Julia Chavez wanted the business, but she wanted it on her own terms. She took a deep breath and continued.

"Well, we do have those dates available for your meeting. We can offer the guestrooms at $99, a reduction from our standard $110 rate, and offer the meeting space you need at $1,000 per day. However, I know that getting high value for your dollar is a consideration for everyone these days, so, if you can be flexible and change your dates to a Wednesday arrival and a Sunday departure, I can offer the rooms to you at $85 and waive the $1,000 charge for the meeting space—if you will hold your farewell banquet with us."

"I can't believe this!" Jon said, his voice rising. "The Salton Hotel down the street has the dates I want *and* they can give them to me at the rate you quoted! Granted, I prefer your hotel overall, but I have to consider my company. This meeting has been set for a long time; some of my people have already made travel plans. We've even scheduled the speakers. I can't go back and change things now! Why are the rates so different later in the week?"

Julia was prepared for this response and answered him as tactfully and honestly as she could. "I'm aware of your concerns and I know it would be difficult to move the meeting, but I wanted to give you the option. Since we're both businesspeople, I know you'll understand that I have to consider my property's financial position in all of this. Our sales history shows that we have our highest occupancy during the first part of the week—between 90 and 100 percent—but later in the week that number declines to around 60 percent; that's why I can give you a lower rate at that time. Because we're sold out or almost sold out from Sunday through Thursday, it doesn't make sense financially for us to offer you the lower rate early in the week."

"Look," Jon said, "I can appreciate where you're coming from, but I don't see how I can change this meeting—even if I can save a lot of money."

"I understand your situation and want to work with you in the future," Julia replied, "but I'm not sure we can meet your needs this time. Down the road, if you bring me your next meeting, I'll throw in a free cocktail party. I think you'd be very pleased with our hotel. We have outstanding food and a very friendly, courteous staff. I hope you'll come and visit us when you're in town."

Jon hesitated. Since he really wanted to stay at the Monte Sereno rather than the other hotel, he didn't want to let the matter drop. "What about this, Julia: if I agree to the higher rates and choose you over a competitor, will you do a few things for me? I'll pay the $99 room rate if you'll throw in the meeting space for nothing. I also want that free cocktail party you just mentioned. In addition, I'd like you to give us turndown service throughout our stay, a free *USA Today* in every room, and, waiting for my account reps when they arrive on Sunday, a mint and a welcome note from me in every guestroom."

Discussion Questions

1. Do you think Julia should agree to host the meeting on Jon's terms? Why or why not?

2. How could Julia further negotiate each of Jon's demands and end with a win-win conclusion?

Case Number: 370CB

This case was developed in cooperation with Bill Flor and Randy Kinder, authors of *No Vacancy: A Tried & True Guide to Get More Rooms Business!*; The No Vacancy Company; Jacksonville, Florida; toll free 1-888-976-7653.

Case Study

Don't Just Tell It—Sell It!
or
Needs Satisfaction Selling: Booking Business by Turning Features into Benefits

Sales at the 112-room Goodsleep Inn have been down lately. The number of room nights sold has dropped and, due to turnover, the sales staff is inexperienced. Today, hotshot sales director Sandra Savvy begins training Drew Newbie, one of the new salespeople.

At their first meeting in Sandra's office, Sandra explains, "Drew, to sell our hotel you have to understand what it is you're selling and how it appeals to your potential clients."

"That's easy—we're selling rooms," Drew said.

"That's true," Sandra replied. "But it's not that simple. To be a successful salesperson, you must be able to identify the hotel features that can benefit your potential clients and satisfy their *specific* needs."

"What do you mean?"

"How would you describe the Goodsleep Inn to someone who's never been here before?" Sandra asked.

"Well," Drew said, "it has 112 rooms and is three stories high, with external corridors. Is that the kind of information you mean?"

"That's a start. What else?"

"Hmm, let's see," Drew continued. "We have a swimming pool, and our rates are pretty reasonable. We have a great, free continental breakfast, too."

"Right," Sandra said. "What about the property's location?"

"I think I see what you're getting at," Drew said enthusiastically. "We have a coin-operated laundry for guests. We're in the suburbs near the business district. The area is safe. It's also close to the interstate. And even though we don't have any food and beverage outlets at our property, there are a lot of family restaurants and convenience stores within walking distance."

"Excellent! You're getting the hang of it," Sandra said. "Some other things you may want to mention to a potential client are: recent updates to the hotel, like the $150,000 guestroom renovations we just did; the free movies we offer; and our non-smoking rooms. These may seem like little things, but to some guests they mean a lot. The key is to find out what your potential guests need, then match the property's features to your guests' needs and show them how the property can benefit them."

"So, it's not just telling someone you've got rooms available, is it?" Drew asked.

"No, that's called *tell* selling," Sandra said, shaking her head. "That's what the stereotypical salesperson does—you know, the pushy person trying to sell you a used car you don't want. To really be successful in sales, you have to look for a win-win situation with clients. Find out what they really want, then describe the features of the hotel that match what they want. Keep in mind, though, that it's not just selling them a line. You don't make up stuff about the hotel that isn't true. You merely make the effort to match what you've got to what they want and describe what you have in terms of how it benefits the client. That's the way you can build long-term relationships with clients, which will increase the number of room nights sold in the long run."

Drew thought for a minute. "It sounds like common sense."

"It is. You'd be amazed at how successful you can be by simply listening to what your prospects need, describing how your hotel can meet those needs, and using a little common courtesy," Sandra said.

"Common courtesy," Drew said. "I've got that. I always say please and thank you."

"It's more than that," Sandra said. "There are simple things you can do that will really impress your potential clients and win you business for life. For example, greet potential clients at the front door, or even meet them in the parking lot and walk them to the front door; don't make them ask for you at the front desk. During the hotel tour, introduce them to the property manager and hotel employees. You'd be amazed at how little details like these can set the right tone."

"So, how do you find out what the potential clients' needs are?" Drew asked.

"That's simple—ask them! Also, take the time to get to know your markets. I do a little research before I meet with a potential client so I have some ideas about what he or she might want. Not only does it help me prepare, but it shows that I care about meeting the person's needs, not just making a sale. Then, when you give property tours, simply ask potential clients what's important to them in a hotel and then give it right back to them by describing the hotel features and benefits that fit those needs."

"I guess I have my work cut out for me," Drew responded.

"Yes, Drew, but you're up to the job." Sandra picked up her planner and flipped it open. "I've got an idea. I'm giving three property tours next week. Let me tell you what I've found out about each potential client and you tell me how you would sell the property to each.

"The first tour is for the local terminal manager who handles accommodations for long-distance drivers. These guests often use a room for only eight or nine hours, just enough time to get some sleep before getting back on the road. They want time to unwind, but they don't socialize. They stay in their rooms and watch

TV or sleep. They want king-size beds, clean rooms, and respect. They want to be reassured that you don't look down on them because they drive trucks or buses.

"The next tour is for a youth soccer league organizer from the parks and recreation department. She's responsible for recommending properties to out-of-town soccer teams that come here for games. Team members are usually 12- to 16-year-old boys and girls. Parents, coaches, and chaperons look for safe properties close to affordable restaurants and the soccer fields where the kids play. Luckily, we're really close to the soccer fields and we have a lot of affordable restaurants nearby. These guests want rooms with two double beds and an on-site laundry. Also, the property they choose has to be tolerant of the athletes. Everyone wants to have a good time, and the kids can get pretty rowdy.

"The third tour is for the pastor of a local church that offers a weekend couples conference twice a year. The couples attending this conference are very rate-conscious, but they want safe, clean, well-appointed rooms with king-size beds and some amenities for their weekend stay. They often do some socializing at breakfast and after the conference, although most of their time is spent away from the property."

Sandra closed her planner and looked up. "OK, Drew, it's your turn. We'll generate about 4,000 extra room nights a year if we can win the business of these potential clients. That means $125,000 in revenue. How would you present our hotel to each of these potential clients to win their business?"

Discussion Questions

1. How can Drew show common courtesy to each of these three potential clients?

2. How should Drew present the Goodsleep Inn's features and benefits to the local terminal manager?

3. How should Drew present the Goodsleep Inn's features and benefits to the soccer league organizer?

4. How should Drew present the Goodsleep Inn's features and benefits to the church pastor?

Case Number: 370CC

This case was developed in cooperation with Bill Flor and Randy Kinder, authors of *No Vacancy: A Tried & True Guide to Get More Rooms Business!*; The No Vacancy Company; Jacksonville, Florida; toll free 1-888-976-7653.

🔍 Case Study ————————————————————

Selecting a Salesperson

Sales consultants Claude Wise and Cyril Smarts had a rough time convincing owner/operator Jean Pennypincher that hiring a sales staff for her 12 limited-service properties would revive lagging profits. However, they finally convinced her to hire one part-time salesperson, with no benefits, to work at the Springtime

Inn—the hotel with the greatest potential. Jean agreed that if this person was successful at the property, she would hire additional salespeople for the other 11 properties.

Claude and Cyril advertised the position and narrowed down the applicants to four finalists. From a previous interview with each of them, the following information was gathered (note: some of the information would be illegal to request during a job interview; such information was volunteered by the candidates):

Harriet Fisher

Harriet was looking to re-enter the hospitality industry after a five-year hiatus. She mentioned that both her children will be in school, and she would like to work from 9:00 A.M. to 2:30 P.M. each day. She does not need benefits. She previously worked three years as an account executive for a mid-size hotel. She has one year of junior college.

Juan Carlise

Juan is a senior in a university hospitality program and has completed three-fourths of the curriculum. He also has served an internship as a guest-service representative at a luxury hotel and worked at the front desk of a local mid-size hotel for the past four years. He speaks English and Spanish fluently. He's looking to work 20 hours a week.

Amy Adler

Amy has worked at a retail clothing store for the past eight years. She has a junior college degree. She's interested in a job with better weekday and fewer weekend hours. She's hoping to make enough money to return to school for a four-year degree.

Warren Jordan

Warren recently retired from the navy after a 20-year career. One of his last assignments was Bachelor Quarters Officer, for which he helped implement the BQ Quality of Life standards on his base. He receives military retirement pay and benefits. He's looking for a job with flexible hours that will provide a challenge and some extra money.

Claude and Cyril developed the following ten questions to ask these four applicants during their final interviews:

1. If you were independently wealthy, what would you be doing right now?

2. What was your worst encounter with a salesperson, and how would you have improved that sales experience?

3. I'm sure you've been rejected before in a business situation. What were the circumstances, and how did you handle it?

4. Would you give us an example of a time when you had to be persistent, and would you describe the result?

5. Would you rather sell something or help someone buy?

6. This position is part of a pilot test. If it is successful, we will be hiring a salesperson for each of the other 11 properties. What would you bring to the table that would help us make this pilot program a success?

7. If the pilot test is successful and we hire additional salespeople, do you see yourself managing this sales force?

8. If you could be anything other than a human, what would you be?

9. What do you like to do when you're not at work?

10. You will be given a set of weekly goals, such as 10 personal calls and 20 telephone calls a week. How would you manage your time to achieve these goals?

They carefully designed the questions so that some of them focused on sales and managerial skills while others presented open-ended opportunities for applicants to talk about their personal values, habits, life styles, and more. After interviewing each candidate, they reviewed the audiotapes they made of each session. The answers they received to each of their ten questions follow.

HARRIET FISHER

1. If you were independently wealthy, what would you be doing right now?

"I'd hire a private tutor and take that person and my entire family and travel. I'd make sure the girls got to see all the wonders of the world they only read about now. It'd be a fantastic education for them to meet people from different cultures and see historic buildings and places."

2. What was your worst encounter with a salesperson, and how would you have improved that sales experience?

"The worst salesperson I met was actually at a hotel. This salesperson had described a three-day vacation package to a family that wanted two rooms. What she *didn't* say was that the price was per person, not per room. The father, surprised at what a great price they were getting, asked if she was certain that the quoted price was for all four of them. It was a low-occupancy week, and I'm sure the salesperson was anxious to book the family. Once they arrived at the hotel, the front desk agent told them the price was twice what they expected. Despite the fact that they had traveled twelve hours by car to get to the hotel, the father was ready to walk out and take his family back home, canceling their vacation. The salesperson should have been clear about the package or offered them a less expensive package at rates they were willing to pay."

3. I'm sure you've been rejected before in a business situation. What were the circumstances, and how did you handle it?

"Well, yes, I've been rejected—though I generally try to avoid it! One of the reasons I'm applying for this job came out of a recent rejection. I applied for a personal loan to buy a recreational vehicle. I was turned down because I wasn't employed. They wouldn't let me use my husband's income or my home as collateral. My first instinct was to switch banks. I did apply for a loan for the same amount at a credit union. I haven't heard back from them yet. If I'm turned down there too, I'll bide my time and apply for the loan again after I've worked for several months."

4. **Would you give us an example of a time when you had to be persistent, and would you describe the result?**

"Potty training. I can't think of anything that requires more persistence than that. The result is that my youngest child is going to nursery school in 'big girl' panties instead of diapers—and I assure you, that wasn't a foregone conclusion!"

5. **Would you rather sell something or help someone buy?**

"I'd much rather help someone buy what they want. I really hesitated before taking my first sales job at the Hot Springs Hotel. I never saw myself as a salesperson. But I loved the job because I was able to help people have a successful experience, whether they were on a business or pleasure trip, and really help meet their needs. I always tried to create a win-win situation."

6. **This position is part of a pilot test. If it is successful, we will be hiring a salesperson for each of the other 11 properties. What would you bring to the table that would help us make this pilot program a success?**

"I know the needs of transient and group guests. I can really help them see the benefits of staying at the Springtime Inn. I have experience in hotel sales, and I'm confident I can surpass the goals you outlined."

7. **If the pilot test is successful and we hire additional salespeople, do you see yourself managing this sales force?**

"I can see myself managing the process—at least initially. I have strong organizational skills and could help set up processes to be copied by other people. As much as I enjoy working with people, though, I'd prefer not to be a manager. My last job was very high-stress and, while I enjoyed the challenges, I'm at a different stage in life now. When I go home, I don't want to take my job with me or worry about the performance of my employees. I'm no longer on the high-powered, career-at-all-costs track."

8. **If you could be anything other than a human, what would you be?**

"I'd want to be a cat. They're loving, yet independent. They communicate blissful happiness, but aren't afraid to hiss and stick up for themselves when threatened."

9. **What do you like to do when you're not at work?**

"What *don't* I like to do would be an easier question to answer! My oldest daughter is active in competitive ice skating, and I take her to a lot of practices. I also make her outfits and help sew outfits for several other girls. I like to ski, go sledding, hiking, rappelling, fishing, and canoeing. I used to be involved in Habitat for Humanity when the girls were younger, but I no longer have the time."

10. **You will be given a set of weekly activities and goals. How would you manage your time to achieve these goals?**

"I would start out by breaking the weekly goals into daily goals. I would then sort my calls geographically. I really believe that for every five minutes spent planning your work, you save ten. I would want to arrange my calls and visits so that I have a half hour free at the end of each day. That way, if something runs longer, I wouldn't have to push whatever I was working on at the end of the day to the next day. And if that half hour ends up empty, I could spend it preparing for the next day."

JUAN CARLISE
1. **If you were independently wealthy, what would you be doing right now?**

"I'd set up a fellowship in my name at the university to pay the tuition of hospitality students who show a lot of promise. Then I'd buy a hotel that could double as a training school for the university."

2. **What was your worst encounter with a salesperson, and how would you have improved that sales experience?**

"It was a car salesman—surprise! I was all ready to buy a car. All I wanted to do was take the paperwork home and fill it out. I had a date that night and I really wanted time to go home and get ready—I didn't want to hang around the dealership after I'd made up my mind. But the salesperson kept hounding me, telling me that if I didn't sign right now, the model I wanted might be sold out by the next afternoon. I said if he could sell all those cars, then bully for him—he didn't need me to buy. Then he said I might not get the color I wanted. I think I told him three times I was willing to chance it. Finally, I got so disgusted I gave him back his paperwork and left. He could have sold me a car if he hadn't kept up the high pressure, 'gotta-have-it-now' sales pitch. Now he'll never have me for a customer. He'd have been much better off to let me leave with the paperwork and then follow up with a phone call the next afternoon."

3. **I'm sure you've been rejected before in a business situation. What were the circumstances, and how did you handle it?**

"Hey, you've got to be cool about rejections. I was rejected for two internships before I got a really great one last summer at a luxury hotel. I handle rejection by learning why I was rejected, how to prevent it the next time, and by trying again somewhere else."

4. **Would you give us an example of a time when you had to be persistent, and would you describe the result?**

"Persistence is my middle name. I had to be persistent to get into college and to get an internship. I have to be persistent every day at work to get the room attendants to report room status in a timely manner."

5. **Would you rather sell something or help someone buy?**

"I like to sell. I enjoy being a salesperson and bringing in high occupancy rates. Certainly, you want to help the customer buy your services. And I definitely don't believe in badgering customers beyond their tolerance. However, it's important to ask for a sale. A good salesperson can find at least one property service to sell to just about anyone."

6. **This position is part of a pilot test. If it is successful, we will be hiring a salesperson for each of the other 11 properties. What would you bring to the table that would help us make this pilot program a success?**

"I bring a good education, motivation, and excitement. The first thing I'll do to help you meet your goals is meet my goals. Then I can provide an analysis of how my sales techniques can help your other properties excel. I'll also make sure I generate more business than I could possibly support alone—especially part-time."

7. **If the pilot test is successful and we hire additional salespeople, do you see yourself managing this sales force?**

"I've spent several years preparing myself for a managerial position in hospitality. I believe that once I graduate, I'll be ready to manage the other people you hire and lead them through the same growth process that I'll be leading this first hotel through."

8. **If you could be anything other than a human, what would you be?**

"I'd want to be a book. That way I'd be immortal and constantly contributing to other people's knowledge and enjoyment."

9. **What do you like to do when you're not at work?**

"I enjoy fixing up old houses. I've got some buddies who have carpentry and electrical skills, and we contract out our services to fix up old homes. We're currently restoring a house built in 1885. It's got some great woodwork and an unusual root cellar. By the time we're done with it, it'll look like new—at least, what new was a century ago."

10. **You will be given a set of weekly activities and goals. How would you manage your time to achieve these goals?**

"I'd make a to-do list with each of the goals and the tasks needed to complete those goals. Then I'd prioritize them and start working on them according to priority. I'd start with the 'A' task and work at it until it was done, then go to the 'B' task, and so on until I was through my list."

AMY ADLER

1. **If you were independently wealthy, what would you be doing right now?**

"I'd buy an island up north where it snows a lot and live in a huge log cabin with a large fireplace. I'd have food flown in every week, and just curl up and read, watch television, and knit."

2. **What was your worst encounter with a salesperson, and how would you have improved that sales experience?**

"It was a telephone solicitor. He called at eight o'clock in the morning. I'd been doing inventory at the store the night before and hadn't gotten home until 2 a.m. The last thing I wanted was for the phone to ring at eight o'clock. I was half asleep when I answered the phone and didn't fully wake up until the solicitor asked for my credit card number. I told the caller I didn't want to buy anything. He said I'd already agreed and the conversation was taped. I told him again I didn't want anything and hung up. A week later I received a cellular phone and a bill. I sent it back, but it took months to get them to stop sending me threatening letters. How would I make it better? Well, I'd certainly be sure that the customer I was talking to was fully awake and understood the purchase conditions—I wouldn't just read a script. Neither would I be rude to customers and tell them that they *have* to buy whatever I'm selling."

3. **I'm sure you've been rejected before in a business situation. What were the circumstances, and how did you handle it?**

"When we were opening the outlet store, I had a great idea for setting up a perpetual inventory. It was rejected because of silly politics. Once I realized the new manager liked doing things her own way, I just put my idea in a memo and did what I was told."

4. **Would you give us an example of a time when you had to be persistent, and would you describe the result?**

"We were opening a store at the mall down the road from here. I was temporarily relocated to help the store set up. The person I was working with had never opened a clothing store before and had a lot of strange ideas about how clothes should be displayed. I had to be very persistent and diplomatic to make sure everything was set up in a way that would be conducive to sales."

5. **Would you rather sell something or help someone buy?**

"I prefer to sell; I'd much rather have an item and try to sell it than waste a lot of time with customers who are uncertain of what they want. You can make a lot more sales when you work at selling something specific."

6. **This position is part of a pilot test. If it is successful, we will be hiring a salesperson for each of the other 11 properties. What would you bring to the table that would help us make this pilot program a success?**

"I've been a salesperson for a number of years. I've helped open new stores and helped turn around low-performing stores. I'll be able to do the same with your hotels. I'll bring my experience with start-ups to help your hotels find new markets and meet the needs of those markets."

7. **If the pilot test is successful and we hire additional salespeople, do you see yourself managing this sales force?**

"I think I could. I'm very good at working with people. In retail, you get all types. I've always enjoyed solving problems for employees and customers."

8. **If you could be anything other than a human, what would you be?**

   "I'd want to be a cruise ship. Except for a few days in ports, I'd be spending most of my time out on the seas—and that seems like a wonderfully peaceful and relaxing existence."

9. **What do you like to do when you're not at work?**

   "I like to make crafts. I have several nieces and nephews I enjoy making things for. I also enjoy renting videos. I especially like British comedy."

10. **You will be given a set of weekly activities and goals. How would you manage your time to achieve these goals?**

    "Those sound like very reasonable goals. I'd plan to do two personal calls a day and four telephone calls."

WARREN JORDAN

1. **If you were independently wealthy, what would you be doing right now?**

   Probably not much different than what I'm doing now. I'd probably get a bigger house, a new car, all that sort of stuff. I'd still be looking for a challenge, though. Granted, I wouldn't be applying for this job; instead, I'd probably open my own business."

2. **What was your worst encounter with a salesperson, and how would you have improved that sales experience?**

   "My worst experience by far was trying to buy an engagement ring for my wife. The jewelry store salesperson at the first place I went to refused to show me a moderately priced ring. I was on a military salary and didn't want to go into debt for the ring. The salesperson kept telling me that it was an investment, and that I'd be showing how much I loved my fiancée by the size of the diamond I picked. When I asked to see a smaller ring, she said, 'Why are you marrying her if you don't love her enough to get her a decent ring? You want her to be embarrassed?' I walked out at that point. Fortunately, I found another salesperson at another store who was helpful. It's this person who epitomized how I would handle the situation. She asked me what my budget was and then showed me a number of different rings with different settings. She asked about my fiancée's style and taste. Then she offered to engrave the ring with our wedding date, once we set the date. She did such a nice job that I went back to that store the next year when I got a bonus and bought my wife a pair of diamond earrings."

3. **I'm sure you've been rejected before in a business situation. What were the circumstances, and how did you handle it?**

   "The situation that is most memorable was the first time I was turned down for a promotion to lieutenant in the navy. I smarted for about a day, but then I met with my commanding officer and asked him why I had been turned down. He helped me outline the steps I could take to make sure I qualified next time. Then I followed those steps."

4. **Would you give us an example of a time when you had to be persistent, and would you describe the result?**

"When I was manager of bachelor housing, I had a building manager who acted as though his budget was just a guideline, not a requirement. As a consequence of his poor budgeting, several of his building's requirements went unfunded. At first, I thought he just didn't understand the importance of the budgetary process, or that perhaps he didn't know how to fill out the budget forms. As it turned out, he was just biding his time until he was rotated to another position. That may have been fine for him, but I found it unacceptable. I had to hound him continually to fill out every form and make sure he could justify his numbers. I had to take measures with him that none of my other building managers required, but the end result was that I got an accurate budget out of him to submit to navy command."

5. **Would you rather sell something or help someone buy?**

"I'd rather help someone buy. It's of no value to sell people something they don't need. There are many more long-term benefits to finding out what customers want and meeting those needs than to selling them something they don't need or want. The latter philosophy leads to too many one-time customers."

6. **This position is part of a pilot test. If it is successful, we will be hiring a salesperson for each of the other 11 properties. What would you bring to the table that would help us make this pilot program a success?**

"I bring to you strong organizational skills and the expertise of someone accustomed to managing people and resources. I'll help you reach your goal by being so successful that it won't be necessary to justify hiring other salespeople to the hotel owner. Instead, she'll wonder how she lasted so long without them."

7. **If the pilot test is successful and we hire additional salespeople, do you see yourself managing this sales force?**

"I think I would be the ideal person to help you select and supervise your new hires. As I mentioned before, I have extensive experience managing people, and I'm very good at establishing and implementing processes."

8. **If you could be anything other than a human, what would you be?**

"Hmmm, that's a hard one. I guess I'd want to be a mountain. That way I can be kind and gentle, yet strong and powerful."

9. **What do you like to do when you're not at work?**

"I'm the vice president of a local hospital board. We have several projects I'm currently working on. I chair the publicity committee, and we are promoting a fundraising campaign that starts next month. I also like to take the kids fishing and go golfing."

10. **You will be given a set of weekly activities and goals. How would you manage your time to achieve these goals?**

    "First I'd determine when the best time is to reach each client I wanted to contact. Then I'd schedule my calls according to premium success times. I'd also analyze how I spent my time so that I could eventually look for ways to increase my output by a given percentage each month."

Discussion Questions

1. What are the strengths and weaknesses of each applicant?

2. Which applicant would you hire? Why?

3. Which applicant do you think Claude and Cyril hired? Why?

Case Number: 370CD

This case was developed in cooperation with Bill Flor and Randy Kinder, authors of *No Vacancy: A Tried & True Guide to Get More Rooms Business!*; The No Vacancy Company; Jacksonville, Florida; toll free 1-888-976-7653.

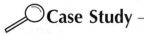 **Case Study** ─────────────────────

Sales Slump in Sun City

Sun City—how could anyone be unhappy in this vacation paradise where tanned natives and sunburned tourists basked on white sand beaches all year round? But Gregory Earle, general manager of the 122-room Sun & Surf Inn, was unhappy as he gazed out of his office window. Why aren't those tourists at my hotel, he wondered as a sleek, silver tour bus cruised past his property. "Headed for the Beachcomber, I'll bet," thought Greg, picking up the latest sales report from his desk. Tour groups made up only five percent of the Sun & Surf's business, and occupancy was down eight points from budget. Greg couldn't help but think the two were somehow related.

Greg had been general manager of the Sun & Surf Inn for only three months. This was his first position at a travel destination property; the other hotels he'd managed in this national chain drew most of their business from commercial travelers, not tourists. His predecessor left for a new opportunity, followed closely by the resignation of the hotel's sales director, who took with her a couple of profitable accounts with tour operators and wholesalers. Now, Greg's sales staff consisted of his new director of sales, Kendra Wilson, who was promoted from the sales position she held with the hotel for the past two years. Greg called Kendra to his office, hoping she could help him get a handle on their sales picture.

"Kendra, why aren't we pulling in the tour groups the way the Beachcomber does?" Greg asked. "Our rates are comparable, we've got the same amenities, and we're actually closer to the beach than they are. So why are we only doing five percent in tour group business?"

Kendra looked uncomfortable. "Well, we lost a couple of key tour accounts when the director of sales left, and she had to work hard to keep them before then. The last general manager wasn't always real good about paying commissions to the tour companies on time. That, and we haven't sent anyone to the Pow Wow or Florida Huddle for a while. We were always arguing over whether trade shows were worth the expense," she said.

Seeing Greg's confusion, Kendra explained that trade shows like the Pow Wow and Florida Huddle, as well as the National Tour Association (NTA) trade show, were good places to consider for soliciting business from tour companies and wholesalers, which contract with a hotel for a certain number of room nights which they build into tour packages.

"It sounds like we need to get back on the trade show circuit if we're going to boost our occupancy rate," said Greg. "Kendra, I'd like to have you look into those shows and spend some time meeting with tour operators and wholesalers as part of your marketing plan. That should get us back on track."

Kendra shook her head. "It's not that easy, Greg. It takes time to build strong relationships with tour operators and wholesalers. Besides, these folks book their business a year in advance. Even if I start now, we won't see the results on our books until sometime next year. I'm willing to take on the challenge, but we'll need to look at some other marketing strategies that will show results sooner than later."

Greg rolled up his sleeves. "All right, where do we start?"

Kendra showed him her marketing plan. She met regularly with the local Convention and Visitor's Bureau to keep on top of events that were bringing groups into town. She read the business pages of the daily newspaper to find new businesses that were coming into the area, and called on them to make them aware of the hotel and to ask for their business. The hotel was listed with two local colleges, that recommended the property to students' families during orientation and commencement, as well as to visiting athletic teams. Kendra had also recently updated the hotel's two billboards, which were located in prominent positions along the two major highways leading into Sun City. "We're listed in the AAA book, too," Kendra said.

"That's great," said Greg. "How big is our ad?"

"I didn't say we had an ad; I said we were listed," Kendra replied.

"Oh. Well, how about any of the coupon books for our low-demand dates? At my last property, we were in a couple of travel club programs, like Entertainment Card. No? Maybe you should look into that," said Greg.

"Okay. I've tried to put together some attractive packages to bring in people during our low demand times, but they don't seem to work very well," said Kendra.

Greg asked if the reservation agents were actively selling those packages, and if their chain's central reservations office had an updated listing of the hotel's special rates.

"I don't know," said Kendra. "I gave the information to Luis. I figured it's his job as front office manager to take it from there. I never thought to check out what happened after that."

"Thanks, Kendra," said Greg. "Why don't you meet with Luis about those packages, and we'll all get together to discuss this further."

Discussion Questions

1. What are some of the problems Greg has inherited from the previous general manager, and what will he have to take to remedy them?

2. What issues will Kendra need to consider as she begins to solicit business from tour group operators and wholesalers?

3. What are some additional marketing activities the Sun & Surf Inn can implement to increase occupancy in the short term, while the director of sales is building the hotel's wholesaler and tour group business?

4. What are some of the issues that should be discussed with Luis, the front office manager?

Case Number: 370CE

This case was developed in cooperation with Lisa Richards of Hospitality Softnet, Inc., a marketing resources and support company (Sixty State Street, Suite 700, Boston, Massachusetts 02109; tel. 617-854-6554).

Case Study

Reviving Revenue Management

The Hearthstone Suites Hotel is an all-suite property with 250 rooms. A new property, the Fairmont Hotel, opened near Hearthstone Suites three months ago. Several months before the opening of the Fairmont, Laurie, the GM at the Hearthstone Suites, pushed all her front office and reservations staff to sell as many rooms as possible. As she put it, "Whatever it takes, to stay competitive." The director of sales, Pat, supported the plan from day one, but Jodie, the front office manager, had misgivings from the start. Jodie was concerned that the revenue management program managers implemented a year and a half earlier, would be totally useless because of the push for occupancy.

The most recent profit and loss statement indicates that Jodie's fears were fulfilled. Though the occupancy is at budget year-to-date, the average daily rate (ADR) is down by $6.00. Also, the mix of commercial business is lower than planned—40 percent of guest mix instead of 50 percent. Also, the SMERF segment is higher than it should be—15 percent of guest mix instead of 5 percent. SMERF is a catch-all term for group business at substantially low rates—Social, Military, Educational, Religious, and Fraternal groups.

Jodie, Pat, and Laurie are in a meeting to discuss these latest figures.

Laurie opens the meeting by saying, "Well, we've weathered the storm caused by the opening of the Fairmont. We managed to hold on to our occupancy level. But it looks like we have some regrouping to do. I trust you've each received the profit and loss statement I sent you. I'm concerned about the fact that we've lost so much of our share of the commercial business. And our ADR is much too low."

"I agree," says Jodie, "but I was just following orders when I had my staff focus on selling rooms. Our good occupancy rate has come at the cost of both yield management and revenue. It will take quite awhile to regain our former position."

"We all sat down and agreed months before the Fairmont opened that we should do our best to keep our occupancy numbers, and that's what we've done," says Pat. "You and your staff have worked hard and are to be commended, Jodie."

"Hear, hear," says Laurie. "And now we have some time to re-evaluate our position and start targeting that corporate segment again."

"I just hope it's not too late to win it back from Fairmont," sighs Jodie.

Later that day, Jodie gathers her front desk and reservations team to brief them about re-implementing the revenue management program. "I know you've all been putting a lot of extra effort into filling rooms over the past several months. I'm proud of you; the whole management team is. We've met our occupancy goals. The down side is that our guest mix is off. We've lost some of our commercial segment and gained too much of the SMERF segment. And our ADR is down a full $6. It's time we reviewed the revenue management program we use…"

"The revenue what?" blurts Jack, a fairly new front desk agent. "You never told us about that."

"Now hold on a minute," counters Jodie, "some of you are so new that you haven't been fully trained in this program, but I know I've talked about it to some extent with all of you."

"Sure, you told me a little about it," offers Tracey, a reservationist. "I never have been comfortable with it, to tell the truth. One day I quote a guest $85 and he books a suite. A month later he calls back to book another and I quote $105. Then the guest asks why the rate went up—what am I supposed to say?"

"Well, there are things you can tell guests who ask that, but we're not going to get into that right now," says Jodie.

Bill, the most experienced front desk agent, speaks up. "I've been using the yield management program all along, just like you showed me." He turns to his co-workers. "It's really not unreasonable when you look at the big picture of the hotel's revenue. I just tell inquisitive callers that our rates depend on their arrival dates. Some periods are busier for us than others, and that affects rates."

"Bill, it's good to hear that you continued using the yield management program," Jodie says. "We can get into more detail on applying it in formal training. We've had a lot of changes since the push for volume began—changes in personnel and even changes in the yield management program itself. It's clearly time I evaluated training needs in our department in the area of yield management program execution. You can be confident, Tracey—and all of you—when you quote rates that they are competitive for what we offer. That reminds me," and here Jodie pauses a moment, "how many of you have actually been inside some of our suites?"

Three of the six employees raise their hands. "How many have seen rooms at the Fairmont or at any of our other competitors?" continues Jodie. Only Bill raises his hand. "So almost none of you have seen the difference between our suites and the single rooms other properties are offering?"

"There hasn't been time to look at what we're selling," protests Jack.

"...much less to look at what anyone else is selling," adds Linda, another reservationist.

"That's what I was afraid of," says Jodie. "In the next two weeks or so, as I'm re-evaluating training needs, I'm going to have each of you spend time gaining an appreciation of the value we offer—especially in comparison with the value of Fairmont's offerings and those of our other competition."

"Are we still going to be offering the $84 supersaver rate?" asks Tracey. "We've had a lot of repeat business because of that rate."

"I've had callers tell me we're the best deal in town," Linda says.

But Bill cautions, "We won't need to use it next week. The Home Builders convention is in and every room in town will be booked. We can afford to charge more next week."

"That's good thinking, Bill," says Jodie. "I know it's nice to be popular with guests, and it's easy to use that discount whenever a potential guest shies away from a quoted rate; but the supersaver rate is intended to be used only as a last resort or in other special cases. We shouldn't be offering it too frequently. We also need to adjust our selling strategies when special events come along like this convention."

"Speaking of selling strategies, when are we going to get to go through that training module on selling skills you were talking about?" inquires Linda. "I've heard about it but I haven't gone through it yet."

Discussion Questions

1. How can the management team address the problem of low ADR?

2. What are some ways Jodie could make employees like Jack and Tracey more familiar and comfortable with a yield management program?

3. What selling skills should training focus on for the Hearthstone Suites Hotel staff?

4. How can the Hearthstone Suites Hotel regain some of the commercial business it has lost?

Case Number: 370CF

This case was developed in cooperation with Lisa Richards of Hospitality Softnet, Inc., a marketing resources and support company (Sixty State Street, Suite 700, Boston, Massachusetts 02109; tel. 617-854-6554).

🔍 Case Study

Distributing Sales Functions Between a Hotel's Sales and Catering Departments

Carla Mills is the general manager of the Woodfield Plaza, a 400-room first-class/suburban hotel. It's early July, and Carla has just reviewed the forecasted year-end profit and loss statement. A couple areas concern her. First, assuming the hotel will hit budget the rest of the year, banquet food sales will be down $60,000 to budget. Also, the audiovisual revenues and room rental revenues will miss budget by $30,000. Carla calls a meeting with her director of catering, Alan Jenkins, to discuss ways to remedy the situation.

Carla opens the meeting by contrasting the forecasted statement with the budget and asks Alan what he plans to do about the decrease in banquet food sales.

"You've been here sixty days now, Alan. You should have a good feel for the property and the community. Tell me, why are sales down in your area?"

Alan shifts in his seat. He thinks about the question for a moment, then responds. "Well, I think ultimately it comes down to a problem with selling," he says. "The sales staff knows how to sell guestrooms, but they don't seem to sell function rooms. They don't seem to be aware of opportunities to sell catering, or how to take advantage of those opportunities. I can't remember one event since I've been here that was generated by sales. And from what I've seen in past reports, this has been an ongoing problem."

"OK. That's a legitimate point," Carla replies. "Salespeople certainly could take advantage of those kinds of opportunities. Sales and catering aren't often as united as they could be when it comes to selling our services—"

"It's just that no one in sales will take ownership for selling catering," Alan interrupts.

"Then you take ownership of it," replies Carla. "Look, in fairness to sales, it's not their job to sell function rooms and banquet events, primarily. Their job *is* to sell guestrooms. In some situations they could probably work a little harder on selling function rooms. But the responsibility for selling catering events ultimately belongs to catering, not sales… and since you're so concerned about *sales* selling *functions*… how many *guestrooms* has *catering* sold? The street goes both ways."

Alan sits back in his chair, thinking about what Carla has said. "Not many, actually," he finally says. "As far as catering taking responsibility for its own sales… you're right. We need to. But we're so busy taking the calls coming in, and we're trying to process them as fast as we can. We haven't had time to focus on increasing our sales skills."

"You can't continue to be just order-takers and expect your sales to do fine," Carla says. "You need to take responsibility for your sales. You need to take an active role in this. In your own words, you need to take ownership of it. Let me ask you: Do you know where you're losing business, and why?"

"Not offhand, no."

"Do you know how you're going to solve the problem?"

"Well, I think I can come up with a solution," Alan replies.

"I know you can. And I know your staff is capable. What I'd like you to do is come up with a plan as to how you'll sell catering, and how you'll work with the sales staff to sell catering. Could you get that to me… let's see," Carla looks at her calendar. "Two weeks from today?"

"I think I can do that."

"Great. Now on to my next concern." Carla holds up the forecasted statement. "As you can see from this forecast, by the end of the year audiovisual revenues and room rental revenues will miss budget by $30,000—that's if all goes well the next six months. Now, what do you suggest we do about *that*?"

Alan thinks about the problem. "With the room rentals, I think the problem is that we're giving function space away to book more room nights. I understand we have to do this, to some degree, but we're losing money doing it."

"But don't you think that's a worthy trade-off, to get more room nights?"

"It would be if it were necessary. But I don't think it is."

"What do you mean?" Carla asks.

"I think we can keep the room nights without losing the room rental completely, if we institute a sliding-scale function fee."

"Yes," Carla nods.

"For example, if the customer picks up 80 to 100 percent of a room block, there's no rental. If they pick up 50 percent of the room block, they'll get 50 percent off the rate, and so on."

"Excellent idea. That should increase room rental revenues. You may want to consider putting a similar scale in place for catering revenues."

"Hmmm… come to think of it, my staff does seem a little too eager to lower rentals. Maybe scales will help them deal more effectively with that issue."

"Good. Now, what about audiovisual rentals?"

Alan pauses. "I need to look into that. I know there are several ways to increase the A.V. revenues, as well as additional ways to increase room rental revenues. How about if I think about the problem in the next couple of weeks, and include my proposals in my plan?"

"I trust your judgment. Let's get together again in two weeks and see what you've come up with."

"Great. I'll see you then."

Alan leaves the room. Both he and Carla feel that they made some progress in solving their budget problems. And they're confident that in two weeks they'll have a plan in place to help prevent similar problems in the future.

Discussion Questions

1. In an ideal situation, what should the distribution of sales functions between a hotel's catering and sales departments look like?

2. Given the responsibilities of a hotel's catering department, what challenges will the director of catering face as the department shifts from simply being production-focused to being sales-focused?

3. How could the catering department at the Woodfield Plaza recover more audiovisual and room rental revenues?

4. What steps should the director of catering at the Woodfield Plaza take to identify the specific causes of his budget problem? Once the specifics of the budget problem have been identified, how should he address the problem?

Case Number: 370CG

This case was developed in cooperation with Lisa Richards of Hospitality Softnet, Inc., a marketing resources and support company (Sixty State Street, Suite 700, Boston, Massachusetts 02109; tel. 617-854-6554).

🔍 Case Study

Sales Underperforms Even While Meeting Budget

The Christopher Hotel is a 180-room economy/business property of a national chain located in a booming suburb of a major city. Tony, the regional director of operations, is orienting the property's new general manager, Janice.

Generally, the hotel is close to meeting most its budgeted targets. However, when Tony compares the hotel's activity with competing hotels in the area, the picture changes dramatically. Other hotels are enjoying much higher occupancy levels than the Christopher and they are selling rooms at higher rates. The Christopher's market penetration is only 84%, when its baseline goal should be to achieve at least 100% of its fair share of the market. Tony calculates penetration rate by dividing the hotel's actual market share by its fair share (based on the proportion of rooms available in the local market).

Tony and Janice also review the Christopher's group business. Year-to-date, the hotel sold 4,796 group room nights—short of the budgeted target of 6,500 group room nights. The average room rate (ADR) for group business is down $4 from the budget.

Tony tells Janice, "While I'm here I want to investigate these problems with you and help come up with an action plan to address them. How can we increase the Christopher's penetration rate, Janice?"

"I'd start by examining what kind of new business—group and otherwise—is being generated," says Janice. "What is the mix of corporate, leisure, government, or educational groups that is looking for rooms? I bet that new college is putting together a sports program; visiting teams will need someplace to stay."

"You could be right," says Tony. "The school is so new that you might be too early on that idea, but it couldn't hurt to get a start with the sports program developer. Let's see what the hotel has historically done with groups." He pulls out some reports. "They've got corporate groups contributing 3,000 room nights and other groups contributing the rest of their total 4,796."

"'Other groups'? Is that how it's listed—'other groups'? Aren't there classifications within that 'other' category?" asks Janice.

Tony responds, "That's how it's listed."

Janice shakes her head and asks, "Do we have a group rooms control log to look at so we can see how individual group segments are performing? How about a pace report so we can see how group bookings kept up with budgeted amounts?"

Tony shuffles some of the papers and replies, "The previous GM did keep a GRC log and a pace report. He may not have used them to fullest advantage. He also could have kept better track of what the property's competitors were doing. That information is crucial to success, especially in this local area. In the next few months, I would like you to keep up to date on what our competitors are doing and how they're doing it."

"How good a networker was the previous director of sales?" asks Janice. "Did he have relationships with area churches, mosques, and synagogues for wedding and other special ceremony business? Was he in touch with the manager of the local convention center? How about city officials?"

"He focused more on officials of agencies serving the whole metropolitan area than on officials of this suburb." Tony replies. "Maybe he was hoping to land some of the business for conventions held downtown. He was using the right technique but on the wrong people. Our competitors here keep in touch with the city Department of Parks and Recreation. As far as wedding and ceremony groups, there's been no sales effort specifically targeting them, though some large bookings have come from that segment. I'd encourage you to pursue that option with the staff. And don't be shy about using the yellow pages of the phone book. So many salespeople use that as a last resort. Just think about all the kinds of business represented there..."

"It does sound like this is a very competitive area." Janice offers. "I wonder if our sales contacts with those buyers for groups are everything they should be. How experienced are our sales staff?"

"I'm not sure, but that's another good area to look at. Now how about this problem of the group ADR?" asks Tony.

Janice picks up a management binder labeled Rate Guidelines from the GM office bookshelf. "It's great that they had some of these, though having guidelines and making sure staff know and use them are two different things. Hmm, it doesn't have a date listed; do you know when it was last updated?"

"No, I don't," replies Tony.

"That could be important; I'll check on it. Maybe we also need to change our rooms inventory management guidelines to make sure we sell out on every night when there's potential to do so," Janice responds.

Tony closes with, "I think you've got a good handle on the most pressing issues facing the Christopher Hotel, Janice. Why don't you draft an action plan in the next couple of days and we'll refine it together."

Discussion Questions

1. What factors should Janice consider when planning to increase the hotel's market penetration rate?

2. What factors should Janice consider in relation to increasing group business?

3. What initial steps should Janice take to evaluate the low average room rate for groups?

4. How can Janice find out what the competition is doing and how they're doing it?

Case Number: 370CH

This case was developed in cooperation with Lisa Richards of Hospitality Softnet, Inc., a marketing resources and support company (Sixty State Street, Suite 700, Boston, Massachusetts 02109; tel. 617-854-6554).

Case Study

Leadership at the Hamilton: Impasse Between the General Manager and Director of Sales

It was hard for Susan Fontenot to keep her mind on her driving as she made her way through the city's early morning rush-hour traffic. She was on her way to a potentially difficult meeting with Thad Johnson, the director of sales for The Hamilton, a 500-room first-class hotel right in the heart of downtown. Susan was a marketing consultant that the general manager of the Hamilton, Rick Martin, had called last week, all in a dither. "I can't believe it," Rick had said. "I just got this month's profit and loss statement, and occupancy year-to-date is down four percent, while marketing expenses are over budget by $55,000. How can that happen? Months ago I raised the sales-call quotas for our salespeople, started sending them to every trade show in sight, and re-did all of our collateral materials so they are really first class. And still we get these numbers! I don't know what else to do to help Thad—my background is in F&B, not sales. Will you come in and help us come up with a plan to turn things around?"

Susan knew from experience that there were two sides to every sales-are-down story, and this was no exception. When she arrived in Thad's office and sat down across the desk from him, it didn't take him long to get to the point. "Rick doesn't know what he's doing," he said bluntly. "Three months ago, when the occupancy numbers first began to go down, he started bugging me about sales calls. I told him to be patient, things would turn around. But they didn't turn around fast enough for him, and a month ago he raised our sales-call quotas. The only thing raising our call quotas did was raise everybody's stress levels in the department."

"Yes, Rick mentioned raising the quotas," Susan said, taking a yellow pad and pen from her briefcase. "Just how high did he raise them?"

"He wanted each of us to make 50 in-person client calls a week! Two breakfast site inspections, two lunch site inspections, two dinner site inspections, and four other on-site visits in between, every day. He just pulled those numbers out of the air. It's ridiculous."

"How many calls were your salespeople supposed to make before?"

Thad frowned. "I don't believe in quotas," he said. "I came up through the ranks, and I know how much I resented the director of sales I used to work for. She insisted on a certain number of calls every week, with all sorts of end-of-week and end-of-month sales call reports to fill out, and I told myself I wasn't going to operate that way. I trust my people and I don't look over their shoulders all the time. Besides, they're always busy. Because we're a first-class hotel, I emphasize personal service. I make sure the salespeople baby-sit their groups when they're in the hotel. 'Make sure the client sees you all the time and knows you care'—that's my motto. If a client has a problem, the salesperson is right there to take care of it personally."

Susan smiled. "It must make it hard for your salespeople to find time to make outside calls."

"Well, as a matter of fact, it was pretty rare for us to make an outside call before Rick handed down his quotas," Thad replied. "I never had quotas before; our hotel sells itself. Everybody knows what we stand for and what we offer. If someone wants to go first-class in this city, this is the place to stay."

"How close are your salespeople coming to actually making 50 calls a week?"

"To be honest, I don't know," Thad said. "I just told them to do the best they could. Like I said, I don't believe in quotas and paperwork and I'm hoping Rick won't push it."

Susan made some notes on her yellow pad.

"Besides," Thad went on, "we're too busy going to trade shows! That's another thing Rick insisted on. Just between you and me, I think it's because he enjoyed going to the National Restaurant Association show in Chicago every year back when he was a food and beverage director. Now we're constantly packing and unpacking our trade-show booth and making travel arrangements to travel hither and yon. Most of the time these trade shows don't generate any business. People just pick our booth clean of brochures—and that's another thing!" Thad grabbed a brochure sitting on his desk. "Look at this thing! Ten pages, full color! Back at the beginning of the year Rick insisted that all of our collateral materials be in color, so he scrapped everything except for this brochure and a 30-page banquet menu collateral piece we send out to prospective banquet clients. That used to be a two-color piece, but now it's full color too. He said a first-class hotel should have first-class collateral. That sounds nice, but I don't have to tell you how expensive full-color stuff is."

"Full-color costs money, no question about it," Susan agreed.

"And while we're on the subject of expenses, how fair is it that every manager in the hotel signs for meals and drinks and it gets charged to my department as 'advertising and promotion'? If they are legitimately with a client, that's one thing. But they eat at the hotel because they don't want to eat in the employee break room, or it's raining outside, or they're short on cash this month—they even treat their spouses to dinner, and they sign the bills like it's a management perk or something. And it all gets charged to marketing. If Rick is so concerned about marketing expenses, why doesn't he do something about that? I've complained and complained about it."

"I've seen that privilege get abused at other hotels, too," Susan nodded. "How do you keep track of the other department expenses, like office supplies, sales trip expenses, and so on?"

"Oh, I just wait for the profit and loss statement to come out at the end of the month and see where we are. If we're over one month, I try to cut back the next."

Susan made a note, then tapped her pen on her chin. "Let's backtrack for a moment. I'd like to know more about your staff—Rick didn't go into details with me. How many people do you have and what's their experience level?"

"I'm lucky—when I came on board two years ago, I inherited a staff of four veteran salespeople. Two had been with the hotel for five years, the other two had just come on board but had worked for other hotels for a number of years." Thad smiled. "I didn't have to do any training or coaching, I was able to just do my job and let them do theirs."

Susan smiled. "Sounds like you're pretty confident in their abilities. Have you ever gone out on a call with them?"

"No, why should I?"

"Well, because you're so confident in them, I was wondering if you had actually seen them in action, selling to a client."

"No. Up until this year, we've always made our numbers, and, like I said earlier, we didn't make many outside sales calls anyway. People know our hotel's reputation. Most of our clients call us."

"So you don't provide your salespeople with sales targets to meet or action plans to follow?"

"Not really. Like I said, they're busy fielding all the incoming calls and taking care of clients. They're good people and they know what they're doing."

"I see." Susan made some more notes on her pad. "Well, as you know, Rick has asked me to make some recommendations to help the hotel raise its occupancy numbers. Four percent doesn't sound like much, but I'm sure you are as aware as anyone that, with your hotel's average daily rate and budgeted occupancy levels, a four-percent shortfall comes out to about $700,000 below budget for the year. I have some preliminary notions about what might be helpful, but do you have any ideas for turning things around?"

Thad leaned back in his chair and thought for a moment. "To tell you the truth, I think Rick overreacted to the situation," he said finally. "Of course I'm willing to take a look at any ideas you come up with, but I think the numbers would eventually have come up on their own if we had just stayed our course. To my mind, personal service is the key to this market. A continued emphasis on really serving our clients once they get to the property will keep them coming back, and word-of-mouth from happy clients will keep our phones ringing." Thad paused. "I think Rick's directives are doing more harm than good, so my suggestion would be to call off the call quotas and cut way back on the trade shows."

Susan nodded and returned her pad and pen to her briefcase. "You have a point about the trade shows," she said. "Rick wants to bring marketing costs down and increase occupancy. From my discussions with you and Rick, I think I'm going to concentrate on three marketing expense areas: the trade show issue, the hotel's collateral materials, and the advertising and promotion expense account. On the occupancy side, I'm going to look at ways to help you determine whether your salespeople have the sales skills they need to meet the booking objectives, and I'm probably going to recommend that you give your salespeople more direction as to where you want them to focus their efforts."

Susan rose and shook hands with Thad. "I know it can be difficult to have an outsider come in to look at what you're doing, but my job really is to just try to be helpful and look for ways to make sales targets easier to make. I'm going to schedule a meeting with both you and Rick sometime next week, and I hope you'll be happy with the recommendations I come up with for you."

Discussion Questions

1. What are some recommendations Susan can make for decreasing the hotel's marketing expenses?

2. What are some recommendations Susan can make to Thad to help him evaluate his staff's sales skills?

3. What are some recommendations Susan can make to Thad to help him give his staff more direction to ensure that their efforts are focused and targeted?

Case Number: 370CI

This case was developed in cooperation with Lisa Richards of Hospitality Softnet, Inc., a marketing resources and support company (Sixty State Street, Suite 700, Boston, Massachusetts 02109; tel. 617-854-6554).

Case Study

Overcoming Rate Resistance—Among the Sales Staff

Conversations stopped as Fran walked into the meeting room where the sales staff of the 263-room Park View Hotel had gathered. The director of sales surveyed the anxious faces that turned toward her as she approached.

"Lighten up, folks," Fran said reassuringly. "This is a strategy session, not a wake. I know you're all aware I had a meeting with the general manager last week, and he'd like us to make a few changes to our marketing plan. I'd like us to sit down together and brainstorm ways to solve some problems we identified in our meeting."

Fran passed around a handout as the sales people took their seats. The objections started as soon as they began reading the agenda.

"Get rid of 5,000 room nights of our corporate contract business? That's crazy!" said Angela. "Most of my best accounts are corporate preferred. I worked hard to get those accounts and I'm not dropping them now."

"Where are we going to find the customers to replace these 5,000 room nights?" Michael asked. "You can't just expect that kind of new business to come strolling through the door right away."

Murmurs of agreement filled the room. "And how am I supposed to break it to my accounts that they're not going to get their preferred rate any more?" asked Tanisha. "I wouldn't know what to say, and I don't think I could sound real convincing."

Fran raised her hands. "Let's take this one step at a time. Here's the situation. The hotel has too much contracted business at a low rate. Some of these accounts have had the same rate for the past two years. We need to replace about a third of this business—about 5,000 room nights—with higher rated transient and group business. I'm not saying we're going to get rid of all our contract business. I just want to evaluate which accounts we should keep, which ones might accept a higher—but still discounted—rate, and which ones don't make good business sense to keep."

Fran stood up next to a flip chart and uncapped a marker. "Let's set up some criteria for reviewing our contract accounts. What kinds of things should we look at? I'll start." She wrote, "Keep accounts with attractive arrival/departure patterns."

She continued to write as the staff began calling out ideas.

After a coffee break, Fran called the group together again. "Great work, folks. Now let's think about how we're going to replace that contract business with some new business that will bring in more revenue. I'd like to make a list of market segments and sources we could solicit more strongly. Then we can evaluate which areas we should concentrate our sales efforts on. Any ideas?" Fran worked the flip chart again.

That job done, Fran turned to the issue Tanisha brought up earlier: how to tell clients about the change in the hotel's corporate preferred rate policy. Together, the staff decided they would be more comfortable and effective if they had scripts to work from.

Fran assigned two of the sales staff to write some scripts that everyone could use when talking with their accounts, whether they were increasing their rate or eliminating their preferred rate. As the meeting adjourned, Fran still heard grumbles from some of the sales people. "My work's not done yet," she thought, and began planning her next steps for helping her staff accept these new rate changes.

Discussion Questions

1. What are some of the criteria the sales staff could use to evaluate whether a corporate contract account should be retained or dropped?

2. What factors should the staff consider when determining new sources of business to replace the displaced contract business?

3. What would the scripts look like that the sales staff could use when talking to clients about the rate change.

4. How can Fran help her staff become comfortable with the changes in the hotel's rate structure?

Case Number: 370CJ

This case was developed in cooperation with Lisa Richards of Hospitality Softnet, Inc., a marketing resources and support company (Sixty State Street, Suite 700, Boston, Massachusetts 02109; tel. 617-854-6554).

Index